Educational Psychology

'002

6th EDITION

Educational Psychology

N. L. Gage
STANFORD UNIVERSITY

David C. Berliner
ARIZONA STATE UNIVERSITY

HOUGHTON MIFFLIN COMPANY

BOSTON   NEW YORK

To Margaret Burrows Gage and Ursula Casanova

Senior Sponsoring Editor: Loretta Wolozin
Associate Editor: Lisa Mafrici
Packaging Services Supervisor: Charline Lake
Senior Production/Design Coordinator: Jill Haber
Senior Manufacturing Coordinator: Sally Culler
Marketing Manager: Pamela J. Laskey

Cover design: Cathy Hawkes, Cat and Mouse Design
Cover art: Max Bill, *Rhythm in Four Squares,* 1943. © 1998 Artist
Rights Society (ARS)/Pro Litteris, Zurich.

Printed in the U.S.A.

Library of Congress Catalog Card Number: 97-72473

ISBN: 0-395-79794-2

23456789-DW-02 01 00 99 98

Brief Contents

PART ONE

Educational Psychology: Some Background   1

CHAPTER 1   Educational Psychology's Purposes and Methods   3

CHAPTER 2   The Tasks, Standards, and Objectives of Teaching   28

PART TWO

Student Characteristics   47

CHAPTER 3   Cognitive Abilities   49

CHAPTER 4   The Development of Cognition, Language, and Personality   96

CHAPTER 5   Human Diversity and the Schools: Culture, Gender, and Exceptionality   150

PART THREE

Learning and Motivation: Theories and Applications   205

CHAPTER 6   Behavioral and Social Views of Learning   207

CHAPTER 7   Cognitive Learning: Processes and Strategies to Make Meaning   251

CHAPTER 8   Motivation and Learning   312

PART FOUR

Teaching Methods and Practices   363

CHAPTER 9   Lecturing and Explaining   365

CHAPTER 10   Teaching Small Groups: The Discussion Method and Cooperative Learning   397

CHAPTER 11   Individual Instruction   427

CHAPTER 12   Classroom Teaching: The Orchestration of Methods   452

PART FIVE

Assessment   507

CHAPTER 13   Basic Concepts in Assessment and the Interpretation of Standardized Testing   509

CHAPTER 14   The Teacher's Assessment and Grading of Student Learning   550

Contents

Preface   *xix*

PART ONE

Educational Psychology: Some Background   1

CHAPTER 1

Educational Psychology's Purposes and Methods   3

The Purpose of Educational Psychology: How Does Ms. Eugster Do It?   **4**

Educational Psychology and the Tasks of Teaching   **8**

Passion and Educational Psychology   **8**

Educational Psychology in Action   **8**

Are the Results of Research in Educational Psychology Obvious?   **9**

The Concepts and Principles of Educational Psychology   **10**
Concepts and Variables   **11**   Principles   **13**

Using Concepts and Principles in Explanation, Prediction, and Control   **14**
An Example of Explanation   **14**   An Example of Prediction   **14**   An Example of Control   **15**   The Interaction of Explanation, Prediction, and Control   **15**   In Short   **16**

Methods for Studying Relationships   **16**
Correlational and Experimental Methods   **16**   Qualitative Research: Interpretive Methods   **22**   Replication and Meta-Analysis   **23**

Using Research to Guide Practice   **23**

CHAPTER 2

The Tasks, Standards, and Objectives of Teaching   28

What Are the Major Tasks of Teaching?   **29**

Why Do We Need Standards and Objectives?   **31**

How Standards-Based Reform Has Affected Objectives   **32**

The Content of Instruction **34**

Decision Making at the National, State, and Local Levels **34**   The Teacher's Role in Determining Content **34**   The Students' Role in Determining Content **36**

Thinking about Objectives in Terms of Student Performance **36**

General Objectives **37**   Specific Objectives **37**

POLICY, RESEARCH, AND PRACTICE

Is It Preferable to Use Specific or General Objectives in Order to Facilitate Learning? **38**

Multiple Perspectives 1

APPLICATION

Formulating Your Own Objectives **41**

Classifying Objectives **41**

Identifying Three Domains **41**   Focus on the Cognitive Domain **42**

POLICY, RESEARCH, AND PRACTICE

The Knowledge versus Intellectual Skills Debate **43**

The Performance-Content Matrix **44**

PART TWO

Student Characteristics 47

CHAPTER 3

Cognitive Abilities 49

The Definition of Cognitive Ability **51**

The Measurement of Cognitive Ability **51**

Cognitive-Ability Tests and the Normal Distribution **53**   The Stability and Reliability of Cognitive-Ability Test Scores **54**

The Organization of Cognitive Ability **55**

POLICY, RESEARCH, AND PRACTICE

Why the Classroom Teacher Needs to Know about the Organization of Cognitive Ability **57**

Cognitive Ability and Success **58**

In School **58**   On the Job **59**

Heredity and Environment in Cognitive Ability **61**

Do Genetic or Environmental Differences Affect IQ Differences More? **63**

Heritability Is Not Genetic Determination **64**   Heritability Is Not Unchangeability **65**
The Changeability of IQ **66**

POLICY, RESEARCH, AND PRACTICE

Can Schools Get Along without Intelligence Tests?   69

Two Recent Conceptions of Intelligence   71
Practical Intelligence, or Common Sense **71**   Multiple Intelligences **75**

APPLICATION

Consider How Your Own Multiple Intelligences Operate Together   77

Group Differences in Cognitive Ability   80
Socioeconomic Status Differences **80**   Urban-Rural Differences **81**   Ethnic
Differences **82**   The Nature-Nurture Issue and Conservatism-Liberalism **83**
Explanations of Group Differences **84**

Improving Cognitive Ability   87
The Home Environment and Cognitive Abilities **87**   School Influences on Cognitive
Abilities **90**

CHAPTER 4

**The Development of Cognition, Language,
and Personality   96**

The Development of Cognition   97
Piaget's Stages **97**   The Developmental Process **105**   Dissenters from and
Alternatives to Piagetian Theory **106**   Bruner's Theory of Cognitive Growth **109**
Vygotsky's View of Cognitive Development **111**

POLICY, RESEARCH, AND PRACTICE

Teaching from a Context of Diversity   113

APPLICATION

Instructional Implications of Piaget, Bruner, and Vygotsky   115

The Development of Language   118
Stages of Development **118**   Adults' Influence on Language Development
and Literacy **121**   Language Issues and Schooling **122**

The Development of Personality   127
Erikson's Theory of Personality Development **127**   The Development of Moral
Reasoning **131**   The Organization of Personality: A Profusion of Traits **136**

APPLICATION

Making Use of Thinking Guides in Problem Solving   142

CHAPTER 5

Human Diversity and the Schools: Culture, Gender, and Exceptionality 150

Cultural Differences 151

Defining Culture and What Constitutes Cultural Differences **151** Enculturation by Socializing Agents **152** Historical Background **154** Developing a Cross-Cultural Perspective **155**

POLICY, RESEARCH, AND PRACTICE

Culture and Readiness to Learn in School 159

Developing a Multicultural-Education Classroom **165**

Gender Differences 168

Personality Differences **170** Differences in Academically Relevant Capabilities **170** Socialization of Gender Expectations and Behaviors **171**

Exceptionality 173

General Definitions **173** Categories of Students Who Are Eligible for Special Education **174** Students with Physical and Sensory Disabilities, Impairments, and Challenges **177** Students with Cognitive Disabilities or Brain Dysfunctions **184** Students with Serious Emotional and Behavioral Disorders **188**

POLICY, RESEARCH, AND PRACTICE

Is It Preferable to Have Children with Emotional Disorders in the Regular-Education Classroom? 192

APPLICATION

Some Classroom Adjustments for ADD/ADHD 194

Students with Multiple Disabilities or Other Developmental Problems **196** Students Who Are Gifted and Talented: Another Category of Exceptionality **198**

Multiple Perspectives 2

General Concerns and Recommendations for Teachers 202

PART THREE

Learning and Motivation: Theories and Applications 205

CHAPTER 6

Behavioral and Social Views of Learning 207

Learning 208

A Definition of Learning **208** Three Behavioral Learning Theories **209** Foci of This Chapter: Operant Conditioning and Social Learning **214**

Operant Conditioning **214**

Positive and Negative Reinforcers **215**   Primary and Secondary Reinforcers **216**
Schedules of Reinforcement **217**   Contingency Management **221**   The Elimination
of Responses **226**

APPLICATION

Unintentional Reinforcement   227

Ethical Issues and Limits of the Theory **231**

Social Learning Theory **234**

How Learning Occurs through Observation **234**   A Social-Learning Analysis of
Observational Learning **237**

POLICY, RESEARCH, AND PRACTICE

**Are Systematic Training Programs an Effective Way to
Change the Imitation of Aggressive Behaviors Modeled
by the Media?   240**

A Note on Cognition **241**   The Teacher and Modeling **242**   Self-Regulation of
Behavior and Its Processes **243**   Mentoring **246**

POLICY, RESEARCH, AND PRACTICE

**Are Systematic Training Programs an Effective Way
for Students to Regulate Their Own Behaviors?   247**

CHAPTER 7

Cognitive Learning: Processes and Strategies to Make Meaning   251

Underlying Assumptions of Cognitive Learning **253**

Contrasting Views of Learning: The Behavioral versus the Cognitive **253**   Shared
Characteristics and Beliefs among Cognitive Theories of Learning **255**   The Role
of Strategies in Cognitive Learning **256**

Cognitive Models, Perspectives, and Strategies **258**

An Information-Processing Model of Learning and Memory **258**   Strategies for
Processing Information and Enhancing Memory **264**   Metacognition **270**
Cognitively Active Learning **273**   Constructivist Perspectives on Learning **276**
Problem-Solving Approach to Learning **278**

POLICY, RESEARCH, AND PRACTICE

How Do Teachers Develop Expertise?   281

Situated Cognition **284**   Strategies for Promoting Cognitive Learning and Higher-
Order Thinking **288**

POLICY, RESEARCH, AND PRACTICE

Overcoming Student Misconceptions in Science   297

Transfer of Learning **299**
A Glance at Traditional Views **300**   Contemporary Views of Transfer **301**
Teaching for Transfer **303**

APPLICATION

Enhancing Our Own and Our Students' Mindfulness   305

Instructional Ideas and Strategies for Promoting Transfer **306**

A Look Ahead to Chapter 8   **307**

CHAPTER 8

Motivation and Learning   312

The Crucial Role of Motivation in Behavior and Learning   **313**
Motivation Determines What Makes a Reinforcer **314**   Motivation Accounts for Goal
Orientation **314**   Motivation Determines the Time Spent in Different Activities **315**
Motivation and Achievement **316**

Conceptions of Motivation and Their Implications   **317**
Four Conceptions **317**   Implications for Education **318**

Achievement Motivation: A Cognitive Composite   **319**

APPLICATION

**Conduct Your Own Survey of Young Children's Changing
Motivation   320**

Relationship between Need for Achievement and Performance **320**   Classifying
Achievement Attributions **321**

POLICY, RESEARCH, AND PRACTICE

Internal and External Attributions and Emotion   324

The Relationship of Self-Worth and Need for Achievement to Classroom
Structure **328**   How Other Motives Interact with the Need for Achievement **331**

Intrinsic and Extrinsic Motivation   **333**

Operant Conditioning and Motivation   **336**
Stimulus Control and the Role of Reinforcers and Incentives **337**   Frustration and
Motivation **338**

Changing Motivational Patterns   **339**
Cognitive Approaches **340**

POLICY, RESEARCH, AND PRACTICE

**Are Attribution Training Programs an Effective Way
to Change a Student's Perceptions about Why He or She
Succeeds or Fails?   341**

Environmental Approaches **343**

Self-Efficacy and Achievement Motivation **348**
Developing Self-Efficacy **349**   The Self-Efficacy of Teachers and Schools **351**

Motivational Techniques in Classroom Teaching: Guidelines for Teachers **352**

PART FOUR

Teaching Methods and Practices   363

CHAPTER 9

Lecturing and Explaining   365

The Lecture-Method Paradox: Strong Condemnation, Wide Use   **366**
Defense of the Lecture Method **367**   Research Evidence on Effectiveness **369**

POLICY, RESEARCH, AND PRACTICE

What Are the Proper Uses of Lecturing?   370

Important Considerations for Using the Lecture Method   **371**
Preparing a Lecture **371**   Low- versus High-Inference Variables **373**
Cognitive Load: A General Rationale **374**

APPLICATION

Reducing Cognitive Load in Your Own Learning   375

The Introduction to the Lecture   **375**
Appealing to Students' Interests **375**   Providing Motivational Cues **376**
Exposing Essential Content **376**   Helping Students Organize Content **377**

The Body of the Lecture   **378**
Covering Content **378**   Providing Clear Organization **378**   Organizational
or Outlining Forms **379**   Explanations **383**   Clarifying the Organization **385**
Clarifying the Content **387**   Maintaining Attention **389**

Multiple Perspectives 3

POLICY, RESEARCH, AND PRACTICE

The Role of Humor and Enthusiasm in Lecturing   392

The Conclusion of the Lecture   **394**
Functions of the Conclusion **394**   The Summary **395**

Interlecture Structuring   **395**

CHAPTER 10

Teaching Small Groups: The Discussion Method and Cooperative Learning   397

Rationales: Social Learning and Distributed Cognition   **398**
Social Learning Theory **398**   Distributed Cognition **398**

The Discussion Method **399**
Objectives of Discussion-Group Teaching **399** Considerations in Using Discussion **400** Before the Discussion Group Meets **402** During the Meeting **405**

APPLICATION

Experimenting with Using Questions versus Nonquestion Alternatives 407

POLICY, RESEARCH, AND PRACTICE

How Do a Teacher's Actions Stifle or Stimulate Student Discussion? 409

After the Meeting **412** Intellectual Pitfalls **413** Social-Emotional Pitfalls **415**

Cooperative Learning **419**
Some Cooperative Learning Schemes **419** The Role of Computers in Cooperative Learning **422** The Effectiveness of Cooperative Learning **422**

POLICY, RESEARCH, AND PRACTICE

Computers and Cooperative Learning 423

CHAPTER 11

Individual Instruction 427

A Rationale for Individual Instruction **428**
Promoting Independent Learning **428** Adapting to Individual Differences **428**

Ways of Promoting Independent Learning **429**
Homework **429** Study Skills and Strategies Training **431** Independent Study **433**

Ways of Adapting to Individual Differences **435**
Ability Grouping **435** Mastery Learning **436** Tutoring **439**

POLICY, RESEARCH, AND PRACTICE

What Are the Benefits of Peer Tutoring? 441

Using Computers for Learning in the Classroom **442**
Programmed Computer-Assisted Instruction (CAI) **443** Further Uses of Computers in Today's Classrooms **446**

APPLICATION

Making the Computer Work for You 448

The Teacher's Role with Computers **449**

CHAPTER 12

Classroom Teaching: The Orchestration of Methods   452

The Pattern of Classroom Teaching   453

Distinguishing Characteristics of Classroom Teaching **454**   Reasons for the Prevalence of Classroom Teaching **457**

POLICY, RESEARCH, AND PRACTICE

Does Smaller Class Size Improve Achievement?   **461**

The Planning Phase of Classroom Teaching   462

Types of Planning Needs **464**   Planning for Classroom Discipline and Management **464**

APPLICATION

Becoming Aware of Your Own Unintentional Biases   **472**

The Interactive Stage of Classroom Instruction   477

Direct Instruction **477**

POLICY, RESEARCH, AND PRACTICE

Redirecting Questions and Probing   **487**

POLICY, RESEARCH, AND PRACTICE

How Can Teachers Improve the Academic Learning Time (ALT) of Students?   **494**

Constructivist Teaching **496**   A Synthesis of Direct Instruction and Constructivist Teaching **503**

PART FIVE

Assessment   507

CHAPTER 13

Basic Concepts in Assessment and the Interpretation of Standardized Testing   509

Assessment with Tests   510

Systematic Procedures **510**   Measuring **512**   Behavior **512**   Sample **512** Evaluation **513**   Standards and Norms **513**

Norm-Referenced Testing   514

Using a Local Norm Group **514**   Using a National Norm Group **514**

Criterion-Referenced Testing   515

Reliability **518**

■ Multiple Perspectives 4

Test-Retest Reliability **519**   Internal-Consistency Reliability **521**   The Standard Error of Measurement **522**   Improving Reliability **524**

Validity **524**

Content Validity **525**   Criterion Validity **525**   Construct Validity **526**

Evaluation **528**

Formative Evaluation **529**   Summative Evaluation **529**

Standardized Tests in the Assessment Process **530**

Advantages and Special Uses of Standardized Tests **530**   Disadvantages of and Concerns about Standardized Tests **534**   Types of Standardized Tests Used in Schools **535**

POLICY, RESEARCH, AND PRACTICE
Is It Fair to Publish Standardized Achievement Test Scores? **537**

APPLICATION
Taking a Test to Understand It **540**

Administering Standardized Tests **540**   Interpreting Standardized Tests **541**

POLICY, RESEARCH, AND PRACTICE
High-Stakes Standardized Testing Can Have Some Very Undesirable Consequences **543**

What Does the Future Hold for Standardized Testing? **546**

CHAPTER 14

The Teacher's Assessment and Grading of Student Learning **550**

Informal Assessment **551**

Sizing-Up Assessments **551**   Assessment during Interactive Teaching **552**

Formal Assessment: Determining What Kinds of Achievement Are Important **554**

Domain-Referenced Testing **555**   The Table of Specifications **555**

Types of Formal Tests and Test Items **557**

Performance Tests **559**

POLICY, RESEARCH, AND PRACTICE
What Are the Problems and Prospects of Performance Testing? **566**

Essay Tests **567**   Short-Answer Tests **570**

APPLICATION

Using Guidelines to Write Good Multiple-Choice Questions   574

Getting the Advantages of Using All Kinds of Questions **577**   Using the Computer in Classroom Assessment   **578**

From Assessing to Grading: A Difficult Transition   580

Establishing a Frame of Reference for Grading Judgments **581**   Two Common Questions about Testing, Grading, and Marking **582**

POLICY, RESEARCH, AND PRACTICE

How Can Tests and Grades Be Used Sensibly and Humanely in the Assessment Process?   584

Sources of Information for Grading Decisions **586**

POLICY, RESEARCH, AND PRACTICE

What Factors Actually Go into Teachers' Grading Decisions?   591

Considering the Toughest Grade of All: Nonpromotion **592**

Using Portfolios in the Assessment Process   593

Appendix   Standard Deviation   601

Glossary   603

Author-Reference Index   625

Subject Index   661

Preface

Purpose

We have prepared this sixth edition to update and otherwise improve what, judging from the widespread use of the fifth edition, has proved to be a beneficial introduction to educational psychology. We still aim at giving future and present-day teachers—and also administrators, counselors, and specialists of all kinds—an interesting, memorable, and certainly practical look at what contemporary educational psychology has to offer. Accordingly, this book is full of the organized facts, concepts, and principles that emerge from educational research. The book continues its groundbreaking and still extensive treatment of teaching, while introducing new applications and accessibility for novice students.

Organization

The book is organized around a logical five-component model of the teaching process. The model begins with the *objectives* of teaching and the *student characteristics* that should help in determining those objectives. Second, it goes into the processes of *learning and motivation* that must be fostered to help students achieve the objectives. Third, it presents what is educational psychology's hitherto neglected contribution to the scientific basis of the art of *teaching.* It ends with a treatment of the *assessment* of student achievement.

We continue the 14-chapter organization that proved successful with the fifth edition. But we have taken into account recent advances in educational thinking. So we have given small-group teaching methods a chapter of their own. The treatment of humanistic education has been replaced with one of constructivism. And we have combined into one chapter the discussion of assessment's basic concepts, principles, and standardized tests.

What's New: Features of the Revision

The years since the fifth edition have witnessed a host of important new ideas—the results of intensive scholarship, research, and analysis. We have sifted these to take advantage of their contribution to our book's purpose. Consequently, much of the book has been carefully rewritten. The many new references show how the literature since the fifth edition has been used. The following summaries mention only a few of the major new items of substance in this edition.

Part One, Educational Psychology: Some Background. In Chapter 1, Educational Psychology's Purposes and Methods, we begin with a new sketch of how Ms. Eugster, a sixth-grade teacher, goes about teaching one topic for one hour. The story takes the student, in the process, through our book—all of its sections and chapters—showing how they bear upon what Ms. Eugster thinks and does. We also emphasize the concept of effect-size over statistical significance as the important concern of experiments in the social sciences. In Chapter 2, The Tasks, Standards, and Objectives of Teaching, we introduce the concept of standards, which has received renewed and re-emphasized attention in the present decade. We also go into and resolve the lively controversy between advocates of higher intellectual-process objectives and advocates of knowledge objectives: high-level thinking requires knowledge.

Part Two, Student Characteristics. Chapter 3, Cognitive Abilities, recognizes *The Bell Curve* controversy and cites recent research that questions some of that book's premises. Carroll's massive reworking of many factor analyses of cognitive-ability tests is described. The recently made distinction between heritability and genetic determination is applied. Ceci's evidence on the powerful role of education in determining intelligence is summarized. Recent evidence on the improvability of cognitive ability is presented. Chapter 4, The Development of Cognition, Language, and Personality, gives new attention to the work of Vygotsky and the importance of culture in the development of thinking. The "Big Five" factors of personality are also described. In Chapter 5, Human Diversity and the Schools: Culture, Gender, and Exceptionality, we present new material on understanding the culture of the educational system and the curriculum, the socialization of gender expectations and behaviors, and the inclusion of children with disabilities in regular classroom settings. We also explore the acceleration versus enrichment controversy in educating gifted and talented children.

Part Three, Learning and Motivation: Theories and Applications. Chapter 6, Behavioral and Social Views of Learning, presents recent research on reinforcement schedules and the rationale for using reasoning as an alternative to punishment. Systematic training for changing media-modeled aggressive behavior and for improving students' ability to regulate their own behavior are also discussed. Chapter 7, Cognitive Learning: Processes and Strategies to Make Meaning, provides a new treatment of the underlying assumptions of cognitive learning, goes into strategies for information processing and enhancing memory, and introduces the new thinking on situated cognition. The treatment of transfer has been increased to present new material on learning strategies. Chapter 8, Motivation and Learning, includes new material on the relations of self-worth and need for achievement to classroom structure, ways of conducting one's own survey of children's changing motivations, attribution training programs, and self-efficacy and achievement motivation.

Part Four, Teaching Methods and Practices. Chapter 9, Lecturing and Explaining, introduces the reducing-cognitive-load rationale for making lectures, and any cognitive message, easier to understand and remember. It improves the treatment of a model for explanations with a new illustrative subject matter and diagram. The treatment of humor and enthusiasm has been strengthened. Chapter 10, Teaching Small Groups: The Discussion Method and Cooperative Learning, introduces the theoretical frameworks of social learning and distributed cognition. The treatment of teacher questioning and its values and dangers is expanded. Teachers' actions that stifle and stimulate discussion are elaborated. In the treatment of cooperative learning, computer-assisted methods are introduced, and their positive effects and possible shortcomings are described. Chapter 11, Individual Instruction, has a new section on ability grouping, its forms and effects on achievement and self-esteem. The effectiveness of tutoring is given further support. The treatment of computer-assisted instruction (CAI) is buttressed with recent information on the prevalence of computers in schools and on the effectiveness of using technology to improve achievement. The status of the intelligent-tutoring-system movement is updated. Chapter 12, Classroom Teaching: The Orchestration of Methods, has a new section on constructivist teaching and an updated treatment of many of its previous topics.

Part Five, Assessment. Chapter 13, Basic Concepts in Assessment and the Interpretation of Standardized Testing, contains new treatments of the fairness of publishing achievement test scores and the consequences of high-stakes standardized testing. The future of standardized testing is also discussed. Chapter 14, The Teacher's Assessment and Grading of Student Learning, introduces new and more extensive treatments of performance testing as an alternative to the essay and multiple-choice testing that have long predominated. Extensive examples of portfolios are also featured. The importance of sensibility and humaneness in evaluating student achievement is considered.

Pedagogy-Enhancing Features

New Policy, Research, and Practice Features

These boxed features appear in every chapter and show how research throws light on policy issues that have important implications for classroom practice. Examples of these features include:

The Knowledge versus Intellectual Skills Debate (Chapter 2)
Computers and Cooperative Learning (Chapter 10)
What Are the Benefits of Peer Tutoring? (Chapter 11)
What Are the Problems and Prospects of Performance Assessment? (Chapter 14)

These discussions are presented from the perspective of classroom teachers and the decisions they make.

New Application Features

These boxed features provide illustrative detail on applications to teaching, for use by classroom teachers. Examples include:

Consider How Your Own Multiple Intelligences Operate Together (Chapter 3)
Making Use of Thinking Guides in Problem Solving (Chapter 4)
Enhancing Our Own and Our Students' Mindfulness (Chapter 7)

Chapter Outlines

Each chapter opens with a detailed outline of major content headings. These outlines serve as advance organizers that preview chapter content. Students can use these outlines as aids in finding their way around a chapter.

Chapter Overviews

The chapter overviews provide a concise introduction to the most important topics in each chapter. The authors pose questions about the material to be covered and encourage students to start thinking about what they already know in each area and what they can expect to learn from each chapter.

New Margin-Placed Thought Questions

Questions in the margins of chapters provide students with prompts for critical thinking, applying ideas to themselves, and making comparisons with other points of view.

New Chapter Summaries

Summaries in the form of numbered lists aid students' review of key concepts and self-testing.

Glossary

A glossary at the end of the text provides readers with brief definitions of the key terms that appear in boldface type in the text.

Author/Reference Index

This index lists alphabetically by authors and occasionally annotates the sources used in the preparation of the text. It provides an excellent list of resources for further study in every area of educational psychology. The pages on which each item is cited are given after each entry.

Subject Index

A detailed subject index makes it possible to find the pages on which a host of the book's ideas can be found.

New Full-Color Inserts on Multiple Perspectives

These inserts link today's classroom practices and ideas in educational psychology with quotations from modern and classic thinkers, educators, philosophers, and poets. These pithy quotations, along with their visual representations in the form of photographs and graphics, cast multifaceted reflections on the entire teaching-learning process and encourage further thought about the text's content.

Study Guide

This edition, like its predecessors, is supported by a *Study Guide* designed to help students understand the most important points of each chapter of the book. Each *Study Guide* chapter provides (1) focus questions, (2) chapter objectives, (3) chapter overviews, (4) definitions of key concepts, (5) projects and activities that call for application of key concepts, (6) multiple-choice tests for students to use in monitoring their understanding of each chapter, (7) suggestions for term papers, and (8) (*new*) crossword puzzles. All these *Study Guide* features call on students to make active use of the material they have learned in each chapter.

Instructors interested in more information on materials that support the text can contact the Houghton Mifflin Faculty Services Center at 1-800-733-1717 or visit the College Division home page at http://www.hmco.com.

Acknowledgments

We wish to thank the following reviewers for their helpful suggestions and contributions to the content of this edition:

Edward J. Caropreso, Clarion University
Christopher M. Clark, Michigan State University
Libby G. Cohen, University of Southern Maine
Theodore Coladarci, University of Maine
Margaret Desmond, California State University, Hayward
Kenji Hakuta, Stanford University
William M. Hopkins, State University of New York College at Cortland
Dinah Jackson, University of Northern Colorado
Fayneese Miller, Brown University
Antoinette Miranda, The Ohio State University
Mustafa Ozcan, Clarke College
James A. Reffel, Dickinson State University
Richard E. Snow, Stanford University

We also would like to thank Dr. Sharon McNeely of Northeastern Illinois University, for contributions made to the revision of Chapter 5,

Human Diversity and the Schools: Culture, Gender, and Exceptionality, and Dr. John Bing of Salisbury State University, Maryland, for revising Chapter 6, Behavioral and Social Views of Learning.

We are especially grateful for the unstinting attention to substance, design, format, detail, schedule, and much else, provided by Loretta Wolozin, Lisa Mafrici, and Jean Zielinski DeMayo of Houghton Mifflin Company, and for the thorough editorial development work of Merryl Maleska Wilbur. Our thanks also to Nancy Benjamin of Books By Design, Inc. And, for this edition especially, we are deeply grateful to our wives, Maggie and Ursula, who gave us every moral support.

Educational Psychology

PART ONE

Educational Psychology: Some Background

Psychology is the study of the thoughts and actions of individuals and groups. Educational psychology is the study of those thoughts and actions as they relate to how we teach and learn. From that study, we have identified principles and methods that can improve teaching and learning. In Chapter 1, we examine some of the broad ways in which educational psychology can help educators in general and teachers in particular. We also look at how researchers go about gathering the scientific knowledge on which the principles and methods of educational psychology are based. In Chapter 2, we talk about educational standards and goals, the first concerns in teaching, and examine the ways of thinking about them that have been developed by psychologists and other educational researchers.

Educational Psychology's Purposes and Methods

Overview

THE PURPOSE OF EDUCATIONAL PSYCHOLOGY: HOW DOES MS. EUGSTER DO IT?

EDUCATIONAL PSYCHOLOGY AND THE TASKS OF TEACHING

PASSION AND EDUCATIONAL PSYCHOLOGY

EDUCATIONAL PSYCHOLOGY IN ACTION

ARE THE RESULTS OF RESEARCH IN EDUCATIONAL PSYCHOLOGY OBVIOUS?

THE CONCEPTS AND PRINCIPLES OF EDUCATIONAL PSYCHOLOGY

Concepts and Variables

Qualitative and quantitative variables

Alterable and unalterable variables

Principles

USING CONCEPTS AND PRINCIPLES IN EXPLANATION, PREDICTION, AND CONTROL

An Example of Explanation

An Example of Prediction

An Example of Control

The Interaction of Explanation, Prediction, and Control

In Short

METHODS FOR STUDYING RELATIONSHIPS

Correlational and Experimental Methods

Defining correlational relationships

Examining the differences between correlational and causal relationships

Methods for determining correlational relationships

Methods for determining causal relationships

Qualitative Research: Interpretive Methods

Replication and Meta-Analysis

USING RESEARCH TO GUIDE PRACTICE

Summary

OVERVIEW

You may be wondering, What is psychology? What is educational psychology? We want to give you some short, preliminary answers: Psychology is the study of the thoughts and actions of individuals and groups. Educational psychology is the study of those thoughts and actions as they relate to how we teach and learn, particularly in school settings. In this chapter we first present an introduction to educational psychology and look at the nature of the research on which the field of educational psychology is based. We examine the basic concepts and relationships among concepts that educational psychology, like other sciences, uses to interpret significant concepts and events. These concepts and relationships help us explain, predict, and control phenomena related to teaching and learning.

Then we discuss the empirical methods (methods relying on experience, as against pure logic or faith) used by educational psychologists to understand the concepts and determine how they are related. Throughout this book we refer to the research-based underpinnings of the concepts and relationships within educational psychology.

But some people insist that educational psychology tells us only what we already know—that it yields only common-sense generalizations about teaching and learning. We hope to convince you that the evidence shows otherwise. In this chapter we look at several of these "common-sense" generalizations and see how people can misunderstand them.

The Purpose of Educational Psychology: How Does Ms. Eugster Do It?

Let us start our journey through educational psychology by looking at a teacher—one teacher with one class for one hour. At 7:45 A.M. one Thursday, Lillian Eugster gets started on her job at the Neil Armstrong Junior High School. Her sixth graders will not be arriving for another 30 minutes, so she has time to finish the overhead transparencies—on what causes the seasons—that she began preparing the night before.

She has given some thought to the choice of understanding the seasons before she decided to devote an hour to it. The understanding would get her class into some astronomy (the earth's motion and the inclination of its axis) and also some physics (spread or concentration of radiation and hence of heat). It would also give the class some practice in visualization of spaces and angles.

Furthermore, the topic was suited to the students' intellectual capabilities—something they could learn and grasp at this stage of their development. And, as with the weather, it was a universally interesting topic. So it was highly likely to have some attention-grabbing appeal. And the right answer was not obvious.

This book and educational psychology deal with the hopes and fears of human beings.
(© Spencer Grant/ Monkmeyer)

Her class consists of 13 boys and 16 girls. Of these, 13 are of European-American descent; six, African-American; six, Hispanic-American; and four, Asian-American. The students come in about equal numbers from blue-collar and white-collar family backgrounds. So, she thought, her choice of topic in this case is unlikely to leave anyone out because of gender or ethnic or social-class differences in interests, but she does have some concern about sex differences in spatial-visualization ability.

After the class arrives, she gets the usual preliminary chores of attendance and the like out of the way. Then she introduces the topic with a minilecture about the importance of seasons, the weather, and the mystery of what causes them. Next she calls for students' own ideas about what causes the seasons. Kyung Chul Woo is the first to volunteer, and he offers the idea that the earth varies in its distance from the sun as it revolves once each year. Ms. Eugster takes the answer seriously and calls for more. Billie Washington raises her hand, but then thinks better of her idea and lowers it again. Joe Applegate suggests that cloud cover moved by the winds might cause the seasons. This seems enough to get the class thinking. Ms. Eugster then breaks up the class into four nearly equal-sized groups, who are to talk over the problem for seven minutes, form hypotheses, and choose a spokesperson. After a quiet minute or so the groups begin to buzz, and when the class reassembles four different "hypotheses" are set forth by the groups' spokespersons.

Ms. Eugster watches and listens during these proceedings. Larry seems to be doing too much of the talking. Amado and Nancy seem uninvolved. As usual, Rosalie Espinosa has been chosen as a spokesperson. Ms. Eugster is not surprised at the roles taken by most of the students, but Amado's withdrawal does seem unusual.

Now that the exercise is well underway, Ms. Eugster drops a hint about the inclination of the earth's axis and how that inclination stays the same as the earth takes its annual journey around the sun. The class ponders this clue for about a minute, the silence being interrupted only by a few mutterings. Then Nancy asks if she can go to the chalkboard. Permission granted, Nancy draws a big circle for the sun and two smaller circles for the earth at two opposite positions in its annual orbit around the sun. The right answer quickly emerges, and the class throws out comments showing understanding and drawing inferences about differences between the northern and southern hemispheres and about the relative smallness of the differences in the earth's distance from the sun owing to its elliptical orbit. Ms. Eugster then shows her transparencies, which tell the story with a bit more clarity and detail.

Ms. Eugster inevitably evaluated her students during these proceedings. She could not help but notice the quality of the thinking, interest, and social behavior displayed by various students. A week later, when she asks her students to write a paragraph about what causes the seasons, most of them have it right, but there were some disappointments.

This sketch of one teacher's work with one class on one morning on one lesson contains in miniature much of what this book is about. In choosing a topic Ms. Eugster acted out the task of deciding on the content and performance she wanted her students to learn. As you shall see in Chapter 2 on the content and goals of teaching, she did not do so alone. Looking over her shoulder were the many political, economic, cultural, and professional institutions and organizations—in the nation, the state, and the local community—that agonize about educational standards and how to think about them.

She also inevitably had in mind the characteristics of her students. We deal here with students' cognitive abilities and stage of development, both as a class and as individuals who come from different cultural backgrounds and homes. Here Ms. Eugster can be guided by the kinds of ideas set forth in Chapter 3 on cognitive abilities and Chapter 4 on the development of cognition, language, and personality. And with students as heterogeneous as hers, in her particular school, in its particular neighborhood and community, she was bound to think about how they resembled and differed from one another and from other kinds of students and communities. Chapter 5 on human diversity and the schools presents these issues, helping teachers think about cultural and gender differences and about relative extremes (exceptionality) in physical and mental characteristics.

When it comes to learning, Ms. Eugster was bound to be guided by some ideas of her own about how it takes place. Here she was able to benefit from the theories and research of psychologists for whom the learning process is a central problem. As set forth in Chapters 6, 7, and 8, these conceptions of learning, memory, and transfer (how learning one thing affects the learning and performance of other things) provided useful bases for her personal theories and teaching practices. The same was true of her thinking about the perennial major problem of motivating students—how to get them energized and directed. Obviously, they should be interested in the learning that school is all about. Here, Chapter 8 on motivation and learning lays out these pertinent ideas.

When Ms. Eugster got into the teaching of her lesson on the causes of seasons, she realized she had many choices—lecturing and explaining (Chapter 9), discussion and other small-group methods (Chapter 10), individual-instruction approaches (Chapter 11), and the combination of all these that educators call classroom teaching (Chapter 12). She made quick decisions on these alternatives, but those decisions were nonetheless complex. She had to take into account the underlying techniques, pitfalls, advantages, and costs of these teaching methods. And she had to do so not only in relation to the subject matter and her students but also in relation to her own skills with the methods and what she knew about how to make them work.

At the end of the hour, the day, the unit, and the school term, Ms. Eugster had to evaluate and assess—engage in a "conversation" with herself, her students, their parents, and her school's authorities about how well the students had done. How well had they learned what they should have learned? How could she find out? How should she let them know the results of her evaluative efforts? This part of her teaching is indeed sensitive, involved with issues of fairness and justice. The issues and

Teachers evaluate students' learning and their achievement of educational objectives.
(© Paul Conklin)

How does Ms. Eugster's class compare with your own sixth-grade class?

methods involved in using tests, both standardized and teacher-made, and in giving grades, are spelled out in Chapters 13 and 14.

We expect that taking this journey with Ms. Eugster has helped you to recognize the tasks teachers face whenever they enter a classroom. We believe that your work with the concepts and ideas in this book will help you understand these same tasks and challenges. Most of all, we hope that your work with this book will help you in your own journey toward conducting education in ways that students (and much research) identify as characteristic of good teaching—which, when you think about it, will probably be more like the teachers you remember as good teachers. Underneath it all, this is the purpose of including educational psychology in programs that prepare teachers.

Educational Psychology and the Tasks of Teaching

The challenge of teaching begins before the first day of school and continues every day thereafter. You spend a lot of time preparing yourself on what you want to teach and how to teach it. Then you walk into the classroom, put your books and things on the desk, probably print your name on the chalkboard, and turn around to face the class. Whether this is your first class or your thirtieth, the moment is exciting and challenging. Your students may be second graders or high schoolers. They may be with you for the whole day or for just 50 minutes. You may be teaching a variety of subjects or only one. Whatever your situation, the tasks you must deal with raise problems that teachers have always had to face. And these problems arise in some form not only on the first day but every day you teach.

Educational psychology serves teachers, in fact all educators, by helping them deal with these problems. Sometimes educational psychology leads directly to a solution. More often it is only part of the solution, a basis for it. In other words, educational psychology serves as a discipline underlying education just as the physical sciences underlie engineering.

Your knowledge of educational psychology can give you insight into many aspects of educational practice. It can give you important ideas about learning and about how the family, business, industry, and the community influence learning. It also can improve your thinking about school administration, curriculum development, counseling, and other educational activities. But this book is most directly concerned with teaching and learning processes in classrooms. More precisely, we deal primarily with the problems that arise when you carry out the tasks of teaching.

Passion and Educational Psychology

Like most textbooks, we wrote this one in a neutral, academic style. But do not let that deceive you. Like a song from the Grateful Dead or Mahler's Second Symphony, this book deals with things that are loaded with feelings and emotions—the hopes and fears, the joys and sorrows, the loves and hates, the successes and failures, the glorious clarities and desperate confusions of human beings. Beneath what is discussed in these chapters, there lie the emotional depths and heights of education: the transformation of classrooms from boring to exciting; from failing to successful; from institutions where parents are alienated to those in which parents cooperate; from schools that foster cultural isolation to those that develop cultural acceptance. It is easy to feel passionate about educational psychology because it is woven into the activities that make schools and classrooms such exciting places.

Educational Psychology in Action

Let us look at an example of how research in educational psychology combined with a concern for practice can help teachers meet the challenges of their job. Consider the problems of classroom management faced by all teachers—especially novice teachers, who realize that some reasonable level of order is necessary for learning but worry about their ability to create that order.

This problem has been attacked by many researchers. One successful approach was developed by researchers (Anderson, Evertson, & Brophy, 1979) who were interested in improving reading achievement in first-grade classes serving middle-class children in a small city in Texas. They focused on how to run a reading group in an effective way. They became familiar with the objectives of reading instruction at that grade level in that community, studied the characteristics of the students in the schools, and observed how the students were motivated and went about their learning. They also observed the teaching practices and styles of the teachers in the community's first-grade classes during reading-instruction periods. Especially, they analyzed the differences between the practices of teachers of high- and low-achieving classes. Finally, they familiarized themselves with the tests and other ways of evaluating the pupils' reading achievement.

On the basis of what they knew about previous research findings and the schools with which they were working, the researchers devised a training program to help teachers learn about the successful teaching practices found through their research. (These research-based practices are described in Brophy & Good, 1986). And they found that a *new* set of classes whose teachers used the research-based teaching practices scored a lot higher on a reading achievement test than did the classes of teachers who did not get the research-based recommendations. The research informed teachers about more effective ways to manage reading groups, and the teachers were influenced by that research to change their practices. Their new ways of teaching caused much higher levels of achievement. This kind of improvement is, of course, a major purpose of research in educational psychology. Educational psychology provides teachers with information that will help them make better decisions.

Are the Results of Research in Educational Psychology Obvious?

Some people think the results of psychological studies of teaching and learning are really quite obvious. A newspaper article on a government document entitled *What Works*, which discussed research findings considered potentially helpful to schools and teachers, was headlined "Researching the Obvious" (*Arizona Daily Star*, March 8, 1988). And in the June 1990 issue of *The Atlantic Monthly*, Cullen Murphy said, "A recent survey (by me) of recent social-science findings . . . turned up no ideas or conclusions that can't be found in Bartlett's or any other encyclopedia of quotations" (p. 22).

Let's look at two generalizations from research on teaching:

1. When teaching reading, some third-grade teachers make greater use of paper-and-pencil activities, such as textbooks and workbooks,

whereas others rely more on manipulatives, such as games and toys. Reading achievement is higher when teachers use more manipulatives and fewer paper-and-pencil activities.

2. In grades 1 to 9, students were found to get better scores on achievement tests in classes with less teacher control and more student freedom to select activities.

In one experiment on obviousness, about 1,200 people were asked to rate these research findings on a four-point scale: (1) extremely obvious, (2) obvious, (3) unobvious, (4) extremely unobvious. *Obvious* was defined as "self-evident . . . the researchers were almost certain to find what they did."

Before you read further, you might rate these two propositions, just as the subjects did in this research.

The people did indeed rate each of these findings (and many others not given here) as obvious. But what is interesting is that they rated the "finding" as obvious *both when it was the actual finding and when it was the opposite of the actual finding.* Half the people in this study had gotten the actual finding to rate and half the opposite of the actual finding. It was the *opposites* of the actual findings that were stated in the list above. The *actual* findings from educational research are these:

1. When teaching reading, some third-grade teachers make greater use of paper-and-pencil activities, such as textbooks and workbooks, whereas others rely more on manipulatives, such as games and toys. Reading achievement is higher *when teachers use more paper-and-pencil activities and fewer manipulatives.*

2. In grades 1 to 9, students were found to get better scores on achievement tests in classes with *more teacher control and less student freedom to select learning experiences.*

In short, this study, by Wong (1995), showed that people tend to consider research findings obvious regardless of whether the "finding" is what was actually found or the opposite of what was actually found. The same result was obtained by Baratz (1983) for social research findings in areas other than teaching.

As the famous sociologist Paul Lazarsfeld (1949) commented after a similar discussion, "Obviously something is wrong with the entire argument of 'obviousness.'" Almost any flat statement, delivered with conviction—without ifs, ands, or buts—strikes us as not only unquestionable but also obvious. This effect occurs especially in areas like human behavior and education, with which everyone is familiar. "The feeling that a research result is obvious is untrustworthy" (Gage, 1991, p. 15; see also Myers, 1993).

The Concepts and Principles of Educational Psychology

What does science look like when it is applied to the field of educational psychology? Like any science, educational psychology develops concepts and principles based on certain methods. Here we focus on the concepts and principles; later in this chapter, we discuss the methods.

The **concepts** in educational psychology refer to our characteristics, behavior, mental processes, and environment as we become involved in

The educational psychologist pores over data on students' learning and achievement and on teachers' methods and practices to formulate the concepts and principles of the field.

(© Elizabeth Crews/Stock Boston)

Name a few concepts of the kind you would teach in some subject area.

What are some comparable principles in a field you know well?

educational activity. Here are some of the concepts we will be getting into: cognitive ability, students' academic learning time, transfer, attribution, constructivist learning, low-inference variables, test reliability, attention, encoding, and memory.

A concept is the organized information we have about an entity. Everything we know about cognitive ability or memory constitutes our concept of cognitive ability or our concept of memory.

The **principles** of educational psychology describe relationships between concepts. For example, "Cognitive ability is positively related to school achievement," or "Cooperative learning environments improve student attention" are both principles. When we link concepts by stating some kind of relationship, we are developing a principle.

Concepts and Variables

Concepts may take the form of **variables**—attributes that vary among individuals or events. The concept of cognitive ability, for example, is a variable because human beings vary in cognitive ability.

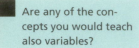

Are any of the concepts you would teach also variables?

What we mean by a concept is partly a matter of definition and partly a matter of the methods of studying the concept, or measuring the corresponding variable. In the case of the concept of cognitive ability, the usual definition rules out moral considerations since people with high cognitive ability may or may not be kind or honest. On the other hand, cognitive ability usually emphasizes speed and correctness in solving problems expressed in symbols—verbal, mathematical, or spatial (e.g., diagrams).

Psychology deals with many concepts and variables not much studied by other sciences. Much of this book is concerned with the concepts that have been especially developed by educational psychology. You will be looking at broad concepts such as cognitive ability, learning, attitude, and motivation. You will also get into more specific concepts such as contingent reinforcement (which refers to how behavior is controlled or maintained by its linkage to some positively valued event), content validity (whether subject-matter questions on an achievement test deal with what students have been taught), and pedagogical content knowledge (teachers' knowledge of subject matter such that they can teach it sensibly and effectively).

Qualitative and Quantitative Variables   How do you identify and define variables? Often they come from your experience—either informal or arranged. The **qualitative** researcher describes events. The **quantitative** researcher measures characteristics of events. Both kinds (discussed further below) contribute variables for teachers to consider. What is important is to analyze both the inner thoughts and the outer behavior of people under study in ways that are valuable to education.

Alterable and Unalterable Variables   Educational psychology has some choice as to what kinds of variables it wants to be concerned with. Education is aimed at bringing about wanted *changes* in people—in their knowledge, understanding, skills, and attitudes. So the discovery of ways to cause these changes has great practical importance. Accordingly, as Bloom (1980) pointed out, educational psychologists should be more interested in **alterable variables** whenever possible, rather than those that seem unchangeable or static. For example, the number of days in the school year is usually determined by school law. It is not nearly as easy for a teacher to change as "time-on-task," which the teacher can increase through certain teaching practices.

But **unalterable variables** are also worth studying. Even if these variables cannot be manipulated to improve education, they can help teachers understand education. Suppose someone studies student gender, obviously an unalterable variable, and discovers that girls tend to do less well than boys after instruction on certain spatial tasks, and that boys tend to do less well than girls after instruction on certain verbal tasks (see Chapter 5). Knowing these tendencies from studies of the unalterable variable "student gender" allows a better understanding of some educational problems. Alterable variables, such as time-on-task, become very important after teachers identify educational problems.

Name some alterable and unalterable variables you might be especially concerned with as a teacher.

We need to learn how variables unalterable by classroom teachers, such as home environment, are related to educational processes.
(© Laura Dwight/Photo Edit)

Compared to boys, girls may need a bit more time studying tasks that call for spatial abilities; compared to girls, boys may need a bit more time on tasks that call for verbal abilities. It is in this way that many gender, social-class, and ethnic differences, which appear to be unalterable, can be significantly modified.

Principles

Besides dealing with concepts, you will be concerned with descriptive principles, or statements that describe the relationships between variables. For example, classes that have more "academic learning time" (defined in Chapter 12) tend to have higher achievement. This is a principle because it describes a relationship between two variables—academic learning time and achievement. If a principle is firmly established, it is called a *law*. Scientific principles and laws serve as guidelines for practice. For example, students with high need for social acceptance (a concept or variable) tend to achieve more (a relationship) with teachers who show a lot of warmth (a concept or variable). So you can infer that you should display more warmth with students who have such a need.

Scientific principles, including the relationships between the variables of educational psychology, are not simply matters of definition, as they are in logic or mathematics. They must be empirical—*based on observations, on experience.* Educational psychology is an empirical science; that is, it accepts a relationship as a principle or law only if that relationship agrees with the facts of experience as determined by systematically collected data.

Using Concepts and Principles in Explanation, Prediction, and Control

The objectives of educational psychology, like those of any science, are to explain, predict, and control the phenomena with which it is concerned. To **explain** is to account for relationships between variables in ways that are reasonable, logical, and justifiable. That is, the relationships make sense in terms of everything known at that time. To **predict** is to state, with better-than-chance accuracy, the future value of one variable given knowledge of the earlier value of the same or another variable. To **control** is to change (to administer in varying amounts) one variable in such a way as to change (or, in education, to improve) the value of another variable. When we try to improve our students' level of learning, concentration, or memory, we are trying to control these variables. Let us look at examples of how research has attained all three of these goals in educational psychology.

An Example of Explanation

As an example of explanation, we can use the work of educational psychologists (summarized by Berliner, 1990) who set out to discover why some classes achieve much more than others in reading, mathematics, and other subjects. The researchers, observing in the classrooms, gradually developed a tentative explanation of what made the difference between the high-achievement and low-achievement classes. They got the impression from their observations and other sources that class time was being used differently in the various classes. Some teachers allocated more time to, say, reading and mathematics than other teachers did. Also, some teachers appeared to use **allocated time** more efficiently, so that their students were engaged with the subject matter for a much higher percentage of the allocated time. The researchers developed theories in which instructional time was a key concept, and they made logical arguments, based on observations, about the importance of time in learning. They identified logical and empirical relationships between the variables—relationships that helped in explaining student achievement.

> Name a principle you consider to be particularly well explained. Name another you consider poorly explained. How do they differ?

An Example of Prediction

The explanation above concerning instructional time seemed plausible. But educational psychologists realized the idea would be on firmer ground if it could be found to have predictive power, that is, if instructional time turned out to predict achievement. So the researchers measured allocated time and engaged time in reading in several dozen classrooms at the same grade level. Later in the school year, they measured reading achievement. They found that the earlier-in-the-year measures of allocated and, especially, engaged time in the classrooms actually predicted end-of-year gains in reading achievement. They had found a pre-

> Can you think of an example of at least moderately accurate prediction in education? On what basis is the prediction made?

dictive relationship between the variables. The predictions held up even when other factors, such as the students' cognitive-ability level and the average-income level of the classes' families, were held constant. The predictive power of the measures of how teachers employed time supported the use of this concept to explain differences in class achievement.

An Example of Control

For an example of control, let us turn to the work of educational psychologists who wanted to see whether changing teaching practices would improve (that is, exert control over) class achievement. We noted one study of this kind, above, when we described educational psychology in action. Actually, there have been 15 experiments of this kind (summarized by Gage & Needels, 1989; and Needels & Gage, 1991). In each study, a team of researchers picked teaching practices that had turned out in earlier studies to predict student achievement. Then they educated one group of teachers—the **experimental group**—in the use of those practices. Another group of teachers—the **control group**—who were similar to the experimental group, received no instruction in the teaching practices until the study was over. The similarity between the two groups was brought about by **random assignment,** that is, by putting each teacher into one group or the other on some chance basis, such as flipping a coin. The two groups of teachers were carefully observed as they went about their classroom work. It turned out that, in all but one of the 15 studies, the experimental group used many of the recommended teaching practices much more than did the control (uninstructed) group. And, most important, the classes of the experimental-group teachers did much better on achievement tests. So the use of the teaching practices that predicted achievement also had value for controlling, that is, improving, achievement. The researchers had found a **causal relationship** whereby one variable caused (influenced, determined, brought about) change in another variable.

Later, when the effective teaching practices were examined to discover why they might have increased achievement, it seemed that they improved the use of time in the classroom. The effective practices worked because they reduced disruptive behavior, captured and maintained student attention, induced students to participate in learning activities, reduced the time students had to wait to have their written work checked, and so on. This explanation, then, provided logical understandings about why some variable can predict achievement or can control (cause a change in the level of) achievement.

> Control in education is usually intended as improvement. What variables can you control in order to get certain effects?

The Interaction of Explanation, Prediction, and Control

So far, we have discussed explanation, prediction, and control primarily as separate goals of scientific research. But they are somewhat interdependent and also somewhat independent of one another. They are interdependent in that all three depend on relationships among the same variables. They are somewhat independent because we can have one without the other two.

- Sometimes we can at least partially *explain but not predict or control,* as in the case of earthquakes and volcanoes.
- Sometimes we can *predict and explain but not control,* as in the case of the return of Halley's comet.
- Sometimes we can *control and predict but not explain.* This was true, until a few decades ago, of headaches, which we could control with aspirin and thus predict, although scientists could not explain for 90 years why aspirin worked.

Scientists, including educational psychologists, want especially to reach the goal of *explanatory theory* as much as possible. But the nature of such theory is a complex, largely philosophical matter.

> Can you think of original examples of explanation without prediction? without control? of prediction without explanation or control? of control without explanation or prediction?

In Short

Whether in physics or educational psychology, the three goals of scientific effort are always the same—explanation, prediction, and control. Achieving these goals depends on finding certain kinds of relationships among variables.

- Explanation depends on rational, sensible, logical relationships.
- Prediction depends on temporal (time) relationships.
- Control depends on cause-effect relationships.

As already noted, the three kinds of relationships are not the same; we can have one without the others, at least to some degree. As we study teaching and learning, we shall use all three kinds of relationships— logical, predictive, and causal. Each has value for certain purposes.

Methods for Studying Relationships

Now that we have classified the relationships among variables according to whether they are logical, predictive, or cause-effect, let us examine the three main ways researchers study these relationships: correlation, experimentation, and interpretation.

Correlational and Experimental Methods

Defining Correlational Relationships   A **correlational relationship** indicates that certain values of one variable tend to be found together with certain values of another variable. For example,

- Students who score high on a cognitive-ability test tend to achieve higher grade-point averages than students who score low.
- Students from wealthier families tend to have fewer absences from school than students from poorer families.

> What are two educational variables that are correlated *but probably not* causally related? correlated *and probably* causally related?

Correlations may or may not reflect a cause-and-effect relationship. If variable A correlates with variable B, it may be because of the various possibilities, among many others, shown in Table 1.1.

TABLE 1.1

Alternative Explanations of a Correlation between Variables

Causal Possibility	Symbols	Example
1. A determines B.	A → B	Studying (A) determines Achievement (B).
2. B determines A.	A ← B	Achievement (B) determines Studying (A).
3. A and B determine each other.	A ↔ B	Studying (A) and Achievement (B) determine each other.
4. C determines A and B.	C ⤳ A ⤳ B	Home Environment (C) determines both Studying (A) and Achievement (B).
5. E determines C and D, and C determines A, and D determines B.	C → A, E, D → B	Parents' Expectations (E) determine Home Environment (C), which determines Studying (A); (E) also determines Students' Background Knowledge (D), which determines Students' Achievement (B).

The correlational method—determining whether certain values of one variable tend to be found with certain values of another variable—is good for determining whether concurrent or predictive relationships exist. A concurrent relationship is one between variables measured at the same time, for example, how the number of hours that have now gone by since your last meal relates to the strength of your present hunger pangs. A predictive relationship is one between a variable measured at time *1* and another variable measured later, at time *2*, for example, how students' cognitive ability measured in the fall of their senior year in high school (perhaps with the SAT or ACT tests) predicts end-of-freshman-year grade-averages obtained by the same students in college two years later.

Examining the Differences between Correlational and Causal Relationships   It is important to remember that a causal relationship exists where change in one variable brings about (results in, influences, effects, determines, produces, causes) change in the other. The best, but not the only, way to determine whether two variables are causally related is to perform an experiment. The term **experiment** has a specific meaning here. It is not synonymous with research, investigation, study, and the like; it refers to a particular kind of research or study—a study in which the researcher manipulates one variable, the **independent variable,** then measures the values of another variable, the **dependent variable.** If the dependent variable is found to have changed as a result of the deliberate manipulation of the first, the change is said to result from a causal relationship. An obvious example: Suppose one group of students is taught algebra but another, similar group is not. Being or not being taught algebra would be the independent variable, the one manipulated. The students' knowledge of algebra would be the dependent variable. If the taught group has greater knowledge than the group not taught, we could say that the teaching *caused* the greater knowledge. Educators knew from the studies of instructional time, reported earlier, and from experience, that the more time spent studying algebra the higher achievement in algebra is likely to be. That is, educators were pretty sure that study time and achievement were *correlated.* But they were not sure, until they did the controlled experimental study, whether study time was one of the factors that cause, or determine, school achievement.

Whether a relationship is causal or just correlational can have immense practical importance. The relationship between exercise and health is a case in point. Physiologists demonstrated long ago a positive correlation between exercise and health. Exercise is measured with questionnaires, interviews, or observations. Health is measured with all sorts of laboratory tests and medical examinations. But does the exercise *cause* the better health? Or does the better health cause the exercise? The correlation is ambiguous as to the direction of the causality here. It is plausible that healthier people feel more energetic and more inclined to engage in physical activity. This ambiguity is where experiments become necessary, and they show that exercise causes health, not the other way around (e.g., Eaton, 1992).

In teaching, it was long ago observed that more orderly classes tended to have higher achievement. But which caused which? It was reasonable to suspect that achievement determined orderliness—higher-achieving students were less frustrated by their lessons and so less inclined to misbehave. But it could also be argued that orderliness determined achievement—higher orderliness interfered less with the teaching and learning processes, wasted less time, and thus brought about higher achievement. Fortunately, here again experiments reduced the ambiguity: training teachers in ways to have more orderly classrooms brought about such classrooms, which had higher achievement. The degree of order in a classroom *determines* achievement (see reviews by Gage & Needels, 1989, and Needels & Gage, 1991).

Methods for Determining Correlational Relationships   How do we determine whether a correlational relationship exists? First, the researcher needs some basis for *pairing* the values of one variable with those of the other. For example, to determine whether IQ and scholastic achievement are correlated, individual students are the basis for pairing. That is, we pair some numerical indicator of each student's IQ with a numerical indicator of the student's achievement. We would need to obtain measures of the two variables by testing a number of students with an IQ test and determining for those same students their grade-point average. If the two variables are, say, class size and class achievement, our basis for pairing them would be at the level of the classroom. We would pair the number of students in the class with the class's average achievement, for a number of different classrooms.

Second, we would treat the numerical values of the two variables for the group of students by a statistical method that yields a correlation coefficient, a statistic that tells us whether a relationship exists. Correlation coefficients are numbers that range from -1.00 through zero to $+1.00$. They tell us the *direction* and *strength* of the relationship between the two variables. The closer the correlation coefficient is to -1.00 or $+1.00$, the stronger the association between the two variables. The closer a correlation is to zero, the weaker the association between the two variables. At zero, two variables are said to be uncorrelated—independent of each other. For example,

- Body weight and school achievement show little relationship to each other. Statistically, they have a correlation of around zero.
- High school grade-point average and college grade-point average show a substantial relationship to each other, usually yielding correlations of between $+.40$ and $+.60$.
- Temperature in Fahrenheit and temperature in Celsius are perfectly correlated; that is, the correlation is $+1.00$. If we know one of the two temperatures, we can easily and exactly compute the other with a simple equation.

Coefficients of correlation give us very useful information. Figure 1.1 shows contrived scatterplots for various levels of correlation. A scatterplot is a good name for these different examples. They are the plots obtained when we take a single point (one of the dots in these graphs) to represent a person's (or a class's) position on the two variables we are correlating. The dot could, for example, represent the grade-point-average (GPA) of a high school senior and that same student's GPA at the end of the freshman year in college. Or it could represent the average socioeconomic level of the occupations of the fathers of students in a class and the average achievement of the students in that class. The points representing all the students in a class fall into the kind of scatterplot shown. Those points scatter around some average value, which is the straight line shown in each graph. This line is called the *regression line*, and it is determined by statistical formulas that need not concern us here. Notice how the numerical value of the correlation coefficient, shown in the lower right-hand corner of each box, gets lower (nearer zero) as the dots become less closely clustered along the straight line. Low correlations result from lots of scattering, indicating no strong trend in the data. Higher correlations result from much less scattering of the points around the regression line and indicate a stronger trend in the data. The labels for the two axes of the scatterplot name the variables being correlated. We have chosen these labels as plausible examples of different kinds of correlation. Positive correlations are shown in the top six scatterplots in the figure.

Notice that the scatterplot in the lower right-hand corner in the figure illustrates a negative correlation: the higher the rate of spelling errors, the lower the teachers' grades for the essays tend to be. Negative correlations are interpreted just like positive correlations—the closer they are to -1.00, the stronger the relationships are. Instead of a higher score on one variable going with a higher score on the other, when we have a negative correlation, a higher score tends to go with a lower score. Thus,

FIGURE 1.1

Scatterplots illustrating higher and lower correlations, and positive and negative correlations

Adapted from L. J. Cronbach (1984), Essentials of Psychological Testing, *5th ed. (New York: Harper & Row), p. 138. Copyright © 1990 by HarperCollins Publishers, Inc. Reprinted by permission of Addison-Wesley Educational Publishers, Inc.*

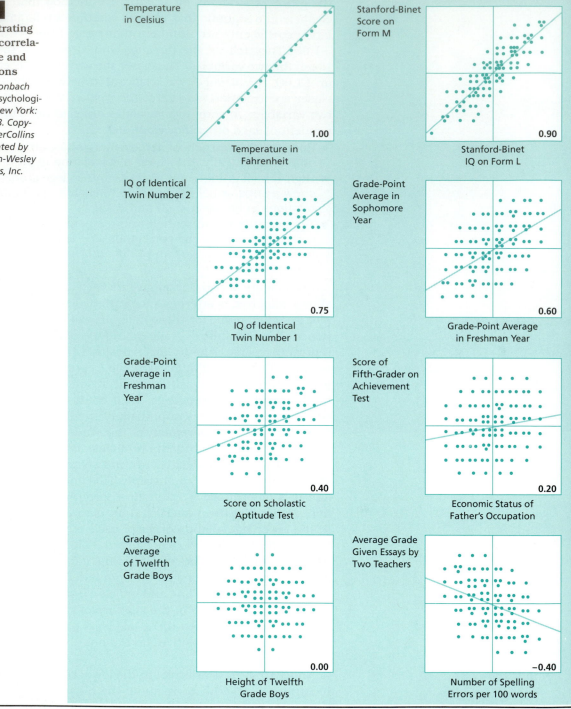

students' higher rates of spelling errors tend to go along with lower grades for those students on essay assignments, and classes with lower average family incomes tend to have higher rates of absence.

Coefficients of correlation are one of the most important tools of the social sciences. Correlations, said the father of American educational psychology, E. L. Thorndike, "are destined to play somewhat the part in the social sciences that equations do in physics, chemistry, and engineering" (1939, p. 42).

Methods for Determining Causal Relationships As noted above, to determine whether changes in one variable cause changes in another, we should, if possible, conduct an experiment. For example, suppose we give each of four groups of students a different explanation of the same subject matter—say, the addition of simple fractions—and suppose we then measure understanding with a test. We would be conducting an experiment. We have manipulated one variable (type of explanation) and have measured the values of another variable (amount of understanding). If the test scores of the four groups have different average values corresponding to changes in the type of explanation, we can infer that the differences in the independent variable (type of explanation) caused the average differences in the dependent variable (understanding).

Random assignment is important in experiments in the social and behavioral sciences and education. This means assigning students, classes, schools, or whatever, randomly to the different treatments we are studying. We do this to balance out the groups so that none is likely to have an initial advantage over the others. Random assignment tends to balance out, from one group to another, all the variables (such as age, sex, cognitive ability, social class, and beginning achievement) that could affect our experiment. Unless we balance things out, we may infer a causal relationship that does not really exist; the differences among scores might be due to differences in one of the variables we failed to balance out.

Implementation is also important. This means trying to make sure, perhaps through observation, that the independent variable is actually used (implemented) as it should be. If the experiment concerns teaching practices, does the experimental group of teachers actually use the practices recommended? Does the control group use them much less? We try to observe both groups of teachers before and after we manipulate the teacher training intended to give the experimental group understanding of and practice in using the recommended ways of teaching. With proper design we try to control all the factors that might mislead us in our search for causal relationships.

Statistical analysis follows the collection of data. In most experiments we use statistical analysis to obtain estimates of whether our findings—differences on the dependent variable—are **statistically significant,** that is, so large as to reflect a *probably nonchance* difference between the experimental and control groups on the dependent variable. If the differences are not very large, or if they are so small as to be easily due to chance, they are called *statistically nonsignificant.* When statistics tell us that the findings are statistically significant (that something besides chance is at work), we can say that a causal relationship is probably operating. We say this with more or less confidence, depending on the size of the groups studied as well as the size of the difference between the groups on the dependent variable.

Even more valuable than knowing the statistical significance of the result is knowing the size of the difference (Cohen, 1994). For this purpose, measures of **effect size** are used. They are independent of the units of measurement. This means that the results of experiments by different researchers are comparable even if they used different achievement tests (tests with 10, 50, or 500 questions) or different kinds of scores. Effect size can tell how much larger (or smaller) than the average of the control group is the average of the experimental group. For example, we might state the effect size of an experiment as follows: "The average of the experimental group fell at the 73rd percentile rank of the scores of the control group. That is, the average member of the experimental group was higher on the test than 73 percent of the members of the control group."

Experimental methods in educational psychology, like those in any science, require technical ability and artistry. Good experiments, those that allow for clear causal interpretations, are less common than we would like. Nevertheless, when random assignment, good implementation, and appropriate statistical analysis are used, the findings are likely to be trustworthy. Educational psychology, active for a century now in promoting the use of scientific methods in the study of education, has accumulated much trustworthy knowledge that can be used to help explain, predict, and control (improve) educational processes (Berliner & Calfee, 1996).

Qualitative Research: Interpretive Methods

Qualitative research, the rich, field-based description of events, sometimes uses correlational and experimental methods, but this kind of research looks for something different. It tries to understand the meaning of relationships to the people involved, to describe the many interacting forces at work, to look at relationships from the perspective of the participants themselves—of say, teachers and their students.

Imagine you are a researcher observing a class in the Southwest. The teacher asks the students—a group of American Indian children—several questions and gets no answers. If you are a qualitative researcher, it is not enough to report these facts. You want to understand the relationships at work here. Does the teacher feel he is a failure? Does he feel frustrated? Does he think the students are rude or ignorant? And what about the students? Are they confused by someone who asks questions to which he already has the answers, something no one in the students' community would do? Are they confused by a situation that asks them to violate their family and neighborhood customs by showing off (if they give the correct answer) or by shaming themselves (if they give the wrong answer)?

This interpretive approach—developed originally by anthropologists—is most useful when it is important to understand local conditions rather than state or national trends. The method would be helpful for studying the meaning of teacher dissatisfaction in a particular school, for example, but not the problems of teacher dissatisfaction throughout the profession. The interpretive approach is also useful for understanding a one-time event, say a teachers' strike in a particular city, or for understanding a complex situation, such as how a change in the enrollment boundaries of a school affects student achievement, teachers' expectations, parents' views of the school, resale values of homes in the area, and administrators' roles.

Both the quantitative and the qualitative styles of research try to make sense of some phenomenon. But their users approach their goal with different questions, different ways of collecting data, and even different beliefs about what it means to make sense of a phenomenon. The two approaches should be regarded as complementary, not competitive. Each has advantages and disadvantages.

Replication and Meta-Analysis

How many replications of the study of the correlation between class size and student achievement have been performed? You can find out by looking into ERIC (Educational Research Information Center).

People in all of the sciences are skeptical about the results of any single investigation. They do not really believe those results until researchers have confirmed the results by a repetition, or **replication,** of the study. And often some of their skepticism remains until there have been many replications.

How do we synthesize the findings of many different studies of the same relationship? Certainly we must read each study and summarize its results. With many replications—many studies of the same phenomenon—however, it becomes difficult to keep all the results straight and then to form a valid impression of what they mean. It is like trying to remember the exam scores of thirty students; the numbers begin to blur.

For this reason, statisticians, especially Glass (1976), invented what is called **meta-analysis,** the quantitative synthesis of results, usually by averaging the results, across replications. Meta-analysis is applied to the many studies of the same relationship, either correlational or causal. Throughout this text, we describe the results of meta-analyses of various sets of replications. For example, in Chapter 11, we discuss a meta-analysis of many experiments on whether homework improves achievement (Cooper, 1989a). Such meta-analyses give us a better way of estimating the relationship between two variables because they summarize results across many different studies, making more intelligible the results of a number of replications.

Using Research to Guide Practice

Throughout the book, we will be telling you about many relationships between variables—between cognitive ability and achievement, between gender and interests, between age and personal concerns, between so-

Teaching is an opportunity for shared learning experiences and discoveries. One goal of qualitative research is to understand the personal meanings of an event.

(© Susan Lapides)

cial class and aspirations, between teaching practices and achievement, between testing methods and fairness. What should you do with this information, especially the information that implies what you should do as a teacher?

The relationships we describe are never perfect. That is, there are always exceptions to these relationships, to the trends that less than perfect correlations describe. For example, in the area of health, the relationships between diet and cancer, and between cholesterol level and heart disease, are far from perfect, that is, far from correlations of $+1.00$ or -1.00. The same is true of relationships between teaching practices and student achievement. What the teacher and the physician can do with their knowledge about relationships is fairly similar. They can use this knowledge "reflectively"—think about it, take other factors into account, weigh the costs and benefits of any course of action, try to estimate the likelihood of exceptions to the trend, and keep in mind the usefulness and the inadequacies of the knowledge the scientific method has yielded (Gage & Berliner, 1989).

Some people react to the imperfections of scientific knowledge in the social sciences, including educational psychology, by rejecting outright the whole idea that teaching can benefit from this kind of knowledge. Our own position, however, is the same as that of the famous American philosopher Josiah Royce (1891):

> It is vain that the inadequacy of science is made a sufficient excuse for knowing nothing of it. The more inadequate science is when [used] alone, the more need of using it as a beginning when we set about our task. . . . Instinct needs science, not as a substitute but as a partial support. . . . When you teach, you must know when to forget formulas, but you must have learned them in order to be able to forget them.

By *instinct,* Royce meant our natural impulses and common sense. By *forget,* he meant knowing when to make exceptions to what is implied by statistical trends. Sometimes we should make exceptions; sometimes we should not. The art of teaching is in knowing, with the scientific knowledge that educational psychology provides, when to make exceptions.

Research in the social and behavioral sciences, including educational psychology, is often of high quality. Despite popular belief to the contrary, the consistency of results of such research compares favorably with that in some important areas of the physical sciences (Hedges, 1987). The relationships between variables are often even stronger than those on which some important medical practices are based (Gage, 1996).

Nonetheless, classrooms and other social systems are less consistently uniform than the things studied in the physical sciences. Thus, when A causes B in a physics experiment in Switzerland, it also does so in Kansas City. We cannot be sure, however, that the relationship between C and D in classrooms in suburban San Francisco holds in urban Houston. It might. It is probably a good bet, especially if the relationship has been found in many replications in many settings and summarized through meta-analysis. Certainly the research finding is worth taking seriously. But it does not provide us with as much confidence as an engineer has, from one setting to another, in applying the findings about, say, the weight-bearing strength of concrete or the lubricating efficacy of oil.

As someone who cares about education and who may be planning to make it a profession, you should take seriously the research findings presented throughout this book. But at the same time you, and officials who evaluate teachers, should be wary of becoming overzealous about these findings. We need to avoid turning findings worthy of reflection into rules that must be obeyed. Research findings should be used to guide thinking about teaching; they should not be used to dictate ac-

Can you think of good reasons to make an exception to some desirable policy or practice?

tion. Sometimes the simple, straightforward implication of a relationship between, say, teaching practice *A* and wanted outcome *B* should be followed. But often it should not. Knowing the difference is what distinguishes the wise and effective teacher from the rest.

SUMMARY

1. Educational psychology uses scientific method, but it is not often the basis for inflexible prescriptions or rules. Its major purpose is to provide information to help teachers and other educators make wiser decisions.

2. Educational psychology, like the other social sciences, is often criticized for finding only the obvious. But close examination reveals that intelligent judges tend to regard as obvious even the opposite of actual research results.

3. The concepts, or variables, that we study are aspects of our behavior and mental processes as we teach and learn. Their meaning, boundaries, and relationships are defined by our experience and knowledge. Some are alterable; others are not. But all have a relationship to how we teach and how our students learn.

4. The principles derived from the study of educational psychology depend on the application of scientific methods to determine relationships between concepts. Principles help us explain, predict, and control the phenomena of teaching and learning. Explanation depends on a logical relationship between variables; prediction, on a temporal relationship; control, on a causal relationship.

5. To move toward these goals, to uncover the relationships between variables, we use three methods—correlation, experimentation, and qualitative research (primarily interpretive inquiry).

6. Correlation tells us that certain values of one variable tend to be found with certain values of another variable. It does not tell us whether the values of the first variable cause or determine the values of the second; that is, it does not show cause and effect. Correlation, then, helps us to describe relationships between variables but not necessarily to explain or control them.

7. Experimentation allows us to determine logical, time, and, most important, causal relationships. In an experiment, we manipulate an independent variable, then measure the values of a dependent variable. If those values have changed, we can, under the right conditions, conclude that the change in the independent variable caused the change. The right conditions include random assignment (which balances out many other characteristics of the individuals in the two or more groups being studied in the experiment), sound experimental design, and valid statistical analysis.

8. Qualitative research, the third method we use to determine relationships between variables, often rests on interpretive inquiry. It is not enough to simply observe and record an event. In interpretive work the researcher must look deeper and attempt to describe the many relationships at work and the feelings of the people involved.

9. The development of educational principles does not stop with one correlation, one experiment, or one interpretation. The skepticism inherent in science demands replication (another trial to see if the same results are obtained, then another, etc.) and meta-analysis (a synthesis of the findings of the various similar studies). What we end up with is reasonably trustworthy information. It is simply the best information available about teaching and learning that we have, even if it is not 100 percent guaranteed to work in your classroom as it did in the classrooms that were the subjects of the original studies.

10. It is important to realize that the principles of educational psychology are just that, principles. They are guidelines with which to work, not hard-and-fast rules. It is critically important to understand them; it is just as important to know when—and when not—to follow their implications.

The Tasks, Standards, and Objectives of Teaching

Overview

WHAT ARE THE MAJOR TASKS OF TEACHING?

WHY DO WE NEED STANDARDS AND OBJECTIVES?

HOW STANDARDS-BASED REFORM HAS AFFECTED OBJECTIVES

THE CONTENT OF INSTRUCTION

 Decision Making at the National, State, and Local Levels

 The Teacher's Role in Determining Content

 The Students' Role in Determining Content

THINKING ABOUT OBJECTIVES IN TERMS OF STUDENT PERFORMANCE

 General Objectives

 Specific Objectives

POLICY, RESEARCH, AND PRACTICE

 Is It Preferable to Use Specific or General Objectives in Order to Facilitate Learning?

APPLICATION

 Formulating Your Own Objectives

CLASSIFYING OBJECTIVES

 Identifying Three Domains

 Focus on the Cognitive Domain

POLICY, RESEARCH, AND PRACTICE

 The Knowledge versus Intellectual Skills Debate

THE PERFORMANCE-CONTENT MATRIX

 Summary

OVERVIEW

What does a teacher do? One answer lists five tasks: (1) choose *objectives* (2) in the light of an understanding of your *students* and (3) with an understanding of their *development and learning processes,* then (4) select and use *ways of teaching,* and finally, (5) evaluate your *students' achievement* as a basis for beginning the process all over again, either with the same students or a new group.

This chapter first shows how later text will help you prepare for these tasks. Then it goes into questions related to choosing objectives—the content and performances you want your students to achieve. That is, what information, knowledge, content, concepts, principles, themes, and so on, do you want them to learn? And how should they be able to perform (think, feel, move) in relation to that content after you have taught?

Notice the two parts of what teachers teach, namely, content and performance. **Content** refers to domains like reading, English, mathematics, history, art, physical education, and science. And within each of these, content also includes enormous numbers of subtopics and sub-subtopics. **Performance** refers to what you want students to be able to do with content, such as remember, comprehend, analyze, and solve problems. Or, in terms of emotions, you may want students to enjoy or appreciate content. Or, focusing on movement, you may want them to be able to play an instrument or dance a certain step.

Content and performance deal with curriculum and educational objectives. A curriculum can be a whole set of courses, or what is taught within a single course. An objective is a wanted outcome. Near synonyms include standard, goal, aim, purpose, end performance, or intention. Learning can occur just from daily life, of course. But formal teaching means someone has an "objective." We usually use the term *objective* because it is widely accepted as a technical term in education.

Behind all teaching is the question, "What do you want students to learn?" So, logically, a statement of curriculum and objectives is the first step in the educational process. Whatever the scope in question—a nation's or state's educational system, a school's curriculum, a single course, a class session, or a one-minute explanation—it is necessary to decide, early, on what *content* to teach and what *performances* students should become capable of.

Content and performance standards are what nations and groups of professional educators worry about. Content and performance objectives are what teachers worry about. Although the specificity may differ (more general for a nation, more specific for a teacher), both nations and teachers need such goals.

So we talk about choosing objectives, the most effective ways to state objectives, how objectives are classified, and how objectives are developed in one of these classifications—the cognitive domain. Finally, we provide a tool—the performance-content matrix—for organizing ideas about objectives.

What Are the Major Tasks of Teaching?

The instructional process involves five primary tasks:

1. Choosing objectives (content and performances)
2. Understanding student characteristics
3. Understanding and using ideas about the nature of learning and motivation
4. Selecting and using ways of teaching (methods and practices)
5. Evaluating student learning

It is helpful to think of each task as a set of problems for both teachers and their students. Educational psychology can help teachers make wiser decisions as they formulate solutions. Figure 2.1 shows how these five tasks (and problems) relate to the chapters of this book. The model applies equally well to a day's or a year's instruction. Although we present the tasks as a chronological list, the instructional process is actu-

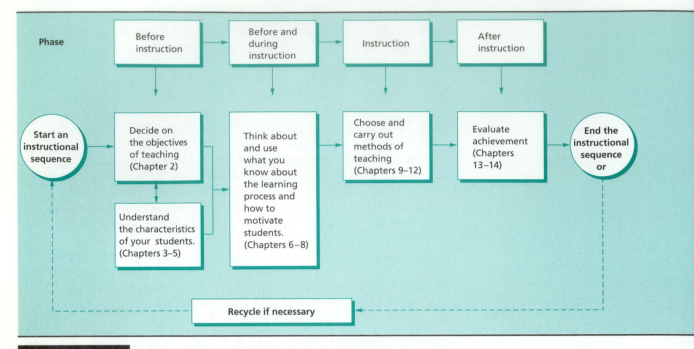

Phase

Before instruction → Before and during instruction → Instruction → After instruction

Start an instructional sequence → Decide on the objectives of teaching (Chapter 2) → Think about and use what you know about the learning process and how to motivate students. (Chapters 6–8) → Choose and carry out methods of teaching (Chapters 9–12) → Evaluate achievement (Chapters 13–14) → End the instructional sequence or

Understand the characteristics of your students. (Chapters 3–5)

Recycle if necessary

FIGURE 2.1

A model of the instructional process, showing how the sections of this book fit the model

ally a *cycle*, which goes back and forth between these tasks. According to the model,

1. The teacher begins with some idea of *objectives* concerning the content that students should be helped to learn and the performances they should be helped to acquire for that content.

2. In choosing objectives, the teacher uses information about the important *characteristics of the students.* As Figure 2.1 shows, Tasks 1 and 2 occur simultaneously, and interact. You need to understand your students' stage of development and their abilities, strengths, and weaknesses. In the students' words, "The teacher should know us and then treat us appropriately. For example, she should realize how much we do (and don't) know."

3. Next the teacher must understand *learning and motivation* so as to understand and choose teaching methods and practices that fit what is known about students' learning and motivation. Teachers can apply knowledge about learning and motivation both before and during instruction.

4. After all the preinstructional decisions, the teacher selects and uses *teaching methods and practices,* such as lecturing, explaining, discussing, showing movies or videotapes, tutoring, providing computer-assisted instruction, leaving students alone, or some combination of these activities.

5. Both throughout the process and usually at the end of a cycle the teacher *assesses* students' achievement of educational objectives. Students need to be told when they are (or are not) doing a good job. They need guidance on how to improve, for example, by being told to check their comprehension by putting an idea into their own words. Students demand fairness in how they are assessed and graded.

If assessment shows that students have achieved the objectives, the teacher can go on to new objectives. But if assessment reveals that some or all of the students have not learned the content and performances that were taught, the teacher will need to reflect on why and adjust instruction accordingly. Remember that the process is a cycle; "recycling" is expected.

Why Do We Need Standards and Objectives?

People involved in all kinds of educational tasks—not only teaching but also curriculum designing and achievement testing—insist that statements of standards and objectives are helpful, even essential. Unless they think about objectives, teachers tend to focus primarily on the *content* of instruction classroom activities and ignore how students should learn to *perform* with that content.

Think about your own experiences as a student. Have you ever wished a teacher had told you more clearly what you should have been learning and why? Without the teacher's focus on students' performance goals, students often assume that they need only to remember content. A history teacher, for example, may want students to be able to see connections between historical and present-day events. But if the teacher does not explain this intention to the students, they may assume that they should simply remember what they read rather than trying to look at contemporary problems in historical perspective.

Objectives can apply to education as a whole or only to teaching. Many educational objectives—self-fulfillment, appreciation of the nature of a good life, love of knowledge—are broader than any single teacher can hope to achieve. In this chapter we focus on the objectives of teaching—what *you* as a teacher want your students to achieve as a result of your efforts. We will focus on objectives in content-general terms, ways that cut across subject matters and can also be used in thinking in content-specific terms, that is, in reading, mathematics, physical education, or any other content area.

How Standards-Based Reform Has Affected Objectives

In recent years critics of American education have argued that the achievement of U.S. students falls below that of students in other countries with which the nation must compete economically. These critics place much of the blame for these shortcomings on what they consider to be the inadequate standards of achievement set by American educators.

So a new focus on **educational standards** has motivated educators to reexamine the ways in which objectives are formed and used. This focus has led to the standards-based reform movement (O'Day & Smith, 1993) and the development of new curriculum standards in various subject-matter fields. The standards emerging from educators and professional organizations in art, social studies, mathematics, and other professions, which are intended to guide our states, districts, and teachers, set forth the contents and performances considered most important. For example, for mathematics, science, and social studies, respectively, the National Council of Teachers of Mathematics (1989), the National Research Council (1996), and the National Center for History in the Schools (1994) have each issued content standards. Table 2.1 presents sample standards from each of their lists.

We provide this information about the use of standards in educational reform because it is receiving considerable attention. The question is whether these statements of standards and objectives will improve education across the country. However, we must add an important caution. Not everyone in education believes that all the criticisms of American schooling are justified; Berliner and Biddle (1995), among others, have challenged the validity of many of the test results and assumptions on which the criticisms are based.

The same educators point to the importance of opportunity-to-learn standards as well as content and performance standards (Berliner & Biddle, 1996). Opportunity-to-learn standards have to do with the quality of educational resources provided—the teachers available, the amount of time available for learning, the availability of computers for learning, and all the other characteristics of schooling that provide students with the opportunity to meet the standards and achieve the objectives. If

> Look at a national curriculum statement in a content field of interest to you. What is it like?

2.1

Sample National Standards in Mathematics, Science, and History

Mathematics

Curriculum and Evaluation Standards for School Mathematics
[Dates given in reference at end of table.]

Part of Standard 1: Mathematics as Problem Solving

In grades K–4, the study of mathematics should emphasize problem solving so that students can

- use problem-solving approaches to investigate and understand mathematical content;
- formulate problems from everyday and mathematical situations;
- develop and apply strategies to solve a wide variety of problems; . . .

Science

National Science Education Standards

A sample from the secondary-school content standards
Content Standard A: In grades 9–12, all students should develop

- Abilities necessary to do scientific inquiry
  —Identify questions and concepts that guide scientific investigation. . . .
  —Design and conduct scientific investigations. . . .
- Understandings about scientific inquiry. . . .

Physical Science Content Standard B: In grades 9–12, all students should develop an understanding of

- structure of atoms
- structure and properties of matter
- chemical reactions
- motions and forces
- conservation of energy and increase in disorder
- interactions of energy and matter

History

National Standards for United States History

An example of these standards refers to the American Revolution:
Standard 1

- Students should understand
  —the causes of the American Revolution, the ideas and interests involved in forging the revolutionary movement, and the reasons for the American victory.
- Students should be able to
  1A Demonstrate understanding of the causes of the American Revolution by
  —explaining the consequences of the Seven Years' War and the overhaul of English imperial policy following the Treaty of Paris in 1763, demonstrating the connections between the antecedent and consequent events. [Marshal evidence of antecedent circumstances]

From National Council of Teachers of Mathematics (1989, p. 23); National Research Council (1996, pp. 173, 175, 176); National Center for History in the Schools (1994, p. 10).

How do these statements of standards fit in with your knowledge about the schools you went to? Are they specific enough to help teachers?

those opportunities to learn are not equal for all of America's children, then school improvement through standards-based reform may occur only in the schools that can afford to implement the opportunity-to-learn standards. Children attending schools in poorer districts may have trouble meeting the new national content and performance standards.

The Content of Instruction

Let us look at approaches to the *content* that students should be helped to learn. In a later section, we deal with the *performances* students should be helped to acquire for that content.

American school systems do not give teachers a free hand in determining the content to be taught. The whole society takes part in deciding what is taught (and, sometimes, how it is taught) in the public schools. Curriculum policy is made at many levels.

Decision Making at the National, State, and Local Levels

At the national level, Congress and its committees on education, as well as the executive branch's Department of Education and National Science Foundation, exert great influence. They support standards and curriculum development in the natural sciences, mathematics, foreign languages, and early-childhood education, among other fields. Textbook publishers and national testing agencies also influence curriculum. Foundations, organized labor, and business corporations support or oppose trends in curriculum. And national professional organizations, such as the Association for Supervision and Curriculum Development, continually debate curriculum issues.

At the state and local levels, state legislatures, departments of education, accrediting associations, and subject-matter associations affect the curriculum. Within cities and counties, the school board, the superintendent, the principal, and sometimes the school's department chairpersons, along with various city or county associations of educators, have an effect. And the American political system permits, even encourages, local citizens' organizations, conservative and liberal, through their influence on elected and appointed officials, to try to shape what is taught in the classroom. On the question of what we should teach our children, everyone has an opinion!

The Teacher's Role in Determining Content

The curriculum handed down from "above" has seldom been so specific as to spell out all the details of how the content should be formulated, what emphases should be given to its various topics, what learning tasks should be set, and what performances should be acquired. No two teachers ever teach the same "handed-down" curriculum in exactly the same way; the teacher has plenty of room to use judgment in filling in the specific details. So some educators (e.g., Clandinin & Connelly, 1992) argue against seeing the teacher as a mere conduit who transmits curriculum without influencing it. Others, such as Hirsch (1996), call for greater specificity and uniformity of content within each grade level. In any case, the teacher is inevitably a curriculum *maker* whose own content knowledge, sense of what is important, ideas about students and teaching, and capabilities as a teacher have an effect on what is taught.

The textbook is obviously one major way in which the curriculum is determined. Sometimes teachers can help in textbook choice, and when they do, they act as curriculum makers. But even when they do not, they still make curriculum by using the textbook in different ways (Doyle, 1992). They differ in how they use time; emphasize various topics; employ practice materials, the textbook's various chapters, and the teacher's guide; arrange discussions; ask (or avoid) questions during discussions; and in many other ways.

So even when the teacher's choice of content is heavily influenced by the textbook and the textbook was chosen by others, the teacher has many content-related decisions to make. Some of those decisions may be made unconsciously, in the sense that the teacher is acting on deep-rooted preferences, of which he or she may be unaware. Sometimes the choices are philosophical, in the sense that they come from the teacher's convictions about the purposes of education and the nature of the good life and the good society, to which education should contribute.

At the same time, the teacher's decisions about and choices of content will often be guided by the concerns of educational psychology. Some psychological guidelines are as follows:

> Think of one teacher you remember favorably. To what extent did he or she stick to a textbook? Do you wish that extent had been different? Why?

1. *Appropriateness in difficulty.* The content's difficulty should be appropriate to the students' ability, maturity, and level of background knowledge, so that the teacher does not demand more (or less) than they are capable of learning at their level.

Teachers too often expect too little of their students, particularly poor and minority students, and underestimate what they are capable of learning. And much research (e.g., Dusek, 1985) demonstrates that teachers' expectations, both positive and negative, affect students' achievement. (You will find a good deal of what psychology offers for understanding student ability and developmental level in later chapters, especially Chapters 3, 4, and 5.)

2. *Appropriateness to learning processes.* What we know about the various ways in which learning can take place (as set forth especially in Chapters 6 and 7) should be used to choose and shape the content. Such knowledge helps a teacher to avoid content that conflicts with natural learning processes, and can be used to help students use those processes to foster achievement.

3. *Appropriateness to students' motivations.* Content should be chosen in the light of students' motivations. Motivations include interests, appreciations, aspirations, and ambitions, and all of them affect learning. So understandings about motivation (discussed especially in Chapter 8) should provide bases for the decisions teachers must make in choosing content (and methods of teaching) that will engage their students.

4. *Appropriateness to teaching methods.* Choices of content depend in part on what teaching methods and practices are feasible. Some kinds of content are better taught to some students, in some situations, by one kind of teaching—a lecture, cooperative learning, or

a hands-on exercise—rather than another. In turn, some kinds of teaching are more feasible than others. (Chapters 9 to 12 treat these critical factors.)

5. *Appropriateness to assessment.* Finally, choices of content may be influenced by what educational psychology says about ways of assessing student achievement. Achievement can be measured in many different ways, ranging from multiple-choice tests to portfolios containing products of student work. Good assessment practices are themselves determined by psychologically sound ideas about the nature of desirable achievement, so they are tied closely to the teacher's content decisions.

All five factors will help you as a classroom teacher to determine what content to teach. The best thinking and experience of those who focus primarily on what should be taught—curriculum specialists, textbook authors, committees of teachers, and many others—do not exempt you, the individual teacher, from thinking about content choice.

The Students' Role in Determining Content

Sometimes it is possible and desirable to give students a voice in determining content, with a gain in student interest and without sacrificing the integrity of objectives. If a film (e.g., *Nixon*) might serve as well as or better than a textbook chapter as a basis for discussing political lawlessness and impeachment, give students that choice. If students can use paper squares rather than a drawing to demonstrate the Pythagorean theorem, let them choose. The possibilities are endless.

Some educational philosophers (progressive and open educators) have argued for giving students a strong role in choosing content. Students should often be able to choose among topics for essays, designs for posters, novels for independent reading, laboratory exercises on a scientific phenomenon, or ways of studying how newspapers treat opposing politicians.

But the students' role must be balanced against society's standards. Students should not be given a choice as to whether they will learn to read (a choice A. S. Neill, 1960, advocated), or do arithmetic, or understand government at their level. Such "freedoms" might eventually deprive students of more important freedoms (e.g., to participate in their society).

Thinking about Objectives in Terms of Student Performance

Statements of objectives act as maps guiding teacher and students. To find a city, we do not need a road map that specifies every village and creek; in fact, such specificity could get in the way. But to find a house, we need a street map. Similarly, in teaching we may need general or specific objectives, or both.

General Objectives

No teacher should be required to base instruction on the hundreds of objectives and subobjectives that could be specified for a unit of instruction. General objectives can describe the broad outlines of what students should achieve in a given content area.

Objectives in any content area can be visualized as forming a pyramid. At the apex is a single term (reading, algebra, world history). Just below that are various divisions of that area (in reading: decoding skills, word identification, etc.; in algebra: understanding the equation principle, etc.; in world history: political, cultural). Below that level, still more specific subdivisions can be identified (in decoding skills: pronouncing vowels; in equations: linear and quadratic equations; in cultural history: a day in the life of ancient Rome, etc.). The specification can go on indefinitely.

But where to draw the line? The teacher, using objectives as a road map, must decide. It depends on how well the teacher knows the "territory." When teaching content for the first time, the teacher may need much specificity, just as the newcomer to a state needs both a state road map and a town's street map. But the teacher (traveler) who has taught the content before (knows the state) may need only specific objectives (a street map) to find his or her way. And the veteran needs neither objectives nor maps.

For most teachers, as they gain experience the amount of specificity they need diminishes. But beginners may need specific reminders.

Specific Objectives

Within each of the general objectives, teachers may have to develop more specific objectives. When doing so, they find the advice of Mager (1975) useful.

1. *State objectives in terms of performances*—what teachers can see or hear students do once they have learned. Performances include mental processes—ways of thinking and feeling, and evidence of these ways in the form of products such as what students have done, said, written, enacted, drawn, or built. For instance, a general objective for students reading this book might be "understanding educational psychology." To state part of the objective in terms of performances, we could state that students should "be able to grasp the significance of empirical methods in education." Or that students should "know and appreciate the concepts and principles of educational psychology." But we must then spell out how students should be able to *perform* when they "understand," "grasp significance," "know," or "appreciate."

Think of the objective as stating the **terminal performance**—what the student will be able to do at the end of instruction. We specify performances more when we say that students should be able to

- differentiate among the correlational, experimental, and interpretive methods in educational psychology (Chapter 1).

POLICY, RESEARCH, AND PRACTICE

Is It Preferable to Use Specific or General Objectives in Order to Facilitate Learning?

A LOOK INSIDE THE CLASSROOM

It is 3:20 and her last student has just rushed back in and out for a forgotten glove. The room is quiet for the first time in seven hours. Ms. Jacobsen settles in at her desk and immediately opens her plan book. Whenever possible, she likes to spend some time at the end of each day looking ahead to the next day's lessons. Based on the way the day has just gone, there are almost always adjustments to make to the original plans. When she is about through, she looks up to see a new teacher, Mr. Gould, standing in her doorway. She invites him to pull up a chair; as they chat, the new teacher's eyes fall on the open planning book. He can't help but notice how different it looks from his own. He decides to ask Ms. Jacobsen a direct question about planning, particularly about using objectives. "Do you think the kinds of specific objectives we all learned about in college really help? I mean, don't you think they can be too restricting? I'm still trying to work this out." Ms. Jacobsen explains that she is a great advocate of using specific performance objectives, emending the district-wide objectives and tailoring them to her own class's needs. She believes that, by telling students what they should learn, the specifically worded objectives help students achieve those objectives. Is she right, or does Mr. Gould have a point?

A LOOK AT THE RESEARCH

How can research help us answer this question? Klauer (1984) analyzed 23 studies involving 52 comparisons between (a) students given specific objectives, learning directions, or questions before reading an instructional text and (b) students who did not receive these guides. He found that students who received objectives tended to learn more of the relevant material—that is, material related to the stated objectives—but they learned less of the material not relevant to the objectives. Apparently giving students instructional goals and objectives influences their intentions; it directs their attention to those parts of the material that are most related to achieving the stated goals and objectives. However, it is also true that students do pick up a considerable amount of incidental information, even when guided by specific objectives. Another reviewer independently reached the same conclusions (Hamilton, 1985).

MULTIPLE PERSPECTIVES 1

These quotations and visual representations are selected from many sources to encourage your further thought about the content in this text. Most quotations cast multifaceted reflections on the entire teaching and learning process discussed in chapters throughout the book. We direct your attention intermittently to specific chapters having direct bearing on a particular quotation. We selected quotations from educators, philosophers, scientists, and poets—underscoring the point that serious thought about education comes from multiple perspectives. For complete sources of these quotations, see the author-reference index at the end of this book.

"Education is a kind of continuous dialog, and a dialog assumes . . . different points of view."

Robert M. Hutchins, Chancellor, University of Chicago, *Time*, December 8, 1952.

How should we learn?

Critical thinking

Academic knowledge

Pro   **Con**

"Our public education system has not successfully made the shift from teaching the memorization of facts to achieving the learning of critical thinking skills."

John Sculley, 1989.

"Street-smart children in the Bronx and elsewhere demonstrate outside school that they already possess higher-order thinking skills . . . what these students lack is not critical thinking but academic knowledge."

E. D. Hirsch, *International Herald Tribune*, September 8, 1993.

"To be literate is to undertake dialogue with others who speak from different histories, locations and experiences. Literacy is a discursive practice in which difference becomes crucial for understanding not simply how to read and write . . . but also to recognize that the identities of "others" matter as part of a broader set of policies and practices aimed at reconstruction of democratic life.**"**

Paolo Freire and Donaldo Macado, *Literacy: Reading and the World.*

"Any educator that aims at completeness must be at once theoretical and practical, intellectual and moral."

Aldous Huxley, *Words and Their Meaning*, 1940.

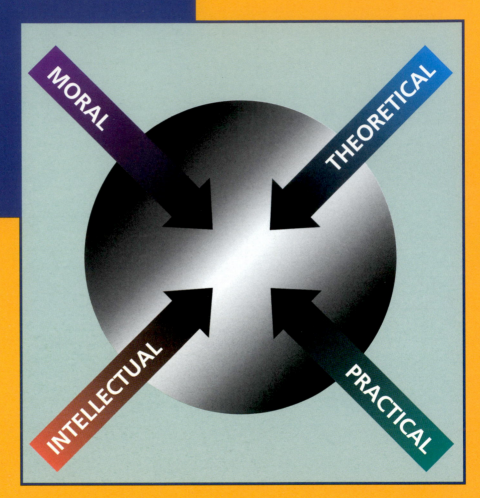

MORAL

THEORETICAL

INTELLECTUAL

PRACTICAL

REFLECTIONS FOR YOUR OWN CLASSROOM

What can you learn from the questions the two teachers were discussing and from the research findings? Perhaps the most important point is that it is a good idea to provide students, in advance, with instructional objectives or statements about the specific objectives of learning when the goal is focused, targeted learning—whether this learning be from the text students are using or from lectures, discussions, and other oral forms of instruction. However, at the same time, you should bear in mind that when you give students specific information about what you want them to learn—while it is likely to improve that particular learning—it may also detract from their learning about things you have not defined. Thus, in situations in which you want them to pick up more incidental information or when general enrichment is the goal, you should use objectives that are more general.

- give original examples of situations calling for general only and for both general and specific objectives (Chapter 2).
- make up a 10-item multiple-choice test (following procedures described in Chapter 14).

Each of these objectives is more precise than general objectives that merely use words like *understand* or *appreciate*. Differentiating, *describ-*

It is more respectful to let students know what they should be learning.

(© Suzanne Szasz)

ing, and *making up original examples* tell us what performance to look for and describe terminal performances clearly and explicitly.

2. *State conditions of performance*—the situation or setting in which the student should be able to perform. That is, simple statements of wanted performance may not be enough. Often we should also specify the important conditions under which the performance is expected to occur. For example, suppose our objective is, "Students should be able to contrast the correlational and experimental methods of research." We might want to add to it such *conditions* as "using provided (or student-identified) examples of actual research articles"; "with or without class notes (or the text)"; "at home (or in class)"; "orally (or in writing)."

Wording that informs students about conditions is easy to recognize. For examples, look at Table 2.2. The first phrase or clause of each objective states a condition.

3. *State acceptable levels of performance*—what will be considered adequate achievement. Should you refer to a necessary rate of speed? Should students be able to solve only one type of problem? or three? or four out of six? questions in only one form? in several forms? That is, how can you make clear to the student what you will consider to be the standard for judging the learning to be a success?

For example, it may not be enough to say, "Students should recognize the writing style of Ernest Hemingway." It might be better to say, "Given ten pairs of short prose passages, each pair having one selection by Ernest Hemingway and one by a different author, students should be able

TABLE 2.2

Examples of Teaching Objectives

Government. When given a series of instances of government activities, the student should be able to identify the instance as the proper interest of the legislative, judicial, or executive branch of government. (8 out of 10 correct)

Economics. Using no references, the student should be able to write five ways in which socialist and capitalist countries are alike and five ways in which they differ.

Statistics. Without notes, the student should be able to recall, without error, the formula for computing the rank-difference correlation coefficient.

Music. Given the name of a note and the scale, a member of the chorus should be able to sing the note accurately 9 out of 10 times.

Physical Education. On a level surface, the student should be able to do 30 push ups in three minutes.

Arithmetic. Given an electronic calculator, the student should be able to call out the answers to 100 percent of the multiplication and division items containing numbers up to seven digits.

Art. When presented with pairs of paintings, the student should be able to choose the painting of the impressionist period 7 out of 10 times.

Algebra. The student should be able to solve 8 out of 10 quadratic equations of the type $AX^2 + BX + C = 0$, in class without any aids.

Formulating Your Own Objectives

You might want to use the examples provided above and in Table 2.3 on page 45 as a guide to try formulating some of your own objectives. Be sure to keep these criteria in mind:

1. Does the objective describe how students should be able to perform when they have achieved the objective?

2. Does the statement describe the conditions under which you want students to be able to demonstrate their achievement?

3. Does the statement indicate at least the lower limit of what you will consider acceptable performance?

to choose *at least nine of the ten* selections written by Hemingway." Look again at the examples in Table 2.2 and see if you can find the part of each objective statement that expresses the level of performance expected.

To apply and illustrate what we have just said: we could state our objective as, "Given this introduction and one hour's time, you will be able to construct ten objectives in a subject-matter area of your choice, at least eight of which meet the criteria listed above."

Classifying Objectives

What kinds of objectives are there? Educators and psychologists have developed **taxonomies** of objectives. These are classification schemes for making distinctions to help teachers organize their thinking about objectives. They also help in teaching students and evaluating their achievement.

Identifying Three Domains

One major set of distinctions draws upon the differences among cognitive, affective, and psychomotor performances.

1. **Cognitive objectives** (Bloom, Engelhart, Furst, Hill, & Krathwohl, 1956) deal with intellectual processes such as knowing, perceiving, recognizing, thinking, conceiving, judging, and reasoning. When a teacher is concerned about Josh's inability to spell words correctly, she is referring to an objective in the cognitive domain.

2. **Affective objectives** (Krathwohl, Bloom, & Masia, 1964) deal with feelings—likes and dislikes, emotions, attitudes, appreciations, interests, values, and the like. When the teacher worries about Josh's boredom with reading, she is dealing with the affective domain.

3. **Psychomotor objectives** (Harrow, 1972) deal with skilled ways of moving, such as handwriting, typewriting, dancing, and blowing glass for a chemistry experiment.

These three kinds of performance are never *completely* isolated from one another. But it often is useful to focus on one at a time.

Focus on the Cognitive Domain

Because the cognitive-domain taxonomy is the only one that has been widely used and discussed, it is the only one we deal with here. But you might want to look up the taxonomies for the other two domains, particularly if you are to teach art, music, or physical education.

The cognitive taxonomy identifies six major areas within which cognitive objectives can be classified.

1. **Knowledge** is the ability to remember—or recall or recognize—ideas, facts, and the like, in a situation in which certain cues, signals, and clues are given to bring out whatever knowledge has been stored. *Examples:* Students should be able to provide the dates of the last three American wars . . . to name the continents . . . the elements in cooking salt . . . the houses of the U.S. Congress . . . the three components of a performance objective.

2. **Comprehension** is the ability to receive what is being communicated and make use of it, without necessarily relating it to other materials or seeing its implications. This is generally what people mean when they say they "understand" something, although it is a minimal kind of understanding. *Examples:* Students should be able to explain the causes of the Civil War . . . translate a paragraph from Spanish to English . . . give examples of protein-rich and protein-poor foods.

3. **Application** is the ability to use abstractions, rules, principles, ideas, and methods in particular and concrete situations. *Examples:* Students should be able: to use barometers to predict weather . . . to find unknowns in equations . . . to correctly pronounce words of the type consonant-vowel-consonant (*D-O-G*).

4. **Analysis** is the ability to break down some communication into its constituent elements or parts. *Examples:* Students should be able to distinguish between the different parts of a research article . . . compare and contrast the sonnet and limerick . . . distinguish statements of fact from statements of opinion.

5. **Synthesis** is the ability to work with pieces, parts, and elements, combining or putting them together in some way to form a whole or constitute a new pattern or structure. *Examples:* Students should be able to do something unique, such as propose a plan for the governance of the class . . . write a story on their school district's parks and playgrounds . . . combine what they know about adding one-digit numbers with what they know about place value in order to develop skill in the addition of two-digit numbers.

6. **Evaluation** is the ability to make quantitative and qualitative judgments about the extent to which materials and methods satisfy criteria. According to the builders of the taxonomy, this is the highest level of cognitive ability. Examples: Students should be able to judge the merits of a story or play . . . argue the case for or against welfare programs . . . decide whether physical violence is ever justified and, if so, when.

What would you consider to be a *knowledge* objective for a lesson you might teach?

Write a *comprehension* objective for a lesson you might teach.

Are there *application* objectives in a lesson you might teach? Name one and justify it.

What kind of *analysis,* if any, would you aim at teaching your students to be able to do? If there is such an objective for the content you might teach, state it.

What kind of *synthesis* would you try to enable your students to do in a content area you might teach?

Would you ever be interested in having students become able to think evaluatively in a content area you might teach? Give an example.

POLICY, RESEARCH, AND PRACTICE

The Knowledge versus Intellectual Skills Debate

QUESTION: SHOULD SCHOOLS DEEMPHASIZE KNOWLEDGE AND FOCUS ON INTELLECTUAL SKILLS?

Knowledge is often a controversial objective. Some educators and students downplay the value of knowledge of facts, dates, ideas, and formulas, which can always be "looked up." Knowledge is "mere" and "rote." Objectives such as comprehension and analysis are "higher-order"; knowledge seems "lower-order."

PRO KNOWLEDGE

Defenders of knowledge see it as required for the other objectives. Students cannot achieve comprehension, application, synthesis, and so forth in a vacuum. They need the knowledge in order to comprehend, apply, or synthesize the knowledge.

So *domain-specific knowledge* is important. No one can master the applications of mathematics without handling addition, multiplication, and fractions completely automatically. And one can acquire "an intimate and instinctive knowledge of numbers" only by rote (Effros, 1989). Domain-specific knowledge is important for actors (lines), football players (signals), mathematicians (common integrals), and so on.

General knowledge was emphasized by Hirsch (1987) as **cultural literacy:** specific, communally shared information. Although rarely detailed or precise, cultural literacy is needed by every member of a society for participating fully in its affairs. Some examples from Hirsch's 5,000 items, shown below, illustrate his conception of cultural literacy—ideas that people should know about.

Sample Items from Hirsch's List of Things Americans Should Know About: 1492, Archimedes, biofeedback, cabinet (government), composite materials, *Death of a Salesman,* diffraction, Emancipation Proclamation, The grass is always greener on the other side, Grimm brothers, Joshua, *memento mori,* paragraph, relative humidity, Stalinism, V-E Day.

PRO INTELLECTUAL SKILLS

On the other side, educators argue for *higher-order skills* such as (1) critical thinking ("Evaluate Clinton's first administration"), (2) problem solving ("How to save Social Security"), (3) deep understanding ("What forces act on a tossed coin?"), (4) expertise ("French cooking," "hang gliding"), (5) the ability to translate ideas across media ("Convert the words

continues

Can you nominate a few items of knowledge that would be part of cultural literacy in one of your own subcultures? Why these?

into graphs"), and (6) strategies for monitoring one's own learning ("Do I really understand why I carry remainders?").

CAN WE ACHIEVE GENERAL INTELLECTUAL SKILLS?

But note that all the kinds of higher-order skills listed above depend on specific knowledge. They are therefore specific to particular domains. Critical thinkers and problem solvers in one field usually fall short in others. The chess champion may be a duffer in politics; the brilliant logician may be simple-minded about ethics. The reason is that enormous amounts of time are necessary to acquire the knowledge required for expertise in any complex domain (Berliner, 1992, p. 229). Thus it becomes unrealistic to hope for any great accomplishments as a result of general, not-domain-specific training in critical thinking and problem solving. Training that produces good thinkers across many different domains has yet to be validated.

So the problem becomes, Beyond *domain-specific* higher-order cognitive skills, can teachers hope to teach domain-general skills—skills that can be applied across a wide range of domains? If so, the good thinker will be adept in everyday life and also in science, art, literature, politics, and so on. Although this has been a fond hope of teachers for centuries, as yet it remains unrealized.

The Performance-Content Matrix

The definition of objectives should refer to both content and performance. The kinds of content can be stated in highly general terms (American history, general science) or more specific ones (the Bill of Rights in the Constitution, the laws of the lever). The kinds of performance (knowledge, comprehension, evaluation, etc.) are illustrated by the categories of the cognitive taxonomy. You can put **performance-content** combinations into a **matrix,** a gridlike table with rows and columns. An example is shown in Table 2.3.

The performance-content matrix shown in the table has six different performances and three content areas. The performances—listed in the rows—refer to six kinds of cognitive processes: knowledge, comprehension, application, analysis, synthesis, and evaluation. The columns define three content areas: Chapter 1 of this book, the novel *The Sun Also Rises,* and the legislative process of the federal government. The cells of the matrix are filled in with illustrative (but incomplete) objectives.

The rows will be labeled with types of performance, such as the ability to recall, comprehend, apply, analyze, synthesize, or evaluate. The columns will be labeled with categories of content, such as periods of American history, types of national life (political, economic, social), or topics in general science (sound, light, heat). The cells of the matrix, where the rows and columns intersect, specify combinations of perfor-

Can you evaluate any of the cells in Table 2.3? How worthwhile is the objective specified in that cell? Defend your opinion.

TABLE 2.3

A Performance-Content Matrix with Three Examples

Performance	Content		
	Chapter 1 in Educational Psychology	*Hemingway's The Sun Also Rises*	*Legislative Processes of the Federal Government*
Knowledge (to recall, recognize, acquire, identify, define)	Students should be able to define *correlation* and define *negative* and *positive correlation*.	Students should be able to recognize a passage that uses *irony*.	Students should be able to draw a chart of or describe how a bill is voted on in Congress.
Comprehension (to translate, transform, put in own words, rephrase, restate)	Students should be able to interpret the statement that the correlation between high school and freshman college grade-point averages is between .40 and .60.	Students should be able to describe the main idea of the story.	Students should be able to describe the roles of the two houses of Congress.
Application (to generalize, choose, develop, organize, use, transfer, restructure, classify)	Students should be able to use the concept of correlation in interpreting a news item about age differences in science achievement.	Students should be able to write one or two paragraphs about the Vietnam War in Hemingway's style.	Students should be able to write a letter to their congressperson about a current bill, arguing a position in a persuasive manner.
Analysis (to distinguish, detect, classify, disseminate, categorize, deduce, contrast, compare)	Students should be able to distinguish between correlation and causation.	Students should be able to describe the personality flaws in the character of Brett Ashley.	Students should be able to distinguish between Democratic and Republican positions on a bill.
Synthesis (to write, tell, produce, constitute, transmit, originate, design, formulate)	Students should be able to design an experiment identifying the independent and dependent variables.	Students should be able to provide other plausible endings, given the major themes in the story.	Students should be able to describe the arguments of Democrats and Republicans for and against a bill and predict its final form.
Evaluation (to judge, argue, validate, assess, appraise, decide)	Students should be able to describe the weaknesses and advantages of correlational, experimental, and interpretive inquiries.	Students should be able to evaluate the novel, given the author's goal.	Students should be able to evaluate the wisdom of Congress's action on a particular bill.

mance and content. For example: Students should be able to *recall* (performance) the approximate beginning and end years of the precolonial period (content). Or, students should be able to *comprehend* (performance) tables containing statistical data on the growth of the American economy during Reconstruction (content).

By specifying the performance you want from your students and outlining the subject matter you plan to teach, you can develop your own performance-content matrix. Creating a justifiable performance-content matrix can be a challenge. It demands skill, practice, and time. But once developed, a matrix can guide your instructional activities and your students' learning activities. Of equal importance, it can tie instruction to evaluation. If you share the matrix with students, parents, and administrators, and if you build assessment methods tailored to the matrix, you will improve in ratings of fairness by your students.

SUMMARY

1. Before teachers begin to teach, they have to have some idea of what they want to teach. Standards and objectives help to define the instructional program. Objectives of high quality have three characteristics, which describe the end product of instruction: (a) what the teacher wants students to *know and be able to do* at the end of the unit or course, (b) the *conditions* of performance, and (c) the *acceptable levels* of performance.

2. Standards and objectives should refer to both subject matter (content) and performances.

3. Working from national- and state-level standards, teachers generally need to formulate a reasonable number of clearly stated *general* objectives and, at least until they gain experience, some illustrative *specific* objectives.

4. The three domains of objectives—cognitive, affective, and psychomotor—reflect the three kinds of skills and attitudes teachers may want to influence in their students. Taxonomies have been developed for each domain.

5. The taxonomy in the cognitive domain helps teachers to aim above mere memorization, to focus more clearly on how students can process information through comprehension, application, analysis, synthesis, and evaluation.

6. A performance-content matrix, a table that shows what you want students to be able to do in each content area, functions in two ways: (a) guiding your performance and that of your students, and (b) helping you assess what has actually been taught.

We are now at the end of Part One, which provides background on educational psychology. We have presented a view of educational psychology as a foundation discipline that helps to accomplish the tasks of teaching. We have discussed the content and the methods that educational psychology uses to help in gaining reliable information about educational problems. Finally, we have presented ideas about instructional objectives to help think about the goals of teaching and education.

PART TWO

Student Characteristics

So far we have discussed the content and objectives of teaching. Now, following the model of instruction shown on page 30, we turn to the nature and characteristics of students. We concentrate here on just a few of the characteristics, although there are literally thousands that could concern us.

In Chapter 3 we deal with cognitive ability—one of the most thoroughly researched, educationally significant, and controversial characteristics in educational psychology. We go into what causes individual and group differences in cognitive ability, as a basis for understanding the important controversies that surround them. We discuss as well the many efforts to increase measured cognitive ability and achievement, especially in certain social groups.

In Chapter 4 we talk about cognitive development as children grow into adolescence and adulthood, and how language, a critical part of that development, evolves. We discuss also how personality develops over the years from childhood to old age. The developmental changes in cognition, language, and personality that result from experience and maturation have fascinated parents, novelists, and psychologists alike. These changes have a lot to do with teaching as well.

In Chapter 5 we look at individual differences—that is, differences between individuals—that are due to culture, gender, and exceptionality. We discuss how teachers should think and act given the cultural differences among contemporary students. We also examine gender-related differences in abilities and how sex roles develop. We consider, too, the school's role in fostering gender stereotypes and some ways to avoid them. We also look at those individual differences that create the need for special education.

Cognitive Abilities

Overview

THE DEFINITION OF COGNITIVE ABILITY

THE MEASUREMENT OF COGNITIVE ABILITY

Cognitive-Ability Tests and the Normal Distribution

The Stability and Reliability of Cognitive-Ability Test Scores

THE ORGANIZATION OF COGNITIVE ABILITY

POLICY, RESEARCH, AND PRACTICE

Why the Classroom Teacher Needs to Know about the Organization of Cognitive Ability

COGNITIVE ABILITY AND SUCCESS

In School

On the Job

HEREDITY AND ENVIRONMENT IN COGNITIVE ABILITY

Do Genetic or Environmental Differences Affect IQ Differences More?

Heritability Is Not Genetic Determination

Heritability Is Not Unchangeability

The Changeability of IQ

The Flynn effect: Massive changes in IQ

POLICY, RESEARCH, AND PRACTICE

Can Schools Get Along without Intelligence Tests?

TWO RECENT CONCEPTIONS OF INTELLIGENCE

Practical Intelligence, or Common Sense

Tacit knowledge

Measuring practical intelligence

Research evidence

Criticisms of practical intelligence

Multiple Intelligences

APPLICATION

Consider How Your Own Multiple Intelligences Operate Together

Multiple intelligences and factor-analyzed intelligences

Multiple intelligences in the schools

GROUP DIFFERENCES IN COGNITIVE ABILITY

Socioeconomic Status Differences

Urban-Rural Differences

Ethnic Differences

The Nature-Nurture Issue and Conservatism-Liberalism

Explanations of Group Differences

Selective migration

Environmental influence

Test bias

IMPROVING COGNITIVE ABILITY

The Home Environment and Cognitive Abilities

Adoption studies

What processes do have influence?

School Influences on Cognitive Abilities

The argument for early intervention

Early education programs

The Abecedarian Project

Summary

OVERVIEW

Public interest in cognitive ability climbed in the mid-1990s with the publication of *The Bell Curve* (Herrnstein & Murray, 1994). This book about intelligence, or more generally, cognitive ability, became a best seller and aroused great controversy (see, e.g., Fraser, 1995; Jacoby & Glauberman, 1995). Its 800+ pages—full of references, statistical analyses, and other earmarks of scholarship—argued that cognitive ability is important for success and for prevention of personal and social problems in American society. It also argued that cognitive ability is largely inherited and therefore unalterable. So the lower average cognitive-ability scores of certain groups creates grievous problems for both those groups and American society as a whole—problems that cannot be solved through education, affirmative action, or other present-day social policies. What will emerge, the researchers predicted, is a "custodial state" based on acceptance of the intrinsic, native, cognitive inferiority of those groups.

The book was extensively and often technically reviewed. Whole issues of some periodicals (e.g., *The New Republic*) were devoted to it. This chapter deals with much of what *The Bell Curve* was about.

We go into the definition, measurement, and organization of cognitive ability. We also look at two recent conceptions of cognitive ability whose roots differ from those that gave rise to traditional IQ tests. We deal briefly with current practice in cognitive-ability testing and the doubts that have been raised about that practice.

We discuss what is still, after a century of research and debate, a controversial issue: the relative importance of the roles of heredity and environment in determining variation among people in cognitive ability. Evidence suggests, although even this is somewhat controversial, that, within a group sharing a similar cultural environment, *individual* differences in cognitive ability are in good part genetically determined. But *group* differences in cognitive ability and scholastic achievement have been the subject of even greater controversy.

So we examine the evidence on the causes of both individual and group differences in cognitive ability. People with different social and political ideologies interpret the evidence and the causes differently. But we believe that the degree to which group differences are hereditary cannot be determined by any known methods, and that the critical question is whether such differences in cognitive ability and achievement—whatever the reasons for them—can be reduced or eliminated. We know that average height, a highly hereditary group characteristic, has been altered through improved diet and other means. It seems reasonable, then, that educators will also be able to improve cognitive ability and achievement once psychologists understand intellectual growth as well as nutritionists understand nutrition. Indeed, improved nutrition has been linked to improved intellectual growth (see p. 67).

So we look at the variables in the home environment that seem to make a difference in the intellectual achievement of children. We go on to the ways in which schooling, especially at the earliest levels, can help. We review the arguments and evidence for early intervention and the role of language in intervention programs. And we look at how direct academic instruction in preschool and the early grades affects the achievement of children from low socioeconomic status (SES) homes.

The Definition of Cognitive Ability

Everyone knows what cognitive ability is. It is brightness, sharpness, the ability to understand things, solve problems, figure things out quickly, and learn from experience. Cognitive ability explains part of why some students seem to learn readily, while others in the same class, with the same books and teachers, have great difficulty.

The definition and measurement aspects of cognitive ability go hand in hand. In fact, the traditional definition of cognitive ability evolved through the development of ways to measure it. This original hit-or-miss approach to the definition and measurement of the concept has been improved on. But no complete consensus about its nature in Western culture has yet been reached.

There is agreement on certain elements, however. Snyderman and Rothman (1987) asked a group of experts in psychology and education to rank important aspects of cognitive ability. The group agreed overwhelmingly on three elements.

The ability to deal with abstractions (ideas, symbols, relationships, concepts, principles) more than with concrete things (mechanical tools, physical objects).

The ability to solve problems—to deal with new situations, not simply to make well-practiced responses to familiar situations.

The ability to learn, especially to grasp and use abstractions of the kind involving words and other symbols.

> What are some desirable and important characteristics *not* included in cognitive ability?

Estes (1982) brought these ideas together in a brief definition of cognitive ability, or **intelligence,** as "adaptive behavior of the individual, usually characterized by some element of problem solving and directed by cognitive processes and operations" (p. 171). Anastasi (1986) pointed out that definitions such as this one emphasize that cognitive ability "is not an entity within the organism, but a quality of behavior" (p. 19).

The Measurement of Cognitive Ability

We measure cognitive ability with **tests** that use questions or exercises calling on the individual to make responses. The questions are arranged in groups that increase in difficulty.

> Make up a cognitive-ability test item for a 6-year-old; a 15-year-old.

At the 6-year level of the Stanford-Binet scale, there are several items like these: "A table is made of wood; a window of _____"; "A bird flies; a fish _____"; "The point of a cane is blunt; the point of a knife is _____"; "An inch is short; a mile is _____." Another subtest, designed for an older group, asks students to repeat backward a series of digits that increases in difficulty. The person being tested may start with 1, 3, 7 and try to advance to 1, 5, 4, 2, 8, 6, 3. Paper-and-pencil tests often include (1) a vocabulary subtest requiring definitions of a word such as *pen* at the beginning and *alienation* at the end, (2) paragraph comprehension, (3) arithmetic reasoning, and (4) mathematical knowledge.

Some cognitive-ability tests measure ability at spatial visualization of a kind not taught in school. The respected Ravens Progressive Matrices

The individual testing of intelligence—a scene repeated tens of thousands of times each year.

(© Meri H. Kitchens/ The Picture Cube)

Test requires seeing a pattern of changes from one set of three figures to another set that change according to the same rule and then applying that rule to select the correct choice to complete a third set of three figures. Figure 3.1 shows an example of this kind of problem.

Most general cognitive-ability tests include several different kinds of content, which make up a number of subtests. The responses to these tests are usually scored right or wrong and given a certain number of points. All the points earned are added, the total making up the individual's raw score. The raw score is then converted into a more meaningful standardized score, such as a number in which the mean, or aver-

FIGURE 3.1

Example of a problem similar to those that appear in the Ravens Progressive Matrices test. Which of the four figures below the line would belong in the lowest right-hand box above the line?

From E. Hunt, Will We Be Smart Enough? A Cognitive Analysis of the Coming Workforce. *Copyright © 1995. Reprinted by permission of Russell Sage Foundation.*

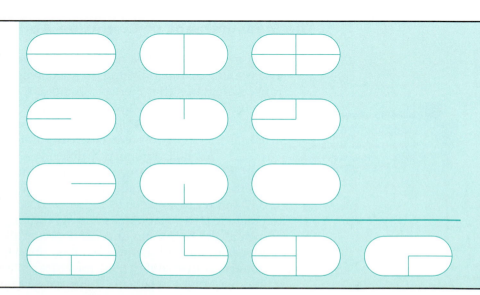

age, of a representative group of students is set at 100 and the standard deviation, a measure of variability, is set at 15. The meaning of any standardized score can be interpreted in light of the test's norms. The norms for a test show the frequency with which various scores have been obtained by the members of some norm group, say, a representative sample of five-year-olds in the United States, adults, or high school seniors taking the SAT.

Cognitive-Ability Tests and the Normal Distribution

During the first half of the twentieth century, large, representative samples of children and adults took millions of cognitive-ability tests. Partly because of the way the tests were made and partly because of the way human cognitive ability is distributed among people, the resulting raw scores (e.g., total number of right answers), or their equivalent standard scores, fell into the so-called **normal distribution,** which has the bell shape shown in Figure 3.2. A **frequency distribution** shows the number of people (the vertical dimension) who get a given score (the horizontal dimension). The bell-shaped curve has been found for the frequency distribution of many human characteristics, such as height, weight, or head circumference, in representative samples of human beings in a given category, such as five-year-old boys of Norwegian descent. Mathematically, a normal frequency distribution occurs whenever the magnitude of a variable is determined by many independent factors of

FIGURE 3.2

Normal curve with corresponding standard scores

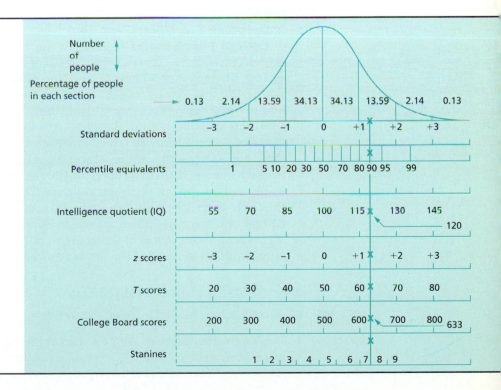

roughly equal importance. *Normal* in this sense does not mean *healthy;* it means "similar to the mathematically defined bell-shaped curve."

Why do IQ scores tend to be normally distributed? Is it simply because the test is so designed? Partly, but not entirely. Remember that the test consists of many items, each designed to differentiate among individuals. That is, the test is written so that on some items only about half of a given age group responds correctly, while on other items a higher or lower percentage of that age group responds correctly. Also, the goal of test developers is to have each item measure an ability that correlates only moderately with the ability measured by any other item. Someone's raw score is determined by responses to many items, and whether each response is correct correlates only moderately, but positively, with the correctness of the other responses. In this situation, a normal curve results. Height is also determined by many relatively independent (anatomical) factors. So both measured cognitive ability and height—and many other characteristics—are normally distributed in the general population (say adult U.S. females) and within any specific age, ethnic, and gender group (such as 12-year-old Japanese boys).

Using age-group norms, the test authors prepare one or more tables for converting raw scores into percentile ranks or one of the various kinds of standardized scores—**z-scores, T-scores,** or **stanines** (described in Chapter 13). Figure 3.2 shows the percentile ranks associated with various IQ scores that have a mean of 100 and a standard deviation of about 15. (The Appendix explains standard deviation further.) Percentile rank—a widely used standardized score because it is easy to understand—tells what percentage of the norm group has scores lower than the score of any given rank. The other types of scores, discussed later, have specified means and standard deviations.

College Board scores (e.g., those on the well-known SAT) are raw scores converted to scores with a mean of 500 and a standard deviation of 100. The score of 500 represents the mean of all high school seniors taking the test. Scores of 600 and 400 are 1 standard deviation above and below the mean, respectively. If the scores fall into the kind of distribution shown in Figure 3.2, it is easy to interpret standard scores in terms of percentile ranks. The figure shows several percentile ranks and their equivalents in various standard-score systems. The *X*s indicate where someone with an IQ score of 120, or a College Board score of 633, would fall on the various distributions. This person would be at about the 90th percentile rank. Roughly, this means that an IQ of 120 on an IQ test or a score of 633 on a College Board examination is higher than 90 percent of the scores of those in the norm group used as a reference; only about 10 percent of the norm group does better on either test.

The Stability and Reliability of Cognitive-Ability Test Scores

Is cognitive ability stable? Or does it change from day to day, season to season, year to year? The evidence comes from many longitudinal studies of cognitive-ability tests given to individuals. (Longitudinal studies are those in which the same people are studied at intervals over a considerable period of time.) These studies (e.g., Bloom, 1964; Gustafsson, 1992) showed how the correlation between cognitive ability first measured at a given age and that at maturity (ages 16 to 18) increases as the first age increases. The correlations are below .70 before age 7 but higher afterward. This means that for most people cognitive ability begins to be stable by age 7. By age 12, cognitive ability is very stable. And the rank-order of individuals in cognitive ability at age 12 is much the same as their rank-order at any subsequent age.

This degree of **stability** also means that cognitive-ability tests are highly reliable. **Reliability** is a technical concept (discussed in Chapter 13) that refers to the degree of consistency, dependability, or stability in a test's results. The correlation between scores on two or more testings of the same characteristic determines the reliability of a test. If the correlations are high, the rank-orders of individuals on the two testings are very similar.

Most standardized tests of general cognitive ability (or intelligence, scholastic **aptitude,** mental ability, and the like) are highly reliable. That is, few individual scores shift dramatically from one testing to another. But some do; a 20-point shift in IQ score from one testing session to another for a particular individual is not unheard of. For younger children, the reliability of the tests is not as high as it is for older ones. Petty and Field (1980) found that as many as 50 percent of their sample of 235 Australian children in grades 3 through 6 changed as much as 16 points in IQ scores in consecutive years, and 69 percent changed that much between any two years in those grades: 14 percent changed as much as 32 IQ points. At older age levels, the amount of fluctuation decreased. For 10 percent of the children, the changes from grades 3 to 6 were steadily upward; for another 10 percent, steadily downward. What teachers need to remember is that, for the majority of people, IQ (and other cognitive-ability) scores are highly stable, but for particular individuals such scores may vary considerably from one testing to another.

The Organization of Cognitive Ability

Is cognitive ability a single, general mental ability? What about the people who are good at handling language but not mathematics? What about those who can see complex spatial (e.g., mechanical) relationships readily but not complex verbal relationships between words and sentences? Do people tend to show the same relative level of ability in dealing with verbal, mathematical, and spatial problems? Or is ability in one area somewhat independent of ability in the others?

Most psychologists believe that there is a **general** mental ability, or **general intelligence,** which they call **g,** because all tests of cognitive ability tend to correlate positively with one another. That is, people who are good at one kind of ability tend to be good at all other kinds as well. The tendency to go together—for there to be positive correlation between two abilities—may be strong or weak, but it is always there. And this finding holds for all tests of cognitive abilities, whether they differ in content (verbal, mathematical, spatial) or reasoning process (memory, deduction, induction, analogy, discrimination).

Researchers have also discovered that tests of mental abilities can be grouped into clusters that are highly intercorrelated, that is, tend to go together more within their own cluster than with other clusters. These clusters of related tests are called *group factors.* For example, tests of vocabulary, verbal analogies, reading comprehension, and dozens of other tests that rely on language are highly intercorrelated, or cluster together and form the verbal factor. Researchers have consistently identified verbal, numerical, and spatial group factors.

We certainly can think of each group factor as a specific ability—a distinct kind of cognitive ability; remember that the scores a student gets within each area are usually correlated positively. But they also correlate positively, although not at such high levels, with scores in other areas. This means that all scores probably have in common *g*, the general mental-ability factor, as well.

The most comprehensive study of the organization of cognitive ability is *Human Cognitive Abilities* by Carroll (1993; see also Gustafsson & Undheim, 1996). Carroll performed the statistically complex operation called **factor analysis** on 468 sets of intertest correlations that had appeared over several decades (feasible only because of modern computers). His results led to a three-stratum theory, wherein there are three levels of generality.

Do you know anyone who seems to have the *same* level of ability (high, medium, or low) in all three of the Stratum-II abilities shown in Figure 3.3? Someone who has very *different* levels of these three kinds of ability? What are the bases of your opinions?

Stratum I. In the first stratum, containing the narrowest abilities, the set of abilities identified so far number around 60. One example is general-sequential-reasoning-ability, which involves "tasks or tests that require subjects to start from stated premises, rules, or conditions and engage in one or more steps of reasoning to reach a conclusion" (Carroll, 1993, p. 245). A second example is printed-verbal-language-ability, consisting of vocabulary knowledge and reading comprehension. A third is spatial-relations-ability, or "speed in manipulating relatively simple visual patterns by whatever means (mental rotation, transformation, or otherwise)" (p. 363). These are all relatively discrete, narrow abilities needed to function in particular contexts.

Stratum II. In the second stratum, a broader one, abilities numbering "perhaps as many as a dozen," (Carroll, 1993, p. 638) are found. The measures of competency within each of these broad-stratum factors correlate more highly with one another than they do with measures of competency in other broad-stratum factors. Among the abilities in the relatively small number of broad-stratum factors are (1) **crystallized intelligence,** such as reading skills and general information (*crystallized* applies to contexts or materials *previously learned* in school or on the job; a good deal of verbal activity requires crystallized ability); (2) **fluid intelligence,** or complex induction, reasoning, and problem solving (*fluid* applies to solving problems in different contexts and using different or *novel* materials; a good deal of mathematical reasoning requires fluid ability); and (3) visual perception ability.

Stratum III. In the third stratum, or general stratum, some form of *g*—general mental ability—is needed to explain why the scores on all relatively distinct second-stratum abilities correlate positively with one another.

POLICY, RESEARCH, AND PRACTICE

Why the Classroom Teacher Needs to Know about the Organization of Cognitive Ability

Does it really matter how you think of cognitive ability? Why do you need to know about the organization of mental abilities? Understanding how cognitive ability is organized is important because of what it means for educational practice.

If a single, general ability accounted for most of the differences teachers see among students, they could expect that the rank-ordering of students as to ability in any one kind of task would be similar to their rank-ordering on any other kind of task. Some would have more ability, some less.

On the other hand, if group factors are at work, you probably would look for, and fully expect to find, individuals who are relatively stronger in mathematical than in verbal or spatial skills or vice versa. If you have high verbal ability, you may do better in verbal occupations, such as law and journalism. High mathematical ability improves chances of success in engineering and science; and high spatial ability helps in art, architecture, engineering, and mechanical work. High ability of these kinds suggests better likelihood of success in particular kinds of work. An overall IQ score conceals these kinds of intraindividual differences.

To get an overall estimate of academic aptitude, it is common for educators to add together students' scores on verbal and mathematical measures of such tests as the SAT, which is used widely as a part of the college admissions process. But to estimate separate abilities, they also use the two kinds of scores separately. Both kinds of information are useful.

Some combination of the general mental-ability conception and the group-factor conception is what you need to keep in mind as you think about educational alternatives for your students. Do not disregard the general cognitive ability so necessary for abstract reasoning. At the same time, do not neglect the more specific (group-factor) abilities. Remain aware of the potential of each student in some area, whatever his or her ability in other areas.

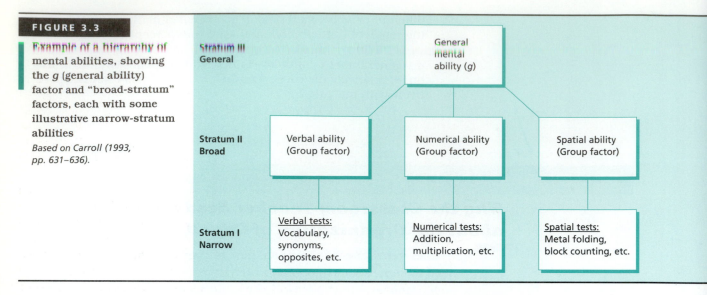

FIGURE 3.3

Example of a hierarchy of mental abilities, showing the *g* (general ability) factor and "broad-stratum" factors, each with some illustrative narrow-stratum abilities
Based on Carroll (1993, pp. 631–636).

Figure 3.3 represents how psychologists currently think cognitive abilities are organized. It shows the three strata in a hierarchy, with **Stratum III** at the top, representing *g*. In the middle is Stratum II, where three of the dozen broad but less general factors are named. At the bottom is Stratum I, representing the many narrow kinds of abilities described by the different tests people take.

Cognitive Ability and Success

In School

From the historical sketch just given, you might guess that cognitive ability correlates with school success, and you would be right. Whether school success is measured in terms of grades (marks), grade-point averages, or achievement-test scores, there is always a positive correlation between general cognitive-ability test scores and school-success measures. Thousands of such correlations have been computed throughout the twentieth century, and we know of none that has been zero or negative. Depending on how varied the students are in terms of their cognitive ability (here often called *scholastic aptitude*), the correlations range from about .2 to about .6, with an average value of about .4. (Look at the scatterplots in Figure 2.1 to see what such correlations look like.) Within the same class, course, or curriculum, students with higher scholastic aptitude tend to get higher grades.

If scholastic success is measured with achievement tests rather than grades, the correlations tend to be somewhat higher. This is so partly because both variables entail skill with paper-and-pencil tasks and partly because test scores are less affected by nonintellectual factors (e.g., participation and conduct in class) than grades are.

One question about the correlation between cognitive ability and school success is whether the content of the cognitive-ability tests is too similar to the content of what is taught in school and measured by achievement tests. Vocabulary, paragraph comprehension, and mathematical knowledge and problem solving seem to be required in both cognitive-ability tests and achievement tests, so no wonder they correlate! But this criticism can be answered by the fact that cognitive-ability tests of the kind not taught in school also correlate, almost as strongly, with school success. One such test is rearranging scrambled sentences (e.g., "by quarter game the team won our the last was in"). Another such test is the Ravens test, illustrated in Figure 3.1. Such tests get at skill with novel kinds of problems rather than the kinds directly taught in school.

The correlations of cognitive ability with school success are not so high as to rule out the possibility that some students with high scholastic aptitude can get low grades (perhaps for lack of motivation) and others with low aptitude can get high grades (perhaps because of strong motivation, or good study habits). The correlations are low enough to leave a lot of room for exceptions to the general trend.

Remember that correlation does not mean causation. The positive correlations between IQ and school achievement do not necessarily mean that IQ level tends to determine or influence achievement level. It may well be that both variables are influenced by a third variable, such as home environment. Homes and parents that provide intellectual stimulation and motivation tend to bring about both higher IQs and higher achievement. It may also be that the higher school achievement, resulting from better teaching and curricula, tends to raise IQs. Keep these ideas in mind as you read this chapter.

On the Job

Do more cognitively able people do better in the "real" world of jobs, that is, in performance on the job, making a living, and producing goods and services? The way to find out is to (1) give a group of workers in the same job a cognitive-ability test so as to obtain a measure of each worker's cognitive ability, (2) obtain a measure of how well each worker is doing the job, and (3) obtain a coefficient of correlation between the cognitive-ability measure and the job-performance measure.

More than 1,000 studies of this kind have been reported, and Hunter (1986) has summarized their methods and results using meta-analysis. He adjusted the obtained correlations so as to obtain estimates of the correlation that would be obtained if the tests and performance measures were perfectly reliable (see Chapter 13). These adjustments made the correlations higher than those usually reported. They represent the upper theoretical limit of the correlations rather than those obtainable in practice with the available imperfectly reliable measures of cognitive ability and job performance. He concluded that general cognitive ability predicts supervisor ratings and training success; it also predicts work performance with even higher validity. He demonstrated that general measures of cognitive ability predict job knowledge ($r = .80$), and that job knowledge predicts performance on the job quite well ($r = .75$). So

Hunter demonstrated a strong link between *g* and skill in performing everyday work.

But the coefficients were lower in 750 studies examined by Hartigan and Wigdor (1989). Those studies looked at the *unadjusted* relationships between cognitive ability as measured by the General Aptitude Test Battery (developed by the U.S. Employment Service) and ratings of job success by supervisors. Here the *r*s were "in the range of .2 to .4" (p. 5). Nonetheless, the fact remains that general cognitive ability is positively and substantially related to job success.

The kinds of jobs for which these generalizations hold vary highly. They include both complex and simple jobs. They hold for mechanical, electronic, skilled services, and clerical jobs. And the correlations are not merely greater than zero, they are high enough to have considerable practical significance.

So the evidence is strong that what is measured by cognitive-ability tests relates not only to academic success but also to job success. More cognitively able workers tend to learn more about their jobs (have greater job knowledge). Those with greater job knowledge tend to do better work. And so those with higher general cognitive ability tend to do better work (Schmidt & Hunter, 1992). We can summarize this as follows:

None of this rules out the importance of other kinds of ability. General cognitive ability tells an important story but certainly not the whole story. But the importance attached to tested cognitive ability by parents, teachers, and people in general is well justified. It is a human characteristic that makes an important difference in how well people succeed in school and on the job.

So far we have talked only about relationships between cognitive ability and success within the same job. What about cognitive-ability differences between jobs? Here, data from a variety of sources show clearly that certain levels of cognitive ability are typically found in some occupations and not in others. Writers, accountants, engineers, and teachers typically average in the top 15 percent on standardized tests of cognitive ability. Teamsters, lumberjacks, and cobblers often average in the lower 50 percent (Ryan, Paolo, & Dunn, 1995; Reynolds, Chastain, & Kaufman, 1987; Nagoshi & Johnson, 1986). Such occupation-related differences in average cognitive ability of adults have been found in England, Hawaii, the former Soviet Union, and the Netherlands, as well as in the United States.

Another way of stating the connection between jobs and cognitive ability is illustrated by Gottfredson (1986):

Data show that at most only 10 to 20 percent of the general population possesses the intelligence level required for minimally acceptable performance as a physician. This contrasts with percentages of around 40 to 80 percent, respectively, for general duty nurse and licensed practical nurse. (p. 385)

So certain occupations seem to require or attract people at certain levels of measured cognitive ability, or academic aptitude. Educators need to keep in mind that if environmental factors keep certain groups from achieving at higher levels, these groups are likely to remain in lower parts of the occupational structure.

It is also easy to see that the economic welfare of a nation depends in part on the cognitive ability of its workers—on whether they are able to meet the intellectual demands of the jobs that produce the country's wealth. In today's competitive world economy, it is important for American workers to be as able as those in competing nations to meet modern demands. This fact led Hunt (1995) to ask, "Will we be smart enough?" to handle the cognitive demands of the economic world of the twenty-first century. Of course, it is also possible that the jobs of the future will employ vast numbers of service workers, requiring of most workers a winning personality and only modest levels of cognitive ability (Berliner & Biddle, 1995).

In fact, recent research has shown that intelligence (general cognitive ability) can sometimes be less important than domain-specific knowledge in correlating with memory, performance, and comprehension in a specific subject matter. In one study (Schneider, Körkel, & Weinert, 1989), German elementary school boys and girls were asked to read a detailed narrative about a soccer game and its young hero's physical and psychological condition after the game. It turned out that their previous knowledge about soccer was much more highly correlated with their memory for and comprehension of the narrative than was their score on a cognitive-ability test. So "rich domain-specific knowledge can compensate for low overall aptitude on domain-related cognitive tasks" (Schneider et al., 1989, p. 311). Other studies have yielded similar results. These studies suggest that low-aptitude learners can do excellent work in domains they know a lot about. So teachers should aim at getting learners to use in academic domains the same capabilities they use in the domains in which they often have great knowledge (soccer, automobile repair, or whatever).

Heredity and Environment in Cognitive Ability

> There is perhaps no issue in the history of science that presents such a complex mingling of conceptual, methodological, psychological, ethical, political, and sociological questions as the controversy over whether intelligence has a substantial genetic component.
>
> *(Block & Dworkin, 1976, p. xi)*

Two kinds of factors determine any human characteristic: heredity (nature) and environment (nurture). Both are indispensable to human development. The question of which factor is more important is meaningless; it is like asking whether the length or width of a rectangle con-

When raised together, identical twins have nearly identical IQs; when raised apart, they show the effects of different environments.

(© Bob Daemmrich/ The Image Works)

tributes more to its area. Without hereditary factors, no food, air, education, or other environmental elements would produce growth. And without the proper environment, hereditary factors would be powerless.

The sensible question is, what is the relative weight of variation in each factor (heredity or environment) in producing variation in a given characteristic? For variation in eye or skin color, variation in heredity makes all the difference. For variation in spoken language (English, Swahili, Tagalog, Swedish), variation in environment makes all the difference.

When there are no variations in hereditary factors—as is the case with **identical twins**—all differences in cognitive ability result from variation in environmental factors. Similarly, if there were no differences in environmental factors—a condition that cannot exist, even for identical twins brought up in the same family—all variation in cognitive ability would result from hereditary factors. One problem in getting clear answers here is that heredity and environment usually vary together, making it difficult to separate their effects. People who are genetically related (parents and their children, siblings, twins) tend to have similar environments. So it becomes hard to tell whether their similarity (in IQ and other cognitive abilities) results from similarity in genes or similarity in environment.

According to some writers (e.g., Herrnstein & Murray, 1994), the degree to which variation in heredity and variation in environment determine variation in human characteristics has major importance for social policy. This position is based on the assumption that highly heritable characteristics are highly unchangeable. If variations in cognitive ability are largely determined by variations in heredity, it seems futile to attempt to increase cognitive ability by improving environment. It then becomes correspondingly futile to try to improve chances for the good life in modern society, insofar as those chances depend on cognitive ability. For example, lower-SES people tend to have lower cognitive-ability test scores. If these scores are determined by hereditary factors, improving the environment (schooling, housing, welfare, family life) may not solve the problems of low-SES people in gaining equal education, jobs, income, social status, and self-esteem. Only insofar as lower cognitive ability is caused by inferior environment can environmental factors be changed to improve cognitive ability and the corresponding ability to acquire the good things, material and cultural, that society offers. At least this is the reasoning of certain writers.

Do Genetic or Environmental Differences Affect IQ Differences More?

Sometimes nature manipulates the genetic and environmental similarity between two people. When that happens, researchers can examine the relative effects of heredity and environment on their similarity in measured cognitive ability. They first list types of pairs of people in order from least different (most similar) to most different (least similar) in heredity and environment. Then they look at the similarities in IQ scores as measured by the correlations between the pairs.

There are nine levels of genetic and environmental similarity, ranging from least different to most different, as shown in Figure 3.4. The most recent updating of the evidence was presented by Bouchard (1993). Figure 3.4 shows the median correlation coefficients obtained in these studies for each kind of genetic and environmental similarity. Clearly the correlations tend to decrease as genetic and environmental similarities decrease. At the highest level of genetic-environmental similarity, that of identical twins reared together, the median of 34 correlation coefficients is .86, almost as high as the coefficient expected from IQ scores of the same people obtained a few days apart.

For identical twins reared apart, the environments differ enough to lower the median correlation to .72. This correlation, based on four stud-

---

FIGURE 3.4

Correlation between IQ scores for different levels of similarity in heredity and environment.

Adapted from McGue, Bouchard, Iacono, & Lykken (1993, Table 1, p. 60).

Category of Relationship	Median Correlation Coefficient
	.00 .10 .20 .30 .40 .50 .60 .70 .80 .90 r
1. Identical twins reared together	.86
2. Identical twins reared apart	.72
3. Fraternal twins reared together	.60
4. Ordinary siblings reared together	.47
5. Parent-offspring reared together	.42
6. Unrelated children reared together	.32
7. Ordinary siblings reared apart	.24
8. Adoptive parents and foster children	.24
9. Biological parents and children reared apart	.24

ies, is so high that many psychologists consider it to be strong evidence of the importance of genetic similarity in determining IQ similarity. Here, apparently, the environments of the twins differ, but the IQ correlations (similarities) remain quite high. The only explanation, many psychologists conclude, is that the genetic similarity (or identity) produces the IQ similarity and so hereditary factors are highly influential in determining IQ.

> Without positing the existence of genetic influences, it is simply not possible to give a credible account for the consistently greater IQ similarity among monozygotic (MZ) [identical] twins than among like-sex dizygotic (DZ) [**fraternal**] **twins,** the significant IQ correlations among biological relatives even when they are reared apart, and the strong association between the magnitude of the familial IQ correlation and the degree of genetic relatedness.
>
> *(McGue, Bouchard, Iacono, & Lykken, 1993, p. 60)*

Studies that deal with children raised from infancy by adoptive parents also reveal a lot about the relative influence of heredity and environment. Whose intellectual status does that of these children resemble—their adoptive parents' or their biological parents'? If environment makes the greater difference, the correlation between the children's and the adoptive parents' IQ scores will be higher. If heredity makes the greater difference, the correlation between the children's and the biological parents' IQ scores will be higher. Figure 3.4 shows that environment and heredity have about equal influence.

Researchers, using complex statistical methods (Chipeur, Rovine, & Plomin, 1990; cited by McGue et al., 1993) have concluded that environmental variability contributes about 49 percent, and genetic variability about 51 percent of the influence on IQ score differences. Devlin et al. (1997) were able to distinguish statistically between hereditary and intrauterine (environmental) effects, which they called maternal effects. Doing so reduced genetic influence to below 50 percent. The implication is that prenatal environment (the mother's nutrition and freedom from alcohol, drug, and cigarette consumption) could raise IQs.

So the evidence simply does not support either complete hereditarianism or complete environmentalism. But it runs directly against the notion that, under present-day conditions, all **individual differences** in cognitive ability are due entirely to environmental factors. In short, although the issue is still controversial (see discussion of Block, 1995, below), the evidence suggests that variations in hereditary factors are about as powerful as variations in environmental factors in producing individual differences in cognitive ability within a single racial or cultural group (specifically, whites in Northern Europe and the United States). But, as you will see below, hereditary and environmental factors cannot at all clearly account for the determinants of **group differences** in IQ scores.

Heritability Is Not Genetic Determination

It is important to distinguish between heritability and genetic determination, as Block (1995) pointed out. Heritability is a statistic, analogous to a correlation coefficient. **Heritability** is the ratio of variability due to genetic factors to the total variability (due to both genetic and environmental factors). That is,

$$\text{Heritability} = \frac{\text{Variability due to genetic factors}}{\text{Total variability (due to both genetic and environmental factors)}}$$

This statistic applies to a population of people or other organisms, not to an individual. As the variability due to genetic factors varies in that population, heritability also varies. If genetic variation is zero, heritability becomes zero. If environmental variation were zero, so that everyone had the same environment, heritability would become complete, or 1.00. But **genetic determination** is

> an informal and intuitive notion that has no quantitative definition. . . . It depends on the idea of a normal environment. A characteristic is said to be genetically determined if it is coded in and caused by the genes and bound to develop in a normal environment. Genetic determination in a single person makes sense: my brown hair is genetically determined. By contrast, heritability makes sense only relative to a population in which individuals differ from one another. You can't ask "What's the heritability of my IQ?"
> *(Block, 1995, p. 103)*

The distinction is important because

> a characteristic can be highly heritable even if it is not genetically determined. Some years ago when only women wore earrings, the heritability of having an earring was high because differences in whether a person had an earring were "due" to a chromosomal [i.e., a genetic] difference, [an] XX [chromosome for women] versus [an] XY [chromosome for men].
> *(Block, 1995, p. 104)*

By statistical methods (which we cannot go into here), correlation coefficients between the IQs of people of different relationships (e.g., identical twins reared apart, unrelated individuals reared together, etc.) can be used to obtain estimates of the amount of influence attributable to environmental and genetic differences.

Heritability Is Not Unchangeability

For educators, the question is whether cognitive ability or, also important, achievement in school and job, can be improved. What many people erroneously assume is that the more heritable a characteristic is, the less it can be changed or improved. Some traits, such as eye color or hair color, are determined by genetic makeup almost entirely and are also unchangeable (ruling out colored contact lenses, hair dyes, and aging). The high heritability of height shows up in a correlation of .86 between the heights of 56 pairs of identical twins reared apart (Bouchard et al., 1990, p. 226). But even this highly heritable characteristic has changed remarkably. Angoff (1988) cited a Japanese study showing an increase of 3⅓ inches in the average height of young adult males in Japan between 1946 and 1982. The average height of U.S. adults is still increasing. For men aged 35 to 44 years, it increased from 68.5 inches in 1960 to 1962, to 69.1 inches in 1971 to 1974, and then to 69.4 inches in 1976 to 1980 (*Statistical Abstract of the United States 1986*, p. 120).

The Changeability of IQ

So a question of major importance is, how changeable is IQ? Major figures in the history of intelligence measurement have disagreed here. The first successful intelligence tester, Alfred Binet, considered intelligence (as he measured it) to be learned and changeable. But others, such as the famous and still highly controversial Sir Cyril Burt, considered intelligence to be unalterable by education or other environmental influences.

The Flynn Effect: Massive Changes in IQ   Flynn (1987) found "massive IQ gains in 14 nations" from one generation to the next. The strongest evidence appeared in the Netherlands, which tests almost all 18-year-old men during military screening. Taking the same test (a form of the Ravens Progressive Matrices Test), the Dutch showed an increase from 1952 to 1982 of about 20 IQ points. The samples of men were comprehensive. The test remained unaltered during this period. The test was considered relatively free from cultural and educational influences. The men tested were relatively mature and so had reached their highest test performance. So Flynn considered the evidence of a "massive IQ gain" from one generation to the next to be verified "beyond a reasonable doubt." Similarly strong evidence was obtained for Belgium, France, Norway, New Zealand, and Canada. The evidence went in the same direction, but not as strongly, in the United States, (the former) East Germany, Great Britain, Australia, Japan, (the former) West Germany, Switzerland, and Austria. Figure 3.5 shows the increase in average IQ in the United States between 1918 and 1990.

Flynn's Interpretation   Flynn reasoned that, if the IQ test gains reflected real gains in intelligence, the countries showing the gains should

---

FIGURE 3.5

Scores from both Wechsler and Stanford-Binet tests rose 24 points in the United States between 1918 and 1989. The scores have been calibrated according to 1989 levels.

From Dimitry Schidlovsky, Scientific American *(November 1995), Vol. 273, No. 5, page 14. Copyright © 1995. Used by permission of the author.*

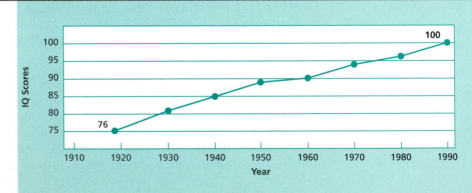

also have shown greater occurrence of outstanding real-life performances. Thus, "a generation with a massive IQ gain should radically outperform its predecessors" (p. 187). The percentage of men in the Netherlands showing IQs of 130 and above increased from about 2 percent in 1952 to about 25 percent in 1982. "The result should be a cultural renaissance too great to be overlooked" (p. 187) if the IQ gains reflect genuine intelligence gains. Yet no such "renaissance" occurred.

As for the causes of the IQ gains, Flynn concluded that they could not have been genetic. No genetic change of such a magnitude could occur in whole populations in a single generation. Flynn posited "unidentified environmental variables" instead (p. 188). In the Netherlands, the data ruled out increases in educational level and socioeconomic status (i.e., father's occupation and educational level) as the causes of any major part of the gain. Similarly, Flynn did not see greater sophistication at taking the test as major cause. "At present, the Dutch data leave unknown the environmental factors responsible for about 15 points of a 20-point gain" (p. 189).

A Nutritional Explanation Lynn (1993) argued that the IQ increases have been due to improved nutrition. (Devlin et al., 1997, noted above, would agree.) The countries in the studies had poor nutrition during the 1930s. Then living standards improved over the next five decades so that people were able to buy better food. And height, head size, and brain size increased over the same period about as much (measured in units of variability) as intelligence. Lynn considered the nutritional explanation more plausible than one based on improvement in intellectual stimulation. First, there is no direct evidence for such an improvement. Second, intellectual stimulation should have increased verbal intelligence more than nonverbal, but the opposite was true. Third, the increases in mental (and motor) development occurred among infants, whom cognitive stimulation would not yet have affected. And fourth, evidence from early-education programs indicates that the effects of intellectual stimulation tend to fade away over time.

A Schooling Explanation Ceci (1991) brought together eight kinds of evidence showing the effects of schooling on IQ.

1. High correlations between IQ and number of grades completed. This relationship is ambiguous, of course, unless testers control for other variables, such as early IQ. But Husén and Tuijnman (1991) found that the increase in IQ was substantial even if such controls were used.

2. The effect of summer vacation on IQ. Children decline slightly but consistently in IQ over the summer vacation, especially low-SES children, whose summer activities least resemble those in school.

3. The effect of intermittent school attendance on IQ. Children who do not go to school regularly, such as transients and those in isolated mountain communities, decline in IQ. And the longer the school-deprivation of siblings within the same family, the greater the decline. When schools become available in isolated communities, IQs go up.

4. Delayed-beginning-of-school effects on IQ. In the Netherlands,

children who started school several years late because of World War II had IQs about seven points lower than those who started at the normal age. Similar effects from delayed schooling were found in other countries, even after social class and parental motivation were controlled.

5. Early-end-of-schooling effects on IQ. In Sweden, when children at age 13 who were similar in IQ, SES, and school grades were tested again at age 18, those who had dropped out of school had lower age-18 IQs, by about 1.8 points for each high school year missed. As already noted, Husén and Tuijnman (1991) studied the IQs of 20-year-old men whose IQs at age 10 were known and could be held constant statistically. The main determiner of their IQs at age 20, after IQ at 10 years was held constant, was the number of grades they had completed. The amount of schooling could not be attributed to their IQ at 10 because it had been held constant.

6. High correlation between achievement-test and aptitude-test scores. Schooling obviously improves achievement-test scores in various school subjects. And aptitude- (e.g., IQ) test scores correlate highly with achievement-test scores. So it is reasonable to expect schooling to improve IQ. The results of many studies bear out this expectation.

7. Schooling variations with age held constant. Consider children who were born within a month before the legal age for admission to school compared to children born within a month after that age. They differ only slightly in age but by a whole year in amount of schooling they have received. When researchers have compared these two sets of children, those born earlier but with a year's more schooling had considerably higher IQs. Similarly, Cahan and Cohen (1989), studying the effects of schooling and age on the IQs of Israeli pupils, found that the differences in IQ were related more closely to amount of schooling with age held constant than to age with amount of schooling held constant. "The effect of schooling is about twice the effect of age" (Cahan & Cohen, 1989, p. 1245).

8. Historical changes in amount and kind of schooling. Soldiers in World War II did much better on intelligence tests than did the soldiers of World War I. But when the grade level achieved by the two groups was held constant, the difference became less than half as great, indicating that the increase in education produced much of the gain between the two wars.

Overall Conclusions The Flynn effect—the many findings of widespread and massive increases in IQ in many countries during the twentieth century—is "most plausibly linked to changes in society (e.g., widespread exposure to media and better nutrition), including large increases in the mean levels of school attendance" (Ceci, 1991, p. 709). What does this conclusion mean for the future of the nation and its educational policies? These findings are important to present-day concerns about groups that score substantially lower, on average, in cognitive ability, school achievement, and occupational status. The problems of socioeconomic disadvantage, and low achievement in American society that are associated with lower scores on IQ tests can be reduced, at least to a great extent, by students in those groups staying in school longer.

POLICY, RESEARCH, AND PRACTICE

Can Schools Get Along without Intelligence Tests?

WHAT RESEARCH TELLS US

The usefulness of group-administered intelligence tests in the schools has been severely challenged in recent decades. At one point, the state of California, for example, stopped using them. Individual intelligence tests for students who need special attention are still being used, but in 1979, in *Larry P. v. Riles,* Judge Robert Peckham ruled that even individual IQ tests should not be used as a basis for classifying children as educable mentally retarded (EMR) because the tests had resulted in the overrepresentation of minority-group children (African-Americans and Mexican-Americans) in EMR classes, and had not been used together with evidence from developmental histories, adaptive behavior, and medical histories. Although the tests were developed so as to eliminate gender differences in average IQ scores, the same effort was not made to eliminate racial and social-class differences (U.S. District Court, Opinion No. C–71–2270 RFP).

Since then, the use of intelligence tests as a part of the basis for assigning children to programs for the educable mentally retarded has continued to face challenges. A series of court decisions have reversed, then reinstated, then reinterpreted the original decision (Macmillan & Balow, 1991). Judge Peckham himself reversed his earlier decision because African-American parents demanded IQ tests so that their children could get needed services.

The policy of using IQ testing has been criticized, in part, on the basis of the **self-fulfilling prophecy** effect of the IQ measure (a prophecy that tends to make itself come true; e.g., if enough people predict that a bank will soon fail, they withdraw their money and make it fail). As one teacher said, "Once you know the child's IQ score, you tend to see him through it, and you adjust your teaching to his ability or level of intelligence—as revealed by the test." In this way, IQ scores may become the basis for self-fulfilling prophecies for both children and teachers.

One estimate by Good (1987) was that a third of the teachers observed in a series of studies showed exaggerated responses to students they believed to be low achievers. Their responses to these children included the following:

- Waiting a shorter time for them to answer questions
- Giving them answers more frequently, or calling on someone else when they were having difficulty; but not giving additional clues or chances to respond, as was often true when students for whom a teacher held high expectations had difficulty in answering a question

continues

Describe some of the teachers you have known as to whether they behaved in any of these ways.

- Rewarding their incorrect answers or inappropriate behavior more often, which sustained, and at times even caused a drop in, their already low performance
- Criticizing them for failure more often
- Praising them less frequently for success
- Failing to give them feedback after they had made a public response
- Calling on them less often
- Interacting with them less, and appearing less friendly in the interactions that did take place
- Smiling at them less often
- Seating them farther away from the teacher's desk
- Demanding less work from them
- Not giving them the benefit of the doubt when answers on a test were borderline

The self-fulfilling prophecy is often a powerful shaper of behavior. Sometimes it is subtle, sometimes obvious. In one classroom, a teacher was overheard saying, "Hurry up, Robyn. Even you can get this right"; in another, "Michelle, you're slow as it is. You haven't got time to look around the classroom" (Alloway, 1984).

When teachers group students (say, for reading instruction) on the basis of IQ scores or achievement, they almost always treat the groups or tracks differently. Students thought to be less able often are given less varied tasks, less thought-provoking work, slower-paced instruction, less choice about what to study, and more drill and practice. And in their groups or tracks, there are more management problems and fewer opportunities to move up. This last is a particular problem. Once a child has been categorized, it may be very hard for him or her to move out of that category. Assignment to a slow group early on can be like a life sentence with no likelihood of parole.

WHAT THIS MEANS FOR YOU AS A TEACHER

Given these findings, it is no wonder that some parents argue against the use of intelligence tests. Because minority-group and low-SES children less often do well on these tests, their parents are right to worry about how the information is used.

Test instructions to teachers usually caution against relying solely on group intelligence tests with children who come from diverse cultural backgrounds or who have verbal, cultural, physical, social, or emotional disabilities. It should not be overlooked, however, that intelligence tests can be used to (1) ascertain that low achievement is not associated with low intelligence, (2) determine whether learning disabilities are general or specific, and (3) discover that a child from a linguistically or culturally different background, or an impoverished one, is enormously talented in one or another cognitive ability.

So the position set forth in *The Bell Curve,* that these problems cannot be solved because they are caused by genetic (and therefore unalterable) characteristics of economically disadvantaged people, is extremely questionable in light of the evidence this section summarizes.

Nonetheless, no explanation of the Flynn effect has won unanimous agreement among experts. The cause(s) of the Flynn effect remained a matter of debate into the late 1990s, as was indicated by a conference on the question (Neisser, 1996). But the idea that IQ is malleable or modifiable as a function of environmental circumstances is no longer strongly challenged.

Two Recent Conceptions of Intelligence

Debate continues about the importance of general mental ability in education and the role of the major group factors or specific factors that make up intelligence. There are not necessarily any wrong or right answers here; the arguments simply focus on different aspects of this complex characteristic we call intelligence.

Two conceptions of intelligence which have emerged recently differ substantially from the various conceptions held by the measurement specialists who design the kinds of intelligence tests described earlier. One of these emphasizes the practical aspects of intelligent behavior; the other makes a case for multiple intelligences.

Practical Intelligence, or Common Sense

Describe a problem requiring practical intelligence recently encountered by you or someone you know.

Think about the problems on a traditional IQ test. They differ, as shown in Table 3.1, from problems in the "real" world (Neisser, 1976; Wagner & Sternberg, 1986). "Except perhaps in television game shows . . . , one is rarely expected to repeat series of numbers, to solve analogies, or to identify well-known figures within a time period of a few seconds in

3.1

TABLE

Differences between IQ Test Problems and Real-World Problems

IQ Test Problems	Real-World Problems
Formulated by others	Unformulated; need to be identified
Of little or no intrinsic interest	Of personal interest
All needed information available	Lacking some needed information
Separated from everyday experience	Arise in everyday experience
Usually well defined	Poorly defined
Have only one right answer	Have more than one right answer
Often only one correct method	More than one correct method

Based on Neisser (1976); Wagner & Sternberg (1986).

order to achieve a social reward" (Kornhaber, Krechevsky, & Gardner, 1990, p. 187).

Now consider intelligent performance as it takes place in the real world.

- Getting a car started and keeping it running with limited equipment, tools, and money
- Handicapping horses at racetracks
- Navigating the open ocean in a small boat without instruments
- Finding the fastest route to the airport at rush hour

All these are tests of intellect.

In recent decades, this kind of thinking has led to the idea of practical intelligence. Is there such a thing, apart from the kind measured by traditional cognitive-ability tests? Those who say yes (e.g., Sternberg, Wagner, Williams, & Horvath, 1995) argue that traditional tests do not predict success in "real life," that is, outside schools and colleges. These writers are fully aware of the kinds of evidence, cited above (pp. 59–61), for how well IQ tests predict success on the job. But they point out that there is plenty of room for improvement in that predictive power. So they have tried to develop definitions, concepts, and tests that are more relevant to real-life performance.

Tacit Knowledge   Sternberg et al. (1995) show that there is often no correlation between people's IQs and how well they solve practical problems. They explain this lack of correlation by pointing to what they call *tacit knowledge,* which differs from formal, academic knowledge in that it

- is action-oriented
- is acquired without help from other people
- helps achieve personal goals
- is procedural (deals with ways of doing things)
- has to be inferred from what people do or say
- is typically unexpressed rather than stated
- applies to a particular purpose or kind of problem

It can consist of a set of complex rules for how to get something done under certain circumstances in real life. Examples are as follows: When and how to

- give the boss bad news
- compare, without a calculator, the unit prices of groceries that come in different-sized containers
- get studying done when you have a noisy roommate
- stick to your proper calorie intake during a party
- get everything you need from a library book that you cannot borrow
- discover whether you and a potential date are likely to get along well

Even if these kinds of goals are important to you, you seldom learn, or are taught, such knowledge by other people in any direct way. You typically pick it up by yourself.

Give an example of what you would consider part of the tacit knowledge of an expert teacher.

Measuring Practical Intelligence   The concept of practical intelligence becomes more useful if there are ways to measure it. So its advocates

Work-Related Situations and Associated Response Items

Academic Psychology

It is your second year as an assistant professor in a prestigious psychology department. This past year you published two unrelated empirical articles in established journals. You don't believe, however, that there is a research area that can be identified as your own. You believe yourself to be about as productive as others. The feedback about your first year of teaching has been generally good. You have yet to serve on a university committee. There is one graduate student who has chosen to work with you. You have no external source of funding, nor have you applied for funding.

Your goals are to become one of the top people in your field and to get tenure in your department. The following is a list of things you are considering doing in the next two months. You obviously cannot do them all. Rate the importance of each by its priority as a means of reaching your goals.

____ a. Improve the quality of your teaching
____ b. Write a grant proposal
____ c. Begin long-term research that may lead to a major theoretical article.
____ d. Concentrate on recruiting more students
____ e. Serve on a committee studying university–community relations
____ f. Begin several related short-term research projects, each of which may lead to an empirical article
.
.
.
____ o. Volunteer to be chairperson of the undergraduate curriculum committee

Business Management

It is your second year as a mid-level manager in a company in the communications industry. You head a department of about 30 people. The evaluation of your first year on the job has been generally favorable. Performance ratings for your department are at least as good as they were before you took over, and perhaps even a little better. You have two assistants. One is quite capable. The other just seems to go through the motions but to be of little real help.

You believe that although you are well liked, there is little that would distinguish you in the eyes of your superiors from the nine other managers at a comparable level in the company.

Your goal is rapid promotion to the top of the company. The following is a list of things you are considering doing in the next two months. You obviously cannot do them all. Rate the importance of each by its priority as a means of reaching your goal.

____ a. Find a way to get rid of the "dead wood" (e.g., the less helpful assistant and three or four others)
____ b. Participate in a series of panel discussions to be shown on the local public television station
____ c. Find ways to make sure your superiors are aware of your important accomplishments
____ d. Make an effort to better match the work to be done with the strengths and weaknesses of individual employees
.
.
.
____ n. Write an article on productivity for the company newsletter.

FIGURE 3.6

Sample practical intelligence test items.

From R. J. Sternberg, K. Wagner, W. M. Williams, & J. A. Horvath, American Psychologist, 50 (November 1995, p. 92). Copyright © 1995 by the American Psychological Association. Reprinted with permission.

have developed tests for this variable. Some of these tests take the form of a practical problem and a set of alternative ways to solve it—ways the individual must rate on, say, a 10-point scale as to their importance in solving the problem. Typical problems are shown in Figure 3.6.

Scores on problems such as those in Figure 3.6 can be obtained by comparing the individual's ratings of the alternatives with those of experts in the kind of practical intelligence being tested. For an assistant professor seeking tenure, the experts would be a group of recently tenured professors. For a young manager seeking promotion, the experts would be successful managers. Sternberg et al. (1995) describe studies showing that scores on such tests are indeed higher for the groups who should score higher because of their known experience, expertise, and success on the job.

Research Evidence In the academic community, the concept of practical intelligence is much less well established than that of general intelligence and the various broad-stratum abilities measured by traditional intelligence and aptitude tests. Researchers have raised various questions about it, such as, is practical intelligence specific to each occupational domain, as a job-information test would be? Or do people who have a lot of it in one domain tend to have a lot of it in other domains? When 60 undergraduates took tacit-knowledge tests in business management and academic psychology, the correlation of their scores on the two tests was .58, showing that the tacit knowledge had considerable generalizability from one domain to the other (Sternberg et al., 1995, p. 920).

Does this generality mean that tacit knowledge is just a new approach to general intelligence rather than basically different? In samples of undergraduates, the correlations between (1) tacit-knowledge scores and (2) verbal-reasoning and cognitive-ability test scores have been very low (.12 and .16). For a group of 45 managers, the correlation was .14. These and other low correlations indicate that the two kinds of tests—tacit-knowledge and general-intelligence—were measuring different things.

How well do tacit-knowledge tests correlate with practical success as indicated by success on the job? Here, the correlations with the success of managers in business (as measured by their salary, years of management experience, employment in a high-ranking or Fortune 500 company, merit-based salary increases, ratings for generating new business) were about .20 to .56, about the same as correlations for cognitive-ability tests. When researchers used tacit-knowledge test scores together with IQ scores, the prediction of ratings of success in a managerial training program increased from .38 to .46, indicating that tacit knowledge accounted for a substantial amount of success beyond that explained by IQ. And a training program for improving "practical intelligence for school performance" produced "greater increases in reading, writing, homework, and test-taking ability over the school year" and "fewer behavior problems" (Sternberg et al., 1995, p. 923) as against students who did not receive the training.

Criticisms of Practical Intelligence Despite this evidence, some psychologists (Schmidt & Hunter, 1993) argue against giving practical intelligence the status of another kind of intelligence as important as general intelligence. They say that practical intelligence is really only a form of job knowledge rather than a form of intelligence. Job knowledge, which

Describe someone you have known whom you would describe as high (or low) in IQ and who had the opposite level (low or high) of practical intelligence.

is determined by both job experience and general intelligence, should correlate more highly with job performance than does intelligence alone—as it actually does. So these critics conclude that its character as a test of job knowledge gives practical intelligence, or measures of tacit knowledge, its success in predicting job performance.

Although further research will clarify such issues, the value of the concept of practical intelligence now is that teachers should be alert to kinds of ability other than those measured by traditional intelligence or cognitive-ability tests. There is more to human ability than what is measured by the traditional tests—which leads us to another major nontraditional conception of intelligence: the theory of **multiple intelligences.**

Multiple Intelligences

Gardner (1983) supplemented the traditional psychometric approaches to intelligence (e.g., Carroll, 1993) by asking how intelligence might be organized if he focused on

- literary accounts of intelligence
- neurological evidence from studies of brain-injured people
- descriptions of genius and deficiency, as in prodigies, autistic people, *idiots savants* (low-cognitive-ability persons with exceptional skills or talents in a special field, such as mental arithmetic), and learning-disabled children
- anthropological reports on diverse people and on practices in different cultures, species, and millennia.

When a certain ability showed up in several of these kinds of literature, Gardner accepted it into his categories of intelligence. His scholarship led him to theorize that there are seven distinct kinds of intelligence, and that they are only slightly correlated or interdependent.

1. *Linguistic intelligence* is seen, in its extreme forms, in the work of the poet or writer, and in the aphasic person, who is unable to speak or understand spoken or written language. It is commonly referred to as **verbal intelligence.** It includes the abilities to use vocabulary, do verbal analysis, understand metaphors, and comprehend and produce complex verbal material.

2. *Musical intelligence* shows up in the genius of a Mozart or a John Lennon, and in the ordinary development of musical talent in ordinary young children. To develop musical talent in 3-year-olds, as the Suzuki method (a musical-talent education program) does, argues well for the idea of that our musical system is "wired in," waiting for the environment to influence it.

3. *Logical-mathematical intelligence* appears, in its extremes, in mathematical genius and the long chains of reasoning in theorizing in high-energy physics and molecular biology. Arithmetic, algebra, and symbolic logic all demand this form of intelligence.

4. *Spatial intelligence* is seen clearly in the work of architects and engineers, who demonstrate unique spatial ability. It can be deduced from the biographies of Rodin and other sculptors, and Picasso and other artists. It is measured by tests wherein subjects look for hidden

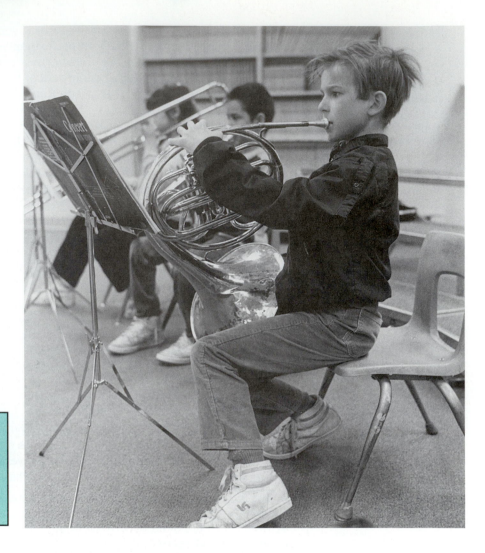

figures in diagrams, or mentally rotate objects in space and describe the changes that they undergo.

5. *Bodily-kinesthetic intelligence* is shown by athletes (especially gymnasts and divers), dancers, and jugglers and can be defined as a high level of awareness and control of one's body.

6. *Intrapersonal intelligence* is the form of self-knowledge often seen in people with unusual awareness of their strengths, weaknesses, feelings, desires, and what they need to be happy. There are currently no tests of this ability.

7. *Interpersonal intelligence,* often called *social intelligence,* is the ability to make use of subtle cues in the complex social environments created through interaction with our families, friends, employers, employees, customers, schoolmates, club members, and neighbors.

Gardner holds that each kind of intelligence uses its own system of symbols as a fundamental unit for the processing of information. For

Consider How Your Own Multiple Intelligences Operate Together

It is overly simple to link single intelligences with specific occupations or types of work. Think about the violinist who needs not only musical intelligence and a good ear but also some types of bodily-kinesthetic intelligence—finger dexterity in the left hand and accurate movements in the right arm—and also logical-mathematical intelligence to understand the complex score, theory, and harmony of a concerto.

Or, similarly, think about how the basketball player's various intelligences, beyond kinesthetic-bodily intelligence, show up in the following description by Bill Russell, once of the Boston Celtics, of how he and another expert, K. C., did their problem-solving. Consider how logical-mathematical and interpersonal intelligences are operating in what Bill Russell describes.

> We decided that basketball is basically a game of geometry—of lines, points, and distances—and that the horizontal distances are more important than the vertical ones. . . . Neither of us needed a blackboard to see the play the other was describing. Every hypothetical seemed real. . . . K. C. has an original basketball mind, and he taught me how to scheme to make things happen on the court, particularly on defense. In those days almost every player and coach thought of defense as pure reaction; that is, you reacted to the player you were guarding. . . . K. C. thought differently. He tried to figure out ways to take the ball away from the opponent. He was always figuring out ways to make the opponent take the shot he wanted him to take, when he wanted him to take it, from the place he wanted the man to shoot. . . . Or he'd let a man have an outside shot from just beyond the perimeter of his effectiveness, and instead of harassing the player, would take off down the court, figuring that I'd get the rebound and throw him a long pass for an easy basket. He and I dreamed up dozens of plays like these and fed into our equations what we knew about the weaknesses of our opponents. . . .
>
> (Russell & Branch, 1979, pp. 92–95)

Now apply this to yourself. Of Gardner's seven intelligences, which would you consider your strongest and most developed? Which two or three other intelligences are also particularly developed in you? What is one activity or pursuit in which your most-developed intelligence is utilized? Can you also identify other pursuits or interests in which you can see your three or four strongest intelligences operating together? Examine this process and try to describe it, on paper or to a friend.

example, musical intelligence, is built up of rhythmic information; spatial intelligence uses a visual symbol system. For Gardner, each type of intelligence is self-contained but connected to others. He also thinks of them as modular, comparable to the systems that make up a car, in which the ignition system is related to, but clearly separable from, the propulsion system, the exhaust system, and the brake system.

His conception means that a single measure of intelligence, such as IQ, is grossly inadequate for describing people's capabilities. If so, even two scores, such as the Scholastic Assessment Test's Verbal and Mathematics scores, are obviously insufficient. Gardner and his coworkers have been developing ways of assessing all seven intelligences. They are using not only paper-and-pencil approaches but also performances with machines (taking apart a meat grinder), social tasks (telling a story), drawing a picture, and dancing.

How would you rate the ideal third-grade teacher on these intelligences? The ideal college teacher of English?

There are good reasons for accepting Gardner's ideas. First is the evidence of remarkable phenomena around us: the people who lose their speech but not their musical talent; those idiot savants who can correctly multiply seven digits by seven digits in seconds in their heads but are developmentally delayed in other ways; the people who can draw beautifully but can barely do anything else. These cases argue for separate musical, mathematical, and artistic processing systems in the brain. And the autobiographies of great musicians, artists, and writers contain descriptions, in their earliest memories, of a special sensitivity to rhythm and melody, color and form, or words and language. It may even be that there are specialized areas in the brain for the different systems.

Multiple Intelligences and Factor-Analyzed Intelligences   How do traditional cognitive-ability researchers regard these multiple intelligences? As Luborski and Benbow (1995) pointed out, such intelligences "possess strong linkages to traditional psychometric conceptualizations of human abilities" (p. 935). Carroll (1993, p. 641) compared Gardner's intelligences with his own list of Stratum II abilities, described above (see Figure 3.3, p. 58). His comparison is shown in Table 3.2. The agreements between the two sets of abilities, which were derived through two radically different approaches, should give us confidence in the validity of at least those intelligences they have in common.

Multiple Intelligences in the Schools   What is important for you to remember, however, is that the theory of multiple intelligences has implications for what a full school program might be if educators tried to develop *all* the talent of all our youth (Kornhaber, Krechevsky, & Gardner, 1990). Right now, schools are designed primarily to develop linguistic and logical-mathematical intelligences. They do not do as well with the musical and spatial forms of intelligence, and treat as extracurricular the development of bodily-kinesthetic intelligence. The two forms of personal intelligence—intrapersonal and interpersonal—are generally ignored in formal schooling altogether. But some educators would say the schools should care as much about the other forms of intelligence as they do for the linguistic and logical-mathematical forms. Nurturing

How would the idea of "going beyond IQ" and into the multiple intelligences apply to you as a teacher?

3.2

TABLE

A Comparison of Gardner's Intelligences and Carroll's Cognitive-Ability Factors

Gardner's Intelligences	Carroll's Cognitive-Ability Factors
Linguistic intelligence	Crystallized intelligence
Musical intelligence	Auditory perception ability (or at least some special subfactors of it)
Logical-mathematical intelligence	Fluid intelligence
Spatial intelligence	Visual perception
Bodily-kinesthetic intelligence	(No direct counterpart; does not recognize psychomotor ability as a central component of cognitive ability)
Interpersonal intelligence	Knowledge-of-behavioral-content factor
Intrapersonal intelligence	(No counterpart)

Based on Carroll (1993, p. 641).

many different kinds of intelligence would allow many more students to succeed in learning, and that success would be a powerful motivator.

Other educators say the school's main responsibility is to cultivate the intellectual outcomes based on linguistic and logical-mathematical intelligences. They hold that other institutions (families, religious organizations, mass media, interactions with peers in the neighborhood and playground) can—and should be relied upon to—cultivate the other kinds of intelligence.

They would also say that the various intelligences have different importances in postindustrial societies, so that demand for the different kinds of intelligence differs. Everyone in society needs some linguistic and logical-mathematical intelligence, but not everyone needs some musical intelligence in order to prosper. They argue that the nation needs teachers, physicians, and engineers more than, say, dancers or athletes. In reply, defenders of multiple intelligences point out that journalists and lawyers, for example, need not only linguistic and logical-mathematical competencies but also interpersonal and intrapersonal strengths. This kind of debate (see, e.g., Kornhaber, Krechevsky, & Gardner, 1990), which raises the issue of values and the curriculum, is now more enlightened in view of the theory of multiple intelligences.

But debate has not stayed at the theoretical level. An entire elementary school—the Key School in Indianapolis—has been organized around the idea of putting the theory of multiple intelligences into practice (Gardner, 1993). It gives equal attention to English, mathematics, music, art, computers, movement, and other subjects. Children develop their competencies in these areas by working as "apprentices," led by teachers with appropriate interests, in small classes composed of chil-

Are the various multiple intelligences equally important to our society?

dren from any grade level. In this way the children can discover their strengths and develop the various intelligences. Each pupil carries out a year-long project on a theme such as "humans and their environment" or "changes in time and space," and the projects are videotaped and evaluated.

The theory of multiple intelligences, or concentrating on the different broad Stratum-II abilities, is sure to give a more multidimensional view of students than that afforded by the *g* theory of intelligence; the wider the view of intelligence, the more likely that society will find talent among diverse students.

Group Differences in Cognitive Ability

Observers have known since early in this century that different groupings or categories of people tend to differ in their average scores on measures of cognitive ability. What are these differences? In this section, we take up socioeconomic status differences, urban-rural differences, and ethnic differences.

Socioeconomic Status Differences

Socioeconomic status (SES) is typically measured by one or more of the following kinds of indexes: parents' occupation, family income, place of residence, and parents' educational level. Most comparisons (e.g., Lubinski & Humphreys, 1996; Ferguson, Lloyd, & Harwood, 1991; Capron & Duyme, 1989) show that middle-SES children have higher average IQ scores than lower-SES children.

The study by Capron and Duyme (1989) is especially significant because they distinguished between the SES influence of biological parents (heredity) and that of adoptive parents (environment). Adopted children were located who fell into each of four groups:

1. High-SES Biological Parents and High-SES Adoptive Parents ($n = 10$)

2. High-SES Biological Parents and Low-SES Adoptive Parents ($n = 8$)

3. Low-SES Biological Parents and High-SES Adoptive Parents ($n = 10$)

4. Low-SES Biological Parents and Low-SES Adoptive Parents ($n = 10$)

Parental SES was measured with two variables: (1) occupation (high: student, physician, senior executive, professor; low: worker, diverse unskilled, small farmer) and (2) number of years of schooling (high average: 15–17; low average: 6.3–6.8).

All parents in the high-SES groups were highly similar in SES and all parents in the low-SES groups were highly similar in SES. Furthermore, there was "no evidence of selective placement: the age of the child at the time of relinquishment and age at adoption did not differ between the

TABLE 3.3

IQ of Adopted Children

		SES of Adoptive Parents		
		High	Low	*Mean IQ*
High	n	10	8	
	Mean IQ	119.60	107.50	113.55
	Variability	12.25	11.94	
	Range	99–136	91–124	
Low	n	10	10	
	Mean IQ	103.60	92.40	98.00
	Variability	12.71	15.41	
	Range	91–125	68–116	
	Mean IQ	111.60	99.95	

(Row label: SES of Biological Parents)

Adapted from Capron & Duyme (1989).

four groups" (pp. 552–553). Health and selection factors were also controlled. The average age at the time of the IQ testing was 14 and did not differ among the groups.

As Table 3.3 shows, children reared by high-SES parents had substantially higher IQs than those reared by low-SES parents, regardless of the SES of the biological parents. Similarly, children born of high-SES parents had substantially higher IQs than those born of low-SES parents, regardless of the SES of the adoptive parents. This small but carefully controlled study supports the previously stated conclusion that both heredity (biological parents) and environment (adoptive parents) have substantial effects on IQ.

Many educators believe that schools in general, and teachers in particular, have a responsibility to eliminate, or at least reduce, the differences in educational achievement between lower-SES and middle-SES students. But how? The traditional view has been that special educational treatments—enriched curricula, new teaching methods, and the like—should be given to students from lower-SES homes. These treatments should improve the students' scholastic aptitude, and reduce and eventually eliminate their disadvantages as indicated by lower average IQ scores. This approach is reflected in Project Head Start and Project Follow Through on a national scale, and in many comparable programs in various cities and states.

Urban-Rural Differences

It is typical to find urban-rural differences in cognitive ability and achievement. In general, students in metropolitan areas show higher achievement than do those outside them. In their huge (and still-relevant) 1966 study, Coleman et al. found these differences at all the different grade levels studied (grades 1, 3, 6, 9, and 12) and on all the measures used—verbal ability; nonverbal ability; reading comprehension; mathematics achievement; and general information in practical arts, natural sciences, social studies, and humanities.

Ethnic Differences

The term *race* is impossible to define as a biological concept. As such, it typically refers solely to such behaviorally unimportant physical characteristics as skin color, eye shape, and facial configuration. So the term *ethnicity* has come into use to refer to the psychological and social-cultural differences among human groups—differences that are caused by and in turn influence the social forces operating in societies.

Are there ethnic differences in cognitive ability? Certain facts are clear. In the United States, African-Americans have consistently scored substantially lower on average than whites on cognitive-ability tests. Shuey (1966) reviewed approximately 380 studies that dealt with all age levels, in all regions, using many different tests. In the vast majority of the comparisons, the mean IQ score of the African-Americans was 10 to 20 points lower than that of the whites. This difference is now seldom disputed. It is the *cause* of the differences that is in doubt.

Hereditarians argue that (1) cognitive-ability differences within whites in the United States and Northern Europe have high heritability (see the

Some definitions of intelligence include social competence and social skills.

(© Jean-Claude Lejeune)

FIGURE 3.7

Heritability can be high within each of two groups even though the difference between the groups is entirely environmental.

Reprinted from N. Block (1995), "How Heritability Misleads about Race," Cognition, 56, p. 110. With kind permission of Elsevier Science, NL, Sara Burger-hartstraats 25, 1055 KV Amsterdam, The Netherlands.

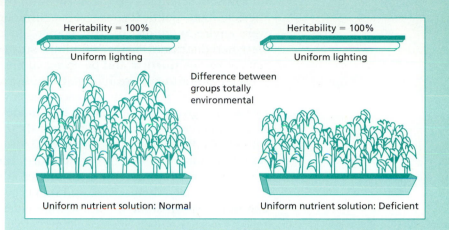

discussion of twin studies above) and (2) therefore the group differences among ethnic groups are probably also largely determined by hereditary factors.

But the substantial heritability of differences *within* a group, such as whites, does not necessarily indicate any heritability of differences *between* groups, such as whites and African-Americans. This fact is readily understandable from Lewontin's example, as summarized by Block (1995) and illustrated in Figure 3.7.

> Suppose you buy a bag of ordinary seed corn from a hardware store. This is ordinary genetically variegated (not cloned) corn. You grow one handful of it in a carefully controlled environment [e.g., hydroponically]. . . . The corn plants will vary in height and since the environment is uniform, the heritability of height will be 100%. Now take another handful of corn from the same bag, which you grow in a similarly uniform environment but with a uniformly poor nutrient solution. The plants will vary in height again but all will be stunted. The heritability of height in both groups is 100%, but the difference between the groups is entirely environmentally caused.
>
> (Block, 1995, pp. 110–111)

Furthermore, the Flynn effect and Ceci's information showed that (1) the environment can have substantial effects on IQ and (2) African-Americans have been, throughout American history and are still, on average, seriously worse off than whites in SES—the kinds of environmental factors (schooling, nutrition, housing, job opportunities, and others) that make a difference in IQ.

The Nature-Nurture Issue and Conservatism-Liberalism

You should be aware that there are questions about scientific objectivity in this area. Pastore (1949) looked at the positions of 24 American and British scientists on the **nature-nurture** issue, comparing them to the scientists' political conservatism or liberalism. Of the 12 liberals, 11 were environmentalist in their stance, and of the 12 conservatives, 11 were hereditarians. Pastore's findings suggested a link between views on nature versus nurture and basic social and political issues.

Related findings were reported by Sherwood and Nataupsky (1968). They surveyed 83 American researchers who had studied race differences in cognitive ability. Some had made hereditarian interpretations of the differences; others interpreted their findings along environmentalist lines. When the two groups were compared, it turned out that the hereditarians more often were firstborn, had grandparents born in the United States, had parents with higher educational levels, had higher grades in college themselves, and had grown up in homogeneous, rural communities. In some ways, the differences suggested that the hereditarians were themselves more conservative and advantaged. Perhaps for this reason they tended to believe that cognitive ability is innately determined, their own good fortune being a natural right rather than the result of a good environment to which others might have equal rights.

More recently, similar tendencies for conservativism to go along with hereditarianism and liberalism to go along with environmentalism were found by Furnham et al. (1985) in England and Nilsson and Ekehammar (1989) in Sweden. So it is interesting to note that a statement by 52 "experts in intelligence and allied fields," expressing neither a hereditarian nor an environmentalist position, was published in the (conservative) *Wall Street Journal*.

> There is no definitive answer to why IQ bell curves differ across racial-ethnic groups. The reasons for these IQ differences between groups may be markedly different from the reasons for why individuals differ among themselves within any particular group (whites or blacks or Asians).
>
> *(Wall Street Journal, December 13, 1994)*

Explanations of Group Differences

Psychologists have proposed three explanations for the group differences just described: selective migration, environmental influence, and test bias.

Selective Migration   The explanation based on selective migration says that more-able people move into the more-advantaged social statuses, occupations, and communities. Their superior intellectual ability makes them better at competing for social advantage, and more able and interested in the kinds of activities and situations found in these more favorably placed parts of society. According to this explanation, the differences in cognitive ability exist *before* a group or individual moves into the more-advantaged social category or location. Evidence in favor of this explanation would show that initially more-intelligent people migrate from lower-SES to middle-SES life situations, from rural to urban communities.

Anastasi (1958), after summarizing the evidence, concluded that "in general, studies on adults do show a tendency for migrants from rural to urban areas to constitute a superior sampling of the rural population" (p. 530). Even in a small country like Denmark, regional differences in cognitive-ability test scores and educational levels showed up. But these differences seemed to be due not to selective migration but to regional urbanization and population density and the correspondingly better educational resources available (Teasdale & Owen, 1988).

In any case, these results do not necessarily support hereditary explanations because the initially superior groups may have had an environmental advantage in their original rural setting as well. Also, in some situations, selective migration might operate so that those who migrate are less able. For example, in the Great Depression of the 1930s, it was the mountain-area dwellers and sharecroppers who headed toward the cities, not the landed or higher-income individuals. Those who are more able have achieved an advantageous position in their communities so that, when there is a famine or a depression, they have less incentive to migrate.

Environmental Influence According to the environmental-influence explanation, urban or suburban, middle-SES communities and families provide better environments than rural or low-SES communities and families for developing the abilities measured by cognitive-ability tests. These environments more often expose children to the stimuli—sights and sounds, words and ideas, problems and solutions—that nourish the skills and knowledge measured by cognitive-ability tests. But the exact nature of this stimulation is still unknown in any detail. No research has yet pinpointed the specific experiences that give city children an advantage in cognitive ability over farm children.

Two of the environmental factors that lower cognitive ability can readily be imagined: neglect and abuse. So Perez and Widom (1994) studied 413 adults who had been abused and neglected when they were children, matched to a control group of 286 adults who had not been so treated. Both groups were on average about 28 years old. Even when age, sex, race, and SES were controlled, the previously abused and neglected young adults showed lower intellectual ability and academic attainment.

Test Bias The **test-bias** explanation of group differences in cognitive ability rests on a belief that cognitive-ability tests involve types of content and processes that are more accessible to children in advantaged groups. Fairer test content and processes would reduce group differences.

How is test bias detected? Among the methods that psychologists use (see Berk, 1982) are

- making judgments about the content and behaviors called for by test items
- doing experiments to see whether different kinds of test content (e.g., content reflecting African-American culture and white culture) cause differences in the performance of African-American and white students. For example, a test of reading comprehension based on

content identified with the white culture could be about the topic of food in restaurants. A second test, measuring similar skills, might be based on a black woman's reflections on her Civil War experiences (Schmeiser, 1982).

■ statistically analyzing the kinds of items that are more difficult for one ethnic group than another and items that do not produce such differences.

■ determining differential test validity, that is, seeing whether tests have less accuracy in predicting school or occupational success for minority groups than for white groups.

These methods are used because the words, ideas, and problems in standardized tests are suspected of being drawn from situations of the kind more likely to be met by white, urban children in middle-SES families. For example, an item intended to call for abstract thinking requires knowledge that lower-SES children do not typically have. Tests do not have to use items such as "Symphony is to composer as painting is to (artist)" when they could use "Corn is to farmer as cake is to (baker)." If we want to measure reasoning ability rather than knowledge, we have to free tests of their most obvious middle-SES, white, urban and suburban bias—we have to use more **culture-free tests** (sometimes called *culture-fair tests*). And, in fact, tests have been getting better in this sense. The most blatant forms of bias against woman, minorities, lower-SES children, and others have been essentially eliminated.

It seems obvious, however, that group differences in cognitive ability might disappear, or at least become much smaller, if all the bias in test content were removed. But here a problem may come up. Cognitive-ability tests are intended to measure what is important to success in contemporary American society; and that society is itself oriented toward middle-SES and urban concerns. Removing "bias" from the tests would make them less relevant to their purpose, a point emphasized in *Equality of Educational Opportunity.*

> The facts of life in modern society are that the intellectual skills, which involve reading, writing, calculation, analysis of information, are becoming basic requirements for independence, for productive work, for political participation, for wise consumption. . . . Such tests are not in any sense "culturally fair"; in fact, their very design is to determine the degree to which a child has assimilated a culture appropriate to modern life in the United States.
>
> *(Coleman et al., 1966, p. 218)*

So middle-SES bias has proved much more difficult to eliminate than was anticipated. For tests of the intellectual abilities useful in modern American society, a "middle-SES" and "urban" orientation may constitute not bias, but relevance. An emphasis on verbal facility and the ability to solve abstract problems may be just what postindustrial, technical, mercantile, urban societies require. So educators may not want to change the tests so much as change the environments that promote low test performance.

What do you think? Are most cognitive-ability tests biased or relevant?

Improving Cognitive Ability

Can cognitive ability be improved by changing environment? This is the major question in today's studies of cognitive ability. There are as yet no methods for increasing cognitive ability as substantially and dependably as improving, say, knowledge of French or auto mechanics, that is, by simply teaching those subjects in a way appropriate to the level of the students. As yet, no one has developed successful, clearly defined methods that can be repeated by other researchers and get the same results.

This can also be said, but with less assurance, about achievement in school. The same socioeconomic status, rural-urban, and ethnic differences found for cognitive abilities are also found for achievement. The problem, then, is one of reducing or eliminating group differences in school achievement as well as in cognitive ability. The problem has been explored, progress has been made, and additional work may be expected in the years ahead. The social and educational problems at stake are so important that educators and psychologists should understand what is being done.

Are there ways to manipulate environmental variables—both at home and in school—to reduce or eliminate major between-group differences that put a given segment of society at a disadvantage? The social concern with group inequalities in cognitive ability and achievement arises from ideals of social justice. When whole groups—various minority groups, rural, or lower-SES children—are found to be handicapped by lower average cognitive ability and achievement, it is plausible that broad social forces are at work. For African-Americans, these social forces include tragic parts of American history—slavery, home and school segregation, job discrimination, and persecution. Many of the same factors have influenced Latino-American citizens. As these injustices are eliminated, minority-group disadvantages in average achievement should lessen. For educators, the task becomes improving education to make up for centuries of deprivation and neglect.

The Home Environment and Cognitive Abilities

Much evidence indicates that home environment can affect IQ scores. We have already noted (p. 85) the negative effects of abuse and neglect. But what about positive effects of the home?

Adoption Studies   Here the evidence is what happens when low-SES children are adopted into what seem to be advantage-providing homes. One appraisal of that kind of influence was that "Whereas compensatory educational programs involve the child for a few hours per day . . . adoption alters the entire social ecology of the child. Parents, siblings, home, peers, school, neighborhood, and community—the child's rearing environment—are transformed by adoption" (Scarr & Weinberg, 1976, p. 736). Good adoptive homes and adoptive parents, it was believed, can

Reading to children and discussing what is going on in the books is probably the most important contribution parents can make to their children's reading development.

(© Paul Conklin/PhotoEdit)

turn out children whose IQ scores are substantially higher than would be predicted from the biological parents' IQ scores. This belief was based on such studies as that by Scarr and Weinberg (1976), who studied 130 African-American or interracial children adopted by socioeconomically advantaged, white families. The adoptees scored on the average 106 in IQ and at the 55th percentile in achievement—well above the mean IQ score and mean school achievement of both African-American children reared in their own homes and the white population. Early-adopted children did even better. "This mean represents an increase of 1 standard deviation above the average IQ of 90 usually achieved by black children reared in their own homes in the North Central region" (Scarr & Weinberg, 1976, p. 736).

Similar findings occurred in a study in France (Schiff et al., 1978) of the children of 32 "working-class" mothers who had abandoned their infants. These children were adopted before 6 months of age into upper-middle-SES families. In that group, the rate of school failures (repetition of grades or placement in a class with a simplified curriculum) was only 13 percent, much lower than that of 39 children of the same mothers who had not been abandoned, namely, 56 percent. Only 17 percent of the adopted children had IQ scores below 95, while 49 percent of the children who had not been abandoned had IQ scores below 95. The researchers subsequently reported that the estimated increase in IQ score for the adopted children was 14 points (Schiff et al., 1982). Recall that the study by Capron and Duyme (1989, pp. 80–81) yielded similar results. Here again we see that both nature and nurture play a strong role in determining the intelligence of adopted children—and, by implication, all children.

What Processes Do Have Influence?   The evidence says that home environment affects cognitive ability, but it reveals relatively little about the processes involved. Just what variables in the home make the difference? If we knew, we could try to help other parents use them and try to incorporate them into our classrooms.

Researchers have made sophisticated attempts to analyze the home-environment variables that affect cognitive development. They measure home environment by having observers rate such things as how often and well parents

- speak to the child
- provide the child with a variety of games and toys
- avoid restriction and punishment
- organize the child's time and space
- provide warmth and affection
- provide variety in the people with whom the child interacts (see Whiteside-Mansell & Bradley et al., 1996)

Each of these categories of parental behavior or home environment contains six to ten highly specific kinds of behavior or environmental elements to observe. Scores on such measures typically correlate about .30 to .40 with children's IQs (Gottfried, 1984).

But any correlation between home-environment variables and cognitive ability may not reflect purely environmental cause-and-effect connections. Parents influence their child's IQ both genetically and environmentally. As Figure 3.8 shows, the correlation may result from any or all of the following:

1. The environmental effect of the parents' abilities, values and behaviors, which lead them to provide a more or less stimulating home environment

2. The genetic effect of parents' cognitive ability on their children's cognitive ability

3. The reactive effect of the children in shaping their own environment

In Figure 3.8, Diagram 1 means that the parents' IQ determines, in part, the home environment, with higher-IQ parents tending to provide more stimulating environments, which in turn leads to their children's having higher IQs. Diagram 2 means that higher-IQ parents genetically tend to have higher-IQ children, who seek out and so cause their own environments to be more favorable to intellectual development. "Thus, the mother's treatment of the child may be shaped by the characteristics

> Make up a little scenario to fit each of the possibilities shown in Figure 3.8.

FIGURE 3.8

Three ways in which parents can influence the IQ of their children

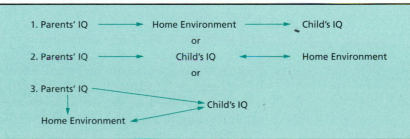

[such as IQ] of the child. The direction of influence is ambiguous" (Brody, 1992, p. 170). Diagram 3 illustrates how the parents' IQ, operating genetically, and the parent-IQ-influenced home environment, operating environmentally, both have an influence on the child's IQ. It is always hard, however, to determine what factors are operating in real families, in real homes.

Despite the difficulty, in recent years the home life of Asian-American students has been analyzed because of the high average IQ scores and school achievement among these students. More than 20 percent of the freshmen at highly selective colleges, such as the Massachusetts Institute of Technology and the University of California, Berkeley, are Asian-Americans, despite their constituting only about 2 percent of the American population. The source of Asian-American achievement apparently is related partly to family factors (Stevenson, Lee, & Stigler, 1986). Asian-American mothers, for example, stress hard work and the economic benefits of school success, hold high expectations for performance, and are regularly dissatisfied with their children's level of performance. They expect children to get and do homework, they limit television viewing, and they delay dating. They are much more likely to provide their children with a desk at home and mathematics and science workbooks they have purchased themselves. These parental behaviors reflect the strong education-oriented values in Asian-American culture, and Asian-American student performance reflects this heritage. These kinds of parental behavior would seem to support children's academic success in any cultural group.

The parental behaviors associated with student intellectual achievement can also serve as guides for teachers. Whether certain parental behaviors are causally related to a child's intellectual development remains to be seen. Certainly some home advantages result from the parents' own cognitive ability, which influences both their style of life and their child's inherited cognitive ability. But some of the variation in children's IQ scores and achievement probably results solely from variables in the environment, variables that parents do have control over.

School Influences on Cognitive Abilities

The research discussed above is important to educators because it says that IQ and achievement can be improved, at least to some extent. Of course, teachers cannot intervene directly in the homes of their students, except through programs of parent education and involvement. But they can accomplish a great deal by what they do at school.

The Argument for Early Intervention   It has long seemed reasonable that attempts to improve cognitive ability will be more effective at earlier ages. That is why many programs focus on nursery school children.

Economic deprivation means inadequate opportunity for the stimulating and varied experiences that promote the ability to learn. Crowded homes may provide these kinds of experiences during the first year of life, but they can suppress intellectual growth in subsequent years. Also,

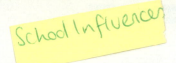

exposure to books and print at an early age is often limited in low-SES homes. The clear implication is that preventive measures should be taken during the early years, and that early schooling in an enriched environment should enable children to enter first grade without academic impediments.

This evidence and reasoning led to the proposition that early schooling can prevent children from low-resource families from entering the first grade handicapped in achieving adequately in that grade and later. With early schooling, the preschool child can and should learn to handle language, evaluate information, use probable cues as well as completely certain ones, and otherwise grasp general principles and methods of successfully dealing with the environment. Exposure to a rich environment and taking part successfully in problem-solving activities should further the learning that leads to later success in school or on the job.

Early Education Programs   The most widely used of the preschool programs is the federally supported Project Head Start. According to a meta-analysis of comparisons of Head Start and control children (McKey et al., 1985), the program has had many positive effects on children's social and emotional development, physical health, families, and communities. Studies have shown that Head Start children are more likely to be promoted to the next grade and less likely to be put into special education classes. But the good, immediate educational effects on cognitive abilities have seemed to disappear by the end of second grade. So evaluators have raised questions as to whether Head Start is sufficiently early (in starting only at age 2 or later), intensive (in hours per day), or long-lasting (in number of years).

The Abecedarian Project   The Abecedarian Project has produced the most recent report on an educational experiment aimed at improving cognitive ability. (*Abecedarian* means someone who learns the alphabet or anything basic and fundamental.) It is one of several major long-range follow-up studies of the effects of early education on IQ and achievement (e.g., the Milwaukee Project [Garber, 1988], and the Perry Preschool Project [Schweinhart & Weikart, 1980]).

The Abecedarian effort, begun in 1972, differed from others in starting the intervention in very early infancy and being more intensive. Abecedarian staff worked with and studied 90 African-American children, who were randomly assigned to four groups as shown in Figure 3.9.

> The random assignment of children to the various treatment conditions is a very important feature of this study because it permits the investigators to attribute group differences to the treatment, rather than to differences in family factors. This procedure avoided one especially important confound—that of systematic differences [in motivation, values, and abilities] among low-income families who sought full-time child care for their infants compared to those who do not.
> *(Campbell & Ramey, 1995, pp. 747–748)*

(Note, however, that Herrnstein and Murray (1994, p. 407) objected that the small size of the groups ($Ns = 9$ to 15) may have made random as-

Design of the Abecedarian Project
Reproduced, with permission, from Ramey & Campbell (1991), p. 192.

School-Age Intervention

		Yes	No
Preschool Intervention	**Yes**	*PS + SA* Birth to age 8 Intervention	*PS* Birth to age 5 Intervention
	No	*SA* Age 5 to 8 Intervention	Controls

The PS + SA group (N=25) received an intensive preschool (PS) program from infancy to age 5 *and also* an enriched school-age (SA) elementary-school program in grades 1–3.
The PS-only group (N=22) received only the preschool program.
The SA-only group (N=21) received only the school-age program.
The Control Group (N=21) received neither the PS nor the SA program.

signment less effective in making the initial characteristics of the four groups equivalent, and that the best-achieving group also had the highest initial scores.)

The preschool intervention began in the first half of the child's first year. The curriculum provided intensive experiences in cognitive and fine-motor development, social and self-help skills, language, and gross motor skills. Teachers placed special emphasis on language development and preliteracy skills to develop sociolinguistic competence (see Chapter 4). In addition to the preschool treatment, one group also received the school-age intervention, which enhanced parental involvement, with a home-resource teacher providing parents with activities to be conducted at home to strengthen the reading and mathematics ideas taught at school. The parents were asked to conduct these activities for at least 15 minutes daily. IQ results showed that

> Children who received preschool treatment had higher IQ scores over time than children in the preschool control group. The average IQ-score advantage for individuals treated in preschool was 8.8 points, with [an advantage] of 16.4 points at age 36 months [changing] to [an advantage of] 4.5 points at age 8; the final difference, at age 15, was 4.6 points.
>
> *(Campbell & Ramey, 1995, pp. 756–757)*

So the effects on IQ were larger in the early years than at age 15. The effects on age-15 IQ, while positive, were not as great as the effects on academic achievement. Achievement-test results in both reading and mathematics showed big advantages for the preschool-treatment groups over the nonpreschool-treatment groups at ages 8, 12, and 15. Furthermore, "through 10 years in school, children who had the Abecedarian preschool treatment made better school progress, in terms of fewer retentions in grade and fewer assignments to special education programs, than those in the preschool control group" (Campbell & Ramey, 1995, p. 761).

The Abecedarian Project was performed with high levels of control and rigor, in ways unmentioned in this brief account. Also, it allowed a

Offer a hypothesis as to why the school-age intervention did not have the same kind of effect that preschool intervention did.

comparison of the effects of treatments in preschool only, in grades K–3 only, and in preschool plus grades K–3. And its results were followed up through age 15. So it is an important study. It showed that an intensive (full-day, year-round) preschool program, beginning in the first half-year of life, can have highly beneficial and long-lasting effects on intellectual development and achievement in reading and mathematics, prevention of retention-in-grade, and reduction of need for special education. It also found that "the early education [preschool] treatment itself was responsible for the benefits found. . . . As the present study shows, early failure among this [African-American] population can be significantly reduced with an intensive [five-year] preschool program" (Campbell & Ramey, 1995, p. 764).

So, can IQ be raised? The answer seems to be yes. But both the question and its answer may be less important than was originally thought, in light of the effects of intensive preschool education on achievement, general adjustment to school—and, perhaps most important, adult adjustment.

On the subject of adult adjustment, the Perry Project has provocative evidence (Schweinhart, Barnes, & Weikart, 1993), based on the 123 low-SES African-American children whom it followed to age 27. Here, the children who participated in the preschool program, compared with the control group, turned out at 27 to have significantly higher earnings, to own their own homes more often, to have gone further in school, to have been arrested less often, and to have required less help from social service agencies. The authors claimed that for every dollar spent on the preschool program more than seven dollars had been saved by taxpayers. Educators must keep reminding the public that investments in education are not just a moral commitment by a just society. Those investments pay off in terms of decreased costs to maintain poorly educated people and of increased tax revenues paid by productive, wage-earning citizens.

SUMMARY

1. Cognitive abilities are the intellectual skills and capabilities used for dealing with abstractions, solving problems, and learning.

2. They are measured with tests that pose questions and problems, sometimes dealing with content similar to what is taught in school and sometimes with novel content and situations.

3. Scores on such tests for culturally homogeneous groups of people tend to fall into a normal frequency distribution, which has most people in the middle of the range and decreasing numbers toward the extremes above and below the middle. The relationships between scores and their frequency lend meaning to various derived, as against raw, scores on the tests.

4. Scores on cognitive-ability tests tend to be highly reliable, so they change little from one testing to another, and fairly stable, so that an individual's standing is unlikely to change very much from year to year, especially after late childhood.

5. Cognitive abilities correlate positively with one another, giving rise to the concept of a single general cognitive ability, called *g*, which is usually estimated with an IQ test. But the abilities also fall into less highly correlated groups of abilities, such as verbal-crystallized, mathematical-fluid, and spatial-visualization abilities.

6. Both the general and less-general cognitive abilities correlate positively with school and job success and so have value for predicting such success.

7. Whether the determiners of cognitive abilities are genetic to any degree has been investigated through correlations between the test scores of pairs of individuals differing in genetic and environmental similarity. The most similar are identical twins raised together by their parents; next most similar are identical twins raised apart. Then come siblings raised together and apart, and the least similar are unrelated pairs raised apart.

8. The average correlations between the scores tend to decrease as the closeness of the relationship between paired individuals decreases. The most relevant data come from identical twins reared apart, since their genetic similarity seems separable from environmental similarity, but even here there are ambiguities.

9. The data from these correlations are used to estimate heritability, which is the ratio of genetically determined variability in IQs to the total variability (genetic + environmental). Current opinion puts this heritability at about 50 percent, meaning that variability in environment accounts for the other half of the variability in IQ. But one recent study distinguished between genetic influence and intrauterine (environmental) influence, which is substantial. If so, genetic influence is reduced.

10. The research is equally clear that these findings apply only to individuals within culturally homogeneous groups, not to differences between groups.

11. Heritability does not mean unchangeability; even highly heritable characteristics have changed markedly for nongenetic reasons. That IQ is also highly changeable, whatever its heritability, is indicated by the Flynn effect: massive IQ increases in many industrialized nations during the past 30 to 50 years. The cause of these increases may be improved nutrition, but some eight kinds of evidence strongly suggest that schooling improves IQ. So it is also probable that better schooling has contributed to the Flynn effect.

12. Current practice is to use intelligence tests to select, place, and counsel students because the tests predict success in educational programs. Intelligence tests differ from achievement tests, which measure actual performance in school subjects. The content and skills required by intelligence tests are usually not taught directly; the content and skills required by achievement tests are, or certainly should be, taught in school. Yet there is a high correlation between the results of the two kinds of tests.

13. Many people argue that intelligence tests create a self-fulfilling prophecy—that children who receive low IQ scores are taught in ways that prolong poor achievement. Whereas low scores on achievement tests are interpreted to show a need for improved teaching and more

effort in learning, low scores on intelligence tests are often interpreted fatalistically, as if nothing can be done to help the child with a low IQ score.

14. It is probably a good idea, then, to get along without intelligence tests except as part of a diagnostic process, along with other components, to identify the need for special education.

15. Two new conceptions of intelligence go beyond the present-day tests. One, the idea of practical intelligence, focuses on tacit knowledge, not formally learned, of the kind that amounts to common sense in handling real-life as against test-question problems.

16. The second new conception of intelligence, the idea of multiple intelligences, has used a wide range of evidence to identify seven relatively autonomous intelligences, which turn out to resemble somewhat the special abilities found through analyzing correlations between different tests. The multiple-intelligences conception implies that schools should broaden their definition of intelligence to tap the potential of as many students as possible.

17. There are ethnic and social group differences in measured intelligence. The average IQ score is lower for African-Americans than for whites, for students from lower-SES homes than for those from middle-SES homes, and for those from rural areas than for those from metropolitan areas. Why? Whatever the heritability of individual differences *within* cultural groups, the relative importance of heredity and environment to differences *between* groups is not determinable.

18. The heritability of a characteristic tells nothing about its genetic determination, which is a different matter.

19. Hereditarians use the concept of selective migration to explain why some social advantages are related to measured intelligence. Environmentalists argue that environmental deprivation and test bias are responsible for the lower IQ scores of certain ethnic, social, and geographic groups.

20. There is evidence that the home environment can affect both measured intelligence and academic achievement. The difficulty is determining which variables, genetic or environmental, are at work. Using correlations with IQ scores, researchers have identified several factors that seem to relate positively with measured intelligence: parental pressure for achievement and language development, and the provision of general learning opportunities outside school.

21. Studies of Asian-American homes and comparison of Asian and American cultures suggest, but do not prove, the importance of home environment in fostering intellectual achievement. The effect of home environment on intelligence and achievement is important because it says that change is possible and gives clues to the kinds of changes educators must make in schools.

22. To overcome the educational effects of economic deprivation among children, intervention must take place very early. Evidence over many years indicates that preschool programs do improve both intelligence and achievement.

The Development of Cognition, Language, and Personality

Overview

THE DEVELOPMENT OF COGNITION

Piaget's Stages

First stage: Sensorimotor (birth to age 2)

Second stage: Preoperational (ages 2 to 7)

Third stage: Concrete operational (ages 7 to 11)

Fourth stage: Formal operational (ages 11 to 14)

The Developmental Process

Dissenters from and Alternatives to Piagetian Theory

Questions about Piagetian theory

Neo-Piagetian and other alternative theories

Bruner's Theory of Cognitive Growth

Vygotsky's View of Cognitive Development

POLICY, RESEARCH, AND PRACTICE

Teaching from a Context of Diversity

APPLICATION

Instructional Implications of Piaget, Bruner, and Vygotsky

THE DEVELOPMENT OF LANGUAGE

Stages of Development

The one-word stage

The two-word stage

The more-than-two-word stage and metalinguistic awareness

Adults' Influence on Language Development and Literacy

Language Issues and Schooling

Nonstandard English

Bilingualism

Sociolinguistic competence and schooling

THE DEVELOPMENT OF PERSONALITY

Erikson's Theory of Personality Development

The Development of Moral Reasoning

Kohlberg's levels and stages

Gilligan's model

Fostering moral thinking

The Organization of Personality: A Profusion of Traits

Honesty

Creativity

APPLICATION

Making Use of Thinking Guides in Problem Solving

The teacher and trait theory

Self-concept

Summary

OVERVIEW

As we saw in Chapter 3, intelligence tests were originally developed to resolve a practical problem, and they served that purpose fairly well. But the developers of the tests did not describe coherently the ways in which mental functioning at one age differs from that at another. A thorough description of these kinds of developmental changes was in large part the contribution of the Swiss psychologist Jean Piaget, whose work began in the 1920s.

Piaget's theories have helped us understand how one behavior must develop in order that another can follow; how children incorporate experience into their own very personal conceptions of the world; how children's moral values develop sequentially; how imagination is formed and how it changes; how logical thought (such as scientific thought) develops; how the ability to categorize, generalize, and discriminate grows with children's experience; and how children learn symbol systems.

Cognitive development has also been described by Bruner (1966) and Vygotsky (1978), and we present their ideas in this chapter as well. Then we examine recent work on the development of language. As Piaget, Bruner, and Vygotsky would agree, when language is learned, cognitive development is changed. The development of this sophisticated symbol system makes possible the complex reasoning that is characteristic of humans and so important to the learning process.

But cognition is only one part of personality, which is the integration of all our traits, abilities, and motives as well as our temperament, attitudes, opinions, beliefs, emotional responses, cognitive styles, character, and morals. In fact, the concept of personality encompasses all aspects of human behavior, and so we also need to understand how aspects of personality other than cognition develop.

We begin by examining Erik Erikson's theory of how personality is formed, a general theory that describes personality development from birth to old age. Erikson believed that personality develops through a series of "crises." He focused especially on the crisis of adolescence and the development of identity, but he described also how youngsters develop trust, autonomy, and initiative. Next we talk about a more specific theory of personality, which focuses on one aspect of personality development—the growth of moral reasoning.

Then we look at the aspects of personality called *traits*, which for most people are the names used to communicate our descriptions of one another. We examine the traits of honesty and creativity. And we emphasize both the variability and the modifiability of personality traits as we encounter them in the classroom. Finally, we look at how self-concept— our beliefs and evaluations about ourselves—affects behavior.

In this discussion of personality, then, we move from the general to the specific. We go from an all-encompassing theory, to a theory concerned with the development of a single aspect of personality, to individual personality traits and our concept of self. The variability and changeability of these characteristics is highlighted.

The Development of Cognition

Piaget's Stages

Beginning in the 1920s, Piaget observed and interviewed children, presented them with intellectual tasks, and recorded their answers. He reported his sensitive insights, unique data-gathering procedures, and wide range of interests in many volumes, among them *The Language and Thought of the Child* (1926), *Judgment and Reasoning in the Child* (1928), *The Child's Conception of Physical Causality* (1930/1951a), and *The Moral Judgment of the Child* (1932).

Piaget was trained as a biologist, a fact that explains his way of looking for how one behavior fits within another and evolves in ways to help the organism adapt to its environment. If young children engage in some activity, that activity must serve a function. By carefully watching children we may learn how they come to see themselves as different from their environment and why that differentiation is important for the later development of their image of self. For instance, we may learn the ways in which the manipulation of objects—the sheer joy children take in repetitive activities with objects—helps the development of skilled motor performance and, later, symbolic thinking. Piaget was searching for patterns in behavior, for the ways in which even the simplest behavior of an organism is organized and adaptive.

Piaget's most enduring contribution was perhaps the recognition that children do not have reality neatly impressed on their brains. They construct reality for themselves—knowledge is built by the knower (Beilin, 1992). This is the root of contemporary interest in **constructivism**—the theory that each learner is an active maker of his or her own meanings. Constructivism asserts that knowledge cannot simply be handed over to someone else, though too many teachers act as if knowledge were a sticky note to be pasted onto the brain of the learner (Strauss, 1996). Piaget has taught us that teachers who think of knowledge as some kind of entity to be deposited into the brain of a student hold an incorrect model of how minds work. All learners, Piaget held, construct knowledge for themselves.

Piaget saw intellectual development as having four main stages in its advancement to logical reasoning: sensorimotor, preoperational (which he subdivided into preoperational and intuitive), concrete operational, and formal operational, as shown in Figure 4.1 (see also Flavell, 1963; Ginsburg & Opper, 1988; Gruber & Vonèche, 1977; Wadsworth, 1989). The age designations for each stage are approximate, not hard-and-fast. Moreover, a stage does not end suddenly; rather it trails off. A child may still think mistakenly in some areas while performing logically in others (de Ribapierre & Rieben, 1995).

First Stage: Sensorimotor (Birth to Age 2)   Covering roughly the ages from birth to 2 years, the **sensorimotor stage** is characterized by the child's growth in ability in simple perceptual and motor activities. This stage covers the period during which children move from a newborn's reflexive activity to a more highly organized, goal-directed kind of activity. In this stage children learn to

- see themselves as different from the objects around them
- seek stimulation in the light and sound around them
- try to prolong interesting experiences
- define things by physically manipulating them

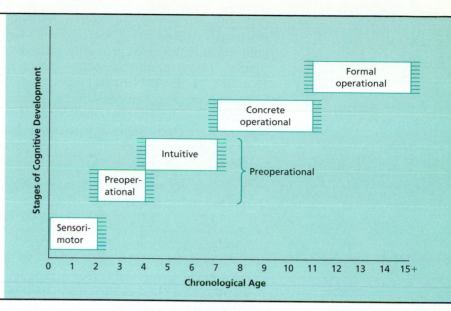

FIGURE 4.1

Piaget's concept of stages of cognitive development at various chronological age ranges

- regard an object as constant despite changes in its location or in their own point of view

One example of how behavior changes in the sensorimotor stage is that of an infant who tries to suck from the bottom of her bottle when it is given to her upside down. Perhaps just a month or two later the baby learns to turn the bottle right side up because she sees the bottle as the same object, regardless of the way in which it is given to her. Similarly, a baby at the age of 5 months stops looking for a ball when it rolls under a blanket. But at 8 months he continues to look for it, having learned that objects do not cease to exist when they suddenly go out of his direct observational field. This important feat is called the development of **object permanence.** When you think about it, some remarkable achievements take place in the sensorimotor stage. Children change enormously through **maturation** and learning during this stage.

You may be wondering why we sit back and watch children change. Does it really matter that a baby turns a bottle around? What children do, from the simplest graspings through the most complex examinations of things, is designed to give them mastery over the world. In part they acquire this mastery by building internal (mental) representations, or schemata (sing., **schema**), for the objects and events they experience in the external world. These early and primitive schemata for "eating," "traveling to grandmother's," or "bicycle riding," as well as conceptlike schemata that determine the boundaries of categories such as "animals" and "relatives," form the basis of conceptual thought. Without these broad schemata we would be quite limited in our thinking skills.

Second Stage: Preoperational (Ages 2 to 7) In the **preoperational phase** of the second stage, which covers the ages from 2 to 4, children are busy using language to help themselves develop concepts. Their concepts are very private and often unrealistic, and experience is crucial for learning linguistic forms. You may say to a child, "Too much water. You'll spill it!" and the child promptly spills it. Is the child testing your patience? Or is the child incapable of understanding a complex relational term like "too much" until a later stage, after much experience with the environment? Piaget insists that children need extensive experience to understand complex relational terms. Because our own thought patterns are relatively sophisticated, we overestimate the depth of understanding of young children. In the preoperational phase of development, children

- are markedly self-centered—egocentric—and often incapable of putting themselves in another person's shoes, that is, taking another person's point of view in perceiving the physical world
- can classify objects on the basis of a single conspicuous feature (redness, all metal objects)
- are unable to see that objects alike in one respect may differ in others—green squares and green triangles are grouped together. (The inability of a child in this phase to handle multiple classifications is seen in the nursery school child who meets her teacher in the supermarket and either fails to recognize her or is shocked to discover that she also eats!)
- are able to collect things according to a criterion, including a shifting criterion
- can arrange things in a series, but cannot draw inferences about things that are not adjacent to each other in the series. They cannot usually infer from the facts that if John is taller than Sam and Sam is taller than Manuel, then John is taller than Manuel.

In the **intuitive phase** of the preoperational stage, which covers the ages from 4 to 7, children reach conclusions based on vague impressions and perceptual judgments that are not put into words. These give ground, but only slowly, to more logical, rational understanding. Perception without words—that is, without symbolic mediation—often leads children to misunderstand events in the world around them. As language becomes more and more important, more mediation can take place.

Slowly, perhaps by age 7, children learn to react to symbol systems in a reliable way and to override their intuitive perceptual impressions. More important, by age 7 children can use symbol systems to transform the contents of their minds. But this can happen only if they have had extensive experience with the world at large.

In the intuitive phase of development, then, children

- become able to form classes or categories of objects, but are not necessarily aware of them
- become able to understand logical relationships of increasing complexity
- become able to work with the idea of number
- start acquiring the principle of **conservation,** that is, the idea that the amount of something stays the same regardless of changes in its shape or the number of pieces into which it is divided. Children begin to acquire the conservation of mass at about age 5, weight at

Engage children of varying ages in a classification activity. Do the differences in classifying ability you observe jibe with Piaget's predictions?

about age 6, and volume at about age 7 (see Figure 4.2). They may not completely master these concepts, however, for a year or two.

To study the conservation of mass (see Figure 4.2a), Piaget gave a child some clay to roll into a ball the same size as another clay ball. Then he rolled one of the balls into a long cylindrical shape. At the age of about 4, the child believes that the longer of the two objects contains more clay. But at the age of about 5, roughly half of the children recognize that the amount of clay is the same. In studying the conservation of weight, an understanding acquired at about the age of 6, Piaget first asked a child to balance two balls of clay on a scale (see Figure 4.2b). After changing the shape of one of the balls, Piaget noted whether the child realized that the ball whose shape had been changed would still balance the round ball. In studying the conservation of volume (Figure 4.2c), Piaget first showed a child that balls of equal size make the water level in a cylinder go up by the same amount. Then he asked the child whether a clay ball whose shape had been changed, perhaps elongated, would cause the water to rise the same distance. Typically, about half the chil-

FIGURE 4.2

Examples of conservation tasks

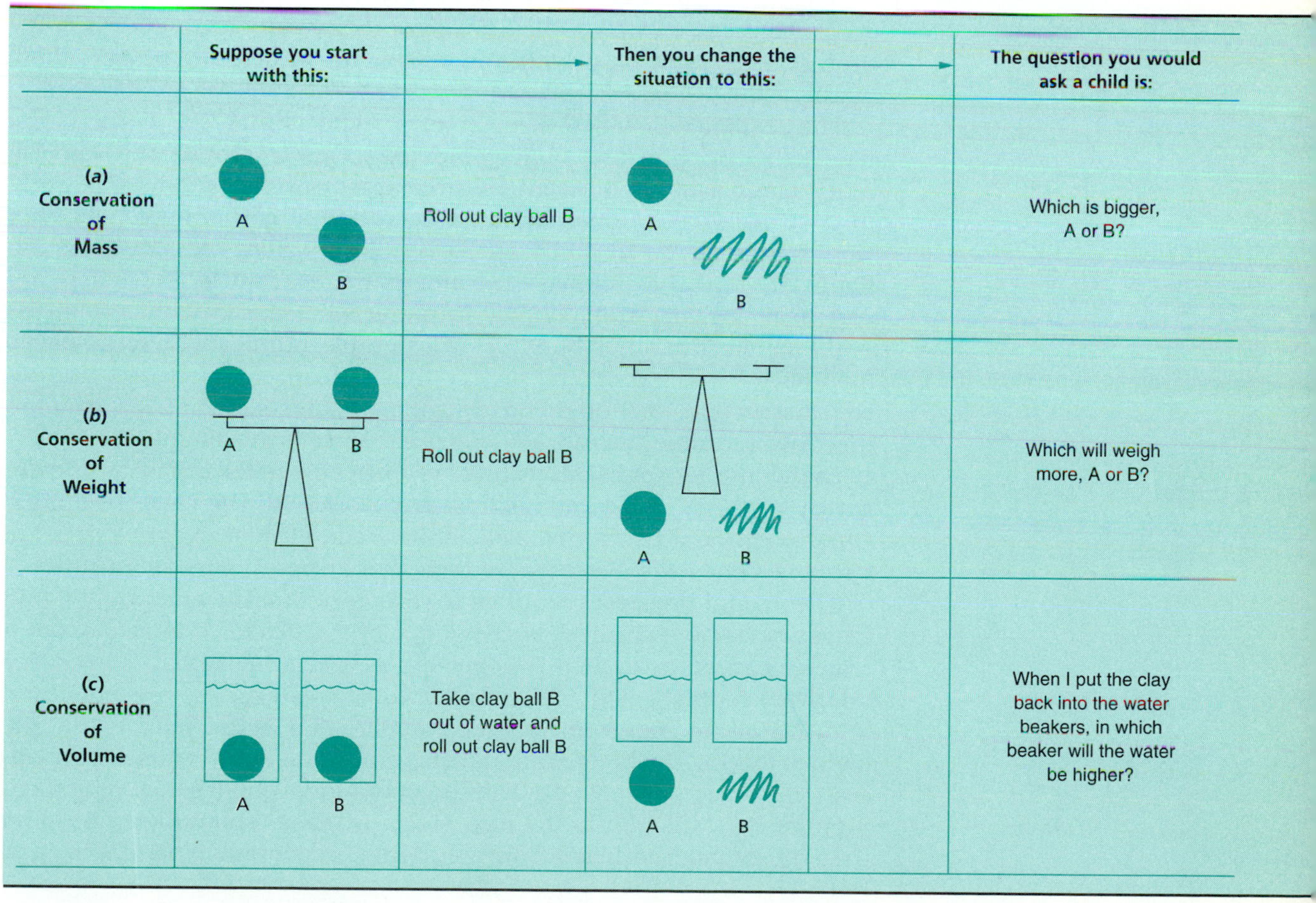

	Suppose you start with this:	→	Then you change the situation to this:	→	The question you would ask a child is:
(a) Conservation of Mass	A B	Roll out clay ball B	A B		Which is bigger, A or B?
(b) Conservation of Weight	A B	Roll out clay ball B	A B		Which will weigh more, A or B?
(c) Conservation of Volume	A B	Take clay ball B out of water and roll out clay ball B	A B		When I put the clay back into the water beakers, in which beaker will the water be higher?

Sets in mathematics are a problem of classification—so easy for adults, so difficult for children.
(© Gale Zucker/Stock Boston)

dren gave the right answer, demonstrating the principle of conservation, at about the age of 7.

The sequence in which these kinds of conservation are learned (first mass, then weight, and finally volume) seems to remain the same in many studies and in different cultures. It is possible, with a lot of work, to train children to understand conservation at earlier ages than they would normally do so. But Piagetians point out that the process is difficult and that the children's learning is fragile, that is, they easily revert back to their rudimentary thinking when faced with a complex problem. On the other hand, a considerable number of psychologists (neo-Piagetians and others) believe that exposure, experience, and direct instruction can and do have significant effects on a child's capabilities. (We examine their ideas in later sections of this chapter.)

In the intuitive phase, the child becomes able to form classes or categories of objects, see relationships, and work with the idea of number. Children are not usually conscious, however, of the categories they are using, which is why we describe their thought processes as intuitive.

The mental processes required to recognize that the amount of liquid stays the same regardless of the shape of the beaker it is in, or that a teacher can be a teacher, a homemaker, *and* a basketball player, are relatively sophisticated. The initiation of the categories, concepts, and minitheories to engage in complex thought such as this tells us that the child is leaving the preoperational stage of thought and entering the operational stage. As they work with preoperational children, helping them prepare for transition to the next stage, teachers should keep in mind that these children benefit from enriching, concrete experiences, and from work with language and concept development. Experiences such as field trips to the police and fire station, the zoo, and parks, together with a focus on the naming of things and concepts, help prepare children to develop more advanced thought and ready them for concrete operational thinking.

Third Stage: Concrete Operational (Ages 7 to 11)   In the **concrete operational stage,** which covers roughly the ages from 7 to 11, children become capable of various logical operations but only with concrete things. Children around this age are not good theorists; they are very much practical-minded, earth-bound, and fixated on the reality before them (Flavell, 1985). But now they begin to use operations—and this is a great leap forward in cognitive development. An **operation** is a type of action—a manipulation of objects or their mental representations. It calls for transforming information so that it can be used more selectively. Operations make trial and error unnecessary because the child can think through certain actions and the results of those actions. Operational thought replaces the impressionistic leaps from data to conclusions with a series of small-scale reversible steps, each of which can be judged as reasonable or unreasonable. If information is concrete, comparisons can be made accurately. Thus children are not taken in by changed beaker shapes as liquid is poured back and forth. They can imagine operations and anticipate results. For example, until this stage is reached, a child cannot tell you with any conviction what the other side of the moon is like. But in the stage of concrete operations a child can "manipulate" the moon, turning it around in her mind, and can tell you that it probably looks just like this side of the moon.

During this stage children become able to handle classification systems like the one shown in Figure 4.3. This means that children become able to handle complex logical ideas.

> **Composition.** The idea that whenever two elements of a system are combined (e.g., gasoline-engine cars, A, and other cars, A′), another element of the system (i.e., cars, B) is obtained. Or if we combine cars (B) and other means of transportation (B′), we obtain means of transportation (C).

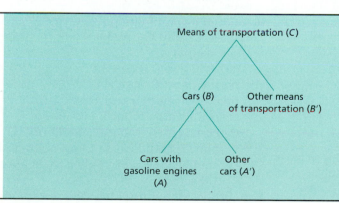

FIGURE 4.3

Classification scheme showing kinds of operations that a child can handle in the concrete operational stage

Associativity. The idea that the sum is independent of the order in which things are added. In the example above, A + A′ = B, and A′ + A = B.

Reversibility. The idea that not only can we add noncars (B′) to cars (B) to obtain means of transportation (C), but we can also subtract noncars (B′) from means of transportation (C) to get cars (B).

Children in the concrete operational stage can handle classification, grouping, and ordering problems. No longer centered on salient perceptual characteristics, they can think through a number of problems independent of the perceptual dimensions involved. The limitation of this stage, however, is that the children need concrete representations to tie to their thinking; they are not yet fully aware of the principles involved. So the seven- to eleven-year-old child still has problems with highly abstract thought.

As a teacher of children in this age group, you would do well to use visual aids and materials to illustrate concepts—for instance, timelines in history; number lines, blocks and balance beams in mathematics; or balls or globes to illustrate how the earth revolves. You might plan a visit to the mayor's office to demonstrate how governments work. As children manipulate objects or directly experience events for themselves, they gain concrete exposure that broadens and deepens their formation of schemata. The rule for teaching at this stage: always go from the concrete to the abstract.

> List additional objects and activities that might be particularly helpful to a teacher of children in the concrete operational stage.

Fourth Stage: Formal Operational (Ages 11 to 14)   In the **formal operational stage,** which covers the ages of about 11 to 14, children become capable of logical thinking with abstractions—that is, with the "possible" as well as the "here and now." They can think scientifically, drawing conclusions, offering interpretations, and developing hypotheses. Their thought has become flexible and powerful. Children in the formal operational stage can

- work out all logical possibilities without having to determine which ones actually occur in the real world. This capability is more than simple imagination; it is the systematic exposition of logical alternatives.
- conduct a combinational analysis of possibilities. Given two possible causes, C_1 and C_2, and a result, r, students can formulate the possibilities that
    either C_1 or C_2 causes r
    both C_1 and C_2 cause r
    neither C_1 nor C_2 causes r
    C_1 could cause r but C_2 could not
    C_2 could cause r, but C_1 could not
    C_1 and C_2 could cause r, but neither one alone could
    C_1 could cause r, but only if C_2 is absent
    —and so on
- do propositional thinking. Youngsters in this age group can take propositions like the ones about C_1, C_2, and r and combine them

into new, higher-order propositions ("either p_1 or p_2 can be true, but not both").

■ generalize from propositions based on one kind of content, say, clay or beads, to many other kinds of content, say, water, wood pieces, physical objects in general, all liquids, or all numerically denotable quantities.

If a child reaches formal operation thought, he or she ought to be capable of (Wigfield, Eccles, & Pintrich, 1996)

■ abstract thinking, thinking about possibilities beyond concrete reality
■ propositional thinking, thinking that is logical and consistent
■ combinatorial thinking, the synthesis of ideas
■ hypothetico-deductive thinking, that is, scientific thinking
■ metacognitive activity, the monitoring of his or her own thinking (see pp. 270–272)
■ self-reflective thinking, concern about identity, morality, and personal relationships

Notice our use of the word *if* in the first sentence of the paragraph above. These characteristics of "mature" thought do not automatically develop for many students at 11 to 14 years. This highest level of formal operational thought may be beyond the abilities of many students. Only through experience and maturation does this kind of reasoning develop. For some this advanced cognitive development occurs when they are older adolescents or even adults, particularly if they attend college and have their intellect "stretched" (Wigfield, Eccles, & Pintrich, 1996).

There are two somewhat paradoxical lessons that you as a teacher can draw from all this: First, realize that the teaching methods recommended for concrete operational thought might be appropriate for *every* age group. Second, be sure you model scientific thinking and build in hypothetical questions as part of the curriculum for every youngster in this age group. It is not likely that formal operational thinking will ever develop without some prodding by adults who themselves display formal operational thought.

The Developmental Process

Children develop progressively more complex intellectual capabilities through the process of seeking an equilibrium between what they presently perceive, know, and understand on the one hand, and what they see in any new phenomenon, experience, or problem on the other. If their present condition can handle the new situation, their equilibrium is not disturbed. But if it cannot, then some intellectual work is necessary to restore the equilibrium. That is, the organism must adapt in some way to the new environment.

Adaptation takes two forms—**assimilation** and **accommodation**—which occur simultaneously. Assimilation is the process of changing what is perceived so that it fits present cognitive structures (the representation, in cognition, of a concept, say, man or car or food); accommodation is the process of changing cognitive structures so that they fit what is perceived. Suppose you have never seen a bat, and one flies by you for the first time. If you had to tell a friend what you saw, you would probably describe something like a bird. You would *adjust* your perception to fit an existing cognitive structure. This is the process of assimilation. Suppose your friend, after hearing your description, tells you about bats. Now you would have to change your cognitive structure of the concept "mammal" to include a new characteristic—flight. A flying mammal requires accommodation—changing cognitive structures to fit what was perceived.

> Describe examples from your own learning of assimilation and accommodation.

Assimilation is like chewing and digesting food in order to transform it into something the body can use. It transforms new ideas into something that fits into already-existing cognitive structures. Accommodation is like the adjustments the body makes in eating and using food: opening the mouth; contracting the muscles of the throat, esophagus, and stomach; and secreting digestive juices. In the same way, an existing cognitive structure must be modified, extended, or refined to come to grips with a new or unusual idea.

Assimilation and accommodation can be hard to tell apart. They go on simultaneously, and in the processing of ideas, they are two sides of the same coin—the process of maintaining equilibrium between people and their environment. When people interpret, construe, and structure, they are changing the nature of reality to make it fit into their own cognitive structure. This is assimilation. When people adjust their ideas, they are changing their cognitive structure—calling up a memory, a similarity, or an analogy in order to make sense of reality. This is accommodation.

The processes of assimilation and accommodation have somewhat lasting effects on cognitive structures. As ways by which an organism adapts to its cognitive environment, they are comparable to the biological processes of adaptation that affect the structure and functions of the organism's body. So children's schemata, that is, their cognitive organizations and structures, gradually change as a function of experience, as they go through the four stages of cognitive development.

Dissenters from and Alternatives to Piagetian Theory

In recent years, a number of respected researchers have raised questions about some of the basic tenets of Piagetian theory. We list some of the more well known of these and then look at the ideas of several relatively new groups of cognitive psychologists, whose work relates to but goes beyond Piagetian theory.

Questions about Piagetian Theory   Brainard (1978a, 1978b) claimed that Piaget's stage theory is just descriptive, that it does not explain anything. He noted that multiplication ability always follows the development of the ability to add, but no one presumes that this sequence has any biological origins. Piaget's stage theory, then, may have little to do with biology.

Many researchers have pointed out that Piaget often underestimated the complexity of children's cognitive achievements at a particular age (Bauer, 1996; Boden, 1980; Carey, 1985; Gelman, 1985). Dozens of studies have shown, for example, that newborns can display more complex behavior than Piaget (or the rest of us) believed possible. "Not only do children understand more than previously thought, they also can learn more" (Siegler, 1991, p. 53). Piaget also made much of children's egocentric speech and perception. But many researchers have now demonstrated that children can be very social in speech at very young ages and, when given appropriate instructions, are able to take different perspectives in perception. These are characteristics that Piaget believed to come much later in development.

Another issue being reexamined is the role of motor experience in cognitive growth. To Piaget, early motor activities are the basis for cognitive growth. Yet multiply-disabled children who have little motor experience in infancy show normal cognitive development.

An additional issue has to do with Piaget's definition of formal operations. Only a small percentage of the general population appears to have formal operational abilities as Piaget defined them. One problem here seems to lie in Piaget's use of abstract tasks in investigating formal operational thought. For example, on two tasks requiring exactly the same logical processes, one presented abstractly and the other with concrete referents, the percentage of people showing formal operational thought increased from 19 to 98 (Boden, 1980).

This kind of study reveals the crucial role of **contextualization** in people's judgments. Different tasks, instructions, social settings, and the like influence greatly whether researchers find different kinds of thought processes when they study children's thinking (Gelman, 1985; Nagy & Griffith, 1982). In fact, it may be only children's lack of knowledge in particular domains that leads people to conclude that they think differently than adults. Carey (1985) believed this to be the case, concluding that young children and sophisticated adults really think alike—but one just knows a lot more than the other, and this difference in knowledge confuses the issue. The ability of children to take on complex knowledge, as did a 4½-year-old who was fascinated by and became an expert on dinosaurs, is evidence of developmentally advanced, complex scientific thought, in that domain (Chi, 1985). The implication for teaching here is clear. Our students (and we, their teachers) may act like sophisticated thinkers in one area of the curriculum and be less able to engage in sophisticated cognitive processes in another. Development is a spotty phenomenon. Cognitive processes in various areas of the curriculum do not change at the same rate.

Finally, research raises questions about Piaget's training studies, once thought to demonstrate that children cannot really be taught certain kinds of things before they reach certain ages. This age requirement now appears not to be true. Carefully designed training programs show that concrete or formal operational thought can occur much earlier than Piaget thought possible (Brainard, 1978a; Case, 1978; Scandura & Scandura, 1980; Siegler, 1991).

Neo-Piagetian and Other Alternative Theories   The foregoing problems with Piagetian theory have led to alternative theories about the development of children's thought (Siegel & Brainard, 1978). For example, one branch of cognitive psychology (discussed in Chapter 7) uses information-processing theory as an alternative to Piaget's thinking (see Case, 1991, 1993; Klahr, 1980; Pascual-Leone, 1980).

This view considers the **information-processing** demands of a task, such as the *number of bits of information* that must be carried along to solve a problem, the *number of transformations of data* necessary, the *number and complexity of the rules* to be learned, the *number of items that must be in working memory simultaneously,* and so on. These demands are thought to be more important in the production of logical thought than are the mental structures that the child has built up developmentally. Piagetian theory emphasizes the nature of the child's internal mental structures more than the demands of the task. So information-processing theory and Piagetian theory differ most in their relative emphasis on the roots of problems in the development of logical thought: The information-processing theorist more often emphasizes the nature of the tasks to be mastered; the Piagetian tends to stress the structure of the individual's thought process.

Neo-Piagetians (e.g., Case & Griffin, 1990; Case, 1991) have merged these different views. They believe that central ideas, or conceptual structures—in mathematics, social relations, physics, geography, time, and so forth—change with age and experience. These central conceptual structures are mental entities consisting of meanings, representations, concepts, and their relationships to each other. Similar to schemata, but neither biological nor logical, as in Piaget's system, these central conceptual structures are semantic (i.e., meaning-based) in nature. The meaning of, say, the concepts "hour" or "uncle," are built out of experience in a particular domain and the state of the information-processing system at a particular stage of development. Thus, 4-, 6-, 8-, and 10-year-olds display different abilities in different areas depending on their experience and their central conceptual structures. The structures develop in an ordered way but are acquired through socially mediated processes (see the discussion of Vygotsky later in this chapter) and are potentially teachable.

The issue of whether conceptual structures are believed teachable is perhaps the most important difference between Case and Piaget. Although constrained by the information-processing system at certain stages (e.g., available memory), there is no need in Case's theory to believe that advanced levels of thinking (Piaget's formal operational thought) are unlikely to occur if instruction is appropriate. Piagetian theorizing allowed for underestimation of ability, or promoted the idea that teachers must wait for certain developmental characteristics to emerge. But Case returns responsibility to parents, teachers, and schools. And that, we believe, is appropriate. We think that Piagetian theory has focused too much on what children cannot do, and not enough has been made of the impressive collection of cognitive abilities they do possess (Brown, 1994).

One final important question about Piagetian theory: Is it, after all this criticism and reevaluation, still valid? The answer is a definite yes. Piaget's ideas are being refined and clarified, but because they form a remarkably adaptive theory, they are still robust after sixty years of development (Beilin, 1980, 1992).

Bruner's Theory of Cognitive Growth

Jerome Bruner (1966) also examined the development of cognitive functions and proposed his own theory. Criticizing Piaget, he said (1973, pp. 143–145), "If the child only takes in what he is 'ready to assimilate' why bother to teach before he is ready, and since he takes it in naturally when he is ready, why bother afterwards?" To Bruner a "developmentally appropriate curriculum," as recommended by many educators, seems to slow down growth. Bruner believed that any idea or concept can be taught in some intellectually honest way to a child of any age—an important counterpoint to the Piagetian idea that some things are beyond a child's grasp. Bruner also claimed that thinking and intellectual activity are not merely properties of the developing information-processing system or the individual experience of the child. Instead, he saw thinking as the "internalization of 'tools' provided by a given culture" (1973, p. 22). His theory is based on these beliefs:

- Intellectual growth is characterized by *increasing independence of responses from stimuli.* Children are at first under rigid stimulus control: they respond in set ways to various stimuli. Over time they become increasingly independent of stimuli in the responses they make and the form those responses take, especially as they acquire a language system.

- Growth depends on the *development of an internal information-processing and storage system* that can describe reality. Unless children learn a symbol system, such as language, with which to represent the world, they can never predict, extrapolate, or hypothesize novel outcomes.

- Intellectual development involves an *increasing capacity to say to ourselves and others, in words or with symbols, what we have done and what we will do.* This point really deals with self-consciousness. Without the development of abilities to describe past and future actions, we cannot direct analytic behavior toward ourselves or the environment.

- *Systematic interactions between a tutor and a learner are necessary for cognitive development.* Bruner's point is that father, mother, teacher, or some other member of society must teach a child. Simply being born into a culture is not enough for full intellectual development.

- *Language is the key to cognitive development.* It is through language that others communicate with us, teaching us their conceptions of the world. It is also through language that we communicate our conceptions of the world to others and question the way the world functions. Most important is the fact that as we grow older we learn to use language to mediate, interpret, and reconcile events in our world. This ability to provide linguistic mediation ties one event to

Describe how specific implications for instruction derived from Bruner would be quite different from those derived from Piaget.

another in a causal way, links the new to the familiar, and allows us to code events so that we can deal with these internal representations. (We talk about language development in more detail later in this chapter.)

- Cognitive growth is marked by the *increasing ability to deal with several alternatives simultaneously,* to *perform concurrent activities,* and to *pay attention sequentially* to various situations.

From his observations Bruner identified these three stages of growth in the ways that children come to represent in their minds the world around them:

1. The **enactive stage,** the earliest, in which the child understands the environment through action. For example, there is no imagery and there are no words that can help you teach a child to ride a bicycle. It is *psychomotor knowledge* alone that gives the child mastery of a bicycle. At this stage, Piaget and Bruner have said, objects are what the child does with them. The enactive stage is one where holding, moving, biting, rubbing, and touching provide needed experience with the objects of the world. It is this form of representation of knowledge that is at the root of Gardner's bodily-kinesthetic intelligence (Chapter 3).

2. The **iconic stage** is a great advancement. It is the level at which information is carried by visual and auditory imagery. The child develops visual memory but still makes decisions based on sensory impressions, not language. (Piaget's descriptions of preoperational thought overlap with Bruner's iconic stage.) The child is a prisoner of his or her perceptual world, swayed by brightness, vividness, noise, and movement. It is this form of representation of knowledge that Gardner (Chapter 3) calls *spatial intelligence.*

Looking, hearing, touching, feeling, chewing, squeezing, smelling—the ways in which children in the sensorimotor (and enactive) stage gain their knowledge.

(© Gloria Karlson)

3. The **symbolic stage** is reached as understanding through action and perception give way to understanding of the world by means of symbol systems: language, logic, and mathematics. The symbolic stage allows us to translate experiences into formulas [$F = MA$, $E = MC^2$, $B = f(P \times E)$] and into semantically rich statements ("Too many cooks spoil the broth"). These formulas and sayings, communicated by symbol systems, allow us to condense ideas and so store vast amounts of information we can retrieve easily and use to represent the world accurately. In Gardner's theory of multiple intelligences (pp. 75–80), these are the verbal and quantitative forms of intelligence—the kinds most emphasized by schools. For Piaget, the symbolic stage is the stage where operational thought is possible. Although Bruner believes that the symbolic system usually becomes dominant, he also believes that adults often still code their experiences by enactive or iconic systems. So it is possible that great surgeons, athletes, and violinists have highly developed enactive coding systems, and that great artists are still dominated by their iconic processes.

Remember our earlier comment that Bruner believes culture to be the great molder of thinking, that each culture enables individuals to make sense of and prosper in the world according to that culture. The power of culture to mold cognitive development is even more central to Vygotsky, the theorist we look at next.

Vygotsky's View of Cognitive Development

Russian psychologist Lev Vygotsky (1978; see also Moll, 1990; Wertsch & Tulviste, 1992) attributed a special role in cognitive development to the social environment of the child. He noted that children begin learning from the people around them—their social world—which is the source of all their concepts, ideas, facts, skills, and attitudes. That social world, one's culture, determines which stimuli occur and are attended to.

To help a child or novice go from a social to a personal psychological form of knowledge requires, in Vygotsky's view, that the adult determine two things: (1) the child's actual developmental level, by learning about the child's problem-solving capability as he or she works without any adult help, and (2) what the child can do with adult guidance. When a child is working independently, we see the actual developmental level of the child. When a child is working with an adult, we see the *potential* development of the child under optimum circumstances—learning with a competent, nurturing mediator. The difference between these two levels of functioning is called the **zone of proximal development** (ZPD). Instruction is good, Vygotsky said, only when it proceeds ahead of developmental level. Instruction must awaken and bring to life those functions that are in the process of maturing, that is, those in the zone of proximal development. It is in this way that direct tutelage and other forms of instruction play an important role in the cognitive development of the child (Moll, 1990; Vygotsky, 1986). For example, a child working alone with crayons may produce a strange drawing of a human—one eye, a huge head, and tiny legs. But someone more competent (an older sibling, a teacher) might ask, "How many eyes does a person have? How about ears; do people have ears?" Changes in the child's drawings will reflect this kind of socially mediated learning. The difference between what the child can do on her own and what she can do with some mentoring is the ZPD.

Vygotsky also points out that because each culture selects differently, offering a unique sociocultural patterning of events, individuals from different cultural settings come to see and hear different aspects of the world. Cognitive development, then, has its origins in interaction among people in a culture before the psychological process—representing those ideas, events, attitudes, and strategies in mind—becomes possible for children. All personal psychological processes begin as social processes, shared among people, often among adults and children. Language, of course, is the clearest example of this series of events. Social interactions determine what we find funny and sad. They determine whether we hold cognitive categories (tall, brave, wealthy, and so on) that are very wide or very narrow. That is, personal psychological processes begin as social processes, patterned by culture. And this can have important effects on you, as a teacher, dealing with students of diverse cultural backgrounds in the classroom.

Vygotsky's emphasis on the role of knowledgeable adults or siblings in influencing the cognitive development of children implies that learning is enhanced when children work cooperatively or collaboratively with adults and other children. In Vygotsky's theory, apprenticeship is an important concept. Apprenticeships in learning to be a tailor or a plumber are the ideal model for learning because a knowledgeable adult mediates the learning environment for the novice. Cognitive development during apprenticeships can proceed from other-regulated behavior to self-regulated behavior, which is exactly what we want for our students.

> Teachers, tutors, and master craftsmen in traditional apprenticeship situations all ideally function as promoters of self-regulation by nurturing the emergence of self-control, as they gradually cede external control. In short, in a variety of learning situations, experts model many forms of control over their thinking and problem-solving activities, the controls that others must internalize if they are to become successful, independent thinkers and problem-solvers.
>
> (Campione & Armbruster, 1985, p. 339)

Mediated learning environments occur when an adult or other knowledgeable person intercedes—mediates—between things in the environment and the child. For example, teacher A tells her students to take three or four books from the library on this visit. Teacher B, on the other hand, tells her students that this weekend is the Thanksgiving holiday, so school will be closed and they'll want extra books around to read while they are at home. The children of teacher B learn much more than those of teacher A. Adults or siblings like teacher B explain *why* things need to be done—they provide reasons—and in this way teach plan-

Would peer tutoring, in which older or more knowledgeable students tutor others, jibe with Vygotsky's beliefs? Why or why not?

POLICY, RESEARCH, AND PRACTICE

Teaching from a Context of Diversity

Luria (1979), with Vygotsky's help, worked with uneducated peasants in the 1920s in rural areas of the former Soviet Union. He presented the following syllogism (pp. 78–79) to a 37-year-old villager*:

Q. In the far north where there is snow, all bears are white. Novaya Zemlya is in the far north, and there is always snow there. What color are the bears there?

A. There are different sorts of bears.

Luria repeated the syllogism.

A. I don't know. I've seen a black bear; I've never seen any others. . . . Each locality has its own animals; if it's white, they will be white; if it's yellow, they will be yellow.

Q. But what kind of bears are there in Novaya Zemlya?

A. We always speak of what we see; we don't talk about what we haven't seen.

Q. But what do my words imply?

He again repeated the syllogism.

A. Well, it's like this: our Tzar isn't like yours, and yours isn't like ours. Your words can be answered only by someone who was there, and if a person wasn't there, he can't say anything on the basis of your words.

Q. But on the basis of my words, in the North where there is always snow, the bears are white, can you gather what kind of bears there are in Novaya Zemlya?

A. If a man was 60 or 80 and had seen a white bear and had told about it, he could be believed, but I've never seen one and hence I can't say. That's my last word. Those who saw can tell, and those who didn't see cannot say anything!

At this point, a young Uzbek volunteered: "From your words it means that bears there are white."

Q. Well, which of you is right?

The first subject replied, "What a cock knows how to do, he does. What I know, I say, and nothing beyond that!"

Luria pointed out that these people make intelligent judgments and draw proper conclusions about things in their lives, but being unschooled, their minds are bound to the things their culture offers them to think about. They have no intellectual inability, but they belong to a culture that shapes their thinking, as does the culture we belong to: the cultures

continues

113

associated with our churches, mosques, and synagogues; our political parties and families; our ethnicity, race, and social class; and so forth. Vygotskians claim we have overlooked how powerful the communities we belong to are in shaping how we think.

A related study made this particular point clearer. Cole and Bruner (1971) cited how nonliterate rice farmers from Central Africa and sophomores at Yale University were given tasks calling for estimation of volume and distance. The Yale students were superior at judging distance, the rice farmers superior in judging how much rice was contained in different-sized bowls. The inherent competence of both groups to make estimations is clearly equal. What differs, however, is how this ability is made manifest. Their respective cultures make it likely that inherent abilities will show up in different forms.

The message of the Vygotskian research is that you always must know about the sociocultural/historical background of an individual to understand him or her. Portes (1996) notes that cultural-historical ways of thinking help us to understand ethnic differences—both strengths and weaknesses—which are so obvious in a multicultural society such as ours. Bruner (1990) sums up this line of research by reminding us that human minds are reflections of culture and history, not simply a result of biology.

Excerpted by permission of the publisher from The Making of Mind: A Personal Account of Soviet Psychology *by A. R. Luria, Cambridge, Mass.: Harvard University Press, copyright © 1979 by the President and Fellows of Harvard College.*

ning, not simply obedience. So the simple directions for a visit to the library can be infused with meaning by providing an underlying reason, by mediating or interpreting for children as they interact with their environment. This is not different from explaining what happens when we regroup in two-column addition, or why certain rules of behavior are to be followed in class. One child can learn to regroup and behave by rote, another because he understands the reasons behind regrouping and the rules for conduct. The latter child will develop into a more competent adult, one capable of self-regulation (Kozulin & Presseisen, 1995).

In summary, the key to advancing the cognitive development of the child is to find out the dimensions of the zone of proximal development within which a teacher should work. Schools, noted Vygotsky, leave too much for the child to do independently, and this tendency slows the child's cognitive development. To develop fully, a child must be led systematically into more complex areas. The mastery of more complex kinds of functioning can proceed with the help of an adult or anyone else who has expertise in the area. The more knowledgeable person provides the intellectual scaffolding for the child to climb. In the zone of proximal development, social knowledge—knowledge acquired through social interaction—becomes individual knowledge, and individual knowledge grows and becomes more complex. Ultimately, development leads to a successfully functioning adult *in a particular community.*

Instructional Implications of Piaget, Bruner, and Vygotsky

Understand How Children Think

Children do not think like young adults; they think in ways that adults can no longer remember. They make mistakes most adults have difficulty predicting. Accordingly, educators need to make a special effort to understand the child's mental operations, to see phenomena and problems in the way the child sees them. This kind of intellectual empathy is not easy, but it can be achieved through interviews, observations, and questionnaires.

Use Concrete Materials to Foster Learning

Children, particularly in the preschool and early elementary school years, learn especially well from working with concrete objects, materials, and phenomena. Words and other kinds of symbols are less effective than things in promoting understanding at these ages. Giving children a chance to manipulate, act, touch, see, hear, and feel things helps them acquire an understanding of concepts and relationships more effectively than the more abstract forms of learning that work well later in childhood, adolescence, and adulthood.

In some ways, the subsequent kinds of understanding based on words and symbols require the earlier kinds of understanding based on both direct and mental manipulation of objects. Children who have not acquired a "feel" for the laws of the lever by playing on seesaws may have difficulty understanding those laws in high school physics. Children who have not played with beads, rods, and lumps of clay may have difficulty understanding addition, subtraction, multiplication, and division. To teach the concept of number, for example, we must begin by classifying objects on the basis of color, size, form, weight, or coarseness.

Balance Discovery and Direct Instruction

The effect of Piaget's and Bruner's ideas is to encourage "discovery" and other inductive approaches for teaching young children. In these approaches, children acquire an understanding of concepts and principles through personal discovery. Vygotsky probably would not have argued this point with Piaget or Bruner. He would, however, have stressed the unique role of adults and older children in learning. He might have stressed the important role of direct tutoring. So a teacher must think of balancing the two kinds of educational experience—discovery learning and direct instruction. Overwhelming predominance of either is probably a mistake.

Use Certain Sequences of Instruction to Foster Learning

The idea that cognitive processes develop has implications for sequencing instruction across semesters or even within a small unit in

continues

CONTINUED

your classroom. First, begin instruction of children with a "messing around" stage, a hands-on stage that builds enactive representations. You could do this with visits to rivers or valleys for geography, examining car parts in an auto mechanics class, using wooden block letters in a kindergarten, counting stadium seats for introductory arithmetic, and surveying a field for a class in plane geometry.

Second, focus on developing perceptual clarity. You could point out salient features of objects or events, use audiovisuals extensively, and provide concrete, pictorial, and diagrammatic rather than abstract referents for things. This part of instruction is concerned with building iconic representations, but in a social environment with knowledgeable adults. Using time-lapse photographs to show a flower growing, pointing out the parts of a pictured airplane, and color coding a model of a molecule of salt to show both of its elements are all ways to use iconic representations.

Third, follow these concrete and iconic referents with more abstract information. This segment of the instructional sequence makes use of the verbal stage of development. Verbal discussions provide symbolic experiences for students.

This sequence of instruction, which moves from hands-on experience with objects, to attention to their perceptual characteristics, and finally

Exploration of the environment ("messing around") is necessary for cognitive growth.

(© Stanley Rowin/The Picture Cube)

to verbal discussion of events seems to make sense, particularly for young children. A related idea is that "proximal (nearby) experience must precede distal (far-off) experience" (Elkind, 1976). For children to understand the map of the United States, they must first understand the map of their own school, neighborhood, city, or town. Sometimes a teacher who is having trouble explaining something should think about backing up to enactive and iconic levels of experience. Vygotsky would state it differently, but with similar implications—you must know your students' zone of proximal development and not exceed it.

Introduce New Experiences in Moderately Novel Ways

New experience, whether social or individual, interacts with cognitive structures to arouse interest and develop understanding. A new experience must fit to some extent with what children already know. But it should not fit so thoroughly that it prevents disequilibrium, because the feeling of disequilibrium is what drives a child to assimilate and accommodate. In other words, moderate novelty helps, zero novelty bores, and radical novelty bewilders.

Individualize the Pace of Learning

Children ought to be allowed to learn at pretty much their own pace. They should have some chance to regulate their own learning rather than have it forced. This points toward individualized instruction rather than methods that carry a whole group of students along at the same rate. Some children need more help, different kinds of help, and more time to work alone on their own projects. They must be allowed the time they need to construct their own knowledge. The implication here is that children often need "occasions for learning" more than they need formal teaching. Providing these occasions, or settings, and materials gives the teacher plenty to do. All three theorists would recommend that at least some of the time a teacher should change from "sage on the stage to guide on the side." This is particularly necessary when working in the zone of proximal development.

Do Not Neglect the Social Side of Learning

The teacher must also see to it that the Vygotskian view of cognitive development is represented by attending to the social aspects of learning. Interaction with others—both teachers and other students—has cognitive as well as affective consequences. Young children are very self-centered. This self-centeredness gives way as children are forced, through social interaction, to confront other people's points of view. Because social interaction goes on primarily by means of words, it enhances symbol usage. Furthermore, the "tools" of thinking in a particular cultural setting are passed on through social interactions. So in a fundamental way, social interactions provide opportunities for a child to learn to become (i.e., to think like) an authentic member of his or her own larger cultural group.

continues

CONTINUED

Analyze Errors

Piaget made it clear that there is more information for the tester when the child makes an error then when the child is correct. If you take the time to analyze and interpret the errors of your students, rather than simply informing them that they are wrong, you can learn a great deal about their thinking and how you might help them.

The Development of Language

Stages of Development

Between the ages of 1 and 2 years, the vocabulary of a toddler grows enormously, commonly increasing by a few thousand percent. By about 2 years, the sensorimotor, enactive, and iconic stages of development begin to be overwhelmed by the symbolic—by the power of language. This symbol system tends to replace preverbal ways of knowing. The impact is swift, so that by 4 or 6 years the primary medium of human thinking, learning, and communicating is language. It is this extraordinary tool that makes human experience so different from that of other animals.

There is some evidence that the ability to acquire language is innate (e.g., Chomsky, 1957, 1968). In fact, a language-acquisition device, present in all of us and activated by exposure to spoken language, has been suggested (McNeil, 1970). Whether or not such a device exists, all linguists agree that it is *experience* with language that elicits and modifies language behavior. Variations in environment, particularly in the interactions between the primary care giver and the infant, influence language and thought (Anastasiow, Hanes, & Hanes, 1982). As listeners and speakers interacting with mature language users, children bring to bear their own creativity and logical processes, quickly learning an enormously complex set of rules and an even more complex set of exceptions to the rules (Rosser, 1994).

The One-Word Stage Language in the form of single-word utterances typically starts after the first year of life, give or take a few months. By about 15 months, a 50-word vocabulary is evident. Most of this early vocabulary consists of referents to objects (shoe, milk, cookies, dog, car) and action verbs (go, push, blow). These are the things and events in the environment that the child acts on or that move and demand the child's attention Children's early speech is also characterized by emotion. A child may say "cookie" loudly, meaning "I want something to eat," or "cookie" softly, meaning "I am content." The child at this stage is busy labeling things that have been enactively known and emotionally felt. Many of the action verbs are used as imperatives. The child says "push," meaning "push my swing some more." Or the child says "go," meaning "I want to go now." Sometimes the imperatives are self-directed. As the child moves from one room of the house to another, she might say "go," using the word to define the event because action alone is no longer definable without language.

First words are often overgeneralized because meaning is so difficult for a young child to determine. So "ball" is used to label all round objects, and "dog" describes a horse, a cow, and a rabbit. This period of overgeneralization ends when the child is a little older and deduces something of great importance—that everything has a name. Parents are familiar with the "What's that?" question, repeated over and over, all day long, as the child learns to name his world and build vocabulary.

Children do not, of course, have the detailed and differentiated ideas of adults. But the single-word utterances of a child are said to be **holophrastic,** that is, one-word expressions of complex ideas, equivalent to the full sentences of adults. Even a child's first use of referents, action verbs, and imperatives seems to imply a rudimentary knowledge of grammar.

Differences in the kind of words children first learn appear to be related to their linguistic community, as Vygotsky would predict. In a study of the initial 50-word vocabularies of children, K. Nelson (1973) found that the firstborn of highly educated parents use more words referring to things; later-borns of less educated parents use more words referring to the self and other people. The linguistic community we grow up in affects what we learn, and this fact has implications for education. But our learning and thinking skills—our competence—does not depend on characteristics of the linguistic community. Cognitive development and linguistic competence are not affected by differences in linguistic communities. In this view, the linguistic competence of all speakers is equal; it is linguistic performance that differs from speaker to speaker. Performance is affected by the linguistic community, setting, topic, attention, memory, anxieties, and many other factors. But (except for individuals with extreme disabilities) competence for development of a completely useful language system is not in question. The important lesson for you as a teacher is clear: Never underestimate the competence of someone to think and learn because they use a dialect, have an accent, or do not use the socially approved language of school-board meetings, social gatherings, and so forth. Linguistic performance and linguistic competence are different concepts.

The Two-Word Stage   One-word utterances give the child a sense of the power, social significance, and functional importance of language. Eventually, of course, and usually between 18 and 24 months, children combine words. The child begins to speak in the way adults write telegrams. Instead of saying, "The car broke down," she simply says, "Car broke." When Lourdes wants to claim possession, she says, "Lourdes sock," not "This is my sock." The child also learns to use pivot words ("more," "all gone"), which are easily combined with other words. "More juice," "more ball," and "more giggle" communicate well, even though by means of telegraphic sentences. The common pivot word *all gone*—"all gone sticky" or "all gone milk," meaning "I have cleaned my hands of the sticky stuff" or "I have finished my milk," is a way of expressing nonexistence. Even with beginning utterances, then, a sophisticated concept like the null (nonexistent) set, or empty category, can be communicated. This reflects remarkable growth, cognitively and linguistically,

Why do you think experts say it is not a good idea to correct a very young child's language usage and grammar?

TABLE

4.1

**Examples of the Semantic Relations That
Can Be Expressed by Two-Word Utterances**

Semantic Relations	Examples	Semantic Relations	Examples
Identification	See doggie	Agent-action	Mama walk
Location	Book there	Action-object	Hit you
Repetition	More milk	Agent-object	Mama book
Nonexistence	All gone thing	Action-location	Sit chair
Negation	Not wolf	Action-recipient	Give papa
Possession	My candy	Action-instrument	Cut knife
Attribution	Big car	Question	Where ball?

Source: Adapted from D. I. Slobin, "Seven Questions about Language Development," from P. C. Dodwell (Ed.), New Horizons in Psychology, No. 2. Copyright © P. C. Dodwell and contributors, 1972. Reprinted by permission of Penguin Books Ltd.

for a 2- to 2 ½-year-old child. The range of semantic relations displayed by a typical child in this stage is shown in Table 4.1. This is also the time when adjective use develops. Children's first adjectives are often related to size (little boy), color (red dog), and feelings (pretty baby).

The More-Than-Two-Word Stage and Metalinguistic Awareness The child progresses, but quite unevenly, from the simple "go," to "go car," to the more sophisticated "go car house," which conveys both complex syntax and semantic knowledge. When more-than-two-word chains are formed, a new stage of linguistic development begins, marked by the introduction of inflection. In English an *inflection* is an ending of a word stem that expresses grammatical relationships. The plural *-s* and the past tense *-ed* are inflections. As children learn the rules of inflection, in order of their syntactic and semantic complexity, they overregularize their language. For example, when the child uses *-ed* to express the past tense of break (breaked), come (comed), or go (goed), we see overregularization. Of course, this is also evidence of the child's growing cognitive ability, because he or she is applying rules to unfamiliar words and expressions. It may take the child a number of years to use the rules of inflection correctly.

Between approximately 2 and 5 years, children often display a highly creative use of language. Chukovsky (1968) wrote that beginning at age 2, every child becomes, for at least a short time, a linguistic genius. During this stage a child might say, "I'm barefoot all over!" or "I'll get up so early it will still be late." Children at this stage also love nonsense verse. Chukovsky studied children's love of "topsy-turvies," a special form of nonsense, illustrated by "The rooster goes meow" or "The cow jumped over the moon." These are sources of hilarity to children, ways to play with the cognitive representation of the world and the linguistic system that describes that world. As Piaget noted, this kind of play is really the "work" of children because it provides the experience they need for further development.

By 5 or 6 years, children typically lose some of this linguistic creativity. But children have mastered most of the adult syntactic relations by this age. It is also at about this age that metalinguistic awareness develops.

Metalinguistic awareness is the ability to think at a conscious level and talk about the sounds in words, the ordering of words in spoken or written sentences, and the selection of the form most suitable for conveying a given meaning. Children may implicitly know pluralization and some other rules, and their comprehension and production of spoken utterances may be correct. But they may be unable to state these rules. School tasks, however, may demand an explicit awareness of rules, requiring of students the ability to state them correctly. For example, a child may need to know consciously that the plural of most nouns ending in *y* is formed by replacing the *y* with *ies.* To succeed academically, children must make explicit their implicit knowledge of language. To participate in certain kinds of social encounters also requires metalinguistic skills. For example, to laugh at a pun or a knock-knock joke requires the ability to be playful with sounds or word meanings—a metalinguistic skill (Anastasiow, Hanes, & Haynes, 1982). Metalinguistic awareness is necessary, too, to develop certain creative and scientific responses. Metaphors and subtle distinctions in language usage, so necessary for creative and scientific work, are best understood when metalinguistic awareness has been developed. And that awareness allows students to act on possible rather than actual information. Without some sophisticated metalinguistic awareness, then, children cannot function at the formal operational level.

Adults' Influence on Language Development and Literacy

As with the acquisition of conservation, directed training before certain ages is not as powerful as widespread experience. The research data are sketchy but consistent in indicating that parents' training procedures (modeling, reinforcement, punishment) have little or no effect on young children's grammatical knowledge. Grammatical knowledge probably builds as cognitive and intellectual abilities grow. When they are cognitively able, children can learn and generalize the complex rules of language. But remember that what children pick up is determined by their linguistic community. Models in that community that say, "I went to the store" eventually influence the language of the child that says, "I goed to the store." So children who have language models using rich, complex, and the "approved" language of the school will more easily fit into the culture of the school. It is also clear that children from certain households and neighborhoods enter school with unacceptable linguistic performance, though their competence is not in question. Teachers find it difficult, but not impossible, to replace the language of the home and the neighborhood with more standard forms of English. Fortunately, children are natural language theoreticians and often develop bidialectism—a school language and a home language.

Although direct intervention, correction, and training may have little effect on the acquisition of language by young children, parents and older siblings have a great impact on a related set of processes, namely, those involved with the development of literacy. Language develops naturally, but literacy development requires more thoughtfulness. Emergent literacy, the early skills needed for acquisition of genuine reading and writing, is shaped by the conversations parents and care givers have with children; the modeling of reading behavior (e.g., whether newspapers appear at breakfast every day or are never seen); naming letters on signs or in print material; teaching the child the letters for his or her own name; praising initial attempts at writing; and most important, reading many, many books together. Some children have 1,000 hours of "lap time" with parents before they enter school; others have very little (Paris & Cunningham, 1996). So the pace and quality of emergent literacy depend greatly on those kinds of attention from parents and others in the social environment of children.

> What is the single most important thing you can do with a child learning to read to encourage a love of and interest in reading?

Language Issues and Schooling

Preschool and elementary school teachers, naturally, have the greatest concern with language development. But the crucial role of language in school, and in life in general, requires some additional thinking by teachers about other linguistic phenomena, namely, nonstandard English usage, bilingualism, and sociolinguistic competency.

Nonstandard English In the United States, there are many speakers of Vernacular Black English, or ebonics; the creole of Louisiana; the dialects of French speakers in Northern Maine and Mexican-Americans along the border; those with New York or Southern accents and style. Along with that heterogeneity in language use, there is continuing public controversy about whether nonstandard English is inferior to standard English. To understand the debate, it is important to note that a resolution of the Linguistic Society of America (1997) states that the difference between a dialect and a language is quite arbitrary. Chinese "dialects" are different enough that speakers of one dialect cannot understand another. Yet speakers of Spanish and Italian, two different "languages," generally can understand each other. Historically, standard English has been used by some people to differentiate themselves from others who are less prestigious in class, nationality, or race. Standard English certainly carries with it the most prestige in our society. But there is nothing *linguistically* special about standard English as opposed to any of the other American dialects. The dialect known as black English, or ebonics, for example, is as systematic and rule-governed as any other human language (Bloome & Lemke, 1995; Bough, 1983; Smitherman, 1994). If African-Americans were dominant culturally and politically, ebonics would no doubt be the standard, and Midwestern American English would be considered a "problem dialect" educators must "deal with."

For most linguists, the issue about dialect and language is closed. There has yet to be found a dialect or language that is associated with any cognitive deficiency. No dialect or language is more accurate, logical, or capable of expressing thought and feeling than any other language or dialect. The consensus of linguists is that the surface structure or phonological sound of the language used by any speaker of nonstandard English is different *but not deficient*. So the question is really whether the surface differences in the structural system of the language of nonstandard-English speakers have educational and economic implications. This is a social issue, not a cognitive one.

Bilingualism   The debate on how to teach non-English–speaking students is also a social issue, not a cognitive one. As a teacher you will almost surely come across students whose primary language is not English. The number of non-English–speaking school-age children is surprisingly high. Although most of us are familiar with the large Native American-, Chinese-, and Spanish-speaking communities of the United States, we tend to forget the Russian-speaking settlements of Brooklyn, New York, the Portuguese enclaves in Massachusetts, the Korean speakers of Los Angeles, and the Samoans and Southeast Asian immigrants of the San Francisco Bay area, among others. In the early 1990s, 2.3 million students whose native language is something other than English were enrolled in the schools (Fleischman & Hopstock, 1993). By the time the children of these diverse linguistic communities come to school, they have already mastered most of the complexities of their native language. Then the challenge begins: How can the schools help them master English and other school subjects so that they have a chance to achieve in the economic sphere, *without destroying their native language competence, their self-image, or their cultural identity?*

Educational research, with remarkable consistency, has shown to be false the belief that bilingualism results in lower competence in both languages. Data consistently support the positive effects of bilingual education on students' cognitive abilities and attitudes when it is started early, extends for considerable periods of time, is additive (adds the second language while preserving the first), and is two-way (English speakers and foreign language speakers learn each other's language) (Diaz, 1983; Hakuta, 1986; Ramirez et al., 1991; Thomas & Collier, 1995; U.S. General Accounting Office, 1987). The most effective approach to bilingual education appears to be two-way bilingualism; both groups then end up with high levels of skill in two languages (Thomas & Collier, 1995). Teachers should not see bilingualism, then, as only for minority-group students. It is a better way of educating majority-culture students as well. Moreover, research has shown that age is not as crucial and limiting a factor in learning a second language as was once thought. Clearly, there's a critical period in learning a first language. But second-language learners can achieve high levels of competence no matter at what age they begin (Hakuta & McLaughlin, 1996). So two-way bilingual programs in our schools are recommended.

This research and the desire of many cultural groups to maintain

Have you ever tried to think, or to communicate solely, in another language? What were the challenges you encountered?

their language community and cultural heritage have been part of the force for building bilingual education programs. But the primary factors in the growth of bilingual education are (1) the intense culture shock experienced by non-English–speaking youngsters on entering school, and (2) the academic retardation that takes place when class time is used to teach English, while children's regularly used, already-mastered language is ignored as a medium for teaching reading, social studies, science, and other subjects.

Programs for children from linguistically and culturally diverse backgrounds vary from community to community. A program usually starts in the child's native language and eventually shifts to English. Whenever possible, education is provided initially by bilingual native-language speakers until, after a few grades, more instruction in English can take place. Then special education programs to maintain students' native language and to teach them more about their own cultures should be instituted, but usually are not. In an analysis of recent research, bilingual education showed positive effects on tests of reading, language skills, mathematics, and other curriculum areas when the tests were in English. But the programs also produced higher achievement in mathematics, writing, social studies, listening comprehension, and attitudes toward school when tests were in the student's native language (Willig, 1985). The data from a meta-analysis suggested that the average student in a bilingual program scores higher than 74 percent of the students who speak a foreign language but are placed in an all-English immersion program.

Many Americans—including many politicians—seem to favor English-immersion programs as the proper way to teach foreign-language speakers to speak English (Arias & Casanova, 1993; Crawford, 1992; Garcia & Baker, 1995). But the data do not support this opinion. In two recent studies (Ramirez et al., 1991; Thomas & Collier, 1995), the long-term gains for good bilingual programs were obvious. But the trick is that they must be good. Too often the education of immigrants goes on in classes that are overcrowded, with the least qualified teachers, in neighborhoods with poverty, violence, and other social problems. Neither immersion nor bilingual education works well under these conditions. But when qualified teachers, working under reasonable conditions, implement bilingual education, their students usually perform better in both languages. Furthermore, we now know that bilingual children who have control of both languages are cognitively more adept and have better metalinguistic understanding than monolingual children (Hakuta, 1986; Kessler & Quinn, 1987). In general, monolinguals are at a considerable cognitive disadvantage to bilingual speakers of any two languages.

The teacher's role in bilingual education is typically defined by a committee in charge of the bilingual program. Educational psychology can give us some insights into teaching of this kind:

- Linguistic competence and intellectual competence are not the same. English-language tests of intelligence may seriously underestimate the intelligence of bilingual students. Students with language problems in English may have no difficulties expressing

themselves in their native languages. They are also likely to withdraw from discussion and other classroom activities if teachers or
other students treat them as though linguistic and cultural differences are synonymous with inferiority.

■ Bilingual students are also bicultural students. Particular attention
should be paid to matching curriculum materials and methods of
instruction to bilingual students. For example, it makes no sense to
teach spelling by means of spelling bees and other kinds of contests
to students who belong to certain Native American groups, who look
down on individuals who achieve at the expense of others.

■ Bilingualism enhances economic opportunity. Corporations today
are multinational and need native speakers of other languages. The
tourist industry also requires multilingual personnel.

■ After their transition to English, students need opportunities to
express themselves in school in their native language to help maintain their native linguistic competence and cultural identity. Only
a short time ago teachers in the Southwest would send home

Bilingualism—full
competence in two
languages—enhances
cognitive develop-
ment. It is valuable for
everyone, not just for
those lucky enough to
learn their heritage
language at home.

(© Paul Conklin)

Mexican-American children who "dared" speak Spanish in school. Instead the schools should see to it that facility in students' native language also grows by providing, for example, time for academic discussions in the native language.

Sociolinguistic Competence and Schooling   It is now evident that the language development of many children outside of school may not prepare them for school. This is so because schools have a culture of their own, with special rules for communication. Children who have not mastered the etiquette of language called for in school are not able to understand and participate fully in their own education (Schultz, Florio, & Erickson, 1982). It is like visiting a foreign country—they can probably get by, but they blunder often and miss a lot!

The effects of the home-school gap have received a lot of attention (see Guthrie & Hall, 1983; Phillips, 1983). Educators now understand that a problem exists, for example, if a student has not learned the structure of classroom lessons—a structure that often calls for a teacher initiation act (I), a student reply (R), and a teacher evaluation (E) (Mehan, 1979; 1982). (Such IRE units resemble the structuring-soliciting-responding-reacting units, discussed in Chapter 12 when we consider classroom teaching.) A child may deviate from what is expected when this repetitive recitation pattern is used—responding to a teacher's question with a question, giving too lengthy an answer, or challenging the teacher's evaluative comment. These responses, although perfectly appropriate at home, are not appropriate in the classroom. Students may have to learn a new set of social rules for using language in school.

Sociolinguists see the classroom linguistic environment as rule-governed. Rules tell us how to speak, to whom, when, and for what purpose. But like other aspects of the process of learning language, rules are not posted on bulletin boards—children must infer them from what goes on in the classroom. Not every child does this well. Also, classrooms differ in their rule structures. Some teachers ask "pseudoquestions," in which they have a right answer in mind; others ask "real" questions designed to be truly informative (Morine-Dershimer & Tenenberg, 1981). Students need to learn which kind of question is being asked. The rules also vary according to what teachers think about their students' ability. Low-ability students are not expected in reading lessons to spend much time on content or meaning; they are expected to spend their time on decoding and pronunciation problems (see J. L. Green, 1983). Rules differ, too, for different activities within classes. That is, the rules governing participation in the lesson, and the definition of appropriate content for discussion, differ markedly for large-group instruction in mathematics and small-group instruction in reading.

Many different social rules for discourse in classrooms must be learned by schoolchildren. Being academically talented is not enough. Students need to present information in an appropriate form at the appropriate time (J. L. Green, 1983). Teachers can help in the development of sociolinguistic competence by making explicit the rules for talking out, taking turns, participating in recitations, displaying factual knowledge, responding to comments by others, and so forth (see Morine-Dershimer,

Conduct an informal observation of yourself and your peers as you engage in classroom language and in out-of-classroom language. What differences do you notice?

1987). Some people estimate that it may take a foreign student only a few months to look like an American student (the "right" athletic shoes and T-shirts), a few years to learn passable conversational English, but five or more years to learn the cultural norms of American schools and culture. Clothing and language rules are much more explicit; cultural norms are hidden from view. So the teacher must make these rules of discourse and interaction clear to the students from other cultures.

The Development of Personality

Schools have responsibility for developing more than cognition—they cannot help but be concerned with the "whole child." In this section, we look first at one general theory dealing with personality development throughout the life span, next at different theories that deal with one specific aspect of personal development—the growth of morality—and last at several of the traits or individual characteristics that make up personality.

Erikson's Theory of Personality Development

How do I acquire a sense of what I know to be the "real me"? Erik Erikson (1968) believed that personal identity grows out of certain "crises" in psychosocial development. These crises lead to personality growth, or regression. They influence whether our personality becomes more or less integrated. Erikson's underlying assumption was that as we grow we are forced to become aware of and interact with a widening social community. In the course of these interactions, first as children and later as adults, we have a chance to develop a "healthy" personality—one characterized by mastery of the environment, unity of functioning, and the ability to perceive the world and ourselves accurately. These are the qualities of the self-actualized individual described by humanistic psychologists such as Carl Rogers and Abraham Maslow. Self-actualized persons are those who are happy to be doing what they do and pleased with who they have become.

For Erikson, self-actualization takes place only after the acceptable resolution of certain crises, or basic psychosocial problems (Table 4.2). A crisis is a time of increased vulnerability to a particular psychosocial challenge. Each crisis is related to the others. Each exists in some form before the decisive moment for its resolution arrives. And each, as it is positively resolved, contributes to the ultimate strength and vigor of the growing personality (Erikson, 1963).

The **trust versus mistrust** crisis occurs in *infancy*, roughly from birth to 1½ years. The quality of life during infancy—including love, attention, touch, and feeding relationships—influences the child's fundamental feelings of trust or mistrust of the environment. Order and predictability in an infant's life also give rise to trust. These feelings pervade all of later life. A favorable ratio of trust to mistrust is a form of psychosocial strength, the foundation of traits like optimism and hope.

The crisis of **autonomy versus shame and doubt** occurs during the

4.2

TABLE

Erikson's Developmental Sequence of Crises

Age of Occurrence	Crisis to Be Resolved
Infancy	Trust vs. mistrust
Early childhood	Autonomy vs. shame and doubt
Middle childhood	Initiative vs. guilt
Elementary school age	Accomplishment vs. inferiority
Adolescence	Identity vs. role confusion
Young adulthood	Intimacy vs. isolation
Adulthood	Generativity vs. stagnation
Old age	Integrity vs. despair

Source: Extracted from Identity: Youth and Crisis *by Erik H. Erikson. Copyright © 1968 by W. W. Norton & Company, Inc. Reprinted by permission of W. W. Norton & Company, Inc., and Faber and Faber Ltd.*

toddler and preschool years, roughly between 1½ and 3 years. The child tests her parents and environment, learning what she can control and what she cannot. Developing a sense of self-control without loss of self-esteem is necessary to her feelings of free will. Overcontrol by parents gives the child lasting feelings of doubt about her capabilities and shame about her needs or body. A child's feeling of autonomy grows out of the initial emancipation from her mother. It depends on the earlier development of trust rather than mistrust.

The crisis of **initiative versus guilt** occurs in preschool years and kindergarten, roughly between 3 and 5 years. With a sense of trust and a feeling of autonomy, the child can develop a sense of initiative. He can go on his own into strange places and let curiosity run its course. A realistic sense of purpose emerges along with rudimentary forms of ambition. A healthy resolution of the challenges at this age leads to a sense of personal responsibility. It is at this time that the development of initiative and the consequent experience of guilt begin to form the conscience. The parents deny the child permission to do certain things as part of their response to his unbridled curiosity. As the child transgresses these prohibitions, in reality or fantasy, he feels guilt. The parent or teacher who blocks initiative too often may raise a guilty, constricted child. The parent or teacher who rebukes too rarely may raise a child without a fully developed conscience.

The crisis of **accomplishment versus inferiority** occurs during the years between kindergarten and puberty, roughly between 5 and 12 years. The child must become able to do and make some things well or even perfectly. Being denied feelings of accomplishment leads to the development of feelings of inferiority and inadequacy. Teachers in these years have the responsibility of creating successful experiences for each

> Do you think Erik Erikson would place low value or high value on a preschool teacher's position? Why?

child, of keeping feelings of ineptness from forming. This requires knowing each student's capabilities and controlling her working environment. One particular danger, noted by Erikson, is that doing the work becomes an end in itself, stifling the child's further growth. Children may develop as "good little helpers" or "good little workers" but never develop the idea that work should be pleasing to themselves (Dacey & Kenny, 1994). Healthy resolution of the crisis at this stage leads to a sense of competence for coping with life's problems as they arise.

The crisis of **identity versus confusion** occurs in adolescence, that period of "storm and stress," roughly between 12 and 18 years. At this stage, some delay in the integration of personality elements must take place. Boys and girls are becoming men and women and cannot help but feel estranged and unattached. Their bodies and hormones change so that sexual forces often overwhelm other concerns, capture the imagination, and arouse forbidden desires. A new intimacy with the opposite sex approaches or is sometimes forced on the inexperienced young person, adding to the confusion.

The central problem of this period is establishing a sense of identity. For adolescents, this means a series of problems in clarifying who they are and what their role in society should be. The particular concerns of adolescents seem to fall into four categories: (1) future and careers, so issues such as schooling, tests, and work are important to them, (2) health, including the issues of sex, smoking, alcohol, and other drug use, (3) identity, or their sense of a personal self, and this includes concerns about parents, family, and friends, and (4) social self, also related to friends but including appearance, dating, sports, and other social activities (Violato & Travis, 1995). In fact, during adolescence the social concerns can dominate all the others (Wigfield, Eccles, & Pintrich, 1996).

The inability to come to an understanding of self—a lack of identity—leads to confusion. Failure to resolve this crisis prolongs adolescence and limits the ways in which people function in adult roles. These individuals do not cope effectively with later crises in the life cycle. On the other hand, a healthy resolution of this crisis leads to confidence in oneself and a sense of security that the future is going to be good.

As a teacher you need all the sensitivity you can muster to work with students experiencing the turbulence of adolescence. But you need to remember that not all adolescents are in a negative state of crisis. In fact, most adolescents maintain close and honest relationships with their families, share the values of those whom they live with, do not experience terrible stress, and are as concerned about world affairs and environmental issues as are those with whom they live (Violato & Travis, 1995). Nevertheless, television influences teenagers, and in the area of sexual behavior, in particular, teenagers end up accepting the stereotypes themselves. Television has, in a sense, invented some of the teenage experience (Dacey & Kenny, 1994).

The crisis of **intimacy versus isolation** arises in young adulthood, roughly between 18 and 25 years, after identity is functionally established if not fixed. Can the young adult share by giving some piece of his or her own identity over to another, so that "we" supplants "I" in thinking about the present and future? The inability to develop intimate relationships leads to psychological isolation, which is often less desirable, and perhaps less healthy, for the individual. A healthy resolution of this crisis results in the person's ability to confidently give and receive love.

The crisis of **generativity versus stagnation** is the crisis of adulthood, occurring roughly between 25 and 65 years. *Generativity* refers to creativity, productivity, and an interest in guiding the development of the next generation. Maturity requires a dependent, one for whom you are mature. It also requires caring for and nurturing what is in your environment—ideas, things, and people. Without a certain amount of generative responding, the adult suffers boredom, apathy, pseudointimacy, an impoverishment in interpersonal relationships, and a pervading sense of stagnation. A healthy resolution of this crisis results in a caring, socially involved person.

The crisis of **integrity versus despair** occurs in old age. The personality is fully integrated when an adult develops a sense of acceptance of this one and only chance at life on earth and of the important people in it. People and events must be taken at face value. Her children, spouse, parents, and job are what they are. And most important, in recognizing this, she can say, "I am what I am!" At this stage she can come to have dignity. On the other hand, despair or disappointment with herself and what she has accomplished can lead to a troubled and self-contemptuous end to the life cycle.

Few theories of personality are supported by a firm body of objective and replicated data, and Erikson's theory is no exception. Still, it does have the ring of truth. Embedded in this general theory of development are all the possibilities of personality formation that we see in the people around us. Characteristics such as trust, stinginess, creativity, altruism, complacency, assertiveness, precociousness, and desperation appear to have roots in the various crises and resolutions Erikson described.

As a teacher, you need to be aware of the changes going on within students, particularly at the stage of the adolescent identity crisis. Sometimes the newspapers report a series of teenage suicides. In many cases, family, friends, and teachers did not realize the terrible stress the young people were feeling. They remind us again of how difficult adolescence can be for *some* of our youth. It is worth remembering, also, that adolescence is more stressful for girls (Gilligan et al. 1990) and for racial and ethnic minorities (Dacey & Kenny, 1994). There is evidence that young women lose self-esteem in adolescence, while African-American adolescents withdraw from academic competition, afraid of "acting white" (Ogbu, 1987; Fordham, 1988; Wigfield, Eccles, & Pintrich, 1996). Establishing sexual and cultural identity in a sexually charged and racially tense nation can make a complex process even more difficult.

A teacher's guidance, friendship, and caring can help students through this stressful period. We are in classrooms to do more than teach fractions or the causes of World War I. We are there to foster the social development of our students, to help them develop healthy and integrated personalities.

The Development of Moral Reasoning

How does morality develop? At what ages do we acquire ideas about right and wrong? Does our thinking about moral issues develop in stages, in a process like the one Piaget described? We take a look at two major researchers in this area, Lawrence Kohlberg and Carol Gilligan, and then examine ways in which teachers can enhance moral development.

Kohlberg's Levels and Stages Kohlberg (1963, 1981) identified three levels of moral thought, with two stages of development characteristic of each level. These are detailed in Table 4.3. Notice how the developmental progression of different kinds of moral reasoning closely parallels Piaget's preoperational, concrete operational, and formal operational levels of thought. Kohlberg and Piaget held similar views about the process

TABLE 4.3

Kohlberg's Levels of Moral Development

Levels of Moral Thought	Stages of Moral Development	
A. *Preconventional level.* The child responds to cultural labels of good and bad, but looks mainly at the physical effects of action (pleasure or pain) or at the physical power of the rule givers.	1. *The punishment-obedience orientation.* The individual tries to avoid punishment and defers to power in its own right.	2. *The instrumental-relativist orientation.* Right is what satisfies one's own needs, or sometimes others'. Human relations, as in the marketplace, are strictly a matter of reciprocity (You scratch my back and I'll scratch yours). This is a practical morality.
B. *Conventional level.* Meeting expectations of family, group, or nation is valuable, regardless of immediate consequences. Loyalty to and support of the social order are valued beyond mere conformity.	3. *The interpersonal-concordance orientation.* Good behavior is what pleases or helps others. Much conformity to stereotypes of "appropriate" behavior. Intentions are important. One earns approval by being "nice."	4. *Authority and social order–maintaining orientation.* Right behavior consists of doing one's duty, respecting authority, and maintaining the given social order for its own sake.
C. *Postconventional, autonomous, or principled level.* Effort is made to define moral principles that are valid apart from the authority of persons holding them or one's identification with these groups.	5. *The social-contract legalistic orientation.* Utility of laws and individual rights is critically examined. Societally accepted standards are important. Personal values are relative. Procedural rules for reaching consensus are emphasized. Hence laws may be changed democratically. Rational consideration of laws and rights can improve their usefulness.	6 *The universal-ethical principle orientation.* Right is defined by conscience, in accordance with self-chosen, logical, and comprehensive ethical principles. Right is abstract and ethical (e.g., the Golden Rule), not concrete and moral (e.g., the Ten Commandments). There is emphasis on reciprocity and equality of human rights. There is respect for the dignity of the individual.

Source: Adapted from E. Turiel, "Stage Transition in Moral Development," in R. M. W. Travers (Ed.), Second Handbook of Research on Teaching (Chicago: Rand McNally, 1973), pp. 733–734. Copyright 1973 American Educational Research Association. Also adapted from F. Oser, "Moral Education and Values Education: The Discourse Perspective," in M. C. Wittrock (Ed.), Handbook of Research on Teaching (3d ed.) (New York: Macmillan, 1986), pp. 923–924. Copyright 1986 American Educational Research Association.

of development, particularly the views that young children are virtually incapable of handling the abstractions of the higher stages, and that formal operational thinking is necessary to achieve level C—the level characterized by principled reasoning.

Kohlberg identified these levels and stages from the verbal responses of children and adults to hypothetical moral dilemmas. One of these dilemmas (adapted from Kohlberg, 1984; and Cobb, 1995), is: Tiffany, 14, sees her sister, Jennifer, 10, steal some money from their mother's purse. Tiffany's possible responses to this dilemma, and categorization of those responses, are as follows:

Level A: Preconventional

Stage 1. *The punishment-obedience orientation.* Tiffany: "I can't tell Mom, Jennifer would get me for it." (Perspective: one's own; motive: own needs, avoid punishment; standards: other people's behavior; criteria: consequences)

Stage 2. *The instrumental-relativist orientation.* Tiffany: "I better not tell. Sometimes I do wrong things, too, and I wouldn't want Jennifer telling Mom on me." (Perspective: one's own and another's; motive: satisfy own needs and those of another; standards: other people's behavior; criteria: fairness, reciprocity)

Level B: Conventional

Stage 3. *The conformist orientation.* Tiffany: "It's better to tell on Jennifer. Otherwise, my mom might think I was in on it." (Perspective: another person's; motive: approval; standards: internalized rules of what is proper; criteria: living up to expectations)

Stage 4. *Authority and social order–maintaining orientation.* Tiffany: "Stealing's wrong. I haven't got a choice. I must tell on Jennifer." (Perspective: the community; motive: uphold the laws; standards: the rules and laws for behavior; criteria: compliance with the law)

Level C: Postconventional, Autonomous, or Principled

Stage 5. *The social-contract legalistic orientation.* Tiffany: "I'll try to talk Jennifer into giving back the money. But if she won't, I'll tell Mom, even though I'd hate doing it. But the money's Mom's, and Jennifer just can't go around taking what she wants." (Perspective: society's; motive: maintain the social order; standards: laws, agreements about what is right; criteria: justice)

Stage 6. *The universal-ethical-principle orientation.* Tiffany: "Jennifer needs to see how unfair she is to Mom. Telling on her won't accomplish much. I need to show Jennifer where she is wrong and help her to earn some money so she can pay Mom back, maybe without Mom even knowing it!" (Perspective: society; motive: human rights for all; standards: personal principles; criteria: universal moral code)

Between 7 and 16 years, the percentage of responses to dilemmas that are at Level A goes down, the percentage of Level B responses goes up sharply, and the percentage of Level C responses goes up modestly.

By age 16 about half the responses made to dilemmas are Level B—conventional—and one fourth are at Level C—the postconventional level. That means, of course, that about one fourth of 16-year-olds are still responding to moral dilemmas in preconventional styles of thinking. Similar percentages have been found in places as different as an Australian aboriginal village, a Turkish city, a Turkish village, a Mexican city, and a Mayan village.

Using a different way to assess moral development, the Defining Issues Test (DIT), researchers have done hundreds of studies of moral development (Rest et al., 1985). These have, in general, supported Kohlberg's assertions.

Gilligan's Model   Gilligan (1982; Gilligan & Antanucci, 1988; Gilligan, Ward, & Taylor, 1988) makes the point that women care more about social relationships and responsibility for caregiving than do men, who come to adopt a more abstract view of rights and obligations under law. Table 4.4 presents Gilligan's theory of moral development, the end result of which is the development of an ethic of caring, not the espousal of a legal principle, as is more common among men.

Gilligan sees female responses to the psychosocial crisis of adolescence as different from male responses. In one sense, the three levels described in Table 4.4 describe the different identities girls can choose from as adolescence arrives. A girl can be selfish and self-absorbed (level 1); become the good little conventional girl (level 2); or take on a caring ethic, nurturing self and others (level 3). Gilligan notes that leaving childhood is harder and different for girls than it is for boys, because

TABLE 4.4

Gilligan's Model of Moral Development in Girls and Women

Level 1

Caring for self—A survival orientation. Self-interest and self-preservation are primary. Other people are not considered of great importance. Transition to the next level only occurs when a person realizes that there is a discrepancy between the person she is and the person she would like to be. The young person moves from self-concern to concern for others if she has developed sufficient self-worth.

Level 2

Caring for others—A goodness orientation. Acceptance of social conventions about what is good takes place. Moral judgments rely upon shared norms and expectations. Survival now depends on acceptance by significant others. Females become part of the community by caring for others; that is, they accept the notions of "good girl." Trying to be "good" is as much a problem as just taking care of oneself, as in the first stage. This stage is left behind when women see caring for themselves and others in some kind of balanced relationship.

Level 3

Caring for self and others—A caring orientation. Females at this stage no longer put the needs of others first, but take care of themselves as well. They must, of course, have a vision of what their own needs are. This means being honest with oneself. An ethic of caring represents a balanced concern for others and self.

Debate the pros and cons of Kohlberg's highest level of moral development vis-à-vis Gilligan's. Does your personal experience support the male/female distinction noted here?

girls enter a male-dominated culture characterized by separation from others and a norm of individuality. Girls, however, remain in a culture of attachment and caring, neither separating nor developing individuality. Caring, arising out of women's connectedness to others, is simply not valued as much as the kind of abstract thinking about justice that characterizes male thought. It is the separation of men from family and their greater development of individuality that allows them to stop thinking about particular people and use abstract principles of justice to make moral decisions. So it also is no surprise that they would regard this as the highest level of moral thinking.

Johnson (1988), wondering whether she could test Gilligan's ideas experimentally, gave early and mid-adolescence girls and boys fables to discuss. One required a judgment about whether a guest should stay after beginning to disrupt the daily life of the household. Another was about a dispute over competing rights. The solutions respondents offered were judged to be either caring solutions, taking into account the rights of all parties, or justice solutions, relying on what is right from a legal standpoint. Many more of these adolescent males solved these dilemmas with abstract legal/justice orientations; many more adolescent females solved them with caring-for-the-rights-of-all orientations. So, although both boys and girls are capable of justice- and caring-based ethics, each gender seems to prefer one kind over another when making moral choices.

Gilligan appears to have put her finger on one particular way males and females differ. Note, however, that when educational levels are held constant, adult females actually score higher than adult males on the justice dimension as well (Rest et al., 1985). Apparently women not only think differently about moral issues, but they usually think at a slightly higher level on the dimensions that characterize male thinking if they have had the same educational opportunities as men.

Fostering Moral Thinking   Can we use special school experiences to increase the rate of moral development? The answer at first appeared to be that training programs made little long-term difference. But more recent evidence (Rest, 1994) is far more positive. For example, Schlaefli, Rest, and Thoma (1985) analyzed 55 studies that tried to stimulate the development of moral judgment. They found that when students of junior high school age and up discussed the dilemmas in a program lasting from, say, eight to twelve weeks, a definite change in their moral reasoning occurred. The same effect has been found for programs designed to intensify self-reflection and personal psychological growth, particularly as it relates to how someone interacts with others and society in general. Students in these kinds of programs show more principled reasoning. Average students in a control group would be expected to score at the 50th percentile rank on a test of moral-reasoning ability. But these same students would be expected to score at about the 60th percentile rank after a training program. Rest (1994) notes that some of the most dramatic changes occur in young adulthood—in one's 20s and 30s. In particular, college seems to have a great impact on moral reasoning. And accumulated evidence (Rest, 1994) shows that moral reasoning is correlated with moral choices and moral behavior. So increasing moral reasoning skills *may* increase moral action.

A training program for promoting moral development has been outlined by Oser (1986, 1994). He has suggested moral discussions between teacher and students as the stimulus for raising the level of moral thinking among youth. This discourse should be

- directed toward moral conflict and the stimulation of higher levels of moral thought
- analytical of the student's own beliefs, reasoning, and theoretical positions
- directed toward moral role taking and moral empathy
- directed toward an understanding of shared norms and the meaning of a moral community
- directed toward moral choice and moral action

Certainly, simply discussing moral issues does not automatically lead everyone to act in moral ways. But moral discourse is a way to think critically about the important issues we face as individuals and as a society. To let education in this area happen by accident seems less sensible than to try programs that might move students more quickly to a postconventional level of moral thinking and an ethic of caring as well.

Toward these ends, schools have designed "just communities," with student committees to set rules, hear complaints, administer justice, and discuss the dilemmas faced by young people. Students in schools that have created this kind of community have higher levels of moral reasoning than those in control schools without such experiences (Higgins & Barna, 1994).

Schools have also been consciously designed to be caring places, featuring cooperation and helping behavior. Solomon et al. (1990) have, for example, developed such schools, emphasizing five elements:

- Helping activities
- Rewarding kindness, fairness, honesty, responsibility, and the like—not just academic achievement
- Discourse about understanding—discussions of literature, class meetings, assemblies, and fairs to promote helping, caring, and understanding of others (e.g., people of other cultures)
- Developmental discipline—rule setting and discussion of rules by children to foster self-control and the building of friendships by resolving disputes in an equitable manner
- Cooperative learning—the building of prosocial values and social skills while working to achieve competency in academic content

Assessment of children in this kind of program (Solomon et al., 1990) shows them to actually be "nicer"! That is, they are kinder to each other, more helpful, more cooperative, and more responsible than are children in schools without the commitment by teachers and the students' families to build a caring community. In these troubled times for youth, perhaps we need to acknowledge that schools designed around an ethic of caring, rather than the pursuit of academic excellence alone, have much to recommend them. Noddings (1992, p. xiv) says this well:

Teenage pregnancies nearly doubled between 1965 and 1985; the teen suicide rate has doubled in the same period of time; teenage drinking takes a horrible toll in drunk driving accidents and dulled sensibilities; children take guns to school, and homicide is the leading cause of death among minority teens; a disgraceful number of children live in poverty. And still many school people and public officials insist that the job of the schools is to increase academic rigor. In direct opposition, I will argue that the first job of the schools is to care for our children. We should educate all our children, not only for competence but also for caring.

Moral school settings, through the creation of just and caring communities based on discourse and reflection, are both desirable and possible. It surely takes hard work to carry out these ideas, but moral growth and the development of a caring ethic, in males as well as females, are outcomes as important as achievement in mathematics and literacy.

The Organization of Personality: A Profusion of Traits

Personality is a concept derived from behavior. We observe only behavior. But we create names for that behavior to talk about the different kinds of behaviors we notice. Our names for behavior—honest, aggressive, hot-tempered, cheerful, serene, naive, creative —are often the same as the words we use to describe personality. Psychologists have studied these descriptive words, called *trait names,* to understand the way personality is organized and maintained.

A **trait** is an enduring aspect of a person's behavior, generally consistent across a wide variety of settings and situations. Allport and Odbert (1936) found 17,953 English-language adjectives that could be used to describe traits. Many questionaires and inventories are designed to measure traits. The Gordon Personal Inventory is aimed at measuring "cautiousness," "original thinking," "personal relations," and "vigor." The Edwards Personal Preference Inventory is aimed at measuring some of our social needs, such as affiliation and achievement. The California Personality Inventory is intended to measure "sociability" and "tolerance," among other things. Almost all of these tests are designed to locate people on trait scales so that we can say that Suzi Yee is very "sociable" or Henry Washington is extremely "cautious." Ideally, educators would use these measurements to understand a student's personality, to help them diagnose and prescribe for that student. That is, trait scores should give us additional insights into a student's behavior.

Recently, research has found that the thousands of traits group reasonably well into five clusters—called the **Big Five Factors of Personality** (John, 1990; Snow, Corno, & Jackson, 1996). The statistical technique researchers used to find these five broad factors was factor analysis (the same method as was used to discover the broad Stratum II factors discussed in Chapter 3). Figure 4.4 describes the Big Five factors and some representative traits that help define each factor. Each

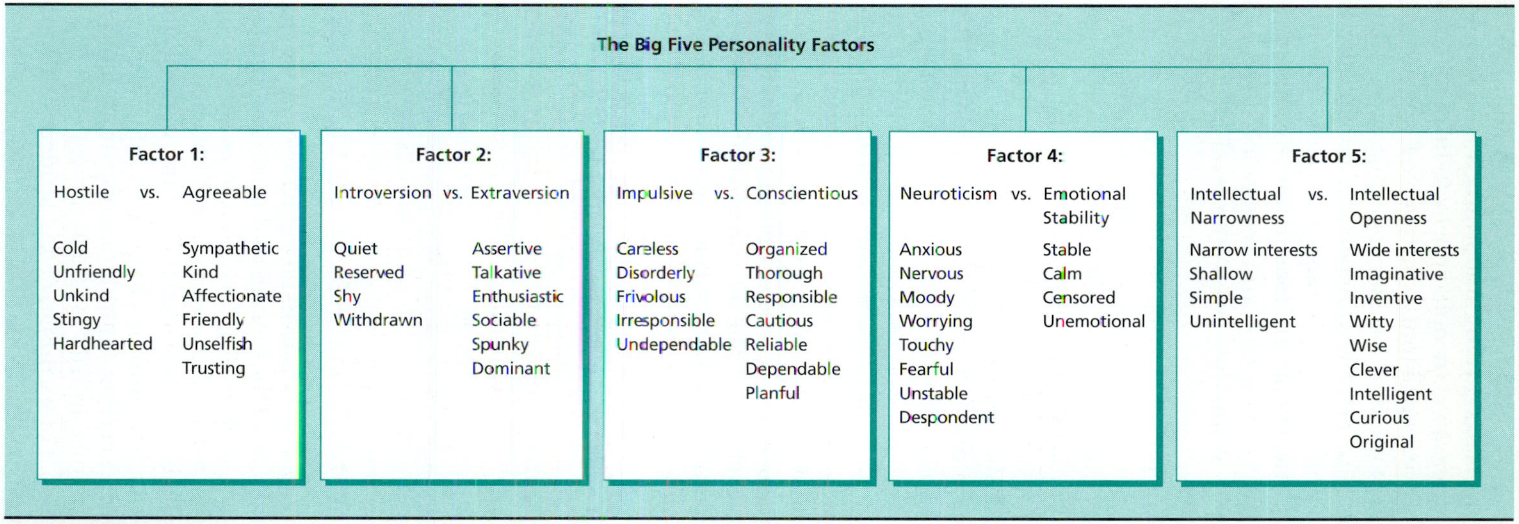

The Big Five Personality Factors

Factor 1:		Factor 2:		Factor 3:		Factor 4:		Factor 5:	
Hostile vs. Agreeable		Introversion vs. Extraversion		Impulsive vs. Conscientious		Neuroticism vs. Emotional Stability		Intellectual Narrowness vs. Intellectual Openness	
Cold	Sympathetic	Quiet	Assertive	Careless	Organized	Anxious	Stable	Narrow interests	Wide interests
Unfriendly	Kind	Reserved	Talkative	Disorderly	Thorough	Nervous	Calm	Shallow	Imaginative
Unkind	Affectionate	Shy	Enthusiastic	Frivolous	Responsible	Moody	Censored	Simple	Inventive
Stingy	Friendly	Withdrawn	Sociable	Irresponsible	Cautious	Worrying	Unemotional	Unintelligent	Witty
Hardhearted	Unselfish		Spunky	Undependable	Reliable	Touchy			Wise
	Trusting		Dominant		Dependable	Fearful			Clever
					Planful	Unstable			Intelligent
						Despondent			Curious
									Original

FIGURE 4.4

Five personality factors and related trait names

factor can be considered as having both a positive and a negative side. But there is something important about factors and traits to keep in mind. At one level, people appear to be consistently agreeable or hostile (factor 1) or consistently introverted or extroverted (factor 2). But at a more "molecular" or more specific level—say concerning the traits of honesty or creativity, aspects of personality that teachers care a lot about—people vary a lot more from time to time and place to place than was thought. People are reasonably, but not perfectly, consistent at one level—the broad level—and reasonably inconsistent but not totally inconsistent at another level—the level of the traits that make up these five factors.

It turns out, then, that behavior is a function of *both* personality and environmental factors (Mischel, 1973, 1990). The different environments students and teachers find themselves in bring out different kinds of behavior. And for the most part, it is the rewards and punishments in particular environments that influence their behavior. As might be expected, if the rewards and punishments for a given kind of behavior in different situations are largely uncorrelated, the behavior itself should not be similar or stable from setting to setting—and indeed it is not in most empirical studies. Generality in behavior is not high because the consequences for behavior vary so widely from one situation to another. So, on any given day, in any given environment, consistency in a person's behavior may not be evident.

Let us look now at two of the hundreds of student traits that are relevant to teaching—honesty and creativity. We examine their consistency across settings as we describe them, then briefly discuss **self-concept,** people's own assessment of all their various traits and characteristics.

Honesty   Factor 3 of the Big Five Factors is characterized, on the positive side, by conscientiousness, responsibility, and reliability, and that is where the trait of honesty probably fits. The opposite and negative side of that factor is characterized by the traits of impulsivity, undependability, and irresponsibility, which is where the trait of dishonesty probably fits. Needless to say, teachers value honest children—those who do not take money from a teacher's wallet, steal chalk or pencils, cheat on tests, or lie. The classic studies of honesty and deception in children were conducted by Hartshorne and May (1928) and reexamined by Snow, Corno, and Jackson (1996). Among the tests used were these three:

Copying. For example, giving IQ tests to children, collecting the tests, secretly scoring and recording the answers, giving the tests back, and having the children score their own tests. The discrepancy between the experimenter's secret scoring and the child's self-scoring provided a measure of cheating.

Peeking. For example, asking a blindfolded child to pencil some dots within certain boundaries drawn on a piece of paper. Good performance in this task can almost always be attributed to peeking.

Stealing. For example, giving students the opportunity to remove some coins from a box in the belief that only they can tell how many coins should be in the box.

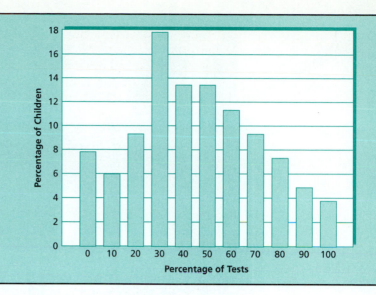

FIGURE 4.5

Percentage of tests on which children cheated

Percentage of Children (y-axis: 0, 2, 4, 6, 8, 10, 12, 14, 16, 18)

Percentage of Tests (x-axis: 0, 10, 20, 30, 40, 50, 60, 70, 80, 90, 100)

What are some instructional implications of the point that consistency in personality traits is not as great as many people assume?

The intercorrelations among these three kinds of tests are positive but low. This indicates that a student who cheats by changing an IQ score is not likely to peek or steal. Yet the correlations do indicate some consistency, so a general trait of honesty probably does exist (Snow, Corno, & Jackson, 1996). The point is that consistency in the trait in children, from setting to setting, is not as great as everyday usage of the term "honesty" implies.

Over the series of tests, the number of times some form of deception—cheating, peeking, stealing—took place is shown in Figure 4.5. Fewer than 8 percent of the students never cheated, and about 4 percent of the students cheated at every opportunity. For the remaining 88 percent of the students, honesty was not an all-or-nothing trait, consistent across all situations. Rather, it was behavior that depended, in ways no one understands, on the interaction between environmental circumstances, particularly the immediate demands of the task, and previously learned behavioral tendencies.

This emphasis on the dependence of behavior on both personality and environmental variables is important for teachers: Be careful about the labels you apply to students. Herman may cheat in your English class but not in science class. Luanne may steal some pennies from Ms. Murphy's class fund but would not peek in the blindfold task. Honesty, like many traits, may be fairly consistent over similar situations but more changeable in different situations. We reexamine these points later in this chapter in the section on the teacher and trait theory.

Creativity Creativity is another trait name commonly used to describe behavior. The positive end of factor 5 (see again Figure 4.4) is where the trait of creativity seems to fit. We have tests of creativity and special programs in creative art, music, writing, and mathematics. The school, like society in general, values and feels it must nurture creativity.

Creative work in writing, architecture, mathematics, problem solving, or sculpting all share the same qualities—originality, suitability, validity, and somehow elegance, or being "just right."
(© Robert Kalman/The Image Works)

Important elements in the definition of creativity include *flexibility* in thinking and *fluency* in the production of ideas. But central to the idea of creativity is *originality*. What people consider to be creative may vary greatly, from a new way of solving a problem in logic; to a new tool or chemical process; a new-style musical composition; a new-style painting; a new way of reasoning in law, philosophy, or religion; or a new insight into a social problem. Creative work is original, suitable, valid, and somehow elegant, or just right (Sternberg & Lubart, 1996).

Creativity and General Intelligence   Is **creativity** the same as intelligence? Torrance (1967) concluded from a review of the literature that the best estimate of the correlation between creativity and general intelligence was about .20 when verbal IQ measures were used, and .06 when nonverbal intelligence measures were used. But this estimate may have been too low. The prevailing view is that creativity is partially independent of intelligence, with correlations between measures of each usually under .50 (Getzels & Jackson, 1962; Hattie & Rogers, 1986; Sternberg & Lubart, 1996).

Following the lead provided by Gardner's ideas about multiple intelligences (Chapter 3), we can state that creativity, like intelligence, has a domain-specific quality. That is, creativity in a field such as music, art, literature, or auto repair is not likely to be highly correlated with creativity in other fields. Sternberg and Lubart (1995) found that to be the case. So creativity is best thought of as a characteristic of a student (or teacher) that applies only to their behavior in some domains, but not others.

Fostering Creativity   At one time, researchers believed that creativity was a relatively unmodifiable trait, highly consistent from one situation to the next. Now we know that environments that elicit and reward original behavior can produce original behavior on tasks that are different from the ones on which a person trained. Teachers need to remember this when a student makes an original, creative response in class. Dacey (1989), who studied creativity among adolescents, says that the greatest inhibitor to creative thinking is the fear of being wrong. That is a fear teachers can influence by their behaviors when students attempt creative responses. Over time, classroom environments that reward creative attempts are environments where more creativity will be seen.

Despite their stated values, many teachers do seem to stifle creativity. For example, beginning teachers may be told, "Be ready to use the first minute of class time. If you get your students busy right away, they have no time to cook up interesting ideas that might lead you astray or delay the start of instruction." This kind of "helpful hint" does make classes more manageable, but many educators would see something perverse in sacrificing students' "interesting ideas" for the sake of discipline.

Teachers may do better in fostering creativity if they adopt the idea of creativity as problem solving. For example, Covington et al. (1974) developed their Productive Thinking Program in the form of 16 cartoon-text booklets designed to teach fifth- and sixth-graders to think like imaginative scholars, detectives, or scientists. When students got stuck on a problem, they were told to consult the thinking guides—presented here in the "Application Feature" (Covington, 1992). These are good bits of advice for teachers to give students when they get stuck. It helps students find both **convergent,** or prosaic, solutions to problems, and solutions that are creative, **divergent,** or original.

The Productive Thinking Program did improve problem-solving skills applicable to a broad range of tasks. Students exposed to this program generated more "good" ideas and showed better planning than students

> In your own experience as a student, have you ever felt your creativity stifled by a negative teacher? Think of specific ways you can avoid this in your own teaching.

Making Use of Thinking Guides in Problem Solving

Presented below is a list of 16 suggestions for solving a problem that you or your students might confront. Try putting it to use now by applying the suggestions to a real problem that you are currently dealing with. Give it some time. Which steps seem to help the most? Does the overall process help? Can you think of ways in which students would be able to put this process to work?

1. Reflect on the problem before you plunge in. Decide exactly what the problem is.

2. Get all the facts of the problem clearly in mind.

3. Pick out all the important elements of the problem, and think carefully about each one.

4. Plan to work on the problem in some systematic way, not haphazardly.

5. Pick out some general approaches to solutions before you analyze the bits and pieces of the proposed solution.

6. Generate many ideas about how to solve the problem; don't stop at just a few.

7. Let your mind wander as you search for ideas. Almost anything around you might trigger a solution.

8. Purposefully try to generate unusual ideas.

9. Don't jump to conclusions too soon. Keep an open mind.

10. If you get an idea you think is unlikely, test it out before you throw it away, trying to see how it might work.

11. Check your ideas against the facts of the situation so you don't spend too long on poor ideas.

12. If you run out of ideas, try looking at the problem in a new and different way.

13. Be on the lookout for oddities, puzzlements, things that don't quite make sense. They may hold the key to a solution.

14. When several oddities in a problem exist, see if you can link them together in some way.

15. If you are stuck, go back and make sure you really understand all the facts. You might have missed something important.

16. Keep at it. Don't be discouraged or give up.

Adapted from Covington, Making the Grade. *Copyright © 1992. Used by permission of Cambridge University Press.*

who were not trained in thinking in this way. The trained students seemed to have developed an executive ability, an ability to oversee the processes needed to solve problems. This allowed the less intelligent class members to acquire the tools to think well that more intelligent children seemed already to possess (Covington, 1992).

Direct observation of master teachers of the gifted by Silverman (1980) indicated that these teachers provide less information to their students.

They spend more time questioning their students than instructing them. They often refuse to answer students' questions, turning them back to the students by asking, "What do you think?" Their questions are often divergent ("What would happen if . . . ?"). They often ask students, "What made you think that?" They have a habit of not giving judgmental feedback. In short, they are not so much information givers, trainers, and evaluators as they are mentors or counselors, and this seems to be a key in the development of creative individuals.

In a 22-year longitudinal study of creative achievement, Torrance (1986) found that mentors make a big difference in the life of youngsters, particularly those from minority-group and low-income families. B. S. Bloom (1985), looking at similarities in the upbringing of extremely successful swimmers, pianists, surgeons, mathematicians, and sculptors, noted the crucial role of teacher-mentors in the development of an individual's unique talent. Different kinds of mentors are needed at the beginning, middle, and later stages of the development of an Olympic swimmer or world-class mathematician. But in all cases the personal involvement of a caring, knowledgeable teacher—a mentor—makes a big difference.

But perhaps the most important point of all is that creative thinking can be taught and creative activity can be enhanced. Your role as a teacher is critical in this regard.

The Teacher and Trait Theory   As a teacher, you should use caution in dealing with all categories of behavior, or traits—not only honesty or creativity but the dozens of other characteristics your students demonstrate, from shyness, to bullying, care giving, and so forth. There is evidence that expert teachers understand this principle. In a comparison of expert teachers with novice teachers, the experts paid almost no attention to the notes left by a previous teacher about students they were planning to teach. Why? Apparently because they understood that each child may act differently in each class. Novice teachers tried to learn all they could about students before meeting them, apparently believing that a previous teacher's notes are valid and student behavior is consistent across settings (Carter, Sabers, Cushing, Pinnegar, & Berliner, 1987).

This does not mean that we have to give up the notion of consistency in human behavior. We still need to be able to predict behavior on the basis of past behavior. But you should not infer from limited observations of behavior in unique environments that your students have broad dispositions to act a certain way. You may not only be wrong, but, worse, you may communicate your unfavorable beliefs through your behavior and create a self-fulfilling prophecy—that is, exert subtle pressure on your students to play out their attributed role as sneak, dummy, clown, or aggressor.

We need to be especially careful about labeling others. Generally, humans tend to overattribute consistency to the behavior of others. As Jones and Nisbett (1971) pointed out, "Actors [in the sense of persons behaving] tend to attribute the causes of their behavior to stimuli inherent in the situation while observers tend to attribute behavior to stable dispositions of the actor" (p. 8). For example, Amalia says, "I tripped because it was dark," while her teacher says, "Amalia tripped because she is clumsy."

The distinction here is a crucial one. Since these kinds of behavior are often specific to a given situation, labeling a student as honest, creative, or anything else could amount to a false generalization. Most traits can be changed, depending on environmental factors that call forth and reinforce the kinds of behaviors identified with trait names. If teachers think a kind of behavior is bad because it interferes with a student's and others' achievement of educational objectives, they should try to modify the behavior before labeling the student.

Self-Concept Individuals tend to develop an organized concept of themselves based on all their characteristics, at least as *they* see them. This self-concept determines how they feel about themselves, what they might do in the future, and how they might evaluate their own performance. Teachers (and parents) have as a goal that students develop a positive general self-concept as well as positive specific beliefs about, say, their talent in at least some fields, such as mathematics, science, or art. For example, we can infer a part of self-concept, in the area of mathematics ability, from a student's response to this question:

> How do you rate yourself in mathematics ability, compared with others in your class?
> a. I am among the best.
> b. I am above the average.
> c. I am at the average.
> d. I am below the average.
> e. I am among the poorest.

If we change *mathematics ability* to *general academic ability*, we could use the same item to measure a part of general academic self-concept.

We can think of self-concept as a hierarchy, as shown in Figure 4.6. At the top of this hierarchy, at level 1, is general self-concept, the set of beliefs we hold about ourselves, beliefs that are relatively difficult to modify. At the next level, there are two major areas of self-concept for students: academic and nonacademic (social and physical). The latter, as we have noted, is extremely important to adolescents. The third level holds the more specific areas of self-concept, related directly to a subject matter or a kind of activity. These specific self-concept areas are probably the most likely to change as a function of everyday experiences. They are not nearly as stable as one's general self-concept. If students' performances in mathematics or dating or baseball improve, their attitudes toward themselves in these areas are also likely to improve. Self-concept, then, is also related to self-esteem, self-efficacy, and feelings of self-worth (Covington, 1992; Snow, Corno, & Jackson, 1996). But the important point is that all these related visions of ourselves *are* modifiable. If we get better or worse at doing something, we know it, and our self-image improves or deteriorates.

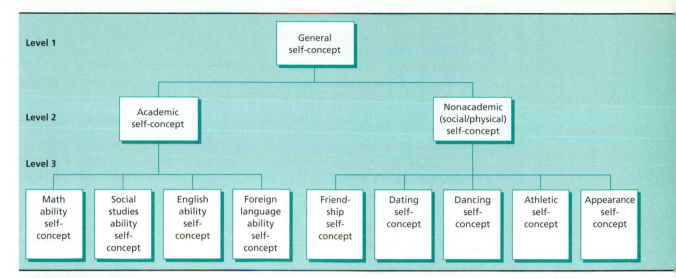

FIGURE 4.6

Three levels of self-concept for students

Adapted from Shavelson, Hubner, and Stanton, Review of Educational Research. © 1976 American Educational Research Association. Used by permission.

Short-term behavioral changes in ability do not always affect self-concept, however. In fact, students who have acquired low self-esteem in some areas seem to reject their own success at first. Presumably they do so because these experiences are not congruent with their self-concepts. But long-lasting behavioral changes in areas of concern do lead to changes in self-concept and self-esteem.

Changes in verbal behavior about oneself can change self-concepts, as illustrated by the simple method reported by Homme and Tosti (1971). In this case the "behavior modifier" (teacher) identified a child with good academic potential but low academic self-esteem. The teacher announced recess and let everyone go outside except this child. The child was told, "You cannot go outside and play until you say something good about your work in school today." If the child then said something like, "Today I really understood my English grammar lesson!" he was allowed to go out and play. Valid positive statements about self plus reinforcement (reward) for making those statements resulted in a more positive self-concept and a higher level of self-esteem.

So invalid negative self-statements take their toll ("I can't do math"), and valid positive self-statements promote achievement, as in the story of the little train that could ("I think I can, I think I can"). Helping students eliminate untrue negative statements about themselves and replace them with valid (or true) positive statements can raise their self-esteem. That is, changes in self-esteem follow changes in verbal behavior expressing self-concept *only* if the words accord with reality. Procedures to induce change work best when low self-esteem is unrealistic. It is difficult, unwise, and perhaps unkind, to try to develop high self-esteem about physical attractiveness or agility when an individual is really homely or clumsy.

For teachers, an important question is: Do feelings of self-worth, self-esteem, self-efficacy, or overall self-concept affect educational outcomes? Or do educational outcomes affect feelings of self-worth, self-esteem, self-efficacy, and overall self-concept? Correlational studies show substantial positive relationships between achievement and these kinds of measures (Byrne, 1984). But such data cannot tell us which variable is causally affecting the other. The evidence is persuasive, however, that level of school success, particularly over many years, predicts beliefs about one's ability and level of regard for self (Bridgeman & Shipman, 1978; Kifer, 1975), whereas level of self-esteem does not predict level of school achievement nearly as well. The implication is that teachers need to concentrate on increasing the academic successes and decreasing the academic failures of their students. It is the students' history of success and failure that gives them the information to assess themselves with. This is consistent with Erikson's notion of the crisis of accomplishment versus inferiority, which takes place in the elementary school years. A sense of inadequacy and inferiority can arise if children do not receive recognition for their efforts. The recognition of genuine accomplishment by parents and teachers often leads to positive self-concept and its correlates—positive feelings of self-worth, self-esteem, self-efficacy, and general competency (Covington, 1992).

> Based on this information, which would it be preferable for a teacher to do—offer a great deal of praise to a low-achieving student or provide opportunities to succeed at specific learning tasks?

There is an important lesson here for teachers and school administrators. Programs designed to promote self-worth, esteem, efficacy, and so forth, without providing for accomplishment—some kind of genuine physical, social, or academic achievement—are probably wasting time. Students evaluate themselves positively when there is objective reason for such a positive evaluation. It should follow that teaching that improves achievement should also improve self-concept; and in fact it does (Crawford et al., 1978). From students' self-appraisals it was learned that better teaching was positively associated with higher student self-esteem and attitude toward school, and a reduction of anxiety (Corno, Mitman, & Hedges, 1981). So the best teachers can do for students' self-concept, whether as mathematician, historian, or writer, is to teach them well and to help them to honestly evaluate their accomplishments.

SUMMARY

1. The importance of Piaget to teachers arises from his analysis of thought processes in children and adolescents. He built a cohesive and persuasive theory that identifies four stages of intellectual development.

2. Important behaviors that take place in the first stage, the sensorimotor stage, are the base from which more complex behaviors can emerge. In the preoperational stage children are conceptually confused. Although they talk and apparently reason, in fact they are not often able to think operationally. That is, children before about age 7 cannot usually transform and manipulate the world mentally; they usually do not have the symbolic representations with which to engage

in abstract, logical, and scientific thinking. Some of this ability appears in the concrete operational stage. But it is rudimentary, and the experience gained is only a prelude to the development, from about age 11, of formal operational thought.

3. An important contribution of Piaget's theory is the idea that development goes on through a process of constant adaptation to the environment. When a new phenomenon disturbs the equilibrium of their environment, children restore balance by assimilation (changing what is perceived to fit what they already know) and accommodation (changing cognitive structures to fit what is perceived).

4. Neo-Piagetians' important point is that rich experiences and good instruction can influence the complexity of a child's thinking. They note that the limits on thinking by children are more likely to be related to the limits of their memory than to some lack of ability to think logically and deductively.

5. Bruner described three stages of representation of information, which overlap considerably with Piaget's developmental stages. In the enactive stage, which is much like Piaget's sensorimotor stage, knowledge and action are synonymous. In the iconic stage, knowledge is coded by perceptual characteristics, much as it is in Piaget's preoperational stage. In the symbolic stage, understanding comes through symbol systems, especially language.

6. Vygotsky pointed out the importance of children's social community in the development of cognition. The directed learning he advocated demands an understanding of what a child can do alone and what he or she can do under the guidance of a knowledgeable tutor. The difference between these two levels of functioning is the zone of proximal development. And the key to enhancing the child's cognitive development is determining the dimensions of the zone in which to work.

7. The theories put forth by Piaget, Bruner, and Vygotsky have implications for how teachers teach. They emphasize the importance of understanding how children think, of using concrete materials in teaching young children, and of sequencing instruction. And they give insight into the ways to introduce new material and set the pace of learning.

8. The development of language is probably the most important factor in the development of cognitive abilities. Humans appear to have an innate system that allows us to determine implicitly the rules operating in our language community. As we develop and interact with others in that community, our language becomes more complex. There is a progression from one-word holophrastic speech, to two-word telegraphic speech, to multiple-word inflected speech.

9. Although development of competence in a language may be biologically based, language performance is affected by experience. Children acquire their linguistic competence from adult models in their community. Adults who engage in direct instruction have little impact on the process of language development. But adults do influence the child's views of literacy. Language is more naturally acquired, while emergent literacy is more directly affected by parenting behavior and other adult influences.

10. Most linguists agree that no dialect or language is any more or less accurate, logical, or capable of expressing thought than any other. For teachers, the issue of nonstandard English centers on educational and economic implications, not cognitive ones.

11. Concerning bilingual students, the challenge is to help them master English and other subjects but without destroying their cultural identity and stopping development of their heritage language. Bilingual programs offer an effective means for developing metalinguistic awareness, and two-way bilingual programs offer the best means of producing the largest number of bilingual students for the nation.

12. Teachers should not think of children as younger versions of adults. Children's ways of thinking and their ability to communicate are very different at different ages. They need a wide variety of experiences, including interaction with others and a good deal of time, in order to develop formal operational thought and a linguistic system for expressing that thought. Remember that thinking is a process that develops over time. Your methods and expectations must match the level of cognitive development of your students, or lead it.

13. Simultaneous with the development of language and cognition is the ongoing process of personality development. Erikson believed that psychosocial development is a response to crises we face at different stages in life. Proper resolution of these crises allows us to develop a "healthy" personality. In infancy we learn trust rather than mistrust; in early childhood, autonomy rather than shame or doubt; in middle childhood, initiative rather than guilt; and in the elementary school years, accomplishment rather than inferiority. In adolescence we face a special crisis: the development of an identity.

14. Who are we? What will become of us? These are the kinds of questions teens ask and need to resolve, if only in a preliminary way. If you work with high school–age students, remember that many of them are going through a time of turmoil, in part determined by how the media view them. Understanding their confusion is an important part of helping them learn. Remember, too, however, that many other adolescents do not undergo any great agony in adolescence. Once again, large individual differences in how people respond to similar events are evident.

15. In young adulthood comes another crisis—the challenge of sharing our lives with someone else. To resolve this in times of changing roles and social values is a difficult problem. Many beginning teachers face this crisis at just the time they begin their careers, and it is often a source of great stress for them. In adulthood, we face the problem of generativity rather than stagnation; and in old age, integrity rather than despair.

16. Although we cannot prove them objectively, Erikson's insights appear to have validity as we look around and analyze the ways we and our families, friends, and students function.

17. Moral knowledge also grows as the child progresses through stages of development. Young children are governed by a primitive system of morality, their behavior motivated by avoiding punishment or getting something in return. The conventional level of morality is held by most people from about age 13. It is characterized by conformity and a sense of doing one's duty. As a result of experience and growing

older, but also as a result of further education, an increasing percentage of people develop a principled morality, governed by legal and ethical beliefs.

18. Contrary to earlier work, it appears now that teachers can influence the moral development of their students, that they can foster higher levels of moral thinking. The developmental paths to moral thinking and behavior may, however, be different for men and women. An ethic of caring, the highest level of moral concern for women, is a worthwhile goal for the men in this society, as well.

19. Five broad personality dimensions have been identified. With relative consistency, people may be placed on continua going from (1) hostility to agreeableness, (2) introversion to extroversion, (3) impulsivity to conscientiousness, (4) neuroticism to emotional stability, and (5) intellectual narrowness to intellectual openness.

20. But these broad classifications are made up of many traits, and traits are not as consistent as many people believe. Our honesty or creativity at a particular time, for instance, depends in part on the environment in which we are operating. Therefore, teachers can modify traits by changing factors in the environment.

21. It also means that labeling a student could harm that student. A student may be dishonest, shy, or anxious under certain circumstances. But by attributing the general trait of dishonesty, shyness, or anxiety to that student, teachers could be exerting subtle pressure on the student to become what they believe him or her to be.

22. The sum of children's developing characteristics and personality contributes to their self-evaluation. Self-concept and related terms—self-worth, self-efficacy, and self-esteem—grow out of genuine achievement. The best way for a teacher to develop positive self-esteem and a healthy self-concept in a student is to develop that student's competency in the academic, social, and/or physical realm.

Human Diversity and the Schools: Culture, Gender, and Exceptionality

Overview

CULTURAL DIFFERENCES

Defining Culture and What Constitutes Cultural Differences

Enculturation by Socializing Agents

Historical Background

Assimilationism

Cultural pluralism

Developing a Cross-Cultural Perspective

Understanding an individual's acquisition of culture

Understanding the culture of the school classroom and the individual within that culture

POLICY, RESEARCH, AND PRACTICE

Culture and Readiness to Learn in School

Understanding the culture of the educational system

Developing a Multicultural-Education Classroom

Parent and community roles

GENDER DIFFERENCES

Personality Differences

Differences in Academically Relevant Capabilities

Mathematical ability

Verbal ability

Physical ability

Socialization of Gender Expectations and Behaviors

Socialization by parents

Curriculum

Teacher-student interactions and expectations

EXCEPTIONALITY

General Definitions

Categories of Students Who Are Eligible for Special Education

The Individuals with Disabilities Education Act (IDEA)

Mandates and processes of identification and qualification for services

Labeling and educational relevance

Students with Physical and Sensory Disabilities, Impairments, and Challenges

Students with visual impairments

Students with hearing impairments

Students with disorders in speech and language

Students with orthopedic, neuromotor, and other health impairments

Students who have traumatic brain injury

Students with Cognitive Disabilities or Brain Dysfunctions

Students with mental retardation

Students with learning disabilities

Students with Serious Emotional and Behavioral Disorders

Attention Deficit Disorder (ADD) and Attention Deficit-Hyperactivity Disorder (ADHD)

POLICY, RESEARCH, AND PRACTICE

Is It Preferable to Have Children with Emotional Disorders in the Regular-Education Classroom?

APPLICATION

Some Classroom Adjustments for ADD/ADHD

Students with Multiple Disabilities or Other Developmental Problems

Students with autism and pervasive developmental disorder

Students who have experienced prenatal or early-childhood substance exposure/abuse

Students Who Are Gifted and Talented: Another Category of Exceptionality

Acceleration

Enrichment

A debate over accommodation

GENERAL CONCERNS AND RECOMMENDATIONS FOR TEACHERS

Summary

OVERVIEW

Every student is a unique individual. Each of us has a variety of characteristics—ways of behaving, sets of expectations, attitudes, and beliefs—which contribute to our uniqueness

Contributions to the revision of this chapter were made by Dr. Sharon McNeely of Northeastern Illinois University.

and to human diversity. Psychology refers to these as individual differences. Chapters 3 and 4 were concerned with some of this variation, describing individual and group differences—and their sources—in cognitive abilities, language, and personality. In this chapter, we take a closer look at other sources of individual and group differences, those stemming from culture, gender, and exceptionality. We look especially at the research that contributes to understanding the instructional needs of an increasingly diverse student population in classrooms.

First, we look at culture, its definition, current emphasis on individuals within cultural contexts, and researchers' explanations of some aspects of behaviors and expectations from cultural perspectives. We look at some studies of culture that have an impact on what we do in schools. We also look at how school programs and processes that respect culture typically improve the academic achievement of culturally diverse students. Second, we consider research on gender-related differences, especially those that have implications for classroom instruction. Third, we consider the full range of exceptionality, considering students with disabilities and those who are gifted and talented. We consider pivotal concepts and legal mandates regarding the inclusion of students with disabilities or special talents in regular classrooms. We look at the basic information used to screen and assess individuals who are categorized as exceptional. Finally, we make some general recommendations about teaching that take into account the needs of diverse students.

Cultural Differences

Defining Culture and What Constitutes Cultural Differences

When a group of people share beliefs, symbols, and ways of interpreting the meaning of things, they share a **culture.** Cultural knowledge, concepts, and values are shared through the group's own systems of communication (Banks, 1993; Bullivant, 1993), which are also ways in which group members share their ways of thinking about and engaging in behavior. The degree to which an individual within a group accepts and practices these behaviors is called the *degree of enculturation*. An individual may be highly enculturated to one culture, or have various degrees of enculturation to multiple cultures.

Culture is powerful. It influences many aspects of our behavior, including the cognitive and verbal skills that we emphasize in schools. The knowledge and skills we possess, how and when we use them, and how we value them are all part of our culture. The language we use, how we use it, with whom we use it, when we use it, and how much we use it, are also part of our culture. Even the ways we stand, how close we stand to others, the ways we use our bodies, and the ways we interpret and

Can you identify three behaviors that are more appropriate in your culture and less so in others?

react to others' behaviors are all a matter of our culture. A behavior that is acceptable, or considered normal, in one cultural group may not be in another. For instance, looking and speaking directly at an older person may be desirable in one culture but considered an affront in another. Standing very close to someone when talking may be considered rude in one culture but necessary in another. Asking questions may be expected in one culture but offensive in another. So what you may consider "normal" behavior as a teacher may not be considered "normal" by students or their parents who do not share your cultural heritage.

Cultural groups are often defined in terms of membership within particular groups, such as a nationality, social class, religion, ethnicity, and exceptionality. A student's degree of enculturation to a particular group and of socialization into that group is important for understanding and explaining the student's behavior in the classroom. Although students may identify with and be socialized into a particular cultural group, they are not completely passive. Students also choose the extent to which they actually follow and practice culturally appropriate behaviors and the extent to which they develop individuality within a culture (Banks, 1993).

In education, the term **ethnicity** is often used for identifying a major source of diversity within the student population. Ethnic diversity in the nation has increased dramatically in recent decades as a result of immigration and the increasing globalization of trade. Because of a democratic commitment to inclusionary practices, our schools have an increasing range of ethnically (and therefore culturally) diverse students. For instance, in 1976, 24 percent of the students in U.S. schools were nonwhites, that is, not of white European descent. By 1984, this figure had climbed to 29 percent. By the year 2000, nonwhite students are expected to account for about one third of the school population. By the year 2020, when you will be a seasoned teacher, nonwhite students will account for 46 percent of the population (Hodgkinson, 1985; Cushner et al., 1996). In some states, and in many communities, the nonwhite public school population is already a majority. This is particularly important because the teaching profession in 1995 was overwhelmingly (87 percent) white. Black teachers make up about 7 percent of the teaching force; Hispanics 4 percent; Asian/Pacific Islander teachers 1 percent; and Native American/Alaskan Native teachers add another 1 percent to the total minority population of teachers (U.S. Department of Education, 1995a). Obviously, the potential for cultural misunderstanding exists.

Being a member of the global society carries responsibilities to respect diversity. How can a teacher show respect for student diversity?

Enculturation by Socializing Agents

The United States is a culture of many cultures. Compared to many other countries, such as Japan and Finland, we have a wide range of ethnic groups that share within-group beliefs, knowledge, and values. Schools are one of the many socializing forces that help to create a common cultural bond between diverse groups. Other socializing agents include family, church, community, neighborhood, peer group, electronic and print media, sports, the workplace, and the arts (Cushner et al., 1996). Our ethnic diversity and the plethora of socializing agents challenge teachers in several ways. One challenge is to try to determine the culture each individual student is primarily acculturated into. Another is to determine the primary culture(s) of the parents or care givers of each student and their expectations for enculturation of the student. Yet another is to try to develop a culture in the classroom that will help individual students achieve success in the mainstream, national culture and yet *not* conflict with desirable customs of the culture of the students' home.

Individual students also face many cultural challenges. Each has been enculturated to a particular way of thinking and behaving at home, at child care and preschool centers, and in their neighborhoods. When the student gets to school, the thinking and behaviors that are required may not be the same as those already learned elsewhere.

Sometimes school-required behaviors are compatible with the individual's culture. Other times, they are directly the opposite or otherwise incompatible. In this case, the students are faced with trying to learn a new culture, appropriate behaviors in that new culture, and the ways to resolve the conflicts between the cultures of their parents and their school. One example of this was encountered by a teacher we know. Family expectations for a child of recent immigrants to the United States included working in the small family restaurant after school hours and joining the business on a full-time basis after high school. The teacher, however, expected more homework and less participation in the family business, and school counselors were helping the student prepare for college, not the business. As you might expect, conflicts between home and school occurred. Another case we know of involved an overnight trip by a class to a country camp for nature study. But the parents of a Muslim girl would not allow her to go on such a mixed-sex outing, though it was chaperoned and integral to the science curriculum. Again, the culture of the home and the culture of the school were in conflict. Similarly, as contemporary schools try to institute a "thinking skills" curriculum, requiring that students learn to challenge the texts they read, fundamentalist Christian parents become alarmed. Believing in the inerrancy of the Bible, they become very concerned if the school teaches that texts should be challenged and that the meaning of a text is constructed by the student rather than residing in the text itself. In this situation, too, school and home cultures are in conflict.

Today, students also have the additional challenge of learning about multiple cultures and ways to interact with each other that are acceptable across cultures. This challenge also can arouse psychological conflict. As students learn about other cultures, they may accept or reject certain practices of those cultures. Acceptance of new behaviors, ways of thinking, styles of dress, and so forth, may conflict with their home cultures, which parents may be intent on preserving. And rejection of some new behaviors may lead to conflict with the school or majority culture. On the other hand, new behaviors may be easily integrated into families that want their children integrated into the majority culture, as many do. The best advice about the education of ethnically diverse children is that teachers should attempt to achieve two goals: (1) help

What conflicts might a student face if her parents expect her to maintain her culture of origin and not enculturate to the school's culture?

153

Two goals for schooling: Help students retain their heritage culture and ensure integration into the mainstream culture.
(© Pat Greenhouse/ The Boston Globe)

children retain their heritage culture and language and (2) simultaneously ensure the child's integration into the common, mainstream culture and language as well. The African-American, Asian-American, Irish-American, Italian-American, Jewish-American, and Mexican-American are all very much Americans. The hyphen reminds us, however, that they have other cultural characteristics as well. These other characteristics—language, arts, family relations, ways of thinking, dietary preferences—can be preserved only if they are valued by the schools and the mainstream culture. The trick for the nation is to foster assimilation of our immigrants and minorities while prizing their diversity. Historically, this has not been done.

Historical Background

Assimilationism   Ever since various European groups started migrating to the United States, the nation has had cultural pluralism. Many different groups have taken various perspectives on education. For instance, some religious groups have believed in separate education based on religion (e.g., Catholic schools). Some have believed in separating groups based on country of origin or the skin color of the students (e.g., separate schools for African-Americans). Some have believed in separating males from females. Generally, those promoting separate education systems have wanted to preserve cultures and cultural communities.

While the United States promoted separate education systems, it also promoted a public education. One task of public education in the past was to enculturate children into "American" ways of thinking, valuing, and behaving, to teach children that they should give up their original cultures in favor of "American" culture. Usually this culture was described as white, middle class, Anglo-Saxon, and Protestant in character. The idea that one type of culture is best for society is called a *monocultural perspective*, or an **assimilationist ideology.** From the 1870s until recent years, the assimilationist ideology was typically followed in our schools. This meant that students from different cultures had to adapt to the school and the dominant culture, to become part of the "melting pot." Students who were not culturally adapting to school—that is, not achieving to expected academic standards—were perceived as being disadvantaged, as having a deficit of some kind. Education in the 1950s and the 1960s was, perhaps unintentionally, a patronizing effort to provide so-called compensatory education to try to compensate for the assumed deficits some students faced because of cultural differences.

Cultural Pluralism   By the 1950s, however, some educators realized that the idea of the United States as a melting pot and the "deficit" model of minority-student education were not in keeping with democracy. They proposed that a political democracy must also be a cultural democracy (Banks, 1993). This idea, called *cultural pluralism*, holds that society is strengthened when different cultures are present and maintained within the larger society. Under cultural pluralism, individual differences are valued. In a pluralistic school, differences in students' learning styles, interactions, histories, and cultures are recognized and addressed. The metaphor of the "salad" replaces the metaphor of the melting pot.

In the 1960s and 1970s, the U.S. government legislated many educational programs. These were part of the larger human and civil rights legislation growing out of a desire for greater cultural pluralism in our society at that time. Society had come to recognize that there was discrimination and unequal opportunity, that not all people were recognized as having educational and other rights. The major legislation important to education included the Voting Rights Act of 1963, the Equal Pay Act of 1963, the Civil Rights Act of 1964, the Bilingual Education Act of 1968, Title IX of the Education Amendments of 1972, and the Education of All Handicapped Children Act of 1975. This legislation promoted access to and equity of public education for all children, regardless of racial, ethnic, religious, gender, or disability status. Schools, as one of the primary socializing agents, were asked by legislators to solve the problem of unfair treatment of some children by society. Educators continue to struggle to implement these laws sensibly and humanely.

> The U.S. government mandates equity of public education for all children. How do you know if equity is being achieved in your school?

Developing a Cross-Cultural Perspective

Understanding an Individual's Acquisition of Culture   The cultural-pluralism movement, combined with supportive legislation, gave impetus to the development of various kinds of multicultural education, that is, educational programs that address the needs of various minority students. Typically the goals of multicultural education include

1. recognizing that social and cultural changes are ongoing in our society

2. understanding that differences both between and within groups are important, and that learning about these differences helps us better understand people

3. improving intragroup and intergroup interactions by teaching students about cultures and ways to interact with students from other cultures

4. teaching cross-cultural understanding and skills to students so that they are able and willing to participate in our interdependent, multicultural world (Cushner et al., 1996).

The challenge to teachers is to reach these goals in the classroom. Pederson (1988) recommends that teachers who will be trying to provide multicultural education use principles derived from cross-cultural psychology to study and learn from the cross-cultural interactions in their classrooms. Some cross-cultural principles are:

1. People usually communicate their cultural identity to others in the broadest possible terms (the clothing of a skateboarding teenager, the skullcap of an orthodox Jew, as well as the obviousness of color differences)

2. Because we are all multicultural, our cultural identity is dynamic and changing

3. Although culture is complex and variable, it is nevertheless patterned

4. Interactions with other cultures can be viewed as a resource for understanding

5. Behavior should be judged in relation to its context

6. People holding a multicultural perspective continually strive to find common ground among individuals.

Cross-cultural interactions are any communications or exchanges, both verbal and nonverbal, between two or more people who have different cultural backgrounds. Given current demographics and the number of different cultural groups to which a person may belong, every classroom has a wide variety of cross-cultural interactions.

As you recognize and study the cross-cultural interactions in the classroom, you need to keep in mind that your own cultural identity influences how you learn and how you teach. These sources of cultural identity may be stable, or they may change with time, experiences, and learning. Cushner et al. (1996) have identified 12 sources of cultural identity, illustrated in Figure 5.1. Each source contributes to how people think and learn. The development of cultural identity in the individual is influenced, to varying extents, by the communication of views, attitudes, and expectations from socializing agents present in our society. These too are illustrated in Figure 5.1. The challenge you face is understanding how each of the parts interacted in the development of your

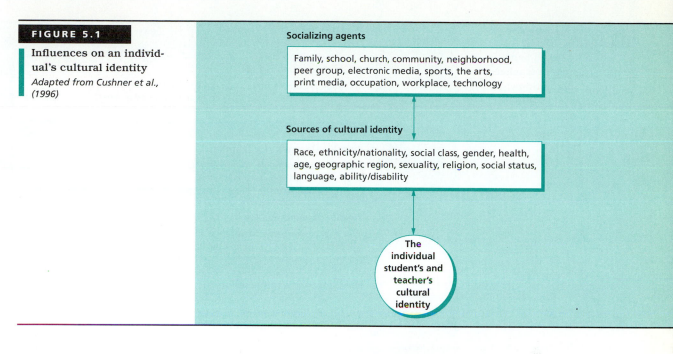

FIGURE 5.1

Influences on an individual's cultural identity

Adapted from Cushner et al., (1996)

Socializing agents

Family, school, church, community, neighborhood, peer group, electronic media, sports, the arts, print media, occupation, workplace, technology

Sources of cultural identity

Race, ethnicity/nationality, social class, gender, health, age, geographic region, sexuality, religion, social status, language, ability/disability

The individual student's and teacher's cultural identity

What is your current cultural identity?

cultural identity, as well as the identities of each of the students in your classroom. It will be hard to optimize learning without thinking about these issues, though there are no ready prescriptions about what to do once you have thought deeply about how cultural identities are formed.

Understanding the Culture of the School Classroom and the Individual within That Culture   Understanding your own culture, and the culture of your individual students, is a key factor in successful multicultural education. But you should also be concerned with understanding the culture of the school classroom itself, and how cross-cultural interactions occur in that environment. In most schools, the majority of teachers are Euro-American females (Cushner et al., 1996), and the majority of administrators are Euro-American males. So, in some schools, this leads to what might be considered a culture mimicking the dominant American culture, or what some call mainstream or Eurocentric culture. Students comfortable in that culture can do well in the schools, but those who fit into that culture less easily are likely to have a harder adjustment to the schools.

You need to think about how schools work, what types of cross-cultural interactions (exchanges between people) are valued at home and at school, what kinds of cultural knowledge and behaviors are expected of you, and what you can expect from your students.

Figure 5.2 diagrams some of the culturally based behaviors that have an impact on any teacher-student interaction. But be warned: You should not assume that because someone has a particular cultural label he or she will think and behave in a particular way. You should also not anticipate or assume that cultural labels imply that someone cannot or will not do certain things. However, you do need to be aware that

FIGURE 5.2

Culturally based behaviors that affect teacher-student interactions
Adapted from Hall (1976)

Teacher ◄ - - - ► Student

Adult-child relationships

Do people treat each other as empowered or helpless?
Do people treat each other in a caring or a detached manner?
Do people know about each other's personal lives?

Emotional context for learning

Are emotions acceptable, displayed, valued?
Is it proper for people to be emotional in the classroom?

Physical communication

How much space between people is acceptable?
Are pats on the back, hugs, or any other touches considered appropriate?

Mental/cognitive interaction

Do people speak directly, look directly, at each other?
Do people repeat themselves to make their thinking clear?
How do people share what they are thinking?
How do people prefer to learn material, alone or with others, aloud or silently, hands-on or symbolically, etc.?
How do people share what they are learning?
Is it appropriate to work on more than one task at a time or to change tasks every few minutes?

Social interaction

Do people cooperate and share information or compete and withhold information?
Does someone display self-knowledge or encourage others to show their knowledge?
Does someone feel that his/her behavior reflects only on self, or also on the larger social group, or both?
What types of social interactions are appropriate, and what are considered to be conflicting?
Is it proper for people of different ages, genders, etc., to interact?

within various cultural groups there are certain expectations for how someone is to behave and how he or she shows capability. The expectations discussed here come from a wide range of sources and are meant to provide you only with a general cross-cultural perspective (Hall, 1976). They do not focus on any particular cultural group.

One interactional variable is adult-child relationships, that is, how adults and children behave toward each other. How a child is treated and how personal the adult is with the child are typical classroom considerations. Another interactional variable is the emotional context for learning. This includes the range of emotions considered appropriate in the classroom, not only as reactions to emotional events but also as motivators. Physical communication involves such aspects as how you stand, how close you get, and whether you touch a student. Given the heightened awareness of child abuse and concerns about improper touching

POLICY, RESEARCH, AND PRACTICE

Culture and Readiness to Learn in School

The people in one of the communities studied by Heath (1983) are black; members of the other community are white. Although these people live only a short distance apart and most of the adults work in the same textile mill, children in the two communities learn very different sets of rules as they learn to speak.

The researcher asked residents in both communities to explain how children learn to know and talk. In the black community of Trackton, Annie Mae explained,

> He gotta learn to know 'bout dis world, can't nobody tell 'im. . . . White folks . . . hear dey kids say sump'n, dey say it back to 'em, dey aks 'em 'gain 'n 'gain 'bout things, like they 'posed to be born knowin'. You think I kin tell Teegie [her grand-child] all he gotta know to get along? He just gotta be keen, keep his eyes open. . . . Gotta watch hisself by watchin' other folks. Ain't no use me tellin' 'im: "Learn dis, learn dat. What's dis? What's dat?" He just gotta learn, gotta know; he see one thing one place one time, he know how it go, see sump'n like it again, maybe it be de same, maybe it won't. He hafta try it out. If he don't he be in trouble; he get lef' out. Gotta keep yo' eyes open, gotta feel to know. (Heath, 1983, p. 8)

Annie Mae's thinking is in sharp contrast with that of Peggy, in the white community of Roadville:

> I figure it's up to me to give 'im a good start. I reckon there's just some things I know he's gotta learn, you know, what things are, and all that 'n you just don't happen onto doin' all that right. Now you take Danny 'n Bobby, we, Betty 'n me, we talk to them kids all the time, like they was grown-up or something, 'n we try to tell 'em 'bout things, 'n books, 'n we buy those educational toys for 'em. (pp. 127–128)

In Trackton, Heath concluded, adults talk of children "comin' up"; in Roadville, they speak of "bringin' up" their children. The two communities hold different concepts of childhood and development, and each provides roles for adults and children that fit their notions of who can and should teach children to listen, talk, read, and write. By the time they go to school, the children have learned their own community's ways of using language to get along and to attain social goals (Heath, 1983).

The adults' assumptions influence the language development of children in these communities. In Trackton, children have rich and varied experiences with language, but their perceptions of things and events are not guided by adults. They have to find their own patterns in the complex, multichannel stream of stimuli that surrounds them because time, space, and talk are not set aside especially for the children. Parents in Roadville do set aside special time and space and talk for their children, but they focus the children's attention mostly on labels and descriptions. They give them opportunities for extended narratives, creating new contexts, or manipulating elements of an event or item.

continues

159

Trackton children come to school with a well-developed ability to contextualize—to understand an item or an event in relation to the context in which it occurs. This ability has served them well in their community, but it is useless in the school, where correct responses require students to lift items and events out of their context, to decontextualize. So Trackton children have a problem separating letters and their sounds from words, and words from sentences. And they learn to read slowly. Their ability to contextualize could help them in upper grades, where relationships become important to understanding. But the initial difficulty they experience in school discourages them from further developing their skills.

When they first enter school, Roadville children experience success. Their home world and that of the school appear well matched. They have been accustomed to a structured, linear world, where time is divided into blocks and there are limits on the use of space. They know about bedtime stories and coloring books. But theirs is a limited readiness that does not prepare them for higher-level academic tasks—tasks that demand an understanding of relationships, an ability to predict outcomes, and a synthesis of knowledge. They know less about how to contextualize.

Heath (1983) and the teachers who participated in the study of language development in Trackton and Roadville attempted to use the knowledge they gained to improve the effectiveness of their instruction. One example is the work of Mrs. Gardner, who was assigned a class of nineteen black first-graders. All the students had been designated "potential failures" on the basis of reading-readiness tests. Mrs. Gardner visited her students' communities before school started and made simple maps of them. She picked up old tires and, with the help of some parents, attached them to pieces of wood to make letters and scattered them around the yard outside the classroom. The children had many opportunities to play with these "toys" informally.

Mrs. Gardner used the knowledge gained from the research and her visits to the communities to develop a program that built on her students' skills at noticing similarities between items and events. An example of her efforts to integrate students' early learning with school activities was the way in which she formally introduced the letters of the alphabet. She did not limit herself to presenting them as only symbols on paper; they appeared in structures all around the children: I's as telephone poles, L's as upside-down streetlights, and, of course, the toys in the schoolyard. The children were encouraged to search for the letters all around them and bring their findings to the classroom.

Instruction in that first-grade classroom was drastically changed by the teacher's knowledge of her students and her integration of their skills into the instructional effort. Her goal was academic excellence. She did not change her goal; she only modified instructional practices. She met her students halfway.

Mrs. Gardner's efforts were amply rewarded. By the end of first grade, all but one of the potential failures was reading at grade level. (The one exception was a child diagnosed as having serious emotional problems.) Six of her nineteen students were reading at second-grade level, and eight were reading at third-grade level!

What are your cultural beliefs about touching a student? What kinds of touching are appropriate?

today, you should be very sensitive to this interactional variable, concerned about how your physical communication is perceived and received in the school and by the students. The mental/cognitive interactional variable involves all of the above variables to some extent, but also includes how you promote thinking, how you connect through eye contact or speech to get your students thinking.

You should understand how eye contact works in the culture(s) of your classroom, and how teachers are expected to impart knowledge and build skills in students. The idea of social interaction for learning, or the social context of interaction, is also important. Social context refers to the ways that people are expected to interact with each other, such as whether they are to cooperate, compete, work alone, and so forth. There is research to suggest that certain groups, such as females and Hispanics, learn well in cooperative learning activities (see Chapter 10). On the other hand, for white males brought up in a competitive, individualistic environment, cooperative-group instruction may be a less compatible learning environment. It is not that learning in a competitive environment is a disaster for females, or that learning in a cooperative environment harms males. But each group may have a slight advantage when learning one way rather than the other, so that a teacher

There are few gender and cultural differences among children whose school work is interesting, captivating, or perplexing.
(© Grant LeDuc/Monkmeyer)

who uses one mode of teaching regularly may be biasing instruction for or against some groups.

Understanding the Culture of the Educational System   All states provide for a free public education in grades 1 through 12. Some states provide kindergarten and prekindergarten experiences as well. Most educational systems are required to assess students' skills and knowledge when they start school, and assessments continue throughout schooling. Based on how students perform on these assessment instruments, they are placed into various classes and given various opportunities in the school system. These common characteristics of U.S. education are intimately tied to four important areas of culture: language, developmental readiness, the nature of assessment itself, and the choice of curricular content.

Language   Some school districts have programs to assess students' use of language in their native tongue, such as Spanish or Vietnamese. But even then, the assessment they use may lack cultural appropriateness because it may simply have been translated from English, with no consideration of differences in how language is used or the meaning of particular words in their cultural contexts. Some school districts lack language assessments for students who do not speak English. These districts do not get an adequate picture of a child's overall language knowledge and skill. The federal government requires that schools provide education in the native language of students who do not speak English; however, the requirements do not have to be met until schools have certain percentages of their populations that need the services. So tens of thousands of children from language-minority backgrounds get improper assessments and no special services. Under these circumstances, the chances of misunderstanding a child's abilities are quite high.

An example of such misunderstanding occurs when teachers confuse a child's language skills with his or her academic competence (Diaz, Moll & Mehan, 1986). Many immigrants are literate in their native language. But instead of giving these students instruction at a level of comprehension comparable to that achieved in their native language, teachers sometimes begin English instruction using simple texts of the type used to teach much younger children. The message to immigrant students, although unintentional, is that they have not learned anything worthwhile in their native languages.

Developmental Readiness   Development is typically assessed by giving students a variety of tasks and evaluating their responses. How easily students interact with each other, how well they follow directions, whether they know colors and how to count, whether they can identify letters of the alphabet, and so forth, are just a few of the tasks given to assess readiness. But the nature of the tasks chosen to judge a child's competence makes a big difference in judging whether he or she is ready to learn. This was demonstrated decades ago by Serpell (1979), but each generation of teachers needs to be reminded of this phenomenon. Serpell examined the conclusions that African children lack certain general cognitive abilities. These conclusions had been drawn from studies re-

> How do you think a student feels the first week of attending school when he/she is new to the U.S. and does not speak any English? How will you welcome that student? How will you communicate with that student?

quiring the children to reproduce patterns using paper and pencil or blocks. Serpell's study incorporated four perceptual tasks:

- *Mimicry*, which required the children to copy the position of the researcher's hands
- *Drawing*, which required copying two-dimensional figures using pen and paper
- *Molding*, which required constructing copies of two-dimensional objects using strips of wire
- *Modeling*, which required the children to use clay to copy three-dimensional objects.

Serpell chose these particular tasks because he knew that the two cultural groups he wanted to compare had had different opportunities for prior experience with each of them. He predicted that a group's prior experience would affect performance on each task.

The results of this study, which compared British and Zambian children, showed that the two groups of children performed similarly well on those tasks in which they had comparable experience—mimicking hand positions and modeling with clay. British children had the advantage in the drawing tasks, which required the use of pencil and paper. Zambian children performed better on the wire-molding task, an activity common to them but not to British children.

What is the moral here? Students from an immigrant or minority culture may simply not have had exposure to the tasks being used to assess them. This does not mean they have an inability. That judgment might be correct, but only if the task assigned cannot be done after repeated exposure to it in its cultural context. It is wise to remember, too, that roughly 75 percent of all recent immigrant children—such as Guatemalans, Russians, Bosnians, and Haitians—have had interrupted educations (Igoa, 1995). They may not yet know some things that would be easily learned if they were simply given the opportunity to learn them. Their silence in class may reflect the trauma of immigration and the sudden inability to communicate, not incompetence.

Cultural differences may also lead to judgments of developmental incompetence when what is actually occurring is adherence to valued cultural norms. For example, asking questions of some Native American students may be met with silence. To show off knowledge in front of a group by answering a teacher's question is inappropriate. So the silence is not inability, it is respect for one's own native culture. But this culturally appropriate behavior becomes a problem when dealing with European and U.S. models of education, which rely on question asking and answering as teaching and assessment techniques.

A decision that some child is not "school ready," or has some inability, is always difficult. But when an immigrant or minority child is the object of study, such decisions should be made with even more than the usual caution. All teachers are gatekeepers; they have the power to open or close doors for students. So you must learn to recognize the influence of such factors as lack of opportunity to learn on your decisions about students' competence.

Assessment   Testing is ubiquitous in the schools of the United States. The skills assessed are typically those that the dominant culture holds as necessary for school achievement, and so assessments are likely to reflect a monocultural perspective. That is, what students must do to show they have learned, the ways they are supposed to demonstrate learning, and even the circumstances under which they are supposed to display their accomplishments are all embedded in the mainstream culture. That culture typically values the success of the individual student competing against everyone else, and taking pride in what he or she achieves individually. In other cultures, competition is not as valued, and may even be considered undesirable. Although most U.S. schools seem to value, above all else, linguistic and mathematical thinking, and try to assess aspects of those, some cultures value politeness to elders, handcrafts, or interactions of the body in harmony with the environment at least as much. In these cases, students would find cognitive assessments strange, and they might not quite know how the dominant culture expects them to show they have learned. The result may be that the educational system decides incorrectly that these students are not ready for or capable of "normal" schooling.

Historically, many students from immigrant and minority cultures were assumed to be somehow "inferior" in their ability to learn. Based on the results of mainstream cultural assessments, these children were placed in special-education classes and denied equal educational opportunities and access to other aspects of the public educational system. Although educators like to think, and hope, that students today have an equal chance of participating in the educational system, the reality is that the system may not recognize the ways a minority-culture child has been raised, the expectations students and their families bring to the system, and the difficulty in taking on the understandings that allow one to function as a bicultural individual.

> Western industrialized societies are commodity oriented, and commodities are easily discarded and quickly replaced. Consciously or unconsciously, school professionals tend to transfer the commodity model onto that of culture, believing that children can discard their old cultural values and replace them with new ones as easily as they throw out their old shoes and get a new pair.
> *(Igoa, 1995, p. 44)*

We expect greater understanding of these issues in the next generation of school leaders.

Curriculum   As you learned in Chapter 2, the educational-reform movement has promoted the development of standards or objectives for student learning. The schools also have series of textbooks and other materials you are expected to use with students. Chances are high that these texts, materials, and learning objectives are all developed on the basis of mainstream, or centrist, culture. Students from, or comfortable with, the mainstream culture may have only minimal problems with

Can you describe four different ways students can show their learning without taking an individual test?

these materials, but students from minority cultures may have more serious ones. For instance, there may be a lack of involvement with a particular learning objective. Why should students of African-American, Mexican-American, or Native-American descent learn only about dominant culture themes and views, and only about certain heroes? When the great writers and artists of the nation are studied, does the curriculum mention the Harlem Renaissance? Is the sad story of the Trail of Tears discussed when we study Native Americans, or are they portrayed unidimensionally, as savages who attacked wagon trains and stood in the way of progress? When the western expansion of the nation is studied, does the curriculum present the dilemma modern historians debate: whether General Custer was an American martyr or a cruel and foolish leader. Was the Alamo a great victory for Texas heroes and a slaughter by the Mexican army, or from a different perspective, could it legitimately be seen as needless martyrdom, easily avoided through negotiation?

One main idea of multiculturalism is to ensure that no one in a nation as diverse as ours is left out as educators set about designing schools to provide morally and intellectually educated adults. The standards and objectives we choose can allow for various perspectives of an event instead of just one. Except for nations and cultures that have engaged in crimes against humanity, there are praiseworthy heroes and role models to be found in every culture, for every culture. Given the current demographics of the nation, you will probably need to think about transforming the learning objectives provided to you into meaningful multi-cultural-classroom interactions.

Developing a Multicultural-Education Classroom

Educators who specialize in multicultural classrooms consistently ask several questions to determine whether they are multicultural in their perspective. These questions are listed in Table 5.1. As teachers and schools have recognized the need to become more multicultural in nature, they have developed various ways of integrating multicultural perspectives into schooling. Banks and Banks (1993) have identified four levels of such integration. These descriptions, presented in Table 5.2, can be used to evaluate the schools in which you teach.

It is important to remember that no matter how well developed the curriculum content, a truly multicultural education provides a variety of learning experiences for the students, building on cultural expectations and helping them develop a range of learning strategies. Cooperative learning (see Chapter 10) is typically cited as one method of instruction appropriately used in multicultural classrooms. This involves students working together in small groups, preferably groups of mixed cultures and various achievement levels, to attain a common learning objective. The use of peer tutoring and cross-age tutoring (see Chapter 11) is also typically recommended. These involve students working in groups of two, with the tutor being either of the same age/grade level (peer) or older

Can you remember things you were required to learn that caused you cultural conflicts? How did you feel?

Why might it be important for a teacher to know basic greetings and classroom directions in multiple languages?

TABLE **5.1**

Questions to Determine Whether a Classroom Includes Multicultural Perspectives

What learning objectives and materials do you provide to students?
- Do the objectives and materials value various cultures and multiple perspectives?
- Do they take into account your students' prior knowledge and experiences?

Are multiple types of intelligence valued and encouraged in your classroom?
- Do you recognize that, in addition to verbal and analytical skills, there are other skills and intelligences that are important?

What learning behaviors do you encourage and value in your students?
- Do you encourage students to speak to each other, to learn with others, to move around as needed?
- Do you encourage them to practice alone as well as with others?

What is the setup of your classroom?
- Are there learning areas and chances for students to choose tasks?
- Given the interests, experiences, and needs of your students, do they have chances to share and interact on the basis of their common grounds as well as their diverse backgrounds?

What languages do you promote in the classroom?
- Are students encouraged to talk to each other in native languages to help each other learn?
- How do you react when students speak to each other and you don't understand the language?

How do you monitor student progress, and what type of feedback do you give to students?
- Are students encouraged to show progress through more than pencil-and-paper tests when appropriate?
- Are students told how well they are doing verbally or nonverbally or both?
- Do you compare each student to a set standard, the learning objective, or to other students?

What types of signs and displays for learning are in your classroom?
- Are they respectful of a variety of differences?
- Do they use multiple languages when appropriate?

What are the routines and structures you give to students?
- What are your expectations about students' setting up their own routines?

In what ways do you present information?
- Is it global, step by step, or both? Is it meaningfully integrated for the learner, or isolated bits?
- Is it mainstream-culture information only, or is the information balanced for multiple perspectives?

(cross-age). Tutoring programs are usually helpful when students need to have large-group instruction supplemented. Individual instruction (Chapter 11) is also suitable for multicultural settings. It may be too demanding when teachers in some situations need time and materials to prepare for each student. However, when used properly, and sometimes with technology, it can be effective for attaining some learning objectives.

TABLE

5.2

Levels of Integration of Multicultural Perspectives

Typically schools and teachers start at Level 1. They may or may not advance through the other levels. What is the level of your school? What level will you be using in your teaching?

Level 1: The Contributions Approach

Some contributions of some minority groups are presented, usually in a haphazard manner, such as for a holiday or other cultural event. A hero, an issue, an event, or a cultural story is presented in isolation. Students are provided isolated opportunities to learn minimal knowledge and skills associated with the contributions. There is almost no opportunity for students to consider the content's full significance or to engage in higher-level thinking. There is little opportunity to develop a true understanding of the culture being presented. Cultural stereotypes may be reinforced if the information is misinterpreted or poorly presented.

Level 2: The Additive Approach

Some content is changed and some themes and concepts are added, usually in a segmented manner, for discrete parts of the overall schooling processes and curriculum. The additions augment schooling but do not change the curriculum or the nature of the schooling. Students have some opportunities to interact with the added materials but generally do not get to consider the deeper significance of the materials. There is little opportunity to develop understanding of the culture being presented, which may prevent students from developing attitudes and background knowledge to appropriately respond to the material.

Level 3: The Transformation Approach

The perspectives of the curriculum are changed, as are the fundamental goals and structure of the curriculum and schooling processes. Students are provided ample opportunities to study content through a variety of perspectives. They have frequent opportunities to choose which cultural groups to include in their studies, and to think about the impact the various groups have had on the concepts being studied. There are more opportunities to develop a deeper understanding of the cultures and to reduce stereotypical thinking, but it takes a great deal of the teacher's time to develop appropriate materials and change the schooling processes to properly support this approach.

Level 4: The Social-Action Approach

This approach assumes that the transformation approach has been developed and put into place. The added component is action based on the learning. The students build their decision-making skills and use them to help effect social change. In many schools, the time it takes to complete a unit is greater because of the breadth and depth of the material covered in this approach. Despite getting students deeply involved in their learning, there is some risk of their feeling like failures if the actions they take have little or no effect on social conditions.

Based on J. A. Banks and C. A. M. Banks, Multicultural Education: Issues and Perspectives, *2d ed. Copyright © 1993. Reprinted by permission of the author.*

Parent and Community Roles More and more educators are coming to realize that even though a school may have its own unique culture, it is still part of the larger culture of a community. You should recognize the importance of being an actor in that community, whether or not you are of its dominant culture. Parent and community involvement acknowledges that student learning does not occur only in the classroom. Par-

Describe how your local school encourages community involvement.

ents are the children's first and most powerful teachers. Each ghetto, barrio, and 'hood—each homogenous cultural setting—has within it people and institutions with enormous power to influence the lives of children in positive ways. For example, black churches in African-American communities, the Catholic church and the bodega owners in Hispanic communities, and the council of elders in Native American communities can all be enlisted to foster multicultural identities and a desire by their children for school success. No parents or communities want their children to do poorly in school, though many parents and communities do not understand what it takes to guide a student to a successful life. When working with some shared vision and understanding of the students, the school, family, and community can help more children achieve well.

Though not always without conflict, increased parent involvement with the school improves student achievement and helps to accomplish many social goals as well (Campbell, 1992; Casanova, 1996). For example, a school may have a volunteer program in which parents and other community members tutor and provide other support services for students. The school may run mother-daughter computer laboratories, father-son cleanup activities, and so forth. Student learning improves, and the intergenerational and crosscultural interactions may also lead to greater trust and fewer conflicts in the community (Comer, 1986; 1991).

Any plan for parent and community involvement, however, should face the fact that cross-cultural understandings need to be developed by all involved parties. Some cultural misunderstandings seem inevitable. Contributing to these are the differences in expectations by parents and teachers of females and students with exceptional needs. Problems of equity and access continue to be an issue for these groups, and we turn next to the accommodation of these sources of individual differences.

Gender Differences

Every culture has gender-based expectations for student behaviors. In most cultures it is assumed that males and females are supposed to act differently and learn some things differently. Some cultures expect that males or females cannot learn particular things, or cannot excel at certain things, because of their gender. But it is very hard to figure out what differences between the sexes are rooted in culture, which makes it equally hard to know whether any of the differences are genetically based. In any case, it is important to remember that whether the roots are genetic or environmental, differences *within* a group are almost always greater than the differences *between* groups. That is, within groups of males or females are wide ranges of differences so that some girls are better at, say, basketball, than some boys, and some boys are better at, say, art, than some girls. These *individual differences* tend to be much greater than the *average* differences between males and females.

Gender is an extremely salient characteristic among people. Have you ever forgotten a person's face? his or her name? where he or she lives? If you are like most people, the answer is yes. But have you ever forgot-

Limiting a person's choices about what to excel in, based on gender, simply wastes talent.

(© Elizabeth Crews)

ten whether someone was male or female? Probably not. It is something we code and remember quite well. In recent years, the idea of gender schema—an organized knowledge base containing information about the sexes—has been used to explain not only why this is so but a range of individual differences attributable to gender. A gender schema develops from the child's innate tendency to classify and simplify information, and because knowledge of gender is so important to survival of the species (Eisenberg, Martin, & Fabes, 1996). Gender schemata develop in each of us and influence what we notice, remember, and learn. But perhaps most important is that the gender schemata influence how we behave. Students typically attend to and remember information that is schema-consistent (Carter & Levy, 1988). In addition, students may distort information that is inconsistent or neutral, making it fit their own schemata (Martin, 1991). These are the processes of assimilation and accommodation that Piaget described (see Chapter 4, pp. 105–106). Because of this tendency toward cognitive consistency, gender stereotypes may continue in a cultural group even after students are given disconfirming information (Martin & Halverson, 1983).

Personality Differences

In most cultures, boys and girls experience considerably different environments and expectations. These differences, particularly in toys and activities, influence their development and behavior. The differences influence personality development, but make it difficult to know whether the two genders develop different average personalities because of genetic differences or environmental differences.

Until the early 1970s, this section of the book might have included a long list of personality differences between the sexes. At that time, researchers were designing experiments and collecting data in ways that today are no longer considered gender-sensitive. Since the mid-1970s, however (see Maccoby & Jacklin, 1974; Spence & Helmreich, 1978), researchers have learned to question the types of measures used (e.g., are they designed by males? do they use male vocabulary? are males the group used for determining "normal" responses?). They have also questioned the design of the studies (e.g., Are females expected to do "traditionally male" tasks? Do females have to do the task in front of males, with the help of or with males, or with other females?). As a result of this questioning, and by conducting new studies, most researchers now agree that there are few personality characteristics associated with gender that seem to be consistent across cultures. Of these, aggression is the only one that may substantially affect the teaching-learning process. In most cultures, males are more aggressive than females. There may be hormonal or other biological reasons for this, in addition to cultural expectations. Regardless, you are likely to find that males are usually more dominant, assertive, energetic, active, hostile, and destructive (Eisenberg, Martin, & Fabes, 1996). But recognizing these differences in the classroom does not mean that you should excuse aggressiveness as "biological" and allow inappropriate behavior by males any more than females.

Differences in Academically Relevant Capabilities

A great deal of research has tried to determine what, if any, gender differences exist when it comes to intelligence, problem solving, verbal and mathematical ability, and achievement in school. Recent cross-cultural studies have changed previous conceptions. Now, most researchers conclude that gender differences in these areas are slight, if they exist at all, and are not uniformly found across cultures. So again, it is important to remember that within-gender differences are typically as great as between-gender differences.

Mathematical Ability   It used to be thought that there were significant differences in mathematical ability between the genders, but recent research has limited these differences to a couple of select areas. Males tend to do better than females on problem-solving tests in high school and college. They also tend to outperform females on math that is related to measurement, science, and sports. They may still have an advantage in spatial ability, a related cognitive skill, but that research is less convincing now than it once was. Females tend to outperform males on math that is related to aesthetics, interpersonal relationships, and some traditionally female tasks such as sewing (Eisenberg, Martin, & Fabes, 1996). It is also true, given cultural expectations, that males tend to take more mathematics courses than do females when these are electives. So, when assessed later in their scholastic careers, males tend to show greater levels of achievement. Most of their advantage, therefore, seems to be related to the greater amount of mathematics coursework and not to innate ability. When exposure to mathematics coursework is equal, differences seem to disappear.

Verbal Ability   After meta-analysis of a variety of research, Hyde and Linn (1988) concluded that there are no substantial gender differences in language competence. However, as with mathematics, there are contextual differences: Males tend to do better than females on questions of verbal content in science and political affairs; females tend to do better than males on questions of aesthetics. Females also seem to develop their verbal skills earlier than do males.

Physical Ability   Thomas and French (1985) meta-analyzed 64 studies related to physical-ability differences. They concluded that the differences favoring males—other than strength—were due to environmental influences, with the exception of the male superiority in ability to throw. Smoll and Schutz (1990) found gender differences on a variety of motor tasks. But they concluded that with increasing age, these differences became more a function of environment than of biology. However, it should be noted that puberty plays a large role in some differences. Following puberty, males tend to have greater muscle mass, so that they tend to perform better on skills that involve power, size, and strength (Thomas & Thomas, 1988).

Do any of the facts about gender differences surprise you? Were you holding stereotypes that are not accurate?

Socialization of Gender Expectations and Behaviors

Socialization by Parents   Parental behaviors and expectations influence not only how they treat their children but also what the children in turn believe about their own abilities and performances. Parents who believe that the gender of a child matters when it comes to abilities and how one achieves tend to have children who bear out those expectations (Jacobs, 1991). For example, if a boy's parents believe he should do well in math, he probably will. Likewise, if a girl's parents believe she should do well in math, she probably will. The cultural significance of the subject area and the expectations for a particular child play a big part in determining the attitudes your students bring to the classroom. It is important that you not challenge parental expectations directly, but instead consider all the ways in which you and the school may provide your own set of expectations for the students in the environment over which you have control—your classroom.

Curriculum   Until recent years, researchers found that school texts and curriculum materials, tests, and activities for learning provided the mainstream stereotypes of gender. Males and females were depicted in particular roles, and with particular abilities. Texts, tests, and materials used the term *he* instead of balancing it with *she* or using neutral terms like *one* or *they.* Most texts also used familiar cultural stereotypes and failed to present variations to adequately represent males and females from different cultures.

In recent years, responsible school-materials publishers have made improvements so that many common stereotypes are not presented and are even challenged by examples directly counter to stereotypes (e.g., a woman fighting a fire or flying a jet). Some texts try to be nonspecific by presenting green or purple "people" with no identifiable gender. You should be aware of the recency of the materials you use in class and the examples they present. Most educators want students exposed to curriculum materials portraying a wide range of roles for both males and females.

Title IX of the Education Amendments of 1972 states that "no person in the United States shall, on the basis of sex, be excluded from participation in, be denied the benefits of, or be subjected to discrimination under any education program or activity receiving federal financial assistance." So schools should provide and encourage equal access to courses and other educational opportunities. However, in reality, in addition to materials, curriculum access by both genders is also a concern. Even in early grades, there are differences in how much time teachers spend providing mathematics and science instruction to boys versus girls. Parents, school counselors, and teachers may encourage boys to take particular courses, such as shop, and encourage girls to take home economics. This kind of influence may be lessening, but even if students have equal access to all subject areas initially, teachers also need to be concerned about their receiving equal treatment once they have gained access to the classes.

Teacher-Student Interactions and Expectations   Although you may repeatedly vow that you will not treat boys and girls differently, the chances are pretty good that you will because you bring your cultural expectations with you to the classroom. In most cultures, boys and girls are expected to interact differently with the teacher, and to perform differently. You will undoubtedly try to change your beliefs and attitudes to enhance learning for all students, but you also need to be aware of, and watch out for, the mainstream cultural expectations teachers commonly bring into class. These include pushing for individual achievement instead of group achievement, fostering competition rather than cooperation, accepting more raucous behavior from boys than from girls, and assigning more girls to teacherlike activities than boys, among others.

Researchers have learned that teachers tend to give boys more positive attention in the classroom, and tend to provide boys with more positive feedback about the intellectual content of their work. Though there are wide variations among teachers, in general they uphold stereotypes about ability and performance, providing different kinds of tasks and feedback about learning to males and females. Over time, with repeated

Describe how the gender stereotypes you were raised with may impact your teacher-student interactions and expectations.

exposure, students may come to accept these expectations and interact as they believe the teacher, and the school, want them to. In this way stereotypes continue to be upheld. Remember also that the gender schemata that students hold affects their learning, and simply providing information that challenges their stereotypes may not be enough to change them. You need to provide active engagement in a variety of activities that enhance new thinking about gender roles and personal expectations (Bigler & Liben, 1992).

Exceptionality

General Definitions

In all cultures, there are children who have unique blends of characteristics that affect their ability to learn from traditional ways of teaching in the traditional classroom environment. For some students, the unique blend results in what might be considered a "limited" ability to learn. For others, the unique blend results in giftedness—an enhanced ability to learn. The characteristics include ways of mentally processing information, ways to sense or perceive information, ways of or problems with communicating orally or in writing, ways of interacting with society, neuromotor or physical challenges, long-term emotional problems, or a combination of multiple problems and challenges.

In the United States, students are considered exceptional under federal laws and guidelines when they (1) meet a set of criteria for being classified as such and (2) require modification of school practices, usually special-education services, to develop to their maximum capacity (Ysseldyke & Algozzine, 1995). **Exceptional children** includes those considered gifted and talented as well as those who have disabilities. Currently, the term *challenge* is used as a synonym for the term *disability*. Legally, the term *disability* is used when someone has a medical, emotional, cognitive, social, or learning difficulty that significantly interferes with his or her normal growth and development. Prior to the implementation of PL 94–142, the Education for All Handicapped Children Act, in 1978, most students who were disabled were placed in special-education schools, or segregated special-education classrooms. Today students with disabilities are to be educated in the "least restrictive environment," and there are such students in almost every classroom receiving a variety of services in regular education settings. Far fewer students are in segregated special-education classrooms or institutions than was the case in previous decades. The movement to normalize education for exceptional children emerged from both the civil rights movement and the special-education research community. The movement's success means that you will work with a broader range of students and a greater number of professionals in your classrooms than ever before. To do this effectively, you need basic information about exceptionality. This section of the chapter covers the categories of disability, then the area of gifted and talented.

Categories of Students Who Are Eligible for Special Education

In many schools, the term *special education* is used to refer to the instruction of students considered legally disabled under Public Law 94–142. The term *disabled* is used because of the legal definition. It is important to note that for many of these categories, terms such as *challenged* or *outside of the normative sample* may be more accurate but could lead to confusion. To keep it simple, we use here the language used in the law. Note also that gifted students qualify for special education, but that type of education is covered under a different set of laws, and is discussed separately later in the chapter.

The Individuals with Disabilities Education Act (IDEA) In 1975, after years of advocacy by parents and others concerned about children, Congress passed Public Law (PL) 94–142, the Education for All Handicapped Children Act. This act was designed to "assure that all handicapped children have available to them a free and appropriate public education." In 1990, Public Law 101–476 was passed; it was an updating of the previous legislation and called the *Individuals with Disabilities Education Act (IDEA)*. IDEA requires the specification of procedures for identifying and labeling students as exceptional, descriptions of the categories (labels) of specific exceptionalities, and the procedures for appropriately dealing with these students and their parents. The many components of IDEA, and its status as a federal law require that you be careful to follow it faithfully and act in the best interests of the child.

Mandates and Processes of Identification and Qualification for Services The regulations that accompany the IDEA relate to screening, referring, assessing, labeling, and placing a child into special-education services. A series of tests are required before a child can be labeled *exceptional.* A parent can request that his or her child be tested, or a school or medical professional can request the testing. If the parent makes the request, the school has a limited time to react and begin the processes prescribed under the law. So it is always important for you to immediately provide a written memo to your administration if a parent tells you that he or she wants testing for a child. If you suspect a problem yourself, you need to talk with your special-education coordinator and administration about the best ways to handle the procedure. How parental permission is obtained for the testing, and how the school proceeds legally if a parent refuses testing, depends on state laws as well as IDEA mandates.

Regardless of who makes the referral for testing, you are asked to provide information about the classroom behaviors and learning progress of the child. You are asked to document specific behaviors, to fill out various forms, and to implement some specific interventions to note the child's reactions. It is likely that the special-education teacher, school psychologist, or school social worker will visit the classroom and observe the child. It is also likely that school administrators will call for an

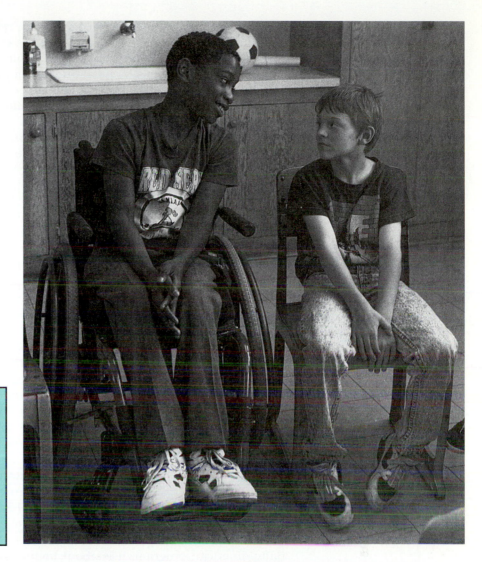

Disabled students are more like other "regular" students than they are different from them. They smile, laugh, pout, and respond like other students. And they can learn.
(© Elizabeth Crews)

initial consultation meeting to determine how best to proceed—if the school is to make a thorough case study of the child.

A case study typically involves testing of intelligence and personality, classroom observations, and other cognitive and educational assessments of the child. It is typically expensive because the school psychologist, social worker, nurse, special-education coordinator, and other professionals may all take time to work with the child. In each case, the types of assessments used are determined by the reported problems. Typically, unless the child has a severe problem, the school does not seek neurological or other highly specialized testing because the school would have to pay for it. In all cases, children have the right to be tested in their native language. In addition, parents have a right to have all information translated and an interpreter provided. Under no circumstances can a child be categorized using the results of only one test. You need to inquire how the IDEA mandates are carried out in your district. These processes can be traumatic for a family, and you would not want to add to their problems by providing inaccurate information.

When all of the testing is done, the school professionals get together with the parents, and if appropriate, the child, to discuss the results. At that time, a determination is made about whether the child qualifies under the law for special-education labeling and services, or whether other intervention strategies might be used instead. The major categories of disability are discussed in more detail below. If the child is labeled, that is, assigned to a category, then the instructional team needs to develop an Individualized Education Plan (IEP). The label and the severity of the problem determine the kinds and levels of special services to be provided. These may include time with the special-education teacher, physical therapy, occupational therapy, speech therapy, adaptive physical education, and counseling. In all cases, it is assumed that the student is to remain in the regular classroom, which is considered under IDEA to be the "least restrictive environment," unless it is determined otherwise. If the child cannot be in a regular classroom all day long, the number of minutes that the student is to be out of the classroom and where he or she is to be placed need to be specified. You will be asked to help develop a list of learning objectives for the child and describe how progress towards those objectives is to be assessed. The group also determines when the services are to start and when they are to be reviewed. Under IDEA, the IEP must be updated at least once a year, and every three years a new evaluation must be made if it is determined that the child still needs special services.

Few teachers are happy about having children with special needs in their classrooms. Their presence almost always means more work for the teacher, and possibly less time and attention for other students. Many parents also oppose having special-needs students in regular classes with their "normal" children; they too fear a loss of the teacher's attention to the regular-education students. But IDEA is a quintessentially American program. It is about inclusion rather than segregation. It is about trying to normalize life for children with difficulties, not treating them as outcasts. This educational philosophy arrived during the 1970s. U.S. public schools excel over those of other nations in the commitment to help disabled fellow citizens, and that commitment is proper in a society dedicated to educating all its citizens to the best of their abilities. The challenge is to teach teachers how to cope with various forms of exceptionality so that classrooms function well with such children present. Some of these techniques are noted below.

Labeling and Educational Relevance   Years ago, it was unusual to consider the culture of a child when he or she was being considered for services. Consequently many children were inappropriately tested, labeled, and placed in special education. Sometimes children were so placed because of their race, ethnicity, or non-mainstream language (Heller, Holtz-

Would an IEP be useful for every student in a class?

How do you feel about having special-needs children assigned to your classroom?

man, & Messick, 1982; Cummins, 1986). Although testing in the native language is required, there still are many problems with testing and placement. Often the tests used are not culturally sensitive but simply translations of mainstream-culture tests into other languages. As a result, children may be falsely labeled, or mislabeled. You need to remember that the purpose of the label is to generally describe a set of characteristics and behaviors in order to qualify a child to receive special-education services. But labels can bias our perception. So you need to get to know the child and his or her unique characteristics and needs, not make assumptions based on the label assigned to the child.

You need also to remember that different labels are given for different reasons. Sometimes children are born with physiological, biological, biochemical, or genetic abnormalities that lead to their need for special-education services. Sometimes the home environment of the child, or special circumstances the child encounters, contributes to the child's having problems in school and needing special-education services. Educators used to say that genetics could not be changed but that circumstances could. But with the rapid expansion of genetic research and technological advances, some chromosomes may now be changed. You need to keep an open mind rather than assume that a label is permanent, or that, once given a label, a particular condition cannot be remedied.

Even after you or a parent makes a referral for evaluation, you need to remember that the student's age, how long the problem has been exhibited, the extent of the problem, and cultural expectations for how the child should act and be treated are important not only for the evaluation and labeling of a child but also for your work with the child in the classroom. A thorough evaluation takes time, and while that is ongoing you are still expected to continue to work with a child. Your work and the reactions of the child are important and should be carefully and objectively documented.

Below are most of the major categories of exceptionality covered under IDEA. Here we use the terminology found in the law, although you may discover that it is not used in your school or in society. As you consider the categories, remember that whenever the law is updated they may change. In addition, with educational, medical, and technological advances, the criteria applied to label a child within a category may also change. You need to stay current in your knowledge of this field as you work with these students in your classroom.

> Have you ever been labeled a trouble-maker, a clown, gifted, "nice," etc.? Did your behavior change as a function of that label?

Students with Physical and Sensory Disabilities, Impairments, and Challenges

Students with Visual Impairments   A student whose vision is impaired so that he or she cannot function normally in the classroom without help is labeled as having a visual impairment. The student may be able to see and read print, but the print may need to be a particular size or color. The student may not be able to see and read print but may see some shapes and colors. Whatever the case, you are likely to have students with visual impairments in your classroom.

Students so labeled have typically had rehabilitation and support services that have provided them with orientation and mobility services, canes, guide dogs, sensor devices, tape recorders, optical instruments, or other devices. You should be aware of the student's needs when arranging seating. With the advancement of technology in recent years, many people who are visually impaired have obtained scanners and speech synthesizers that "read" materials to them. In the United States, the response to a student who is visually impaired may be sympathy and offers to help, but you also need to remember that most likely the student needs to learn functional skills for engaging in daily living and learning activities by him- or herself. The American Foundation for the Blind has recorded books and magazines, various kinds of equipment, and informational materials available to help the student and you make decisions about the teaching and learning process. See Table 5.3 for a list of general accommodations teachers are expected to make.

Some students in your classroom may have unrecognized or slowly developing visual impairments. It is important that you recognize the

How will you help your students interact with a child that has sensory disabilities?

TABLE 5.3

General Teacher Accommodations for Special-Education Students

Although the school system may provide specialists to furnish adaptive services or technology, you are expected to modify your teaching and the classroom to accommodate the students. Typically you are expected to

- get to know the student as an individual, and identify and respect the capabilities he or she brings to the classroom.
- get to know the specific medical and emotional needs of the student, and what happens when he or she is ill or medicated, or has missed medications.
- learn to order materials that meet special needs, such as large-print books, closed-captioned videos, and the like.
- provide a physical environment and seating assignment that allow for assistive technology, interpreters, note-takers, and so forth; and access and easy mobility.
- if needed, learn and use sign language and finger spelling, and teach other students sign language so they can interact with students whose most important language is sign.
- provide experiences allowing for interactions with the physical environment and other students.
- provide opportunities allowing all students to interact appropriately, and specifically teach other students the appropriate interactions you expect.
- allow the student to initiate, choose topics, and lead conversations.
- respond to student-initiated behaviors in appropriate ways.
- learn to describe class activities and interactions for those who cannot see what is happening.
- demonstrate interactions, ways of thinking, how to solve problems, and other cognitive strategies you want the student to learn to use.
- train and use peer helpers when the student can benefit from them.
- recognize that stress, anxiety, novelty, and the like may have an impact on the student that influences interactions and learning.
- privately discuss any self-stimulating movements, or other concerns, with the student, and develop a private cueing system to help reduce these movements.
- not encourage stereotypical behavior on the part of the student or his or her peers.

signs and behaviors of a possible visual impairment. If you suspect an impairment, talk to the school nurse and, perhaps, advise the parents to have the student's vision tested. Typical physical signs or symptoms of a possible visual impairment include

- eyes that are red or watery or have a discharge, have unevenly sized pupils, move excessively, do not follow text, cross, or do not move together
- eyelids that are red, crusty, swollen, have sties, droop, blink excessively, or stay closed longer than average
- squinting, blinking, shutting, or covering one or both eyes
- moving toward or away from light or to or from materials during visual activities
- reporting eye pain, headaches, dizziness, or nausea
- frequently losing place in sentences, confusing letters or words, improperly spacing or using lines when writing (Gearheart & Weishahn, 1984).

If you suspect a problem, you should talk with the student and try to provide support in the classroom, noting any modifications that help.

Students with Hearing Impairments   A student whose hearing is impaired so that he or she cannot function normally in the classroom without help is labeled as having a hearing impairment. The student may be able to hear sounds, but the sounds may need to be enhanced. The student may be able to hear only certain ranges of sounds, or certain types of sounds. The degree and type of hearing available to the student determines whether he or she is labeled deaf or hard-of-hearing. Given classroom inclusiveness, you may have students with hearing limitations in your classroom.

Students who are deaf or hard-of-hearing typically have had rehabilitation and support services providing them with hearing aids and interpreters. With the technological advances, some students may also have devices that put spoken words into print. You need to help a hearing-impaired student determine the best way to function in the classroom. Obviously, sitting the student where he or she can see you, anyone else who speaks, and the interpreter is important. If there is no need for an interpreter, seating the student so that distracting noises are minimal is important.

In the United States, the most common responses to a hard-of-hearing student are to shout, overdramatize physically, or simply avoid interactions. None of these responses optimizes student learning. Perhaps the student needs to learn to lip-read and sign manually, so that he or she can engage in independent-living activities. If you do not know manual sign, such as the American Sign Language or Signed English, you should at least learn basic symbols and finger spelling. Additionally, you should teach your students signs so that they can interact with each other. The American Association for the Deaf has a variety of materials to help you make decisions about the processes you use for teaching. The general recommendations in Table 5.3 also apply.

In recent years, some hard-of-hearing people have gained additional hearing through new medical interventions, including implants. Others

Do you know where to go to receive sign-language training in your community?

regard their hearing status as a different ability, not a disability or challenge. They argue that they have their own language (sign) and culture, and should be allowed to live in and develop this culture. This group of people may reject some school services or medical interventions that could improve their capacity to hear in order to stay tied to the deaf cultural community.

Some students in your classroom may have unrecognized hearing problems, or they may be slowly losing hearing capabilities. It is important for you to recognize the signs and behaviors that may indicate a hearing problem. If you suspect such, talk to the school nurse and perhaps advise the student's parent to have his or her hearing tested. Remember that young children often get ear infections, commonly otitis media (a middle-ear infection), for a short time. Infections can lead to short-term or permanent hearing loss if unattended (R. W. Heath, 1992). Because more children now grow up without adequate medical insurance than in previous decades, your vigilance can help prevent the development of a hearing disability.

You should look for the following signs and behaviors that may indicate someone is hard-of-hearing:

- Sharp body or head movements toward various noises or to see the lips of a speaker
- Not responding to auditory stimulation that others attend or react to
- Complaints of headaches, earaches, dizziness, ringing in the ears, or difficulty hearing
- Shouting or using a very loud voice when talking to others, or consistently pronouncing words improperly

If you suspect a problem, you should take action quickly.

Students with Disorders in Speech and Language Although students who have visual or hearing limitations may have some problems with communication, there are also people who have impairments in the use of language or speech without showing other problems. The use of language includes both receptive (receiving and interpreting messages) and expressive (developing and sending messages). The vocalizations of language are called *speech.* There are many kinds of language and speech impairments. Generally these are all included under the label of *communication disorders.* Such learners account for the second largest group of exceptional learners served under IDEA.

Students who are disfluent have problems with the flow and rhythm of speech. They may repeat or prolong sounds, words, or phrases. They may hesitate or pause exceptionally long times. They may stutter or mutter their words. They may engage in mouth, lip, or facial distortions; blink excessively; or make extraneous body movements when they try to speak. Learners who have voice disorders have difficulty with pitch, volume, and timbre quality. Children with articulation disorders have problems producing language sounds. Students may also have other language disorders, such as absence of language, delayed language, and other deviations in language development (Shea & Bauer, 1994).

Students with such communication impairments may receive speech or other therapeutic services. They may get help from a communication specialist who assists with individualizing technological devices to help with recording or producing language. Sometimes the student may need augmentation of communication to promote interactions and facilitate learning. Usually these children are in the regular classroom. Communication may be enhanced if the teacher helps the learner feel comfortable enough to risk communication. Other general ways the teacher may help are given in Table 5.3.

Some students in your class may have an unrecognized communication impairment. Or they may be slowly losing communication abilities as the developmental tasks they face become more demanding, speech becomes more complex, and so forth. It is important for you to recognize the signs and behaviors that may indicate a communication disorder. Typical signs and symptoms include

- actively avoiding communication situations through withdrawal from, or not sustaining, interactions
- refusing to speak in class or in front of others
- speaking unintelligibly or showing difficulty in producing words or putting words together into standard sentences
- making few variations in speech, such as in tone
- relying on physical movements or objects to complete communication

If you suspect a problem, you should immediately begin to document the types of communication errors and problems you observe, and talk to the school nurse and/or the school speech specialist. They can help you decide how best to proceed under the law. You should also talk with the student and try to provide support in the classroom, noting modifications that help.

Students with Orthopedic, Neuromotor, and Other Health Impairments Students who have physical disabilities, challenges, and health impairments or limitations that are severe enough to interfere with their normal participation in daily activities represent a wide range of challenges for the school and the teacher. *Orthopedic*, or *neuromotor*, disabilities are general labels given to the category of students who have less than normal use of hands, arms, feet, legs, and other body parts. Medically, the labels applying to such students may be *paraplegia*, *quadriplegia*, *cerebral palsy*, *spina bifida*, or *spinal-cord injury*. These students may rely on wheelchairs or supportive devices to assist their mobility.

Physical health impairment is a general label for students who have some sort of medically identified chronic illness that interferes with access to the environment. Medically, these students may carry labels such as having *epilepsy*, *sickle cell disease*, *human immunodeficiency virus* and *acquired immune deficiency syndrome*, *juvenile diabetes*, *cystic fibrosis*, *juvenile rheumatoid arthritis*, *muscular dystrophy*, *hemophilia*, *cancer* or *leukemia*, a *heart condition*, *asthma*, *allergies*, or *lead poisoning*. Students in one of these categories typically have supportive medical services. The school nurse may be monitoring or providing specific services. The students may have medications they need to take at certain times of the day, special dietary needs, limitations on the activities their doctors allow them to participate in, and assistive technology that improves their capabilities. Many times these students spend time out of school, living in medical facilities or receiving hospice services, and they may be in pain. As you might suspect, some of these students also suffer from emotional distress, depression, or anxiety because of their illnesses (Nelms, 1989). They may not understand what happens to them or why they are purposely limited in interactions with others. They may also feel that the school is a limiting place if they do not have access to all facilities, or are not allowed or encouraged to participate in various school functions. Some of these students may have been home-schooled, further limiting their interactions with others.

Even though these students may not have any known additional challenges or any cognitive problems, Schlieper (1985) found that they are more at risk for academic failure than their physically healthy counterparts. So as you teach children in this category, you need to be sure they have a chance to acquire the knowledge and skills that might have been missed owing to their illness. This is an obvious problem for the growing frequency of childhood asthma, which results in legitimate school absences. After an asthma attack recedes, the child returns to a class that has moved ahead of him or her. This loss of school learning time academically impairs the asthmatic child or the child with other health problems, and this side effect of illness or impairment is one that teachers should try to minimize.

There are many things the teacher needs to keep in mind when working with these students. First, the students may be scared, angry, confused, or have a variety of other emotional responses to their physical conditions. Even if they have had their condition since birth, there are always new levels of acceptance to attain along with new developmental challenges. The student who is newly diagnosed is going through various processes of denial, rejection, and acceptance of his or her condition. Younger impaired students may not realize that they differ from other children and fail to recognize the impact of their disability, but older students are likely to react in a variety of other ways. As with all the other categories of special need, you should recognize the individual differences among students and keep those in mind. Among these differences, social reactions to illness also become important. You need to remain aware of how you and others react to the child. For most of these conditions, there are national advocacy groups that can provide you with specific information, and link you with educational materials and resources. The general recommendations of Table 5.3 also apply here.

Additional recommendations need to be noted for one group of students, those who have tested positive for human immunodeficiency virus (HIV) and may or may not show signs of acquired immune deficiency syndrome (AIDS)—one of the fastest-growing categories of illnesses among school-age children. When you teach students who have

Have you ever talked with a person with one of these impairments? What did you think and feel? How will you interact with a student who displays these characteristics?

this medical condition, you need to maintain strict confidentiality; in most schools in the United States, you are legally obligated not to disclose this diagnosis to others. In some schools, officials may know but not disclose the diagnosis to you. Throughout the nation it is safe to assume that there are students with this condition whose parents have not told school officials, or students who do not know their own medical status. Many health professionals report that they feel ill prepared to control infectious diseases and lack confidence in their ability to work with individuals who have tested positive for HIV (Shea & Bauer, 1994). Owing to medical advances, the diagnosis of HIV is no longer considered a death sentence. The American Academy of Pediatrics and other advocacy groups have supported unrestricted student attendance for those who test positive. Yet this is one diagnosis that typically arouses fear, distrust, and other reactions, such as discrimination against the student. You need to keep the learning environment as normal as possible for these children. But you must also be sure to know how to deal with the inevitable situation involving a student who loses potentially contagious body fluids in the classroom through paper cuts, nosebleeds, or the like.

Some students in your classroom may have a physical health impairment but are not yet identified as such. You should keep track of any

What will you do if a child with HIV gets injured and bleeds? You might want to think about and discuss this eventuality.

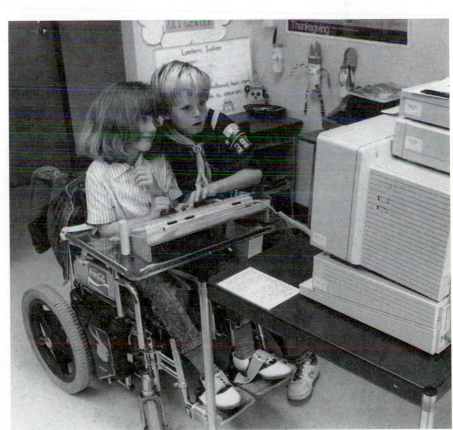

It is not just the child with a disability who learns something in the regular classroom.
(© Richard S. Orton/ The Picture Cube)

behaviors or reactions that may indicate an underlying problem. Typical symptoms indicating a health impairment include

- lapses in concentration or attention
- changes in behavior after eating, after eating certain foods, or at certain times of the day
- complaints of pain or muscle weakness after exercise
- coughing, shortness of breath, rashes, or other reactions to certain stimuli, or at certain times of day
- frequent bruising
- difficulty or decline in performance in balance, posture, coordination, eye-hand coordination, and so forth

Remember, if you suspect a problem you should talk with the student as well the school nurse and, perhaps, the parent or guardian. Simultaneously, you should document the types of problems you notice and modifications that help.

Students Who Have Traumatic Brain Injury   Public Law 101–476 added the disability category of traumatic brain injury as a diagnosis that requires special educational considerations. This disability is defined as a severe trauma to the head that impairs learning, behavior, and motor functioning. Typically, the injury was caused by an external physical force, such as a fall, car accident, or sports injury. In some cases, the injury was caused by an internal occurrence such as a stroke. Traumatic brain injury is one of the leading causes of death for school-age children.

A student labeled as having a traumatic brain injury may have a variety of medical and other support services provided in the school. The student may or may not need to take medications, and may or may not have pain accompanying the injury. The student may be using a variety of technological and medical devices to facilitate daily living and learning. You should know the specific modifications you are expected to make for this student.

Injuries to the brain from sports and car accidents are common. These may go undiagnosed or be misdiagnosed as minor. You may be the one who first spots the changes in behavior revealing the extent of the injury. In addition, there are cases where a child experiences these kinds of trauma at an early age, but specific problems and symptoms do not emerge until later, when there are changes in developmental tasks and demands for more complex performance. Note any instances in which the child is not progressing as expected and speak with the school nurse about him or her. If you find consistent patterns, talk with the nurse about approaching the parents with your concerns.

Students with Cognitive Disabilities or Brain Dysfunctions

Students with Mental Retardation   In one sense, mental retardation can be thought of as a physical disability in that there are problems with brain functioning and sometimes chromosomal abnormalities. But our view is shaped by the definition supplied by American Association on Mental Retardation (1992, p. iii):

> Mental retardation refers to substantial limitations in present functioning. It is characterized by significantly subaverage intellectual functioning, existing concurrently with related limitations in two or more of the following applicable adaptive skill areas: communication, self-care, home living, social skills, community use, self-direction, health and safety, functional academics, leisure, and work. Mental retardation manifests before age 18.

As you will recall from earlier chapters, how intelligence is defined, observed, and measured is culturally based. Within any culture, there are wide ranges of acceptable functioning in intelligence and adaptive behaviors. In the United States, the typical way intelligence is defined is with the intelligence quotient (IQ), a score on a standardized intelligence test. Of course, these tests are highly embedded in the mainstream culture. Although there are variations from state to state, the federal programs are typically based on three or four levels of mental retardation. Someone is labeled as having severe and profound mental retardation if an IQ score is below 40. When four levels of labeling are used, the severe and profound category is divided, with the profound label applied to someone who scores an IQ below 25. The person whose IQ score is between 40 and 55 is typically labeled as having moderate mental retardation, and the person whose IQ score is between 55 and 70 (sometimes 75) is typically labeled as having mild mental retardation. For any of these labels to apply, there have to be particular limitations on adaptive behaviors. IQ scores, alone, do not provide enough information to be very useful. Also remember that such labeling is rarely used in the classroom because it is currently not considered a helpful way to know anything useful about the student. The emphasis should be on the supports the student needs to function both in the classroom and in society.

A student labeled as having severe or profound mental retardation typically requires extensive and pervasive support. This student is not usually placed in a regular-education classroom, but rather in a special-education classroom. Even given the general movement toward mainstreaming and inclusion, it is unlikely for such a student to spend much time in the regular classroom. Usually the focus is on teaching daily living skills and building some work-capacity skills. Many students labeled as having this serious problem spend at least a portion of their lives in a residential facility; they are also likely to have other medical problems or disabling conditions. If you teach a student with this diagnosis, it is important that you work as a team member with the special-education staff and other service providers to ensure that he or she receives appropriate learning materials, and that you help to build and maintain appropriate social behaviors. For many of these students, opportunities to have appropriate interactions with other students who are not so labeled are very important. But their social skills may be limited, and their frustration levels high because of their inabilities. The other side of the inclusionary approach to contemporary special education is that regular-education children should have opportunities to know children with special needs as real human beings—not objects of pity or derision, but as people struggling for dignity like the rest of us.

A student labeled as having moderate mental retardation typically requires limited but ongoing support services. This student may be placed in the regular-education classroom for some of the day and in a special-education classroom or receiving other support services some of the day. Traditionally, this student was called *trainable* and was trained for some vocation that does not require even average-level cognitive functioning. In recent years society has learned that students who fall into this IQ-score range, if they do not have too many adaptive-functioning problems, are usually able to function independently in daily living, learn to do basic reading and arithmetic, and become self-supporting if they live semi-independently. Educators have also learned how important it is for these students to have positive, appropriate interactions with others who are not so labeled, and opportunities to see others displaying acceptable behaviors. If you teach such a student you will undoubtedly work with a team to make decisions about your approaches and expectations.

The student labeled as having mild mental retardation traditionally was called *educable* and requires intermittent support. This student is usually placed in the regular-education classroom at least part of the day and meets developmental milestones in the same sequence as others, but usually later and with the need for more support. You most likely will have to modify somewhat the regular teaching and learning experiences and expectations for this student; however, you can still expect him or her to learn. Again, you should work with the school team to set expectations and define success. Usually these students can graduate from at least primary school and go on to become self-supporting citizens.

As with the other categories of exceptionality, it is important in general that you not let the mental-retardation label automatically change or lower your expectations. Rather, you need to talk with special-education experts and work out a plan for the student to attain success in the classroom. Many of the recommendations made for students who have other categorical labels also apply here.

Federal law now requires doctors, teachers, and others to report students who are at risk for having disabilities as soon as they suspect any. As a result, more and more students in this category (and the others) are being identified before school age. But these days, because of cultural considerations and recognition that intelligence testing is so culture-bound, many teachers are hesitant to recommend a student for testing if he or she is from a minority group. Also, if the student is in a school where many students are achieving at low levels, he or she may not even come to the attention of the teachers as being a candidate for diagnosis. In general, if a student is presenting clear developmental delays in academic and adaptive-behavior skills, you need to consider recommending him or her for diagnostic evaluation. Remember, recommending the student for evaluation does not release you from your responsibility to try to teach this child. And keep notes on the types and results of the various strategies you use with this student.

Students with Learning Disabilities   Students labeled as having a learning disorder or learning disability are not mentally retarded; they have average or above-average intelligence. Indeed, some highly successful people, such as former Vice-President Nelson Rockefeller, have had learning disabilities. Learning disability refers to some specific cognitive dysfunction, a problem with some aspect of learning. The category of learning disabilities is relatively new. As a result, there are several different definitions in the field, most developed by different professional organizations. In general, a student who has a learning disability has

1. a disorder in one or more of the basic psychological processes presumed to be related to a central-nervous-system dysfunction

2. difficulty in learning, specifically in speaking, listening, writing, reading, and/or mathematics

3. no other primary cause for the problem, such as mental retardation, emotional disturbance, or cultural disadvantage

4. a severe discrepancy between apparent potential for learning and actual level of achievement (Lerner, 1997).

How can a classroom teacher help determine that a student has a discrepancy between potential and actual achievement?

It is important to recognize that this category of exceptionality is a broad one, encompassing many different types of disorders and currently the largest category of special needs. Specific labels in this category include *dyslexia* (difficulty in reading), *dyscalculia* (difficulty in arithmetic), *dysgraphia* (difficulty in graphic analysis or creation), and so forth. Regardless of the label, the student typically needs your attention and support in the regular classroom.

Depending on the nature and extent of the learning disorder, various support services might be provided to this student. He or she may need materials presented in larger type or auditorally, in a set sequence, or with prompts. The student may need a peer to provide learning cues, or the teacher to provide specific focus cues. You need to be aware of the exact nature and extent of the diagnosis and areas of concern before making classroom adaptations. In years past, the recommendation was to work on the weak areas, the areas of disability. In recent years, however, teachers are usually advised to provide instruction that helps to maintain and build the student's strengths. You may encourage the student to practice in the weak or dysfunctional area, but you should not rely on that area for primary learning. This change in teaching focus is based on the recognition that such disorders are often not corrected, especially if they are neurologically-based. Rather, disorders can be remedied if the student is taught how to rely on, use, and enhance his or her strengths; compensate for those weaknesses; and in many instances, minimize the presentation of a disability. To help the student learn, you should make explicit the processes and strategies you use that they do not seem to acquire. That is, you should model the processes and strategies you want the student to learn. You can also increase the chances that students will learn effectively if you present information in multiple ways (auditorally, visually, tactilely) and allow the students to demonstrate what they have learned through different means (telling, writing, acting, drawing).

Recognizing that a student has a potential learning disability is a difficult task for any teacher. It is especially difficult for a new or novice teacher who may not yet have a good understanding of the ranges of developmental readiness or appropriate tasks for the students at a particular grade level. Lacking such understanding, you might think that many students have learning disorders, or that none of them do. In reality, we all have strengths and weaknesses in how we learn, but it is the discrepancy between potential and actual achievement that is the important clue for finding students in your class who qualify for this diagnosis. When in doubt, compare the discrepancy over time and discuss it with another teacher or the special-education teacher.

The learning-disabilities category has been expanding. In 1968 only 120,000 students were so labeled, but by the early 1990s almost two million students were in this category. This jump may be due, in part, to misuse of the label. Students who do not easily fit into some other category and are experiencing problems in school may be given this label. Students may be labeled learning-disabled because their parents believe there is something wrong but are not sure what it is, and want their children to have the advantages of untimed achievement tests or special consideration for admission to programs supplying extra attention. Students who seem to have problems paying attention, fidget a lot, or are "easily distractible" may all be given this label. Students who simply do not fit some more specifically defined category are often given this label. So it is important that you not make many assumptions based on this general label. Rather, you need to seek information about the individual student; the label itself does not help you to make many decisions about the teaching-learning process in these cases.

When you work with a student who has a learning disability, or you suspect a disability, you need to observe and document the child's behavior, the nature and severity of the difficulties, and the responses to various teaching and learning methods. There are wide ranges of normality, but it is easy to find differences among students, especially if you look for them. You should recognize that no one teaching method works across all students, or even with one student consistently. You should try new methods, note what works, and the extent of the success. You should approach all learning tasks as things the student can do, not as tasks that cannot be done, and recognize that individual styles of learning may need to be matched with the learning task. Whenever possible, involve multiple senses in the learning task.

Students with Serious Emotional and Behavioral Disorders

Each individual develops a unique personality and ways to express it as he or she grows and matures. Basic characteristics tend to become stable and expressed in fairly consistent ways over time. As a teacher, you face the challenge of trying to learn each student's personality and how it is typically expressed. As you learn about the lives of your students, you should be able to determine which behaviors are normal and which might be indicators of a serious emotional disturbance.

The Individuals with Disabilities Education Act (1990) defined serious emotional disturbance as

> a condition exhibiting one or more of the following characteristics over a long period of time and to a marked degree that adversely affects a child's educational performance:
> a. An inability to learn which cannot be explained by intellectual, sensory, or health factors
> b. An inability to build or maintain satisfactory interpersonal relationships with peers and teachers
> c. Inappropriate types of behavior or feelings under normal circumstances
> d. A general pervasive mood of unhappiness or depression
> e. A tendency to develop physical symptoms or fears associated with personal or school problems.
> The term includes schizophrenia. The term does not apply to children who are socially maladjusted, unless it is determined that they have a serious emotional disturbance.

The diagnosis of serious emotional disturbance is also used for students who present a range of behavioral disorders in the classroom. These students may have a conduct disorder or a mood disorder; be hyperactive, aggressive, or socially withdrawn; oppose authority and others; try to distract others into irrelevant activities, or engage in other behaviors that seem "disordered."

When this diagnosis is applied, the student has had the characteristics over a long period, usually at least six months. Teachers can expect an emotional reaction to a trauma, major stressor, or series of anxiety-producing life events, such as a death in the family, divorce, sexual abuse, and so forth. Under such circumstances emotional problems may be visible. However, in time and with some special support, the student should overcome the emotional trauma and reinstate appropriate behaviors. But when a child has always exhibited the emotional disorder or does not recover from a trauma, he or she is likely to qualify for this categorical label.

It is important to note that a child may have a serious emotional problem but still be functioning appropriately in the classroom. If you suspect something is wrong because a student is just a little more quiet than usual, or suddenly breaks out in anger when none has been shown before, or looks off into space and disassociates more than the usual, then you may need to do some probing to know if in fact something is wrong. Despite coping with school reasonably well, the child may still need counseling and guidance.

Some students who have serious emotional disorders start school already labeled. The serious nature of their behaviors may have already

What clues and signals can you think of that might be shown by a student who is undergoing severe stress?

led their parents, preschool teachers, or others to seek the help of psychiatrists, clinical psychologists, or school mental health professionals. Other students may not exhibit serious problems until they are adolescents, and they will come to your attention then. As with any other suspected problem, you should record the student's behaviors, your methods of dealing with the problems, and the response of the student to them. In addition, you should recognize the following behaviors, especially if they occur frequently, as indicators of an emotional disorder:

- Extensive overactivity; moving frequently, rapidly, and without purpose
- Aggressive behavior directed at a victim and intended to cause harm
- Withdrawn behavior: avoiding social interaction, becoming lost in revery
- Disruptive behavior such as leaving one's seat, touching others, playing, and making noises
- Delinquent behaviors such as stealing, lying, or breaking laws
- Playing alone or failing to interact with others when requested
- Thought disturbances, such as extremely bizarre ideas
- Flat, distorted, or exaggerated emotional responses
- Sudden changes in behavior or mood for no apparent reason
- Attempts to hurt self or others
- Lack of guilt for wrongdoing
- Lack of concern for others' feelings

If you suspect an emotional problem, you may want to talk with school support people, such as the social worker or special-education teacher, to get some input on methods to manage the behaviors while encouraging learning.

Support services offered by the school might include having the student work with a psychologist or social worker. He or she may be placed in the regular classroom, or in a special-education room but in the regular classroom for some activities. If a student is so aggressive as to be potentially dangerous, the school often limits interaction with others in a regular classroom, increasing the time as the student learns to handle him- or herself better. Regardless of whether the student is in a regular classroom or special-education room, there is often a behavior-management plan implemented specifically for the child, based on his or her behaviors and aimed at building appropriate behaviors and strengthening appropriate emotional responses.

Depending on the specific nature of their emotional needs, individual students require different types of instruction and management. However, in general, Rosenberg et al. (1997) recommend that teachers employ well-planned and -structured methods of instruction, including

- clear and consistent management
- step-by-step procedures for new-skill learning
- efficient use of instructional time, including allocating more time to academic activities, rewarding school attendance and punctuality, providing fluid transitions between activities, minimizing classroom interruptions, and increasing on-task rates during lessons
- individualization on the basis of skills students need to be taught

- small-group instruction, which allows practice of appropriate classroom behaviors
- careful selection of what is taught
- presenting skills in a teachable and learnable format
- clearly communicating academic expectations
- planning and organizing learning to optimize student success

Each of these recommendations is applied differently, depending on the classroom environment you have built as well as the individual emotional problems the student presents in your classroom.

Attention Deficit Disorder (ADD) and Attention Deficit-Hyperactivity Disorder (ADHD) School professionals struggle to label and provide services for students who exhibit attention deficit disorders, with or without hyperactivity, because this problem is not a category covered under IDEA. Nevertheless, it is a common problem, occurring in about 3 percent of students. Some professionals label these students as having a learning disability, a neurological problem, or other health impairment. But most commonly, since many of the behaviors are often the same as those of students who have emotional problems, the emotional-disorders label is used for providing services. Students who have ADD typically fail to pay close attention to details, have difficulty sustaining attention, do not seem to listen to or follow through on directions, have problems organizing or finding materials for activities, and are forgetful or easily distracted.

The addition of *hyperactivity* to the label (ADHD) is given when the student talks excessively; moves excessively by leaving the assigned seat, running around, or fidgeting; or is so "on the go" that play or other ac-

Children with ADHD can distract other children.

(© Michael Weisbrot)

POLICY, RESEARCH, AND PRACTICE

Is It Preferable to Have Children with Emotional Disorders in the Regular-Education Classroom?

A LOOK INSIDE THE CLASSROOM

It is 4 pm on Monday and the students have left the classroom long ago. Ms. Herrera sits at her desk, the first time she has sat all day. Benjamin has been in her class for two weeks, the longest two weeks of her life! Prior to joining her class, Benjamin had been in a self-contained special education classroom. However, this year the new principal had been working to try to include all special education students in the regular classrooms. Benjamin's IEP had been rewritten a few weeks ago, and now, with the start of the new semester, he was in her class full-time, with a special-education teacher providing resources for one hour a day.

Since the start of Benjamin's inclusion, Ms. Herrera had tried to note all the incidents in the classroom that had caused her concern. In the first week there had only been five incidents, but last week there had been twenty, and today alone there were six. At this rate, she would be spending all of her time dealing with Benjamin, and never get to teach the class! Just then, Mr. Thild, the special-education resource teacher, stopped at the door and said, "I'll see you tomorrow!"

Ms. Herrera replied, "I don't know about that. I may not come in tomorrow. Benjamin is wearing me out! I just can't believe how much his acting-out has escalated since he came to the class. I thought you told me he had his behavior problems under control! You take my class tomorrow and see how many problems he is causing throughout the day. I wonder if Benjamin will be able to stay in this classroom!"

A LOOK AT THE RESEARCH

How can research help Ms. Herrera know what to do to help Benjamin? Rife and Karr-Kidwell (1995) reviewed the literature on inclusion of children with emotional disorders in regular education classrooms. They recommended that inclusion can work, but it should be done with implementation of other supportive services for both the student and the teacher. Regular-education teachers do need support from special-education teachers. They need to learn how to cue and manage student acting-out behaviors. They need to know how to engage in collaborative teaching with the special education teacher. They need to learn how to involve the student's parents in the classroom, as well as the other students. The emotionally disturbed student may do well in the classroom when the teacher knows how to work with the student, and helps other students learn to work with the student. The teacher may set-up peer tutoring for the student, or social skill training, depending on the needs of the student. The teacher may also set up a judicious management system or another management system, which encourages individual responsibility and conflict resolution (McEwan & Nimmo, 1995).

REFLECTIONS FOR YOUR OWN CLASSROOM

Many teachers are apprehensive when emotionally disturbed students are integrated into their classroom. They feel unprepared to deal with the students, or fear that the students will be disruptive to the classroom. It is important to recognize your feelings, as they may impact your expectations and your behaviors in the classroom. If you feel unprepared or show fear, any student will pick up on those feelings and may take advantage of them. If you feel unprepared, you need to identify what you need to know, and then take steps to learn it. Often, another teacher will be able to answer your questions or provide you with information you need. If you are afraid, you need to think about your expectations and analyze the situation. Most teachers are not afraid of the student, but rather of the changes that might occur in the classroom. Good management is a balance of skill and knowledge, with practice. Practicing new management skills with your students will make any changes easier for you, and for them. Remember to be fair, consistent, and firm in your expectations and management of all students. If you are consistent, it is likely that even the student who tries out various inappropriate behaviors will learn that you are in charge, and will decrease or stop acting-out in your classroom.

tivities cannot be sustained. If the student is also impulsive, he or she blurts out answers, does not wait to take turns, and interrupts others.

Too many of the students labeled with ADD/ADHD are simply exhibiting behavior on the edge of the normal range ordinarily seen among children. It is true that their behavior may cause teachers and parents some stress. But alleviating the stress of the teachers and parents by giving these children medication, such as Ritalin or other drugs that "slow the child down," is often the wrong thing to do.

Medication is an appropriate treatment for some ADD/ADHD children. But most of them also respond well to behavior-management techniques that the teacher or parent can learn to institute. These techniques include using contingency contracts and systematic reinforcement for sustained attention to a task, or when the child stays seated for a five-minute period, or for walking rather than running in the classroom, and so forth (see Chapter 6). School psychologists are trained to provide consultation on these issues. Some of the programs they recommend help students learn to channel their activity needs in useful ways, focus attention, and divide tasks into doable parts. Other programs require

Some Classroom Adjustments for ADD/ADHD

Some of the approaches taken by experts in special education are simply good general teaching practices that have broad utility. The techniques for control of ADD/ADHD recommended by researchers and practitioners seem to be of that type—good teaching strategies that might be useful for all children (see Pfiffner, 1996; United States Department of Education, 1995b)

- *Minimize distractions.* Provide a quiet workspace, away from doors, windows, traffic corridors, and pencil sharpeners. Seat close to children that are good workers.

- *Organize your classroom.* Clutter and disorganization are no problem for the regular child, but the ADD/ADHD child needs more routine. Keep things in the same place all the time. Do not allow items the child uses up and replaces, such as paper and pencils, to run out.

- *Establish classroom routines.* Teach subjects in a predictable order, preferably alternating high-interest and low-interest subjects. Try hard to stick to schedules. Make sure that students know what to do when they finish their work. Schedule regular breaks.

- *Adjust the time needed for assignments.* Shorten long assignments or break them up into smaller pieces.

- *Give unambiguous directions.* Try giving one direction at a time. Be brief. Be specific about what you want. To check that the directions are understood, have the student repeat them. Make sure a direction is seen as a direction, not a question or statement. For example, "Bobbie, get the crayons, please" is a simple command, and less ambiguous than the question, "Bobbie, would you please get the crayons?" It is also less ambiguous than the statement "Bobbie will get the crayons for us." Bobbie needs clarity!

- *Give classroom rules prominence.* Post rules. Use large print and bold colors. Have the students, especially any ADD/ADHD students, help to create the rules.

- *Use peers to aid learning.* Pair ADD/ADHD students with others who are calmer. Have them study together and learn to switch roles from tutor to tutee. Have the peer teach organizational and study skills.

- *Have special-assignment folders.* The ADD/ADHD child may need to have daily or long-term assignments written out to avoid confusion, while others in the class may do fine getting assignments aurally. Folders of assignments, serving as a portfolio, can be used to hold completed work.

- *Use strategic verbal attention to the student.* Praise the child for desirable behaviors—sitting in the seat, not calling out, finishing work. Catch the child doing the right thing! Be specific about what you praise; that is, make sure the child knows what behavior was noticed and worthy of praise.

- *Use incentives and rewards.* Privileges (going to the office on an errand for the teacher) and activities (access to the computer) should be dependent on the display of desirable behavior. Draw up contracts and have the ADD/ADHD students pick their own rewards

CONTINUED

from menus you prepare. Deliver a reward for the achievement of realistic goals as set forth in the contract (see Chapters 6 and 8).

■ *When negative behavior occurs, give only one warning.* Just as you need incentives and rewards for appropriate behavior, you need some form of punishment for unwanted behavior. Do not tolerate it. One warning is all that should be given. Be matter-of-fact and brief in administration of punishment. Use time-outs and response costs as punishments (see Chapter 6).

■ *Involve the parents.* Collaborate with the parents. A daily school report may help in communication. Working with the parents on the reward menu for desirable behavior and the consequences for unwanted behavior may be appropriate. They should administer the same rewards and punishments for the same behaviors as you. Consistency is what is wanted in home-school relations.

■ *Incorporate instructional strategies that may prove useful to the ADD/ADHD student.* In reading, have the student follow along in the book while you read; have him or her make story boards to follow the story you are reading; involve him or her more in computer games for learning spelling and vocabulary. In spelling, have the child learn everyday words in context, as when eating a sandwich, spelling *sandwich;* color-code the hard-to-remember parts of words, as in "alth*ough*"; explicitly teach verbal rules such as "i before e except after c." In writing, have the child keep the assignment out during the task; require proofreading of written assignments. In mathematics, focus on the patterns in mathematical operations; color-code the symbols to make them stand out (e.g., bright red for the +, −, %, etc.); require use of a calculator for checking answers after problems are done; require that word problems be read at least twice; make more use of the number line, manipulatives, and graph paper to help the child visualize mathematical concepts and operations.

In summary, ADD/ADHD students need consistency in their environments and in the use of rewards and punishments. They need regularity, order, extra cues about what to do, reminders, and so forth. They can strain the patience of parents and teachers. But the techniques for managing their behavior are getting better known every year, and you should keep up-to-date on these because you are likely to have one or more students diagnosed with ADD/ADHD in your class eventually. For sure, you will have some children who are merely "bouncing off the wall," that is, acting similarly to those with the ADD/ADHD label, and you need the same techniques for management of their instruction and behavior.

cognitive-behavioral therapy (Braswell & Bloomquist, 1991) in which ADD/ADHD children learn to use private speech—a form of talking to themselves—to control their behavior. For example, they may learn to say to themselves, before an assignment, "If I read this slower, I'll get the meaning," or "Talking out makes teacher pout!" We recommend that teachers learn these behavioral and cognitive-behavioral-management approaches and try them out before medications are used to control a child's behavior—or perhaps instead of medications (Hunter, 1996).

Students with Multiple Disabilities or Other Developmental Problems

Not all individuals fit easily into one label or category of exceptionality for special-education services. The category of multiple disabilities is used for those who have two or more disabilities, such as being hard-of-hearing *and* having mental retardation. For some of these learners it is difficult to determine what support services are most likely to promote learning. This category is often also used for those students who have a particular syndrome that has not been provided with its own category under IDEA but by its nature causes learning problems in the classroom.

Students with Autism and Pervasive Developmental Disorder IDEA classified autism as a separate category of disability in 1990. Before then, it was categorized as a particular kind of serious emotional disturbance, then as a health impairment. The change in categorization reflects a growing understanding of some of the dimensions of this problem. Typically, a student labeled autistic has difficulty relating to others and developing personal relationships; problems with both language and speech; developmental delays in cognitive, social, and motor development; and difficulty in reacting appropriately to environmental events (Simpson, 1992). Assessment to determine whether someone has autism usually includes evaluation of cognitive skills; family and environmental behaviors; neurological, sensory-motor, and medical functioning; social and behavioral abilities; and curriculum interactions and skills.

Depending on the severity of this disability, autistic students may be in the regular classroom for all, most, or a little of the day. Typically they receive special-education services to help them develop communication skills, reduce or eliminate stereotypic behavior patterns, and build life skills. Developments in diagnosis and treatment have meant that today autistic students are more likely to live at home or in group homes than in institutions. They also are more likely to become successful at independent living, especially if they are diagnosed at a young age and provided the support services they need.

Teachers usually react to some of the behaviors of the autistic student by wanting to stop the behaviors as soon as possible. Although punishment may temporarily eliminate a behavior, it does not promote the development of more appropriate behaviors, nor does it foster dignity and respect. Long-term learning of new behaviors and skills requires that you use consistent, systematic approaches that break the learning down into small parts that are frequently practiced and positively reinforced. New technology, including computers, may help the student function in the classroom. Additionally, you should plan on working with a variety of support staff, such as social workers and speech therapists, among others, who will help develop learning plans everyone can follow. For these students especially, everyone should consistently encourage the same behaviors and follow the same plans for achieving their development.

Students Who Have Experienced Prenatal or Early-Childhood Substance Exposure/Abuse In recent years, more school-age children have been presenting multiple problems that apparently originate in their mothers' abuse of dangerous substances before or after conception. Currently, specific groups of problems presented by children born under such circumstances are categorized into syndromes. Some of these are fetal alcohol syndrome, cocaine-exposed syndrome, and lead-exposed syndrome. As various other substances are identified as causing fetal-development problems, and those problems are discovered to be typical across individuals, they are likely to be added to the list of syndromes.

If the fetus survives, prenatal exposure to toxic substances may cause severe birth defects, and it typically leads to the student's being labeled as having multiple disabilities. These include physical-development abnormalities or limitations; neuromotor, neurobehavioral, attentional, spatial, auditory, and memory limitations; emotional disorders; cognitive-processing problems; impulsivity, language disorders, and others. Children exposed to drugs or lead when they are young may also exhibit various problems in the classroom.

If the syndrome, or the potential to develop the syndrome, is identified when the child is first born or as an infant, he or she will probably start school with a variety of support services already in place. Such a child may be receiving physical therapy, nursing or medical procedures, social services, special education, and the like. Depending on the nature and severity of the disorders, the student may spend some time in the regular classroom, a segregated special-education room, or an institution.

As with the other multiple disorders, you would most likely work with a team of professionals to best meet the identified needs and concerns of these students. With these syndromes, it is important to remember that direct brain damage, usually called *brain lesions,* are highly likely. Sometimes the deficits caused by the lesions may be lessened if other parts of the brain can be trained to take over the damaged functions. But in other cases the lesions cause damage that cannot be taken over by other parts of the brain. Unless you have training in neurology and the child has a thorough neurological workup, you are not likely to have access to much helpful information about brain functioning. Usually it is safe to use positive reinforcement and modeling (see Chapter 6) to try to build new, appropriate behaviors. However, you should also realize that if the brain damage is severe enough, you may never see change or developmental growth in some areas. The important points to remember are that there are no good assessments or treatments for some types of problems, so we are not able to neatly clarify their characteristics or how to "fix" them. You should always hold high expectations, treat the student with respect, and not assume that he or she is locked into being disabled because of prenatal activities (if they are the known cause) by the parent. It is also important not to judge the parent or hold any negative feelings you have about the parent against the child. It can serve no purpose, and can impede helping the child.

Although many of the children who have multiple disorders are identified when they are infants or toddlers, some of them will not be identified until they come to school. As with the other disabilities, you need to objectively describe behaviors you see and to note specific responses to different teaching methods. Remember that the culture of the student is an important determining factor as you describe different behaviors and try to teach new ones. Because students in this category are going to present a range of potential problems, some of the problems becoming more apparent with maturation, it is helpful to keep detailed track of dates, times, and durations of problems: Treat each presenting problem as a discrete problem that requires specific help. Try not to consider the problems as building upon each other and so overwhelming that they cannot be solved.

Throughout this section on exceptionality we have emphasized keeping records. The best gift you can bring to a conference with a child's parents, the school psychologist, the speech pathologist and other professionals is a set of detailed notes about what you saw and heard that worried you, and the context in which you saw and heard these things. Simply saying, "Jennifer is acting peculiar lately," or "Quentin is wild," or "Mario cannot handle the stuff I'm teaching now" is inadequate. Record precisely the events and contexts in which Jennifer is acting peculiar, Quentin acts wild, and Mario has trouble learning.

Students Who Are Gifted and Talented: Another Category of Exceptionality

Some students may qualify for special-education services under an entirely different category of exceptionality, that of gifted and talented. In addition to provisions in IDEA, there is Public Law 100–297, the Jacob K. Javits Gifted and Talented Students Education Act (GTSEA). Under this act, the gifted and talented student (1) gives evidence of capability of high performance in intellectual, creative, artistic, or leadership areas or in specific academic fields and (2) requires services or activities not ordinarily provided by the schools in order to develop such capabilities fully. Unlike IDEA, PL 100–297 does not mandate special treatments. However, most states have laws that provide for specific school accommodations.

Every culture has its own beliefs about giftedness and what qualities are embraced by the label, and this is recognized in GTSEA. Each culture can determine for itself what giftedness is by the definitions it applies to the concepts of intelligence, creativity, artistry, leadership, and the academic fields it promotes. Each culture can set the standards for measuring giftedness and talent. And each culture can further decide what qualifies as services or activities for the gifted and talented student. Implicit in GTSEA is the recognition that different cultures value aspects of students that might remain hidden if only the mainstream culture defines what giftedness means.

In many schools, giftedness has traditionally been defined in terms of school-based intelligence and achievement, and maybe some other

"Authority in education is to some extent un-avoidable, and those who educate have to find a way of exer-cising authori-ty in accor-dance with the spirit of liberty."

Bertrand Russell, *Principles of Social Reconstruction*, 1916.

© Dan MacDonald/The Picture Cube

"The shrewd guess, the fertile hypothesis, the courageous leap to a tentative conclusion, these are the most valuable coins of a thinker at work. But in most schools guessing is heavily penalized and is associated somehow with laziness."

Jerome Bruner, *The Process of Education*, 1960.

© John Yurka/The Picture Cube

"To be surprised, to wonder, is to begin to understand."

S. José Ortega y Gasset, *The Revolt of the Masses*, 1930.

"If you believe so firmly in the potential of all your students, you have few ready explanations for their failure. The first line of scrutiny is oneself. "What you do is not necessarily good for everyone," Elena [the teacher] would say. "You have to try different things. You have to ask yourself, 'What can I change that will work for a child that is not learning?'" When a student was not doing well, Elena would assume she was failing and put herself through a rigorous self-assessment. "Why am I not teaching him?" she would ask, her record book open, the child's work spread out in front of her.**"**

Mike Rose, *Possible Lives*, p. 90.

© Frank Siteman/The Picture Cube

characteristics, such as leadership and good behavior. Years ago teachers nominated students for gifted programs. But teachers (and other decision makers) have been known to confuse conformity, neatness, good behavior, and other mainstream cultural expectations of the good student with being a gifted student (Ayers, 1987). Then, traditional intelligence-test scores, achievement-test scores, and other apparently objective criteria were used to place students into gifted programs. In recent years, schools have considered the newer definitions of intelligence and the GTSEA's definition of giftedness to identify students as gifted. Gardner's (1985) multiple-intelligences model, or Sternberg's triarchic theory of intelligence (see Chapter 3) are often mentioned as important considerations in finding gifted students and developing programs for them. However, neither of these recent models of intelligence has produced a reliable assessment instrument, so application of these theories for selection of gifted students is limited. Even after acknowledging that the definitions of who qualifies as gifted should be broader, most programs end up using standardized intelligence or cognitive ability tests as the primary tool to determine giftedness. This leads to limited access to such programs by several types of students, particularly those outside the mainstream culture. Gallagher (1992) pointed out that minority, low-income, variously challenged/disabled, and female students are less likely to be identified or served under current school practices. And it is apparent that black and white students have different rates of mobility into honors sections and advanced tracks when homogeneous ability-grouped classes are available (Hallinan, 1996).

> What can a teacher do to make sure that she is not confusing giftedness with good behavior?

There are three basic program accommodations for gifted students: (1) different curricula, (2) different instructional strategies, and (3) organizational and administrative alterations. The curriculum programs include curriculum enrichment, acceleration of content, making content more sophisticated, or providing novel content (Gallagher, 1992). Programs that provide different instructional strategies typically have teachers engaging the students in advanced problem solving of ill-structured problems; providing simulations, analogies, metaphors, and discovery learning; or having students use computers or other technology. Programs that make organizational or administrative accommodations include those that have gifted resource rooms, special gifted pull-out programs, or separate gifted schools (Keogh & MacMillan, 1996). Of these, acceleration and enrichment are the most widely used in schools.

Acceleration Acceleration programs provide students with advanced content that matches their level of attainment regardless of age. Acceleration programs may include early admission to college or the work force, or both. It may include promotion (skipping) to a higher grade level for all or some of the day (e.g., a fourth grader taking mathematics with an eighth-grade algebra class).

A meta-analysis of 26 studies of acceleration concluded that it benefits gifted students academically (Kulik & Kulik, 1984). But despite the consistent record of positive results associated with acceleration, it is not used as often as enrichment programs. There seems to be a lasting fear that a younger child will become socially maladjusted if promoted into a class full of children well above his or her age. There may be some danger in that, though it may be equal to the danger that the child will be bored when kept behind in a class in which he or she can easily excel. The best acceleration solution seems to be to promote gifted children to the level they should work at in their area of giftedness for part of the day, but to keep them with their age mates for the rest of the day. For example, one fifth grader may work with high school students in science, another may take calculus at the junior college, while a third, with musical talent, plays in the high school band. But the children still study their other subjects—history and literature, say—as well as gym, art, and some time for just plain fooling around, with their age mates.

Enrichment Enrichment includes providing students with a variety of materials or references that elaborate on the basic concepts taught in the standard program. Some enrichment programs provide abstract concepts (content sophistication); others, different content (content novelty) (Keogh & MacMillan, 1996). Some of these programs are provided only for students who meet a strict definition of *gifted*. In others, broader definitions allow many students to rotate through several enrichment opportunities such as special clubs, seminars, and field trips.

Accommodation of giftedness through enrichment can be done individually or in small homogeneous groups. In class, homogeneous ability grouping is increasingly recognized as an accommodation that has some merit. But there are those arguing for separate classes of homogeneous ability (tracking by ability), and this recommendation leads to a passionate debate among researchers, citizens, and parents.

A Debate over Accommodation Culross (1996) reviewed the research on inclusion of gifted students in regular classrooms and the effect of inclusion on self-concept and other nonacademic factors. She concluded that the (limited) research supports homogeneous ability grouping as the most effective approach to meeting the cognitive and affective needs of gifted students, and that the regular classroom may be too restrictive an environment.

Yewchuk (1993) also summarized research in this area and concluded that achievement is highest when, in addition to homogeneous high-ability grouping, the gifted students are provided with a differentiated curriculum and instruction that matches their abilities and skills. Interestingly, this review also concluded that ability grouping and differentiated curriculum helped achievement for medium-ability and low-ability students as well. In addition, many parents of the gifted support the segregation of their children by ability group.

But there are dissenters. Some disagree, first, because inclusion is a democratic goal. Democracy works to break down barriers between people. Why should gifted children be treated separately? That is, the fight for inclusion of special-education children in the regular classroom was to overcome their segregation, but some educators and parents of the gifted want schools to segregate again. Surely, say opponents of tracking, schools can accommodate the individual needs of the gifted child through acceleration or enrichment activities.

A second reason for concern is that evidence in support of homogeneous ability grouping has not been found by all scholars studying the issue. For example, Slavin (1990a), reviewing 15 experiments and 14 correlational studies of ability grouping in the high school years, found no beneficial effects from ability grouping. He also studied ability grouping in middle schools (1993), analyzing 27 different studies, and found few positive effects of ability grouping for low-, average-, or high-ability students. Similar conclusions were reached when he studied elementary schools (Slavin, 1987a). The overall conclusions (Slavin & Braddock, 1993) are that tracking does not work; in fact it is harmful to many and undermines American democratic values; and that there are many other ways to accommodate diversity in the regular classroom (see also Oakes, 1985).

Finally, there is the research of Marsh (e.g., 1988; 1995), who studied the effects of high-ability grouping on the self-concept of academically gifted and talented students. His research repeatedly demonstrates the "big fish" phenomenon. That is, a gifted child in a regular class is "a big fish in a little pond." His or her talents are recognized and rewarded, and his or her academic self-concept is high, and rightly so. But if the same child is put into a highly selective school or a homogeneous high-ability group composed of other gifted and talented students, there will still be some students who excel and some who do not, particularly in the highly competitive schools of the U.S. So some children who are talented may move from being "big fish" to being small ones, in which case their academic self-concept goes down. Their achievement and educational aspirations are often affected negatively as well.

So the field is split, and we cannot give well-supported advice about tracking or homogeneous ability grouping for gifted students. We tend to believe that most goals for gifted students can be achieved through enrichment and acceleration. As a teacher, you have to help make the decisions about how you want to support gifted education in your school. You need to know what the current definition of giftedness is, and what programs the school offers. You need to know whether the school expects you to provide curriculum enrichment or make other modifications for gifted students in your classroom. You need to know how to recommend students for a program, and what information you should provide along with a recommendation. You also need to know the laws of your state regarding gifted education. Many states have additional mandates that require you to provide certain classroom opportunities. Once you become familiar with the way your school handles giftedness, you also need to make decisions about how you define and handle giftedness among your students. Do you recognize that the mainstream cultural definitions you hold may prevent you from identifying many of your gifted students? Do you understand how the programs may not support children from other cultures? It is important to remember that using the newer definitions

Do you know the definition of giftedness in your state? In local school districts?

allows you to recognize a greater number of students as gifted and talented. And once you have identified such students you need to make accommodations that promote the development of their giftedness.

General Concerns and Recommendations for Teachers

Throughout this chapter we have provided a wide range of diversity issues for you to consider in your teaching. Diversity is the nature of humanity. Some of the diversity is cultural/ethnic/racial; some a function of gender differences; and some due to the wide variability of our characteristics in the physical, cognitive, or affective domains. Understanding the issues surrounding a particular kind of diversity, and finding the accommodations needed to adjust the school to the differences, is not always easy. But notice that we are asking the schools to adjust. Historically, it has been the student who has had to adjust to a rigid school system. Now we ask that schools bend as well, and try to meet diversity by accommodating to it.

You will probably find yourself contemplating different approaches and experimenting with different techniques until you find what works for a class or an individual student. Keeping this in mind over a school term and over many years, ask yourself what you know and what you need to know about

- the individual student and how his or her culture has affected, and continues to affect, his or her development and behavior. Take time to get to know the students in more depth, to find out how the students think, and what is important and meaningful to them.

- the school's cultural expectations and how well they match those of the parents and the students. Get to know the parents and caregivers of your students. Find out what they value and what they expect. Compare parental and student expectations. Find ways to show students and parents where there are differences in expectations.

- your own cultural expectations and how they influence your attitudes and behaviors in the classroom. Videotape some classroom segments and watch them at home. Analyze your interactions and reactions. Think about the ways your attitudes are reflected in your classroom behaviors.

- how student diversity is assessed in your school and what differences are labeled. Additionally, once a student is labeled, you need to know how the school responds and how you are expected to respond. Get to know the professional resource staff. Get to know the rest of the teachers and aides. Understand what cultural resources they can offer, as well as how they, as a group, think about diversity in your school.

- what instructional materials and methods are valued across the school and by the parents. If you discover that there are conflicting values, you need to acknowledge them and find ways to help your students understand them without degrading either one.

Obviously, teaching is a task that requires you to think, act, and modify your thinking and actions based on the results of previous interactions. Remember also that Table 5.3 has other recommendations for you.

SUMMARY

1. Group identity has meaning in our lives if our perceptions, thoughts, and behavior are shaped by members of any cultural, language, social, or special-needs groups to which we belong. Membership in groups provides the cultural contexts in which we live, affecting many important aspects of our being, and cultural contexts account for much of the diversity teachers encounter when they work with students in the classroom. Obviously, children bring their cultures with them to the school. But at school, they encounter the culture of the school itself, which typically they must adapt to. The cultural expectations students have at home may be very different from those at school, and these home influences may account for many of their behaviors when they interact with teachers and school administrators.

2. Being aware of your own culture and how it influences your teaching is a first step toward meeting the diverse needs of your students. Recognizing that the cultures of students are not "better" or "worse" than yours, just different, should be helpful in preparing you to address diversity in your class. Finding ways to value and advantageously use these differences, rather than ignoring them or using them to make students feel out of place, should enhance the teaching-learning processes in your classroom.

3. Older curricular materials may reflect mainstream culture, and so they may not provide positive experiences for students of different cultures or for girls. Newer curricular materials may reflect cultural heterogeneity but are not always "real" for your students. Remember that children are differentially enculturated to the mainstream culture. Providing opportunities for them to both value their own cultures and learn about cultural differences allows them to develop thinking skills and determine which cultural values they want to incorporate into their own lives.

4. The gender-related differences found within cultures may not be found between cultures. Knowing the gender-related expectations of a culture and how these match the curriculum is important for understanding your students and their families. Remember that students may have stereotypical expectations based on the definitions of gender in their particular cultural group. Finding ways to provide them with experiences and activities to challenge their stereotypical thinking is valuable for their later success.

5. Exceptional students need education designed to meet their special mental, physical, or emotional needs. Typically it is the responsibility of the regular-education teacher to meet the needs of these students in the regular-education classroom. This is an area of education that is highly charged emotionally, and highly regulated by legislative mandates. You have to follow the mandates and carry out any Individualized Education Plan developed for your students.

6. The kinds of exceptional students you may have in your class include students with physical, sensory, and psychological disabilities—visual and hearing impairments, speech and language disorders, orthopedic and health impairments, neurological and neuromotor disorders, learning disabilities and attention disorders, autistic and de-

velopmental problems, retardation and emotional problems. Humans do not all come perfectly formed, perfectly behaved, and able to learn. The test of a society is how it takes care of its special children—its challenged children, as well as its gifted and talented.

7. As you become more familiar with exceptionality, getting to know the common characteristics of and concerns surrounding each special-education label, you will be better able to help with the proper identification and treatment of each child. With experience, you will find ways to effectively integrate these students into your activities and make them part of the classroom.

8. Teachers need to provide all students with opportunities to learn that allow for individual diversity. Students need to engage in a variety of classroom activities, so teachers need experience with a wide range of teaching methods, not become locked into the one that is most comfortable for them. With practice, making adjustments for every student and every classroom, in every subject, based on the unique needs of your learners is something you can learn to do. Teaching in a multicultural classroom, a multilingual classroom, and a classroom with a wide range of diversity is difficult. But it is also a source of pride and satisfaction for the many teachers who now do this on a regular basis.

PART THREE

Learning and Motivation: Theories and Applications

In Part One we talked about objectives, the importance of knowing where you want to go and sharing that knowledge with your students. In Part Two we talked about students' characteristics and some of the ways in which individuals vary. Now, in Part Three, following the model of the teaching process presented as Figure 2.1 (page 30), we look at how students acquire the behavior, skills, and ideas we want to teach them. Chapter 6 begins with a discussion of **classical conditioning.** This theory explains how we acquire certain kinds of responses, particularly emotional responses. We then examine **operant conditioning.** This theory gives us a method for modifying students' behavior. Although operant conditioning explains a wide variety of phenomena, it does not easily explain how we learn from watching others, how we learn to judge ourselves, how we learn from meaningful prose, or how we solve complex problems. So we also talk about a theory that combines ideas from operant conditioning and cognitive psychology—**social learning theory.**

In Chapter 7 we introduce ideas from **cognitive psychology,** examining how information is processed, remembered, and applied to the solution of a wide variety of problems. Here we explore the meaning of **transfer**—how things learned in one setting are used in another. Transfer is extremely important in education, because schooling is intended to help with life beyond school.

Finally, in Chapter 8, we discuss **motivation,** without which learning rarely takes place. We look at internal motivators—such as the need for achievement—as well as external motivators—incentives and reinforcers. We go into procedures and programs for improving motivation and **attributions,** and conclude with a set of practical techniques. Together these three chapters should help you understand how learning takes place and how your teaching can be made compatible with the learning process.

Behavioral and Social Views of Learning

Overview

LEARNING

A Definition of Learning

Three Behavioral Learning Theories

Classical conditioning

Contiguity learning

Operant conditioning

Foci of This Chapter: Operant Conditioning and Social Learning

OPERANT CONDITIONING

Positive and Negative Reinforcers

Primary and Secondary Reinforcers

Schedules of Reinforcement

Fixed-ratio schedules

Variable-ratio schedules

Fixed-interval schedules

Variable-interval schedules

Recent research on reinforcement schedules

Contingency Management

Contingent reinforcement

Kinds of reinforcers

The contingency contract

The Elimination of Responses

Extinction

Reinforcement of other behavior and of low response rates

APPLICATION
Unintentional Reinforcement

Punishment

Reasoning as an alternative to punishment

Ethical Issues and Limits of the Theory

SOCIAL LEARNING THEORY

How Learning Occurs through Observation

A Social-Learning Analysis of Observational Learning

Attentional phase

Retention phase

Reproduction phase

Motivational phase

POLICY, RESEARCH, AND PRACTICE

Are Systematic Training Programs an Effective Way to Change the Imitation of Aggressive Behaviors Modeled by the Media?

A Note on Cognition

The Teacher and Modeling

Self-Regulation of Behavior and Its Processes

Observing one's own performance

Judging performance

Determining consequences for ourselves

Mentoring

POLICY, RESEARCH, AND PRACTICE

Are Systematic Training Programs an Effective Way for Students to Regulate Their Own Behaviors?

Summary

OVERVIEW

Many different kinds of learning take place under many different conditions. It is no wonder, then, that many different theories of learning have been proposed. We start with three behavioral theories that help explain why we learn: classical conditioning, contiguity learning, and operant conditioning, the most important and well-developed of the behavioral theories of learning. Operant conditioning informs us about practical things: how to create a learning environment that builds and maintains a student's correct responses, how and when

This chapter was revised by Dr. John Bing of Salisbury State University, Maryland.

to reinforce a student for appropriate behavior, how to set up a learning contract, and how to eliminate undesired and inappropriate behavior. We end with a moral question: Although operant conditioning gives us the tools to modify our students' behavior, is it ethical to use those tools?

We are also concerned with **social learning.** Here we use both the external reinforcement and internal cognitive explanations of learning (discussed in Chapter 7) to account for how we learn from other people. Humans are social animals. Through observation of our social world, through cognitive interpretation of that world, and through reinforcement or punishment of our responses in that world, we learn enormous amounts of information and complex skills.

In the social learning view, "people are neither driven by inner forces nor buffeted by environmental stimuli. Rather, psychological functioning is explained in terms of a continuous reciprocal interaction of personal and environmental determinants" (Bandura, 1977, pp. 11–12). Social learning theory emphasizes that the environments we are exposed to are not random; they often are chosen and changed by us through our own behavior. A social learning perspective helps analyze the continuous interplay among environmental variables, our personal characteristics, and our covert and overt behaviors. This perspective gives us interpretations of how observational learning takes place and how we learn to regulate our own behavior—two processes that are important for teachers to think about.

Learning

A Definition of Learning

Before we discuss the different kinds of learning, we need a definition of the term. **Learning** is the process whereby an organism changes its behavior as a result of experience. Figure 6.1 displays the key ideas in this definition.

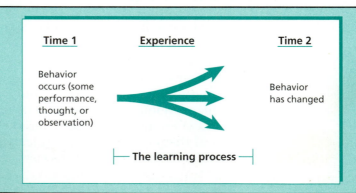

FIGURE 6.1

A representation of learning

Time 1	Experience	Time 2
Behavior occurs (some performance, thought, or observation)		Behavior has changed

├— **The learning process** —┤

The idea that learning is a *process* means that learning takes time. To measure learning, we compare the way the organism behaves at time 1 with the way it behaves at time 2 under similar circumstances. If the behavior under similar circumstances differs on the two occasions, we infer that learning has taken place.

Further, it is a change in behavior that occurs in the process of learning. **Behavior** refers to some action—muscular, glandular, or electrochemical—or combination of actions. One kind of behavior is verbal—our spoken and written actions. The changes of a child from saying "dada" to "father," or of a student from choosing to write an essay about "How I Feel Today" to choosing one about "Public Education," allow us to infer that learning has taken place. The overt behaviors of talking, writing, moving, and the like allow us to study the cognitive behaviors that interest us—thinking, feeling, wanting, remembering, problem solving, creativity, and so on. The overt behaviors of all organisms—human or animal—are always our starting point.

Some psychologists focus exclusively on overt behaviors; they are often called **behaviorists.** Other psychologists use overt behaviors as a clue for inferring what goes on in a person's mind; they are called **cognitive psychologists.** But all psychologists need to observe some form of behavior in order to determine whether change has occurred.

Typically, in school learning, the change in behavior we are looking for is the ability to remember, understand, and apply knowledge and the tendency to have certain attitudes and values, of the kind set forth in our educational objectives. And we want these kinds of learning to be relatively permanent and available throughout students' lives.

The final component of our definition of learning is **experience**—interchange with the environment whereby stimuli take on meaning and relationships are established between stimuli and responses. We exclude from our definition of learning behavior changes due primarily to maturational (biologically programmed) processes, such as a baby's learning to stand and walk and changes in height and weight. We also exclude behavior changes due to alcohol or other drugs. And we exclude purely physiological changes, like the behavior changes that occur when we become tired from exercise.

Three Behavioral Learning Theories

Behavioral psychologists have put forth three relatively distinct theories to describe how we learn. All three theories have applications to learning in schools.

Classical Conditioning   *Classical conditioning,* so termed because it was the first of the modern behavioral learning theories, focuses on changes in muscular or glandular responses. It has never accounted very well for cognitive kinds of learning. Some of the clearest examples of classical conditioning are studies by the Russian physiologist Ivan Pavlov, a Nobel laureate. A review of the procedures he used in his historic studies can help clarify some terminology.

FIGURE 6.2

Model of classical
(respondent) conditioning

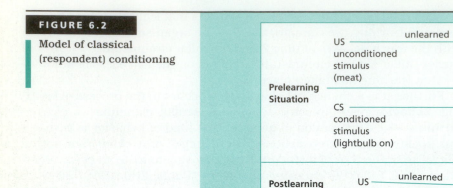

A dog is given some meat and starts salivating as it eats. The meat is called an **unconditioned stimulus (US),** and the act of salivating is called an **unconditioned response (UR).** This particular stimulus (meat) elicits this particular response (salivating). Another name for classical conditioning is **respondent conditioning**—because the responses to certain stimuli are already present. They are "wired in"; they do not need to be learned.

Now suppose we turn on a light in the presence of the dog. Turning on the light has a minimal effect on the dog's salivation. But what if we turn on the light and then quickly give the dog some meat (US)? If we repeated this action a number of times and then, on a particular trial, did not give the dog any meat, we would still notice the salivating response. The light, after several associations with the meat, elicits a response very similar to the one given when meat is presented. The light, previously a neutral stimulus, has become a **conditioned stimulus (CS),** and the response that it elicits is called a **conditioned response (CR).** Figure 6.2 shows the relationships among these terms.

Behavior changed as a result of experience. Learning took place. Now let's move from dogs to people and use this model of learning in a more general form. The unconditioned stimulus-response linkage is operating whenever a stimulus (the US) elicits an instinctive or emotional reaction (the UR), such as salivating, fear, anger, vomiting, revulsion, joy, pleasure, happiness, or ecstasy. Pairing the conditioned stimulus, a previously neutral stimulus, with the unconditioned stimulus leads to a conditioned response (such as fear or joy) to that conditioned stimulus. For example, imagine a five-year-old girl going to school for the first time. She meets her teacher and receives a smile, a hug, and a compliment. In a few days, she begins leaving for school earlier than necessary and tells her mother that she wants to be a teacher when she grows up. In this case the teacher's smile, hug, and compliments can be interpreted as the unconditioned stimulus. They elicit in the child feelings of pleasure, which can be interpreted as the unconditioned response. The pre-

Some children are anxious about school. A caring teacher can soon change that.
(© Elizabeth Crews)

viously neutral teacher, the conditioned stimulus, is associated with the unconditioned stimulus (hugging, etc.) and soon come to elicit the same feelings of pleasure (now, a conditioned response).

But what if this child had come to school and found the teacher threatening, the routine rigid, or the remarks of other children hurtful? The classical conditioning model still helps explain what might happen. The school and all its components—teachers, books, students—might in time come to elicit feelings of fear or revulsion because they have been connected in time and space with the stimuli that induced these feelings. The negative feeling toward traditional schooling held by many students from ethnic and cultural minorities and economically disadvantaged families may have its roots in their perceptions of teachers, schools, and other students as threatening. Teachers must be sensitive to the special needs of these students.

Some students experience nausea as a direct result of test anxiety. Early in their school careers these children learned the linkage between the test result and feelings of failure, real or imagined. They have come to expect disappointment from their teachers and parents, or ridicule from other children. The conditioned stimulus, the announcement of a test, elicits the conditioned response—anxiety.

Virtually anything in the environment can be paired with a stimulus that elicits emotional responses. A teacher's kind or harsh words can elicit feelings of happiness or fear. Associated stimuli—say, mathematics, the gym, the principal, or the school—eventually may elicit a response similar to the unconditioned response simply by closely preceding the unconditioned stimulus. And remember that conditioning often occurs without the student's awareness, making it very hard for the learner to understand how his or her responses were acquired. If you can examine the learning environment with the respondent-conditioning model in mind, you may be able to intentionally condition positive responses by your students to school activities. You may also prevent them from learning unwanted negative conditioned responses.

> **What other school-related emotional responses can be explained by classical conditioning?**

Contiguity Learning The pairing of an unconditioned stimulus and a conditioned stimulus is part of the requirement for classical conditioning. Some learning theorists pointed out that for most animals the simple pairing of events, any events, can result in learning. An unconditioned stimulus-response connection is not necessary. Simple contiguous (close together in time or space) association of a stimulus and a response can lead to a change in behavior.

How does it work? Look at these incomplete statements:

Don't make a mountain out of a _____.
He's crazy as a _____.
May the force be with _____.
Nine times five is _____.

By filling in the words *molehill, loon, you,* and *forty-five,* we demonstrate that we learn things simply because events or stimuli occur close together in time. Sometimes repetition is necessary, but sometimes such learning takes place in a single trial. People change as a result of experiencing events that occur together.

> **When have you used contiguity learning?**

In school situations contiguity learning is used in drill. From repeated pairing, students learn that "2 + 2" on a flash card means "4" and that the written word *cat* is pronounced "cat." A good deal of foreign-language vocabulary is learned this way. Instruction by means of drill, although often tedious, can be an efficient means of learning rote responses to simple questions. And we can make this kind of learning more efficient and less tedious by using contingent reinforcement (for example, giving gold stars, or points that can be used to get some prize, for correct responses) or by building more activity into the learning situation (using games and team competition for learning spelling or mathematics facts).

Operant Conditioning **Operant conditioning** is a form of learning where the behavior of interest is emitted, more or less spontaneously, without being elicited by any known stimuli. In classical conditioning the UR is elicited by the US. In operant conditioning behavior is *emitted* while the organism is "operating" on the environment. The *consequence* of that behavior is the crucial variable in operant learning. The heart of the theory is that behavior reinforced by consequences is strengthened, enhancing the frequency, magnitude, or probability of occurrence. Some emitted behavior changes as a function of experience—the consequences associated with that behavior.

What is a reinforcer? A **reinforcer** is an event or stimulus that increases the strength of a behavior. Admittedly, this is a circular definition. But the fact remains that it is possible to change behavior by manipulating—giving or withholding—reinforcers.

The simplest example of operant conditioning was provided by B. F. Skinner, the famous psychologist closely associated with this form of learning. Imagine a rat in a small enclosure, empty except for a food tray and a lever. When a hungry rat is first placed in the box, it emits a wide variety of responses, or operants—getting up on its hind legs, sniffing around, and trying to climb the walls. Eventually, more or less by accident, it presses the lever. Later it presses it again. Then again. The frequency with which it presses the lever under these conditions, where nothing reinforcing happens as a result of the lever pressing, provides a baseline called the *operant level*—the frequency of this kind of behavior before conditioning.

Now suppose the experimenter delivers a pellet of food into the food tray as soon as the rat presses the lever. The rat, of course, will sniff the food and eat it. Sooner or later, the rat will press the lever again, and again food will drop into the tray. Each time it presses the lever, the rat gets another pellet of food. The reinforcement is *contingent* on pressing the lever. The rate of the rat's lever-pressing response increases. The rat has been conditioned to press the lever by contingent reinforcement with food. In terms of our definition of learning, we see that a change in behavior, an increased rate of lever pressing, has taken place as a result of experience—the contingent availability of food.

The same model applies to humans as well as rats. All of the infinite variety of human behavior or human responses can be made more or less frequent or probable by the use or nonuse of reinforcement, contingent on some response. The response can be anything—an action, a statement, or even inaction. For example, the response may be volunteering to answer a teacher's question or the answer itself. Or the response may be a student's sitting quietly and apparently doing nothing.

If the response is volunteering to answer a question, one likely reinforcer of that response is being called on by the teacher. If the response is the answer to the question itself, the reinforcer is likely to be the teacher's saying "Right" or "Correct" or "That's good." If the response is sitting still and doing nothing, a reinforcer might be the teacher's approval, either in words or by means of a smile. Or it might be relief from the anxiety of being called on and possibly giving a wrong answer.

Foci of This Chapter: Operant Conditioning and Social Learning

Because teachers, especially, find great practical value in operant conditioning, we give much more attention in this chapter to this learning theory than to the other theories of learning put forth by behavioral psychologists. But we also examine social learning theory, which points out that not all learning requires reinforcement. Social learning theorists believe observation is sufficient for there to be learning. They point out that humans learn approximately correct responses from friends, parents, and teachers by observing both their behavior and the consequences of their behavior. So this important theory (also known as *observational learning*) is the second major focus of this chapter.

Operant Conditioning

The major concepts in operant conditioning and their relationship to each other are shown in Figure 6.3 (Skinner, 1953, 1954, 1968, 1973). We begin by looking at reinforcement, a key element in operant learning. There are both positive and negative reinforcers. But whether posi-

FIGURE 6.3

Concept map of operant conditioning

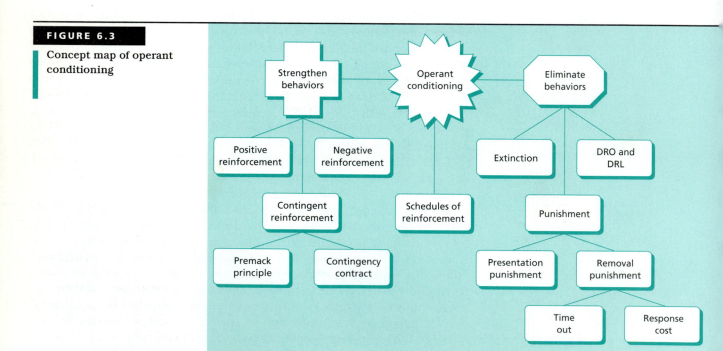

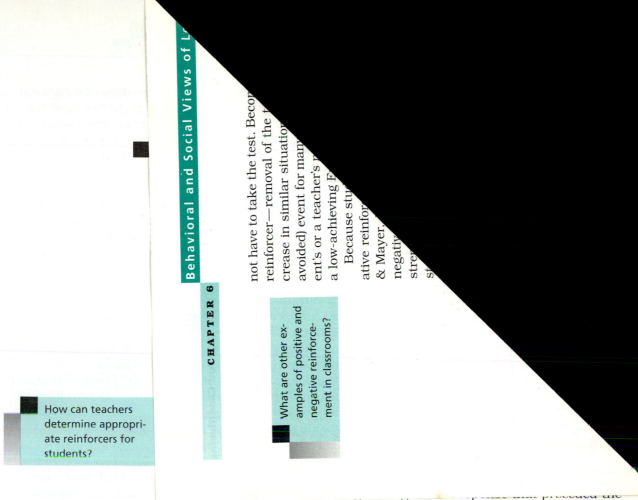

How can teachers determine appropriate reinforcers for students?

What are other examples of positive and negative reinforcement in classrooms?

not have to take the test. Becor[...]
reinforcer—removal of the t[...]
crease in similar situation[...]
avoided) event for man[...]
ent's or a teacher's [...]
a low-achieving F[...]

Because stu[...]
ative reinfor[...]
& Mayer, [...]
negativ[...]
stre[...]
st[...]

removal (see Figure 6.4). Because it strengthens behavior, the event that resulted in removal is a reinforcer; but because it is associated with something unpleasant, something of negative value, we call it a *negative reinforcer*. Examples of things of negative value include harsh criticism and a boring assignment. Whatever new stimulus event is perceived to stop the criticism or end the boredom—such as cleaning your room or making jokes—is likely to be repeated.

Now let us look at a common example of negative reinforcement in school. Suppose that just as a test is about to begin, an anxious child gets sick. What happens? The child is sent to the nurse's office and does

FIGURE 6.4

Types of reinforcement and punishment

		The value of what is given or taken away	
		Positively valued	Negatively valued
What happens after a response is made	Something is given	Positive reinforcement	Presentation punishment
	Something is taken away	Removal punishment	Negative reinforcement

...ing sick has been followed by a negative ...est. We might expect "getting sick" will in... ...s because taking a test is an aversive (to-be-... ...y students. Other aversive events might be a par-... ...agging a student to be neater or being assigned to ...nglish class.

...dents often try to escape from these negative events, neg-...cement is also called **escape conditioning** (Sulzer-Azaroff ...977; 1986; 1991). Responses associated with the removal of ...e events—that is, responses that are negatively reinforced—are ...gthened. For example, if a student became neater and the nagging ...opped, the neatness response would be strengthened. The neatness behavior leads to the *removal* of the aversive stimulus (nagging) so neatness should increase. Neatness becomes the way to obtain the reinforcement—no nagging. Likewise, if a student does not like being assigned to a low-achieving group, and is motivated to work more diligently and achieve more, he may subsequently be moved to a higher-achieving group. Academic achievement is negatively reinforced, and it ought to increase, or at least be maintained at a high level. The behavior that leads to escape from unhappy circumstances usually increases in frequency.

Primary and Secondary Reinforcers

The distinction between **primary** and **secondary reinforcers** is useful. Positive primary reinforcers are stimuli such as food, water, sex, and other events that satisfy physiological needs. By satisfying physiological needs, we can strengthen behavior, particularly the behavior of lower organisms. Human beings, with their elaborate language system and highly developed intelligence, can be reinforced by positive secondary reinforcers like praise, money, gold stars, and movies. Secondary reinforcers may at one time have been linked in some way to the primary reinforcers. That is, money may be a reinforcer because it buys food or shelter. Gold stars may serve as reinforcers because they are linked to a person's basic need for security or safety. If a student is earning gold stars, she is pleasing her teacher and increasing her feelings of security and safety within the classroom environment.

Because money and other secondary reinforcers are powerful reinforcers, the distinction between the two types of reinforcers is blurred when we set out to use reinforcement techniques. The operant conditioner's motto in practice should be "Look for the reinforcer," or find the event that is acting or can act as a reinforcer for a particular person. Whether it is primary or secondary, positive or negative, the appropriate reinforcer can be used by one person to change the behavior of another. If a teacher is the person responsible for student learning, and learning is defined as a change in behavior, then a primary function of a teacher is to change student behavior. Used correctly and for the right purposes, operant techniques can help us change the behavior of students in appropriate ways.

> What are preferred secondary reinforcers for the age/grade level of students you plan to teach?

Schedules of Reinforcement

Reinforcement can be continuous or intermittent. With **continuous reinforcement** we reinforce every response of a given type; with **intermittent reinforcement** we reinforce only a fraction of these responses. If the fraction of responses is based on the number of responses made, it is a **ratio schedule** of reinforcement. We may reinforce every second response, or every tenth response. Or we can use intermittent reinforcement by varying the time interval between reinforcements. This is an **interval schedule** of reinforcement. We might reinforce the first response made after an interval of ten seconds has elapsed since the preceding reinforcement. Or we might reinforce only once every five minutes, or once every hour, regardless of the number of responses made during that time.

Both ratio and interval schedules can be fixed (constant) or variable. So we can use fixed-ratio, variable-ratio, fixed-interval, or variable-interval schedules of reinforcement (see Table 6.1). These and many other possibilities were studied by Ferster and Skinner (1957). They found that the various schedules of reinforcement had different effects on rate of responding, number of responses per reinforcement, and number of responses made after reinforcement was stopped. The Ferster-Skinner research was conducted with rats and pigeons. But it has been found that learning in school is affected in much the same way by the common schedules of reinforcement.

Fixed-Ratio Schedules We might find a **fixed-ratio schedule,** in which a student is reinforced on, say, every fifth correct response, in computer-assisted instruction. For example, every fifth correct answer might be

> What are some classroom examples of reinforcement schedules you have observed?

TABLE 6.1

Types of Reinforcement Schedules Possible in Operant Conditioning

	Ratio	*Interval*
Fixed	Specified number of responses, followed by reinforcement. Continuous reinforcement, a special case of the fixed-ratio 1:1 schedule. Ex.: Have students write 200-word journal entry; follow with reinforcement.	Specified period of time elapses, followed by response and reward. Ex.: Have students read assigned material for 5 minutes; provide reinforcement at that time.
Variable	Varying number of responses occur between rewards. Ex.: Teacher praises student oral responding after varying numbers of questions.	Varying amount of time elapses, followed by response and reinforcement. Ex.: Teacher praises oral responding after students respond on average every 10 minutes.

met with a randomly generated praise statement like "You're doing fine." Fixed-ratio schedules can result in stable responding, particularly when the ratio of reinforcements is low, say, 1 in 100, or 1 in 500 (Ferster & Skinner, 1957). The lower the ratio, the more stable the responding because the individual is conditioned to make many responses in order to obtain reinforcement.

In most situations the goal of the teacher is to phase out the reinforcement. This method forces students to work on their own, or for reinforcers that they control, rather than for those from external sources. To practice this approach, you might start with continuous reinforcement for correct responses, then use a series of decreasing fixed-ratio schedules until reinforcement can be eliminated completely.

A switch from continuous to intermittent reinforcement is necessary in operant conditioning because it is nearly impossible outside the laboratory to reinforce every correct response. Moreover, the use of intermittent schedules in training results in behavior that persists longer without reinforcement than does training with continuous reinforcement. The ratio has an effect on the rate of response too. With a high fixed-ratio schedule, say 1:2 or 1:5, responding is fast, and further responding usually begins right after reinforcement is given. With a lower fixed-ratio schedule, say 1:30 or 1:100, there is a characteristic pause after a reinforcement, as if the person or animal were resting. It is as if the organism knows that it takes a certain large number of responses to earn reinforcement.

Variable-Ratio Schedules   In the **variable-ratio schedule,** responses are reinforced on a certain average ratio, but each individual reinforcement comes after a different number of correct responses. That is, if the individual ratios are 1:5, 1:10, 1:15, 1:13, and 1:7, the variable-ratio schedule averages 5:50, or 1:10. Humans and animals respond at higher rates under variable-ratio than fixed-ratio schedules for the same amount of reinforcement.

In school we might find a variable-ratio schedule in the reinforcement of volunteering behavior. Some children always put up their hands to volunteer to answer a question or perform a task. Suppose 20 of 30 children in a class raise their hands whenever there is a chance for students to respond. One particular child, other things being equal, would be called on 1 time out of 20. Unless the teacher goes alphabetically or by rows, the probability of a child's being chosen is more variable, perhaps *averaging* 1:20, but sometimes 1:3, 1:30, 1:7, or 1:40. In other words, volunteering behavior is reinforced on a variable-ratio schedule. The persistence of hand raising among students may be due to this variable-ratio reinforcement schedule—a schedule that makes any behavior, including hand raising, hard to extinguish. Notice, however, that although it is hard to extinguish this kind of behavior, it is not impossible. By consistently ignoring the raised hands of some students, a teacher can eventually eliminate this behavior on the part of those students. When a behavior is not reinforced, it is less and less likely to be emitted.

Hand-raising behavior is maintained on a variable-ratio schedule of reinforcement.
(© Paul Conklin)

Fixed-Interval Schedules When reinforcement is provided on a **fixed-interval schedule,** a period of decreased responding occurs after each reinforcement. So when a rat is reinforced for the first response made after one minute, the rat is likely to be inactive for perhaps fifty seconds, then respond until reinforced. After this reinforcement, the rat is again

FIGURE 6.5

FIGURE 6.5

Characteristic pattern of responding under a fixed-interval schedule of reinforcement

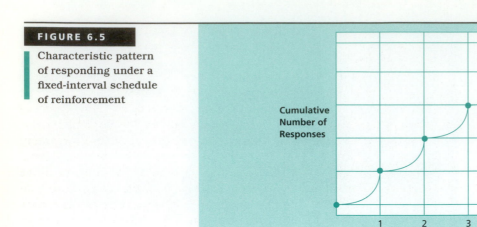

Cumulative
Number of
Responses

Minutes

inactive for a period. Figure 6.5 shows the response curve under a fixed-interval schedule.

We find the same effect in human behavior. Think about the way most students study for regularly scheduled tests. When a midterm and final exam are the only two tests scheduled, the responses required (studying) to get reinforcement (a good grade) increase in magnitude and frequency just before a test. In other words, cramming takes place. Immediately after a test, many students enter an inactive period, rarely studying. The major portion of study behavior occurs at fixed intervals, halfway through the course and again at the end of the course. If tests are given every Friday, it is common to find a cycle of rest (Monday through Wednesday), study (Thursday), and test (Friday). We could change the vertical axis of Figure 6.5 to read "Hours of Study" and the horizontal axis to "Weeks" or "Fridays," and use the same general curve of responding to describe the study behavior of students that we used to show the lever-pressing behavior of rats. Both curves would show the scalloping effect—relatively little responding for some time period, followed by a sharp rise in responding when it is nearly time for reinforcement to take place if a response is emitted, followed by another period of minimum responding.

Variable-Interval Schedules   The fourth reinforcement schedule is the **variable-interval schedule.** An interval of, say, five minutes might be the time span used as an average. Actually the interval during which no reinforcement is given for responding can vary greatly. It may be thirty seconds or ten minutes. The major characteristic of behavior maintained by a variable-interval schedule is its regularity. Stable and uniform rates of responding occur in rats and pigeons on this kind of schedule. Moreover, the response is hard to extinguish; it lasts a considerable time after all reinforcement stops.

A variable-interval schedule might be used in a language laboratory where students respond to audiotaped lessons. Suppose the teacher, by operating a master console, can listen in on students' pronunciation and tell them whether they are doing well or poorly. If the teacher randomly chooses which students to listen to, he or she is creating for a particular student a variable-interval schedule. The student has no way of knowing when reinforcement (being listened to) will take place. In what looks like an effort to ensure reinforcement, the student responds at uniform rates, with no scalloping effect—even when reinforcement does not occur for a considerable period of time. The student has no way of knowing whether the situation has changed or the reinforcement interval has become much longer. So behavior continues long after it stops being appropriate for obtaining reinforcement. We find the same situation in classes where surprise quizzes are given. To be sure that they are prepared, students must study regularly—a very different study pattern from the one we found in a fixed-interval schedule. If a teacher actually stopped giving surprise quizzes after students had taken some, the students would continue to study regularly for a long time. That is, the study behavior would be extinguished only slowly.

You are probably thinking that surprise quizzes are the way to go, and certainly you could use them to keep the study behavior of your students at a high level for extended periods. But there is a danger here of creating high anxiety levels in students. Therefore, you probably should not use surprise quizzes as a general strategy.

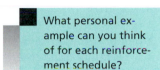
What personal example can you think of for each reinforcement schedule?

Recent Research on Reinforcement Schedules   Skinner's early research on reinforcement schedules was conducted with animals, primarily rats and pigeons, in closely controlled laboratory conditions. Such is not the case in the dynamic interchange of a normal classroom. In a recent review of research on reinforcement schedules, Lattal and Neef (1996) pointed out that the current performance of students is dependent on their past experiences—their entire history of learning, including previous reinforcement schedules. In addition, performance is also affected by the reinforcement schedules and rules that are currently in effect in their classrooms. This means that changing students' responses through operant conditioning is quite a complex job—not nearly as simple as changing the behavior of a rat or pigeon. Nevertheless, contingent management of reinforcers, the next topic we address, demonstrates that operant conditioning provides teachers with a powerful technology for achieving their goal of running an effective classroom.

Also, instructions can modify the effects of reinforcement. Finally, changes in reinforcement schedules can modify their effects.

Contingency Management

Contingent Reinforcement   The term *contingent reinforcement* means that reinforcement depends on certain conditions. When we say, "You will earn one gold star *for every spelling paper that is at least 80 percent correct*" or "I'll allow you to play with others at recess *if and only if you finish your homework at home*," we are making the reinforcement—the gold star or the play activity—contingent on a particular response—spelling correctly or finishing a homework assignment. Research has shown that the clarity of the **contingency** and the consistency with which it is applied have great effects on student behavior.

Contingent reinforcement is simply reinforcement that depends on the occurrence of a certain response. **Contingency management** is providing reinforcement under the proper circumstances and withholding reinforcement when those circumstances are not appropriate.

Kinds of Reinforcers   What kinds of stimuli or events can be used as reinforcers? Long lists of them have been collected by Sulzer-Azaroff and Mayer (1977; 1991) and R. V. Hall and M. C. Hall (1980a). The latters' list consists of dozens of verbal reinforcers (praise, encouragement), physical reinforcers (hugs, smiles), activity reinforcers (listening to records, playing), and token reinforcers (points, chips). Consumable reinforcers can also be used (cookies, candy). Just observing what children like gives us insight into what to use as a reinforcer.

Fantuzzo et al. (1991) surveyed 48 urban elementary school teachers and 98 elementary-age students using a list of 36 rewards. Teachers and students were drawn from grades 2 to 5. The rewards were grouped into four categories (activity, edible, social, and tangible) of nine items each. Results of this descriptive study showed that most teachers (92 percent) used rewards from more than one category and that edibles were used more by teachers in the lower grades. Elementary students preferred activities more than tangibles, and social rewards were preferred over activities, edibles, and tangibles. Students' reward preferences were not gender- or grade-related. Note that Vygotsky (Chapter 4, pp. 111–114) would find it unsurprising for social rewards to be preferred over all others. Teachers should remember that simple access to other children—to team sports, group work with others, play or academic activities with others—is a powerful reinforcer of school work for the very social human beings who are our students.

Premack (1965) offered the principle that an activity more preferred at time X can reinforce an activity less preferred at time X. That is, when people are free to choose their activities, a behavior with a higher probability of occurrence can be used as a reinforcer for a behavior with a lower probability of occurrence. For example, the social activity of playing on a playground with others (high preference or high probability) can be used as a reinforcer for spelling practice (low preference or low probability).

> How have you experienced the Premack principle as a student?

In the classroom, the teacher who says, "Let's play outside now, so we'll be less restless for arithmetic" or "Stop playing around, and do your chemistry" misses the point. We must use the more preferred activity to get students involved in the less preferred activity. The teacher should say, "Let's do a little math now, then we'll go outside and play" or "Let's do a little chemistry now, then everybody can play around." For one teacher we know, this technique succeeded in motivating a group of students from low-income families. The state curriculum required students to read Dickens's *David Copperfield;* the students preferred to read comic books. The teacher, intuitively applying the Premack principle, said, "For five minutes of reading *David Copperfield,* you can read twenty-five minutes of comic books." Soon the contingency was changed to ten minutes of Dickens for twenty minutes of comic books. Eventually, fifteen minutes were given for each activity. As time passed, most of the students became so engrossed in *David Copperfield* that they finished it on their own during the reading period. The students who did not become absorbed in the book were kept at a 50 percent ratio of text reading to comic book reading. It is doubtful that any of these students would have read any of Dickens without the use of contingency management.

A good way to remember Premack's principle is to remember its other name—*Grandma's rule.* For centuries Grandmas have said something like "Eat your spinach, then you can go out and play." Grandma had it right!

The Contingency Contract   Contingent reinforcement gives teachers a procedure to use to modify student behavior. The Premack principle gives us an effective guide for choosing the right reinforcer. We use both in creating **contingency contracts**—written or oral agreements with students and their parents that specify what responses must be made and what reinforcement will be earned.

From behavioral researchers (Homme et al., 1970; Kazdin, 1989; Sulzer-Azaroff & Mayer, 1991) come suggestions for teachers and parents who want to make systematic contingency contracts with students:

1. *Make contract payoff immediate.* The contract payoff (reward) should be immediate, particularly early in the learning situation.

2. *Reward successive approximations.* Initial contracts should call for and reward small and easy approximations of the wanted behavior. This is the idea of shaping behavior by successive approximations. For example, if you want a child to do cursive writing, you might begin by reinforcing any kind of pencil-and-paper contact. Next you reinforce rough approximations of the letters. Then you reinforce fairly accurate imitation of the letters. Finally you reinforce connected letters. Many teachers and parents set first tasks that are too difficult. The result is that no amount of reinforcement can induce a child to accomplish the task. Instead of asking students to do twenty mathematics problems, perhaps a teacher should assign just one or two at first. Instead of offering reinforcement to a child for cleaning an entire room, perhaps a parent should ask that socks be picked up off the floor. The idea is to find an appropriate starting point for shaping the terminal behavior, then, during later stages of training, to change the criterion for reinforcement so that the wanted behavior is approximated more and more closely.

3. *Initially, provide frequent rewards.* In the beginning the teacher should give rewards frequently, though in small amounts. Eventually the teacher may change to a less frequent schedule of reinforcement.

4. *Reward accomplishments.* The contingency contract should call for and reward accomplishment, not obedience. We do not want children to learn to do what we tell them to do in order to get a reward. What we really want to say to them, as clearly as possible, is that for

their *accomplishment* of particular tasks they will be reinforced. The learning situation should be task-oriented; it should not demand obedience to the contingency manager as a person.

5. *Make rewards contingent upon performance.* The teacher should reward the wanted performance *after* it takes place. This first-work-then-play rule is often violated. When a study hall teacher says, "You can have free reading another five minutes, but then you've got to do your homework," the free reading time (a reinforcing activity) does not occur after work on the homework. First work, then play, is a rule that, when systematically used, can help students achieve their goals.

6. *Develop a fair contract.* The contract between teacher and students must be fair. The reinforcement should have a good relationship to the effort required to obtain it. Telling a student that if she passes French you will take her to the movies does not seem fair. The effort to achieve in French is much greater than the magnitude of the reinforcer.

7. *State clearly in the contract what must be done.* The terms of the contract must be clear. Students must always know how much or how well they should perform and what they can expect to receive in return. A good way to see to it that all parties to the contract (teachers, students, and parents) understand what is expected and what will occur is to write out the contract. Use simple language and brief statements. Written versions of contingency contracts often work better than oral versions (Kazdin, 1980).

8. *Be honest about the contract.* That is, the contract must be carried out immediately, as specified.

9. *Use positive reinforcement in the contract.* The shaping of behavior through positive reinforcement is the goal. Certainly contracts can be offered to children where the responses receive negative reinforcement. For example, you can say to a child, "If you do your homework, I'll stop nagging you." This kind of negative reinforcement can work. But it is better to make a contract that takes a positive form: "If you do your homework, I'll take you to the hockey game."

> How could you use contingency contracting with an instructional or management problem?

Kazdin (1980) described a contingency contract for a child named Andrew—a contract that resulted in reduction of fighting in school behavior from nine fights per week to none over an eighteen-week period. The written contract specified what Andrew would do; what his teacher, Mrs. Harris, would do; and what Andrew's parents would do if he could go through a school day without a fight. The behavior was clearly described, and the reinforcers were clearly specified. And the teacher, parents, and Andrew all signed the contract. The contract was never thought of as a legally binding document; it was a commitment of good will among parties who cared about one another. Seven months after the end of the contract, Andrew was still doing well. A sample contract of this kind is shown in Figure 6.6.

OFFICIAL CONTRACT

The contract is between ___Van Thu Hue_____ (student)

and ___Ms. Lepeto_____ (teacher, ~~friend, other~~)

Date: from ___October 1, 1998___ to ___November 15, 1998___

(this date)   (contract expiration)

Following are the terms of the contract:

___Van Thu Hue___ (student) will ___Not engage in any physical fighting on school grounds. All disputes will be verbal. Anger will be discussed with Ms. Lepeto.___

___Ms. Lepeto___ (teacher, ~~friend, other~~) will ___provide to Van Thu Hue 4 movie tickets, the job of school messenger for 1 month, and a chance to work in the school shop during free time.___

When this contract is completed, the contractee will be able to ___control his temper with the other students, respond verbally instead of physically to other students' behavior, discuss freely the feelings of anger generated at school and alternatives to violence.___

___Van Thu Hue___
Contractee

___Virginia Lepeto___
Contractor

___Ho Thu Hue, brother___
Witness

This contract may be terminated by agreement of parties signing this contract. New contract(s) may be negotiated by the same parties.

OFFICIAL SEAL

FIGURE 6.6

Sample contract

Adapted from Achieving Educational Excellence *by B. Sulzer-Azaroff and G. R. Mayer, copyright © 1994 by B. Sulzer-Azaroff and G. R. Mayer. Published by Western Image, P.O. Box 427, San Marcos, CA 92079-0427. Reprinted by permission of the authors.*

The Elimination of Responses

In this section, we talk about several ways to eliminate unwanted responses. Learning how *not* to behave can be just as important as learning how *to* behave.

Extinction   The process by which the rate of occurrence of a response decreases as a result of nonreinforcement is called **extinction.** Being called on reinforces a student's volunteering to recite. The student has acquired the habit of frequent volunteering because, over time, she has been reinforced for this response. But what if she is no longer called on when she volunteers? Her volunteering behavior would be extinguished; that is, it would become less and less frequent, until the behavior returned to its prereinforcement frequency, or operant level.

Extinction is the opposite of response acquisition. It is the weakening of a response by nonreinforcement, just as acquisition is the strengthening of a response by reinforcement. Usually when nonreinforcement begins, there is a temporary increase in the rate and intensity of the response. But soon the rate begins to decline until, if the nonreinforcement continues, the rate of response becomes very low or even zero.

How quickly extinction occurs depends on whether the previous reinforcement has been continuous or intermittent. Again, extinction occurs more slowly after a history of intermittent reinforcement than it does after continuous reinforcement, other things being equal. Among the "other things" would be the amount of positive reinforcement given after each response and the total number of reinforcements received before the beginning of the extinction process.

Examples of acquisition and extinction can be found in many operant-conditioning studies. To show that an increase in the frequency of a behavior is causally related to the reinforcement procedures used, experimenters often include an extinction period in their research design. If during the extinction period the behavior decreases in frequency, then increases again during a period of reinforcement, the evidence is convincing that the behavior changes are causally related to changes in the reinforcement contingencies.

When group contingencies are used, individual members often take on roles to see to it that the group succeeds. For example, members can be quite supportive—reinforcing and helping one another to achieve the reinforcement. But they can also threaten those who endanger the group's chances at reinforcement (Sulzer-Azaroff & Mayer, 1991). The latter side effect does not occur often (Sulzer-Azaroff, 1981), but you should watch for it and eliminate it when you try to shape the behavior of groups.

Reinforcement of Other Behavior and of Low Response Rates   Although it may seem contradictory, reinforcement can be used to reduce or eliminate behavior (Kazdin, 1989). The technique of *differential reinforcement of other behavior* (DRO) requires reinforcement of all kinds of behavior *except* the one you want to suppress or eliminate. If you want to eliminate a student's talking out of turn, you would reinforce every behavior you can that is incompatible with that behavior. You

How could you use a group contingency for students you plan to teach?

Unintentional Reinforcement

Something to watch for when you are trying to shape the behavior of an individual student or a group is **unintentional reinforcement.** Many disruptive classroom behaviors—students getting out of their seats, talking out of turn, pencil tapping—are unintentionally reinforced by a teacher's attention. Sending a student to the principal or yelling at him can have the same effect as praising him, if he is looking for your attention. This is why it seems to teachers that the more they reprimand a student for not raising her hand when she wants to talk, the more she seems to speak without permission.

Apply this principle to your own experiences in two ways. First, think about whether you have ever experienced such unintentional reinforcement yourself. What were the circumstances? What behavior was unintentionally reinforced? How might the other person have achieved his or her goal more effectively with you?

Now think about the class you will be teaching. In addition to the behaviors listed in the text, what student actions do you think you might unintentionally reinforce? How do you think you would wind up doing so?

Once you have thought about all this, react to the following statement:

To extinguish a response, you often do better to ignore it. If attention is the positive reinforcer that maintains the behavior of, say, speaking out of turn, ignoring the behavior will reduce its frequency.

Under what circumstances would ignoring behavior *not* be a good idea? Even when it is appropriate, what might be the greatest challenges to you as a classroom manager in doing so?

might, through attention, reinforce the student when she is writing or staring into space and not talking at all, or reading or doing workbook problems. Over time the unwanted behavior should be reduced or even eliminated.

Differential reinforcement of low rates of responding (DRL) also can reduce or eliminate unwanted behavior. This is the reinforcement of any reduction in unwanted behavior. So when a student who talks too much begins to talk less, using DRL reinforces the reduction in talking. This is a bit like the process of shaping behavior through successive approximations, but instead of trying to use reinforcement to increase a response it is used to help decrease a response.

What is so appealing about DRO and DRL procedures is that they are positive ways of suppressing or eliminating unwanted behavior. Extinction, DRO, and DRL are preferable to punishment, the topic we examine next.

Punishment Another way to eliminate a response is to punish the student when the response occurs. In operant conditioning, punishment takes the form of either presentation punishment or removal punish-

What are some examples of DRO or DRL schedules you have observed?

ment. In either case, punishment results in a decrease in the behavior. Look again at Figure 6.4, which shows the relationship of reinforcement and punishment to stimulus events and their value. Let us examine both kinds of punishment.

Presentation Punishment Presentation punishment is the giving of something of negative value after an unwanted response. Receiving an F on a composition or being suspended from school for fighting are punishments intended to decrease the frequency of a particular response.

Does punishment work? Most recent research shows that, under appropriate conditions, particularly when intense punishment is applied, behavior can be suppressed permanently (Matson & DiLorenzo, 1984). Can punishment reduce behavior? "A definitely affirmative answer may be given" (Azrin & Holz, 1966, p. 426). As Johnston (1972) summarized the evidence, other ways of reducing the frequency of behavior (for example, extinction, DRO, and DRL) have less rapid and enduring effects than punishment properly used.

In some research with human beings, punishment has simply not been severe enough to reduce behavior. In other cases it has failed because, as we noted above, it has satisfied needs for attention, paradoxically serving as a reinforcer. Teachers who pay attention to students only when they misbehave and then provide what they think is punishment may actually be reinforcing rather than punishing.

Although punishment can be effective, is it a good thing? The answer here depends on a variety of factors. If the behavior to be suppressed is dangerous or undesirable enough, then punishment as a way of eliminating that behavior is a good thing. For example, teachers appear to be justified in punishing children who run out of the playground and into the street, continuously violate the rules necessary for orderly classroom work, misuse power tools in shop, bully weaker students, try dangerous activities in the gym, or destroy school property.

A controversy has arisen among people concerned, as either parents or therapists, with retarded or autistic children. Some such children bang their heads in violent, constant, and self-injurious ways. They may hit themselves hundreds or thousands of times per day, injuring their nerves and eyes, and suffering bruises, open wounds, and even detached retinas leading to blindness.

Research showed that 60 percent of such people were significantly improved by means of various kinds of reinforcement, positive or negative. But what about the other 40 percent? Alternatives for them were to (1) permit the self-injury to continue, (2) use heavy doses of tranquilizing drugs, (3) use physical restraints, hand and foot, all day, or (4) use unpleasant, but not painful or damaging, aversive procedures (Rimland, 1990).

One example of the fourth alternative is the Self-Injurious Behavior Inhibiting System (SIBIS). This system uses an electrical shock that is brief and uncomfortable (like a hard pinch), but mild and nondamaging. It works through a device attached to the head. In one study of five cases of head banging, SIBIS greatly helped four with only a few shocks totaling about 2–3 seconds; the fifth case required 3,000 stimulations before reducing head banging to near-zero levels (Linscheid et al., 1990).

Is such use of presentation punishment, in the form of SIBIS, justifiable? Some people say no; only positive or negative reinforcement or removal punishment (see the next section) is justifiable. Others say that when nothing else has been found effective, SIBIS should be used, but only with the consent of the parents or guardians, and only when carefully monitored.

In any case, the example of SIBIS clarifies the issue of punishment. Many psychologists—including B. F. Skinner—who emphasize the desirability of positive approaches nonetheless accept the justifiability of punishment, or "aversive treatments," under such circumstances, namely, when they are "brief and harmless stimuli, made precisely contingent on self-destructive or other excessive behavior, [which] suppress the behavior and leave the children free to develop in other ways . . ." (Skinner, 1987). But in using punishment to suppress behaviors, the punisher (that is, the parent or teacher) can acquire negative stimulus properties. Children who claim to hate their parents and teachers are demonstrating a common response to negatively valued stimulus objects. Another problem here is **stimulus generalization,** whereby the same response is made to stimuli associated with the stimulus to which someone was first conditioned. So a child may extend an intense dislike of the teacher to the teacher's subject matter or to school itself. Then too we have the problem of *avoidance*—the cheating, truancy, lying, sneaking, and hiding that students do to avoid the punishment that goes along with being wrong, failing, misbehaving, or getting caught. All in all, punishment is a weapon that can be as risky for the teacher as it is distasteful to the student.

How should teachers use punishment then? Research indicates that punishment is most effective when

- it is presented immediately after a response.
- it cannot be escaped.
- it is only as intense as necessary.
- an alternative and desirable response is available to the student.

When do you see yourself using presentation punishment in the classroom?

If possible, instead of punishing, warn the student. But if a warning does not suppress the behavior and if nothing positive works, follow the behavior with a punishment. Repeated often enough, this procedure will make the warning effective, eliminating the need for continual punishment. Presentation punishment can be effective, but it must be used carefully to do more good than harm. And because students are so sensitive about it, you must be prepared to use punishment fairly. *All* students who deserve punishment must receive the same degree and type of punishment. Students are quick to spot favoritism and discrimination. Fairness is one of the characteristics of teachers that students prize most.

Removal Punishment Another kind of punishment is generally more acceptable in school settings. As shown in Figure 6.4, removal punishment consists of taking away something of positive value. Here we discuss two kinds of removal punishment: time-out and response cost.

How might you use time-out?

■ **Time-out** is a procedure in which a teacher deprives students of the opportunity to obtain reinforcement if they misbehave (R. V. Hall & M. C. Hall, 1980b). We can deprive a student of an opportunity to see a movie, watch a television program, work on a project in shop, participate in games during gym period, or have some other kind of fun. This kind of punishment often seems more acceptable because it does not force us to impose negative stimuli or events—we simply remove the student from positive ones. Also, physical punishment (presentation punishment) violates present-day ideas about good teacher behavior and makes the teacher a model of aggressiveness.

What particular reinforcers might you remove in your classroom?

■ **Response cost** is another way to use removal punishment. Response cost is the contingent removal of particular reinforcers. The 15-yard penalty in a football game for roughing the passer is an example of a response cost. Because of an inappropriate behavior, some of the reinforcement previously attained is removed, and is unlike presentation punishment, which presents an aversive event for an inappropriate behavior. If the penalty for jaywalking were the shame of a day in jail, it would be an example of presentation punishment—the giving of something of negative value. But if the penalty for jaywalking were a $50.00 fine, it would be an example of response cost—the removal or withdrawal of something of value already earned, a type of removal punishment.

In school, if teachers take away tokens or free time a student has already earned when he or she misbehaves, they are using response cost to control unwanted behavior. For example, Rappaport, Murphy, and Bailey (1982) studied two boys who were being given methylphenidate (Ritalin) to control their hyperactivity. When the researchers chose instead to use behavior-modification procedures, they obtained both increased attention to academic tasks and increased rates of completion of academic tasks by taking away free time from the boys when they did not do their academic work. This response-cost procedure was far more effective than the drug in controlling hyperactivity. Besides, teaching children to depend on drugs to control their behavior cannot be a good practice, common though it is. Behavior modification using operant conditioning often proves superior to drugs in the control of behavior, and it must be considered ethically superior as well. Nonetheless, drug use is still widespread. A survey of Wisconsin teachers (Runnheim et al., 1996) showed 1,300 students (26% of all the students with emotional and behavior disorders) were receiving medication. The controversy over using medication versus psychological alternatives such as behavior modification is passionately contested by advocates for each side (Barabasz & Barabasz, 1996).

Reasoning as an Alternative to Punishment   What about reasoning? Can't we reason with a student who is misbehaving? The answer is yes. Always try rational explanations for behavior. However, as Walters and Grusec (1977, p. 207) asserted, "[A teacher] who relied solely on reasoning as a disciplinary technique would not be very successful in obtaining response suppression. Reasoning becomes effective only when it is supported by a history of punishment."

So what do you do if reasoning and a given punishment do not work? If you find you are using or want to use punishment a lot, you should examine the whole teaching-learning situation. What is causing the unwanted behavior? Is the work too difficult, lasting too long? Is it boring or irrelevant to the student's interests and needs? Are you meeting the student's need for activity? Frequent use of punishment is a symptom of something wrong in your approaches and methods or in the school situation as a whole. The challenge for you as an educator is to discover and correct the problem to reduce the need for punishment.

Ethical Issues and Limits of the Theory

Educational psychologists know that people learn through operant conditioning. But is the process ethical? Some people charge that conditioning techniques are manipulative and controlling. Others insist that it is the teacher's function to arrange and manipulate the environment to bring about learning.

For many kinds of learning, objections to the use of conditioning methods seem unjustified. When a child is cured through conditioning procedures of bed wetting, excessive withdrawal, fighting in nursery school, or stuttering, hardly anyone objects that the child's behavior has been manipulated. When conditioning techniques are used to reduce a child's hyperactivity so that he stays in his seat longer and learns more, almost everyone would agree that the techniques are justified means toward a proper end. But when the techniques are misused—say, to reduce the normal activity levels of children because they make the teacher "nervous"—there is valid reason for complaint.

The greatest objection to conditioning techniques comes when they are used to change attitudes, values, beliefs, and knowledge that should be based on rational, intellectual processes. The process by which a person becomes either liberal or conservative should stem from logic applied to relevant and correct information, not operant conditioning. We shudder at the thought of a person's political views being "shaped" by conditioning processes that the individual is not aware of and cannot control. Such processes smack of brainwashing. Unwanted behavior should not be taught by any method, conditioning or others. And even certain wanted behaviors should not be fostered through conditioning processes. Why? What criteria do we use to make decisions here?

One criterion is that whenever a behavior or attitude can in principle be learned through rational processes, these processes should be used. Certainly teachers can condition children to say, "One of the angles in a right triangle equals ninety degrees" or "Democracy is the best system of government." But instead we should present information and instruction that leads children to understand the defining characteristics of right triangles and what democracy means. These teaching and learning processes, sometimes called *reflective thinking*, are based on the assumptions that human beings are rational and that it is immoral to treat them irrationally. To be moral, the teacher must engage a student's reason; a simple change in behavior is not enough. The change must be brought about intentionally on the part of both teacher and student, and it must be based on rational processes. By this model, "the teacher's prime task is to ensure that when a change occurs in the beliefs or behavior of the students, it occurs for reasons which the student himself accepts" (Nuthall & Snook, 1973, p. 66). Teaching, then, is different from training and conditioning, which focus on performance, not belief and rational action. We do not want students to be patriotic, altruistic, and democratic because they have been conditioned to be so. We want them to arrive at these objectives by considering the issues and reflecting on their meaning.

A second criterion for determining when the ends do not justify conditioning procedures is the degree to which students are aware of the procedures. To be ethical, conditioning must have student cooperation in and awareness of its use to change behavior. (In many instances, effective conditioning actually requires students' willing cooperation.) Of course we assume here that students are capable of understanding conditioning procedures. For young children or those who are mentally retarded, others must decide on the ethics of using conditioning methods.

Behavioral and humanistic concerns can be merged (Thoresen, 1972). Operant techniques are being used to develop self-regulatory mechanisms in people whose freedom of choice has been limited by self-impairing behavior. Bad "habits" that are eliminated through conditioning procedures free people to participate in society more fully. Furthermore, when individuals are fully aware of the procedures being used on them they can learn to apply the procedures to themselves. That is, they can learn to self-reinforce and self-punish. So conditioning procedures can indeed be applied in humanistic ways—ways that respect human welfare, values, and dignity.

A third criterion for some is that conditioning methods should rely on intrinsic rewards and incentives. Rewards are *intrinsic* when they arise in a way that is naturally a part of the learning activity itself. If a student gets the right answer to an arithmetic problem, the intrinsic reward is a feeling of satisfaction at having applied the principles of arithmetic correctly. Many educators argue that intrinsic rewards are better than extrinsic rewards (praise, gold stars, money, high grades) and that extrinsic rewards debase learning. But most proponents of conditioning believe that intrinsic rewards are often inaccessible to students in the early stages of the learning process. Intrinsic rewards do not occur simply because, in many situations, learners cannot make the appropriate response. Should these students go unreinforced? Or should teachers give them an extrinsic reinforcer that will induce them to continue responding, thereby changing their responses in the wanted ways? The answer here depends on what works. Certainly we should not insist on intrinsic reinforcement to the point where students experience prolonged frustration and failure. If intrinsic reinforcers work, fine. If not,

What do you think? Is positive extrinsic reinforcement like bribery?

use extrinsic rewards. (But intrinsic and extrinsic rewards have different motivational effects, as discussed in Chapter 8, pp. 333–336.)

Some educators charge that the use of positive extrinsic reinforcers is a form of bribery. But bribery means using rewards to get a person to do something dishonest or unfair. When positive extrinsic reinforcement is used to promote honest and wanted behavior, with the student's awareness and cooperation, it cannot be considered bribery, anymore than are wages earned for an honest day's work.

Another objection to operant conditioning is that it makes students dependent on others, or subverts their independence. But students can learn to reinforce themselves, to become independent of an external agent. They can also be weaned away from dependence on reinforcers of any given kind (for example, approval by the teacher) by having different reinforcers (approval by their peers) substituted. Finally, students can learn to respond on a very low ratio of reinforcers to responses.

In short, although the issues are complex and not all educators and psychologists agree, we believe that conditioning procedures can be used ethically in educational settings. These procedures offer teachers effective and humane methods for changing student behavior in desirable ways.

Having said this, however, we must add that the operant-conditioning model of learning has distinct limitations. With its focus on how the environment affects the behavior emitted, and its concern with increasing, eliminating, shaping, and improving behavior, this model assumes that no learning takes place without reinforcement or punishment. Can that be true? Don't people learn how to act at a restaurant, airport, hockey game, or wedding without first emitting behavior and then getting reinforced or punished? Didn't you learn to drive a car more by watching other people than by having your behavior "shaped"? How do operant conditioning theorists explain such facts? They try, but we think their explanations are inadequate.

Social Learning Theory

How Learning Occurs through Observation

We also learn from observing others in our social world. We acquire knowledge, skills, attitudes, and culturally appropriate behavior more efficiently and with fewer mistakes when we observe the behaviors and the consequences of those behaviors for parents, friends, and teachers.

If you received a doll or a baseball bat as a child, you probably held it by the correct end, and handled it the way mothers handle babies or baseball players swing bats, right from the beginning. When you first learned to drive a car, most likely you knew where and how to sit and, by observing your instructor, what you had to do to start the car and drive. If you ever go to a formal dinner, replete with extra spoons, forks, and glasses, you will probably wait until some knowledgeable person begins to eat and use that person's behavior to guide your own. These are examples of how we depend on observational learning. Behavior **models**—mothers, baseball players, drivers, people with social graces— guide our behavior. And because our observations change our behavior, we learn through them.

In a classic study, Bandura (1963) illustrated the impact of and conditions for observational learning. He assigned nursery school children to one of five treatments. In treatment 1, children watched a human adult model who physically and verbally attacked a large, inflated soft-plastic doll, called a "Bobo" doll. In treatment 2, children saw a film of the same event. In treatment 3, children saw a cartoon character carrying out the same aggressive actions. The children in treatment 4—the control group—had none of these experiences. Those in treatment 5 saw a human model of subdued temperament, one who was inhibited and nonaggressive toward the Bobo doll. After exposure to one of these five treatments, each child was left alone for a few minutes in a room with the Bobo doll. Through a one-way mirror, observers counted each child's aggressive verbal and physical acts. Figure 6.7 shows the mean number of aggressive responses exhibited by the children in the various treatments. All groups that saw an aggressive model made more aggressive responses than did the control group. The group that saw the inhibited, nonaggressive model made fewer aggressive responses than did the control group. Clearly, observing the model affected behavior.

This and other studies (Bandura, 1969) have demonstrated that exposure to a model can affect a person's behavior in at least three ways: (1) learning new behavior, (2) facilitating already learned behavior, and (3) inhibiting or disinhibiting already learned behavior.

1. *Learning new behavior.* An observer can learn new behavior from a model. In the Bandura study, the children often said things like "Pow" or "Sock 'em," repeating verbatim the aggressive model's unusual language, as they hit the Bobo doll.

What novel behaviors have you recently acquired by observing a model?

FIGURE 6.7

Frequency of aggressive responses by control children and children exposed to aggressive and inhibited models

From A. Bandura, "The Role of Imitation in Personality Development," reprinted by permission from Journal of Nursery Education, *vol. 18, no. 3 (April 1963): pp. 207–215. Copyright © 1963, National Association for the Education of Young Children, 1834 Connecticut Ave., N.W., Washington, D.C. 20009.*

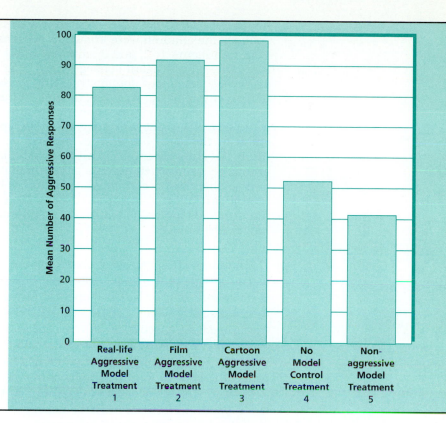

What behavior have you inhibited or disinhibited after viewing consequences to a model?

2. Facilitating already learned behavior. A model can also facilitate the expression of behavior that already exists in the learner's response repertoire. When the model's behavior resembles behavior the learner has previously mastered, the model's performance may simply elicit a previously learned response. For example, aggressive responses appeared in the control group (treatment 4) when these children were confronted with the large, air-filled Bobo doll that seemed to beg to be pushed and pounded. Clearly these aggressive responses were well established and of high frequency. The even higher frequency of aggressive responses by children in treatments 1, 2, and 3 shows that a model, in addition to teaching new behaviors, can elicit more of the behavior that learners already have in their repertoire. These behaviors might not have been performed as frequently had not the model been observed.

3. Inhibiting or disinhibiting already learned behavior. Exposure to a model can inhibit or disinhibit an observer's responses. To *inhibit* is to restrain a response or make it less frequent; to *disinhibit* is to free from restraint and allow a response to occur. Inhibitory and disinhibitory effects are most pronounced when an observer sees the consequences of a model's actions. The model's punishment or reinforcement for the behavior greatly affects the observer's own activities. A comparison of the treatment-5 group with the control group in Figure 6.7 shows that models can inhibit responses. Group 5 made fewer aggressive responses than the control group. Observing the model treating the Bobo doll nicely apparently inhibited the aggressive responses the children were known to possess.

In treatments 1, 2, and 3, children watched aggressive behavior that had no unpleasant consequences. The increased frequency of aggressive responses demonstrated by these children (in comparison to the control group) was due, at least in part, to *disinhibition*. The absence of any constraints apparently removed inhibitions. So it appears that well-established aggressive behaviors are partially held in check by the many constraints imposed by the environment. A particularly forceful constraint on aggressive behavior is the consequence of that behavior when parents or teachers are present. Usually parents and teachers act to extinguish this kind of behavior. When these constraints are absent, as appeared to be the case when the model was not punished for his activities, the inhibitions against aggressive behavior are removed.

One interesting aspect of observational learning is that it is no-trial learning. That is, a response does not have to be made by the learner as is necessary in classical and operant forms of learning. The most likely mechanism by which people acquire behavior through observation is the immediate association of the model's behavior with (1) a cognitive event, say, a sensory event (a visual coding of model, doll, and hitting behavior, for example) or (2) a symbolic response (a verbal coding of the propositions "doll = hitting behavior = okay to do"). The observer records and stores the sensory event or symbolic response at the time of the model's performance. These sensory events or responses serve as cues for later performance, when the learner is called on to make an overt response.

In addition, reward or punishment of behavior can be vicarious, i.e., observed when it is received by another person. Vicariously experienced consequences influence us because we have the ability to mentally substitute ourselves for someone else, experiencing what they experience, which we often do when we see what consequences occur as a function of a model's behavior. But whether through direct or vicarious experience, reward and punishment markedly affect the *performance* of behavior; they do not seem to affect the *acquisition* of behavior. Complex behavior repertoires can be acquired by simply observing another person. The learner need only pay attention to the model's activities—and the model must be credible—but beyond these variables, no others need be offered to account for observational learning.

Studies of observational learning demonstrate that people often learn to do what they see others doing. So teachers need to provide students with models of wanted behavior and reduce their exposure to models of unwanted behavior. Three sources of the latter appear to be television, movies, and video games. Students in recent years have been exposed to many more aggressive and violent models than they were a few decades ago. We look at how this exposure is affecting students' behavior later in this chapter. Now, however, let us see how observational learning in social situations goes on.

A Social-Learning Analysis of Observational Learning

How is observational learning—this basic and pervasive form of learning—viewed from a social-learning perspective? The theory states that there are four phases of learning from models: an attentional phase, a retention phase, a reproduction phase, and a motivational phase (see Figure 6.8).

Attentional Phase Without attention, there can be no learning. Attention is a necessary condition of observational learning in social settings. Research shows that people pay attention to models with high status, high competence, and expertise—attributes that teachers are often thought to have (thank goodness!). Consequently, students are likely to pay attention when a teacher solves a two-column addition problem, decodes a word phonetically, demonstrates a field hockey pass, lists the steps required to identify a wildflower, or dissects a frog. A good deal of what students learn in school they learn by watching their teachers. But more generally, young people also learn in churches, synagogues, and mosques; in shopping malls and at sporting events; and at restaurants and family parties—through what is called *legitimate peripheral participation* (Rogoff, 1990). That is, just by hanging around and taking it all in, both in and outside of school, the young learn complex social behavior.

Students' own characteristics—their dependency needs, self-esteem, and perceptions of their own competence—determine to some extent the likelihood of their paying attention to a model. But often overriding the model's attributes and the students' characteristics as determiners of attending are the incentives for attending (Bandura, 1969; 1977; 1986b). Teachers control rewards and punishments for attending or nonattending. When a teacher says, "This will be on the test," and proceeds to demonstrate how to convert Fahrenheit to Celsius and vice versa, he or she is manipulating the incentives for attention. Making the incentives obvious can override other factors that might lessen attending.

Finally, the distinctiveness, rate, and complexity of the stimuli to be attended to affect whether or not attentiveness can be maintained. Teachers who have their students' attention can make imitation easier by clearly drawing attention to important clues. (For example, "Now notice how I am changing the sign, and taking the numerator and denominator of this fraction and reversing them.") The models' identification of im-

> How has attention played a part in your acquisition of novel behaviors?

FIGURE 6.8

Analysis of observational learning

Adapted from Albert Bandura, Social Learning Theory. © 1977. Used by permission of Prentice-Hall, Inc., Englewood Cliffs, New Jersey.

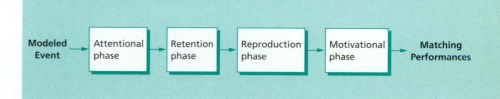

Modeled Event → Attentional phase → Retention phase → Reproduction phase → Motivational phase → Matching Performances

portant aspects of the instruction can greatly facilitate imitative learning. So can repetition. This kind of help is especially important when working with very young children or those with retardation or learning disabilities, who have limited capacity for attention.

Retention Phase   Observational learning takes place by contiguity. The two contiguous events that are necessary are (1) attention to the model's performance and (2) the representation of that performance in the learner's memory. If someone is motivated to learn while observing the dismantling of an engine in automobile shop, the solving of a problem in algebra, or the attempt to figure out how to obtain food in the cafeteria, he or she must represent in memory what is observed. Verbal or visual **mnemonics** (memory aids) and schemata (the mental structures that allow people to learn) must be developed by the observer at the same time that the observer watches how a model takes apart an engine, divides polynomials, or obtains food. These mnemonics and schemata are recalled at a later time, when newly learned behavior is enacted.

We retain material to be learned better when we rehearse it overtly ("All together now, the four phases of observational learning are _____, _____, _____, and _____"). But rehearsal need not always be overt. For example, student teachers preparing their first lesson or lesson segment often use covert rehearsal to practice what they have learned through observation.

> How have contiguity and rehearsal enabled you to acquire a novel behavior?

Reproduction Phase   In this phase of learning from models, the verbal or visual codes in memory guide the actual performance of the newly acquired behavior. Observational learning is most accurate when overt enactment follows mental rehearsal.

A study by Schunk (1981), in which long division was taught to children who had difficulties in learning mathematics, illustrates this point. Modeling was used during instruction and again during the reproduction phase if students made any errors. Compared with a group that had no exposure to models during instruction, the students who learned from models showed greatly improved achievement. They also showed increased persistence and self-confidence when tackling long-division problems.

Note here the importance of corrective feedback for shaping wanted behavior. Knowledge of results—simple feedback—has a strong effect on subsequent behavior. Letting learners know quickly about incorrect or inappropriate responses—before they develop bad habits—is sound instructional practice. This kind of corrective feedback is not punishment. It is crucial in the development of skilled performance. When we tell students to hold their pencils tighter when they write, to remember to count the number of lines in their sonnets, or to spring higher off the board when they dive, we are giving them helpful information.

Motivational Phase   Behavior acquired by observing others is enacted if it is reinforcing to do so. If it is punishing to perform the behavior, it does not usually occur. In this sense, social-learning theory and operant con-

Overt enactment—matching the model—is most important when body-position cues must be learned.
(© Elizabeth Crews)

ditioning are alike. Both recognize how reinforcement and punishment can shape and maintain behavior. But in observational learning, reinforcement and punishment are seen as affecting the learner's *motivation* to perform; they do not account for the learning itself. Moreover, the social-learning view recognizes the importance of covert cognitive activity, not just overt behavior. So the social-learning theorist believes that vicarious reinforcement and punishment—observing the consequences of the behavior of others—can also shape and maintain behavior. When an older sibling is praised for receiving a good report card or sent away from the dinner table for using a vulgar word, the younger ones are often affected as much as if they themselves were being reinforced or punished.

Bandura's experiments showed that learning can occur without any overt responding by the learner. Observing and coding behavior in memory are sufficient to ensure its being learned. The learner's overt performance of what has been learned may occur only when the appropriate environment is encountered later. In social-learning theory, the positive or negative consequences of behavior, then, are not factors in *learning*, as claimed by adherents of operant-conditioning theory, but motivators of *performance*.

One other pair of factors enters into the motivation to perform activities learned from models: self-reinforcement and self-punishment. As we behave, we judge ourselves. In this way we come to regulate our own behavior. (We talk more about this topic later in this chapter.)

POLICY, RESEARCH, AND PRACTICE

Are Systematic Training Programs an Effective Way to Change the Imitation of Aggressive Behaviors Modeled by the Media?

WHAT THE RESEARCH TELLS US

Intuitive understanding of the distinction between performance and learning, and the effects of vicarious reinforcement and punishment, has led many parents and teachers to worry about violence on television and in the movies. Concern about violence began in the earliest days of television. As one author (Levine, 1996) concluded,

> The debate is over.
> Violence on television and the movies is damaging to children. Forty years of research conclude that repeated exposure to high levels of media violence teaches some children and adolescents to settle interpersonal differences with violence, while teaching many more to be indifferent to this solution [violence]. Under the media's tutelage children and adolescents are using violence as a first, not a last, resort to conflict. (p. 3)

Similarly, a leading researcher on television and violence testified before a U.S. Senate Committee as follows:

> There can no longer be any doubt that heavy exposure to violence is one of the causes of aggressive behavior, crime and violence in society. The evidence comes from both the laboratory and real-life studies. Television violence affects youngsters of all ages, of both genders, at all socio-economic levels and all levels of intelligence. The effect is not limited to children who are aleady disposed to being aggressive and is not restricted to this country. (Eron, 1992)

So viewing televised violence and committing aggressive acts are positively correlated in children (Levine, 1996). And experiments show that exposure of some groups to televised violence increases aggressiveness over that of control groups. To explain these clear findings, researchers have suggested, among other processes, observational learning.

Can an instructional program counteract the affects of viewing aggressive media models? The results of a two-year study by Huesmann et al. (1983) indicate that this is possible. Their study identified 169 primary-level (grades 1 and 3) students who frequently viewed violent TV shows. Students were randomly assigned to one of two groups, an instructional treatment and a control group. Some components of the instructional program were "(a) television violence is an unrealistic portrayal of the real world, (b) aggressive behaviors are not as acceptable in the real world as they appear on television, and (c) one should not behave like the aggressive characters seen on TV" (p. 901). Control-group students did not receive the instructional program. At the end of the two-year program, the instructional-treatment group's students' viewing of violence remained unchanged. However, they identified less with violent TV characters, and peer nominations reported that they behaved less aggressively.

WHAT THIS MEANS FOR YOU AS A TEACHER

The social-learning perspective makes it sensible to keep children away from certain films, TV programs, and video games. Parents and teachers should insist that producers end their stories for young people with the villain paying for the crime. Nevertheless, media violence is still pervasive in American culture. Violence enacted by attractive heroes and villains continues to go unpunished, and many parents seem unconcerned that their children are exposed to these shows and games. Keep in mind that from kindergarten through the twelfth grade, the typical student spends about twelve thousand hours in front of a TV set alone, and that a large percentage actually spends over 20,000 hours viewing TV. The medium is "teaching," and the viewer is "learning."

These are facts over which teachers have little control. However, instructional programs similar to those of Huesmann et al. can provide teachers with strategies to help reduce imitation by children and adolescents of aggressive behaviors portrayed in electronic media. So teachers should spend some of their time reminding students that the entertainment media are not reality, that some behaviors seen there are not acceptable in real life, and that aggression is simply not tolerated. Teachers should highlight their own modeling of prosocial strategies for handling conflict and contrast them with the strategies portrayed in movies, television, and video games.

A Note on Cognition

Social learning is affected by how the learner understands the learning event. Learners need sensible reasons to build clear conceptions about what they are doing and why. Modeling is not effective if the observer's beliefs, attitudes, sense of efficacy (competence to learn), and sense of purpose are not congruent with the learning task. In both operant conditioning and social-learning theory, the mechanisms by which people learn are not beyond cognitive control. We exert personal control through reflective self-consciousness. Change in behavior of any lasting kind always means that a change in cognition has taken place. Students think about what they do and what we want them to do, and those thoughts affect what the students do. The idea that the processes of operant conditioning and social learning are mechanical is erroneous. Thoughts are always influencing actions, and actions are always influencing thoughts (Bandura, 1986a; 1986b).

The Teacher and Modeling

A primary definition of teaching is "to show." So we should think about how to show, demonstrate, or model so that we optimize conditions for our students' learning. We often worry more about what we teach than how we teach. But by using information about observational learning, you can do a better job of teaching skills (Schunk, 1996; Zimmerman, 1990; Zimmerman & Schunk, 1989; Zimmerman & Kleefeld, 1977). For example, in one application of social-learning theory, the researchers studied ways of teaching young children to order objects from longest to shortest. One group of teachers read about the instructional task, examined the materials to be used for instruction, and saw a sample of the test items to be used to evaluate how well the children had learned. A second group received the same background information as the first plus simple instructions on how to model when teaching: See that the child is attending, describe each action as you do it, teach memory aids to help learners code activity (for example, "See if the blocks go down in size like stairs"), use the same procedure each time you order a scrambled array of objects, have the child judge his or her performance, and so on.

The children were divided into three groups. Group 1 was taught individually by the first group of teachers and group 2 by the second group of teachers. The third group of children, not taught at all, served as the control group. All children were pretested and posttested on two types of items: judgment items (Is this group of objects in order from longest to shortest?) and ordering items (Can you put these objects in order from the longest to the shortest?). The results showed clearly that teachers who do not know much about how people learn from models do not produce much learning in the children they teach. The students of the untrained teachers showed less learning in judgment items and only slightly better learning in ordering items than did the children who received no instruction at all. The teachers trained in modeling, however, had a great effect on student learning on both judgment and ordering items.

From teachers' helping some students, through modeling or any other communications, classmates develop attitudes toward those students. Indeed, a teacher's help can make classmates think less of the students being helped. This effect showed up in an experiment by Graham and Barker (1990). They showed videotapes of two boys working on math problems, one helped by his teacher or classmates, the other one not. Viewers subsequently rated the helped boy as lower in ability than the nonhelped boy. So a teacher's help may tell classmates that helped pupils are low in ability. Similarly, when children fail on a task, sympathy can tell them that the teacher regards them as having low ability, whereas anger can indicate that the children should try harder.

The same kinds of learning from observation can take place when students observe how their classmates behave toward other students. In cooperative learning (discussed in Chapter 10), students help one another. And being helped makes students be perceived by other students—and by themselves—as having lower ability. These "side effects" of well-intentioned behaviors of the teacher or classmates—praise, minimal criticism, helping, and sympathizing—are phenomena teachers should be aware of.

Self-Regulation of Behavior and Its Processes

Some of the things we do in life are not very important to us, so they do not usually lead to much self-reinforcement or self-punishment. But when the things we do really matter to us, we tend to appraise the behavior that is of interest to us. For example, if someone is concerned about the food he eats, he might evaluate his activities and chastise himself for going to a fast-food restaurant. This self-punishment or self-reinforcement, like direct or vicariously experienced punishment and reinforcement, affects our performance. By means of our cognitive activity and the management of our own environment, we can motivate ourselves through self-generated reward and punishment. In this way we can regulate our own behavior.

Bandura (1978) analyzed the learning of self-regulation, breaking it into three covert processes: (1) We observe our own performance in terms of its quantity, quality, originality, rate, and so on. (2) We judge our performance as to how well we did against our personal standards. (3) We determine the consequences for ourselves: self-satisfaction (personal pride) or self-dissatisfaction (self-criticism). These processes can be thought of as a subset of the motivational phase of observational learning shown in Figure 6.7.

Observing One's Own Performance If a teacher wants to regulate the amount of lecturing he does or a student wants to regulate the amount of time she spends off-task, the first step is observing the responses of interest. We do this by timing or counting the responses. Good record keeping, using graphs or schedules, is necessary to monitor our behavior (or to teach others to do so). Many studies have shown that just knowing about our own behavior can result in behavioral change (Schunk, 1996; Zimmerman, 1989; 1990; Zimmerman & Schunk, 1989). In one study, with secondary-school learning-disabled students, eight students monitored their own daily homework assignments (Trammel, Schloss, & Alper, 1994). The researchers collected records during a baseline phase and then again during a self-monitoring and a self-graphing and goal-setting treatment phase (see Figure 6.9). The baseline phase required teachers to record missing and completed assignments. During the self-monitoring phase, students recorded the number of (1) assignments completed and turned in, (2) assignments incomplete/not turned in, or (3) no assignment. Self-monitoring—a form of observing and reflecting on one's own behavior—resulted in a marked increase in completed assignments. The self-graphing treatment is discussed further in the next section.

Judging Performance Where do people get the standards we judge our performance against? Sometimes they appear to be self-generated, as

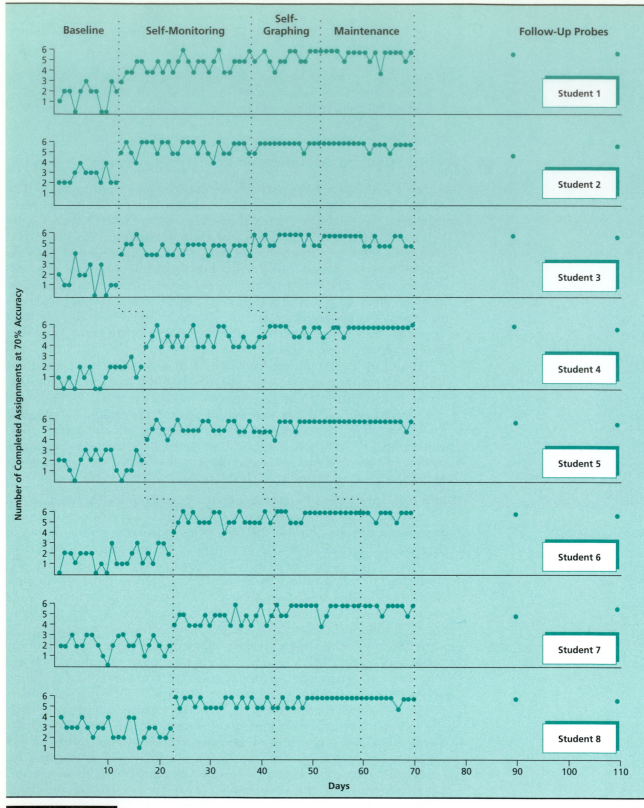

FIGURE 6.9

Multiple-baseline, across-subjects analysis of homework completion under baseline, intervention, and follow-up conditions.

From D. L. Trammel, P. J. Schloss, & S. Alper (1994). Using self-recording evaluation and graphing to increase completion of homework assignments, Journal of Learning Disabilities, 27 (2), 75–81. Copyright 1994 by PRO-ED, Inc. Reprinted by permission.

when a painter, writer, or teacher works over and over to get a painting, chapter, or lesson right.

In the homework-assignment investigation mentioned above (Trammel et al., 1994), students learned to set their own standards. The self-monitoring phase was followed by a self-graphing and goal-setting phase. During this phase, the students graphed the homework assignments completed. Graphs were prominently displayed in the classroom. In addition, students generated their own standards for homework to be completed over the next three days. The goals could be at the same or a higher level as for the previous three days. The results of self-graphing and goal setting were consistently high performance levels. And these levels were maintained after the end of the self-graphing and goal-setting phase.

Social learning theory, however, points out that many of the standards people have for performance are learned, like so much else, from models in our social world (Bandura, 1986; 1989; Schunk, 1996). For example, how long we may be willing to work on tasks that are hard to solve is influenced by models, as shown by Zimmerman and Ringle (1981). Children in their study watched models who tried to solve a problem and failed. The models, however, showed either high or low persistence at the problem and talked aloud, making either highly optimistic or highly pessimistic comments about their problem-solving behavior. The lowest levels of persistence were found in students exposed to models who themselves showed low persistence and who were pessimistic about their chances for success. Models influence our perceptions of our own sense of self-efficacy (discussed at some length in Chapter 8).

A note of caution is in order here. High personal standards are a good thing, but standards that are too high are harmful. Overly rigorous systems of self-reinforcement are sometimes found together with unrealistically high standards and a distorted sense of self-efficacy—an I-can-do-anything! response. Such unrealistic beliefs about accomplishment may be linked to a host of negative feelings—depression, despair, aimlessness, self-injury, or even suicide. People who aspire too high and constantly disparage their own accomplishments live in a state of anxiety and depression. Some students who have received a 99 on a test are crushed that they didn't get 100. These students need as much help in setting high but realistic performance standards as do students who are happy with a barely passing grade.

Determining Consequences for Ourselves

People who reward their own behavior achieve significantly higher levels of performance than those who perform the same activities under instruction but receive no reinforcement, are rewarded noncontingently, or monitor their own behavior and set goals for themselves but do not reward their attainments.

(Bandura, 1978, p. 351)

People who punish themselves, particularly for behavior they do not want to engage in (stuttering, obsessive thoughts) or behavior that will be punished by others (cheating, stealing) can also modify their behavior. You can reward or punish yourself cognitively, consciously saying, "I really did well on that exam" or "I sure acted stupidly." And you can reward or punish yourself by arranging your own environment—going to a movie after you study hard or skipping a meal after you cheat on a diet. The classroom version of this technique would be to give students access to reinforcers (free time, health foods, videogames, comics) when they are satisfied that they have met some behavioral goal. Self-reinforcement and self-punishment turn out to be among the more powerful agents in learning self-control.

Self-reinforcement and -punishment, of course, should take place only after self-monitoring. In professions such as medicine and teaching, self-monitoring in the form of supervision of one's own practices represents a significant portion of professional activity. Using a qualitative, case-study approach, Kilbourn (1991) examined self-monitoring in both medicine and teaching and found that the two professions are characterized by "central points" that distinguish them from each other. The medical profession's central points are the diagnosis and treatment to reduce human suffering while following ethical standards. Teaching's central points are engagement in intellectual acts of lucid thought and reasoning, also while behaving ethically. Many teaching activities, such as explaining, questioning, and reinforcing support these central activities. Other, less visible teaching activities also support these central points. These are the myriad covert intellectual acts that occur during instruction, such as hypothesizing, comparing, interpreting, and justifying behaviors. For Kilbourn, self-monitoring in teaching is the ongoing, personal examination of one's performance relative to the central points of the profession—the standards against which educators judge whether their performance merits self-reinforcement or self-punishment. Educators who self-monitor cannot help but judge themselves and reserve the right to modify their own behavior through self-reinforcement and self-punishment. This is part of the essence of professionalism.

Mentoring

Most of our examples of social learning so far have involved relatively brief observations of others, such as the teacher and classmates, and of oneself. What about learning from many such observations of another person continuing over a period of months or years? Social learning in such situations may constitute learning from a mentor—a wise and trusted senior person. Student teaching experiences in teacher education programs serve as learning experiences featuring a mentor-protégé relationship. Many writers have urged that beginning teachers be paired with experienced teachers who serve as mentors. **Mentoring** can take place in any field—baseball rookies with veterans, graduate students with professors, budding actors with stars, or, in general, mentors and protégés.

POLICY, RESEARCH, AND PRACTICE

Are Systematic Training Programs an Effective Way for Students to Regulate Their Own Behaviors?

WHAT THE RESEARCH TELLS US

Effective self-regulation programs all have common features: self-recording, self-assessing, and goal setting. Such training programs have been shown to be effective for most regular students as well as for those with developmental delays and those with learning disabilities (Rosenbaum & Drabman, 1979; Sawyer, Graham, & Harris, 1992; Trammel, Schloss, & Alper, 1994; Zimmerman & Schunk, 1989; Zimmerman, 1990). Not all programs for teaching self-regulation show effects, and not all programs that do work show that change is maintained over time and in different environments. But the work is promising.

WHAT THIS MEANS FOR YOU AS A TEACHER

The current trend is to educate students with special needs in the regular classroom, so you will be increasingly responsible for educating students with developmental delays and learning disabilities. Self-regulation training programs are beneficial for these students and many others.

To teach self-regulation you should follow these steps:

1. Ensure goal setting. Inform students what the goals of the lesson are and what they are to accomplish. Initially, goal setting may be specified by you but should later come under student control.

2. Provide for student conferencing. As part of the goal-setting activity, provide an opportunity for students to discuss what they understand the goals to be.

3. Ensure accurate self-monitoring. Be sure students are monitoring themselves *accurately.* At first have them compare their records with yours, a resource-room teacher's, or those of another outside observer.

4. Establish contingencies for behavior changes. The consequences for particular behaviors may be successful completion of the task or some other positively valued event.

5. Eventually transfer control of the contingencies to the students. Depending on the instructional program you use, student control of their own schedule of reinforcement may occur either at the start of the program or later.

6. Teach students some verbal instructions and praise statements to use in guiding their own behavior when self-determined contingencies begin to operate. This kind of covert self-talk has been found to improve performance.

7. Withdraw extrinsic contingencies when students are controlling their own behavior.

8. Do maintenance checks. After self-regulation has been established, provide follow-up checks to see if the self-regulation program is still influencing performance.

Not every superior-subordinate relationship is a mentoring one, however. Elements of mentoring include

1. a two-way relationship. In mentoring, the mentor as well as the protégé benefits from the relationship.

2. a work context. Mentoring goes on in relation to some kind of work, that is, in a work environment.

3. promotion of reciprocal advancement. Mentoring fosters advancement of the mentor as well as the protégé. Not just skills but ways of perceiving, thinking, feeling, and acting change in both. The mentor sees his or her ideas of what is important become adopted by the protégé, and the protégé inevitably modifies those ideas in a way from which the mentor also benefits.

4. stages. At the beginning, the two people get acquainted, feel each other out, and make silent judgments about the promise of the relationship. In the middle stage, the relationship is in full swing, with the protégé learning from the behavior, suggestions, and evaluations of the mentor—repeatedly going through the sequence of four steps in observational learning described above—while the mentor is benefiting from seeing how his or her behavior is imitated, suggestions prove fruitful, and evaluations are validated. Finally, the mentoring relationship declines and ends, as the protégé breaks away, strikes out on his or her own, becomes a mature professional, and perhaps begins to serve as a mentor for a next-generation protégé.

Mentoring at the highest level of scientific achievement—that of Nobel Prize winners—can be seen in descriptions of the many instances in which both mentor and protégé have won this honor. Zuckerman (1977), in her book *Scientific Elite*, described many mentor-protégé or master-apprentice pairs. "More than half (forty-eight) of the ninety-two laureates who did their prize-winning research in the United States by 1972 had worked either as students, postdoctorates, or junior collaborators under older Nobel laureates" (p. 100). Fifteen of these forty-eight had had two or more laureates as mentors. And ten Nobel mentors had produced thirty laureates. Clearly it helps to have a Nobel mentor, and Nobel mentors clearly produce more than their share of Nobel protégés.

This Nobel "inbreeding" results from the two-way mentoring process. The mentors seek out and select extremely promising protégés, and the protégés seek out and apprentice themselves to extremely productive, stimulating, demanding, rigorous, and exciting mentors. In mentoring the protégé acquires "socialization": norms, standards, values, and attitudes, as well as the knowledge, skills, and behavior appropriate to a given role, whether it is that of student, adolescent, plumber, mother, teacher, mechanic, ballet dancer, or scientist.

What mentor-protégé relationships have you experienced?

How do mentors foster such learning? (1) By their own example of how good work is done, that is, by providing a model of what is desirable; (2) by expecting such work from the protégé; and (3) by evaluating the work of others according to their (the mentor's) standards. Zuckerman quotes a physicist talking about his teacher: "You tried to live up to him. It was wonderful to watch him at work. Sometimes I eventually did things the way he did" (p. 125).

Whether coaching a girls' basketball team, giving students extra help in math during lunch period, or helping children prepare for a school play, you enter into personal relationships with students, and you inevitably take on a mentoring role. Social-learning theory holds that your students learn from your habits of mind, your ways of solving problems, your standards of performance. You will enjoy being a mentor. But you need to be aware of what you are doing as a mentor and let your students influence you as well. Mentoring—and teaching—are enhanced when influence goes both ways.

S U M M A R Y

1. There are three behavioral theories of learning, each of which applies to some learning tasks but not to others. With *classical conditioning,* a neutral stimulus is paired with an unconditioned stimulus and in time can elicit an unconditioned response. *Contiguity learning,* the kind that goes on with drill instruction, rests on the simple pairing of events. The broadest theory to come out of the branch of psychology called behaviorism is *operant conditioning*—learning as a result of reinforcement. Here behavior is initially spontaneous or an approximation of what is desirable. But with reinforcement that behavior can be strengthened and shaped (modified).

2. There are two major kinds of reinforcement. If we give something of positive value (success, praise, a good grade) after a response (behavior) is made, we are using positive reinforcement. If we take away something of negative value (failure, nagging, a threatening situation), we are using negative reinforcement.

3. A critical part of operant conditioning is choosing a schedule of reinforcement, which affects both the rate of responding and the strength of the response after reinforcement ends.

4. In contingency management, reinforcement depends on a certain response. If that response takes place, we give reinforcement; if it does not, we withhold reinforcement.

5. The Premack principle—that behaviors with higher probabilities of occurrence can be used to reinforce behaviors with lower probabilities of occurrence, coupled with the concept of contingency management—can guide us in making contingency contracts with students.

6. We also need to do something about unwanted responses, such as student misbehavior. Extinction is the process of weakening a response by nonreinforcement. The speed with which we can extinguish a response depends in good measure on whether reinforcement has been continuous or intermittent. It is much more difficult to extinguish a response that has been only intermittently reinforced than one that has been continuously reinforced.

7. There are several other ways to eliminate an unwanted behavior: reinforce other behaviors that are incompatible with the unwanted behavior; reinforce reductions in frequency of the unwanted behavior; or use punishment.

8. Presentation punishment is giving something of negative value (a critical comment, a bad grade) after the response is made. To be

most effective, this kind of punishment must come immediately after the response, be inescapable, be only as intense as necessary, and be used only when an alternative response is available to the student.

9. Removal punishment, generally more acceptable in schools, takes away something of positive value (free time, tokens) after an unwanted response is made.

10. Using punishment requires special vigilance on the part of the teacher. It is very important not to satisfy a student's need for attention when we punish, a kind of unintentional reinforcement of unwanted behavior. And overuse of punishment is a symptom that something is wrong with the educational environment.

11. Social learning, a different but related theory of learning, emphasizes that we learn much by watching those around us. It is based on the principle that learning takes place by simple contiguity and that reinforcement is not a necessary condition for learning. Reinforcement does, however, affect performance in important ways.

12. Models help us learn new behaviors, and they can facilitate, inhibit, and disinhibit behaviors we have already learned.

13. Social-learning theory identifies four phases of observational learning: attention, retention, reproduction, and motivation.

14. Attention is a necessary condition of observational learning. In the retention phase, students use verbal or visual codes to help them remember what they have learned through observation. Rehearsal—both overt and covert—also helps here. In the reproduction phase, verbal and visual codes guide the performance of the newly learned behavior. This phase is especially important where body-position cues are needed to master behavior, as in learning softball or gymnastics. It also allows the teacher/model to identify and correct problems. Corrective feedback has a strong impact on performance, particularly early in the reproduction phase.

15. Students may pay attention to a modeled behavior, try to remember it, even practice it, and still not perform it. The motivation phase focuses on the reinforcement that encourages students to enact a behavior, and on the punishment that discourages them from performing. Effective here are actual and vicarious reinforcement and punishment, and self-regulation. Notice that social-learning theory distinguishes between learning and performance.

16. Our cognitive responses to our own behavior allow us to regulate that behavior. By self-monitoring, we collect data about our responses. With our personal standards, often learned through observation, we judge our behavior. And by rewarding or punishing ourselves, we can effectively control our behavior. We need not be controlled by environmental forces or inner urges. Instead we can learn to become self-directed social beings. Helping students learn the self-regulation process is a critical part of teaching.

17. Mentoring is a two-way relationship between a competent model and a relative newcomer to a field of practice—a relationship in which much social learning takes place. During the course of the mentor-protégé relationship, socialization into the perceptions, beliefs, values, and actions of the profession or other kind of work results.

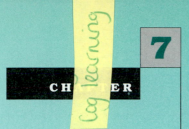

7

cog learning

Cognitive Learning: Processes and Strategies to Make Meaning

Overview

UNDERLYING ASSUMPTIONS OF COGNITIVE LEARNING

Contrasting Views of Learning: The Behavioral versus the Cognitive

Shared Characteristics and Beliefs among Cognitive Theories of Learning

The Role of Strategies in Cognitive Learning

COGNITIVE MODELS, PERSPECTIVES, AND STRATEGIES

An Information-Processing Model of Learning and Memory

Orienting stimuli and responses
Short-term memory and forgetting
Long-term memory
Information storage in memory
Long-term memory and the intertwining of enactive, iconic, and symbolic modes of learning

Strategies for Processing Information and Enhancing Memory

Overlearning
Mnemonic strategies
Reading strategies
Writing strategies
Mathematics strategies

Metacognition

Defining metacognition
Helping students employ metacognitive skills

Cognitively Active Learning

Discovery learning
Generative model of learning

Constructivist Perspectives on Learning

Commonly held beliefs
A different emphasis: Social constructivism

Problem-Solving Approach to Learning

Ill-defined versus well-defined problems
Case knowledge
Distinction between novice and expert

POLICY, RESEARCH, AND PRACTICE

How Do Teachers Develop Expertise?

Situated Cognition

Distributed expertise/cognition
Problem-based project learning

Strategies for Promoting Cognitive Learning and Higher-Order Thinking

Mediation and enhancement
Focus on instructional design
Developing and enriching schemata
Making meaning in mathematics
Schemata and reading achievement

POLICY, RESEARCH, AND PRACTICE

Overcoming Student Misconceptions in Science

TRANSFER OF LEARNING

A Glance at Traditional Views

Contemporary Views of Transfer

Metacognition and transfer
Conceptual models for understanding and transfer

Teaching for Transfer

Teaching for substantive (low-road) transfer
Teaching for procedural (high-road) transfer

APPLICATION

Enhancing Our Own and Our Students' Mindfulness

Instructional Ideas and Strategies for Promoting Transfer

A LOOK AHEAD TO CHAPTER 8

Summary

OVERVIEW

In this chapter we examine a particular kind of learning, namely, cognitive learning, especially from meaningful verbal or mathematical material. Teachers spend much of their time with the facts, concepts, principles, and cognitive skills important in a particular field, such as social studies or physics. So they need to understand the ways *meaningful* information is learned and processed.

251

The study of cognition is the study of mental processes, which are not observable directly. But experimental psychologists have found ingenious ways to make visible some of the mental processes people use. Over the last few decades a voluminous literature describing learning from a cognitive perspective has arisen. We integrate that vast literature by looking, first, at key shared assumptions among cognitive theorists and how students can use strategies in cognitive learning.

We then spend the major part of the chapter looking at six important perspectives on learning gleaned from the research on cognition, examining common threads as well as distinctions. Each of these perspectives has implications for teaching. So, woven throughout the chapter are instructional ideas for teachers and learning strategies for students to use.

1. The *information-processing model,* which attempts to describe how knowledge about the world is acquired, stored, and retrieved from memory, is the first perspective. It uses a model of how the mind works that is similar to a model of how a computer works. Here we also look at the many strategies that promote better learning and retention of meaningful information.

2. Another perspective stresses the need for *metacognitive skills,* which are the monitoring skills people use to judge how they are learning.

3. A model of learning based on a cognitively active mind is the third perspective. Teachers using such a model often have classes that demonstrate greater learning.

4. Constructivism is a perspective in which the mind is regarded as an active entity seeking to make meaning out of the information in the world around it, and to accommodate and assimilate that information in order to construct knowledge for itself. In this view of knowledge, the mind provides no mere replica of the outside world. Nor is there mere transfer of a teacher's words and actions or a book's explanations to a student's mind, where it is stored in some semblance of its original form. In the constructivist view, people do not reproduce information from the world exactly; they always transform it into something personally useful.

5. The attributes of skillful problem-solvers, those who can overcome problems that have not been encountered before, provide a fourth perspective.

6. The perspectives of social constructivists and those who recognize the situated nature of learning provide the sixth set of views we examine. In this perspective knowledge is not completely independent of the environments in which it is acquired. That is, no one can learn, from a book or a television show, the true meaning of love or the proper ways to cook a chicken. Love and cooking are learned best from, and in, social activities. Knowledge is not merely processed or constructed in some disembodied way; it develops in social settings and retains some of the characteristics of the social environment it came from. What people learn is deeply embedded in the social relationships and physical environments in which the learning takes place. In other

words, learning is situated. Communities have an important role in shaping our thinking, as we saw in Chapter 4.

All these perspectives still must deal with the fact that what we learn needs to be transferred to new settings. We study transfer of learning because people recognize that it is almost useless to learn to cook a five-pound chicken and then be stumped when faced with cooking a fifteen-pound turkey! Fortunately, our minds have the ability to work over the knowledge we acquire and come up with reasonable solutions to problems never before encountered. Without problem-solving transfer of knowledge, we would be doomed to live in narrow environments and perform repetitive acts. But humans face new situations every day, and usually succeed in them. Ultimately, that is what school is really about—equipping students to solve new problems and apply their knowledge in out-of-school, real-world situations.

These different but overlapping cognitive perspectives now shape contemporary views of teaching and learning. Older models of the learner as a passive recipient of knowledge are fading, while new models of the learner as an active social constructivist seem ascendant. And with the new models of the learner come new conceptions of how instruction should take place. Some of the controversies in education today result from these newer ways of thinking about learning that novice teachers bring to the schools in which they begin their careers. In education these ideas are controversial, though in psychology they are much better accepted as closer approximations to how people learn. These are exciting times to be studying educational psychology because the ferment of controversy is bound to create new knowledge.

Underlying Assumptions of Cognitive Learning

Contrasting Views of Learning: The Behavioral versus the Cognitive

Let us start our look at the cognitive view of learning by comparing it with the behavioral view, described in Chapter 6. The two positions represent very different emphases in the complex process of learning. The behavioral approach focuses on the environment, particularly how rewards and punishments affect behavior, ignoring for the most part the mental processing of information. The cognitive perspective takes the mental processing as its starting point, not refuting behavioral psychology but thinking it too simple to handle the complexities of meaningful, symbolic materials. The behaviorists emphasize activity, movement, observable behavior rather than the contents of things in the mind. The cognitivists try to understand what happens in the mind *between* a stimulus and a response, attempting to describe the way the mind **processes**

Recall our discussion of schemata in Chapter 4. Who would emphasize schemata development—behaviorists or cognitivists? Why?

information. Of course, cognitivists are concerned with observable behavior too, because the mind can only be understood by its products. But the control of behavior is more likely to be seen as internal to the learner in the cognitivist perspective, and external to the learner in the behaviorist perspective. *Both* perspectives are useful as you think about teaching. Fortunately, teachers rarely personify a pure theoretical position in their classrooms; they are usually the ultimate eclectics—using whatever helps to teach a particular student in an intellectually honest way.

The behaviorist perspective often emphasizes the efficient acquisition of knowledge. Behaviorists may advocate clear goals and statements of objectives for teaching; simple procedures for errorless learning; drill to learn component skills before combining those skills into larger, more complex chunks; and extrinsic rewards to facilitate learning. Assessment is by conventional means since the information learned can easily be evaluated by multiple-choice and recall items.

The cognitive perspective emphasizes conceptual understanding and thinking ability. Its advocates may attempt to teach bigger chunks of knowledge than do behaviorists, and they emphasize the use of strategies to facilitate learning. They often use concrete materials in learning (batteries and bulbs for circuits, simulations of complex systems on the computer) and are concerned with the learner's mental models of the things to be learned. Cognitivists favor assessments that require constructed responses—essays, written reports, projects, portfolios—all of which are claimed to reveal students' conceptual understanding much better than do traditional multiple-choice tests.

Learning in context and in groups is a powerful form of learning!
(© Jeffry Muir Hamilton/ Stock Boston)

Another noteworthy angle on learning is that some cognitivists, called **social constructivists,** emphasize the social context of thinking and learning. This perspective calls for a broadening of ideas about where knowledge can be found and how it comes to be learned by groups and individuals. Cognition, in this view, is shared—distributed across people and tied to the settings in which learning takes place. Social constructivists emphasize the value of learning in collaborative settings and concentrate on students' building positive identities as competent problem solvers in groups. As you will see below, their beliefs are not at odds with other cognitivists; their differences are, again, a matter of emphasis.

Although each of these approaches has something to offer, a teacher's problem remains the same: How do I design curriculum and instruction to fit 30 or so different students, coming from so many different backgrounds? The answer, we believe, is to be eclectic, but one notion merits special attention—putting effort into developing collaborative communities of learners. Only in this way is a teacher free of some of the responsibility for solving every learning problem that arises. It is the very nature of the collaborative learning community to take on some of the responsibility for teaching its own members. It is concerned with induction into the group, mentoring, and the development of attitudes and skills through apprenticeship. This kind of learning is more common in out-of-school settings, such as the Girl Scouts and Boy Scouts. The teacher's role changes from "font of knowledge" to one closer to "coach." Life can be a good deal less stressful for teachers who learn to act, at least part of the time, as "guide on the side" rather than "sage on the stage," participating in group activities where members build knowledge collectively.

Shared Characteristics and Beliefs among Cognitive Theories of Learning

What do the various cognitive perspectives have in common? Most of today's cognitive theories, particularly **constructivism,** assume that people are usually purposive, knowledge-seeking individuals with a highly developed ability to organize information (Noddings, 1990). We make meaning for ourselves by bringing constructive processes to bear on the information that comes our way in the environment. The constructive processes come from either innate structures ("wired in," such as the ability to make sense of language) or those that develop out of interactions with the environments we are exposed to (making sense of postmodernism while working in a community of comparative literature majors).

In the cognitive models, perceptual and **information-processing** activity is loaded with subjectivity. People see and hear and think with their hearts and minds, not just with their eyes, ears, and brain. Nevertheless, there are times when the constructive processes of mind are not very active, as in **rote learning,** simple memory work, and when basic information processing is occurring. But there are also times when constructive processes predominate, as in discovery learning in science and during

As you read through this chapter, try plotting out the various theories and positions on a continuum of weak to strong constructivism.

discussions about politics and values. But whether weak or strong, constructive processes are *always* at work.

Constructivist processes are particularly strong in group settings, where each member must make sense out of the complex social interactions to which he or she is exposed. The role of the community—other learners, the teacher, family members—is to provide the setting, pose the challenges, and offer the support that encourages everyone to acquire useful, appropriate, and morally acceptable constructions of the world. This view of constructivism is the social one, compatible with the Vygotskian claim that all knowledge starts out on the social plane before it becomes individual knowledge.

We humans construct knowledge for ourselves so that we can adapt to the environment. Adaptation (using the mechanisms of accommodation and assimilation—ways of transforming knowledge), says Piaget, is the purpose of the mind. But we are not free to create any kinds of personal knowledge systems we might want. If we did so, we'd probably be locked up. In social constructivism, the adaptations we make that are too far afield (germs don't exist; the sun is pulled by horses across the sky; two plus two equals nine) drop out, and we reach some agreements about what the world is like. So constructivism and related cognitive theories emphasize ways to collectively find agreement on what the world is like while simultaneously making individual meaning of the world.

The cognitive-learning theories are thought by some to be a little overstated, a little too illogical or too obvious, and a little too difficult to refute (see Phillips, 1995; Bereiter, 1994). But they all suggest ways to teach that are different from those emphasized in the past. And the new teaching methods arising out of arguments about which cognitive perspectives are supportable deserve attention separately from the strength of the perspectives themselves (Confrey, 1990).

The Role of Strategies in Cognitive Learning

Highly successful students, those who are motivated and actively involved in their learning, use certain strategies to help them learn. A **learning strategy** is "composed of cognitive operations over and above the processes directly entailed in carrying out a task" (Pressley, Woloshyn, et al., 1990). Reflect for a moment on your own studying of this chapter. If you are judiciously underlining or highlighting, periodically stopping and asking yourself what we mean, and trying to relate the notion of "learning strategy" to your own meaning of "having a strategy," you are using learning strategies. You are more active cognitively than if you were reading without a plan and merely trying to absorb what is before you. Effective learners—whether readers, writers, or mathematicians—are strategy-using learners. They estimate answers before trying to solve math problems, they create mnemonics for memorizing bits of knowledge they need (*Men Very Easily Make Jokes Serve Useful Neighborly Purposes* = Mars, Venus, Earth, Jupiter, and so on), and in other ways are actively (rather than passively) involved in their own learning. More

Observe your own use of learning strategies during the next week. Keep a record. Which work best for you and why?

of these strategies are described below. For now it is worth noting that less effective learners in school settings do not use learning strategies as frequently as do more effective learners.

That may sound like an obvious conclusion about learning, but it is important for you to realize that students frequently have hardly any such cognitive-learning strategies available when trying to master a school subject. Their ability to make meaning out of the symbolic systems—the words, numerals and icons—that are emphasized in school work is limited, though in the practical world outside they may do fine. Although strategies are found to be important tools for learning, virtually no evidence of strategy teaching was found in 13,000 minutes of observation of high school writing instruction (Applebee, 1981) or in 19,000 minutes spent observing general elementary instruction (Durkin, 1979; Moely et al., 1986). Teachers in the past simply have not made explicit the strategies that exist. Before we decide that students do not have the interest or intellectual ability to learn something, we need to be sure that students know how to learn what we are trying to teach them. We all know that the world is filled with people who are smart outside of school but never learn how to do well in school subjects. They may simply never have been instructed in how to learn in school.

So for some students, the explicit teaching of strategies makes schoolwork that was difficult much easier to learn. And for some students with learning disabilities, mastery of strategies can yield substantial gains in regular-classroom achievement. Such strategy-learning programs with special-education students have been successfully validated (Schumaker & Deshler, 1992).

Some people claim that teaching cognitive strategies is not constructivist in orientation; rather, it is more like the skill-based approach characteristic of behaviorist psychology. Pressley and McCormick (1995) reply that strategies are not imposed on students, and learners are expected to modify them and customize them. Moreover, strategies can be taught in ways that are collaborative and evoke understanding. So it is not mere acquisition of the procedures that is the goal of strategy learning. Strategies simply allow students to learn better those aspects of the curriculum to which constructive mental processes will be applied (Resnick, 1987). So we believe that strategies have a particularly important role to play in all the aspects of cognitive learning we discuss in the following pages.

A caution: For students to know a strategy is only half the solution—they also need to know when and where to use it. That is, they must be strategic in their use of strategies. Students need to develop self-management or metacognitive skills to monitor their own learning. Metacognitive skills (discussed later in this chapter) include both the monitoring of cognition (How am I doing?) and the control of cognition (trying to tie what is being learned for the first time to what is already known; recognizing that something is an example of metaphor, say) (Dole et al. 1991). Better students teach themselves to do this kind of metacognitive monitoring as they learn, and bring into play the right strategies, for

> Have you ever met anyone who has had "street smarts"? Are those strategies that are useful for accomplishing things outside, but not inside, school?

particular curricular materials, at the right time. Poorer students need to be taught the same metacognitive skills that better students have already developed.

Cognitive Models, Perspectives, and Strategies

An Information-Processing Model of Learning and Memory

The information-processing model of memory, shown in Figure 7.1, can help you think about how people think. The model differentiates between the external world and internal cognitive events (the area inside the broken line). Information processing often begins with input from the external environment—for example, light, heat, pressure, or sound. In order for the stimulus to work its way through the information-processing system, it must first elicit an orienting response (OR), which focuses attention on the stimulus. This begins the internal (mental) processes.

The information from the environment is stored briefly—less than half a second—in **short-term sensory storage** (STSS). The capacity of the STSS system is probably unlimited, and it may include a separate "store" for each sense. Attention determines what happens next, and this is a particularly important point in the process because what someone is currently processing in working memory is a key factor in determining

FIGURE 7.1

An information-processing model of memory

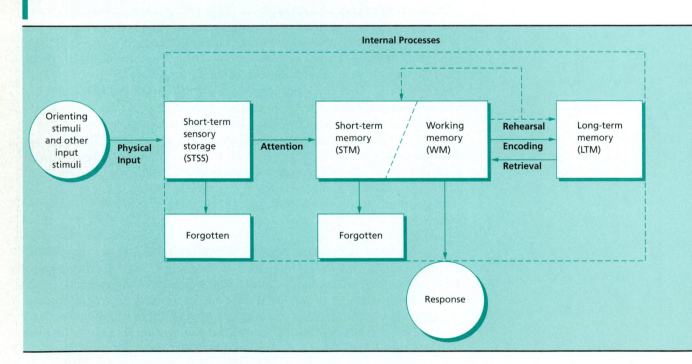

the stimuli she attends to. If the working memory is processing information about dogs, then a bark in the environment will be attended to. But if someone is thinking about his date last Saturday night, the sound of a bark may not even be noticed. If someone does not pay attention to the new information coming in, it is forgotten; if he does pay attention to it, it moves from the STSS to the short-term-memory (STM) and working-memory (WM) storage systems.

Short-term memory is conscious memory—all that people are aware of at one time. The capacity of this store is limited to about seven ± two chunks of information. The information here is not in the raw sensory form in which it exists in the STSS. And it can be bumped out, that is, forgotten, by new information. **Working memory** is very much like short-term memory; in fact, it may be just a part of STM. If short-term memory is conscious memory, then working memory is like a scratch pad someone uses to do mental arithmetic or list the people we want to invite to a party. Information in STM or WM, if rehearsed or encoded, remains the focus of attention or is passed along to long-term memory (LTM). The capacity of **long-term memory,** like that of the STSS, is probably unlimited. The information stored in long-term memory is almost never forgotten, although we may be unable to retrieve it because of a failure in the way we search for it. Any response we might make—say, answering the question "What causes an eclipse?"—comes from working memory, either directly or after some information is retrieved from long-term memory. Let us look more closely at elements of this model.

Orienting Stimuli and Responses   Of the myriad stimuli in the environment, some succeed in eliciting an **orienting response;** others do not. An orienting response arouses interest and curiosity, making us want to know more about the stimulus. It is a response to changes in stimuli or their unique characteristics. Perhaps the simplest way to gain students' attention is to use a command. If a person yells, "Stop!" people usually stop what they are doing and check around them for further commands or more information. The teacher can say, "Now listen closely" or "This is really important" or "Pay attention to this!" All these commands signal that orienting responses—attention—should be paid to what follows.

Variation in the stimuli teachers offer to students also can gain attention. When teachers (like actors) vary their volume, pitch, or rate of speech, they are varying the stimulus in ways likely to arouse the orienting response. When teachers write on the board in

different colors,

or place

words in

unusual

patterns,

students are more likely to pay attention; that is, more of the information teachers want students to attend to ends up in working memory. Emotional stimuli also can capture attention. For example, words like *blood* or *gold* or our own names are likely to elicit an orienting response. Vivid similes and metaphors have the same attention-grabbing properties. Who would not attend further after hearing, "My love is like a red, red rose" or "He was known on the field as Doctor Death!"?

Other attention-arousing stimuli depend for their effect on

- novelty (e.g., the teacher sits on the floor instead of at the desk)
- complexity (the teacher follows a series of two-digit addition problems with one containing five-digit numbers)
- ambiguity (the teacher provides students with a map that names no cities and asks where cities are likely to develop); or
- incongruity (the teacher discusses a mammal that lays eggs, that is, a platypus).

Thinking about the ways to influence your students' attention pays off in getting what you want into their information-processing systems. Teachers and parents are quite right when they say to their children, "Pay attention or you won't learn anything!" Attention is fundamental.

But teachers should use attention-getting stimuli sparingly. All the forms of eliciting attention share a common problem: Once students get used to them, they are no longer effective. Remember that novelty overused becomes commonplace. Students can become accustomed to changing voice levels. And they can lose their emotional responses to words such as *murder* and *ice cream* when they hear or read them often. Use techniques to elicit orienting responses only to attract attention to important information or events.

Short-Term Memory and Forgetting   To move a little further along the path shown in Figure 7.1, let us assume that something in the physical world entered the short-term sensory storage and was attended to. When we pay attention to a stimulus, the information represented by that stimulus goes into short-term memory. This is where we store information that needs to be available for just a few seconds. For example, when you look up a telephone number you are not going to need again, it is stored in STM or WM and forgotten a few minutes or even seconds after you press the keys. This is so unless certain things happen to the information held in STM or WM.

More specifically, unless we **rehearse** or encode what is in STM or WM we fail to remember information. For example, Nickerson and Adams (1979) asked subjects to do the following: "In the circles below draw a penny." Try it before you go on.

The researchers scored responses to eight characteristics of a penny: on the top, Lincoln's head, "In God We Trust," "Liberty," and the date; on the bottom, the pillared building, "United States of America," "E Pluribus Unum," and "One Cent." If you are like most of the subjects in the study, you did not score very high. This is an example of what happens when we do not encode or rehearse stimuli in STM or WM—no matter how often we come across them, we forget them!

Forgetting serves a good purpose. Without forgetting, our minds would become hopelessly cluttered. We really do not want to keep in memory all the information we receive each day. In fact, to survive, people need to forget most of what they initially process. But for teachers, the useful process of forgetting creates a challenge: If we believe the information we teach is worthy of retention, we must combat the natural forgetting process.

Sometimes people are unable to **retrieve** information from long-term memory. That inability may result from new information interfering with attempts to recall old information. Or it may be because there was a quick decay of the memory trace in STM. In either case, much forgetting is desirable (or useful), natural, and universal. Teachers should know that students are going to forget most of the specific facts taught to them—this is the reality of the situation.

Long-Term Memory To get material from short-term memory and working memory into long-term memory is not a big problem. It is necessary only to enhance the material in some way or see that it is held as the focus of attention for some period of time.

But retrieving information from long-term memory is another matter. The problem resembles that of the chief librarian of the Library of Congress. Many documents of many kinds are coming in all the time. Storage facilities in the library are virtually unlimited, particularly since the advent of digital storage. When someone requests a particular document, the main problem for the librarian is not one of storage but of retrieval. A smoothly functioning card catalog (or computer) for locating items is what is needed most.

We can think of long-term memory in the same way. Research has shown that LTM of almost any verbal, visual, or auditory information of real or potential significance can get into long-term storage. And the information in the long-term store is virtually permanently recorded. So storage is not the problem. The problem is one of retrieval, of locating the information in LTM and bringing it up for attention in STM or WM.

Information Storage in Memory How does the brain store information? In pictorial form? verbal form? both? neither? Dual-code theorists believe that all information is tied to sensory input, that is, that things we see are stored in pictorial form and that things we hear or read are stored in verbal form (Clark & Paivio, 1991). This theory has a common-sense ring to it. But then there is the study by Bower, Karlin, and Dueck (1975). They asked their subjects to remember pictures like those shown in Figure 7.2. The subjects in one group used their own pictorial representations, verbal representations, or both, to store and retrieve the pictures. They generally were able to reconstruct from memory about 50 percent of the pictorial stimuli shown. The subjects in a second group were told

What is your reaction to the statement that your students will forget most of the specific facts you teach them? If you find it discouraging, come back to it at the end of the chapter and see if you feel more optimistic.

FIGURE 7.2

Two pictorial stimuli used
by Bower, Karlin, and
Dueck (1975)

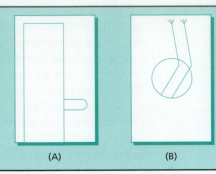

(A)   (B)

that picture A was a midget playing a trombone in a phone booth, and
that picture B was an early bird that had tried to catch a very large worm.
These subjects were able to reconstruct about 70 percent of the pictorial stimuli correctly.

How do we explain this increase in **retention?** It seems that information is stored not only in visual form, verbal form, or both, but that it is
also stored by its *meaning.* The second group of subjects had a meaningful way to refer to the pictures, and they showed the positive effects of
that approach. Regardless of whether the stimulus is visual or verbal, its
meaning to the person determines how it is stored, retrieved, and used.

It is also useful to distinguish among the different forms of knowledge
that might be stored. There are at least three forms worth considering—
declarative, procedural, and episodic (usually called **episodic memory**).
Keep in mind that they are separated here for discussion, but in reality
they operate together. A student's failure to perform well, or a teacher's
failure to teach well, may be due to inadequate declarative knowledge,
inadequate procedural knowledge, or both. And to help that student or
teacher perform better they need to know where the deficiency lies.

Declarative Knowledge **Declarative knowledge** is about factual
things. It includes all the "if-then" knowledge people possess (If it looks
like a duck, sounds like a duck, waddles like a duck, then it probably
is a duck!). Some call this *propositional knowledge* because it seems to
be stored in the form of simple proposition-like relationships between
things. For example, "Michael Jordan may be the greatest basketball
player ever to have played professionally, breaking all scoring records,
and earning the most money for his efforts." This whole bunch of words
is probably stored as something like "Michael Jordan = many points/
many dollars."

Sometimes declarative knowledge is also called *semantic knowledge.*
This points out that the knowledge is organized and tied together in some
way so that units of knowledge are related to each other on the basis of
meaning. So declarative, propositional, or semantic knowledge is concerned with the facts, concepts, principles and theories that schools need
to impart—the characteristics of mammals, or the causes of the Great
Depression, and so forth. Schools are a society's primary institution for

As you read about
the different kinds
of knowledge, think
about ways (in addi-
tion to those listed)
that you might both
assess and tap into a
student's knowledge.

providing the enormous amounts of declarative knowledge needed for contemporary life.

Procedural Knowledge Knowing *how* to accomplish something is called **procedural knowledge.** It includes the many almost automatic procedures we use to go about our business every day—knowing how to start the car or find a word in the dictionary, for example. Although declarative knowledge is typically demonstrated through short-answer tests (such as multiple-choice tests), procedural knowledge is demonstrated by doing something—playing the piano or writing a story. (Performance-based assessment, covered in Chapter 14, is more appropriate for assessing procedural knowledge.) Declarative knowledge has truth value—Michael Jordan is or is not the highest scorer—but procedural knowledge is neither true nor false. Rather, it works or it doesn't work. It is demonstrated by *doing*, and involves both physical and cognitive aspects. Moreover, procedural knowledge is usually acquired through much practice (long division, guitar playing), unlike declarative knowledge, which may be learned all at once (the capital of Canada is Ottawa). Different neural structures may even be involved in the storage of declarative and procedural knowledge (Squire, 1987).

Episodic Memory Episodic knowledge, also known as *episodic memory*, may be thought of as a subset of declarative knowledge that refers to personal, dated, autobiographical, and often emotionally loaded memories. Episodic memory is unabashedly subjective—episodes are people's personal records of events (Martin, 1993). These memories let you go back and revisit personally significant occurrences such as your first kiss, the time you were stopped by the police, or a vacation at a lake. A child's report on a field trip (sometimes including endless description of extraneous material), is evidence of how vivid and filled with visual and verbal information such personal and emotional memories can be. This points out, too, that memory has mood, emotions, and feelings associated with it.

Educational psychologists now know that mood affects learning (Snow, Corno & Jackson, 1996). And they have found that students recall events better if their emotional state during recall matches the emotional state they were in when they learned the material. So it appears that feelings are carried along with some kinds of declarative knowledge. There is also evidence that the absence of negative feelings during learning leads to higher achievement (McCaslin et al. 1994). In addition, positive feelings during learning are associated with increases in interest, motivation to learn, and use of self-regulated strategies for learning. And negative feelings during learning, such as anger or hopelessness, are correlated with decreases in these factors (Pekrun, 1994). These data suggest that emotions evoked during learning affect both the ways people learn and their memories of events.

Long-Term Memory and the Intertwining of Enactive, Iconic, and Symbolic Modes of Learning Remember Bruner's stages of cognitive development (see Chapter 4). The first was the enactive stage, where the child learns to know the world through touch, movement, and chewing—through physical activity. That stage is eventually followed by the iconic stage and shortly thereafter by the symbolic stage—the form of learning that is the focus of this chapter. But the positive effects of incorporating physical activity or vivid imagery into learning do not disappear once the symbolic mode of learning becomes dominant.

So, physically active learning is more likely to result in longer and fuller retention than passive learning. The physical activity may give rise to more associations to code the material with, perhaps simply by focusing attention on the material. As can be seen in Figure 7.1, both attention and enhancement are necessary for storing information in LTM.

So, would learning a foreign language—Japanese, say—be more effective if it were learned by moving appropriately to the commands *Tate* (stand up) or *Aruke* (walk forward)? Yes! Would stripping a little bark off a tree and tasting its bitterness teach about salt water mangroves in a better way than just reading about these processes? Yes! Would reciting out loud the words in a vocabulary list produce better learning than doing it silently? Yes! Would virtually any form of motor enactment during learning enhance that learning? Yes! (R. L. Cohen, 1989). The cognitive process that seems to be at work is **synesthesia,** where images in one sensory system are blended with another, giving rise to enhanced codability and therefore enhanced retrievability. The rule of thumb for teachers is that the more you can get physical, auditory, and visual stimuli combined with the symbolic materials to be learned, the more learning and retrievability are likely to be enhanced.

Strategies for Processing Information and Enhancing Memory

Physical activity aids learning, but so does cognitive activity—and staying cognitively alert can be controlled by the strategies people use during cognitive learning. Here we look at some cognitively active strategies that help with remembering information. Later in the chapter, we examine another set of strategies that work with and build on these.

Overlearning   The process of continuing to study material after it has been mastered is called **overlearning.** Overlearning works; that is, the more time someone spends overlearning, the more likely he is to score well whenever he is assessed on what he has learned. By simply practicing over and over a skill such as piano playing, chess, or even remembering strings of random numbers, people do get better at that skill. Poor musicians get good, modest chess players get to play in tournaments, and people with limited memories develop excellent memories by overlearning—practicing well beyond basic mastery (Ericsson, 1996). Aptitude or talent is certainly important in learning science, math, music, or art. However, recent evidence suggests that massive amounts of deliberate practice—overlearning with constant feedback to correct errors—results in remarkable achievement by people who did not seem to have the talent to begin with.

But repetition does not result only in more learning or simple rote learning; it can result also in different kinds of learning. As students repeat learning trials with unfamiliar, technically complex material, they appear to focus better on the main ideas in the material. The repetitions help them reorganize and transform the ideas and make them more meaningful. In a study of overlearning by Mayer (1983), measures of problem-solving skills and the ability to apply what was learned increased over learning trials. Repetition and overlearning, forms of deliberate practice, then, are likely to have benefits beyond just learning more or learning simple things by rote. Practice may be necessary for real understanding of technically complex material and for learning how to solve problems using that understanding. Expert problem solvers—radiologists, physicists, or chess players—all have acquired extensive knowledge in their chosen domains. So teachers do not need to feel defensive about trying to have students master large bodies of declarative information in, say, chemistry or geography. Problem solving in any domain is without question knowledge-based. The problem is to teach in ways that make the knowledge accessible when it is time to use it (Prawat, 1989).

Mnemonic Strategies Techniques to help people remember are called **mnemonic devices.** Have you ever used the popular strategy of creating first-letter mnemonics to remember something (for example, Roy G. Biv = red, orange, yellow, and so on—the colors of the rainbow)? This and similar cognitive strategies for enhancing memory can be taught directly to students. But careful observation of teachers in classrooms reveals that they actually provide little instruction in how to memorize (Moely et al., 1986). Efficient, routinized memory strategies help students learn basic knowledge in a curriculum area and free them to concentrate on more complex learning. Here we look at three mnemonic strategies: imagery, the loci method, and the keyword method.

Imagery Because most school learning is verbal, students who possess and use an **imagery** strategy have less difficulty with verbal material. Imagery is a useful strategy for generating personal meaning that helps in retrieval. In part this may occur because the storage capacity for pictorial information appears to exceed the very large storage capacity for verbal material.

Evidence suggests that functions relating to verbal and visual coding abilities are separated in the two hemispheres of the brain. Speech is organized chiefly in the left hemisphere; nonverbal imagery, in the right hemisphere. As noted earlier, at least two systems for representing information in the brain may be operating. People may use both an imagery store and a verbal store for encoding input. The imagery system works better for processing concrete and spatial information (the story of Paul Bunyan, geometry), and the verbal system works better for processing abstract and sequential information (a definition of morality). The two systems are richly interconnected. That is, when people can attach verbal material to pictorial images and pictorial images to verbal labels, we can usually retrieve information better.

For example, one way a teacher can help students is to deliberately use concrete (nonabstract) words and point out the associated imagery (Paivio, 1986). Concrete terms such as *zebra* and *house* produce both perceptual and verbal codes, while abstract terms—*justice* and *freedom*—produce only verbal codes. So as a rule concrete terms are easier to learn (R. C. Anderson, 1974). To help your students learn more abstract terms, try to give them images that could accompany the definition or have them generate their own (justice = the blindfolded woman holding scales to weigh the evidence; freedom = the planting of the flag on Iwo Jima; Loneliness = ?).

Can imagery techniques be taught to help children learn more efficiently? Michael Pressley, a leading researcher on strategy learning, holds that instruction in the use of imagery strategies is not helpful before 8 years (Pressley & McCormick, 1995). Above this age, and particularly with adults, these instructions usually have a pronounced positive effect. However, even with young children, if you can get them to draw objects, providing them with motor involvement and pictorial representations as well as verbal coding, you should be able to facilitate learning (Varley et al., 1974).

The Loci Method This trick of ancient orators relies on imagery and can increase recall from two to seven times over customary ways of memorization. To use the **loci method,** first imagine and learn, in order, the location of objects or places, creating a set of "memory snapshots." Figure 7.3 is an example. It shows a "sentimental map" of one person's childhood home and the surrounding area, which could be used to apply the loci method. You could also use the train stops on the subway, a path through the woods that you know well, the different rooms in a house—or virtually any familiar ordering of things with high imagery value.

FIGURE 7.3

A sentimental map of West Avenue, Pawtucket, Rhode Island

From Herbert F. Crovitz, Galton's Walk, p. 43. Copyright © 1970 by Herbert F. Crovitz. Reprinted by permission of Addison-Wesley Educational Publishers, Inc.

Next you place the things you want to remember in these loci. You could place the tragedies by Shakespeare, the 15 different stanzas of a poem, the 21 significant events in a war, or the nations that are permanent members of the United Nations Security Council. Place each image and the verbal label of the new material at one of the imaginary locations in memory. Once you have memorized the loci—a task requiring a good deal of time and effort—it is relatively easy to "walk down the street" or "through the woods," and "pick up" the information you want to remember.

In one example of the power of this method, students studied many lists of nouns (dog, pencil, mountain, etc.), each 40 items long. The subjects were also taught the loci method using 40 familiar places on their college campus. The 40 nouns were studied once, each for 13 seconds. How many of the nouns in such a 40-item list do you think you could remember? For the subjects trained in the loci method, immediate recall averaged thirty correct nouns out of the 40, in serial order! On the next day, delayed-recall scores averaged 34 out of the 40 items (J. Ross & Lawrence, 1968)! In comparison to the scores usually observed in rote-learning experiments, these recall performances are exceptional, if not staggering. Even though demonstrations of the remarkable magnitude of this kind of mnemonic effect are easily found, most people still do not use these strategies. Teachers do not teach them, and students do not use them. But they should. Study-skill centers in universities do teach these skills, and they have established a good record of success.

The Keyword Method   J. R. Levin (1981; Pressley, Levin, & Delaney, 1982) and his associates have developed the **keyword** concept at great length. Suppose you had to learn a foreign word, say, *carta,* Spanish for "(postal) letter." In this method you are taught to find an English keyword that comes to mind when you hear *carta.* Suppose you pick *cart.* You learn to visualize a "cart" and put the "letter" into it. Then when someone says *carta,* you see and can easily respond "letter." This procedure works when students are learning vocabulary in their own language as well. Pressley, Levin, and McDaniel (1987) pointed out that two key stages of the keyword method are an acoustic-link stage and an imagery-link stage. So if a fifth grader were trying to learn the word *persuade,* she might acoustically pull out "purse" and then use as the imagery link a woman being persuaded by a salesperson to buy a purse. The next time she encounters the word *persuade,* the term *purse* comes to mind, the visual image follows, and the meaning is recalled. Mnemonics in general, and the keyword mnemonic in particular, are helpful for poor learners, including students with mild mental retardation or learning disabilities, who usually do not have effective learning and memory strategies of their own (Mastropieri & Scruggs, 1989).

In dozens of studies Levin and his colleagues have shown how the keyword method can improve the learning of foreign language vocabulary, English vocabulary, the presidents of the United States, the 50 states and their capitals, and so on. J. R. Levin (1981) and Bellezza (1981) both make similar comments about mnemonics in education: they (1) are con-

> Has a teacher ever taught you a mnemonic strategy? If so, was it effective? If none of your teachers ever taught you one, why might that be?

sistently effective, (2) show large effects, (3) are usable in many different curriculum areas, and (4) take little time to teach.

Note that simple rote learning of elements is not all that is greatly facilitated by mnemonics. Mnemonic instruction can improve students' problem solving in tasks where creative integration of information is required. This conclusion holds for both analytical-thinking tasks (e.g., figuring out analogies) and formal-reasoning tasks (e.g., predicting results). Efficient memory strategies seem to facilitate students' performance in a number of higher-order thinking and transfer tasks, where success depends on remembering factual knowledge relevant to the task. As noted earlier, higher-order thinking and problem solving, the kind of constructive cognitive activity so highly prized, almost always requires a rich store of basic declarative knowledge (M. E. Levin & J. R. Levin, 1990).

Reading Strategies   Another cognitive strategy is learning to *summarize*, a simple yet marvelously helpful strategy for learning from prose. Many effective school learners have mastered the four major rules of summarization: (1) Identify the main information, (2) delete trivial information, (3) delete redundant information, and (4) relate main and supporting information. When students who did not know how to do such summarization were trained in this learning strategy, they learned more from a text than students who did not use it (Pressley, Burkell, et al., 1990). It may seem unlikely that some people do not know how to do such simple summarization, but they do not! You are, by virtue of getting this far in your academic career, a sophisticated learner, with an extensive repertoire of cognitive learning strategies. But many of your students will not have acquired such strategies. And if students do not learn them, they will struggle needlessly.

Students could also learn another simple strategy, namely, *to ask questions* (see Davey & McBride, 1986; Raphael & Wonnacott, 1985). Those who can ask good questions of text they are to learn often find similar questions on tests later, and then they are ready for them.

Also, students who do poorly on reading comprehension questions can be taught to "*look back.*" For example, students between 9 and 13 years were taught why they should look back in the text and reminded that they cannot remember everything (Garner, Hare, et al., 1984; Garner, Macready, & Wagoner, 1984). The researchers taught them particularly to look back when the questions were factual, when they were about what the author said. They also taught the students not to look back when the questions were about the students' thoughts about and personal responses to the text. Finally, the students were taught to skim the text to find the part that might have the information needed. Students trained in these kinds of "lookbacks" did so more often than untrained students—and they scored higher on a posttest of comprehension of the text. So for some students, what might have appeared to be a deficit in motivation or intellect was simply a deficit in strategy.

Still another learning strategy is based on realization that some students have not acquired the understanding of **story grammar.** Stories have main characters that do and feel things in time and space, and they start and end in particular ways. So you should teach students to keep track of these five questions: Who is the main character? When and where did the story take place? What did the main character do? How did that character feel? How did it all end? In this way, they are able to keep the main points of the story straight, and the story is more memorable for them as well. If some students are unaware that stories are organized in certain recurring ways, they are bound to have difficulty answering comprehension questions. The questions about textual material asked on tests usually are created by someone who assumes that everyone knows how stories are organized. So, students who do not understand story organization are helped by training in identifying the story grammar to do better on tests (Short & Ryan, 1984). A story grammar can also be mapped, as shown in Figure 7.4. Idol (1987) demonstrated positive effects among students who learned the strategy of mapping a story.

Think of a favorite children's book. Apply these five questions and plan out a mini-lesson to teach that story.

FIGURE 7.4

Components of the story map

Reprinted from Idol (1987).

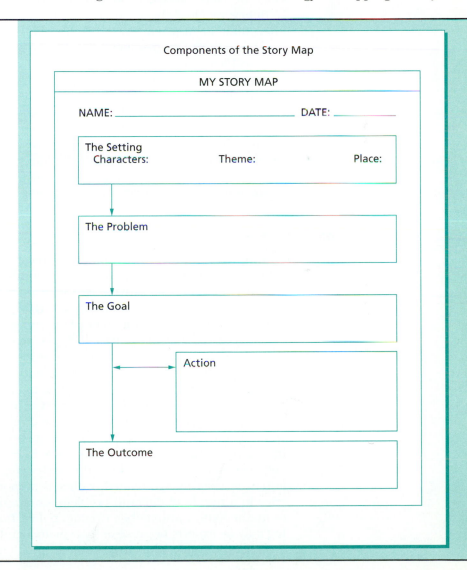

Components of the Story Map

MY STORY MAP

NAME: _____   DATE: _____

The Setting
  Characters: Theme: Place:

The Problem

The Goal

Action

The Outcome

Writing Strategies   One of the writing strategies can be summed up as T-P-W: *Think* (who is my audience? what do I want to say?); *Plan* (use a TREE to plan: T = note *Topic* sentence, R = note *Reasons* for writing, E = *Examine* your reasons, and E = note *Ending*); and *Write* (and rewrite, and rewrite again). Many students have no idea of how to take the perspective of a reader, nor do they understand that writing is a process usually requiring much revision. But such strategic writing skills are teachable and learnable, and result in greater success as a writer (see Fitzgerald & Markham, 1987).

Mathematics Strategies   Strategies for doing mathematics also exist, perhaps the simplest being estimation of an answer as a way of checking whether you are in the right "ball park." For example, the answer to 161.4 − 19.175 has to be around 160 − 20, or around 140; and 96 divided by 18 is like 100 divided by 20, so the answer must be around 5.

Before we close this section, you should be aware that strategies are often difficult to teach (Pressley, Burkell, et al., 1990). Some students find them hard to remember, resent them as extra work, or believe that they will lead to just a little gain for a lot of time expended. Even students who have had successful experiences with learning strategies are remarkably inconsistent in their use of them afterward (Tobias, 1989). Also, many students develop their own successful cognitive strategies. So when they already know how to learn effectively in school, trying to teach them new strategies may interfere with their usual, successful methods. Despite the difficulties, learning more about your students' strategy use and promoting the use of cognitive strategies such as those presented above will almost certainly help your students learn better.

Metacognition

Defining Metacognition   Thinking about one's own cognitive system is called **metacognition.** There are two kinds of metacognition during learning: thoughts about what we know, and thoughts about regulating how we go about learning (A. L. Brown, 1978; Chipman, Segal, & Glaser, 1985; Flavell, 1976). Think about how you might teach a novice to ride a bike, drive a car, or play chess. In apprenticeship settings such as these the teacher usually models for the novice learners. Suggesting strategies for learning in that area, giving a vocabulary to use in describing performance, and training how to regulate and monitor performance are methods you might use. The monitoring part of learning is metacognition.

Too often in schools teachers provide direct instruction only in areas where behavior is easily observed; we spend much less of our time on instruction in metacognitive skills. As A. L. Brown noted, "Metacognitive deficiencies are the problem of the novice, regardless of age. Ignorance is not necessarily age related; rather it is more a function of inexperience in a new (and difficult) problem situation" (1980, p. 475). Experts in mathematics, automobile driving, poker, horseback riding, or teaching may be experts because of their metacognitive skills. Those skills allow them to apply what they know to problem areas, to transfer their

knowledge. Perhaps the greatest benefit of mentoring relationships is that they enable novices to learn how their mentor thinks about problems. It is the mentor's habits of mind as much as his or her factual knowledge that novices need to master. And we are all novices when first learning school subjects such as math, gymnastics, or reading.

Helping Students Employ Metacognitive Skills   Employment of metacognitive skills facilitates learning (Mayer & Wittrock, 1996), and that seems to hold true whether students are high or low in ability. A study of fourth and fifth graders by Swanson (1990) demonstrated that students who possess and use metacognitive skill outperform those without such skills regardless of their ability level.

Metacognitive skills include the ability to ask ourselves, and answer, these kinds of questions:

- What do I know about this subject (this is somewhat like a self-administered achievement test)?
- How much time will I need to learn this?
- What is a good plan of attack to solve this?
- How can I predict or estimate the outcome of this task?
- How should I revise my procedures?
- How can I spot an error if I make one?
- Did I understand what I just read?

Although metacognitive skills usually develop slowly as we get older, the process is not a part of natural development. Experience and explicit instruction seem to play much more important roles in the development of these crucial cognitive skills than does maturity alone. As a consequence, teachers have a responsibility to help students develop their metacognitive skills.

Compared to average students, children who have mild retardation or learning disabilities sometimes show metacognitive deficits (Brown & Palincsar, 1982). So one approach to teaching these children is by instructing them to think in the ways others think when they engage in metacognition. By doing just that, Palincsar and Brown (1981) illustrated the importance of metacognition in learning. These researchers identified some junior high school students with IQs of about 90. The students could decode prose when they read but had comprehension scores at about the 7th percentile rank on national norms. Although they could read words, they seemed unaware of what and how to learn from the words they read. To make up for what seemed to be a lack of metacognitive skills, Palincsar and Brown first gave the students intensive corrective feedback when they tried to answer comprehension questions. They praised the students for correct responding and taught them how to change their responses when they were wrong. Then the students learned study strategies: how to paraphrase main ideas, how to classify information, how to predict the questions that might be asked about certain segments of the prose material, how to clarify what confused them, and how they might solve their own problems. That is, they learned metacognitive skills to use when learning.

The record of one of these children is shown in Figure 7.5. The num-

FIGURE 7.5

Record of the percentage of comprehension questions answered correctly by a student before, during, and after metacognitive training

Adapted from Palincsar & Brown (1981).

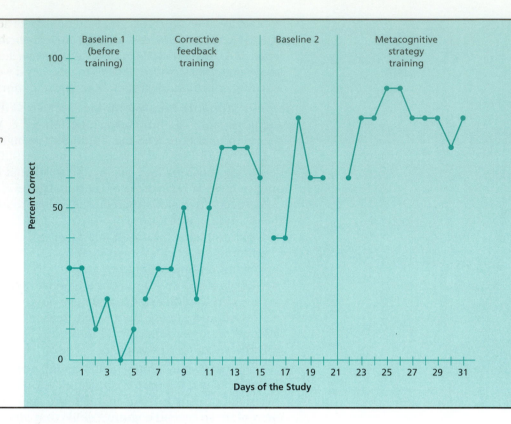

ber of correct responses to comprehension questions was about 15 percent before the special instruction. After corrective feedback, the percentage went up to about 50 percent. And after metacognitive strategies for learning were taught, the student was generally able to answer about 80 percent of the comprehension questions correctly.

In addition, the metacognitive strategies learned by these students transferred to their work in the regular classroom. (We discuss the topic of transfer in greater detail at the end of this chapter.) In fact, after only this short period of special instruction, the students showed improvements ranging from 20 to 46 percent in their regular classroom performance. And evidence for the transfer of learning from the training setting to the real classroom was still present months later.

Every teacher's goal is to have comprehension skills improve and transfer this way, but not every student shows the ability. How did the researchers do it? They assumed, as you can, that many learning and transfer problems are due to deficits in metacognitive skills. Many students need metacognitive training—training in **self-regulation**, self-monitoring, self-checking, problem identification, searching for analogies, and the like. Here are some metacognitive skills students can use to improve learning from textual material (see Tierney, 1985, for additional skills; see also Brown, Armbruster, & Baker, 1985; Brown, Bransford, et al., 1983):

- Make and refine predictions about what they are reading.
- Maintain focus during instruction and problem solving.
- Know how to vary their focus and change their approach when they are doing something wrong.
- Relate ideas to existing knowledge structures.
- Ask questions of themselves.
- Pick out and attend to the important information or characteristics of the text or task.
- Dismiss irrelevant information or characteristics of the text or task.
- Recognize when a relationship occurs or is implied.
- Use visualization when reading and problem solving.
- Consider the worth of ideas.
- Know when to ask for help.

Cognitively Active Learning

We have already discussed how a physically or cognitively active learner learns more than an inactive learner. Here we describe two forms of learning—discovery learning and generative learning—that include in their designs the notion of a cognitively active learner. Stimulating cognitive activity during learning usually improves the effectiveness of the learning.

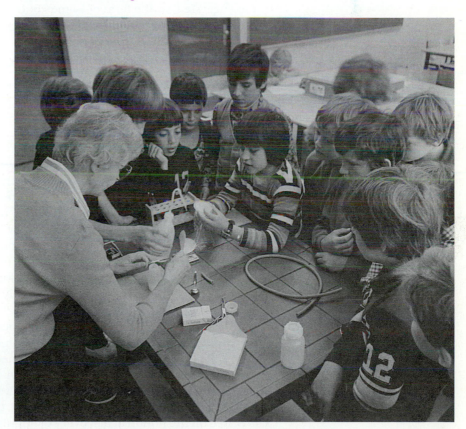

Active learning and heightened imagery result in better learning.

(© Andrew Brilliant)

Discovery Learning Jerome Bruner (1960) recommended that schools use more **discovery learning,** a type of learning preferred by scientists. It involves formulating hypotheses and testing them for yourself rather than just accepting a teacher's statements that something is true. So a student would wonder, Will the addition of chemical A to solution X really blow up? Or a teacher would ask, If you were exploring in Western Pennsylvania, and could settle anywhere, why would you settle in Pittsburgh? Discovery learning is always about the fundamental scientific questions, What would happen if. . . . ? or I wonder why. . . .

Discovery learning is lively, interesting, and meaningful to the individual student. From discovery learning comes practice in formulating general rules and principles, and identifying useful concepts. But it is not just letting students do whatever they want—otherwise the chemistry lab would really blow up and the school's computer would assuredly be used for some nefarious purpose! Discovery learning in schools is orchestrated. That is, teachers *arrange* for students to discover interesting things that they want them to retain. Teachers may ask, What do mammals have in common? What do you think is in cola drinks? Is the bay polluted? How can we know?

> Let it be clear what the act of discovery entails. It is rarely . . . that new facts are "discovered" in the sense of being encountered, as Newton suggested, in the form of islands of truth in an uncharted sea of ignorance. Or if they appear to be discovered in this way, it is almost always thanks to some happy hypotheses about where to navigate. Discovery, like surprise, favors the well-prepared mind. . . . Discovery, whether by a schoolboy going it on his own, or by a scientist cultivating the growing edge of his field, is in its essence a matter of rearranging or transforming evidence in such a way that one is enabled to go beyond the evidence so reassembled, to additional new insights.
> *(Bruner, 1960, p. 22)*

Since new knowledge is best generated by a well-prepared mind, teachers cannot just let discoveries happen as they may. They should be arranged to occur under conditions where teachers have already taught the background needed for the students to discover what has been chosen for them to discover—principles of how certain classes of chemicals interact, or where cities are located, or what makes an animal a mammal.

Teaching with activities that require discovery learning motivates students, actively engaging their minds in seeking the knowledge needed to solve a problem (How do we see?) or simply learning about how things work (How does the sewing machine work?). In fact, the many curriculum programs called the *new math,* developed in the 1960s, all used discovery processes to develop mathematical understandings (Davis, 1990). There is some agreement now that math needs to be taught more as a discovery-oriented set of experiences than as facts and operations to be learned by rote (De Corte, Greer, & Verschaffel, 1996). The whole-language approach to reading, in contrast to the phonics approach, is also based on the notion of discovery of linguistic patterns by the student.

Think of a high school teacher who used discovery learning. Do you think you learned more or less in this classroom than you would have with another approach? Why?

Permeating a good deal of contemporary curriculum, in fact, is the discovery approach, because it is believed to be a teaching technique compatible with present-day constructivist belief in an active, meaning-seeking mind. Discovery learning takes a lot longer than simply telling someone that, say, plants will not grow in the dark. But once learned through discovery, such facts are rarely forgotten. Obviously, discovery learning must be used sensibly because it is time consuming and the learning by each student can be a bit idiosyncratic (Pressley & McCormick, 1995). So "guided discovery" and "scaffolded" instruction (Rosenshine & Meister, 1992) are used to help the learner acquire the appropriate facts and ideas. The scaffold, like the planks in a ladder, are the helpful statements of the teacher that guide and support the next steps in a discovery learning activity. Scaffolding and guidance are recommended over "pure" discovery learning.

Generative Model of Learning　In the **generative model of learning** (Wittrock, 1990, 1991; Mayer & Wittrock, 1996), cognitive learning is seen as taking place when learners actively generate meaning for themselves. This model reminds us that learning is not like digestion—just put stuff in, and the system takes over. It stands in marked contrast to the notion that learning is somehow passive, a view characteristic of educational psychologists and curriculum developers of the previous few decades (Peterson, Clark, & Dickson, 1990). Instead, learning is seen as an active mental process, one in which meaning and significance are bestowed on that which is attended to. Otherwise what is attended to does not get to long-term storage and therefore cannot be retrieved from long-term storage.

More specifically, in this model "instruction involves stimulating the learner's information-processing strategies . . . and stores of relevant specific memories in relation to the information to be learned" (Wittrock, 1978, p. 26). The trick to being an effective instructor, suggests Wittrock, is to identify those students who do not naturally know how to generate relationships between what is to be learned and their own knowledge and experience. By teaching them how to create these associations, we can do much to improve classroom learning. But whenever possible, as in discovery learning, we should remember to let the learner do the work. We could draw a graph, or they could. We could make a table, or they could. We could write out questions, or they could. We can summarize, or they could. The more we involve students in making meaning, the more they are likely to learn. It is they who should draw inferences, paraphrase difficult ideas or passages, draw pictures of the situation, come in with classroom demonstrations, and solve practical problems.

Wittrock refined his ideas after discovering that the insertion of one familiar word into each sentence of a reading text that was in common use in schools increased story comprehension an amazing 50 percent and retention an amazing 100 percent (Marks, Doctorow, & Wittrock, 1974). For example, suppose a story reads: "Nimuk wanted to be a shaman. He wanted to talk with the deities." This could easily be changed to: "Nimuk wanted to be a religious leader. He wanted to talk with the gods." If a teacher asks, "What did Nimuk want to be?" or "Who did Nimuk want to talk with?" he gets very different answers from students who read the first version and those who read the second version. The familiar words make things more meaningful by enabling students to relate the new material to their own personal knowledge base—their schemata on religion. This technique helps learners generate their own meaning, almost always increasing learning. But it is the active generation by students themselves that provides the largest gains.

In one of Wittrock's studies with junior high school students, those generating summaries, constructing topic sentences, or relating what they read to their own experience increased their performance on comprehension and retention tests by about 25 percent—sometimes even by more than 100 percent! These effects were confirmed in other grades, with other samples, including those containing low-ability students. In virtually every case, when students are required to make meaning—to generate paragraph headings, summaries, interpretations, and images and to relate what is read, heard, or otherwise experienced to their preexisting knowledge—comprehension increases significantly.

The views of learning school subjects calling for more discovery and generative activities have something in common: They both stress the importance of the construction of meaning by students for themselves. That continues to be the focus of the next section.

Constructivist Perspectives on Learning

Constructivism is a loosely held together set of cognitive perspectives. At their core is a belief that knowledge is constructed by learners and developed through experience. Knowledge may be received, accumulated, and stored, but the strongest or deepest ways of knowing come from an individual's active construction of meaning through his or her interactions with physical and social environments. The following discussion looks first at the beliefs shared by virtually all the constructivist perspectives. Next, we examine a special kind of constructivism, social constructivism, which is marked more by a difference of emphasis than of philosophy. Throughout, keep in mind that constructivism is both a set of theoretical positions, about which there is much controversy (Noddings, 1990; Phillips, 1995), and a set of practices or methodologies for teaching loosely based on those theories, and worth considering regardless of the theoretical arguments (Confrey, 1990; Noddings, 1990).

Commonly Held Beliefs   When learners construct knowledge for themselves, this knowledge can be idiosyncratic. Personal meanings are attached to information. So someone's knowledge may not bear a close resemblance to what others think of as the real world. Obviously, it would be a problem if everyone had a separate view of the world; it would lead to chaos. That does not happen because there is a convergence of knowledge owing to the fact that we live in social communities. In communities we come to agree that the capital of New York is Albany, not Buffalo,

or that evolution is a viable theory (or not). Learners
ideas of others around them, notably parents, teache
ideas show Vygotsky's influence, and they are the k
constructivism, which we examine below.

When students are viewed as active rather than passive participants
in the learning process, it follows that instruction will more often be
aimed at activating their thinking instead of filling their heads with
knowledge. This results in certain pedagogical decisions. Constructivist
teachers want to enable their students to test new ideas, elaborate on
information, solve the puzzles of daily life, create new responses to situations—in short, to construct for themselves the knowledge they need
to function in their world.

The goals of constructivist teachers are for learning to take place in
rich and meaningful contexts that promote thoughtfulness, reflection,
and critical thinking, and incorporate authentic activities and assessments into instruction (Cognition and Technology Group, 1996). These
teachers choose particular kinds of classroom activities that help students learn to negotiate among themselves for meaning. For example, a
teacher may use projects of depth, complexity, and sustained duration
to enhance motivation and critical thinking. In problem-based project
learning (a topic we cover in a later section), students explore problem-
based situations without "correct" answers to promote thoughtfulness
and to motivate learning. Students work in cooperative settings (see
pp. 419–425), explore ideas publicly, and learn to challenge each other's
ideas (as well as the teachers') to arrive at the *shared* meanings without
which a society cannot function.

In these social interactions, reasons emerge to give up inappropriate
beliefs. For example, in a collaborative science discussion students are
led to discard the belief that the sun rises and sets, substituting for that
"obvious" conclusion the fact that the earth is rotating on its axis. Out
of our social interactions misperceptions that arise from constructing
knowledge for ourselves give way to more accurate kinds of knowledge.
For constructivists, knowledge must be treated as if it is "alive," not inert. It is the act of coming to know, as well as knowing, that is key.

A Different Emphasis: Social Constructivism The fact that learning
takes place in social communities is the focus of social constructivists.
Successful employment of our cognitive processes—thinking, reasoning,
problem solving, and remembering—are achievements of the social system or community we are part of. Except for great original thinkers, we
belong to families, athletic teams, and chess clubs, as well as organizations such as the National Council of Teachers of Mathematics or the Modern Language Association. Our thinking is contextualized (constrained,
enhanced, and controlled by a context) because we choose to belong to,
or are born into, social groups. Here psychology crosses over into anthropology; the study of thinking as it is affected by group membership
and culture is an interdisciplinary problem, requiring researchers from
both disciplines (e.g., Lave, 1988; Lave & Wenger, 1991; Saxe, 1990)

Within the social context, thinking is learned just as eating with uten-

Can you identify any-
one who has *appro-
priately* broken with
a community or fam-
ily on an important
idea? Is this the basis
of creativity?

sils and habits of cleanliness are learned. This can easily be seen in the disputes that have erupted between some religious fundamentalists and those whose beliefs differ from theirs. Some fundamentalists in various religions hold views about child rearing and education at odds with those of the larger U.S. society. Sometimes their views cause conflict at school board meetings (Berliner, 1997).

In communities influenced by constructivist thought, children are encouraged to think for themselves, to be thinking beings, and to question the authority of teachers, books, and scientific knowledge. But some religious fundamentalists, equally concerned citizens, may choose to discourage precisely those forms of thinking. They fear such mental activity would mean that the Bible and other sacred texts are open to challenge. So constructivist teachers may have their teaching methods challenged by fundamentalists.

The point is, different social groups have their own views about what thinking should be like and what thinking is to be about, and they teach these views to their children. We are all apprentices, trying to learn the particular rules of thought and language that characterize our communities, be they religious, political, occupational, or educational. Learning to be a member of an academic community (say, in mathematics or literature) or a social community at school (the "brains," "jocks," etc.) requires the same effort, namely, learning to think in the ways of that social group.

Eventually, some members of the group may depart from those ways of thinking, in desirable or undesirable ways. But they have needed to learn those ways in order to depart from them.

Being a junior member of a community is the way most of our initial political, religious, and moral beliefs are shaped. Apprenticeship in a particular community—of mathematicians or figure skaters—is perhaps the most powerful way to pass on the ways of thinking of that community. Younger learners are introduced to knowledge in advance of where they are developmentally, in accord with Vygotsky's idea of the zone of proximal development (see pp. 111–114). Furthermore, motivation to learn what this community knows and thinks is no problem—the desire to belong to the group is all that is needed to motivate learning to do what the best performers in the group can do.

Of course, the result can be either good or bad. For example, the ways of the street-gang leaders are emulated by the newest members of the gang. Nevertheless, the principle holds: Our thinking is moderated by the groups we choose to belong to. This is the social constructivist position.

Problem-Solving Approach to Learning

There are problems in the world that confound most of us, yet some people manage to solve them better than others. How do they do it? We now look at the nature of problems that teachers and others face, and the ways that experience—particularly reflected-on experience—can help a student become a better problem solver. That experience often comes in the form of case knowledge, and this kind of knowledge is a stepping-stone toward expertise in a field. Here we also discuss what distinguishes a novice from an expert problem solver in a particular domain.

Ill-Defined versus Well-Defined Problems   The problems we encounter in the world arise as either relatively well defined or ill defined. In education a well-defined problem would be to solve a quadratic equation, build a school for up to 500 students, or produce a bus route that takes the least time and uses the least fuel. A less well-defined problem might be to explain the causes of the Civil War, or pick a good school to work in, or find out what makes Roger act so nasty. Each of these seems to have solutions that might help resolve the problem. But at the end of the continuum are the completely ill-defined problems—problems with no easy solutions and no readily available criteria to judge whether a solution is successful or not. For teachers, these might include how to balance the phonics and whole-language approaches to reading, or how to use constructivist strategies—group work, discovery approaches, the project method—and still cover the curriculum they are expected to cover, or how to teach literature in such a way that it instills a love of reading. These problems have no easy answers. But these are the type of problems teachers must deal with most of the time.

In the domain of well-defined **problem solving,** intelligence, perseverance, and some life experience can pay off. Techniques for solving these problems can be learned by most of us. But many fewer learn to solve the more difficult problems that come as ill-defined ones. And teachers and physicians, for example, work in environments that call for these kinds of skills more frequently than do, say, pharmacists and accountants. Do the small number of good problem solvers in ill-defined domains have anything in common? We now know that they do: They have extensive case knowledge and reflect on their experience.

Case Knowledge   So much of problem solving, whether in teaching, auto mechanics, or medicine, depends on the kind of propositions people derive from the cases they encounter. The expertise of auto mechanics, physicians, or teachers is based on knowledge they have acquired from their experience—knowledge of the individual cases (cars, patients, students) they have had in the past (Ericsson, 1996; Berliner, 1994). From working on a hundred Fords, doing a hundred appendectomies, and facing a hundred children with reading or discipline problems, the auto mechanic, physician, and teacher extract information and develop what is called *case knowledge.* They develop propositions such as, "This car (patient, student) is acting like the one I had last year that baffled me until I found a way to handle it. From what I learned then, I should probably do x, y, and z." From the cases they have experienced over the years they derive the kind of if-then relationships characteristic of declarative knowledge—and develop expertise that would not be the same otherwise.

In fact, knowledge derived from cases is what distinguishes the competent practitioner from the novice. How to involve disengaged parents, what to do when a child is disrespectful, how to work with a high school student who works in the evening and falls asleep in class—all are bits

Do you have a negative reaction to the word *problem?* If so, try to reconceptualize the term and to think of it simply as an unresolved situation. Try applying this view to the next problem you encounter.

of knowledge learned from particular past cases that have been reflected upon, and stored in the form of declarative knowledge. So, when an expert teacher encounters something new, he or she can bring to mind a case that appears relevant, and compare the new situation to the old case and its solution. Comparing the new case to the old lets the teacher decide whether there are ways to solve the new problem based on what was learned from the previous similar one. So when a child cheats on a test, as children occasionally do; or when a parent is irate, as they occasionally are; or when students are unable to learn some mathematical concept, as occasionally happens, it is the experience of the past that is the teacher's guide to solving the problems of the present. The problems teachers encounter may have no single right answer, but they can come to wiser solutions if they can learn from past experience.

Two points are worth thinking about, then. First, unless you work hard at reflecting on your practice of teaching you will not learn much from experience. Learning to be a reflective practitioner (Schön, 1987) is what separates the better from the worse auto mechanics, physicians, and teachers. When problems are ill defined, a good deal of reflection about the solutions attempted is needed to turn the problem-solving experience into a learning event for yourself. Journal writing and discussion with colleagues can help you learn from experience.

Second, you will probably not be a great teacher early in your career. Teaching is a very complex activity, one that requires solutions to ill-defined problems every day. You simply cannot have had the experience to sensibly handle all these problems in the first few years of your career. But experience will teach you if you allow it to. Eventually, if you work at it, you can become an expert teacher. Estimates are that it takes five to seven years for a teacher to acquire the skills needed to become an expert problem solver (Berliner, 1994).

Reflect on your reactions to these estimates. Do they seem surprisingly long? Or do you think that any complex work would require this kind of experience? In your own schooling, have the better, more expert teachers been experienced?

Distinction between Novice and Expert   What makes an expert an expert? One answer is that experts have an unusual ability to solve unique problems. That is, they can organize their previously acquired knowledge in such a way that they can apply it to seemingly new situations in order to resolve them.

For example, how do expert chess players differ from novice chess players? Research suggests that one of the ways is that experts, over the years they have played, have stored in long-term memory as many as 50,000 patterns. These perceptually distinct and familiar configurations of the chess board are the expert's "vocabulary" for playing chess. It is like having a vocabulary of 50,000 nouns and verbs for describing your environment. Each of the 50,000 patterns has associated with it certain moves. The expert knows that for a certain kind of game, certain subroutines must be used to win. Furthermore, when playing ten chess games simultaneously, the expert is in fact playing ten distinct patterns. He or she seems to know that on board 1 is game type 6,974 and that it can be won by concentrating on how the bishop moves; or that on board 2 is game type 12,074, which calls for queen and rook attacks if the opponent moves the queen's knight. So each game is classified as a

POLICY, RESEARCH, AND PRACTICE

How Do Teachers Develop Expertise?

The root word of experience and expertise is the same. But not everyone who is experienced deserves to be called expert in their work. So the notion of expertise has become independent of the notion of experience, though the meanings of the terms are still thoroughly entangled. It is probably experience that is the most important prerequisite for the development of expertise.

Experts attain their admirable status through experience of a special kind. In their particular domain, say, chess or driving a car, those who develop into experts learn more from experience than do the rest of us. Their learning is highly motivated and probably reflected upon more than is the learning of others. Experts usually perform appropriately and effortlessly, the hallmarks of exemplary performance, whether it be in chess, physics problem-solving, taxi driving, or teaching. But the transformation from hesitant and frightened novice to confident expert is not swift in a field as complex as teaching. To help beginning teachers know what to expect as they embark on their careers, a five-stage developmental model follows (Berliner, 1994).

Stage 1: Novice level. At this stage, the commonplaces of an environment must be identified, the elements of the tasks to be performed need to be labeled and learned, and a set of context-free rules must be learned. To begin to play chess you learn "This is a rook." To drive a car you learn "The solid line means you cannot pass here." Similarly the novice teacher is taught the meaning of terms such as *higher-order questions, reinforcement,* and *learning disabilities.* He or she is taught context-free rules such as "Give praise for right answers," "Wait three seconds after asking a higher-order question," and "Never criticize a student." The behavior of the novice, including a novice teacher, is usually rational, relatively inflexible, and tends to conform to whatever rules and procedures he or she was told to follow. Only minimal skill at chess, driving, or teaching should really be expected of a novice. This is a stage for learning the objective facts and features of situations. It is a stage for gaining experience. It is the stage at which real-world experience appears far more important than verbal information, as attested to by generations of student teachers. Many first-year teachers as well as student teachers may be considered novices.

Stage 2: Advanced-beginner level. Many first- through third-year teachers are likely to be in this developmental stage. This is when experience can become melded with verbal knowledge, that is, when procedural and propositional knowledge are blended. It is also when episodic and case

continues

knowledge are built up. Without meaningful past episodes and cases to relate to the experience of the present, teachers at this stage are unsure of themselves; they do not know what to do and what not to do. Advanced beginners have difficulty knowing what to do when a child challenges their authority, constantly seeks their attention, or boasts about getting As. Such incidents are understood much better after the second and third time they happen. Similarities across teaching contexts are recognized by the advanced beginner. Strategic knowledge—when to ignore or break rules and when to follow them—is also developed in this stage, as context begins to guide behavior. Although experience is affecting behavior, the advanced beginner may still have no sense of what is important.

Stage 3: Competent level. With further experience and some motivation to succeed, most advanced beginners become competent at what they do (though a few teachers apparently get stuck forever at a less-than-competent level). Many third- and fourth-year teachers, as well as more experienced ones, reach this level. Competent performers of a craft make conscious choices about what they are going to do. They set priorities and decide on plans. They have rational goals and choose sensible means for reaching the ends they have in mind. They can determine what is and what is not important. This is the stage in which teachers learn, through their experience, what and who to attend to and what and who to ignore in the classroom. This is also when teachers learn to make curriculum and instruction decisions, such as when to stay with a topic and when to move on, based on a particular teaching context and a particular group of students. But competent performers are not (yet) very fast, fluid, or flexible in their behavior.

Stage 4: Proficient level. At or after the fifth year, a modest number of teachers move into this stage of development, when intuition or know-how becomes prominent. They develop a more intuitive sense of what they are doing. Out of their wealth of accumulated experience comes a holistic way of viewing the situations they encounter. They recognize similarities among events that novices fail to see. This is the residue of their experience. For example, the proficient teacher may notice, without conscious effort, that today's math lesson is bogging down for the same reason that last week's spelling lesson "bombed." At some higher level of pattern recognition, the similarities between the disparate events are understood. This holistic recognition of similarity allows proficient teachers to predict events more precisely, since they see more things as alike and therefore as having been experienced before. Their rich case knowledge can be brought to bear on a problem. They are faster, more fluid, and more flexible in their behavior. The proficient performer, however, although intuitive in pattern recognition and in ways of knowing, is still likely to be analytical and deliberative in deciding what to do.

Stage 5: Expert level. If the novice is deliberate, the advanced beginner insightful, the competent performer rational, and the proficient performer intuitive, the expert might be categorized as often arational. Experts have an intuitive grasp of the situation and seem to sense in nonanalytic and nondeliberative ways the appropriate response to make. They show fluid performance, acting in an apparently effortless manner. The expert teacher seems to just know where to be or what to do at the right time, almost as if he or she could see into the future.

Experts perform in a *qualitatively* different way than novices and competent performers. An example is the science teacher who reports that the lesson "just moved along so beautifully today" that she "never really had to teach." Experts are not consciously choosing what to attend to and what to do, and this is arational because it is not easily described as deductive or analytic behavior. But the behavior of experts is certainly not irrational. They do things that usually work, so when things are proceeding without a hitch, they are not solving problems or making decisions in the usual sense of those terms. They "go with the flow," as it is sometimes described. When anomalies occur or when things do not work out as planned, they bring deliberate analytic processes to bear on the situation. But otherwise they rarely appear to be reflective about their performance.

This theory of the development of expertise fits a good deal of the data, though like any general theory it does not hold for every individual. However, it serves to inform new teachers that they are embarking on a career that requires time in which to develop expertise. Classroom teaching is a lot more complex than baby-sitting, or even tutoring, one child. Developing competency over the first few years is the first order of business for new teachers, and most achieve it. A few competent teachers, if they work at it, manage to move on to expertise, becoming the Teacher of the Year, grand-masters of the field, the revered and memorable educators that affect students' lives as long as they live.

(Based on Berliner, 1994; Bullough, 1989; Bullough & Baughman, 1997.)

game type, and a first-time-ever-seen configuration is translated into a recognizable "old friend"—a pattern that is already known (see de Groot, 1965).

How do expert physicists differ from novices? One difference is that experts take more time in studying a problem. But once they start to work, they solve problems faster than novices do. The experts also seem more often to construct an abstract representation of the problem in their minds. That is, in their working memory they hold mental representations of the blocks, pulleys, inclined planes, levers, or whatever they need to solve the problem. Expert physicists also tend to classify new problems more frequently. They may decide a problem is type-X, to be solved by using the laws of inclined planes. Or they may see the problem as belonging to the type that deals with forces, pulleys, and blocks, which are always solvable by using some version of Newton's second law, $F = MA$ (force = mass $\times$ acceleration) (Chi, Glaser, & Rees, 1982).

After extensive experience in their areas of interest, experts in chess, physics, and teaching seem able to use old information in a new context to solve problems—by very similar mechanisms! All experts attempt to (1) classify a problem as a particular type, (2) represent the problem visually in their minds, and then (3) use well-known routines to solve the problem.

Classification is very important here. Once someone knows exactly what kind of problem she is dealing with, the solution seems to follow easily. Research on college students solving algebra word problems and physicians solving medical problems, as well as the work on chess and physics experts, shows that experienced problem solvers work with a problem schema. Once they find the schema—the abstract representation of the phenomenon—in long-term memory, it directs the solution. Experts have stored in memory many problem schemata and associated actions that generally produce a solution. They have acquired these schemata as a result of extensive experience (case knowledge) with the phenomena in their fields. Novices, by contrast, do not appear to have developed elaborate schemata. So each problem they face is truly new and therefore extremely difficult.

What does this research mean for teachers? Two important implications stand out:

- Students must have lots of experience with a domain of knowledge in order to learn the skills needed to develop expertise. The "smorgasbord" and "surface" education that schools sometimes give students (one unit of this, one unit of that; one hour of this topic, thirty minutes of that) is not enough to produce expertise. This kind of education develops students familiar with a vast array of events and domains of knowledge but they become expert in none.

- Teachers can help students solve problems by purposefully modeling the problem-solving strategy needed. The teacher might say, "Look everyone! When a block of mass M1 is put on top of a block of mass M2, a horizontal force F1 must be applied. Picture it in your mind! When we face problems of mass and force, we should decide whether the laws of force or energy take precedence. If energy, then . . ."

Teaching problem solving by way of modeling helps the learning of some of these skills. This is why apprenticeship is so important a way of thinking about how we learn in social settings such as classrooms. Making transparent to your students the strategies you use to solve problems will help them learn to solve problems.

Situated Cognition

Situated cognition is one of the newest ways to conceptualize thinking and knowing (Greeno, Collins, & Resnick, 1996). For a situationist, the context or setting within which a particular act of cognition occurs is critical. This context is significant in several ways, and we examine two of these below. The first stresses that the success of an individual's reasoning, thinking, or problem solving is not attributable to that individual alone, but to the system in which he or she lives and works as well. This concept is called *distributed expertise* or *distributed cognition*. The second focuses on the fact that real learning takes place only when situated in "real-world" activities, such as problem-based project learning.

Distributed Expertise/Cognition   In this view, knowledge is not just in the heads of individuals, it is distributed—in the books, tools, computers, artifacts, and ways of interacting that characterize each social group. The communities in which a person functions prescribe and proscribe the ways of thinking and acting that result in successful practices such as solving a math equation or writing an essay on global warming. Knowing how to participate in these various communities plays a crucial role in the development of the skills for reasoning, thinking, and problem solving. In the situated-cognition view, knowing is a property of both the individual (as we ordinarily think about it) *and* the groups we belong to. This is a new way to think about knowledge. Figure 7.6 (from a suggestion by Greeno, 1994) illustrates this concept.

The first photo is Rodin's masterpiece of sculpture, "The Thinker." It has become the iconic representation of what people mean by thinking. This man is a solitary, powerful, greater-than-life-size figure, seriously

FIGURE 7.6

You can never be sure where and when deep thoughts will emerge

(Left: © Gian Berto Vanni, Art Resource, NY; Right: © Elizabeth Crews/Stock Boston)

engaged in a struggle to obtain insight. "The Thinker" implies that thinking is hard, not easy; thinking is serious, not fun; thinking is done alone, not with others. The second photo shows an animated group of students. Are they thinking too? Too often teachers forget that genuine thinking about important things can be easy, fun, and done in a group. Situated learning emphasizes the gains possible when we consider the second photo a legitimate iconic representation of thinking and learning just as the first one is.

When situated learning is the "lens" for viewing the learning process, the teacher-directed classroom is seen as quite limited. From this standpoint, education is deficient when characterized by teachers telling students the things to learn, when lectures are common, when students spend much time filling out workbook pages, when answers are always right or wrong, and the thinking behind the answer is not seen as important. On the other hand, learning is considered better when the students are in an apprentice relationship to the teacher. They get mentoring from the teacher and are afforded opportunities to engage in legitimate peripheral participation as they learn the ways of thinking in the school community.

We are used to the idea of apprenticeships in the trades of plumbing, tailoring, or cooking. In those fields, the apprentice slowly takes on the skills of the master. At first staying peripheral to the activities, the apprentice learns how the master thinks and talks about the work: how to compute the amount of pipe needed, lay out the patterns for sewing, or reduce a sauce. Later, after watching and listening, and with mentoring, apprentices themselves try some parts of the work. Under the watchful eye of the master they learn their trade.

> Have you ever been in an apprenticeship situation? In a community of learners? How did these work?

Cognitive apprenticeships for learning mathematics and science, or writing and art, are no less necessary than apprenticeships for learning plumbing, tailoring, or cooking, or apprenticeships in the arts such as dance and theater (Brown, Collins, & Duguid, 1989; Collins, Brown, & Newman, 1989; Lave & Wenger, 1991). How might such apprenticeships be set up? The key seems to be to develop a community of learners where knowledge is distributed and shared among students and teachers. In such communities students formulate problems as well as solve them, construct and evaluate hypotheses, engage in arguments and arrive at solutions, all under the coaching of teachers and other students who have mastered the forms of argument in that community.

Some communities of this type have recently been formed to teach writing (Scardamalia & Bereiter, 1991; Scardamalia, Bereiter, & Lamon, 1994); to learn how mathematicians think about mathematics (Lampert, 1990); and for general academic work (Brown, Ash, et al., 1993; A. L. Brown, 1994; see also Bruer, 1993). The data are not all in on the latest attempts to develop these interactive, collaborative, learning communities, but initial results are quite positive despite demonstrating at the same time how hard it is to develop and sustain such communities.

Problem-Based Project Learning In problem-based project learning, students explore situations in which there are no "correct" answers.

These projects are more authentic activities than they usually get in school, the kind that simulate real-life problem solving. They seem to promote thoughtfulness and to motivate students. They can be worked on collaboratively, or alone. They are enjoyed more often when they can be done in and by small groups of students.

One such project (given to one of our own children) was to determine whether San Francisco Bay was polluted. It required that a parent accompany his or her child to 11 different sites around the bay to collect water samples. The samples were analyzed in a chemistry class by a team of young scholars, who prepared a report on what they found. In addition, they scheduled a field trip for themselves to an Army Corps of Engineers site, 30 miles away, which had a working model of the bay, demonstrating how water flowed through it. For weeks they sustained interest in a real-life topic with real-life consequences—and they all vowed never to eat any fish caught from the shallow southern part of the bay!

A project for another of our children was to collect data on some social phenomenon and bring it back to class to discuss. This led eventually to her formulating the question: Is lunacy real? That is, she wanted to know if people really do act a little "crazier" during the full moon than at other times of the month. She negotiated access to the admitting records of a county hospital psychiatric ward, and compared admissions for days the moon was full to days when it was not, over the previous three years. She looked at both numbers admitted per day and severity of problems on admission. Over a two-month stretch she carried out her research, analysis, and report writing, then gave her report to the class and led a heated argument about the issue. Everyone in the class disagreed with her conclusion, based on hard data, that there was no relationship at all between acting "crazy" and the phases of the moon in this particular hospital, in this particular community. She learned a number of important lessons that semester, including that people continue to hold beliefs even in the face of data that do not support them.

What is common to these two projects? They allow students to explore a problem that seems real to them. Among the most important things they teach is problem finding, a process that is probably as valuable as problem solving. When children have time for "messing around" in a subject area where there are problems, they learn to recognize many more problems than those they originally set out to deal with. This sustains their motivation to learn.

The problem-based project method also teaches dozens of things simultaneously—much like life. Seldom in real life does one do only two-column addition with regrouping, or writing without any real purpose or audience in mind. So in project-based approaches students use numbers, interpret data, write reports, schedule meetings, try to convince others of their ideas, argue, agree, disagree, and so forth. In other words, school comes to resemble life, and students learn skills that apply to life.

Some technology-based projects offer all these characteristics now, and without even having to leave the school. Computer-based microworlds allow students to see the effects of their decisions on simulated cities, the effects of medical advances on population growth, or the ef-

> Generate a list of a dozen possible problem-based projects. Include several for each of these areas: social studies, science, literature.

fects of economic policies on economic growth. A student can also use a computer as a "lab partner" as he solves problems in heat and thermodynamics, learning along the way to formulate and design experiments for the computer to carry out, compare the results with predictions, and interpret the results in a report of findings (Cognition and Technology Group at Vanderbilt, 1996). At least one multimedia video program allows students to learn mathematics along with archeologist Indiana Jones of the movies, as he searches for the lost Ark.

It is important to emphasize that problem-solving ability can be taught; it is not just inherited. Formal instruction and *real experience in problem solving* can produce better problem solvers (Block, 1994). So simulated environments for solving problems and real-world projects that are problem-based motivate students and teach them interesting things, not all of which are ever represented on the tests ordinarily used to assess them.

Strategies for Promoting Cognitive Learning and Higher-Order Thinking

If a child does not add quickly, you might think about giving her more addition problems to solve in the hope that with more practice her speed will improve. If a child is not reading well, you might break up reading tasks into smaller units so that the subskills can be learned in isolation and combined later. Cognitive psychologists have a very different view of these learning problems from that of the behaviorists or general educational psychologists of just a few years ago (H. Gardner, 1985). Rather than taking the steps described above, cognitive scientists would try to understand the kinds of thinking associated with the particular content to be learned. They would ask what is going on in the minds of these students to understand how they learn to add or read. How are they making meaning—wrong though it may be—from the instruction given? These are the kinds of questions that lead to the strategies we examine in this section.

These strategies are meant to encourage students to think actively as they learn. They should help promote a deeper, stronger construction of meaning because they focus on students' own building of meaning as they engage in analytical and evaluative kinds of thinking. Note, too, that many of the strategies should help students build bridges between what they already know and what is new. The basic instructional rule is: The greater the number of associations, the more meaningful the learning. From what you have already learned about constructivism, you should be able to figure out why this is so.

Mediation and Enhancement   One way to help students make associations is through **mediation,** the process of creating meaningful links between apparently unrelated items or ideas. For students, at least at first, a good deal of what must be learned is apparently meaningless. Mediational strategies are sometimes called *enhancement strategies* since they are ways to enhance meaningfulness. Mediators could involve images or rhymes, say; but however they are constructed, their goal is to help make the second part of a pair of things to be learned more memorable, given the first item in the pair. For instance, suppose a young student is trying to learn the names of twentieth-century leaders and their countries, the names of the northwestern states such as Washington and Oregon; or the capitals of states, as in California: Sacramento. In this kind of learning, called *paired-associate learning,* mediators—connectors, enhancers—can help children remember the pairs more effectively. Children can be encouraged to invent mediators such as: "There's the Churchill of England," "They're Washing the iron ore," or "Cal is in the sack." Some children are able to generate such mediators on their own; others—for instance, students with learning disorders—may need more help from the teacher. However, once learned, mediational strategies appear to help all students remember.

Teachers can help students learn curriculum better by providing mediators that can enhance the associations to what is to be learned. For example, when teaching that Israel is an international diamond-cutting center, the paired associates are "Israel-diamond cutting." To help students connect the two, a teacher might say that Israel receives diamonds to be cut; that diamonds are shipped to Israel and cut there; that uncut diamonds enter Israel and cut diamonds leave; or that Israeli diamond cutters are among the most talented in the world. In each case the teacher is providing a mediator to enhance the link between Israel and diamond cutting. This should help students code, store, and retrieve the information better.

Almost any pairs of things to be learned are more easily remembered when mediators are used. When studying for your next exam, try them. You will probably find that mediational processes (giving yourself some verbal connectors/links/rhymes/images/or any other enhancers) will make declarative knowledge more memorable and help you get the order correct more frequently when calling up procedural knowledge. Having the correct knowledge is the first step in thinking deeper, the issue to which we now turn.

Focus on Instructional Design Here we focus on several additional strategies that involve teachers actively pointing out and working with students on the structural and organizational elements of what is to be learned. Doing so can help students in organizing their understanding, in making better sense of what they are learning, and in retaining what they have learned.

Advance Organizers The **advance organizer,** a technique proposed by Ausubel (1968, 1978), is like a set of general concepts that helps students organize the more specific material that follows. At a somewhat higher level of abstraction than what follows, these oral or written organizing concepts alert students to what is to be presented and how it is structured. The theory is that if teachers give students an abstract, hierarchically structured preview of what they are going to teach, one thought to be compatible with their memory-storage system, they can make new material more meaningful and therefore easier to learn and retrieve.

The advance organizer acts as a kind of mental **scaffolding** for what follows, identifying how the new information is ordered and interrelated, and how it is related, as well, to previous knowledge. Empirical evidence suggests that teachers who begin an instructional session with an advance organizer make new material appear more familiar and meaningful to students, and easier to recall (Luiten, Ames, & Ackerman, 1980). (We return to advance organizers in Chapter 9.)

Hierarchical Structure   Gagné (1985) offered **hierarchical structure** as a way of developing instructional materials. Hierarchical structure is a sequence that orders material from simple learning events (specific, concrete ideas and concepts) to complex ones (abstract concepts and principles). Research on the effectiveness of such sequencing is encouraging. Both Ausubel and Gagné assume that general principles encompass specific ideas, and both use this assumption to make information more meaningful and familiar. But Ausubel's advance organizer works from the top down: By identifying the most general and abstract principles, an advance organizer helps students give more meaning to the specific concepts and facts that make up the new material to be learned. Gagné's theory about the importance of specifying how information is hierarchically organized is compatible with Ausubel's thinking, but it is a bottom-up theory. It creates meaning and familiarity in sequential steps, requiring that students master a lower-order concept before moving on to a higher-order one. Working from the principle that minds do not reproduce reality, but instead, construct it for themselves, Gagné would concentrate on teaching component concepts, for example, distinguishing between the terms *mind* and *brain;* between a "copying" theory of how mind works and other ways information might be coded and transformed; and ensuring that the learner understood the ways constructive processes change a to-be-remembered-idea in certain lawful ways (simplicity, accommodation with, or assimilation to existing knowledge, and so on).

To illustrate an advance organizer here, we could (1) begin by presenting the goals of a constructivist theory, (2) offer the notion that transformations of information may have to occur for information to be remembered, (3) note that ideas need to "fit in" and be ordered in some way to fit the knowledge structures that already exist, and then (4) state that reasonable forms of agreement between people can take place even when we all make our own meanings out of the world.

Both Ausubel and Gagné recognize the effect on retention of familiarity, meaningfulness, and order in instruction. Despite that, one starts ordering from the top down and the other from the bottom up. Both seem sensible forms of instruction compared to what would come from a teacher who has not thought at all about ways to order information to be learned.

Mapping   A special type of organization of to-be-learned information has been studied in many classrooms, sometimes demonstrating remarkable effects. This type uses **semantic maps**—organized visual and verbal diagrams of the declarative and procedural knowledge to be remembered (Lambiotte, Dansereau, Cross, & Reynolds, 1989). Figure 7.7 presents two examples of semantic maps. Maps such as these have been

> Examine this textbook for its structure and pedagogical aids. Which aspects do you find most beneficial to your learning?

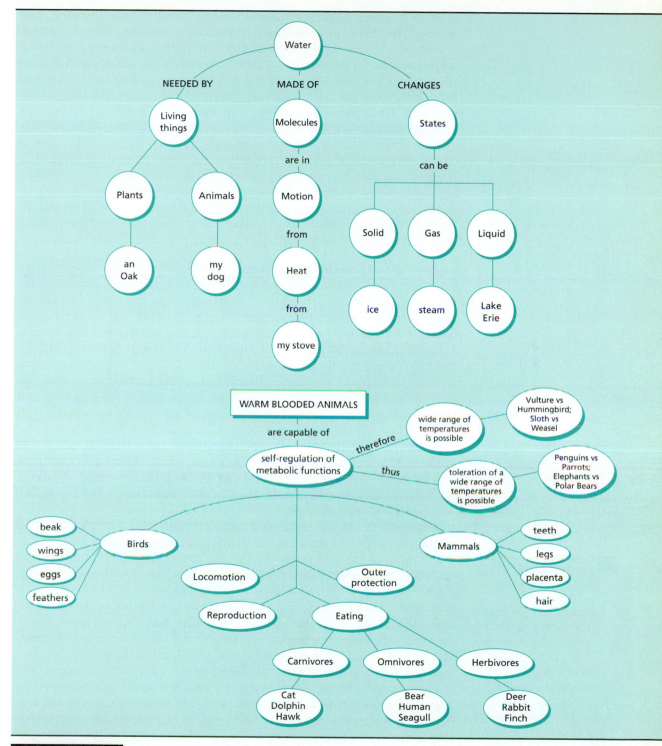

FIGURE 7.7

Two semantic maps: Graphic organizations of knowledge

Source: Adapted from Novak, Joseph D., & Gowain, D. Bob (1984) Learning How to Learn. *Reprinted with the permission of Cambridge University Press; and "Multirelational Semantic Mapping" by J. G. Lambiotte, G. K. Dansereau, D. R. Cross, and S. R. Reynolds,* Educational Psychology Review, *1989, pp. 331–368. Copyright © 1989. Used by permission of Plenum Publishing Corporation.*

used to improve reading comprehension, learning from lectures, and writing. They have been generated by either teachers or students, groups or individuals, and used before or after instruction. Teachers claim such maps are helpful in organizing their presentations, allow them also to spot difficulties in instruction, and useful for designing tests. The best ways to develop and use maps are not yet known. You will have to experiment. But some studies show that they seem to aid in (1) encoding information by adding a visual representation to the verbal knowledge to be learned, (2) retrieval, increasing the cues available to the person trying to remember, and (3) comprehension, helping students see what is important and the relationships between different areas of knowledge. Semantic maps to organize knowledge are particularly beneficial to students with little prior knowledge in an area, those with low general ability, and those with problems in reading comprehension. And that means a lot of students could benefit from greater use of semantic maps.

Developing and Enriching Schemata   Schemata (singular: schema) have been proposed as a way of understanding how the mind organizes information. Schemata are abstract structures that represent the knowledge stored in memory (Rumelhart & Ortony, 1977). For some psychologists, they are the building blocks of cognition—the existing mental structures that allow us to learn new information and guide us through the day, providing the common-sense "theories" and behavioral scripts we need to interpret our world (Rumelhart, 1980; H. Gardner, 1985). We have schemata for eating in restaurants, attending hockey games, and visiting our grandmothers. The full range of knowledge associated with each of these activities is our schema for the activity. That schema also connects with other schemata, and the intersections of schemata define our world. A schema for "student," for example, would intersect with the schemata for "schooling," "reading," and "teaching." It would consist of the information, in an abstract form, of the customary associations we have with the word *student.*

A schema is not the same as a concept: A concept provides a formal definition; a schema underlies the concept. Our concept of "student" is a definition of the attributes of students and nonstudents; our schema for "student" is a more general knowledge associated with the word *student.* The schema contains slots, or place holders into which we fit our experience. For example, we might expect the occupations of an eighteen-year-old and an eighty-year-old to be "student" and "retired" respectively. And our schemata, the knowledge structures we have, about students and retired people contain slots for age, which is customarily associated with these occupational titles. But neither the concept of "student" nor the concept of "retired person" requires age as a defining characteristic. There are some retired eighteen-year-olds and some eighty-year-old students. So our schemata, which we bring to our experience, determine how we interpret that experience.

In fact, some theorists believe that the schemata we bring to an instructional situation are as important as the actual oral or written message that makes up instruction. Here is an example:

Jot down brief descriptions of schemata you hold for two or three concepts—from abstract concepts such as "work" to concrete ones like "car." Ask several friends to do the same for the same concepts. How do you explain the differences?

A general implication for education is that the schemata a person already possesses are a principal determiner of what will be learned from a text. Imagine a section from a geography text about an unfamiliar nation. An adult would bring to bear an elaborate nation schema, which would point to subschemata representing generic knowledge about political systems, economics, geography, and climate. Each subschema would have its own infrastructure and interconnect with other subschemata at various points. . . . The young reader, on the other hand, may not possess a nation schema adequate to assimilate the text. In the worst case, the material will be gibberish. . . . More likely, the young reader will have partly formed schemata that will allow him or her to make sense of the passage but will not permit the construction of mental representatives of great depth or breadth.

(Anderson, Spiro, & Anderson, 1978)

What this implies is that comprehension and meaningfulness depend on engaging appropriate schemata (see also Hiebert & Raphael, 1996). If a relevant schema does not exist, then a teacher needs to provide a schema for what is to be learned. In this way the new material can be assimilated into existing **knowledge structures** and "cross-listed" with other schemata. Unless the teacher provides these schemata, students will come up with their own, which may be inappropriate.

An example of the power of schemata to influence what is learned comes from an experiment by Anderson, Reynolds, et al. (1977). Suppose, like their subjects, you read the following story:

Rocky slowly got up from the mat, planning his escape. He hesitated a moment and thought. Things were not going well. What bothered him most was being held, especially since the charge against him had been weak. He considered his present situation. The lock that held him was strong, but he thought he could break it. He knew, however, that his timing would have to be perfect. Rocky was aware that it was because of his early roughness that he had been penalized so severely—much too severely from his point of view. The situation was becoming frustrating; the pressure had been grinding on him for too long. He was being ridden unmercifully. Rocky was getting angry now. He felt he was ready to make his move. He knew that his success or failure would depend on what he did in the next few seconds. (p. 372)

Is this a story about a prison break, yes or no?

Suppose there were multiple-choice items to test your recall of this story, and one item asked: Was Rocky punished for aggressiveness by (1) being imprisoned or (2) losing points to his opponent? If you think this story is about a prison break, you would choose 1. But, if you were a physical education major (as half the subjects in this study were) you might choose 2, interpreting the story as concerned with a wrestling match. Sixty-four percent of the physical education majors made this choice. Reread the story from that perspective. Only 28 percent of the subjects who were music majors interpreted the story theme as a wrestling match. The point of this and similar experiments (for example, Anderson & Pichert, 1978; Bransford & Johnson, 1972) is to demonstrate how the schemata one brings to a learning experience influence what is learned and what is retrieved. A person's background knowledge—the schema brought to bear on the learning situation—determines what she learns (Hiebert & Raphael, 1996).

Providing schemata or helping learners bring their own appropriate schemata to an instructional situation is an important way in which teachers can ensure meaningful learning. One way to provide schemata is to use similes, such as "Electric current is like flowing water" and "Long-term memory is like a giant card catalog." Similes allow students to incorporate new information into an already-existing schema with only some minor modifications (Ortony, 1975). As a teacher, whatever you can do to tap into the already-existing knowledge structures the learner brings to the instructional situation can help you make the material more meaningful.

Making Meaning in Mathematics   Learning to add can be done a number of ways. Suppose you want to add 2 and 6. You can start by setting a place in your mind at zero, go up 2 units, then go up 6 more, and mentally see what you get. Or you can start with the 2, as given, go up 6 units, and see what you get. Or you can start with the larger number, the 6, and go up 2 units, and see what you get. All three methods give you the correct answer. But a student who learns to add using the first is going to work slowly because that model of arithmetic, although correct, is inefficient. On the other hand, the student who learns the last model works quickly because it is the simplest way to reach the solution. In this case, having a child do more problems would probably not be as effective as finding ways to understand the cognitive strategies used by him to solve addition problems, and then helping him make those strategies more efficient. The point hammered home again and again by cognitive psychologists is that practice and reinforcement are not as likely to increase a student's mathematics skills as is modifying the cognitive strategies the student uses to perform those skills.

Other cognitive studies of mathematics learning find that some kinds of problems that look similar are in reality very different types of problems for young students. For example:

A. Joe has 3 marbles. Tom gives him 5 more marbles. How many marbles does Joe have now?

B. Joe has 3 marbles. Tom has 5 more than Joe. How many marbles does Tom have?

Both of these problems can be solved with the equation $3 + 5 = 8$. But kindergarten and first-grade children who get problem A correct cannot always get problem B right. Type-A problems are of a class called *causing-a-change* problems; type-B problems are called *comparison* problems. Different kinds of thought patterns are needed to solve the two types of problems.

Based on these examples, construct several new mathematical problems. Reflect on the kinds of thought patterns that will be required to solve them.

Cognitive scientists are working to identify the kinds of problems that require different kinds of cognitions (see Mayer, 1986; Nesher, 1986; Riley, Greeno, & Heller, 1983; De Corte, Greer, & Verschaffel, 1996). If teachers can understand how successful and unsuccessful learners think about different kinds of problems, they can do more than just demonstrate mathematics computations, or just provide practice opportunities and reinforcement for their students. They can actually teach students to think in better ways, and they can learn to instruct in better ways. That was demonstrated when a group of teachers learned how to think about students' thinking in mathematics and to understand the different kinds of difficulties encountered in mathematics problems.

These teachers learned a bit about memory problems of young children, as the following dialogue illustrates:

> Teacher: What number equals 2 + 4 + 3?
> Student (7 years old): 2 + 4 = 6. What was the other number?
> Teacher: I said, What number equals 2 + 4 + 3?
> Student: Now, 2 plus . . . uh . . . say the number again, please.
>
> *(adapted from Romberg & Collis, 1987)*

Is this a defect in mathematical understanding or a limitation in the memory span of young children? Probably the latter.

The teachers also learned how children come to adopt strategies to solve problems in school that are completely inappropriate in the real world. For example: It takes Bill 12 hours to cut a lawn. Bob can cut the same lawn in 8 hours. How long will it take them to cut the lawn if they work together and each has his own mower?

Students often answer 10 hours. They look for some key operations to perform, like "get simple average," and do so, because that often works (Schoenfeld, 1985). They rarely seem to check the logic of the answer, apparently finding nothing wrong with concluding that 10 hours of work is needed by two people to cut the lawn, although one of them can do it himself in 8 hours! Learning in school is seen by students as remarkably different from learning and problem solving in the real world (Reed, 1989; Saxe, 1988; De Corte, 1996).

These kinds of mathematics problems associated with childrens' abilities and strategy use were taught to teachers in a program called *Cognitively Guided Instruction* (CGI) (Carpenter et al., 1989; see also De Corte, Greer, & Verschaffel, 1996). The teachers who had CGI began to understand mathematics as students in school might learn it, and these insights into how their students might construct mathematical knowledge affected their teaching. Teachers guided by their new insights into students' cognitions showed (1) increased teaching of problem solving and decreased teaching of number facts; (2) increased encouragement of strategy use by students and more listening to their explanations about how they solved their mathematics problems; and (3) increased knowledge about their students' thinking. As might be expected, significant gains in mathematics learning were achieved by the students of teachers who took this short course in how students construct mathematical knowledge. More practice was not what their students needed to learn better. Greater sensitivity by teachers to how students construct knowledge was the key to improvement.

Schemata and Reading Achievement   What the text presents is important, but perhaps of greater importance is what the reader brings to a reading task. Without rich schemata for incorporating the text, not much will be learned. We find from cognitive studies, for example, that students who do not have a schema for a story often cannot remember stories well. Some children enter school with sophisticated ideas about the nature of stories. They know, for example, that stories have beginnings and ends, are usually presented in chronological order, have a hero or heroine, tell about an obstacle that is put in the hero's or heroine's way, and that the leading character arrives at a solution to the problems presented. A child without a story schema is at a disadvantage. Even if this child could decode and understand every word as well as someone who has a well-developed story schema, he or she would probably comprehend less.

Reading, then, is much more than decoding. There is no doubt that teaching decoding and word-recognition skills—a practice prevalent in schools—is helpful in making reading more automatic (Hiebert & Raphael, 1996). But genuine reading is a sense-making process, with meaningfulness at its core. Strategies for remedial reading, based strictly

What the text presents is important, but perhaps more important is what the reader brings to a learning situation.
(© Mimi Forsyth/Monkmeyer)

POLICY, RESEARCH, AND PRACTICE

Overcoming Student Misconceptions in Science

Suppose we ask a young physicist to imagine a coin being flipped and to freeze the motion about halfway up to the highest level the coin will reach. Now we ask that student what forces are acting on the coin at that moment. A large percentage of second-year physics students would assert that two forces are operating on the coin—a force from the flip, sending it up, and a gravitational force, which acts to bring it down (Clement, 1982). In reality, once set in motion, there is no force acting on the coin other than gravity.

Cognitive scientists say that misconceptions of this kind are widespread. Many children believe that sugar ceases to exist when it is dissolved in water, that styrofoam has no weight, and that shadows are made of "stuff." There are even sophisticated adults who believe that electric current is used up in a lightbulb, that the light from a candle travels farther at night than during the day, or that heavier objects fall faster than light objects. Pressley and McCormick (1995) looked at 2,000 examples of these kinds of scientific misconceptions, or malconstructed bits of knowledge, held by students. Examples: the surface of the sun is solid; rattlesnakes are mean and dangerous; the distance between water molecules does not change when water becomes ice; molecules in solids are still; all living things have blood; people are not animals; environmentally produced effects on an individual can be genetically transmitted to offspring. Although most of these misconceptions are relatively harmless, not all of them are. The kind of knowledge people have about sexually transmitted diseases in general and AIDS in particular is often untrue. In that case, then, we see how misconceptions can literally kill a person.

Intuitively satisfying concepts, wrong though they may be, are held through all kinds of ordinary instruction. Students easily pass through high school and university courses, many with As, still believing that the world operates as they intuit, not as it really does (Carey, 1986; Linn, 1986). If teachers do not interview, question, and probe students to confront their naive theories and misconceptions directly, those wrong-headed ideas may last despite our best efforts at instruction. Roth and Anderson (1990) have evidence that after six to eight weeks of instruction on photosynthesis with fifth graders only 7 percent of them were able to explain that plants make their own food. It sometimes seems as if you have to hit them over the head to get them to give up their beliefs that water or soil or fertilizer, or all of these, are what plants use as food.

continues

To engage in instruction that has conceptual change as its goal, teachers need to develop strategies that (1) reveal the student's misperceptions, (2) create conceptual conflict, and (3) encourage accommodation of new information. Teachers must learn to probe their students' understanding to find out how they have constructed knowledge, and to find out whether students are holding on to misconceptions even after instruction. One way to reveal and repair misconceptions is to set up socially interactive, collaborative science work. In science projects where teams of students work together, misconceptions are more likely to be revealed, challenged, and changed, and a good deal of science is learned correctly (Champagne & Bunce, 1991; Glynn, Yeany, and Britton, 1991; Campione, Brown, & Jay, 1992). In these collaborations, thinking skills, intelligence, cognitive strategies—all kinds of expertise—are distributed. And in collaborative learning groups, where expertise can be distributed, students probe each other's thinking in ways that teachers cannot always do. Moreover, they do this much like scientists do when learning each other's ideas. While we struggle to find ways to overcome students' misconceptions, we can now at least recognize that simply teaching students and then believing that they genuinely understand knowledge as we presented it is inadequate teaching. It is a misconception held by teachers about the nature of teaching and learning.

on having children read bits and pieces of words or do worksheets often devoid of meaning, are probably emphasizing the wrong thing. Yet such strategies are commonly used in instructing low-achieving or low-income children. It seems that the children with the most problems in learning in schools are assigned materials and activities that are harder to learn from. They get the most rote, decontextualized materials to learn from—materials most devoid of everyday meaning.

The social constructivist perspective emphasizes not only that meaning is made in the mind of the student, based on her past experience, but also that meaning is negotiated in the communities to which one belongs (Hiebert & Raphael, 1996). Children can learn to decode the words "re•spect" and "in•di•vid•u•al," but they must have learned their meanings in the past to make sense of those words and the stories they read. Social constructivists point out also that the meaning of these two words differs in different cultures. Different students may have learned different meanings of these terms because of differences in the families, neighborhoods, and cultures to which they belong. So, just working on increasing automaticity is not enough to learn to read better. The developing reader may need genuine literature to read and discuss as often as he or she needs drills in recognizing phonemes and developing automaticity for decoding words (Anderson & Pearson, 1985; Beck & Carpenter, 1986; Brown & Campione, 1986; Paris, Wixson, & Palincsar, 1986; Perfetti & Curtis, 1986).

The same perspective has implications for teaching vocabulary or spelling, which are often taught in rote ways. Since meaning-based instruction is the goal, teachers should probably emphasize the teaching of the vocabulary and spelling words that children encounter and use in their reading, writing, and speaking. It is words in meaningful contexts, not isolated words, that are learned best (Duin & Graves, 1987).

Transfer of Learning

The process that enables people to make previously learned responses in new situations is called **transfer.** Transfer often, but not always, allows us to perform sensibly and adequately in a new task. Learning about pulleys in physics should help a student lift a car engine onto a chassis. Learning how to make a shirt on a sewing machine in home economics should help a student sew a pair of pants at home. Learning English grammar should help a student write English correctly. If not, why is this material in the school curriculum? The things learned in schools are intended to prepare students for life outside the schools. That is, education should foster transfer. As will become clear, this does not happen nearly as often as educators hope. In fact, because learning is situated, people have trouble applying the knowledge learned in one setting, and in one group, to another setting, or in another group. This is a big problem, for if most people do not usually transfer what they know, then running schools is probably foolish. Schooling can only be justified if what is learned there helps someone somewhere else.

To understand transfer we must understand how learning to perform one task gives us the ability to perform another. This problem was ad-

Some claim that chess disciplines the mind by teaching planning, strategy, and complex thinking.

(© Harriet Gans/The Image Works)

299

dressed early in the twentieth century by several eminent American educational psychologists, among them E. L. Thorndike and Charles Judd. Their views of transfer have stood up reasonably well over the decades. We take a brief look at their ideas below.

A Glance at Traditional Views

Thorndike and Woodworth (1901) reasoned, quite sensibly, that if the stimuli in two situations are similar and the same responses are called for, transfer should take place. The more the elements of one situation are identical with those of another, the greater the transfer. This theory of identical elements as the basis for transfer stemmed from a series of experiments Thorndike performed to see whether practice in one test—say, crossing out all the Es on a page—would influence performance on another test—say, crossing out the Ss on the next page. The studies revealed that except for shared perceptual abilities or motor behaviors, or whatever was common to the two tests, no general transfer was present. Positive transfer, such as transfer from playing a piano to typing, takes place only insofar as eye-hand coordination skills are present in both tasks. Thorndike stated his findings clearly: "A change in one function alters another only insofar as the two functions have as factors identical elements" (1913, p. 358).

Thorndike's thinking was very different from the doctrine of formal discipline, which upheld the value of studying certain subjects because they train the mind—for example, that the study of Latin or Greek results in a mind that is disciplined and better able to think. In a series of experiments with real students he disproved these ideas, and the theory of formal discipline almost disappeared after his studies were presented. Thorndike's theory that identical elements account for the phenomenon of transfer was widely advocated, but mainly in its narrowest form—identity of substance, or one-to-one correspondence between the elements of what was studied and what was to be done in real life. So curriculum analysts believed that learning addition helps in learning multiplication only because part of multiplication requires the ability to do addition.

But Thorndike had also pointed out that there could be identity of procedure, whereby the general habits, attitudes, principles, patterns, and procedures people have learned can facilitate performance in a wide variety of situations. Some educators, particularly Thorndike's contemporary, Charles Judd, believe Thorndike's identity-of-*procedures* form is the more prevalent way in which transfer takes place. These educators argue that principles and generalizations are the key elements in the transfer of what is learned in one situation to performance in another.

Sometimes negative transfer occurs: previous learning hinders new learning or problem solving, or leads students to respond incorrectly. Breaking a response set—a tendency to respond in the same way despite new conditions—is hard to do. But unless you make a conscious effort to build into students' lessons some experiences to get them to think more flexibly, they probably will not do so. When teaching students about the characteristics of fish, for example, you should also introduce students to whales and dolphins, to teach the principle that not everything that swims in the sea is a fish. Negative transfer can be avoided only by conscious attempts to teach flexibility in applying principles.

We can conclude from the older studies of transfer that positive transfer takes place when the elements of two tasks are similar. These similarities can occur in simple eye-hand coordination acts or in complex mathematical skills. When two tasks have identities of substance or identities of procedure, there will be positive transfer between them if the learner recognizes the similarities. So an important principle of teaching is to point out the similarities between different tasks so that transfer can take place.

Contemporary Views of Transfer

Cognitive psychologists, studying the thought processes of people who demonstrate an ability to transfer learning, have found that they use certain skills and that some of those skills can be taught.

Metacognition and Transfer   Metacognitive skills are somewhat analogous to the executive in an organization. Metacognitive skills are the supervisory processes—the cognitive activities that check whether all the little jobs are being done right to accomplish a goal. They monitor whether you are thinking well (or not) about a problem. For example, two metacognitive questions that focus on the student's self-awareness of transfer of learning are:

- How is this problem like the ones I solved last month?
- Does anything here remind me of anything I have learned before?

These two questions are important for a student to ask herself because when an analogy is found between the new problem and some other kind of problem successfully solved in the past, transfer can occur. It is not always easy for a student to see, for example, that a word problem about distance and speed of airplanes is not much different from a number problem solved with some ease the previous day (e.g., Gick & Holyoak, 1987; Reed 1987). But a student who consciously looks for similarities between new problems and already-solved problems stands a much better chance of seeing the relationships between them and bringing about transfer. That is also why students who deeply study some worked-out examples in chemistry, physics, or math books show better transfer than students who do not try hard to understand the worked-out examples (Mayer & Wittrock, 1996). New problems usually are analogous to the worked-out problems, though the analogy may not be obvious at first. If worked-out problems are well learned, the relationship between a new problem and the old ones might be spotted. Then it is easy to solve the new problem; transfer has been achieved.

Conceptual Models for Understanding and Transfer   A **conceptual model** consists of the words or diagrams used in instruction to help learners build mental models of what they are studying. Not all the information about, say, how radar works or how brakes work in a car is

Look again at the information-processing model in Figure 7.1. Did this model help you understand the material in that section? If so, how?

worth remembering. A conceptual model is an accurate and useful representation of the knowledge that is necessary to solve problems in a particular domain.

Figure 7.8 shows a conceptual model of how radar works used by Mayer (1989) in an informative series of studies. Conceptual models such as this were taught to some students while students in the control groups received instruction without having conceptual models presented or discussed. In the study concerning radar, both groups heard a lecture. But one group had one minute to study the conceptual model, which featured the main steps and processes in the conversion of time to distance. The model also attempted to make the major elements in the system more concrete: the radar pulse, the remote object to be sensed, the transmitter, the receiver, the clock, and the converter. What did a minute's worth of studying the model yield? Compared to the control group, the students who studied the model before the lecture recalled 57 percent more conceptual information, scored 14 percent lower in verbatim information, and scored 85 percent higher on problem-solving transfer tasks (e.g., answering questions like, How can you increase the area under radar surveillance?). Results from two other instructional situations involving different conceptual models were similar.

FIGURE 7.8

A conceptual model of radar, for promoting transfer

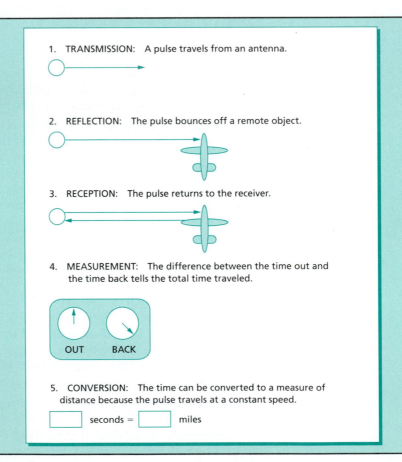

1. TRANSMISSION: A pulse travels from an antenna.

2. REFLECTION: The pulse bounces off a remote object.

3. RECEPTION: The pulse returns to the receiver.

4. MEASUREMENT: The difference between the time out and the time back tells the total time traveled.

   OUT   BACK

5. CONVERSION: The time can be converted to a measure of distance because the pulse travels at a constant speed.

   ☐ seconds = ☐ miles

Mayer's studies are intriguing. They show, of course, that verbatim-information scores may go down when conceptual models are used. Apparently some of the detailed factual information is lost when information is reorganized into a conceptual model for students to remember. Models are, after all, simplifications. But it may not be much of a loss. The studies show also how the models helped students retain the major conceptual information in the area they were studying. Apparently models direct attention to key objects, locations, and events, which is probably more important than attending to all the declarative knowledge in a domain. Most important, the studies reveal that problem-solving tasks requiring transfer are performed remarkably better by students exposed to conceptual models. Students probably use models to build mental representations of great parsimony and power in the domain studied. Students who build personal mental representations based upon conceptual models presented to them, and learn to manipulate those models cognitively, appear to be far better able to solve transfer tasks.

Students who already have a lot of information about some area and those who have a good deal of intellectual ability might find models to be less effective. This might be because such students have developed their own effective strategies for connecting and remembering information important to them. The data confirm this. Using conceptual models primarily affects the performance of those with little knowledge and lower ability in an area. Furthermore, models work best when used before a lesson (like a visual advance organizer) or during a lesson (like an illustration presenting important elements, processes, or events to be learned). Models do not work well when presented after instruction.

Mayer suggested that teachers build models using the "seven Cs" (notice the mnemonic aid) as a guide. That is, such models should be

- complete, having all the important information within them
- concise, not containing an overwhelming amount of information
- coherent, holding together in a rather easy-to-see way, with the logic of the model evident to students who do not know a lot about the area they are studying
- concrete, rather than abstract
- conceptual, that is, explaining something, not just listing things
- correct, that is, really corresponding to the processes or relationships under study (not like some useful but incorrect models, e.g., explaining that electricity is like water flowing—an analogy that under certain circumstances can be misleading)
- considerate, in using a student's vocabulary and an organization appropriate to the student's ability and age.

In sum, conceptual models of this type could enhance transfer of school knowledge for many students. Yet in thousands of hours of classroom observation, investigators have seen little use of such models.

Teaching for Transfer

There are two basic ways of teaching for transfer. Teachers can concentrate on substantive transfer, using the theory of identical elements to guide teaching. A good deal of this kind of transfer is automatic, not requiring much thought. Obviously, if a student has learned how to say *log, fog,* and *hog* he will probably pronounce the word *nog* correctly when he first encounters it tied to the word *egg,* as in *eggnog.* Transfer requiring little mental effort is called *low-road transfer* (Salomon & Perkins, 1989). Or, teachers can concentrate on procedural transfer, using knowledge about how principles and rules can apply across a wide variety of situations. When the student works to transfer principles and rules, investing mental effort, it is known as *high-road transfer.* The high road to transfer is what teachers should take. These two approaches are not mutually exclusive, however; both are important in teaching for transfer.

Teaching for Substantive (Low-Road) Transfer   When teachers concentrate on substantive transfer, they might argue that they try to teach directly whatever it is they want students to learn. If you need computer programming in your job, you should study programming during training, preferably the same type of programming you are going to need on the job. (How much knowledge about the history of computers is necessary for a programmer to be efficient is a highly complex question.) If you want to study Plato in the original, learn Greek—but don't expect that experience to help you much in learning German. To learn German, you would do better to study German directly. Training in statistics might help you solve research problems, because statistics is a tool for solving such problems, but it certainly will not help you to sharpen your general reasoning power, such as your reasoning about ethics.

These statements agree with that part of the theory of identical elements that is concerned with identity of substance. Be careful, then, that curriculum intended to improve students' readiness for learning a particular skill or subject can be defended as having positive transfer for that skill or subject. Often teachers do better to teach children exactly what we want them to know so that transfer is effortless. You might find that the time spent in readiness training is better used for direct training in a curriculum area you want students to master. As Hudgins (1977) noted, sentence diagramming has been defended in the upper elementary grades as preparing students for and improving mastery of sentence structure. Yet the empirical research reveals that "pupils can be taught diagramming rather efficiently, but there is very little benefit in terms of sentence mastery. In fact, in one of the studies . . . the control children actually improved a bit more in sentence mastery than the children who had been taught diagramming" (p. 153). Some myths about transfer linger on despite empirical evidence disproving them.

Teaching for Procedural (High-Road) Transfer   When teachers concentrate on procedural transfer, they often are concerned with how to teach broadly applicable concepts, principles, and procedures. Learning the meaning of words such as *untie* and *unfair* is perfectly appropriate, but notice how much more useful it is to learn that the prefix *un* means "not" or "contrary to." With this knowledge, students can try to find meaning in many more words: *unaffected, unaccompanied, unarmed,* and so on. They can decode the words for themselves. With some mental effort they can apply old learning to new situations. The moral here is, make it a point to teach such highly transferable tools as library skills, the Venn diagrams and truth tables used in logic, and algorithms. All these have wide utility if, and perhaps only if, they are taught in such a way that students can recognize new situations in which the skills are applicable. People's abstract knowledge structures, their schemata, should be built to accommodate the widest possible range of examples and applications. That is, you should always try to present a wide array of examples in which students can see how new principles and techniques can be used. Many of the examples should concern real-world settings. Ultimately, much of what is learned in school must meet some criterion of usefulness or value in the nonschool world.

Procedural transfer often calls for effort, for mindfulness. We usually have to take principles and concepts *deliberately* from one area of knowledge and apply them to another. To do so you have to **decontextualize,** or separate the idea from its original associations, so that you know and understand its essential elements and apply them in a new context (Salomon & Perkins, 1989). For example, you probably learned the concept

Enhancing Our Own and Our Students' Mindfulness

Because transfer across dissimilar contexts requires so much effort, so much mindfulness, people often avoid it. Students who have strategies to help them learn effectively in school do not always use them at home, and vice versa. For example, a student who cooks meals for five siblings and parents at home may not be able to measure at school. He has knowledge that is inert, unusable outside of the context in which it was learned (Brown, Collins, & Duguid, 1989; Cognition and Technology Group at Vanderbilt, 1990). It is now clear that knowledge is usually bound to a single situation and does not easily transfer for use in dissimilar contexts. It is quite situated. To break knowledge free of its context requires mindfulness (Salomon & Globerson, 1987; Salomon & Perkins, 1989).

Our job as teachers is to encourage students to work at generalizing and applying what they know, to be active transferors. Our attempts to foster transfer will be far more successful if we understand and practice mindfulness in our personal and professional lives. With the goal of enhancing your own mindfulness, choose an arena of your life—perhaps your learning in this course, or the way you use your time to study and learn when you are not in class, or a student-teaching experience you are engaged in, or an aspect of your social life. Monitor yourself closely for several weeks. You might keep a daily journal, guided by the metacognitive questions provided earlier in this chapter or others like them. How aware are you of what you are doing and thinking and planning? If you notice what you consider weak spots, try to think of ways to increase your awareness. Make a list of how and why you think such consciousness might benefit both you and your students.

of rhythm from banging a spoon on a plate, or in a music class, very early on. And it was probably not long before you were using the concept to discuss dance, poetry, plays, the graphic arts, the shape of a seashell, and a method of contraception. To apply the concept of rhythm correctly across contexts, you had to decontextualize it, or separate it from its original context.

Instructional Ideas and Strategies for Promoting Transfer

1. Make the training situation as similar to the real-world situation as possible. At the beginning you may teach in a simplified situation, but you are not finished there. If typists usually type in large noisy rooms, don't train them only in a quiet room. You'll end up with a problem of transfer. Don't teach children how to build a sundial only in the classroom, from store-bought materials. Take them to a field, where they'd actually use a sundial, and let them build one out of sticks and stones they find there. Don't ask journalism majors to write a story in 20 days if in the real world they would have only 20 minutes. If you cannot simulate real-world conditions, at least describe them so that students are not confused when they come up against the real-world situation. One factor that prevents novices from solving problems as well as experts is that novices have only encountered textbook problems, not "real" problems. Textbook problems are neat and clean; problems in the real world are often messy and complex. Let your students know what to expect "out there."

2. Provide lots of practice on the original task before you ask students to transfer their learning. This guideline is strictly adhered to in flight training. Landings, simulated and real, are practiced over and over on the training field before a student pilot is allowed to try to land at another field. Experts get to be experts only after much experience.

3. Provide lots of practice on related problems. If you are teaching about contracts, give your students many examples of many different kinds of contracts, with different wording. Make them aware that even in the midst of changing conditions, there are some constants: the contractor, the contractee, the terms, the price, and so on. Try to teach students how to break apart—decontextualize—an idea, to separate its general qualities from the specific situation so that the idea can be applied in more than one situation.

4. Watch for negative transfer when stimuli are similar but required responses are different. For example, to the novice learner, $3 + 2$ and $3 - 2$ may appear to be similar, even though the responses called for are different. Likewise, *Rome* and *Romania* are easy to confuse; so are the words *ethnography, ethnology*, and *ethology*. If you recognize the potential for confusion, you can spot areas where students may have difficulty. When stimuli are similar, spend some time differentiating among them—a process called *stimulus predifferentiation* when it is done early in a sequence of learning. Remember that if students cannot differentiate among the similarities and differences of stimuli, they cannot determine what kind of response to make.

5. Emphasize early learning of prerequisite skills or knowledge. If you are teaching students to identify igneous, metamorphic, and sedimentary rocks, teach the identifications early in the learning unit. Once students master initial required tasks, they can better transfer their knowledge to related tasks. For example, if you teach students how to solve a problem such as 56 ÷ 8, that knowledge can help them solve 93254031.2 ÷ 83274. Learning what happened to the Soviet Union during World War II gives students a basis for understanding Soviet policy during the Cold War. And learning the movements necessary to turn on skis when on a slight grade is immensely useful—that is, these skills do transfer—when students have to turn on a steep and icy ski run.

6. Give your students conceptual models, or have them construct models that capture the essence of what needs to be learned. Models help students in problem-solving and transfer tasks.

7. Whenever you state a principle or generalization, give students a wide variety of examples. If you are teaching the concept of community, you can talk about ants, bees, and Alaskan Natives, as well as a country club, small town, tenants' association, neighborhood association, and Alcoholics Anonymous. When you say that geometry and trigonometry are useful, show students how they can use these subjects to measure distances between places in town, estimate the height of buildings, determine the number of tiles needed to cover the floor of a room, or navigate a boat across a lake.

8. Ask students to make some applications themselves. Have them determine how learning to measure the speed of sound can be used. Ask them whether a new writer resembles anyone else they know, or whether the new novel's plot refers to events they are familiar with. Try to get young students to think of the kinds of measuring they do in their homes and how often they need to measure. In short, help your students link what they learn in the classroom to the world outside of school. Get them to act mindfully. Have them act in a generative manner.

9. Ask students to think aloud when they are trying to solve problems, and use what they say to learn about their metacognitive strategies. What skills do they appear to have? What skills do they lack? If a student has not learned some important self-governing, self-monitoring, and self-checking skills, learning and transfer will be hampered. You can help teach these skills by explicitly modeling how you go about solving problems and getting students to imitate you.

A Look Ahead to Chapter 8

In the last section of this chapter, we emphasized the transfer value of general skills and techniques. But we also must note that attitudes toward self and toward areas of learning are highly transferable. If children think of themselves as competent and of an area of learning as "knowable," teachers can expect them to attack problems vigorously rather than exhibit withdrawn, noncreative approaches to new situations. For this reason, we pay much attention in Chapter 8 to students' attitudes toward achievement in general, and the kinds of explanations (attributions) they make for their own success and failure.

SUMMARY

1. Cognition is examined not through any unified theory but through six major perspectives: the information-processing model of the mind; metacognition; active, meaningful learning models and approaches; constructivist perspectives; a problem-solving approach; and situated cognition.

2. Shared characteristics among the various perspectives on cognitive learning include the belief that people are purposive beings. We are knowledge-seeking individuals with a highly developed ability to organize information. In perception and in thinking, weak or strong constructive processes are always at work. The information-processing model of mind deals little with these constructive processes but acknowledges their existence. Constructivism plays a more important role in all the other cognitive perspectives on learning.

3. Students who are highly successful in different curricular areas are those who are motivated, actively involved in their learning, and typically use learning strategies. Too many students are considered to be lacking in ability when they are really lacking in strategies, which can be taught to them.

4. The information-processing model explains how information from the external environment enters memory. The process begins with a stimulus which elicits an orienting response—a response that makes someone want to know more about the stimulus. Attention is critical here, and often is a result of the psychophysical, emotional, discrepant, or commanding properties of the stimulus.

5. Once we attend to a stimulus, it briefly enters our short-term sensory storage system. Again attention is important. If we don't attend to the information, we forget it. If we do, it moves into short-term memory or working memory. Short-term memory is conscious memory. Working memory, which may be a part of short-term memory, is a sort of mental scratch pad. The information held in short-term memory and working memory must be encoded or rehearsed to move on to long-term memory. The challenge for teachers is to trigger the encoding and rehearsal processes, to get what they want students to learn into long-term memory, then to help them retrieve it. The information is stored in long-term memory in at least three ways—by its meaning, in pictorial forms or images, and in verbal form.

6. The information we have stored seems to be of at least three types: declarative knowledge, the if-then propositions that provide the factual basis needed to run our lives in some sensible way; procedural knowledge, the know-how needed to get things done (e.g., study for a test or write a report); and episodic knowledge, emotionally-laden memories or vivid remembrances of significant events in our lives.

7. Long-term memory is enhanced when the enactive, iconic, and symbolic modes of learning can be blended. The greater the number of associations—verbal, mathematical, visual, and tactile—the easier it

is to retrieve information. So adding a physical activity to learning increases retention.

8. One of the ways to make the knowledge stored away come forth when we need it is to use strategies—a form of procedural knowledge, or step-by-step procedures—for learning the material in the first place. Overlearning, mnemonics (e.g., imagery), the loci method, and the keyword technique are all strategies that aid in coding and retrieving information from memory. There are also learning strategies that are unique to reading, writing, and mathematics, among others.

9. Metacognitive skills are the monitoring processes we use when we learn. They develop through both experience and explicit instruction. They are necessary for classifying problems, representing problems visually in our minds, and retrieving from memory the solutions to problems. Our metacognitive skills function as overseers, coordinating the many and complex parts of the learning process.

10. Discovery learning is about answering questions much as scientists would: What would happen if . . . ? It requires arrangements by teachers so that students are guided and scaffolded to discover what is important. Discovery requires a "well-prepared mind," a student ready to discover. The discovery approach is compatible with constructivism, the notion of an active, meaning-seeking mind. Although discovery approaches usually motivate students, they also take considerable time and therefore must be used sparingly.

11. The generative model of learning suggests that when students generate their own cognitive activity during learning, they learn more and better. The more teachers can get students to actively participate in the learning process, particularly by tying what is being learned to bodies of knowledge they already possess, the more comprehension of various kinds is enhanced.

12. Constructivist perspectives have many assumptions in common. Chief among them is that each of us seeks to make meaning out of the world for ourselves. The pedagogy following from this assumption is that students should be codirectors, that is, actively involved, in their own learning. Constructivists recommend communities of learners, group activities, projects, and real-world authenticity for learning activities.

13. Social constructivists differ in emphasis more than in essential philosophical position from other constructivists. Their beliefs focus on how cognition is influenced by the groups someone belongs to and the materials and artifacts of the culture to which he or she has access. Social constructivists recognize the power of Vygotsky's idea that knowledge is social before it ever becomes private and personal, knowledge that we own. The pedagogy that follows from this uses groups in the learning process more frequently than is customary now.

14. The problem-solving approach distinguishes between ill-defined and well-defined problems. Teaching is sometimes about solving ill-defined problems, for which there is no right or wrong answer. Under those circumstances, expertise develops through experience, but not just any experience. It develops through reflected-on experience and the extraction of propositional knowledge from cases. Developing problem-solving abilities by these means separates the novice from the expert.

15. Situated cognition emphasizes that learning occurs in specific contexts and that the knowledge derived is situated in those contexts.

One important idea emerging from the situated-cognition view is distributed expertise, the notion that knowing is the property of the group as well as the individual. Because learning is situated, apprenticeships are powerful ways to help people learn, particularly in complex and real-life environments. The preferred classroom structure associated with this perspective is the community of learners. Problem-based project learning, emphasizing problem-solving in real-life situations, either simulated or actual, is often used.

16. Certain instructional strategies also promote cognitive learning and higher-order thinking. Teachers make things meaningful by emphasizing the associations related to the material to be learned—by tying something to be learned to something students already know. Mediators, or enhancers of various sorts, create meaningful links between ideas that seem unrelated to the learner. Instructional design—including advance organizers, hierarchical structure, and concept maps—also can help students by emphasizing the structure and organization of what is to be learned. Schemata—abstract structures that represent the knowledge stored in memory—are also important here. If a relevant schema does not exist, the teacher must provide one. There are also specific strategies for making meaning in math, reading, and science. These strategies focus on the ways students think about problems, the schemata they invoke, and the misconceptions they may hold. You should think about your students' cognition and use that to guide your instruction.

17. One major test of knowledge is whether it transfers. Transfer enables people to use previously learned knowledge and skills in new situations. The greater the number of identical elements, in both substance and procedure, the greater the transfer. Principles usually transfer well, but when misapplied they can cause negative transfer, hindering new learning.

18. Metacognition helps transfer by asking students to be aware of whether they are active in trying to transfer what is learned. Metacognitive processes are needed because transfer is mindful and active; it requires work. Simplified visual conceptual models foster transfer because they direct attention to the key concepts, locations, or events to be learned. When conceptual models are used during learning, transfer is especially high.

19. When teaching for substantive transfer, you need to teach exactly what you want students to know. For procedural transfer, you should emphasize principles, broad concepts, and highly transferable skills. Unlike substantive transfer, which is almost unconscious, procedural transfer demands mindfulness. Effort must be made to decontextualize ideas. Ideas need to be free of their contexts in order to move across contexts.

20. Teachers concerned about transferability need to teach material thoroughly and model problem-solving behavior. You can enhance your own mindfulness (and help your students to a greater degree) by monitoring your level of awareness and becoming metacognitive in your own thinking.

21. There are several instructional guidelines and ideas you can use to promote transfer: make the training situation as much like the real-world situation as possible; give students lots of practice on the origi-

nal task and related tasks; guard against negative transfer; emphasize prerequisites of what you want students to learn; teach students conceptual models; give students a wide variety of examples; ask students to make some applications themselves; and get students to think aloud when they are working so that you can "view" their metacognitive processes.

Motivation and Learning

Overview

THE CRUCIAL ROLE OF MOTIVATION IN BEHAVIOR AND LEARNING

Motivation Determines What Makes a Reinforcer

Motivation Accounts for Goal Orientation

Hope and long-term goals

Motivation Determines the Time Spent in Different Activities

Motivation and Achievement

CONCEPTIONS OF MOTIVATION AND THEIR IMPLICATIONS

Four Conceptions

Implications for Education

ACHIEVEMENT MOTIVATION: A COGNITIVE COMPOSITE

APPLICATION
Conduct Your Own Survey of Young Children's Changing Motivations

Relationship between Need for Achievement and Performance

Classifying Achievement Attributions

Students' causal attributions

POLICY, RESEARCH, AND PRACTICE
Internal and External Attributions and Emotion

Teachers' causal attributions
Internal and external attributions

The Relationship of Self-Worth and Need for Achievement to Classroom Structure

How Other Motives Interact with the Need for Achievement

INTRINSIC AND EXTRINSIC MOTIVATION

OPERANT CONDITIONING AND MOTIVATION

Stimulus Control and the Role of Reinforcers and Incentives

Finding the right reinforcers

Frustration and Motivation

CHANGING MOTIVATIONAL PATTERNS

Cognitive Approaches

Achievement-motivation training programs

POLICY, RESEARCH, AND PRACTICE
Are Attribution Training Programs an Effective Way to Change a Student's Perceptions about Why He or She Succeeds or Fails?

Environmental Approaches

Token economies
Motivational contracts

SELF-EFFICACY AND ACHIEVEMENT MOTIVATION

Developing Self-Efficacy

The Self-Efficacy of Teachers and Schools

MOTIVATIONAL TECHNIQUES IN CLASSROOM TEACHING: GUIDELINES FOR TEACHERS

Summary

OVERVIEW

Everyone knows what motivation is, how it makes a difference between resentful boredom at one extreme and ravenous interest at the other. Shakespeare wrote of "the whining school-boy, with his satchel and shining morning face, creeping like snail unwillingly to school." And most of us have known a time of ardent learning, when we could not get quickly enough to the truth of a matter about which we were deeply concerned, when we were altogether entranced. Motivation is what moves us from boredom to interest. It is motivation that arouses us, directs our activity, and maintains our behavior over time.

In this chapter we discuss how motivation affects behavior and learning in our students and our schools. We explore some of the most important of the cognitive motivational variables, particularly achievement motivation—the need to succeed, to be good at something. We also discuss attributions, how teachers and students assign responsibility for their successes and failures at the tasks they try.

After discussing these cognitive motivational factors, we look at motivational variables in the environment, exploring the operant-conditioning approach to the understanding and improvement of motivation, particularly the ways in which the reinforcement contingencies in the environment affect behavior. We also present ideas about the motivating effects of frustration. Like the rest of us, students are energized and directed by frustration, but often that leads toward aggressive behavior.

We then focus on how to change motive patterns by changing either the attributions persons make or the environmental contingencies that shape their behavior. We also examine two behavior-modification approaches—token economies and contracts. Both have been highly effective in improving the performance of unmotivated students. We then discuss self-efficacy—the perception people have about whether or not they control their own fates. Our view of our own efficacy is enormously influential in directing and controlling our behavior. Finally, we present ideas about how to manage certain classroom variables to increase student motivation.

On our way through this chapter we also dispel some myths. We learn that the avoidance of learning is not unmotivated behavior; it is sometimes behavior strongly motivated by a desire to preserve self-worth. We discover the mistakes of those who believe that failure experiences are good motivators. Success experiences are actually a much better basis for building motivation. Although there is a common belief that reinforcement always improves learning, we show that it sometimes undermines motivation to learn. And we also question the belief that a student's ability is the strongest determinant of learning. Sometimes it is the student's sense of efficacy that determines whether, and how much, he or she learns. By creating this little bit of cognitive conflict (between widespread beliefs and research evidence) at the start of this chapter, we are following advice we provide later, namely, that a little unexpected cognitive tension has motivational properties.

The Crucial Role of Motivation in Behavior and Learning

Motivation is sometimes a *means* to educational achievement. In one review of research, the many correlations between measures of motivation and achievement averaged about $+.34$, indicating (to no one's surprise) that high levels of motivation and high levels of achievement tend to go hand in hand (Walberg, 1986). But motivation is also an *end* in itself, one of the purposes of teaching. For example, teachers want their students to become interested in certain intellectual and aesthetic activities and to retain that interest after formal teaching ends. We want adult citizens to be interested in (that is, motivated to participate in) art and music, science, and public affairs. Interests and values of various kinds are outcomes of schooling that we try to foster. So motivation is peculiar in that it is both a means and an end of instruction.

The concept of motivation is useful for understanding and explaining certain intriguing facts about behavior and learning. We need the concept of motivation to account for (1) what makes a reinforcer, (2) the goal orientation of behavior, and (3) the amount of time spent on different tasks.

Motivation Determines What Makes a Reinforcer

Suppose the school newspaper reports that Marcus King, the new center on the basketball team, has received a multivolume set of the *Story of Civilization* from grateful fans for his performance in the first game of the season. And suppose another story tells us that Helen Lee, head of the science club, has been awarded a year's membership at a health club by the alumni boosters for her entry in the state science fair. Sound odd? Yes, because we know that motives determine what makes a reinforcer. If we want behavior to increase in frequency, duration, or magnitude, we need to reinforce the behavior, and to do that, we need to choose as **reinforcers** those things that individuals value positively. It is likely, though not certain, that the athlete would prefer the membership in the health club and the scientist, the books. Their motives (needs, values, incentives, aspirations, attitudes, interests) determine what is and what is not a reinforcer for them. Remember this idea when you are trying to find reinforcers for a particular student. A pat on the head may work as a reinforcer for a child who has a high need for adult approval; it may have no effect on the child with a high need for autonomy; and it may have a negative effect on a child with a high need for peer approval.

Motivation Accounts for Goal Orientation

Apart from its value in determining what operates as a reinforcer, the concept of motivation is required by the fact that behavior is goal-oriented. We behave as if we were "going somewhere." We sit down at a desk, pick up a pen and a piece of paper, write for a period of time, then put the paper in an envelope, which we stamp and address. Later we drop the envelope into a mailbox. All these separate acts are organized into a larger unit that has an evident purpose. In fact, many philosophers point out that one of the distinguishing characteristics of human behavior is that it is purposeful, that is, goal-directed. This is why human behavior can be sustained over much longer periods of time than animal behavior.

> Can you think of three reinforcers and three goals that have affected your motivation this week?

Hope and Long-Term Goals　People with hope, a dream of a future that is to their liking, can sustain behavior over long periods of time. This was proved when a group without hope of a higher education were suddenly given that hope.

In 1981, Eugene Lang, a self-made millionaire, came back to the New York City elementary school he had attended half a century earlier. He was there to give the sixth-grade commencement address. This East Harlem school was filled with extremely disadvantaged African-American children, and in an off-hand remark at the end of his talk Lang promised the children that if they finished high school and got into college he would pay their tuition. Some thought he was making an idle offer, but Lang became intrigued by the challenge his promise represented and decided to help the students take advantage of it. He also thought some of these children might need tutoring, counseling, guidance, and friendship, so he set up the "I Have a Dream" Foundation, which provided these forms of supplementary help (see the section on self-efficacy, pp. 348–352).

So what happened? The program has had amazing effects. By the early 1990s, six of those students had obtained bachelor's degrees and 30 others were attending college. At least 45 of the students graduated from high school or obtained equivalency diplomas. For P.S. 121, one of the lowest-performing schools in a section of the city with many low-performing schools, the record is stunning. School authorities had originally told Mr. Lang he would be lucky if two of the students in his original group graduated from high school (Gugliotta, 1993).

Why has the program had such amazing success? Mr. Lang suggested that the college scholarship he offered was only part of the picture. Indeed, it may not have been as important as the personal involvement of mentors, himself included, who cared for the children from P.S. 121 over the next six years of their lives. Those six dangerous years on the streets of East Harlem were successfully negotiated by this group of young people because someone gave them and their families the hope and resources to help them realize their dreams. Hope and its opposite, despair, are powerful motivators.

Motivation Determines the Time Spent in Different Activities

One of the most important conclusions researchers have drawn from motivation studies is that the relationship of time spent on particular tasks and motivation for those tasks is almost linear. That is, the greater the motivation, the greater the time spent studying. If you are motivated to achieve well in an educational psychology course, you will spend time studying to achieve in that course. The other side of this conclusion is that if you want to know what motivates a student, find out how she spends her time. If she allocates a lot of her time to playing basketball, shopping at the mall, or studying biology, you see evidence of different motive patterns, and clues as to what would be a good reinforcer for this student.

It should not be surprising that the amount of time a student spends in particular pursuits has been found to be one of the better predictors of student achievement in that area, whether the time be spent doing lay-ups in basketball or answering problems in physics (Berliner, 1990). Perseverance (plain old effort, time-on-task, "elbow grease") frequently does lead to success. And perseverance can be increased by increasing the expectations of reward, or the negative consequences of failure, or both. Expectations of reward were part of what motivated the children in P.S. 121, described above. Perseverance in, or time commitments to, academic pursuits can be reduced by lowering the value of completing a learning task (i.e., making no comments on homework assignments turned in), by impairing the self-esteem of the student (informing a student that he is always the last one through), and by making the learning task unpleasant (drilling and practicing decoding skills long after children are reading meaningful prose). Note too, however, that to a clinical psychologist perseverance of a certain kind can be a sign of a problem. Because of neurotic needs to achieve or a kind of **learned helplessness,** a student may spend inordinate amounts of time on an insoluble problem. Here perseverance is a hindrance, not an aid, to learning.

> What might be some signs for the classroom teacher that a child's perseverance was a hindrance to learning? An aid?

Motivation and Achievement

The concept of motivation helps to account for differences in school achievement beyond those that result from differences in intelligence or scholastic aptitude. The correlation between intelligence and school grades—often around .45—is modest enough that teachers often find students of low ability with relatively high achievement, and some students of high ability with low achievement.

> Experience outside the regular classroom can be enriching and motivating for students of all ages.
>
> (© Elizabeth Crews)

These exceptions to the generally positive correlation between intelligence and school achievement have given rise to the concepts of **overachievement** and **underachievement**—achievement that is greater or less than that expected on the basis of someone's intelligence or estimated scholastic aptitude. In the classic studies of students of equal intelligence achieving in school at different levels, the overachieving students were found to have higher motivation to achieve and lower motivation to affiliate. The underachieving students did not fully accept school and parental standards of achievement, but they did value popularity with their peers to a greater degree. Their motive to affiliate was higher than their motive to achieve—a continuing problem in the youth-oriented culture of the United States. In addition, when compared with overachievers, underachievers have poorer study habits and study skills, apply themselves to academic matters less diligently, and set lower vocational and academic goals for themselves. Underachievement among academically talented students, particularly those from lower SES backgrounds, is also a continuing problem for the American educational system. A good deal of that underachievement appears to be rooted in the low value placed on academic achievement by many parents and by adolescent peer groups (Steinberg et al., 1996).

Conceptions of Motivation and Their Implications

Four Conceptions

In this section we briefly present four well-known conceptions of motivation.

1. *Single-motive conceptions.* Some theorize that there is a single, pervasive kind of motivation. Freud's notion of **libido**—a basic kind of sexual energy underlying all human striving—is one example. He believed the libido influences both conscious and unconscious processes in an irrational and instinctual way.

2. *Dual-motive conceptions.* Both scholars and writers (see Hermann Hesse's *Demian,* for example) have used the concept of duality in motivation. They believe that the interplay of two opposing forces—maleness and femaleness, good and evil, yin and yang—give us our energy and direction.

3. *Multimotive conceptions.* Others claim that there are many different types of motives, and offer long lists of them. Murray et al. (1938) offered one of the best-known lists, which included many social needs, among them need for power, need to play, need to affiliate, and need to achieve—a motive of particular importance to teachers and society. We agree with Murray; we believe that many motives exist, and that sometimes they all actively drive behavior at once.

4. *Hierarchical conceptions.* Still another way to think of motives is to group them, as Maslow (1954) did, into a hierarchy (see Figure 8.1). Maslow's hierarchy includes five basic levels of needs. At the bottom, requiring satisfaction first, are physical needs—e.g., needs for food and safety. Once these needs are satisfied, social needs come into play. Once these are reasonably satisfied, various intellectual needs develop,

FIGURE 8.1

A hierarchy of needs
Adapted from a formulation by Maslow (1954) as modified by Root (1970).

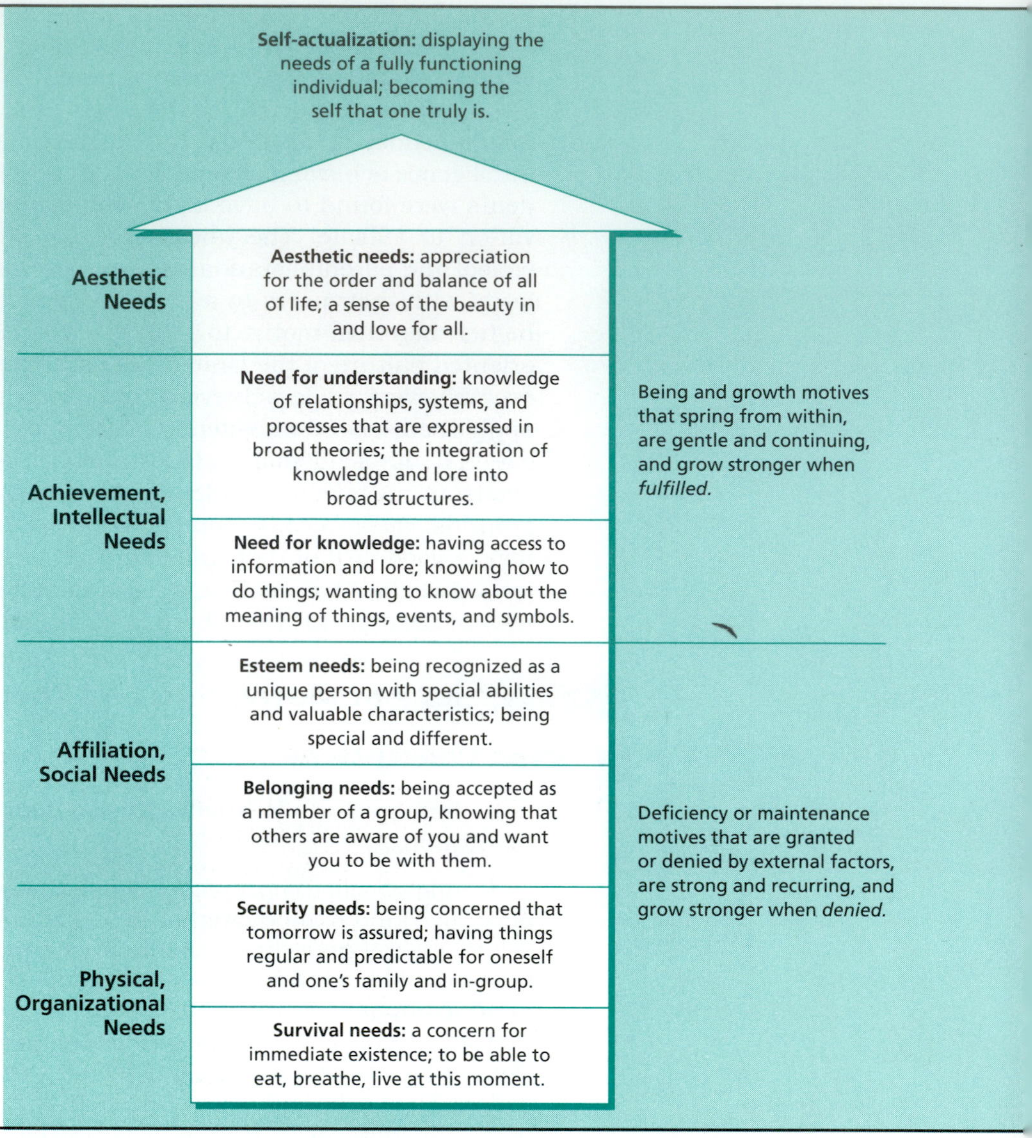

Self-actualization: displaying the needs of a fully functioning individual; becoming the self that one truly is.

Aesthetic Needs

Aesthetic needs: appreciation for the order and balance of all of life; a sense of the beauty in and love for all.

Achievement, Intellectual Needs

Need for understanding: knowledge of relationships, systems, and processes that are expressed in broad theories; the integration of knowledge and lore into broad structures.

Need for knowledge: having access to information and lore; knowing how to do things; wanting to know about the meaning of things, events, and symbols.

Being and growth motives that spring from within, are gentle and continuing, and grow stronger when *fulfilled.*

Affiliation, Social Needs

Esteem needs: being recognized as a unique person with special abilities and valuable characteristics; being special and different.

Belonging needs: being accepted as a member of a group, knowing that others are aware of you and want you to be with them.

Physical, Organizational Needs

Security needs: being concerned that tomorrow is assured; having things regular and predictable for oneself and one's family and in-group.

Survival needs: a concern for immediate existence; to be able to eat, breathe, live at this moment.

Deficiency or maintenance motives that are granted or denied by external factors, are strong and recurring, and grow stronger when *denied.*

followed by aesthetic needs. The highest level is self-actualization, where the need to be everything you want to be is evident in your behavior. The self-actualized person is motivated by needs to be open, not defensive; to love others and self without yielding to aggression or manipulation; to act in ways that are ethically and morally good for society; to express autonomy and creativity; to be curious and spontaneous in interacting with the environment (Maslow, 1971).

Implications for Education

The theory of motivation teachers adopt can affect what and how we teach. Let us examine, for example, the implications of Maslow's theory.

What are some ways in which classroom teachers might work with other school personnel, parents, and people in the community to help address an urban, poor child's needs?

We cannot expect to meet students' intellectual needs, or develop their aesthetic ones, until their physical and social needs have been met. So when a child comes to school hungry, ill, abused, or feeling uncared for, it is difficult if not impossible to motivate that student to achieve academically. Schools may have to become more oriented to children's social welfare than they are now. Until schools address the hunger and medical and social problems of some of the children in their charge, they cannot hope to educate all their students very well. Of all the industrialized democracies in the world, the United States has the highest rate of children in poverty, the highest rate of childhood hunger, and the highest rate of children receiving no medical care (Berliner & Biddle, 1995). Furthermore, not all of our schools are as safe as they need to be for children to be secure. And not all our schools and neighborhoods offer after-school activities allowing children the chance to develop prosocial attitudes and behaviors that emerge from group activities—the boys' and girls' clubs, sports clubs, and service- and church-related clubs (Heath & McLaughlin, 1993; McLaughlin, Irby & Langman, 1994). In this gap, young people join their own clubs—gangs—to satisfy the needs for belongingness and esteem all humans need to satisfy. But gangs typically engage in antisocial behavior, limiting the opportunity for positive growth.

From Maslow's theory you can see that schools and neighborhoods that cannot assure their children satisfaction of their needs at the lower levels of the hierarchy produce children who cannot attain the highest levels of human potential. This is a personal and societal loss that should concern all educators and political leaders. It also explains why some schools feed children, run after-school programs, provide medical exams, and employ security guards, despite complaints of some members of the community that schools are "trying to do too much." These schools recognize that only when the needs at the lowest levels of the hierarchy are satisfied can the intellectual and aesthetic needs of children grow stronger.

Achievement Motivation: A Cognitive Composite

Cognitions, of course, affect motivation as well. One set of cognitive variables that has been studied is of greater importance to teachers and society than many others, namely, those associated with **achievement motivation**—the motivation to succeed, to be good at something. Achievement motivation may be thought of in two ways: (1) *autonomous*, in which we compare our performance against our previous performance, using our own "inner" standards for comparison; and (2) *social*, in which we compare our performance against that of others.

Autonomous achievement motivation develops early and is prevalent until a child enters school. It is the motivation pattern teachers would most like to see in their students and colleagues. As you might predict from our competitive scholastic system, however, social achievement motivation develops after a child enters school. After about second grade,

Conduct Your Own Survey
of Young Children's Changing Motivation

Put together a short list of questions aimed at identifying young children's changing motivations. Focus the questions on what each child is eager to learn and why. Obtain permission from a kindergarten or first-grade, and a third- or fourth-grade teacher (perhaps in the school where you are student teaching) and ask as many children as possible from each class the same questions. From this informal survey, can you detect any changing patterns of motivation across the grade levels? If so, do the changes reflect what is described in the text—that is, from more autonomous to more social? What else can you discover about motivation and learning by asking these questions?

achievement motivation is influenced by social comparisons. Spelling bees, sports contests, as well as tests, capitalize on the competitive drive some children have. From the early grades on, more students are motivated by competition with others than by striving to achieve self-determined standards. This is a real loss, but teachers can do something about it, as will be seen in the discussion of self-worth below.

In any case, it should be clear that the development and maintenance of achievement motivation in students is vital. It is what energizes, directs, and sustains learning activities, and so it determines the productivity level of a student or a school. In fact, there is apparently a relationship between the level of achievement motivation in each generation and the productivity of a society. The evidence suggests that achievement motivation can foster economic and technological progress. So society depends on the schools not just for the teaching of subject matter but for instilling in students the need to succeed throughout life.

Relationship between Need
for Achievement and Performance

However obtained, estimates of students' need for achievement should be reflected in some other measure of their performance. As it turns out, over the years, the strength of the motive to achieve (derived from a test score) has been correlated with a number of performance measures that teachers and society value. For example, suppose a student high in achievement motivation is given a choice of work partners. One of them is friendly; the other is good at the task. The achievement-motivated student tends to choose the person who is good at the task. Students high in affiliative needs but low in achievement needs tend to make the opposite choice. Or suppose a group of students are given a set of complex problems to solve. People with higher achievement needs show much greater task persistence when they encounter difficulty, usually complete more problems per unit of time, and are more likely to reach the correct solutions to the problems they attempt—independent of their ability level. And those high in achievement motivation often see failure as a result of their own lack of effort rather than some external force. So they reason that by increasing personal effort they can perform most tasks. In addition, those higher in achievement motivation are also more likely to perform well even during a "free-time" period, such as Study Hall, when students can determine their own rate of performance. This occurs, in part, because students high in achievement needs maintain high levels of performance without external monitoring. In other words, they do not need to be watched and cajoled as much.

Students with high achievement motivation are able to maintain their goals over longer periods of time, too. And when they are interrupted in their tasks (which is inevitable), they have a greater tendency to complete the interrupted tasks than students who do not have high levels of achievement motivation. High levels of achievement motivation have also been linked with risk taking. Those motivated to succeed more often seek out tasks of intermediate difficulty. Apparently their purpose is to get the maximum realistic estimate of their own ability. With this knowledge they can set goals and plan routes to success more accurately. Those without a strong achievement motive, however, more often choose tasks of low or high risk, avoiding the realistic self-appraisals necessary for sensible goal setting and planning (Heckhausen, Schmalt, & Schneider, 1985).

Classifying Achievement Attributions

Performance is only the visible indicator of achievement motivation. Less observable is the complex system of cognitive and affective activity, including both thoughts and feelings, that accompanies motivated behavior. For example, when we succeed or fail at a task, we almost always think about who or what was behind the success or failure. We look to assign responsibility, to understand the causes of our performance. That is, we make **attributions** about who or what was responsible for how we performed. These attributions turn out to be systematically related to different kinds of subsequent behavior. Attributions are also the source of our feeling good, bad, or indifferent after we succeed or fail—they have emotional consequences. Because attributions about our achievements influence both our subsequent behavior and our feelings, we need to study them more closely.

Attributions can be classified along three dimensions: source of control, stability, and controllability (Weiner, 1986; Graham & Weiner, 1996).

1. **Locus of control.** The locus, or source, of a motivational factor can be internal or external. If you say you did well on a test because you are "good in math," you are attributing your success to an internal characteristic—your ability. If you believe you did well because the teacher was lenient, you are attributing your success to an external factor—the teacher.

2. **Stability.** Some attributions refer to a temporary factor, relating only to a specific task; others refer to more lasting factors, relating to a series of tasks. Suppose you fail an exam. An unstable attribution might refer to your effort (I didn't study as much as I should have); a stable attribution might refer to perceived discrimination on the part of the teacher (This teacher is always tough on girls).

3. **Controllability.** If you believe that the difficulty of the task was responsible for your failure (I didn't do well because the questions were too hard), you're describing a cause that is beyond your control. If you failed the test because you lost your notes and could not study, you're attributing your failure to a factor you can control.

From these three dimensions come eight different categories of attribution listed in Table 8.1. To interpret the table, assume that both teacher and student are assigning responsibility to explain the student's poor performance on a test. The teacher's attributions are included because they too create explanations for their success and failure.

How we classify attributions can affect our performance on future tasks. If you believe a failure is controllable—say, the result of low effort—you may be spurred on by that failure to do better next time. If you believe, however, that you cannot control who or what caused the fail-

> Think of the last time you succeeded at a task and the last time you failed. Use these three dimensions to classify your attributions.

8.1

TABLE

Attributions that Might Be Made by Teacher and Student after Student's Low Performance on a Classroom Test

Characteristic of the Attribution		Teacher's Attributions	Student's Attributions
Internal **Stable**	Uncontrollable	I'm simply not an effective teacher. (ability)	I just have no head for numbers. (ability)
	Controllable	I never prepare well enough to teach this unit. (effort)	I'm too lazy to study much. (effort)
Internal **Unstable**	Uncontrollable	I was too sick that week to teach it right.	When I have to work late, I'm sometimes shot the next morning.
	Controllable	I was too tired from partying that week to teach it well.	I was too tired from partying the night before to do well.
External **Stable**	Uncontrollable	This school's standards for passing a test are too high. (difficult task)	This teacher hardly passes anyone— she's too tough in grading. (difficult task)
	Controllable	These kids don't like me.	This teacher doesn't respect any of us.
External **Unstable**	Uncontrollable	I must have been unlucky in my choice of questions. (luck)	Sometimes you hit it right, when you study, sometimes you don't. (luck)
	Controllable	My aides didn't show up this week to help prepare the students.	Too many people were visiting the family this week.

ure, you may not even try to improve your performance. Failure itself, then, is not harmful; it is attributing failure to causes over which you have no control that does the damage!

Students' Causal Attributions   The research on student attributions reveals that only a small number of categories—effort, ability, mood, task difficulty, and luck being among the most common—are regularly used to account for their success or failure (Bar-Tal & Darom, 1979; Frieze & Snyder, 1980). When the attribution patterns of 743 students from fifth to twelfth grade were analyzed (Fyans & Maehr, 1980), it was found that the students' typical attribution patterns were good predictors of whether they would choose subsequent tasks calling for skill, for effort, or for luck. These cognitions clearly do affect the choices a student makes. Psychologists also know, from the analysis by Whitley and Frieze (1985) of dozens of studies, that children (and adults) usually hold to an egotistical (self-enhancing) attribution system. That is, they ordinarily attribute success to internal factors (effort, ability) and failure to external factors (task difficulty, luck). But some students do not always use this ego-maintaining strategy. Instead they attribute their successes to luck and their failures to lack of ability. And students who perceive lack of ability as the cause of their failure come to expect failure regularly. Since they come to believe they do not have the ability to succeed, they often avoid achievement-oriented activities or fail to work hard on achievement-oriented tasks. Their attributional logic goes something like this: "I failed due to a lack of ability [that is, a stable factor over which I have no control], therefore I am not responsible for my failure [and so in tasks like this I do not need to work hard]" (Weiner, 1994).

What is more, if teachers attribute the students' performance to limited ability, they show sympathy, but they do not urge them on. They tacitly accept the poor performance, confirming the students' poor opinion of themselves. Notice the enormous difference when a child attributes failure to a lack of effort. Then the attributional logic is likely to go something like this: "I failed because I didn't work hard enough (that is, a factor over which I have personal control), therefore I am the one responsible for my own failure (and so the next time I face a task like this I need to work harder)." And, if teachers attribute the students' performance to a lack of effort, they get angry at them, urging them on, confirming the students' opinion that what they need to do is try harder next time. So the attributions of students and teachers clearly have great influences on their subsequent behavior.

Besides attributing failure to an internal characteristic—say, a lack of ability—some students simultaneously attribute their success to an external characteristic—say, the ease of a test or good luck. Students who do this cannot find any sensible reasons to make much effort to succeed in school tasks. Attribution patterns that assign responsibility for failure to a stable internal cause, such as ability, and for success to an unstable external cause, such as luck, are highly maladaptive. Such attribution patterns are most prevalent among people for whom some members of society hold negative stereotypes: members of some minority groups,

Did you ever not do well at something and blame it on a lack of ability or a lack of effort? How did it feel?

POLICY, RESEARCH, AND PRACTICE

Internal and External Attributions and Emotion

A LOOK INSIDE THE CLASSROOM

The two third-grade teachers at Brown Elementary School have color-fully decorated, identical wooden doors next to each other—but opposite reputations. If you fail a test in Ms. Renzulli's class, chances are you'll know she's annoyed with you. In Ms. Messick's class, on the other hand, you'll probably get a long look of sympathy. As an outsider strolling down the hall and hearing about these two teachers' different styles, your intuition might tell you that the students in Ms. Messick's class would be motivated to do better on tests and in classroom performance. After all, who among us doesn't like a little sympathy?

The students' actions and reactions, however, would tell you a different story. They typically try harder in Ms. Renzulli's class; in Ms. Messick's class, they more commonly withdraw after a poor performance, and do not try as hard the next time. If you were to probe into this further, you would find that the students in Ms. Messick's class interpret her expressions of sympathy as arising from her belief that they simply don't have the ability to do better or from some other factor students cannot control. By contrast, the students in Ms. Renzulli's class believe that their teacher gets annoyed because she usually attributes their failure to a lack of effort. Why should these different perceptions of students have such a powerful effect?

A LOOK AT THE RESEARCH

Children learn very quickly in school that there are differences between the concepts of ability and effort (Blumenfeld, Pintrich, & Hamilton, 1986). And studies by Graham (1986; Graham & Barker, 1990) corroborate what the students in the Brown Elementary School know. In her studies, even five-year-olds recognized the link between an attribution of low effort (something within the students' control) with a teacher's expression of anger; and an attribution of low ability (something outside the students' control) with a teacher's expression of sympathy.

Furthermore, children often accept the attribution they think is behind the anger or sympathy (Graham, Doubleday, & Guarino, 1984). That is, they come to believe they have made too little effort or have too little ability to succeed, and they expect to perform accordingly. By attributing a student's failure to lack of effort and expressing anger, a teacher can make the student feel guilty (Weiner, 1986; 1994). That guilt—the feeling that he or she has let self or teacher down—is usually a positive motivating force when the student next attempts a task. But by attributing failure to low ability and expressing sympathy, a teacher ordinarily makes a student feel shame. And shame is not a positive motivating force. Instead it can lead a student to withdraw, to feel inferior and helpless.

REFLECTIONS FOR YOUR OWN CLASSROOM

What can you learn from these observations and research findings that can help you in your own teaching? One lesson is that although sympathy may be a generous emotion, it can backfire. It may be a way of showing caring about the work of your low-achieving students, but it can work against them by demonstrating that you may not believe they have "what it takes" to succeed. But sympathy is not the only emotion that can backfire. So can (1) praise for a student's success and lack of criticism for a student's failure when a task is very easy and (2) providing excessive help, particularly when it is not sought (Weiner et al., 1983).

The moral here is not to encourage teachers to show anger or inhibit praise or even sympathy when it is appropriate. It is to remind you that the self-esteem and self-confidence of learners are built out of the way others treat them, particularly parents and teachers. All parents and teachers make attributions about their children's behavior. More important, all students make attributions about their parents' and teachers' behavior! So as a parent or a teacher, when you criticize, sympathize with, praise, or offer to help a child, you must be sensitive to how he or she might perceive your actions. In sum, you owe it to your students, and to yourself, to give all your teaching actions thoughtful scrutiny. Just as in this scenario, the full picture may be far more complex than you assumed.

students from low-income families, students who are disabled, and women (particularly in science and mathematics), for example. Some researchers argue that more members of these groups reject effort as a causal factor in success or failure. If less-powerful members of society believe that their effort is useless, that it will not give them a chance to succeed because the deck is stacked against them, the schools (and all of society) have a problem. In such circumstances, teachers can expect maladaptive achievement-oriented behavior to be perpetuated across many areas of the school curriculum. Because attribution patterns are fairly stable over time and situations, training programs are necessary to break self-defeating attribution patterns in schoolchildren (Bar-Tal, Raviv, & Bar-Tal, 1982).

Trying to teach children that their failure has more to do with effort than ability isn't easy—but every teacher must try.
(© Harry Cutting/ Monkmeyer)

Teachers' Causal Attributions   Of course teachers also succeed and fail at what they do in schools. To what do they attribute their success and failure? Commenting on test performance, teachers often attribute success to the students' home conditions, effort, and interest, and—as you might expect—their own excellent teaching skill. But when students fail, teachers blame the students' preparation, ability, poor home conditions, and the difficulty of the test (Bar-Tal, 1979). In other words, teachers tend to share credit with students for students' success on a test, but to blame students' failure on external (nonteacher) causes. This tendency is understandable—it is the ego-maintaining mechanism in all of us—but it is probably not appropriate professional behavior.

Ames (1982) noted, however, that teachers can range from low to high in their commitment to excellence in teaching. Teachers who value teaching highly take personal responsibility for student failures. Teachers who have less commitment to excellence in teaching attribute student failure more often to student characteristics. Teachers in the former group increase their effort to help students succeed; those in the latter group do not—they blame poverty, parents, television, moral decay, and other factors for the poor performance of their students.

Internal and External Attributions   Those who generally attribute their success or failure to their own behavior (personal effort or ability) are said to have an *internal* locus of control. Those who generally attribute their success or failure to luck or task difficulty are said to have an *external* locus of control. These relatively stable patterns of behavior are associated with many other personal characteristics.

> Causal attributions in part determine the affective consequences of success and failure. Pride and shame . . . are absolutely maximized when achievement outcomes are ascribed internally and are minimized when success and failure are attributed to external causes.

Thus, success attributed to high ability or hard work produces more pride and external praise than success that is perceived as due to the ease of the task or good luck. In a similar manner, failure perceived as caused by low ability or a lack of effort results in greater shame and external punishment than failure attributed to the excessive difficulty of the task or bad luck. In sum, locus of causality influences the affective or emotional consequences of achievement outcomes.

(Weiner, 1977, p. 183)

Besides having emotional consequences, the degree of internality-externality, like achievement motivation, has been associated with speed of performance, choice of tasks, and persistence on tasks: The higher the internality, the better the performance and decisions about which tasks to attempt. Self-concept as a learner also appears to be related to a student's attribution pattern. The student with an internal locus of control for success (I succeed because I have ability or because I put in the proper amount of effort) and an internal locus of control for failure (I messed up because my luck was bad) enters learning tasks with a positive self-concept (Johnson, 1981).

Learned helplessness, the extreme of a negative self-concept for a learner, is also related to attribution patterns (Dweck & Leggett, 1988). Students with learned helplessness think that nothing they do will lead to success. This is partly learned from their own families, from interactions with their mothers and fathers. For example, Hokoda and Fincham (1995) studied children designated as either "helpless" or "mastery-oriented." With their mothers present, these children were given puzzles to solve. When the child encountered a difficult puzzle and said, "I can't do this one," mothers of the helpless children said, "All right, let's move on to the next puzzle." Mothers of the mastery-oriented children, though, said, "Yes you can do it, stick with it, look . . . ," and then they provided some instructional support. The "helpless" students have developed an internal locus of control for failure (I am dumb!), which induces intense feelings of shame and self-doubt, particularly in the face of cumulative failure (Covington, 1992). Because they believe they do not have the ability to succeed, they often do not even try. There is a kind of sense to this strategy, even though it ensures failure. By not attempting school tasks, their poor performance can be attributed to low effort, which is less shameful in American society than is low ability (Covington, 1992).

Teachers need to be on the lookout for both children with learned helplessness and those who consistently are high in externality. Such students seem to lack the beliefs that make them take responsibility for their academic achievement. But their attribution patterns can be changed, as is discussed below. Those who now avoid school or are failing in school can acquire new ways of coping with the educational system and succeeding in it. Figure 8.2 presents some classroom (or parent) practices that more frequently lead to the kinds of student beliefs that nurture academic achievement.

When teaching a student with learned helplessness, how might you best structure learning experiences so that the student can begin to reverse this belief?

FIGURE 8.2

Enhancing achievement-oriented motivational beliefs

Adapted from D. J. Stipek, "Motivation and Instruction" and used by permission of Macmillan Library Reference USA, a Simon & Schuster Macmillan Company, from Handbook of Educational Psychology, *David C. Berliner and Robert C. Calfee, editors. Copyright © 1996 by Simon & Schuster Macmillan.*

Classroom Practices

Tasks
Design challenging tasks that can be completed with a reasonable amount of effort.
Divide difficult tasks into subgoals that are achievable without excessive effort.
Differentiate among kinds of tasks students are responsible for over time.

Criteria for Success, Evaluation, and Rewards
Define success in terms of mastery and personal improvement rather than performance relative to others.
If competition is used, make sure that all students have an equal chance of "winning."
Provide clear and frequent feedback that informs learners about their developing competence.
Make rewards contingent on effort, improvement, and good performance.

Teacher Behavior Toward Students
Avoid unnecessary differential treatment of high and low achievers.
When someone fails, focus on effort and the learning strategies that were used as the likely cause.
When someone succeeds, focus on effort and ability as the likely cause.
Avoid subtle expressions that communicate a perception of low ability (e.g., overly sympathetic responses after failure, praise for success on easy tasks, unnecessary help).

Mediating Beliefs and Feelings

High expectations for success both in general and in particular task environments (self-efficacy).
Perception of self as academically competent.
Perceptions that achievement outcomes can be controlled, including (1) that rewards are contingent on behavior and (2) that one has the ability to produce the behavior upon which rewards are contingent.
Belief that poor outcomes are attributable to low effort or poor strategy use, and that good outcomes are attributable to personal effort and ability.

Anticipated Student Outcomes

Exerts great effort, uses cognitive learning strategies.
Approaches tasks willingly.
Seeks help when needed.
Persists in the face of difficulty.
Takes pride in successes.

The Relationship of Self-Worth and Need for Achievement to Classroom Structure

Earlier, we talked about the autonomous versus the social need to achieve. There is a parallel in attribution patterns, and it too is linked with age and school. When children are very young, learning on their own, they usually think about their own performance without thinking about how anyone else is doing. They often seem pleased with their own learning. They show what some call **intrinsic,** or autonomous, **motivation** to learn. But once they enter school, they begin to compare their own performance with that of others to determine how well they are doing. The typical child, then, goes from an individual approach to judging his own learning to some kind of social-reference approach for judging learning. The social-reference approach develops because of competition in the classroom, where "winning" and "losing" often seem to be more important than learning. In classes with a competitive structure, a student's ability takes on special status. High-ability students feel pride. But children are not homogeneous—some are not as quick in academic subjects as others. So how does an average or low-ability student feel in a competitive classroom? They ordinarily feel shame, especially when they fail after making a strong effort. In this case, failure is humiliating because it "proves" they do not have ability.

Self-worth theory is about the protection of the self from negative evaluations to preserve feelings of competence. Self-worth can be maintained, then, by *not* trying to achieve. If you try hard and still fail to achieve a goal, it seems that the only reason for that failure is low ability (Covington, 1984; 1992). But if you do not try, then you can preserve your sense of self. Self-worth theory asserts that too many students in competitive classrooms choose to preserve their sense of self-worth by not trying. They are not lazy, docile, passive, or listless. In fact, they are highly motivated. But their motivation is to *not* try because they have learned that in the competitive classroom only a few can win and they are the losers. Self-worth theory suggests, in fact, that schools are set up to ensure that as students progress through the grade levels, most will become turned-off! As Ames and Ames (1984) put it,

> Failing in a competitive setting elicits strong negative affect that is directed at oneself, and because competition necessarily involves a situation of many losers and few winners, most children undoubtedly experience threats to self-esteem. We cannot help but speculate that declines in children's self-perceptions of their ability over the elementary school years may, in part, be a consequence of the competitive nature of many classrooms and the increased emphasis placed on social comparison as children progress through school. (p. 45)

Krumboltz (1990) expressed this trend with more outrage and irony. He said that the United States has designed the perfect system for producing students who hate to learn. Teachers do not involve students in establishing the goals for the class, but then we ask them to perform impossible tasks, such as turning in perfect papers and tests. And when we discover that they are not doing perfect work, we ridicule them by reporting their failures and shortcomings to their classmates and parents. Moreover, if we catch any student helping another with his work, we punish her for cheating. We demand that each student work in silent solitude, separated from every other student in the class. And finally, in our competitive classrooms, when teachers help students, other students interpret that as a sign of the incompetence of the help receiver.

This system seems purposely designed to promote alienation, vandalism, and dropping out of school. It makes teachers the victims of competitive grading too: The student hostility that is a natural consequence

Before reading the next part of the discussion, on alternatives to competitive classrooms, list as many possible solutions as you can here.

of naming the classroom's winners and losers (through tests, report cards, displayed art work, and the like) sours the learning environment for everyone (Krumboltz & Yeh, 1996).

But classrooms do not need to be based on competition or any single notion of ability. There are alternative classroom structures, which increase the number of winners in the class, allowing more students to feel competent. In such environments the effects of failure, even after great effort, are not as devastating. For example, there are classroom structures that emphasize individual learning, where individual learning contracts or mastery approaches (see Chapter 11) teach students that self-improvement comes from self-effort. Standards-based or outcomes-based approaches to school reform (see Chapter 2), inform students, parents, and teachers as to what is to be learned. Although students must master the standards, all who do so are competent, and differentiating among them with grades of A, B, or C is probably not as important to either the teachers or students. What the educational system should seek is not elimination of all competition, but a reduction of it so that students more frequently get to assess their performance using personal guidelines and outside standards. And we should eliminate or vastly reduce systems of evaluation based on comparisons with someone else's performance.

Figure 8.3 shows how the motive to achieve is fostered in classrooms that evaluate learning with reference to the individual, and stifled in those where social-reference groups are used to judge performance. There were 13 teachers in each of the two groups in this study. Researchers measured the achievement motive of 311 students in 26 classes. The data show clearly that over four years the teachers who used a social-reference norm for judging performance had students with significantly lower achievement motivation than did teachers who had

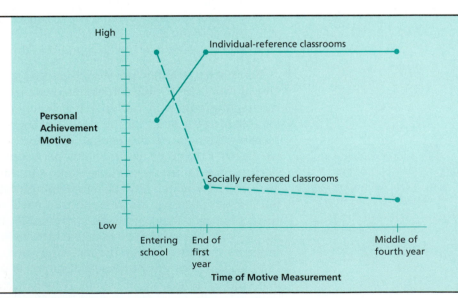

FIGURE 8.3

Effects of two types of classroom structures on the motive to achieve

Adapted from Heckhausen, Schmalt, & Schneider (1985) from data in Trudewind & Kohne (1982).

created ways for children to judge themselves, without comparing themselves to others.

Still another kind of classroom structure that affects motivation is cooperative learning (see Chapter 10). In a cooperative-learning structure, students usually work in small groups for rewards based on the whole group's performance. The high-ability members and the low-ability members of the group must work together to achieve a reward. A key factor in the success of cooperative classroom structures seems to be that genuine cooperation is made to be the only way to get the rewards (Slavin, 1984, 1990c). The effects of failure may be moderated, and can be externalized a bit (We *all* messed up!), which protects feelings of self-worth. And low-ability students can be part of a successful cooperative group (We did it!), building feelings of self-worth. In fact, in such cooperative structures, students may learn that it feels just as good to contribute to the well-being of others as it does to triumph over them (Covington, 1984, 1992; Webb & Palincsar, 1996). Of course this can all backfire as well. The lowest-performing member can be blamed for the group's failure, resulting in scapegoating and ostracism. In some groups there may be "free riders"—those who do not work at all. These phenomena simply illustrate that there is very little teachers can do, cooperative learning included, that *always* works well (McCaslin & Good, 1996; Webb & Palincsar, 1996).

One other kind of classroom structure is worth noting—the **multi-dimensional class.** Rosenholtz and Simpson (1984) have observed that most classrooms are *unidimensional*—all students work on similar tasks most of the time. In this structure social comparisons are common. But in multidimensional classrooms, this view seems to change. Here, students often work at different tasks. While some students are reading, some are doing science projects, and others are painting. Because there are many different academic and social tasks in which a student can achieve, the multidimensional structure allows more different kinds of ability to be recognized, and more students end up feeling competent.

Obviously, schools that track students (that is, put them into homogeneous groups or classes on the basis of academic ability) make academic ability the salient characteristic of the school. In such schools feelings of self-worth are not widely distributed, nor are they equitably distributed. In these cases, the wide array of other human talents possessed by disadvantaged children, immigrant children, or children with disabilities are likely to be ignored (Covington, 1992; Oakes, 1985, 1992). Multidimensional classrooms (and untracked schools) provide more students with chances to feel worthwhile about themselves, and to value the many nonacademic talents, skills, and intelligences they possess, even though their academic ability is not outstanding.

How might multidimensional classrooms be a natural application of the theory of multiple intelligences that you learned about in Chapter 3? Would proponents of this theory find multidimensional classrooms conducive to higher motivation? Why or why not?

How Other Motives Interact with the Need for Achievement

We have concentrated on one motive, the need for achievement in either academic or nonacademic areas, because of its centrality in school success and accomplishment in other areas of society. But a good rule of thumb for teachers to remember is that no behavior is ever controlled by a single motive. The need for achievement and its associated attribution patterns interacts with the need to preserve self-worth and dozens of other motives, such as the need to affiliate, the need for power, or the need for approval. These all influence school performance simultaneously, making it very hard to figure out what the motives for particular actions are. But when researchers study these other motives, separately and in isolation, it is possible to see how they affect behavior.

For example, the **affiliation motive** represents the degree to which students want and need friendly relationships with other people. Students high in affiliative motives ought to do better in classes where the teacher is warm and friendly, and they do. Furthermore, almost all students are motivated by affiliative needs, and these probably move them to attend school much more frequently than do chances to achieve in physics (Urdan & Maehr, 1995). It may be the affilliative motive that energizes a child of Southeast Asian immigrants, who seeks the approval of her family by achieving well in school. And it may be the same motive—affiliation—that accounts for poor achievement among some African-American students. Fordham (1988) and Ogbu (1991) found that some African-American youth reject school achievement in order not to appear "white." Apparently they fear that their affiliative relationships with other black students would be strained by doing too well in the white-majority-run school system. The same affiliative motive is at work, energizing, directing, and maintaining behavior, but in the two different cultural contexts—Southeast Asian and African-American—it leads to very different school outcomes.

Then there is the **need for power**—the need to influence other people. The teachers who encourage students to volunteer their ideas freely in class give students an outlet for their need to influence others. So students who have a need to influence others ought to do better in their classes. And, among male students, that is the case. In the case of both need for affiliation and need for power, a teacher's characteristic behavior appears to interact with a student's motivational system. When the match is right, some students thrive. But the match can also be wrong—say, when affiliative students are placed with emotionally distant teachers, or students with a high need for power are placed in classes where the teacher discourages volunteering—and it is the teacher's job to be sensitive to such mismatches. The environment created by the teacher and the motive patterns directing a student determine whether or not the student thrives.

Another motive that has consequences for schooling is the **need for approval** or recognition. Although all of us need some approval, some individuals are overly dependent on it; they are highly conformist and submissive to authority. These students are affiliation-oriented, but they are often disliked because they are so needy for others' approval. The child who informs on others, tries to be the teacher's pet, or seeks to do well on tests only for the accompanying approval may be inappropriately motivated. These students—as well as those who exhibit other extreme

Think up some strategies for dealing with a conformist student in the classroom.

behaviors such as verbal or physical aggression toward themselves or others—all require the teacher's understanding. The origins of these motives and the training that can reduce their intensity are not as well known as those for achievement motivation.

But as we have already seen, factors in the immediate environment can influence motivational levels and subsequent behaviors. Cognitions are not independent of surrounding environmental stimuli. As you might expect, operant conditioning, with its focus on environmental contingencies, has much to contribute in this area. To discuss the operant conditioning approach, we must first examine the concepts of intrinsic and extrinsic motivation in greater detail.

Intrinsic and Extrinsic Motivation

At times behavior appears to be unaffected by environmental variables. A person seems to maintain energy and direction simply as a result of some unknown drive, without apparent reinforcement from outside. Motivation without apparent reward is sometimes called *intrinsic.* Some claim that intrinsically motivated behavior is better than extrinsically motivated behavior, which depends on observable rewards. These

Intrinsic motivation to learn is wonderful to behold. But its roots often lie in extrinsic reinforcement, received when the activity was first started.

(© Jerry Berndt/Stock Boston)

critics of operant methods say things like "Rewarding children spoils them; it makes them work only for rewards," "Paying children to read or play the piano destroys their chance to develop their own love of reading or piano playing," and "Reinforcement is bribery!"

We believe that people are motivated in large part by the reinforcing consequences of their own or an observed model's past behavior. Often reinforcement is obvious, but even when it is not, it is there. No one reads books or plays the piano without reinforcement. A reader or pianist who appears to be motivated from within actually has developed self-reinforcement processes derived, perhaps, from earlier external reinforcement. Initially, the reading or piano playing may have been fostered by the social approval of parents or teachers—a hug for reading the words *cat* and *hat,* applause from a small but important audience when the first song was played. From these external rewards, the reader or piano player generated a self-reinforcement system. Eventually the fascinating facts about Hemingway's life or the pleasure of playing the piano so as to produce beautiful music replace the hug and the applause. At the latter stage the person has intrinsic motivation. It is the kind of motivation teachers like to see in their students.

If children take to reading or piano playing without any sign of external rewards, as some children do, teachers (or parents) will probably undermine their intrinsic interest in reading or piano if they offer to reward them for what they like to do on their own. But the rest of the students we encounter—perhaps the vast majority—may need some extrinsic rewards to get them started.

If we see ourselves as the cause of our own behavior—that is, if we believe we are "origins," in control of our own behavior—then we believe we are intrinsically motivated. But if we believe our behavior is determined by external forces, that we are "pawns," we think of ourselves as extrinsically motivated. Our perceptions of our motivation for a particular behavior are important because they affect subsequent behavior in interesting ways. In one series of studies (Lepper, Greene, & Nisbett, 1973; Lepper & Greene, 1975), the researchers measured children's initial interest in an activity, after which they were allowed to continue the activity. The children in one group were told they were going to be rewarded for their efforts. Other groups of children either got no reward or were rewarded unexpectedly. The group who came to expect a reward showed a relative drop in performance. It was as if their intrinsic motivation was somehow eroded by the reward. Their attributions may have changed from thinking of themselves as origins to thinking of themselves as pawns, or from enjoying the activity for its value as "fun" to regarding it as a means toward a reward.

> To the extent, for example, that many of the activities we ask children to attempt in school may be of some initial interest to at least some of the children, the effect of presenting these activities in the context of a system of extrinsic incentives . . . may be to undermine that intrinsic interest in those activities. Unwittingly, these studies suggest, we may often turn activities of initial interest into drudgery

which children engage in only when external pressures are present to force or lure them to do so.

(Lepper & Greene, 1975, pp. 484–485)

The effect of extrinsic rewards on performance is a contentious issue. One recent meta-analysis of the studies in this area concludes that teachers have nothing to fear from putting extrinsic reward systems into their classrooms (Cameron & Pierce, 1994; Eisenberger & Cameron, 1996). Simply put, the authors say that extrinsic rewards work for most of the people, most of the time, under most conditions. The power of extrinsic motivation is proved to be successful everyday in ordinary life. The criticism of this position, however, is also convincing (Lepper, Keavney & Drake, 1996; Kohn, 1993; 1996). Experiments have demonstrated that some students, in some situations, actually show decreases in performance because of extrinsic rewards. This decrease is most likely to occur when initial interest is stimulated by the complexity or novelty of a task (Lepper & Greene, 1975).

As a result, teachers must realize that the effectiveness of rewards may depend on circumstances. A good rule to remember is that verbal or tangible rewards that are perceived as attempts to control behavior are not effective; but rewards that provide information about performance are effective (Weiner, 1990). For example, we may undermine a student's interest if we say, "Thanks, that's the way I like the job done," and we may foster that interest when we say, "Thanks, you're doing a fine job. You are neat and fast." Control statements lead to an external orientation and lower motivation; informational statements lead to an internal orientation and enhanced feelings of competence and self-worth (Deci, 1975; Deci & Ryan, 1985). Applying this principle to schooling, we can see how a teacher's task-related comments about a student's performance (informational statements) would enhance the intrinsic motivation of that student more than would grades (which imply external control). Similarly, getting a gold star, unexpectedly, while working on some project will probably motivate a student—it is a form of feedback about progress being made. But getting the same gold star for turning in work that is due, an expected reward for compliance, is likely to undermine the student's intrinsic motivation to work on that kind of task; the reward in the second case is likely to be perceived as a controlling device (Ryan & Deci, 1996). These predictions have been confirmed many times (e.g., Butler & Nisan, 1986)

Our point is not that rewards are bad. For the most part, when used and monitored carefully, they are usually effective. And we think their negative effects have sometimes been overstated. But that does not change two facts. First, it is still more desirable to develop intrinsically motivated students, and extrinsic rewards are not ordinarily appropriate for that. Some classroom processes that have been associated with building intrinsic motivation to learn are given in Figure 8.4. Second, the deleterious effects of extrinsic rewards have been clearly demonstrated over and over. If extrinsic rewards are used with tasks students would have done anyway, they are likely to undermine motivation. Fur-

Think of one instance from your own experience in which you learned something just because you wanted to, and another in which you learned something for a reward. Did the learning feel "stronger" and stay with you longer in one situation or the other?

FIGURE 8.4

Classroom processes for enhancing intrinsic motivation

Adapted from D. J. Stipek, "Motivation and Instruction" and used by permission of Macmillan Library Reference USA, a Simon & Schuster Macmillan Company, from Handbook of Educational Psychology, *David C. Berliner and Robert C. Calfee, editors. Copyright © 1996 by Simon & Schuster Macmillan.*

Classroom Practices

Use of Rewards
Use of rewards only when necessary.
Emphasize the informational rather than the controlling purpose of rewards.
Make rewards contingent on mastery, meeting a performance level or standard that students can achieve with effort (so that positive information about competency is likely).
Minimize practices focusing students' attention on extrinsic reasons for engaging in tasks (e.g., competition with others, salient deadlines, threats of punishment, close monitoring).

Evaluation
Deemphasize external evaluation, especially for challenging tasks.
Provide substantive, informative evaluation based on mastery rather than social comparisons.

Tasks
Give moderately difficult tasks.
Vary format and nature of tasks, chosen so that different children get to excel at some and the same children don't excel at everything.
Give tasks that are personally meaningful.
Allow choice in tasks.

Mediating Beliefs and Feelings
Perception of self-determination.
Feelings of competence and self-worth.

Anticipated Student Outcomes
More intense engagement.
More enjoyment.
A search for conceptual understanding.
More creativity.
More cognitive flexibility.

thermore, students who are already intrinsically motivated do not become more so through the use of extrinsic rewards. Extrinsic rewards may be most beneficial to those whose level of intrinsic motivation is initially quite low (Lepper & Hodell, 1989; Stipek, 1988; Lepper, Keavney, & Drake, 1996).

Operant Conditioning and Motivation

Strictly speaking, psychologists who adhere closely to operant-conditioning concepts regard the term *motivation* as superfluous. Motivation shows up as a response—weak, moderate, or strong. Teachers can talk about a student being motivated to achieve if they like, say the behaviorists (see Chapter 6), but what they are really saying is that the student is achieving well or not. The behavior, the student's response, is the only thing that is important. Like any other responses, those that lead to achievement are strengthened through reinforcement. So finding the reinforcers that might control behavior is the first order of business for those who choose to act as a behaviorist might. What follows is their approach to motivation.

Stimulus Control and the Role of Reinforcers and Incentives

Chances are, if you are teaching arithmetic and make the sum of the homework grades equal 50 percent of the final grade, your students will do their problems (that is, make the desired responses) regularly. By simply bringing a student's behavior under the control of a reinforcing stimulus you can strengthen his or her production of arithmetic. Manipulating stimuli in the environment is enough to change behavior. These stimuli in the environment are called *motivators*. And when we respond to them in particular ways, we are under stimulus control.

Stimulus control—bringing behavior under the control of a stimulus—can be exerted by reinforcing stimuli or incentives. An incentive is not the same as a reinforcer. An **incentive** is the promise or expectation of reinforcement. The expectation of praise is the incentive; the praise itself is the reinforcer. Expectations of receiving grades, money, or social approval are powerful incentives.

What makes something an incentive is a history of association with reinforcement. So incentives in classrooms include all the events that promise reinforcement. An approving glance as the teacher passes by could be a contingent reinforcer for some activity a student is engaged in. Or it could serve as an incentive—a cue that the student is liked and can expect to receive attention and friendship from the teacher. If the student is under stimulus control, the expectation of reinforcement provided by the approving glance or its equivalent is a motivator.

Finding the Right Reinforcers   One method of determining the appropriate reinforcers for children is to observe them. According to the Premack principle (see Chapter 6, pp. 222–223), what children do on their own initiative can be used as a reinforcer for activities they do not engage in spontaneously. You might also simply ask them outright in an informal discussion. Still another way to determine reinforcers is to develop a reinforcement menu, listing lots of activities, tangible items, and consumable items that a teacher can provide. The students consult the menu and choose a reinforcer before they take part in productive activities.

Theoretically, reinforcers must be determined for each individual child. But in practice children may be very similar in what reinforces their behavior. A few cautions: The procedures for determining reinforcers are far from infallible. Students are not always able or willing to talk about what is reinforcing for them. Also, motivational systems change over time. And it is important that the reinforcers be in line with your own values. Do you really want to reinforce a young student with an A or candy? You may prefer to play down adult approval or consumable rewards, substituting free time for reading or some other reinforcer more compatible with your values. The idea is to find a simple way to

What's a good reinforcer for you, a friend or a parent? What incentives are associated with these reinforcers?

FIGURE 8.5

Questionnaire for determining rewards and incentives for upper-elementary grade levels and older students

After Whisler & McCombs (1992); McCombs & Pope (1994).

- The things I do for fun are: _____
- The type of present I would most like to receive is: _____
- My hobbies are: _____
- The types of things I like to do with other people are: _____
- I feel good when: _____
- I spend money every week on: _____
- If I had $100.00 I would: _____
- Of all the things I do every day I would most hate to give up: _____
- I am happiest when: _____

uncover the preferences of individual students, then tailor incentives so that the students are motivated by them. Figure 8.5 presents some sample questions teachers can use to find out what their students might regard as appropriate incentives and rewards.

Frustration and Motivation

Incentives provide control because the expectation of reinforcement is usually followed with actual reinforcement. What happens when expected reinforcement does not come or reinforcers cannot be obtained? The student is frustrated. This frustration motivates student behavior, but not in good ways. (If nonreinforcement continues, the behavior is eventually extinguished, a process described in Chapter 6.)

Frustration can stem from many sources. Several common sources are:

1. *Material that is too difficult for students to complete.* Examples: homework too difficult to do independently, classroom questions too hard to answer during recitation, or worksheets too complicated to finish quickly and accurately. In these cases, students aren't allowed to succeed, and success is important here. High success rates in the classroom predict high student achievement (Marliave & Filby, 1985; Rosenshine & Stevens, 1986). Low success rates are a predictor of continued lower achievement as well as a likely source of frustration for students.

2. *A teacher's failure to provide reinforcement.* If you do not take the time to go over students' papers, they cannot receive the expected reinforcement—a grade they were expecting or the praise they were hoping for.

3. *A teacher's preventing completion of responses that lead to reinforcement.* If you move a student from a group in which she is doing well to one in which she does less well, you are keeping her from receiving reinforcement. If you do not allow a student to finish a task he is engrossed in because time has run out, you are frustrating him.

4. *An unintended by-product of preventing an activity that would lead to reinforcement.* For example, if you excuse a student from a spelling contest because she is a good speller, you are preventing her from making responses that will obtain reinforcement.

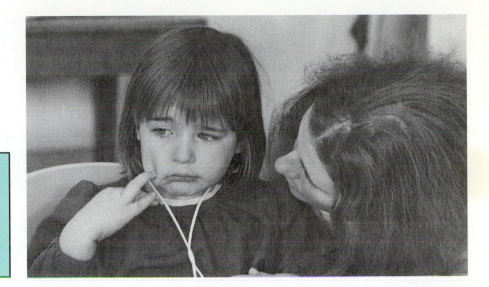

Frustration can lead to aggression. But gentle probing may reveal the problem that is preventing goal attainment.
(© David S. Strickler/ Monkmeyer)

How does frustration, from whatever source, show up in students' behavior? In a classic study by Barker, Dembo, and Lewin (1943), 30 children (2 to 5 years old) were allowed to play with desirable toys. After a period of time the children were frustrated by being moved into another area with a wire-net partition that blocked them from (but let them see) the toys. The researchers recorded, among other things, the constructiveness of the children's play. Following frustration, the children regressed; that is, they showed behavior patterns characteristic of a younger age level. Their play after frustration was, on average, like that of children about 1.5 years younger. They showed less free expression, less friendly conversation, and fewer signs of happiness. There was more restlessness, loud singing and talking, stuttering, thumb sucking, hitting, and the like.

Frustration happens, then, when expected reinforcement does not take place. Frustration does motivate: It does change students' energy level and direction. But it usually weakens wanted behavior and motivates unwanted behavior. It has proved to be a source of emotionality, withdrawal, regression, hyperactivity, and particularly aggression (Lawson, 1965). When teachers see these behaviors in students, they should recognize them as symptoms of frustration, caused, perhaps, by some problem in the reinforcement system. If we can identify the source of frustration, we can work to rectify it.

Changing Motivational Patterns

Because achievement-oriented behavior typically helps a student perform well in school, educators have asked the obvious question: How can it be enhanced? The answer is twofold: On the cognitive or internal side, by helping a student increase achievement motivation or change self-defeating attributions into ego-enhancing ones; and on the environ-mental or external side, by changing the contingencies and rewards for desirable behavior.

Cognitive Approaches

In this section, we look at the cognitive side of the change process, examining two training programs aimed at improving achievement-oriented behavior. Both focus on helping students change the way they think about themselves and achievement. The first is based on the achievement-motivation approach and the second on the attribution approach.

Achievement-Motivation Training Programs   Many successful demon-strations of achievement-motivation training with adolescents have been reported. One program, for lower-SES students, developed (1) spe-cial case studies to be read and discussed, (2) achievement-oriented games and exercises to try out new ways of thinking and behaving, and (3) ways of having the teachers involved model the behaviors and ex-pectations needed to achieve well. They conducted this achievement-motivation course for 21 high school juniors chosen from 56 potential dropouts. A year later, only one of the 21 students had dropped out of school, while eight of the 36 untrained students used as a control group had dropped out. The average grades of the trained students went up about half a letter grade, despite their taking more difficult courses than the untrained students. Furthermore, members of the trained group re-ported more new interests and activities, reflecting a greater feeling of control over their own lives, than did those in the control group (see Alschuler, 1967; 1973; Aronoff, Raymond, & Warmoth, 1965).

DeCharms (1976) also concentrated on changing motivation, in chil-dren from low-income black families. His program emphasized becoming an "origin" rather than a "pawn," and focused on aspects of personality similar to the internal-external locus of control variable. The students were helped to (1) learn their own strengths and weaknesses, (2) choose goals realistically, and (3) determine concrete actions they could carry out immediately to achieve their goals. From the first year's training, the children improved in achievement motivation, realistic goal setting, and freedom from feelings of helplessness. They also showed less absentee-ism and tardiness. Data on vocabulary, reading, language, and arith-metic achievement for students with two years in the training program showed that the training was effective in important ways. Follow-up of these low-income students found that the training had significantly increased the probability that they would graduate from high school (DeCharms, 1980; 1984). A program with similar goals and positive out-comes, designed by teachers of at-risk ninth graders, has been described by Derrickson (1995).

Summarizing about 20 years of these kinds of motivation-change studies, Heckhausen et al. (1985) pointed out that they often result in

POLICY, RESEARCH, AND PRACTICE

Are Attribution Training Programs an Effective Way to Change a Student's Perceptions about Why He or She Succeeds or Fails?

WHAT THE RESEARCH TELLS US

People tend to see the causes of their success and failure in systematic ways. The goal of attribution training programs is to change those ways if people's interpretations are leading to counterproductive emotions and behavior (see Fosterling, 1985; Weiner, 1982, 1986). Table 8.2 shows the wanted and unwanted attribution patterns we are referring to.

Changing unwanted patterns into wanted ones is probably what made Dweck's (1975) attribution training program successful. Dweck tried to change the attribution tendencies of children manifesting learned helplessness, or resignation to failure. After daily exercises over a period of 25 days, Dweck's subjects took more responsibility for their failures in mathematics problem solving, having learned to attribute their failure to insufficient effort. Andrews and Debus (1978) extended and verified Dweck's work. It now appears that some aspects of internality can be learned from teachers who systematically reinforce and model internal

TABLE 8.2

Wanted and Unwanted Attribution Patterns Following Success and Failure

	Event →		Attribution →		Emotion/Expectation →		Behavior
Unwanted Pattern	Success	→	Luck	→	Indifference/minimally increased expectation of success	→	Lack of willingness to engage in achievement tasks
	Failure	→	Lack of ability	→	Shame, incompetence, depression/decreased expectation of success	→	Avoidance or lack of persistence at achievement tasks
Wanted Pattern	Success	→	High ability	→	Pride, self-esteem/increased expectation of success	→	Willingness to engage in achievement tasks
	Failure	→	Lack of effort	→	Guilt/relatively high expectation of success	→	Persistence and willingness to engage in achievement tasks

Source: Adapted from F. Fosterling, "Attributional Retraining: A Review," Psychological Bulletin, 98:495–512, 1985. Copyright © 1985 by the American Psychological Association. Adapted by permission.

continues

attributions. Furthermore, Andrews and Debus (1978) found that training effects endure and that these attribution-change strategies are generalizable to a wide range of school activities. From his review of 15 studies, Fosterling (1985) concluded that attribution training programs work.

WHAT THIS MEANS FOR YOU AS A TEACHER

There is an important lesson here. When a child seems resigned to failure and appears to lack a sense of personal responsibility, you should set up a program of systematic reinforcement for that child so that he or she can learn to attribute problems to his or her own lack of effort. Diener and Dweck (1978) have pointed out how the kind of self-monitoring, self-instruction, and self-reinforcement strategies discussed in Chapter 6 can also be used to teach children with faulty attribution patterns to "talk to themselves" in ways that might be more appropriate. Fowler and Peterson (1981) showed that this approach can increase persistence at reading tasks. The verbal behaviors of the children change, and eventually so does their actual performance. They appear to be more achievement-oriented. Similarly, Rohrkemper (1986) described how students talk to themselves while solving mathematics problems. The messages they send themselves as they work (Try harder, or Try a new strategy versus I give up, or I'll never solve this) are crucial factors in their motivational systems. Teachers need to know about these thoughts and feelings and the attribution patterns they reflect in order to change those that are maladaptive.

Nowhere is the need to change unwanted personal attribution patterns clearer than in studies of children with mental retardation. Many of them have learned to be helpless, given the expectations held for them by others and their own difficulties in achieving because of real deficits in ability. Yet changing their attribution patterns can result in surprising increases in performance (Gold & Ryan, 1979). Effort, not just ability, can accomplish a lot! In fact, all members of groups that must fight stereotypes of low ability—African-Americans, Native-Americans, Latinos, women, students with learning disabilities, and others—can profit from attribution improvement.

In summary, if teachers are given just a little training or opportunity for study on their own, they can probably improve the attribution patterns and achievement motivation of their students. What teachers say and do can indeed influence those attribution patterns (Bar-Tal, 1982).

more realistic goal setting, less fear of failing, increased hope for success, higher opinions of the student's own competence, and less general anxiety and dislike of school. The point is, the motive to achieve is not fixed. It can be changed, perhaps not easily, or in everyone, but under the proper conditions many who are not now motivated to achieve can be transformed.

Environmental Approaches

In this section, we look at two different kinds of motivational approaches—token economies and motivational contracts—that have been shown to be effective in many learning situations over the years. Both emphasize the environmental variables affecting student motivation.

Token Economies Imagine you have been given responsibility for teaching 36 teenage boys, 85 percent of whom are school dropouts and all of whom have been found guilty of serious crimes. Their achievement in five curricular areas at the beginning of your program is shown in the "before" columns of Table 8.3. What would you do if you had between three and 18 months to work with these boys? Would you expect the improvements shown in the "after" columns?

The impressive data on achievement gains for institutionalized boys shown in the table were reported by H. L. Cohen (1973). His program consisted of a learning environment in which academic achievement, as measured by regular tests, bought points that could be exchanged for goods, services, and special privileges. The students had to pay "fees" to get into a course. That is, the students used points advanced to them in order to gain admittance to a course in which they could earn additional points by performing well. The boys could use the earned additional points to purchase desirable items such as mail-order supplies, private showers, or recreational time in a lounge. They could even purchase time out of the institution to shop, go sightseeing, or visit their families. This system motivated the students to achieve at a level unprecedented for alienated and deviant youth. Cohen went on to translate his original system into a system for troubled youth in regular schools. One year of the program brought about remarkable changes in achievement, and the students involved also became less disruptive, attended school more, and improved on a wide range of other social behaviors.

TABLE 8.3

Percentage of Deviant Boys Achieving at Particular Grade Levels in Five Curriculum Areas Before and After Training

Achievement (Grade Level)	Reading		English		Science		Mathematics		Social Studies	
	Before	After	Before	After	Before	After	Before	After	Before	After
1–4	22	3	97	8	22	14	72	14	33	6
5–7	36	28	3	33	78	28	28	8	67	36
8–10.5	39	39	0	25	0	44	0	53	0	19
10.6–12	3	30	0	33	0	14	0	25	0	39

Source: Adapted from H. L. Cohen, "Behavior Modification and Socially Deviant Youth," from C. E. Thoresen (Ed.), Behavior Modification in Education: Seventy-Second Yearbook of the National Society for the Study of Education, *72 (Part I). Copyright 1973. Used by permission.*
Note: N = 36

Explain in your own words why getting the behavior under the student's own cognitive control is the ultimate goal.

Although there is some concern about the deleterious effects of reward on performance, almost all researchers agree that when none of the desirable behavior you seek is evident, these powerful behavioral approaches can elicit the wanted behavior. The trick is to eventually get the behavior under cognitive control. That is, ultimately such students must make attributions that lead to achievement because they desire to achieve well and because some of their academic tasks have become intrinsically motivating.

The system Cohen used is called a **token economy,** and it has often been found to be effective in improving the academic and social behavior of students of many kinds. Typically, a school-based token economy includes (1) a set of behaviors that earn tokens, (2) a set of rules by which students exchange their tokens for wanted reinforcers, (3) a set of rules for awarding the tokens for appropriate behavior, and sometimes (4) a set of rules for taking back tokens for inappropriate behavior. The systems in use have proved to be generally effective in public schools, easier than teachers think to implement and manage, relatively inexpensive, compatible with most school and community attitudes, and liked by the students. But these programs have not often been used. Perhaps you will find a time and place to try out such a program with students who cannot be persuaded to achieve through other means.

If you work with adolescents, you face particular challenges because so much of what matters to high school students—dates, cars, money, sports, fashion, hair styles, music—is outside your control. You may want to enlist parents' help in motivating some of the older students. For instance, you might want to involve parents in a system incorporating home-based incentives and reinforcers, such as use of the family car or permission (and the money) to attend a rock concert. You can use tokens, check marks, or points as a way of keeping track of acceptable student performance and keep parents up to date with notes or phone calls on when reinforcers have been earned. But remember that concern with "extrinsic" reinforcement does not mean less concern for you about your primary job: making schoolwork more interesting to your students and giving them sensible reasons for learning. A token economy is something you should view as merely a powerful supplementary approach.

The effects of token economies appear to be long-lasting if attention is given to making them generalizable. One study of a token economy among fifth- and sixth-grade students, for example, then evaluated their eighth-grade achievement. They had not been in a token economy for at least two years at that point. Still, because of naturally occurring reinforcers in their environment (parent and teacher praise, special privileges for academic performance, and the like), the students maintained their high achievement to a significantly greater degree than did the control students (Dickinson, 1974).

Despite the effectiveness of token economies, if rewards become excessive they destroy intrinsic motivation. If we want children to enjoy reading for itself, apart from someone's approval or the school grades that might reward it, we must gradually withdraw extrinsic rewards as they learn about the fun of reading for its own sake. We must also reward the children's expressions of competency and self-efficacy as learners.

Motivational Contracts The kind of systematic approach developed by Cohen often involves formal or informal contracts between teachers and students. The pay for fulfillment of the contract takes the form of points or tokens, consumables, or simply praise. Contracting of various types, for different ends, and with students of all age levels seems to be an unusually promising educational invention.

Contracting for Mathematics in the Elementary Grades One of the original motivational contracting systems, in the form of a game, was developed as part of a method for improving achievement motivation. Each child in the class was advanced $2,000 in play money. Children could "get rich" or "go broke" by playing the game. Table 8.4 shows the schedule of payments. The greater the risk—say, trying to get 100 percent of the problems attempted correct—the greater the payoff. Students lost "money" for incorrect answers, for revising their contracts, and for late work, which incurred the severest penalty. The contracts were drawn up like the one shown in Figure 8.6, with the teacher the government contract officer.

The children kept their own achievement charts; the teacher never saw them. End-of-year prizes (gerbils, slot cars, and the like) chosen by the class were given to the six highest money winners. All students who finished the problems in their text received an award. The children were encouraged to take moderate risks, revise their plans on the basis of feedback, and make their own decisions about assignments, pacing, and the need for help from friends and teachers. The teacher's job was to coach—

TABLE 8.4

Schedule of Payments for Mathematics Game

Percentage of Problems Done Correctly	Cost to Try Problem Set	Return to Investor for Success	Rate of Return
100	$500	$2,000	4:1
90	$450	$1,350	3:1
80	$350	$700	2:1
70	$250	$400	8:5
60	$150	$250	5:3
50	$100	$150	3:2

Source: Adapted from A. S. Alschuler, "How to Increase Motivation Through Climate and Structure." Cambridge, Mass. Achievement Motivation Development Project. Graduate School of Education, Harvard University. Working Paper No. 8, 1968.

FIGURE 8.6

Math contract
From Alschuler (1968).

The undersigned will attempt to do correctly _____ percent of the problems in Chapter _____.

The sum of $_____ has been deposited with the government of the class for materials and franchise.

I understand that 10% of the gross return will be deducted from my payment for each day the contract goes unfulfilled after _____.

I also understand that the contract may be revised at any time prior to one week before due date for a fee of $10.00. One percent of the gross return will be deducted for each wrong answer below the number intended.

Date: _____

_____
Contractor

_____
Govt. Contract Officer

not to give information—to provide the social approval necessary for building and maintaining achievement behaviors. The teacher was to be warm, friendly, and encouraging, and to concentrate on helping children "win" at the game.

Did the game work? During the fourth grade, 17 percent of the students achieved gains on a standardized mathematics test equal to or greater than that expected (that is, 1.0 year of grade-equivalent growth). During the fifth grade, when the contracting game was instituted, 100 percent of the students exceeded the national norm for expected gain. Indeed, an average gain of three years' growth for one year's work was demonstrated. These impressive results are in line with what has been obtained by others.

> Children who did nothing in mathematics in fourth grade, except under duress, suddenly began taking their books home on weekends. Very few deadlines were missed. Many students began assessing themselves more optimistically, yet realistically, and they performed up to those standards. One boy fidgeted through the entire year in mathematics in fourth grade. Threats and stern words could not focus his attention, nor could they keep him in his seat. His total output reflected a small percentage of his ability. Within the new structure, however, he chose his first goal of 70 percent with two weeks to finish the contract. Within three days he revised his goal upward to 100 percent, paid the extra fee, and did all the problems with only 11 errors out of almost 400 problems. A student was considered by the teacher to be mathematically slow in the fourth grade. She was consistently at the bottom of the class and seldom handed in assignments at all. Her 100 percent contract for the first chapter was the first completed and with only six errors. Her error total was the lowest in the class. . . . It was the teacher's impression that in the

first half of fifth grade, enthusiasm was generated more by the game than by intrinsic interest in mathematics. However, in the second half of the year, buoyed by new-found competence, the game, prizes, and play money became more or less irrelevant while the pace of work continued. Mathematics itself had become more interesting. (Alschuler, 1968, pp. 57–58)

We do not know whether these students will become successful entrepreneurs, but we do know they have become better mathematicians. And we can see how intrinsic motivation develops out of systematic application of contingent reinforcers, an extrinsic motivation system. Our guess is that motivating games of this kind are not harmful and can be altogether beneficial.

Contracting for Reading in the Elementary Grades Another approach to bringing about behavior change through contracting is called *individually guided motivation* (Klausmeier, Sorenson, & Ghatala, 1971). It makes much use of conferences between the teacher (or a teacher's aide) and the student. In the conferences, the teacher and student arrange contracts, and the student is reinforced for completed work, receives feedback, and sets new goals. The program aims at students' developing academic self-direction. They work with the teacher or aide to set realistic goals, to learn why it is important to do work outside of school, and to express their learning in words.

This procedure depends heavily on a one-to-one relationship. In one study, materials and books for various reading levels were made available in the school library and classroom. Rewards (crayons, pencils, erasers) were given first for reading two books, then for reading five books. Individual conferences, conducted by adult volunteer aides who visited the classroom, took place once a week. The aides worked for five to fifteen minutes with each child, listening to the student read, receiving a synopsis of the books read, and finally setting, with the student, some goals for the following week.

The results of the program were clear. Over one school year, 72 third-grade inner-city students read an average of 21 books each. These children had been doing almost no independent reading before the program began. But despite the success of such programs, they are rarely used in schools.

The two contracting systems discussed above were undertaken with young students. The token economy for adolescents devised by Cohen used a contracting system. And doctoral studies in Britain often rely on a similar kind of contracting system, along with one-to-one tutoring. In short, some version of contracting has a place at all levels of schooling. The evidence is abundant that contracting systems, with clearly stated objectives and personal contact between teacher (or other adult) and student, improve motivation and achievement. This occurs even among those students who are predicted to perform poorly.

In the one-to-one setting, it may be that goals are established and reinforcement given freely and often for task-oriented behavior and actual goal attainment. But it is also likely that the affiliative motive comes into play—that the positive relationship between tutor and tutee itself becomes a powerful motivator of achievement-related behavior. Having someone believe in you and expect you to try hard and do well is a strong motivator! In fact, there is evidence that programs incorporating a one-to-one tutoring relationship for children almost always have some success (e.g., the Success for All program of Slavin et al., 1996; the Reading Recovery program described in Pinnell et al., 1994; and others described in Wasik & Slavin, 1993). What may be developed in all these programs is a highly important characteristic: self-efficacy. Let us examine this characteristic.

Self-Efficacy and Achievement Motivation

Bandura (1993) reviewed a good deal of research on individuals who are low and high on measures of **self-efficacy** (SE), the perceptions we have of our own ability to succeed in particular tasks. Concerning one set of studies, he reported how certain task conditions affect SE. For example, one set of group leaders were informed that their group was improving more than other groups trying the same series of tasks. Over time, those leaders showed increased SE, more efficient problem solving, and higher performance. Other group leaders received information that their members' performance was worse than other groups'. These leaders showed a reduction in SE, more erratic thinking, and progressively lower performance. So making people believe that their performance is not good in comparison to others undermines SE and future performance. We discussed this issue above when we noted the effects of competitive classroom structures.

In another series of studies, some group leaders were told they had achieved 75 percent of the goals expected, that they were on the way to meeting the standards that had been set for their group. Their *progress* was highlighted in the feedback they received. Another set of leaders were informed that they were 25 percent short of the goals expected, that they were not achieving the standards that had been set. Their *deficiency* was highlighted in the feedback they received. Note that, objectively, all the leaders of the groups received the same information—either 75 percent complete or 25 percent short of mastering the goals set for them. But the effects of these two different messages on behavior were quite different.

Those leaders who received feedback emphasizing their progress showed higher SE, higher aspirations for further achievement, more efficient analytic thinking, greater self-satisfaction, and higher subsequent performance. Those who received feedback highlighting their shortcomings showed all the opposite effects: lower SE, lower aspirations, less analytic thinking, lower satisfaction, and lower performance. Standards and goals are a part of sensible instructional systems and can indeed be used to promote achievement (see Chapter 2). However, their effects on learning seem to depend on how feedback in meeting those standards and goals is communicated. People can be made to feel incompetent or competent, depending on the type of feedback they receive. SE can be manipulated by what occurs in the environment. And SE in turn affects a wide range of the motivational variables covered in this chapter.

Bandura reported that students of the same ability in mathematics get dramatically different scores on math tests depending on whether they are high or low in SE, for example. Children who thought well of their own abilities in general had more positive attitudes toward mathematics, were quicker to abandon faulty strategies when trying problems, and got higher scores than children judged to be their equals in mathematical ability. In other research, those high in SE made greater efforts to learn, and as a result they learned more than those who were low in SE. In addition, those high in SE who achieve their learning goals, subsequently set even higher goals for themselves. They do not accept low levels of performance, as is true of those with low SE. Self-efficacy even enters into career choices, with those having higher levels of SE keeping open more options for careers, preparing themselves better for those careers, and both staying with and succeeding at careers generally considered to be difficult. One important aspect of their achievement is that those high in SE are generally also high in self-monitoring and use of learning strategies (see Chapter 7). So students high in SE are primed to achieve—they enter learning situations believing they can learn, and they bring to bear all the resources they have to accomplish it (see Schunk, 1991a; 1991b; Schunk & Zimmerman, 1994; Zimmerman, 1995). Another way to say this is that persons high in SE are *volitional*. They act; they commit to accomplishing the goals they have selected (Corno, 1993; Snow, Corno, & Jackson, 1996).

Self-efficacy seems to be related to every aspect of motivation we have discussed. Parents, students, and teachers who have low self-efficacy tend to shy away from difficult tasks because they are seen as personally threatening, likely to result in some loss of self-worth. Parents and teachers with low SE expect less of their children, and students with low SE set lower standards of achievement for themselves. All people low in SE have weak commitments to the goals they do choose. They dwell on their deficits and limitations in the tasks they attempt, focus on the obstacles they will encounter, and hypothesize all kinds of doom and gloom as outcomes. When difficulties do occur in their pursuit of some goal, they slacken their efforts and give up easily, often attributing their failure to lack of ability, and they are slow to get back feelings of competency and SE after defeat. With these kinds of feelings, they more readily experience stress and depression. Low SE is definitely *not* what teachers want to develop in their students.

Developing Self-Efficacy

So what can we do to develop high but appropriate SE? For one thing, SE in any given domain arises out of successful performance in that domain. So tasks that allow students to succeed, if they are willing to put

What is your reaction to the idea of permitting students who have failed an assignment or a test to redo it? If you see potential problems (for example, other students perceiving unfairness), can you think of ways to resolve them?

in some effort, need to be part of classroom life. Classrooms that are task- (work-, mastery-) oriented, rather than ego-oriented (competitive); and promote mindfulness and deep learning through their tests and grading procedures, rather than shallow, surface learning, are likely to foster the development and maintenance of high SE. In these kinds of classes, genuine effort can be expected to yield genuine achievement, which is perhaps the most important lesson a school can teach. And when students do not do well on some task, a teacher who takes the building of SE seriously allows them a chance to redo the task (assignment or test) to make it better. As simple as this may seem, what it communicates to students is quite profound, namely, that failures are inevitable but no one has to live with them. Mistakes can be seen as simply a part of learning, not a cause for lowering of self-efficacy, if the opportunity to correct mistakes is available. Unhappily, not all teachers run their classrooms this way. Figure 8.7 lists six target goals for schools attempting to develop more efficacious students.

Feedback to students during their work is obviously important too. A teacher who says, "Come on, dumbo, time's almost up," even in jest, is likely to have far different effects on SE than one who says, "You're almost there, give it your best shot and you may get it done in time." Feedback from others, as well as self-evaluations (feedback to ourselves about how we are doing), determines SE. In addition, prestigious social models who tell students they can achieve—that they are efficacious, that they are origins and not pawns—are another way to build high SE. That is, teachers, parents, and other respected individuals who believe that students can achieve well help to develop students with high SE. Mr. Lang, through his *I Have a Dream Foundation* (described at the beginning of this chapter), told a group of students who were low in SE that they really could aspire to a college education. He helped them to change their perceptions, and most subsequently achieved more than anyone had thought they could. Apparently, as their SE in school subjects increased, so did their motivation to achieve, and so did their actual achievement.

It is interesting to note that a good deal of contemporary criticism of schools is that they spend too much time on self-concept, self-esteem,

---

FIGURE 8.7

Target goals for schools to develop efficacious students

Adapted from Maehr & Anderman (1993).

Teachers and schools should shoot for a **TARGET** to develop more motivated and self-efficacious students:

Tasks chosen should be important, meaningful, challenging (but doable), and interesting.

Autonomy of the students ought to be a goal, and students should have some choices about what tasks they engage in.

Recognition for progress as well as achievement ought to be given. Effort deserves recognition.

Group students for collaborative instruction more, so that they benefit from distributed abilities. Emphasize individual assignments less.

Evaluate progress and teach self-evaluation; avoid social comparisons that pit one student's achievements against another's.

Time should be sufficient for students to learn at the pace they need given the material they are studying. Time is also needed for the development of interdisciplinary units of instruction.

Do you think teachers really spend too much time on building students' self-esteem, self-efficacy, and self-concept?

and other affective concerns of their students. Although some teachers and schools may sometimes overdo it, or do it wrong, it is clear that concern for students' self-efficacy—their self-concept as learners, and their self-esteem and self-worth as people—is not in the least misplaced. The achievement motivation of students is related to the beliefs they hold about themselves, so it is altogether proper that teachers concern themselves deeply about these issues.

The Self-Efficacy of Teachers and Schools

Students' SE is also affected by their teacher's SE, and even the collective sense of efficacy held by a school. Teachers' belief in their instructional efficacy predicts students' performance at the end of the year. For example, a study by Midgley, Feldlaufer, and Eccles (1989) described the transitions of a large group of young adolescents as they moved from the sixth grade of an elementary school to the seventh grade of a junior high school. The students went from teachers who were low and high in SE as instructors of mathematics, to other teachers who were low or high in SE as math teachers. What happened was in line with predictions. Students who went from sixth-grade teachers with high SE to seventh-grade teachers with low SE

> ended their first year in junior high school with lower expectancies for themselves in math, lower perceptions of their performance in math, and higher perceptions of the difficulty of math than the adolescents who had experienced no change in teacher efficacy or who had moved from low- to high-efficacy teachers. These effects were especially marked among the low-achieving adolescents. By the end of the junior high school year, the confidence that those low-achieving adolescents who had moved from high- to low-efficacy teachers had in their ability to master mathematics had declined dramatically—a drop that could well mark the beginning of the downward spiral in school motivation that eventually leads to dropout for so many low-achieving adolescents. It is important to note, however, that this same decline was not characteristic of the low-achieving adolescents who moved to high-efficacy seventh-grade math teachers.
>
> (Wigfield, Eccles, & Pintrich, 1996, p. 164)

Teachers with high SE are also motivated to devote more time to academic learning, give more time to students having difficulty learning, and praise their accomplishments more. Teachers with low SE as instructors spend more time on nonacademic matters, readily give up on students having difficulty in achieving, and criticize those students more for their failures. Those with low SE as teachers seem to favor extrinsic motivation, use negative sanctions (criticisms, threats) to get students to study, and express a custodial orientation rather than one oriented toward fostering genuine learning (Gibson & and Dembo, 1984; Ashton & Webb, 1986; Woolfolk & Hoy, 1990).

When a school's collective sense of efficacy is assessed, it seems to predict school achievement quite substantially, even better than do the characteristics of the student body (Bandura, 1993). The higher the school's collective sense of efficacy, the higher its achievement, even for low-income children. Educators know how to design schools to promote the self-efficacy of teachers and students (Maehr & Midgley, 1991), yet schools rarely employ all these principles.

The body of research on institutional and personal efficacy should be reflected on. If at any time during your teaching career you think that you are making little difference in the lives of your students, that you simply are not effectively teaching or benefitting them much, you ought to seek earnestly to improve and get help, or leave teaching. And if the school you work in does not really believe it can be efficacious—at its core it fundamentally believes it cannot help its students to achieve because of poverty, parental values, race, ethnicity, or any other factors—then that school needs to be transformed. Quickly. The motivation to succeed is at least as important to nurture among teachers and schools as it is among students. We are sure that teachers with poor perceptions of themselves as instructors, and schools that reflect similar beliefs, cannot and do not teach students well.

You have undoubtedly noted that, in some circles, teachers and schools have been under intense criticism over the past few years. Their alleged failures are reported regularly. Under such negative conditions, it is hard for them to develop or maintain a sense of instructional efficacy. True, many teachers and schools should improve, but intense, and at times unwarranted, criticism is likely to be counterproductive (Berliner & Biddle, 1995). If the critics undermine the teachers' and schools' sense of efficacy, they are likely to have a negative effect on students' motivation to achieve.

> Have you read or heard any such criticisms in the media during the past year? If so, how have they made you feel as a prospective teacher?

Motivational Techniques in Classroom Teaching: Guidelines for Teachers

Classroom teachers can increase student motivation in a number of ways. Some of these ways are well researched, and some derive from the experience of veteran educators. We offer here some guidelines for teachers and the reasons for them.

1. **Begin lessons by giving students a reason to be motivated.** When Brophy et al. (1983) looked at six upper-elementary-grade classrooms eight to fifteen times each, they never heard a teacher say a student might receive some personal satisfaction from a task. Only about a third of the comments teachers made to introduce new tasks were motivating (I think you'll like this—and it will come in handy at home as well!). Most new tasks were introduced neutrally or even negatively (I know you won't like this, but . . .). Brophy (1987) noted that, in general, even teachers who are usually effective do not do and say the things that could motivate their students to learn academic content.

Newby (1991) studied 30 first-year elementary-school teachers responsible for 770 students. He found that "those classrooms in which there was a higher incidence of giving reasons for the importance of the task . . . showed a higher rate of on-task behavior" (p. 199). Since time spent in learning is an indicator of motivation, this is a teacher activity with an important payoff. But this activity is not seen in schools often enough.

Students really do deserve a reason to be motivated. We owe it to them. Try to tell them what the tasks they are doing are good for, how the tasks prepare them to do other things, and why they are important and interesting.

2. **Tell students exactly what you expect them to accomplish.** Energizing and directing student behavior calls for a clear statement to students of what you expect them to accomplish. In many classes, teachers do not give clear directions about what must be done (Berliner, 1982). They plunge into a task without telling students what the goal of the task is and what students need to do to complete the task successfully. The students of teachers who do not provide this kind of information perform less well than do those of teachers who do so. No matter how well motivated students are, if they do not know what is expected of them, they start slowly, feel uneasy, may feel anxious, and may do the wrong tasks.

Guidelines 1 and 2, together, mean you should start out, as often as you can, with clear statements of your expectations for students and some reason for why they should want to meet those expectations. Teachers want students to engage in learning tasks because they perceive benefits to themselves, not simply because they were ordered to. Some motivational theorists think of students as either relatively ego- or task-involved in schooling (e.g., Nicholls, 1984). Those who are predominantly ego-involved seek good evaluations of their competence and minimize their chances of receiving poor ones. They ask themselves questions such as: How smart will I look? Will I be able to beat the others? Ego-involved students usually take less challenging course work, ensuring their attainment of high grades. Task-involved students seek mastery, asking themselves: How can I do this? What will I learn that is useful to me? They are willing to take greater risks to learn more. Taking the time to explain to students (1) what is expected and (2) why they should be learning the material they are assigned are important parts of giving them a task orientation toward learning.

In American secondary schools, though, ego-involved goals seem to predominate. Too many students have learned to seek a passing grade just to get a diploma, or to compete against others for high grades so as to get into prestigious universities. Task-involved learning, learning for mastery, learning that is intrinsically motivated takes a back seat to learning for grades (Wigfield, Eccles, & Pintrich, 1996). It will never be easy to overcome this cultural problem, but taking time to explain why the things they learn are important is compatible with the task orientation toward learning teachers should seek to develop. Another way of counteracting the pressures against the task orientation is to have a sensible testing and grading program in place.

3. **Use tests and grades judiciously.** Despite the many strong criticisms of tests and grades, we believe they should be used. The fact that tests and grades are bases for various kinds of social rewards—approval, promotion, graduation, certification, admission to colleges and professional schools, better jobs, higher prestige, more money, more interesting work, greater responsibility—gives tests and grades

motivational power. Good grades become incentives and reinforcers. Students quickly learn that there are benefits associated with getting high grades. So giving tests and assigning grades come to have the effect of motivating students to learn.

Nevertheless, the criticisms of tests and grades have a good deal of merit. One of the most important criticisms is that evaluation of student outcomes has a potentially harmful effect on continuing motivation—the tendency to return to and continue working on tasks away from the instructional context in which they were initially addressed (Maehr, 1976). Teachers face a problem of balance when trying to use tests and grades in their assessment system, a problem discussed in greater detail in Chapter 14.

4. **Have students set short-term goals.** Bandura and Schunk (1981) studied 40 elementary-age students with substantial deficits in and an intense dislike of mathematics. Some learned to set short-term goals for learning; some set long-term goals; and some had no goal-setting practice. At the end of seven learning sessions, the students who set short-term goals found they actually liked the activities they once thought were so dreadful. They were dramatically higher in measured intrinsic interest and substantially higher in measures of self-efficacy and mathematical skill (Zimmerman, 1989). Morgan (1984) also obtained this result with college-age students. Once again, attainment of short-term goals seemed to enhance both learning and motivation. A sense of mastery, of attaining goals, apparently makes tasks once seen as drudgery much more interesting.

Goal setting should show the so-called *A-B-C-D pattern.* That is, the goal should be Achievable: reasonable for students of a particular age and ability; Believable: students must believe they can reach it if they try; Concrete: clearly stated and measurable, so that it can be unambiguously understood and later reliably judged to have been successfully completed; and Desirable: students should want to achieve it. The closer goal setting approaches the A-B-C-D ideal, the more likely the goal will have motivational effects and actually be reached by students.

5. **Use spoken and written praise judiciously.** In many cases, tangible reinforcement is not as important as a teacher's spoken praise. Saying "Good," "Great," "Wonderful," or "Fine work," contingent on appropriate performance or approximations of appropriate performance, can be a powerful motivating device. Social approval strongly influences achievement, particularly with young children.

Praise is also the easiest to use and most natural of the motivational devices available to a teacher. Most important, praise contingent on a certain behavior increases the frequency of that behavior. In other words, social approval in its many forms is a relatively consistent reinforcer or incentive. Remember, however, that too much praise is counterproductive. Praise can be so much a part of communication in some classes that it loses its utility as a motivating force. And there is "good" praise and "bad" praise (something we talk about again in Chapter 11). Brophy's (1981) study of how praise is used in classrooms yielded guidelines for its effective and ineffective use, which are listed in Table 8.5. Study them carefully.

One set of studies showed that teachers' written academic comments have a small but positive effect on subsequent test performance (Page, 1958; Elawar & Corno, 1985). Although the effort required is

TABLE

8.5

Guidelines for Effective Praise

Effective Praise	Ineffective Praise
1. is delivered contingently.	1. is delivered randomly.
2. specifies the particulars of the accomplishment.	2. is a general positive reaction.
3. shows spontaneity, variety, and other signs of credibility; suggests clear attention to student's accomplishment.	3. shows a bland uniformity suggesting a conditioned response.
4. rewards attainment of specified performance criteria (can include effort criteria).	4. rewards mere participation without consideration of performance processes or outcomes.
5. provides information about competence or the value of accomplishments.	5. provides no information at all or only gives students information about their status.
6. orients students toward better appreciation of their task-related behavior and thinking about problem solving.	6. encourages social-reference comparisons.
7. uses prior accomplishments as the context for describing present accomplishments.	7. uses the accomplishments of peers as the context for describing present accomplishments.
8. recognizes noteworthy effort or success at tasks that are difficult (for *this* student).	8. is given without regard to effort expended or meaning of the accomplishment.
9. attributes success to effort and ability, implying that similar successes can be expected in future.	9. attributes success to ability alone or to external factors (luck, ease of the task).
10. leads students to believe that they expend effort on the task because they enjoy the task and/or want to develop task-relevant skills.	10. leads students to believe that they expend effort on the task for external reasons (to please the teacher or win a competition or reward).
11. focuses attention on students' own task-relevant behavior.	11. focuses attention on the teacher as an external authority figure who is manipulating students.
12. fosters appreciation of, and wanted attributions about, task-relevant behavior after the process is completed.	12. intrudes into the ongoing process, distracting attention from task-relevant behavior.

Source: Adapted from J. E. Brophy, "Teacher Praise: A Functional Analysis," Review of Educational Research, 1981, Vol. 51:5–32. Copyright 1981 American Educational Research Association, Washington, D.C. Used by permission.

substantial and the effects small, we agree with Page that "when the average . . . teacher takes the time and trouble to write comments (believed to be 'encouraging') on student papers, these apparently have a measurable . . . effect upon student effort, or attention, or attitude, or whatever it is which causes learning to improve, and this effect does not appear dependent upon . . . student ability" (p. 181).

Simulations and games motivate students. They can instruct if they sustain attention and require information to be processed at more than a surface level.

(© Michael Zide)

The kind of social approval, social reinforcement, praise, and encouragement that Page studied showed that students can be motivated by these practices. Sometimes teachers forget how important their comments are to students. Some teachers indiscriminately praise all sorts of student behavior, and others never seem to say a good word to students. Both extremes are inappropriate. You need to remember, too, that some students are less responsive to praise than others. But in general, social approval contingent on wanted behavior can serve you well when academic achievement or academic behavior needs to be improved.

6. **Capitalize on the arousal value of suspense, discovery, curiosity, exploration, control, and fantasy.** We talked about the arousal value of novel stimuli when we discussed cognitive learning in Chapter 7. Stimuli that are novel, surprising, complex, incongruous, or ambiguous give rise to a kind of cognitive arousal that Berlyne (1965) called *epistemic curiosity.* This is behavior aimed at acquiring knowledge, the means to master and understand the environment. When epistemic curiosity is aroused, someone is motivated to find ways to understand a novel stimulus.

Berlyne categorized some of the ways in which epistemic curiosity can be aroused:

Surprise. For example, if you slip a brass ball through a metal ring, then heat the ball and try to do it again, it will not fit. (Heat expands the ball.) Another example is furnished by Strober (1990), an economist: You could borrow a dollar bill from a grade-school student and announce that you will cut it up into little pieces with scissors. As you are about to start, the children will begin to wail. Then you can ask them why that piece of green paper is any different from other pieces of green paper. From there it is easy for you to begin a discussion of what money means and the kinds of trust a society needs to use paper as a medium of exchange.

Doubt, or conflict between belief and disbelief. For example, ask students whether the interior angles of triangles always total 180 degrees.

Perplexity, or uncertainty. This condition arises when a number of possible solutions are available but none seems absolutely right. For example, have students try to predict where crime is most prevalent in a city, given only various sociological and economic facts about its different neighborhoods.

Bafflement, or facing conflicting demands. For example, Duncker (1945) described a classic problem: How can a radiotherapist treat a patient's tumor with radiation strong enough to kill the tumor but not so strong as to harm adjacent tissues? (The solution: Focus weak x rays from different directions onto the tumor so that the amount of radiation where the rays intersect is great and that on intervening tissues is much lower.)

Contradiction. This is a finding that seems to fly in the face of a general principle or common sense. One example is the notion that resistance to extinction is greater after partial reinforcement than after continuous reinforcement (see Chapter 6). Or, as discussed in Chapter 3, intelligence is both heritable *and* modifiable.

When teachers use surprise, doubt, perplexity, bafflement, or contradiction, they arouse a kind of cognitive conflict. The motivation lasts until the conflict is resolved or until students give up. Remember, if students cannot resolve the conflict, they will become bored or frustrated, and then these methods will eventually fail to arouse any positive responses in them.

Control and fantasy. Lepper and Hodell (1989) discussed how school tasks, such as learning geometry, can be embellished to increase intrinsic motivation. They noted how Berlyne's ideas plus two others can produce increases in motivation and achievement. One of these ideas is about control. Students who feel they can control the situation for learning (where, when, how) and the outcomes of learning (the level they want to achieve) are more intrinsically motivated. Students have this kind of control when they use computers for learning. In addition, when learning tasks involve fantasy, intrinsic motivation is often aroused. So trying to determine how "space invaders" can find the distance from their spaceship to the tower of knowledge is more interesting to most students than doing a workbook page with geometry problems devoid of meaning.

7. **Occasionally do the unexpected.** Here also you can take advantage of epistemic curiosity. Modify whatever has become ordinary and usual into something extraordinary and unusual. Attempting to cut up dollar bills certainly qualifies (see above). If students have been talking about their own learning problems, suddenly talk about your own. If the discussion has been at an extremely "applied" level in a class in science, give it a theoretical turn. If you usually prepare test questions, ask the students to prepare them. If you usually test your students, have them give you a test. An occasional departure from what students have come to expect has the effect of attracting their attention and getting them involved.

Imagine you are trying to build in each of Berlyne's points to a series of social studies lessons. Come up with an example for each category. Then do the same for science and mathematics.

8. **Whet the appetite.** Give students a small sample of the reward before they make an effort to learn. Show them what social approval is so that they know what they are working for. Read to them so that they know the enjoyment of reading. Use a reinforcer early in the learning sequence in the same way that you plan to use it later in the sequence. This procedure gives the reinforcer incentive value that can influence performance.

One implication of this idea is that you should make the early stages of learning a task easy. Design a sequence of instruction so that students have some initial success—an important motivator. And be sure that all students get an opportunity to receive a "taste" of reinforcement. Brophy and Evertson (1976), for example, found that third graders learned more when teachers called their names first, then asked questions, instead of waiting for volunteers. By calling names first, the teachers were able to control participation (and therefore reinforcement). So the brighter and more eager students did not get a disproportionate share of opportunities to respond and be reinforced.

9. **Be cautious about competition.** Beware of contests, "bees," and games that require some students to "lose," unless you can predict that the same students will not always be the losers. This theme has applications in the design of curriculum and the assignment of grades, and we have mentioned it frequently above. To develop motivation to achieve, the curriculum should make room for a variety of talents and skills. And the grading system should avoid distribution curves that allow only a fixed number of students to pass or earn an A, or that require some students to get a C or D.

10. **Use familiar material for examples.** When you give examples, use things that are familiar. If you are making up arithmetic word problems, use the name of a teacher or student, not the hackneyed John Jones or Mary Smith. In teaching students how library catalogs are alphabetized, use titles from books the students have read or list biographies of their sports or movie heroes. Remember that familiarity, meaningfulness, and associations can improve learning and retention (see Chapter 7). Newby (1991), for instance, discovered that classes where students were encouraged to relate the tasks they were learning to familiar experiences had a higher rate of on-task behavior. And remember that time spent learning is an indicator of motivation and actual achievement. So tying what you teach to things that are familiar in students' lives is good instruction based on how the mind is thought to construct knowledge (see Chapter 7), and it is motivating as well.

11. **Use unusual and unexpected contexts when applying concepts and principles.** Apply the law of supply and demand to the price of tickets at a music concert. Apply the inverse-square law to the number of decibels of sound at various distances from the stage of a rock group. Notice the difference between this point and guideline 10. When you want to build interest, use familiar things to motivate the students. For applications, after learning has taken place, use the unique and unexpected to keep students' interest high and to help them transfer what they have learned.

12. **Make students use what they have previously learned.** By forcing students to use what they have learned before, you reinforce previous learning, or strengthen previously acquired responses. You also build the expectation that what is currently being learned has some

subsequent use. Try not to limit instruction to new learning. Whenever possible, call for previously acquired facts, concepts, and principles.

13. **Use simulations and games.** Simulations and games motivate students, promote interaction, present relevant aspects of real-life situations, and make possible direct involvement in the learning process. In the past few decades, teachers have increased their use of games and simulations. And as competency with computers increases among teachers, they are bound to find more opportunities to use instructional gaming. (See problem-based project learning in Chapter 7, for example.) Many games that do not require computers are also available. For example, *Disunion* is a three-week game that simulates the constitutional crises in the United States between 1776 and 1789. Research activities and role playing help students learn parliamentary procedures, speech making, the problems of the 13 states, and early political philosophies. The game seems to involve students in a way that traditional history teaching does not.

There are two good questions you should ask to help you decide whether a learning game is effective—that is, whether it improves learning:

1. Does the game increase and sustain attention?
2. Is the student keenly involved in the game, processing information and making responses where more than just a surface kind of commitment is called for?

If attention is high and processing deep, chances are the game enhances learning (Lepper & Chabay, 1985). One reminder, however: Any game or activity can be played too long at a time or used too often. Watch out that enthusiasm does not turn to boredom or that the game is played solely to win, not to learn from.

14. **Minimize the attractiveness of competing motivational systems.** Sometimes students feel pressure to put down the teacher, do poor schoolwork, cut classes, smoke, or otherwise defy authority in order to gain acceptance by other students. What can you do to make these behaviors less desirable from the students' point of view? Getting student leaders involved in activities (for example, administering tests or representing the school at a science fair) can help. Concentrating on keeping the most prestigious and popular leaders of a clique from smoking and using drugs is likely to be more effective than trying to convince a regular member of a clique not to conform to the group.

To minimize the attractiveness of competing motivational systems, you might have to use punishment for inappropriate behavior, along with reinforcement for appropriate behavior. The important task here is to identify and analyze competing motivational systems. Then use that information to strengthen positive motivation or to reduce the influence of the competing systems. For a particular student, the need for acceptance by fellow students may be competing with the need for approval by teachers and other adults. Or the need for achievement in athletics or hobbies may compete with schoolwork. Or the need for money can cause a student to take a job when there is homework to be done. By analyzing a student's competing systems, you may be able to devise ways of reducing their antieducational effects.

15. **Minimize any unpleasant consequences of student involvement.** Positively reinforce students' involvement with the subject mat-

TABLE

8.6

Common Characteristics of Classrooms That Can Detract from Achievement Motivation

Loss of self-esteem (from failing to understand an idea or solve a problem correctly)

Physical discomfort (sitting too long, straining to hear in a room with poor acoustics, peering at a blackboard or screen that is too far away for the size of what is being shown)

Frustration from not being able to obtain reinforcement

Being told that one is unlikely to understand something

Having to stop work in the middle of an interesting activity

Taking tests on material and ideas that have not been taught

Trying to learn material that is too difficult for one's present level of ability or understanding

Having a request for help go unmet

Having to take a test made up of trivial or incomprehensible questions

Not being told how well one is doing except at the end of a course, when it is too late to remedy problems

Having to go too fast to keep up with students better than oneself at what is being learned

Having to compete in a situation where only some of the students can succeed (e.g., get an A or B) no matter how well one learns or achieves the objectives of a course; in short, being graded on a curve

Being grouped in a section of lower-achieving students

Having to sit through a presentation that is repetitive, boring, or unchallenging (A teacher's reading aloud from a textbook or manuscript is aversive in most instances.)

Having a teacher who seems personally uninterested in the subject matter

Having to behave in a way other than that in which a prestigious model (teacher or student leader) behaves

ter. And minimize the factors or events that have aversive—that is, disliked—effects on their involvement. What are these aversive effects? Table 8.6 presents some of them. Once pointed out they are obvious, but you can still see them in classrooms all across the United States.

SUMMARY

1. Motivation is what energizes, directs, and maintains our behavior. It is what teachers use to explain how a student performs the same task in different ways under different conditions; and why students with the same aptitude and learning history perform the same task differently.

2. Among the many conceptions of motivation developed are these four types: (1) Freud's belief that a single motive—the *libido*—influences all human behavior; (2) that two opposing forces (for example, yin and yang) motivate behavior; (3) that many different motives exist—dozens or scores of them; and (4) that motives are formed in a hierarchy, such as that proposed by Maslow.

3. Maslow's theory groups into categories many different motives, from basic physical needs at the lowest level, to self-actualization at the highest level. Implications of Maslow's theory for education include a belief that teachers of low-income and troubled students corroborate: Until students' lower-level needs are met, we cannot hope to be effective in helping them acquire knowledge, understanding, or appreciation of the world around them.

4. The measurement of the motive to achieve in the classroom is difficult. Teachers must usually estimate the needs of students by careful observation coupled with intuition and common sense. Why do this? Because educators know that high achievement motivation goes hand in hand with academic behaviors we deem important.

5. A primary influence on students' achievement is their attribution pattern—how they attribute responsibility for their successes and failures. Students who attribute their successes to internal factors (effort, ability) and their failures to external factors (task difficulty, luck) are using an ego-maintaining system. They believe they can control performance. Students who attribute their successes to external factors and their failures to internal factors often believe they do not have the ability to succeed. The result is they come to expect failure and often will not even try to succeed.

6. Another important angle on attribution concerns the teacher's attributions of students' successes and failures. Expressing annoyance at a poor performance can be a means of communicating that students can do better—that it is their effort, not their ability, that led them to fail. Expressing sympathy, however, runs the risk of making students feel that they cannot do better. What is important here is what the students consider your anger or sympathy to mean.

7. Classroom structure affects students' self-concept (and related characteristics called self-esteem and self-worth). A competitive structure, although reinforcing for the few who are "winners," can be a source of humiliation for the many "losers." Individual learning, cooperative learning, and multidimensional classrooms reduce competition, and in the process promote greater feelings of self-worth in students.

8. Teachers play an important role in helping students meet their needs for affiliation, power, and approval. What is important is matching the teaching environment to students' motive patterns. For one student you might increase social reinforcement; for another, arrange group work; and for still another, talk about his tendencies toward overdependence.

9. The distinction between intrinsic and extrinsic motivation is important. What appears to be intrinsic motivation—not depending on external rewards—probably has its roots in extrinsic reinforcement systems. Intrinsic motivation derives directly from the behavior itself, such as reading an interesting book. Extrinsic motivation derives from

rewards not intrinsic to the activity, such as reading a book for money, a gold star, or praise. Over time, external reinforcement gives way to self-reinforcement. Both intrinsic and extrinsic motivation affect self-perception. When someone is intrinsically motivated, extrinsic rewards can have a negative effect on performance.

10. Within the operant-conditioning framework, where extrinsic reinforcement systems are used, the key element is to bring learners under some sort of stimulus control: responding when certain stimuli (signals) appear. Incentives are controlling stimuli because students work to attain the reinforcer implied by the incentive. Learning about a student's preferences—sleeping late, making jewelry, or collecting baseball cards—can help you design a motivational program tailored for any student.

11. Frustration is a motivator, but generally promotes negative behaviors such as aggression, regression, emotionality, withdrawal, and hyperactivity. When you find these behaviors, you should examine the environment you have created. Perhaps the material is too difficult; perhaps you are preventing students from finishing or even starting reinforcing activities. Once you find the source, you can attempt to remedy the problem.

12. Motives can be systematically changed through cognitive learning. For example, the motive to succeed can be trained. By helping students learn their own strengths and weaknesses, choose realistic goals, plan to reach those goals, and evaluate their work, you can help them take control of their behavior. Attribution patterns can also be changed; you can teach and model self-monitoring, self-instruction, and self-reinforcement strategies.

13. Motives can also be changed by emphasizing environmental (external) factors. One way is to set up a motivational system that uses incentives and reinforcers; it is called a token economy. Another is to create a contracting system for groups of students or individual students. Results from these kinds of programs indicate that they can be enormously effective when used properly. These programs do make use of extrinsic rewards, but only to induce students to take part in a learning activity that they would otherwise avoid. As soon as intrinsic rewards, those inherent in the activity itself, begin to appear, you should withdraw the extrinsic rewards so that students will learn to enjoy the activity as much as possible for its own sake.

14. A good deal of the motivation to succeed is based on self-efficacy: the perception of oneself as capable of succeeding. Teachers, parents, and students who feel efficacious behave in ways that lead to success. Raising efficacious, achievement-oriented youth requires home and school environments that foster success and the cognitions and strategies that helped make that success possible.

15. Many motivational techniques can be used with students. You must be alert to what is going on in your classroom and how you feel when you teach a given topic in a certain way. Make your teaching experience cumulative. Do not be afraid to experiment, but be sure to learn from the experience. Keep records. If something works, use it again; if it does not motivate your students, drop it. Teaching is a process that demands constant and careful revision. It is not nearly as easy a job as some media critics think.

PART FOUR

Teaching Methods and Practices

The material in this part provides many answers to the question, How should teachers teach? As you are probably aware, there are many different teaching methods and practices—indeed, a bewildering variety. To help you organize your thinking about them, we group them according to the number of students they are appropriate for, as shown in the table below.

What is a teaching method? It is a recurrent pattern of teacher behavior, applicable to various subject matters, characteristic of more than one teacher, and relevant to learning. The term *pattern* refers to a set of behaviors that occur simultaneously or in a unified sequence. *Recurrent* means that the pattern is repeated over intervals measured in minutes or weeks. *Applicable to various subject matters* means that a teaching method is more than a behavior useful for teaching only, say, the addition of fractions or the nature of a chemical bond. And these behaviors must be usable by more than one teacher; they cannot depend on the talents or traits of a unique individual.

The specific things teachers do that make up a teaching method are called *teaching practices*. So the teaching method called *lecturing* consists of teaching practices such as structuring, clarifying content, explaining, and summarizing.

Organization of Part Four: Number of Students Taught and Corresponding Teaching Methods and Chapters

(Approx.) Number of Students Taught	Appropriate Teaching Methods	Chapter
20+	Lecture method, explaining	9
5–20	Discussion method	10
2–4	Cooperative methods	10
1	Tutoring, computer-assisted instruction	11
15–30	Classroom teaching (combination of various methods)	12

What method of teaching is best? This question really has no answer unless the characteristics of the students (age, cognitive abilities, motivation, previous learning and achievement) and the objectives (content and desired behaviors with that content) of the teaching are specified. Some methods yield better results for students with certain characteristics; others produce better achievement in students with different characteristics. Individual instruction works best for some objectives, the discussion method for other objectives, and the lecture method for still other objectives. Adding to the complexity is that, within any given method, there are scores of different practices that can be applied.

So, we cannot give you a list of methods and practices and tell you that some always work and others never do. But we do give you some general guidelines to help in your decision making. Chapter 9 examines lecturing and explaining. Chapter 10 looks at methods for teaching small groups. Chapter 11 deals with methods for teaching one student at a time. Chapter 12 discusses classroom teaching, blending all the material in this part together.

Does knowledge of teaching methods and practices do any good? The answer is *yes,* and it is based on much research. For example, Metcalf (1992) developed a "clarity training program" based on a collection of teaching practices found, in previous research, to be associated with higher student achievement. He gave the program to a group of trainees in teacher education and withheld it from a control group. The trained group was observed to use the training-program practices to a greater degree than the control group. But more important, the students of the trained group did much better on achievement tests than did those of the control group. This and many similar studies (summarized by Gage & Needels, 1989; Needels & Gage, 1991) suggest strongly that knowledge and understanding, *along with appropriate practice in using these methods,* of the research-supported teaching methods described in Part Four can improve your teaching. The chapters here deal with good teaching practices one at a time for the sake of clarity of presentation. But experiments such as Metcalf's show that when these practices are combined, they are effective in improving learning.

After you finish studying this part, you will know much about effective teaching methods and practices. Your knowledge will stand you in good stead when you begin (or go back to) teaching. Remember, though, what we said in Chapter 1 about the importance of critical, practical, and artistic thinking as you go about applying that knowledge.

Lecturing and Explaining

Overview

THE LECTURE-METHOD PARADOX: STRONG CONDEMNATION, WIDE USE

Defense of the Lecture Method

Rewards to teachers and students
Administrative advantages
Appropriate grade levels and subject matters

Research Evidence on Effectiveness

POLICY, RESEARCH, AND PRACTICE

What Are the Proper Uses of Lecturing?

Lectures versus other teaching methods
The equalization effect

IMPORTANT CONSIDERATIONS FOR USING THE LECTURE METHOD

Preparing a Lecture

Do you know your subject well enough?
Are you comfortable lecturing?
Is there time to prepare?
Will you use media?

Low- versus High-Inference Variables

Cognitive Load: A General Rationale

APPLICATION
Reducing Cognitive Load in Your Own Learning

THE INTRODUCTION TO THE LECTURE

Appealing to Students' Interests

Providing Motivational Cues

Exposing Essential Content

Helping Students Organize Content

Previewing, including advance organizers
Asking questions to prompt awareness of relevant knowledge

THE BODY OF THE LECTURE

Covering Content

Providing Clear Organization

Organizational or Outlining Forms

Component (part-whole) relationships
Sequential relationships
Relevance relationships
Transitional (connective) relationships
Comparisons and contrasts
Combinatorial devices

Explanations

Explanations as minilectures
A model for organizing explanations

Clarifying the Organization

Explicitness
Rule-example-rule technique
Explaining links
Verbal markers of importance
Structural support
Visual aids

Clarifying the Content

Giving examples
Avoiding vagueness
Using rhetorical devices

Maintaining Attention

Varying the stimuli
Changing communication channels
Introducing pauses
Using humor and showing enthusiasm
Asking questions
Student self-questioning
Note taking

POLICY, RESEARCH, AND PRACTICE

The Role of Humor and Enthusiasm in Lecturing

Using handouts

THE CONCLUSION OF THE LECTURE

Functions of the Conclusion

The Summary

INTERLECTURE STRUCTURING

Summary

OVERVIEW

A great deal of teaching still takes the form of solo performance. There you are, all alone, lecturing and explaining, pointing out relationships, giving examples, correcting errors—for one student or several hundred, for an hour or a minute. How do you go about establishing rapport ("connecting") with your students? Can you motivate them? Can you get them to pay attention to what you are saying? Can you organize your thoughts coherently? Can you put them in understandable terms?

In this chapter we talk about these problems and many others and discuss ways to resolve them. We examine both *lectures*—the relatively long, mostly uninterrupted talks frequently used by college and university instructors—and **explanations**—the shorter talks, lasting anywhere from a few seconds to several minutes, frequently used in elementary and secondary school classrooms. We deal in turn with (1) objections to the lecture method and the reasons it has managed to survive despite them; (2) the preparation process; and then the lecture's (3) introduction, (4) body, and (5) conclusion. A word of caution: The lecture can be a valuable instructional tool, but it must be the right tool for the material, the educational circumstances, and most of all, the individual teacher.

The Lecture-Method Paradox: Strong Condemnation, Wide Use

Despite what hundreds of writers have said for hundreds of years, the lecture method is a widely used **teaching method** at all levels. One major study, of a sample of 38 schools in seven states in all regions of the

The lecturer can give a framework, overview, and criticism unlike that found in any printed material.

(© Walter S. Silver)

United States (12 senior high schools, 12 junior high or middle schools, and 13 elementary schools), concluded that

> the data from our observations in more than 1,000 classrooms support the popular image of the teacher standing or sitting in front of a class imparting knowledge to a group of students. Explaining and lecturing constituted the most frequent teaching activities, according to teachers, students, and our observations. And the frequency of these activities increased steadily from the primary to the senior high school years.
>
> *(Goodlad, 1984, p. 105)*

The same is true at the college level. A questionnaire filled out by 820 teachers in 80 colleges showed that "lecturing proved by far predominant over all other teaching methods combined" (Thielens, 1987, p. 7).

These two studies are representative. There is no reason, despite many innovations and reform efforts, to suppose that the picture has changed. Lecturing and explaining are widely used, but they should not be the only methods of teaching (as we see in later chapters).

Lectures have been said to be out of date, no longer appropriate in an age of books, television, and computers. They have been criticized for fostering a passive role for students—the student just sits there—in the learning process. Students regularly argue that lectures are boring, poorly organized, irrelevant, or redundant. And they insist that lectures not only limit their involvement but fail to take into account their individual differences.

These may not be valid criticisms of the method. It may be the fault of the lecturer, not the method itself, if material is boring, poorly organized, or irrelevant. The failure to take individual differences among students into account is indeed a problem of the method—but it is a problem with many other teaching methods as well. We do not dismiss such methods out of hand; we try to adapt them.

So, although criticism has been loud and hard, the lecture method is still widely used. Why?

Defense of the Lecture Method

Those who defend lecturing say that it is valuable for

- *combating students' passivity,* because the process of following a lecture can be anything but passive. Just because students are silent and almost motionless does not mean they are inactive. They may be working hard cognitively to follow the arguments, comprehend their logic, judge their validity, evaluate the facts and evidence, separate the essential from the less important, and in other ways "run alongside" lecturers as they talk.
- *surveying a whole field* of knowledge through the medium of a person.
- *arousing active interest* that leads students to understanding.
- *allowing lecturers to repeat material in different words,* something books rarely do.

■ *making it possible to introduce material not yet in any book,* such as something from this morning's newspaper, or something a year away from publication in a journal or textbook.
■ *compensating for an overabundance* of books in some fields and a scarcity of books in others.
■ *giving students a framework,* an overview, a critique unlike anything in any available printed material.
■ *bringing the lecturer's own enthusiasm* and aesthetic pleasure to the material.

Rewards to Teachers and Students   Lectures can give teachers and students a kind of reward, or reinforcement, not available from other educational procedures. So, to give rewarding lectures, teachers are motivated to pull together their otherwise scattered ideas on a topic. Furthermore, there can be other pleasures in lecturing. A professor of art wrote,

> I enjoy the lecture method. It is the most dramatic way of presenting to the largest number of students a critical distillation of ideas and information on a subject in the shortest possible time. The bigger the class the better I perform intellectually. How else in teaching can you share with so many a lifetime of looking at and loving art? You stand on a stage in front of a screen on which the whole history of art is projected. You can be an explorer of African art, an interpreter of Greek sculptures, a spokesman for cathedral builders, an advocate of Leonardo, a political theorist for palace architects, an analyst of Picasso and philosopher of Sung painting. No other subject is as visually exciting in the classroom, and this is what keeps me turned on lecture after lecture, year after year. With that supporting cast and if he knew his lines, who wouldn't want to perform in front of a large audience?
>
> *(Elsen, 1969, p. 21)*

What rewards can lectures give to students? The rewards can be

■ the knowledge and comprehension acquired.
■ the beauty of the lecturer's logic and reasoning.
■ the lecturer's warmth, humor, drama, intensity, enthusiasm, and attention.
■ the sense of security that comes from doing the right thing at the right time (being at a lecture), paying attention, perhaps taking notes, and responding with interest.

Administrative Advantages   Whatever its faults and whatever its benefits, the lecture method has persisted, probably because it makes administrative sense. It is economical and adaptable.

First, the method can be *cheap;* it allows a single teacher to instruct a very large number of students. If the teacher is in great demand, only the lecture method allows him or her to reach a large number of students—live rather than through a recording. Second, the method is *flexible;* it can be adapted on short notice to a particular audience, subject matter, time, and set of equipment (projectors, books, tapes, CD players, or computers).

FIGURE 9.1

Hypothetical appropriate duration of lectures or explanations for students of different grade levels

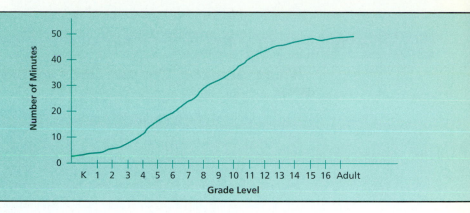

Appropriate Grade Levels and Subject Matters   The usefulness of lectures varies with grade level and subject matter. Let us look at each of these in turn.

Grade Level   The grade-level differences are fairly obvious. Longer lectures become more appropriate as students go from the early grades to the middle school to the high school and the undergraduate level. The relationship of appropriate lecture-duration to grade level may be hypothesized to look like the curve shown in Figure 9.1—short one-minute "lectures" in the early grade levels and longer ones as students become more mature. But even at the college level, lectures seldom go on uninterruptedly for a full class period. Lecturers interrupt their talk more or less often with questions from themselves or invited questions and comments from their students. So you should not necessarily consider the term *lecture* to mean 45–50 minutes of uninterrupted talk by a teacher.

Subject Matter   Any analysis of the value of lecturing should take into account the degree of consensus on the subject being taught. Some subjects are highly agreed upon—their major concepts, principles, and methods are so well established that no competent person in the field could raise serious doubts about them. At the introductory level in mathematics, chemistry, physics, biology, medicine, and engineering, just about everyone agrees on what is important, how the disciplines are organized, and basic concepts and principles. In the social sciences and humanities, however, there is not at present (and in principle may never be) a high degree of consensus. So in psychology, sociology, anthropology, history, economics, political science, literature, music, and art, educators do not agree nearly so much about what is important, good, true, or beautiful. There are schools of thought—and controversy even at the introductory level—about how these fields should be organized. What one teacher teaches in an introductory course in a low-consensus field may not even resemble what another teaches.

What is the earliest grade in which you remember a teacher "lecturing"? In retrospect does it seem appropriate? Why?

Research Evidence on Effectiveness

Whatever its disadvantages, the lecture method would probably not be used at all if experience and research indicated that it is completely

POLICY, RESEARCH, AND PRACTICE

What Are the Proper Uses of Lecturing?

Should school systems, schools, or departments within schools have policies regarding use of the lecture method?

WHAT THE RESEARCH TELLS US

Many educators (Bligh, 1972; McKeachie, 1994; McLeish, 1976; Verner & Dickinson, 1967) have reviewed the studies on the lecture method. With some exceptions, they have concluded that the lecture method tends to be suitable when (1) the basic purpose is to disseminate information; (2) the material is not available elsewhere, is too scattered, or is otherwise unavailable in an appropriate form for a particular audience; (3) the material must be organized and presented in a particular way for a specific group; (4) it is particularly necessary to arouse interest in the subject, or (5) it is necessary to provide an introduction to an area or directions for a learning task to be taught through some other teaching method.

The reviewers have also tended to agree that lecturing is inappropriate when (1) objectives other than acquisition of information are sought; (2) long-term retention is necessary; (3) the material is complex, detailed, or abstract; (4) learner participation is essential to achievement of objectives; or (5) higher-level cognitive objectives (ability to analyze, synthesize, evaluate), using knowledge already acquired, are especially the teacher's goals.

REFLECTIONS FOR YOUR OWN CLASSROOM

The lecture method is probably here to stay. To choose whether to use it or not to use it, you should think about factors like those described here and earlier. It is equally important to separate faults you might have as a lecturer from faults of the method. Not everyone is likely to be an engaging lecturer. If you are not, lectures should be used more sparingly. But if you are good at lecturing, you can convey not only a lot of knowledge about a subject but the ways you personally think about it—your love of ancient Greece or the immensity of Picasso's creativity. Remember that genuine education is as much in learning how teachers think about and feel about some subject as it is in mastering the knowledge of the subject. Lectures can provide your students with ample opportunity to learn how you think and feel.

ineffective. But such evidence has not been forthcoming despite scores of experiments.

Lectures versus Other Teaching Methods   In numerous experiments, college students taught by the lecture method have been compared with those taught by other methods, especially the discussion method, as to their achievement on final examinations. Typical recent studies include one by DaRosa et al. (1991), who found that independent study was superior to the lecture approach in producing learning as measured with tests. But Harrison (1995) found that medical students taught with either lectures or independent-study readings did not differ consistently a year later in knowledge loss or class performance. Similarly, Martens et al. (1995) found no differences in learning outcomes among 502 Belgian college students who were taught statistics in three different ways: interactive learning environments (computers), printed materials, and face-to-face lectures. Although college students and environments are not the same as those found in the precollege public schools of the United States, the evidence suggests that lecture methods will not prove vastly superior or inferior to other methods in most educational environments.

A different approach in examining these studies is to compare the lecture and discussion methods on different criteria: (1) knowledge of factual material, (2) retention and higher-level thinking, and (3) attitudes and motivation (McKeachie, Pintrich, Lin, & Smith, 1990). On factual knowledge (whose importance may be great), the lecture method is at least as effective as discussion. On retention, higher-level thinking, attitudes, and motivation, the discussion method tends to be superior.

The Equalization Effect   You should note that most of these studies run into a methodological problem. Students who know they are going to take a final exam compensate for the inadequacies of the methods by which they are taught, whether lecture or something else. This compensation reduces differences in the effects of the various teaching methods on student achievement. This is called the **equalization effect.** "Irrespective of differences due to the teaching methods used, the work which students do for themselves in preparation for an examination will tend to bring their scores close to equality" (McLeish, 1976, p. 271).

Important Considerations for Using the Lecture Method

Lectures and short explanations have their place throughout the curriculum. We now turn to ways in which lectures can be made effective.

Preparing a Lecture

How long you intend to lecture determines how or whether you should prepare. For a longer, formal lecture, you must prepare thoroughly. For shorter, spontaneous, less formal explanations you cannot prepare at all or must prepare in a different way. We talk about explanations and "preparing" for them later in this chapter. Here we concentrate on the formal lecture.

For the longer lecture, you should think about four factors: (1) your knowledge of the subject, (2) your comfort with the lecture method, (3) the time available for preparation, and (4) the use of media.

Do You Know Your Subject Well Enough?   It seems obvious that lecturers should have content knowledge—teachers must know their subject.

Have you ever heard a lecture on a subject that would have been better "taught" by a discussion? Have you ever been "taught" by a discussion method on a subject that would have been better taught with a lecture?

But what does it mean to know the subject "well enough"? At the minimum, *knowledge* can mean that you have read the textbook one step ahead of your students. In this case you are limited in what you can offer. You will be shaky on other ways to present the material, on fresh examples and applications, on flexible ways of explaining the ideas, on metaphors (or similes, analogies) and other rhetorical devices that may light up the content for students. You will be weak on what Shulman (1987) called **pedagogical content knowledge,** that is, knowledge of how to teach the content knowledge you have.

At the maximum, you have a lot of pedagogical content knowledge and can "move around" in the subject matter comfortably and flexibly. In other words, you know

- *the main, or most frequently taught, topics* in the content area
- *different conceptions of your subject,* such as how it has been changing over time, what topics have recently become prominent, and which ones are on the way out (Fernandez-Balboa & Stiehl, 1995)
- *metaphors,* similar to a simile without the "like." Example: For elucidating the Bill of Rights ("It's the Ten Commandments for Congress")
- *analogies,* such as one for clarifying the Pythagorean theorem ("It is to right triangles as πr^2 is to circles—an important mathematical relationship")

> Give an example of pedagogical content knowledge in a content area you know well. Be sure to make it different from mere content knowledge or mere pedagogical knowledge.

- *examples,* such as those of inherited and acquired characteristics (inherited: eye color, skin color, height, number of fingers; acquired: the language one speaks, religious beliefs, prejudices, political opinions)
- *mnemonics,* or memory aids, for remembering such things as the sonnet's rhyming scheme (three quatrains followed by a couplet—abab, cdcd, efef, gg)
- *the difficulty of various topics,* especially which ones are hard to understand and why.

Pedagogical content knowledge can make a big difference in how well teaching is done. As your teaching experience increases, you will, and should try to, accumulate such knowledge so that your second effort at lecturing benefits from your first and so on.

Are You Comfortable Lecturing?   Many people are apprehensive at the idea of public speaking of any kind. Such "communication apprehension" reduces ability to communicate (Allen & Bourhis, 1995) as well as resulting in reticence, shyness, and unwillingness to communicate.

Communication apprehension can be overcome, however. Interactive video instruction (Cronin, Grice, & Olsen, 1994) has been found effective in this regard. Learners first respond to a videotaped lesson on the nature of speech fright and the rationale for cognitive restructuring (changing how they think about it). They then learn to identify and test the validity of their negative self-statements about public speaking, replace negative with positive self-statements, and use additional ways of managing speech fright. Learners who have gone through the program have shown a greater reduction in speech fright over a four-week period than have students in a control group.

Is There Time to Prepare?   Organizing a good lecture takes time—for collecting information, determining emphases, organizing the sequence of ideas, and creating incisive and fresh examples. Teaching methods other than lecturing may require a more general, less specific kind of preparation, namely, acquiring a broad knowledge and background in the whole curriculum area. Such general preparation allows explanations and examples to come readily to the teacher's mind in a spontaneous, seemingly unplanned way. The lecture, however, should be planned better.

Will You Use Media?   Are films, television, slides, or tape recordings available to help you teach? Many teaching aids exist, and it is usually worth the effort to examine catalogs of films and tapes to see whether appropriate materials can be had. Preview any material and evaluate its relevance and cost. Or, prepare your own materials for an overhead projector or for computer projection.

Low- versus High-Inference Variables

In preparing for lecturing (as well as other teaching methods) we try to focus on **low-inference variables** rather than **high-inference variables.** These terms refer to the amount of inference, interpretation, or extrapolation from cues that researchers or teachers must make to judge or act on the variable. Teacher warmth, clarity, and enthusiasm, for example, are high-inference variables because a researcher or teacher would need to infer a lot in going from cues (what the teacher is doing or saying) to a judgment about these characteristics of the teaching. Then a teacher does not know specifically what to do or say if she wants to act in such a way so as to be warm, clear, or enthusiastic. It is easy to tell an observer to judge these teaching dimensions, but one judge may infer very differently from another on the basis of the available cues that reflect these dimensions. It is easy also to tell a teacher to be warm, clear, and enthusiastic, but such high-inference advice is not very helpful (see, for example, Chilcoat, 1989).

So in the sections and chapters that follow, we try to talk in low-inference terms. When we talk about "clarity," for example, we try to boil clarity down to the kinds of things teachers can do or say in order to be clear. The risk of our talking in low-inference terms, though, is that the "essence" of the high-inference variable may be lost—the very complexities and subtleties that result in clarity. But we think the risk is worthwhile, especially compared to the opposite risk of talking in high-flown, resounding, but not very helpful abstractions.

> Name a high-inference variable that might be important for teaching effectiveness in a content area of interest to you. Then try to formulate some low-inference variables that would be components of that high-inference variable.

Cognitive Load: A General Rationale

Underlying much of what we say about improving lectures is the idea of reducing students' **cognitive load** (see, for example, Sweller, 1994). This amounts to increasing the ease of seeing, remembering, understanding, and applying what is being taught. Researchers on cognitive load have identified some of the factors in (nonlecture) teaching that can unnecessarily increase the load. Some of Sweller's examples of them are

split-attention requirements in tasks, such as having to pay attention to what a text is saying while at the same time trying to understand what is being shown in a diagram, unless the two are highly integrated.

interactive elements in tasks, that is, concepts or ideas that cannot be understood one at a time because the meaning of one depends on the meaning of one or more others. For example, if the parts of the heart are meaningless when separated and the student must integrate them to understand them, the student must carry an additional cognitive load.

conventional problem solving in math or science, as against studying worked-out examples. Solving problems can require attending to aspects of the problems that are unrelated to the learning objectives. Studying worked-out examples can allow students to reduce cognitive load by focusing more directly on the problem-solving method.

Sweller (1994) has repeatedly shown that reducing these elements of cognitive load improves achievement. So as you study the features

Reducing Cognitive Load in Your Own Learning

As you study the rest of this chapter, apply the idea of cognitive load. See how various teaching practices increase or reduce it, and check how you can use the concept to help your own teaching.

The following teaching practices (elements) are discussed later in this chapter: rule-example-rule, explaining links, verbal markers of importance, and signals of transition. As you learn about them, think about how they help reduce cognitive load during a lecture. Reflect on your own reading and learning to observe in exactly what ways your understanding is enhanced by the use of these teaching practices. You might try to analyze a lecture in one of your college courses from this perspective. Did the lecturer make use of procedures that reduced the cognitive load of his or her students? Did it seem to help comprehension?

described in the rest of this chapter, try to see whether thinking in terms of cognitive load helps you understand why these features improve lectures.

The Introduction to the Lecture

Every lecture has an introduction, a body, and a conclusion. The introduction serves several functions:

- Arousing interest
- Motivating students
- Exposing essential content
- Helping students to organize content (by previewing and questioning)

Although the techniques we talk about here are used primarily in the introduction to a lecture, they can also be put to work whenever you introduce a new topic.

Appealing to Students' Interests

Lectures should be relevant to students' goals—whether good grades, the solution to an intellectual problem, success in a career, satisfaction of curiosity, the ability to help other people, or a chance to earn more money. Lectures that are relevant to students' motives become motivating in themselves—they elicit intrinsic motivation (see Chapter 8).

To make a lecture relevant, teachers must first determine, or make judgments about, what students find interesting. This is not always an easy job. Students can have very different interests depending on their age, sex, socioeconomic status, level of ability, previous educational experiences and success, ethnicity, nationality, and religion. Other key factors include

- the times in which they live
- changes in their circumstances and conditions of living
- events in the world of art, politics, science, and technology

These factors have to be taken into account whatever the subject of the lecture—Hamlet, the laws of electricity, or inflation. As we noted in Chapter 8, your choice of words, examples, analogies, and supporting evidence should be drawn from fields that touch students' interests.

Providing Motivational Cues

Telling students that certain ideas are important and that some ideas or techniques are difficult provides cues that motivate learning. And informing students that they will be tested on the content of a film or other presentation tends to make them learn more.

It may be surprising, but it is probably better to tell students in lectures (and other teaching situations) that a topic or problem is difficult but understandable than, in an effort to be encouraging, to say it is easy. Think about it. If you say it is hard and students do manage to understand the topic or solve the problem, their self-reinforcement is greater; and if they fail, their loss of self-esteem is less. But if students succeed with what they have been told is an easy topic or problem, their self-reinforcement is less; and if they fail, their loss of self-esteem is greater. As we noted in Chapter 8, the attributions students make are important. If they attribute success to their own ability, not to the easiness of the task, or if they attribute failure to the difficulty of the task, not to their own lack of ability, their attributions can increase their subsequent effort.

Creating a feeling of puzzlement or imbalance by suggesting that a topic is novel, or challenging students with one or more provocative questions, can also motivate students. For example, you might begin a lecture on lecturing by saying, "Lecturing is the most criticized teaching method in colleges. It is also the most widely used. Why?"

Exposing Essential Content

In a paragraph, the essential content is a topic sentence; in a lecture, it is an announcement of the topic. For example:

Our subject today is the bimetallic standard.
This lesson is about the various kinds of money used during the history of our country.
In this lesson, you will see that circumstances have forced our country to use many different kinds of money.

You can also summarize the main points of the lesson (two to four, at least) or define terms related to the lesson topic here.

A statement of objectives (At the end of this lesson you should be able to understand five causes, besides slavery, of the Civil War) can also be part of exposing essential content.

When different teachers lecture on the same content, those that produce higher student achievement are also rated by students as higher in the "clarity of aims" of the lecture. A high rating in clarity of aims means that teachers have made explicit the objectives of the lesson they were teaching.

Helping Students Organize Content

Previewing, Including Advance Organizers   It is usually a good idea to give students a preview of the lecture's content and organization, its focus and purpose. The preview can include ideas about how the lecture relates to what has come before and what will follow.

Advance organizers (Ausubel, 1960) are ways of telling students beforehand how a lecture is to be organized. They tend to improve students' comprehension of and ability to recall and apply what they hear (see Chapter 7). Luiten, Ames, and Ackerman (1980), in a meta-analysis of the results of 135 studies, concluded that the "average advance organizer study shows a small, but positive effect on learning and retention" (p. 217). This average effect appeared in all grade levels and subject areas, from both oral and written presentations.

Advance organizers can be rules of organization that underlie a body of apparently unorganized ideas. For example, a lecturer could tell students that most psychological research reports are organized according to "purpose, method, results, interpretations, and conclusions." This advance organizer would help students comprehend the typical research report in a psychological journal.

Advance organizers can also take the form of higher-level propositions. For example, the lecturer could tell students that the economic depressions of 1919 to 1920 and the 1930s can be understood as instances of the general (i.e., higher-level) phenomena of "primary and secondary postwar depressions." This advance organizer would help students hearing a lecture on depressions in American history.

> Suppose you were going to lecture to tenth-graders on the U.S. Constitution. What might you use as an advance organizer?

Asking Questions to Prompt Awareness of Relevant Knowledge   Asking questions—orally or in a short, written pretest—is another way to help students organize material, to make them aware of what they already know that can help them with new learning, and what is important. In addition, the answers give teachers an idea of the students' level of knowledge, as well as a basis for modifying the teacher's instruction.

What students already know determines a lot about what they are ready to learn. So teachers should determine that knowledge and teach their students accordingly. A similar idea is that a major factor in learning is the learning of **prerequisite capabilities.** For example, understanding addition is a prerequisite capability for understanding multiplication. Likewise, you may be able to appreciate poetry the first time you hear it, but you are unlikely to understand poetry well without prior understanding of meter.

A third idea is that of schemata—the ways in which knowledge is stored in memory (see Chapters 4 and 7). Coding information to be learned appears to be more effective when appropriate schemata are deliberately brought to mind as learning begins. For example, before a lesson on kinship, you might ask all your students to think about their relatives and how they are related to one another. Or, before viewing a film on the Russian Revolution, you ask everyone to think about the life of serfs in Europe. In each case, one's organized knowledge about some phenomenon—one's schema—is brought up from memory to help in contextualizing the new information. So, from three points of view (prior knowledge, prerequisite capabilities, schemata) you need to bring forth your students' related knowledge and experience before you begin your lecture.

The Body of the Lecture

After the introduction, the teacher moves to the body of the lecture—covering content, creating order, clarifying both organization and content, and maintaining students' attention.

Covering Content

It is obvious that lectures should cover what teachers want students to learn. Many experiments have manipulated the degree to which teachers cover the material. These experiments have found that students regularly do better on tests when content has been covered better. Another way to say this is that most of what you lecture about (though certainly not all) should be aligned with the outcomes that are used to assess learning. So lecturers should provide the content—facts, concepts, principles—that they want students to learn, especially if the lecture is the students' only source of this content. Content coverage is always an important factor in learning.

The other side of this coin is that you should avoid irrelevant and extraneous content that distracts students from what the lecture or explanation is really about. Such material merely increases cognitive load unnecessarily. Students typically have enough to do to follow and understand important content without being led off on tangents. So teachers should *almost* always resist the temptation to digress into irrelevancies, depart from a logical progression, or talk about themselves. The problem for teachers, however, is that sometimes everything seems related to everything else; and it is not always bad to point out those relationships as you perceive them. If you cover only the content that is on the tests, you might overly narrow your curriculum.

Providing Clear Organization

Almost everyone would agree that a lecture should be well organized. All of us have heard them: lectures whose structure made good sense, that held together in a logical way, and that were going somewhere. We all have also heard lectures that were hard to follow because the teacher repeatedly jumped from one idea to an unrelated one. Communication is easier to follow if ideas are connected with one another, that is, are well organized and have some kind of "narrative flow," with clear transitions.

Organizational or Outlining Forms

You can organize the body of a lecture, and therefore its outline, in many different ways:

- Component (part-whole) relationships
- Sequential relationships
- Relevance relationships
- Transitional (connective) relationships
- Comparisons
- Combinational devices
- Explanations

Component (Part-Whole) Relationships   Using **component (part-whole) relationships,** the lecturer shows how a large idea is made up of several smaller ones. Once students understand this relationship, it is easier for them to understand not only the larger idea but also the smaller ones related to it. For example, if you were lecturing about fishing as a hobby, you might talk about (1) why people like to fish, (2) the equipment needed for fishing, and (3) the best fishing spots. Under the heading (1) *Why people like to fish,* you might include the facts that (a_1) it is an outdoor sport and (a_2) it is relaxing. Under *Equipment needed,* you might discuss (b_1) the casting rod for bait casting, (b_2) the cane pole for still fishing, and (b_3) the fly rod for fly fishing. And under *Best fishing spots,* you might point to (c_1) Smith's Pond for panfish and (c_2) Blue Lake for bass. Figure 9.2 shows how these topics and subtopics could be arranged. Notice the *sub*-subtopics under the casting-rod subtopic.

> Illustrate the component-relationship organization in a content area you know well.

This kind of organization is called a **classification hierarchy** (Bligh, 1972). It groups together various items (facts, concepts, principles) under a common, unifying heading. The grouping reduces the number of separate items, making comprehension easier. If the number of items under a single heading becomes too large—more than about seven—it is a good idea to create new clusters if logic allows.

Add **signals of transition** when you use a component organization. That is, be sure to let students know when you are moving to a new ma-

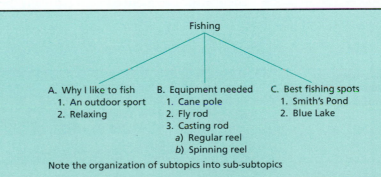

FIGURE 9.2

A component organization for a lecture on fishing

Fishing

A. Why I like to fish
  1. An outdoor sport
  2. Relaxing

B. Equipment needed
  1. Cane pole
  2. Fly rod
  3. Casting rod
    a) Regular reel
    b) Spinning reel

C. Best fishing spots
  1. Smith's Pond
  2. Blue Lake

Note the organization of subtopics into sub-subtopics

jor heading. You can begin by announcing all of the major headings and saying that you are now going to deal with the first of them. When you have finished with the first heading, give students an indication that you are going to talk about the next heading now. Say something like, "We are through with that topic; now let's turn to the second major theme (topic, heading, purpose, problem)." Within each major heading, you may want to list each of the subheadings to keep students continuously informed of the level at which you are speaking.

Sequential Relationships **Sequential relationships** have some sort of order—chronological, cause and effect, building to a climax, or "con-pro"—as their basis (see Figure 9.3). Once students understand this basis, the sequence is easier to remember. For example, you might say,

> In considering a problem for informal group discussion, we should proceed through the following steps in the logical order indicated. First, we should *examine the facts* out of which the problem arises. Second, we should *state and define the problem.* Third, we should *consider the criteria* to be used in evaluating solutions. Fourth, we should *examine and appraise solutions.* And fifth, we should *consider the steps to be taken* in carrying out the adopted solution.

In this case, you begin with a set of facts that create a question or problem. You then present information about and arguments for each of several possible solutions. Finally you adopt a solution and talk about its implementation. Such problem-centered lectures can be highly motivating. And you can heighten interest through *rhetorical questions*—questions you do not expect students to answer—skillfully timed introductions of new pieces of evidence, and careful explanations of the way in which a hypothesized solution follows from evidence.

The **con-pro sequence** can build suspense. First, you lay out all the arguments against your own position, as strongly as possible, perhaps including quotations from your opponents. Your students will wonder how you can answer these arguments. Then in the second part of the lecture, you present your evidence (logic and data) against your opponents' position and in favor of your own. Finally, you sum up by indicating, as evenhandedly as possible, what remains to be done to buttress either your position or that of your opponents. Gage (1991), for example, used the con-pro sequence in a lecture on the obviousness of social and edu-

Give an example of a sequential relationship in a content area you know well.

Think of a controversial issue in your content area. Then outline a con-pro lecture on that issue.

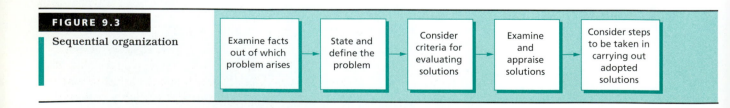

FIGURE 9.3

Sequential organization

Examine facts out of which problem arises → State and define the problem → Consider criteria for evaluating solutions → Examine and appraise solutions → Consider steps to be taken in carrying out adopted solutions

cational research results. He started with quotations from authoritative arguments that the results of social science research are obvious, then proceeded to refute each of them, and ended with a buttressing of his own position.

Relevance Relationships   Having a central, unifying idea and a criterion that determines whether or not other ideas should be included as part of an argument illustrates **relevance relationships.** You begin by identifying the criterion. Then you show how its application results in including some ideas and excluding others. For example, suppose you were trying to convince an audience that American farmers should have price supports. Your most relevant argument—your central idea—is that stable farm prices influence the stability of our whole economy. It is relevant, then, that farmers are large-scale purchasers of the goods of others, that they provide food for all of us, and that they have as much right to economic aid as anyone. It is irrelevant that agriculture is a scientific and mechanical business that requires expensive machinery, technical knowledge, and hard work.

Transitional (Connective) Relationships   Using relational words and phrases to define the structure of your organization shows **transitional relationships.** Make students fully aware of it. By repeating certain phrases, you teach students about the component parts of a series. You should also use a phrase of some sort to indicate that a summary is coming. For example:

> Teaching *can be analyzed* in many different ways for different purposes. *It can be analyzed according* to the components of the learning process (e.g., attention, reinforcement) that it influences, when teaching is being related to the learning process. *It can be analyzed according to* the time sequence of the logical steps involved, when one is planning a teacher education program. *It can be analyzed according to* grade level or subject matter, when one is planning to speak to teachers of different grade levels or subject matters. *To repeat*, teaching can be analyzed in different ways for different purposes.

The repeated phrase *It can be analyzed according to* shows the parallelism of the series of ideas. The phrase *To repeat* signals the summary.

Comparisons and Contrasts   Comparing two or more things requires that you make explicit the bases of the comparison. That is, **comparisons** require bases, or dimensions, on which they are made. Your organization, then, takes the form of listing or defining basis 1, illustrating it, then indicating whether the things being compared are similar or different on basis 1. Then you list or define basis 2, and repeat the process, and continue this way until you have dealt with each of the bases for comparison. Figure 9.4 shows how to organize a comparison-lecture organization.

For example, suppose you are comparing tutoring (thing A) with film presentation (thing B) for teaching some concept. You might note that on the basis of the medium they are dissimilar: the first is highly verbal; the

FIGURE 9.4

Organization of a comparison

Basis of Comparison	Thing A on Each Basis	Thing B on Each Basis	Conclusions as to Similarity or Difference
1	_____	_____	_____
2	_____	_____	_____
3	_____	_____	_____
4	_____	_____	_____

Overall conclusions as to similarity or difference between Things A and B: [_____]

second, highly visual. On a second dimension—say, whether the experiences they provide are transient events or persistent (like a text or photograph)—you would note that they are alike: both are transient. You continue this process until you have examined all the bases for comparing thing A (tutoring) and thing B (film presentation). Then you rate their overall similarity or difference. The rating can use phrases such as "quite similar" or "highly dissimilar."

Combinatorial Devices Whenever two or more distinctions can be applied to the same subject matter, they can be combined. Once a combination is made, new insights into the structure and organization of the subject matter may emerge. This procedure can be seen in the 2×2 tables, also known as $N_1 \times N_2$ tables, like those shown in Figure 9.5. Here the two sets of distinctions are combined to yield $N_1 \times N_2$ categories. A lecture using this **combinatorial device** deals with each of the categories in turn, telling students each of the main distinctions and each of the combinations to which they lead.

When you want to consider each of a number of things (facts, concepts, principles) in relation to each of the other things in a set, **organi-**

FIGURE 9.5

Combinatorial organizations

	Men	Women
Married		
Single		

An Organization for Describing Sex Roles

	Types of Team Sports	
	Noninteractive with Teammates	Interactive with Teammates
Contact	wrestling	football
Noncontact	gymnastics	volleyball

An Organization for Describing Team Sports

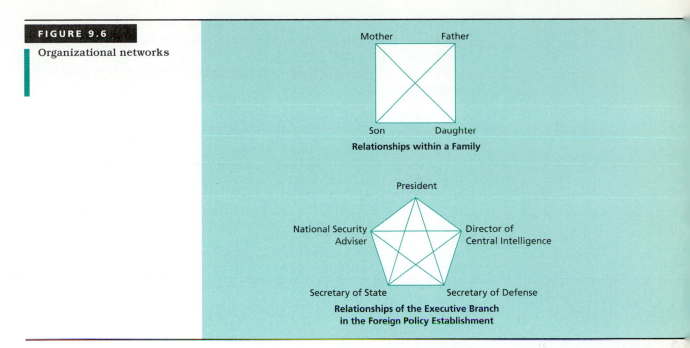

FIGURE 9.6

Organizational networks

Mother   Father

Son   Daughter

Relationships within a Family

President

National Security
Adviser

Director of
Central Intelligence

Secretary of State   Secretary of Defense

**Relationships of the Executive Branch
in the Foreign Policy Establishment**

zational networks of the kinds shown in Figure 9.6 may also be useful. These devices help speakers organize the material they want to cover. They also provide visual images and mnemonic systems that help students remember what they have learned.

Explanations

Questions about when, where, who, what, why, and how often arise in lecturing. Sometimes the questions merely call for simple answers: When? June 6, 1944. Where? Normandy. Who? Eisenhower. What? The invasion of Europe by the Allies. But sometimes, especially in answer to why and how things happen or how to do things, **explanations** are called for.

Explanations as Minilectures   The nature of explanation is a major topic in philosophy. Here we consider it only as an aspect of teaching. As we use the term, explanations are shorter than lectures and have a narrower purpose. They are properly used to (1) define, clarify, account for, or reveal the cause of some single concept, event, or instance; or (2) describe a procedure—how to do something. Explanations can stand by themselves as well as be part of a lecture.

So *Explaining* refers to the brief statements—minilectures and microlectures—that teachers make as they work toward getting students to *understand,* not just remember, the ideas they need in any discipline or subject matter. In this sense, explaining takes place not only in lectures to large groups but also in other kinds of teaching—discussions, tutoring, classroom teaching, recitations—which we talk about in later chapters.

How do we know when an explanation is a good one? It is good to the degree that

1. it follows the rules of logic, or fits the scientifically established facts, or both.

2. students have a feeling that they understand it. What do people mean when they say they understand something? Helmstad and Marton (1992) found that people had three meanings of *understanding:* (a) the individual's relation to things in the world (e.g., It's dangerous to ride through a red light); (b) the individual's relation to another individual's relation to things in the world, or what things look like to another person (e.g., Why my friends talk so much about their new apartment); and (c) the individual's discernment of the component parts of a phenomenon and the relations between those parts (e.g., How a gearbox works in terms of the component gears and how they mesh with each other).

3. students can do what has been explained. That is, they can apply a definition, use a concept, follow a set of directions, solve a problem, or use a tool.

As always, the good explanation is appropriate to students' maturity, possible misconceptions, and prior knowledge of related matters and terminology. A good explanation of the seasons for a six-year-old is not necessarily a good one for a fifteen-year-old.

A Model for Organizing Explanations   It helps to have a model to follow in organizing an explanation. The **covering-law model** attempts to show how the relationship between two or more concepts, variables, or events is an instance of a covering law—a more general relationship or principle.

Suppose you want to explain why it is warmer in summer than in winter in the northern hemisphere. You would go through this series of steps:

Step 1. Be sure you *understand the question* that a student has asked or that you have raised in your lecture. What is the student's concern? What are you hoping to teach?

Step 2. Identify the "things" (elements, variables, concepts, events) involved in the relationship to be explained.

Step 3. Identify the relationships between the things identified in step 2.

Step 4. Show an instance of a covering law—how a relationship identified in step 3 is an example of a more general relationship or principle.

Using the covering-law model, explain something in your content area.

Figure 9.7 illustrates the covering-law model as it applies to why it is warmer in summer than in winter in the northern hemisphere. (The level might be suitable for a ninth-grade class in general science.)

FIGURE 9.7

An example of an explanation that fits into the covering-law model

Step 1. What is the question?
Why is it warmer in summer than in winter in the northern hemisphere?

Step 2. What are the elements, variables, and so forth in the relationship that need to be explained?
The variables are (a) time of year and (b) mean daily temperature in the northern hemisphere.

Step 3. Identify the relationship between the variables identified in Step 2.
The relationship to be explained is that between time of year and mean daily temperature on the earth's surface in the northern hemisphere.

Step 4. Show how the relationship identified in Step 3 is an instance of a covering law—a more general relationship or principle.
The covering law is that, in general, the heating effect of any source of heat (such as the sun) on any surface (such as the earth's surface) is greater the closer the surface is to being perpendicular to the heat rays, because then the rays are spread out over a smaller area when they hit the surface.

Time of year determines where the earth is in its revolution around the sun. The earth's axis is not perpendicular to the plane in which it revolves around the sun; rather it is tipped, and the direction and angle of the tipping stay the same as the earth continues on its annual trip around the sun. The sun is, of course, the source of the heat that warms the earth.

In each hemisphere, how close the earth's surface is to being perpendicular to the sun's rays depends on the time of year, or where the earth is in its revolution around the sun. During the summer season in the northern hemisphere, the earth's surface is closer to being perpendicular to the sun's rays, less tipped away from the sun, than during the winter season (see below). That is why the earth's surface is warmer during the summer season than during the winter season in the northern hemisphere.

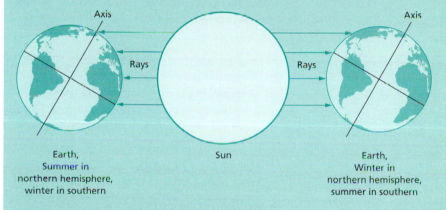

Earth,
Summer in
northern hemisphere,
winter in southern

Sun

Earth,
Winter in
northern hemisphere,
summer in southern

The earth's axis of rotation stays the same in relation to the sun as the earth revolves around it. This shows why the northern hemisphere receives the sun's rays more directly in its summer than in its winter.

Clarifying the Organization

It is not enough for a lecture to be well organized. The organization must be made clear to students. Several tools—signals of transition (mentioned above), explicitness, the rule-example-rule technique, explaining links, verbal markers of importance, and structural support—can help you do just that.

Explicitness Giving students instructions that were explicit and detailed yielded better performance on tasks by eight-year-olds (Van der Will, 1976) and fifth graders (Roehler et al., 1986). *Explicit* meant full, specific, definite, precise, clear-cut, and unambiguous, This did not involve just the amount of time taken; even when shorter instructions were presented more slowly, to take as much time as the explicit instructions, the explicit ones yielded more correct performances. It is more effective, then, to say

> Pick up your blue pen. First draw a big blue circle and then draw a little blue circle next to it.

than to say

> In blue, after you have drawn a big circle, draw a little one by it.
> *(Van der Will, 1976, p. 195)*

It might seem obvious that this is so, but transcripts of teachers explaining things to students makes it clear that not every teacher is explicit. And when they are not, they increase the cognitive load for their students a great deal.

Rule-Example-Rule Technique   Explanations of highly effective lecturers contained many more instances of the **rule-example-rule** sequence than did those of less effective lecturers (Rosenshine, 1971a). For example, in explaining aspects of Turkish foreign policy, a highly effective teacher might say,

> Although it is an Islamic nation, Turkey wants to increase peaceful, friendly relations with the European Economic Community. How? By increasing trade, exchanging ideas, and arranging personal contacts with people in the other nations of Europe. The country's leaders believe that better relations must be established between the nations of the European Community and those in the Muslim world.

Here, the first and last sentences are rules. The material in between provides examples.

> Use the rule-example-rule technique to describe a concept in your content area.

Explaining Links   Good explanations also make use of **explaining links** (Rosenshine, 1971a). These are prepositions and conjunctions that indicate the causes, means, consequences, or purposes of an event or idea. Examples are *because, with* (by means of), *in order to, if . . . then, therefore, consequently,* and certain usages of *by,* and *through.* Explaining links tie phrases together either within or between sentences so that one part of the sentence elaborates and expands on another part. The following four sentences contain essentially the same content, but only the last two make use of explaining links (in italics):

> United States culture permeates all of Canada, and it is a threat.
> United States culture permeates all of Canada, but it is a threat.
> United States culture is a threat *because* it permeates all of Canada.
> *By* permeating all of Canada, the United States culture is a threat.

> Write two sentences on the same content—one without an explaining link and one with.

Explaining links are important *because* (an explaining link!) they serve to tell us that a relationship is being presented.

Verbal Markers of Importance   To cue students to material that is especially important, use **verbal markers of importance.** The cues act like commands, letting learners know they should pay close attention perhaps eliciting an orienting response from learners.

Examples are *Now note this . . . , It is especially important to realize that . . . , It will help you a great deal to understand this if you remember that . . . ,* and *Now let me turn to the most significant point of all, namely, that . . . .*

Structural Support   Things that show the organization of your lecture are **structural supports.** In printed matter, headings make it easier to understand and remember the content. Similarly, in lecturing—whatever organizational scheme you use—you should consider structural support to make it explicit at the outset. Example: "First, I'm going to talk about. . . . Second, I'll take up. . . . Finally, ..." Providing this kind of insight is not necessarily incompatible with maintaining some suspense. You can still add details that are vivid, apt, and engaging.

Visual Aids   Chalkboards, charts, handouts, projected materials, and the like can reveal your organization all at once. Or you can write or project each heading and subheading as you come to it. One experiment (Cheong, 1972) yielded clear evidence of the value of revealing structure progressively, as the lecture unfolds. This approach may be more effective than revealing the underlying structure entirely at the beginning of the lecture.

Clarifying the Content

Almost everyone would agree that lectures should be clear. But how do we go about making them clear? How do we go about converting this abstract advice into concrete behaviors? Researchers have studied two suggestions: (1) give examples and (2) avoid vague language.

> Choose a concept or principle and then give two positive examples and two negative examples of it. Remember, the negative examples should be similar to the positive ones, except in some crucial characteristic.

Giving Examples   Students learn more and rate lectures more favorably when lectures contain examples of the concept or principle being taught (Evans & Guyman, 1978; see also Pugh et al., 1995). The examples should be both positive and negative. That is, they should illustrate what the concept or principle *is* and what it *is not.* Example: A mammal is an animal that suckles its young. It is not necessarily a land animal or four-legged." The negative examples should resemble the positive ones in every respect except the crucial one that makes the difference between things that are examples of the concept and those that are not.

Avoiding Vagueness   Words like *almost, generally,* and *many* are imprecise, indefinite, ambiguous. Several studies have shown that this kind of ambiguity, measured by the number of vague terms, tells students that the teacher is unsure of the subject. Also, it is associated with lower student achievement on tests of understanding of what a teacher has presented. Several studies (Hiller, 1968; Smith & Cotten, 1980; Williams & Buseri, 1988) have shown convincingly that vagueness hurts student achievement and attitude. So teachers should not only know their subject but also avoid words and phrases that give an impression of vagueness. Let us state this another way: "Teachers, you know, should sort of know the subject, and I guess, generally, avoid words and phrases that kind of give an impression that you might find vague." If such vagueness characterizes your speech, you should modify it.

Using Rhetorical Devices   Lecturing, like writing, can benefit from the same **rhetorical devices** that writers on composition have described for many centuries. Rhetoric in this sense is not empty or overblown language but rather the study of the elements used in composition or lecturing—elements of the kind we have been describing. A rhetorical device is any arrangement of ideas that makes an argument (a lecture) more persuasive. Such devices were taught in ancient Greece and Rome (Broudy, 1963) and are still part of what is taught in composition courses. Table 9.1 shows some of these devices.

They suggest that your language need not always be literal, plain, unadorned, prosaic, matter-of-fact. They can help you make your lectures lively and give them flavoring, zest, and gusto. As with food (a simile!), nutritive value (metonymy!) need not be sacrificed when you add flavor. But, of course, a little seasoning (a metaphor!) may be better than a lot.

> Give an example of irony. Of metonymy. Of synechdoche.

9.1

TABLE

Rhetorical Devices That Can Be Used to Enliven Lectures and Explanations

Simile   A statement that something is like or similar to something else. (Some lectures are like long nightmares. His explanation was as clear as plate glass.)

Metaphor   A simile without the *like* or *as*. (His lecture was a long nightmare. That explanation is a jewel.)

Allegory   A statement making an abstract point (most often spiritual or moral) using fictional people or animals as symbols. (The tortoise sure beat the hare on that test. She has the Midas touch.)

Hyperbole   An exaggeration or extravagant statement. (This book weighs a ton. That third-grader was a giant in his ingenuity.)

Irony   A statement the opposite of what you mean. (I just yearn to hear a lecture full of verbal mazes—half-sentences that lead me into a jungle. I was, of course, fascinated by the emptiness of his words.)

Metonymy   An idea used to stand for the idea it is associated with. (He abandoned the laboratory [science], and took up the pen [writing]. She doffed the apron [homemaking] in favor of picking up the briefcase [an executive career].)

Synechdoche   A word substituting the part for the whole or vice versa. (The school had a total of 1200 [students]. Pretty soon, the law [a policeman] appeared on the scene.)

Climax   A series of words, phrases, or clauses in order of increasing importance or intensity. (She was a woman of beauty, dedication, productivity, rigor, and to cap it all, integrity. A lecture ought not merely to fill an hour; it should be interesting, capture attention, enlighten, and, if really exceptional, inspire.)

Maintaining Attention

Even the best organizational structure is wasted if you cannot maintain the attention of your audience. You will no doubt find your own favorite techniques, but we introduce some here.

Varying the Stimuli Always speaking in the same tone of voice, never moving or gesturing, or using monotonous grammatical structure, an overly predictable pattern of speech, and lots of clichés—all these are good ways to lose an audience's attention. **Stimulus variation** has motivational effects. Rosenshine (1971a) found that a lecturer's changes—in movement and gesturing—correlated positively with student achievement. Whatever the lecturer can change fairly often, without making the change so extreme that it distracts from the subject of the lecture, probably helps students to pay attention. Video cameras are easily come by. Have yourself videotaped and critically analyze your lecturing. Remember, however, that stimulus variation can be overdone. Too much (a vague phrase!) has lowered achievement (Wyckoff, 1973).

Changing Communication Channels One form of stimulus variation is the use of slides, graphs, and pictures by means of projectors, chalkboards, and other visual media. By switching the **communication channel** from oral to visual, even momentarily, you cause changes in the response patterns and attention mechanisms of students. Adults seem to prefer visual information. And there is evidence that as children grow older, they pay relatively more attention to visual information and less attention to auditory information in films. But on achievement outcomes and preferences, there is no clear evidence that the addition of visual information to written or oral presentations has any effect.

Studies suggest that the simpler the graph, figure, or table, the better. As a general rule, if you use visual aids, they should convey information quickly and simply, in summary form (Wainer, 1992). Wainer's examples, shown in Figure 9.8, make the point about the possible advantages of graphics over words.

Remember, however, that graphs are almost sure to confuse young students. They need to become familiar with this form of representation and learn the conventions that are used to make graphs. After they have acquired those ideas, the efficiency and stimulus changes that result from using these visual aids make them worthwhile additions to a lecture or explanation.

Introducing Pauses Research supports the idea of pausing occasionally, at strategic moments, for a period of three to thirty seconds. In that way, you can recapture attention, break monotony, and give students time to think, catch up, and take notes. The longer pauses can tell students that you are changing the topic, moving to a new part of your organization.

During lectures, you can give students pauses of four minutes or so for summarizing what they have just heard; doing so improved student achievement (Davis & Hull, 1997).

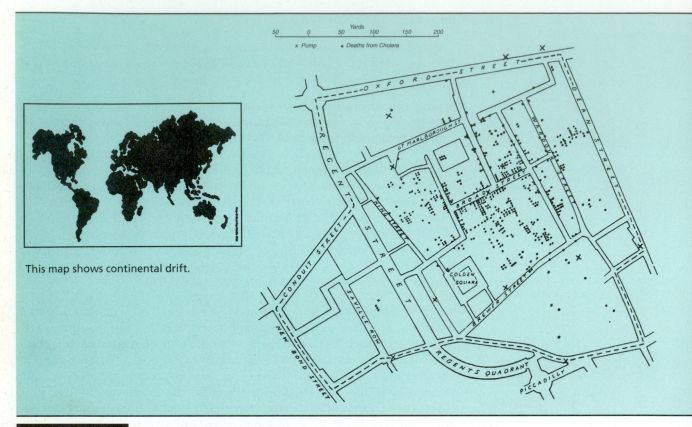

Yards
50   0   50   100   150   200

x Pump   • Deaths from Cholera

This map shows continental drift.

FIGURE 9.8

Two illustrations that show the potential value of nonverbal displays during lectures. *Left:* Continental drift is the theory, now accepted, that the western and eastern hemispheres drifted apart from an earlier, single land mass. *Right:* The 1854 map of London shows where cases of cholera (dots) occurred and where water pumps (Xs) were located. When the Broad Street pump was shut off, the cholera epidemic ended.

Source: Reprinted, with permission, from "Understanding Graphs and Tables," by Howard Wainer, Educational Researcher, *21 (1), pp. 14, 15. Copyright 1992 by the American Educational Research Association. Reprinted by permission of the publisher.*

Using Humor and Showing Enthusiasm   Interesting research demonstrates that humor, in moderation, has a place in education. Thank goodness! Research has also demonstrated that enthusiasm, as everyone believes, is catching.

Asking Questions   We do not usually think of lecturers as asking questions and students answering. But in fact students must be "responding" to lectures, if only in an effort to follow and understand. Beyond this, the teacher can insert questions into an ongoing lecture or explanation. Such questions do increase achievement, probably because they serve a number of functions (Berliner, 1968), including:

■ *Emphasis.* Questions inserted into a lecture can emphasize points in the material that deserve special attention.

■ *Practice.* Responding to questions allows students to practice recently acquired knowledge.

■ *Self-awareness.* Questions can help students become aware of whether they really understand something.

■ *Attention.* Questions that require students to respond may heighten their attention during a lecture.

■ *Diversion.* Questions are a form of stimulus variation, like a coffee break at work. Such diversions also reduce the rate of new input, allowing more time for processing.

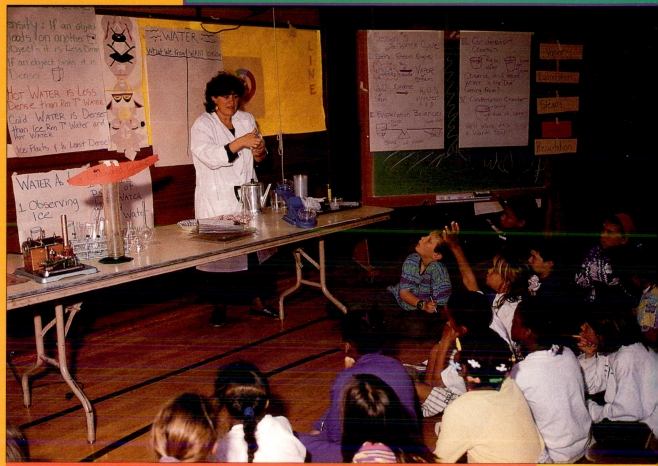

© Elizabeth Crews

"The art of raising challenging questions [in teaching science] is easily as important as the art of giving clear answers." And I would have to add, "The art of cultivating such questions, of keeping good questions alive, is as important as either of those." Good questions are the ones that pose dilemmas, subvert obvious or canonical "truths," force incongruities on our attention.**"**

Jerome Bruner, *The Culture of Education*, 1996.

> **"**The Lecture Method of Instruction is the single most common- ly used teach- ing method in the world and by far the old- est existing method—and one of the least effective, if improperly used.**"**
>
> Martin M. Broadwell, *The Lecture Method of Instruction,* 1980.

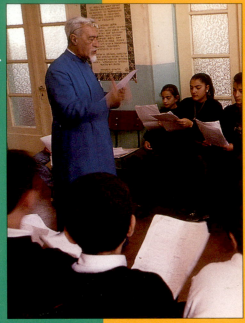

© Nubar Alexanian/Stock Boston

© Irene Perlman/Stock Boston

© Owen Franken/Stock Boston

© Nubar Alexanian/Stock Boston

"[There is] growing agreement that there is no one and only orthodox way of teaching and reading—this greatest of all the arts, in which ear, mouth, eye and hand must in turn train the others to automatic perfection.**"**

S. G. Stanley Hall, *How to Teach Reading and What to Read in School*, 1887.

"Because of the way knowledge has developed in different disciplines, children come to learn about themselves and their world piecemeal. If they get through college, most are introduced to mathematics, chemistry, physics, biology, geography, history, sociology, anthropology, economics, art, music, literature, language, and more. But they rarely learn to relate one area to another."

Robert Ornstein and Paul Ehrlich, *New World, New Mind*, 1989.

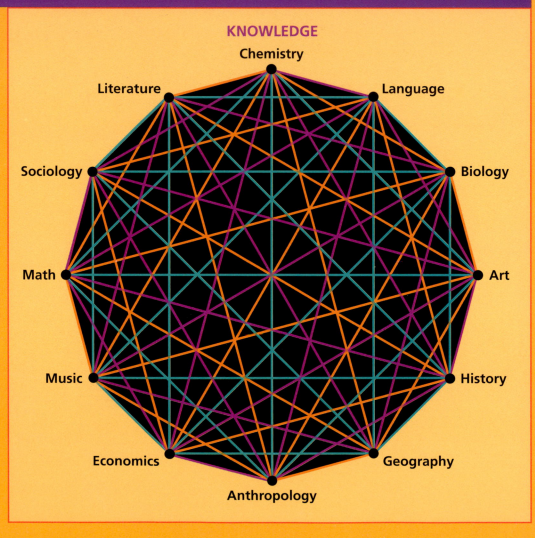

KNOWLEDGE

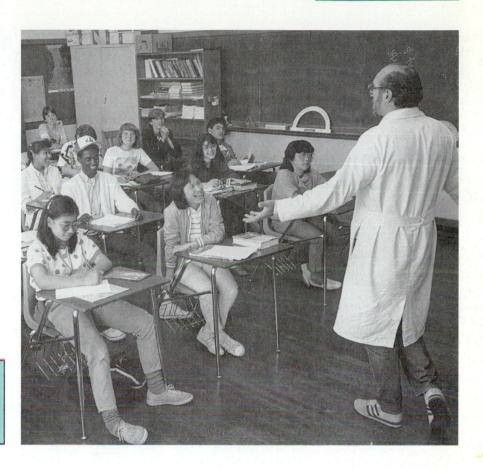

Students' evaluations of their teachers are correlated with their teachers' humor.
(© Elizabeth Crews)

- *Review.* Questions can force students to review what they have been learning, to mentally "scan" all the material the lecturer has presented up to the point at which a question is asked.

Student Self-Questioning   Students can also be trained to ask themselves questions—a metacognitive strategy—while listening to lectures. Such questions can take general forms, such as "What is the main idea of . . . ?" "How does . . . relate to . . . ? What conclusions can I draw about . . . ?" College students, in a remedial reading and study-skills course, were given training in such self-questioning, or in another metacognitive strategy—either summarizing, or taking their own notes and reviewing them (King, 1992). The self-questioning students actually did less well on an immediate posttest than students trained in summarizing, but they did better than the summarizers on a posttest given a week later. The untrained notetakers/reviewers did least well. So teaching students both self-questioning and summarizing should improve learning from lectures.

Note Taking   Many teachers prefer that students take notes while they listen to a lecture. Perhaps it is reassuring for the lecturers to know that

POLICY, RESEARCH, AND PRACTICE

The Role of Humor and Enthusiasm in Lecturing

A LOOK INSIDE THE CLASSROOM

As a student himself, Mr. Atticus—now a new sixth-grade teacher—had always been disappointed when a teacher began the year by saying something like, "I'm not here to win any popularity contests." That phrase seemed to portend a dour year ahead, and all too often the prediction would come true. The hubbub and excitement of a group of students milling about together would seem to dry up at that teacher's door; the clock appeared stuck during class time. But Mr. Atticus was a born punster, and had a lot of energy and love for the subjects he taught. He told himself that as soon as *he* stood in front of a class of his own, he'd liven the place up. He would win the kids over with humor and enthusiasm! Was Mr. Atticus's instinct right? Or are there disadvantages to a teacher's being funny, lively, and passionately engaged in class?

A LOOK AT THE RESEARCH

Researchers have looked into the value of a teacher's use of both humor and enthusiasm. Use of humor—jokes, riddles, puns, funny stories, and humorous comments—has been examined specifically for whether it promotes comprehension and retention, creates good classroom atmosphere, holds students' attention, and enhances students' and teachers' lives. Overall, in about two dozen studies reviewed by Powell and Andresen (1985), the effects on attitude and atmosphere were fairly consistently positive: attention and interest were improved by humor. But the impacts of humor on recall, comprehension, and retention were inconsistent. Sometimes humor helped; sometimes it did not.

"Communicating enthusiasm" has been standard advice for teachers and lecturers for many years. And indeed the value of enthusiasm has been validated experimentally. The behaviors of the enthusiastic teacher (see, e.g., Murphy & Walls, 1994) include gesturing, varied intonation, maintaining frequent eye contact, moving back and forth across the "stage," and using humor and lively examples. But enthusiasm in a broader sense may simply mean communicating feeling and conviction. Even lecturers who look serious or simply read notes are enthusiastic if they communicate a deep sense of the importance and fascination of the subject.

Students of teachers expressly trained in using enthusiasm-conveying behaviors rated their instructors and instruction more favorably (Larkins et al., 1985; see also Brigham, Scruggs, & Mastropieri, 1992; Streeter, 1986). Effects on student achievement, however, have been inconsistent: in some studies students did not learn more than the students of teachers rated lower in enthusiasm. The consistent advantage of teachers' enthusiasm, then, lies more in students' attitude than in their intellectual achievement. This is still an important advantage, of course.

Some evidence also suggests, however, that enthusiasm can have negative effects, in the earlier grades. In an experiment with fourth-graders (McKinney et al., 1983), achievement was unaffected but classroom discipline was worse with highly enthusiastic teachers. Many students in the low-enthusiasm groups exhibited boredom, but one of the teachers said the children in the high-enthusiasm groups were "climbing the walls." So elementary school students appear to behave more appropriately when the teacher conveys a medium level of enthusiasm.

REFLECTIONS FOR YOUR OWN CLASSROOM

When all of the evidence is weighed, it seems that Mr. Atticus was on the right track in following his instinct to be humorous and enthusiastic during instruction. However, there are potential pitfalls he—any teacher—needs to be aware of. As with so many aspects of teaching, striking a balance is probably the most effective course. So it might seem plausible that humor can improve students' creativity by reducing anxiety. But it is equally true that too much humor can boomerang, lowering a teacher's credibility and status. And it is clearly prudent not to expect miraculous achievement from your students just because you are passionately enthusiastic about your subject. However, showing your own eagerness for learning and for the topic at hand probably has a genuine, positive effect on your students' own attitudes toward learning. But here too, displaying a moderate amount seems the wisest course, especially if you teach younger students.

What if you are not a naturally humorous person, though? As it turns out, teachers can definitely be taught to use humor. You can find help in collections of humor—both general and subject-specific (social studies: Mugleston, 1989; science: Flannery, 1993; Matthew, 1991; mathematics: Gleason, 1991; Moldavan, 1993; Schacht et al., 1990)—and in anecdotes in the biographies of well-known individuals in the arts and sciences. And what if you feel awkward about exhibiting enthusiasm? As noted above, teachers can learn enthusiasm-conveying behaviors. In the studies cited, trained groups of teachers showed these behaviors to a greater degree than did untrained teachers. In sum, a new teacher can take heart if humor and enthusiasm do not flow naturally at first. And there is a lot to be gained from a balanced display of enthusiasm for your subject and a sense of humor in the classroom.

students are valuing what they say. But empirical evidence does not always support the value of note taking during lectures (Hartley & Davies, 1977). The issues concerning the effectiveness of note taking seem to revolve around what notes are taken and whether note taking helps in encoding (during the lecture) or in remembering (reading the notes before a test).

The evidence suggests that some students take notes that relate directly to achievement-test questions, and some do not. Obviously, those students who can pick out what is most important in a lecture do better on subsequent achievement tests. So, if a teacher gives students cues about what is important, using some form of cueing or verbal markers of importance, students should obtain higher achievement-test scores. Research has confirmed this (Moore, 1968).

The research also suggests that note taking during a lecture has only a small effect on comprehension. It is not much of an aid in the encoding process so necessary to moving information from short-term to long-term memory. Note taking's positive effect is as an aid to memory of the content of the lecture, through studying the notes before an exam. So a teacher's notes shared with students, or the notes of an official note taker, or even borrowed notes are all likely to improve achievement if the notes are studied before a test. It appears that actually taking notes during a lecture is not the important factor, then. It is attending to the lecture and studying a good set of notes before an examination that enhance learning from lectures. Accordingly, more teachers should themselves furnish their students with outlines and notes.

Using Handouts   Outlines that show the organization of a lecture, and other handouts, can improve student achievement (Hartley, 1976). However, in one study *incomplete* handouts, which omitted twenty key words or phrases (indicated by a line), produced better achievement than either a complete handout or no handout at all. The generative element in learning (see Chapter 7) would seem to explain this finding.

The Conclusion of the Lecture

Once you have finished the body of a lecture, then what? How do you tie it all together? How do you finish up?

Functions of the Conclusion

A lecture should be timed so as to allow for an adequate conclusion. Perhaps one-fifth of the total time available should be left for serving the purposes of conclusions. From his analyses of videotape recordings of what some teachers actually did, Shutes (1969) identified a number of functions that conclusions can serve:

- *Interact with students on a social level.* The conclusion offers an opportunity to say something relaxing and positive. ("It's been a pleasure to teach you something about this important topic.")

- *Check whether students understand the material.* The conclusion can give you a chance to get some feedback by asking the students to recall specific ideas or give examples, definitions, or applications. ("I've talked about several learning theories. Can you name and describe them?")
- *Clear up misunderstandings.* The conclusion can allow you to answer students' questions. ("No, punishment and negative reinforcement are not the same because . . .")
- *Act as a kind of "postorganizer."* The conclusion can let students know what they should have learned and identify key points in the lesson. ("And you should now understand the various parts of a lecture—introduction, body, and conclusion—and the functions each part serves.")

The Summary

Should summaries come at the end of a lecture, or at the beginning? At the beginning they help prepare students; at the end they act as reviews. A summary differs from an advance organizer not only in position but also in *not* being more abstract, general, and inclusive than the lecture or learning material that follows or precedes it.

Although results (e.g., Hartley et al., 1979) are conflicting, and often based on printed rather than oral deliveries, the research tends to favor summaries at the end. When students were given a 1,000-word article to read, they did better on tests of factual knowledge when the summary came at the end than when it came at the beginning or was omitted altogether.

Interlecture Structuring

Clearly you should do your **interlecture structuring** at the beginning of a course—the series of lectures should be planned at the outset. Also, students should be given the program for the whole series right at the beginning so that they can see the structure of the array of lectures.

The end of one lecture should both tie the material to the preceding one and hint at the nature of the next. Lectures should form a chain, and the connections between the links should be clear. It is the teacher's job, then, to describe interlecture structure as well as intralecture structure. For example:

> As you will recall, *this lecture is the fifth* in the section of this course that deals with ecology. *Last time* I dealt with the concept of an ecological niche, which led up to what I have discussed today. *Next time,* I'll go into the ways in which human beings have affected ecological niches. Those ways were suggested by the conclusions I reached today, on the fragility of the niche for most organisms.

Interlecture structuring of this kind can give students a sense of direction that helps them tie the whole series of lectures together into a coherent whole.

In your own content area, write out the titles of a series of lectures so as to illustrate the concept of interlecture structuring.

SUMMARY

1. The teaching method that is most maligned and yet most used at the college level and also at the secondary and even the elementary school levels is lecturing (and explaining). Clearly, it is an important method.

2. But the lecture method has drawbacks. First, it is easily misused: it can be used too often, at too great a length, and too much to the exclusion of other methods. It is best suited to knowledge objectives. It can encourage passivity and dependence on the part of students. It can be used for the wrong purposes (e.g., to save money) rather than for fostering the achievement that students want and need. In heterogeneous classes, lectures can be aimed at too narrow a range of students, missing those for whom it is too elementary or too advanced.

3. The lecture method has value, however, because of its flexibility, the reinforcement it offers both teachers and students, and its administrative benefits. Research indicates that it can be an effective teaching method under certain conditions.

4. Preparing a lecture calls for taking a look at your own motivation and how much time you can devote to the preparation. It also requires making decisions about audiovisual media.

5. The introduction of a lecture serves to motivate through arousing students' interest and providing motivational cues. It should also expose essential content, and help students structure that content with advance organizers and questions to spark recall of related ideas they already know.

6. The body of the lecture covers content. It creates order, using one or more organizational forms and explanations; makes the content clear, using explicit phrasing, the rule-example-rule technique, explaining links, verbal markers of importance, structural supports, and avoiding vague terms; and maintains attention by varying stimuli, changing communication channels, using humor, showing enthusiasm, and asking questions. The teacher can help students take notes by pausing, pointing out what is important, or by providing handouts of the structure and major points of the lecture.

7. The conclusion allows time for asking and answering clarifying questions, reviews key points and allows interacting with students on a social level. This is also where the teacher relates a lecture to those before and after it.

8. Teachers should not use the lecture method if a better alternative is available. And they should not use the method at all if their personalities are simply unsuited to its demands.

Teaching Small Groups: The Discussion Method and Cooperative Learning

Overview

RATIONALES: SOCIAL LEARNING AND DISTRIBUTED COGNITION
  Social Learning Theory
  Distributed Cognition
THE DISCUSSION METHOD
  Objectives of Discussion-Group Teaching
  Considerations in Using Discussion
  Arranging discussion in large classes
  High consensus versus low-consensus fields
  Controversiality and attitudes
  The teacher's personality
  Before the Discussion Group Meets
  Choosing a topic
  Establishing common ground
  During the Meeting
  The teacher's role
  The effects of teachers' questions

  ▪ **APPLICATION**
  Experimenting with Using Questions versus Nonquestion Alternatives

  The students' role
  When should the teacher intervene?

  POLICY, RESEARCH, AND PRACTICE
  How Do a Teacher's Actions Stifle or Stimulate Student Discussion?

  After the Meeting
  Notes and records
  Evaluations
  Intellectual Pitfalls
  Biasing the discussion
  Encouraging yielding
  Withholding crucial information
  Sticking to a dead topic

  Social-Emotional Pitfalls
  Nonparticipation
  Uneven participation
  Hurting students' feelings
  COOPERATIVE LEARNING
  Some Cooperative Learning Schemes
  The Role of Computers in Cooperative Learning
  The Effectiveness of Cooperative Learning
  Positive effects

  POLICY, RESEARCH, AND PRACTICE
  Computers and Cooperative Learning

  Criticisms
  Summary

OVERVIEW

In this chapter, we first look at a rationale for small-group teaching—that is, teaching groups of two to twenty or so students. You can use both the discussion method and cooperative learning in small-group teaching. Then we go into the objectives of discussion-group teaching—critical thinking, democratic skills, and other complex cognitive abilities—and the conditions under which this versatile method works best. Next we look at the process of teaching a discussion group— what to do before, during, and after a meeting. Finally, we consider the intellectual and social-emotional pitfalls of the discussion method. In the second major section of the chapter, we turn to cooperative learning, describing several techniques and their effectiveness.

Rationales: Social Learning and Distributed Cognition

To develop a rationale for small-group teaching that can help your understanding, we show how it follows from Bandura's and Vygotsky's theories of social learning and development and the recently developed concept of distributed cognition.

Social Learning Theory

Visualize the social interaction of a group as a tennis game, with the ball going from one player's racquet to every group member, one of whom hits it—again to every group member—and so on. How does this image resemble and differ from a group discussion?

Recall that Bandura's and Vygotsky's ideas (see Chapters 4 and 6) emphasized the role of the social environment—people and their culture—in learning. All of us, not only children, learn from the people we interact with and whose culture—ways of thinking—we experience. In that social context we acquire our own concepts and ways of perceiving, thinking, making distinctions, and solving problems.

Teaching through discussion, especially, sets up a social context, one in which students learn not only from the teacher but from one another. This kind of learning goes on through **social interaction** in which what one student says sets the occasion for responses by all the other students, including that of the speaker. Each student's response triggers another round of responses, either silent or spoken, by other students or the teacher. Whether speaking or not, everyone is participating.

Discussion typically takes place among peers—students of the same grade level. As a result, it is likely to occur in what Vygotsky called the *zone of proximal development*—the zone between what students can already do alone, without help, and what they can become capable of doing or understanding with guidance from a more knowledgeable person in the subject. So discussion is well-grounded in learning theory.

Distributed Cognition

To clarify distributed cognition for yourself, think of its opposite: individual cognition. Give examples of each from your daily experience.

The concept of **distributed cognition** (e.g., Resnick et al., 1993; Salomon, 1993) refers to the existence of knowledge, understanding, and skill in a group apart from the way it can exist in any given individual. The distributed cognition of a group amounts to something different from, and greater than, the sum of its parts, i.e., the cognitions of the individual members. For example, a group may be able to solve a problem that cannot be solved by any individual member working alone. In this case, members' ideas develop in interaction with the ideas and things, such as devices and materials, other people have developed. In other words, "People appear *to think in conjunction or partnership* with others and with the help of culturally provided tools and implements" (Salomon, 1993, p. xiii).

From the distributed-cognition point of view, thinking, problem solving, comprehending, and other cognitive processes are largely collaborative activities involving division of labor, sharing of ideas, and one person activating another. The "participants" involved need not be only people; they can also include computers, books, and other tools. The distributed-cognition character of mental processes means that what goes on in discussions resembles quite realistically the ways people in general—not just students in the classroom—actually go about their daily lives. So the concept of distributed-cognition allows us to see how discussion comes close to the heart of what education ought to be.

The Discussion Method

Criticism of lecturing (or teacher talk, teacher-dominated teaching, etc.) has long led educators to think about the possibilities and advantages of small-group teaching. Here was an approach that brought students together face to face. Here one student could talk to another, who could then respond. Other students could also enter into the discussion. The teacher usually hovered over the whole complex interaction, acting when appropriate as chairperson, guide, initiator, summarizer, and referee.

Because discussion allows students more activity and feedback, it is, according to comparisons, more effective than lectures in promoting an understanding of concepts and the development of problem-solving skills. But information is transmitted more slowly in discussion classes than in lecture classes. So the lecture is more effective in promoting the acquisition of information.

As might be expected, students sometimes reject discussion-group teaching just as they reject lecturing. Some may say, "I didn't pay all this money (give all this time) to listen to students who are just as ignorant as I am." Or, "I'd rather hear a poor lecture by an expert (a great woman, a renowned scholar, a professional teacher of the subject) than a lively discussion by my fellow students who don't know any more than I do."

Objectives of Discussion-Group Teaching

Nonetheless, teaching through discussion is useful in fostering important abilities:

1. *Ability to think critically, do higher-level thinking, acquire desirable attitudes and motivation.* Recall the research described in Chapter 9 showing the frequent superiority of discussions over lectures in fostering *retention, higher-level thinking, attitudes, and motivation* (McKeachie, Pintrich, Lin, & Smith, 1990). Discussion allows students more activity and feedback, promoting greater understanding of concepts and the development of problem-solving skills.

2. *Ability to speak so as to support opinions with reasoning based on facts, logic, definitions, concepts, and principles.* A discussion almost by definition brings forth challenges to someone's own opinions, attitudes, positions, points of view, values, and solutions to problems. In the process of confronting these challenges, students must evaluate them in relation to their own positions. Are the opposing ideas superior? If so, a student can yield or modify what he has in mind. If not, he can persuade the others of the merits of what he has offered. In either case, the give-and-take teaches the student a lot.

Small-group teaching is useful in fostering critical thinking.
(© Paul Conklin/Monkmeyer)

3. *Ability to participate in democratic discussions.* In an undemocratic setting—whether a nation, a committee, a school, or a classroom—the ability to reason together with others is not essential. But in a democratic setting, skill in the free and rational examination of ideas is important. Working together in groups demands skills that must be learned, and discussion seems especially suited for such learning. Our ability to listen to others, evaluate their arguments, formulate our own view in the give-and-take, resist the influence of personal likes and dislikes and of pressure to conform, focus on the problem at hand despite emotional forces—these skills are all learned in discussion.

But beyond all these objectives, as McCaslin and Good (1996) have pointed out, discussion and small-group methods can

- make school work resemble real-life tasks that involve more than one person
- spread knowledge from more to less knowledgeable participants
- foster positive attitudes toward cooperation
- let students provide models for other students
- give students practice in learning from others
- help students, through interacting, to recognize genuine understanding that goes beyond merely getting correct answers to problems
- enable students to improve their understanding of themselves and others.

Considerations in Using Discussion

You may need to give some thought to various kinds of problems or concerns that can arise in teaching with discussion.

Arranging Discussion in Large Classes   Although people associate discussions with small groups, such teaching can also be arranged in large classes—from more than 20 students to hundreds—by breaking the class into small groups of 5 ± 2 students (Bergquist & Phillips, 1989).

The resulting small groups may be called *buzz groups, panel discussions, symposiums, debating teams, role-playing teams,* or *circles* (of discussants) *within circles* (of audience members). Whatever the arrangement, it results in groups small enough to allow everyone to talk. What the smaller groups do often consists of formulating questions or topics, answers or solutions, analyses or syntheses, and prepared or spontaneous points of view. These small-group products can then be shared with the whole reassembled class either on paper or orally. Sometimes the small group is asked to select a spokesperson to present its ideas to the class.

In short, large classes need not rule out small-group teaching methods. The objectives of such teaching can still be achieved in large part. But since the teacher cannot usually observe and participate in all of the small groups, there are still advantages in having a single small class of about 10 to 20 students.

High-Consensus versus Low-Consensus Fields   Any analysis of the value of discussion-group teaching should take into account the degree of consensus in the subject being taught. As you may recall from Chapter 9, in mathematics, the natural sciences, and engineering, just about everyone agrees on most of what is important, how the fields are organized, and basic concepts and principles. But, as we noted in Chapter 9, in the social sciences and humanities—psychology, sociology, anthropology, history, economics, political science, literature, music, and art—the level of consensus is much lower. Schools of thought exist in these fields, and there is controversy even at the introductory level.

In **high-consensus fields** a major objective is to convey knowledge. In **low-consensus fields** students also need knowledge, but they need a broad sense of the nature of the field as well. They need to be able to find their way around in it. They need to understand the controversies. They need to be able to develop and defend reasonable positions of their own. It follows, then, that one-way communication from books and lectures may serve better in high-consensus fields. And discussion is more suitable in low-consensus fields. Only discussion can give students the kind of practice they need in formulating a position, examining different points of view, and marshaling facts from their reading and experience to defend a point of view. We are not saying that only lectures should be used in high-consensus fields or that only discussions should be used in low-consensus fields. By all means, use different methods; build variety into your instructional program. But remember what we have talked about here when you are creating a balance of methods.

How should a good small-group discussion in a school resemble and differ from a bull session in a student lounge?

Controversiality and Attitudes   Discussion-group teaching may also be better suited than the lecture method for changing students' attitudes and behavior. Discussions are public. Participants who make a decision, who take a stand, are committing themselves publicly to a course of action. This kind of commitment is missing in the lecture form, no matter how forceful the speaker. Research on this question has not yielded consistent conclusions, but the evidence suggests that group discussion, with its public commitment to do something, can lead to attitude and behavior change.

> Group discussion has been successful in causing mothers to give their children orange juice and cod liver oil, workers to increase their rate of productivity, students to volunteer for experiments, juvenile delinquents to improve their behavior patterns, and parents to change their expressed attitudes toward mental retardation.
> *(Gall & Gall, 1976, pp. 201–202)*

And discussion has been found to promote positive attitudes toward Native Americans among fifth-graders, greater change in attitudes toward ecological concepts among sixth-graders, and greater expressed tolerance for racial groups in other grades (Gall & Gall, 1976).

The Teacher's Personality   As with the lecture method, the success of discussion-group teaching depends on the teacher's personality. First, some teachers are better suited temperamentally than others for this kind of teaching. The teacher's ability to tolerate a low degree of **structure** and organization can be important. If you are uncomfortable when discussion is not always organized, logical, and relevant, chances are the method will require some changes in your conception of teaching and your proper role as a teacher.

Second, the discussion-group teacher needs "intellectual agility"—the ability to follow the twists and turns of a discussion without losing track of the argument or losing patience with its complexity. The teacher must be able to show students how to pull scattered points together and bring them to bear on the problem at hand and, when appropriate, let students do these things for themselves.

Third, the teacher using discussion must be willing to relinquish some authority over what goes on in the classroom. During a lecture, the teacher has complete control over the ideas under consideration. But in a discussion, every participant is able to take off in a new direction. The teacher must share the authority to decide what is relevant and where the argument should go. Because not all teachers are comfortable with the idea of sharing authority, some may need to revise their ideas about the proper use of their power.

Before the Discussion Group Meets

Before you meet with students for a discussion, you need to do some of the same kind of planning that is needed for any kind of teaching. Planning (1) the topic and (2) ways to establish common ground are especially important.

Choosing a Topic   To your students, your objectives may seem to consist merely of the topics you choose, which can take any of the infinite forms of human concerns. But topics for discussion have a number of dimensions that make them different.

Either noncontroversial or controversial topics can be used. On noncontroversial topics all informed people agree, so the teacher's function may be to get students to arrive at the same position that is held by informed people. You might say that if acquiring knowledge and understanding is the objective, then the discussion method is not the best way to teach. (Remember, lectures may be more effective for this kind of learning.) But something can be gained from having students arrive through discussion at an uncontested, correct position by themselves. A discussion is a forum in which students can practice expressing themselves clearly and accurately, hearing the variety of forms that expressions of the same idea can take, and criticizing and evaluating successive approximations to an adequate statement.

Here is an example of a discussion of a noncontroversial topic, based on one used by Hatano and Inagaki (1991): Will a lead sphere weighed on a balance scale consisting of weights connected to a lever, weigh more, less, or the same on the moon as it would on earth? Students' votes before the discussion are almost evenly divided between "more," "less," and "the same." The discussion brings forth a variety of hypotheses, references to personal experiences, and analyses of how those experiences relate to the problem. One student offers the idea, from watching astronauts bounding around on the moon, that the moon's gravitational force is weaker, and so the weight will be less on the moon. Another student argues that the moon's gravitational force will affect the lead weight more than the steel balance scale, and so the sphere will weigh more on the moon. A third student argues that because the moon's gravity will affect both the sphere and the components of the balance scale to the same degree, the sphere and the scale will not therefore change their relationships. So the weight will stay the same as on earth. By the end of the discussion, the great majority have moved to the correct answer: the same. A subsequent test shows that the students' right answer is based on correct knowledge and reasoning. The group's discussion of this noncontroversial topic has had genuine instructional value for the individual members.

Controversial topics—topics in which there is no single true or correct position accepted by all competent judges—are especially appropriate for discussion. The value of discussing controversial topics does not lie in establishing one right answer. Presumably, if a single truth about major problems could be achieved through discussion, it would have been arrived at long ago, and the topics would no longer be controversial. Rather, the value of discussions of controversial topics arises from (1) their motivational effect, (2) the need they create to withstand the pressure of another person's logic and information, and (3) the resultant process of sharpening students' understanding of their own logic, information, and position.

The motivational effect of topics takes the form of epistemic curiosity, which we discussed in Chapter 8. The conflict between ideas forces students to find new information, reorganize their thinking, and resolve the conflict.

Topics that create a need to withstand another's logic and information can lead to greater understanding of another person's perspective. Kurdek "found that good cognitive perspective-taking skill was related to

> Suppose you experienced discussion-group teaching in a high-consensus field—a science or math class. Do you think you would learn well from it? Why?

quarreling and arguing with peers and students in grades one through four" (cited in Johnson & Johnson, 1979, p. 54).

Sharpening the understanding of the students' own logic, information, and position results from the interaction with others. When children who understand the principles of conservation of matter (discussed in Chapter 4) are paired with children who do not, and the pair are given conservation problems to solve, conservers usually prevail not because of their social dominance but because of the "greater certainty and superior logic of the conservers" (Johnson & Johnson, 1979, p. 55). So the nonconservers learn from their controversy with the conservers. Similar results have been found in experiments with controversy-arousing discussions of moral dilemmas. "Taken together, the . . . studies do provide evidence that controversies among students can promote transitions to higher stages of cognitive and moral reasoning" (Johnson & Johnson, 1979, p. 55; Oser, 1986).

Unfortunately, teachers often stay away from controversial topics. What happens if teachers refuse to deal, even at appropriate grade levels, with sex, politics, drugs, and schooling? When discussion always centers on trivial issues, students get less useful practice in clarifying values, weighing evidence, hypothesizing, and relating facts. Democratic ends may be served by hearing opinions about whether earnings from a car wash by a ninth-grade class should be used for a party. But this issue probably would not generate as much passion and hard thinking as would a discussion on abortion, grading, gender roles, teaching fifth-graders about safe sexual practices (as was advocated in 1987 by the U.S. Surgeon General), or African-American separatism—topics that are seldom discussed in schools.

> How does the high-consensus–low-consensus distinction differ from the noncontroversial-controversial distinction?

Establishing Common Ground   After you have set the topic for discussion, you need to give your students and yourself some **common ground** from which to work on that topic. The common ground often comes from a reading assignment, but it can be anything that provides information, perspective, or understanding on the topic—a film, television program, or field trip to a factory, museum, farm, or laboratory.

You should also help students focus on the specific material you will be discussing. For example, if the common ground (the reading assignment) is *Hamlet,* you might tell the class that discussion is going to center on, say, Ophelia's sanity or Hamlet's conflicting loyalties to his father and his mother. If you are using the film *Birth of a Nation* in a U.S. history class, you might suggest that students pay close attention to how blacks were perceived by the dominant population in the United States during the first quarter of the twentieth century. Or if you are showing a film of marbles falling through a grid to form a normal distribution, you might ask students to focus on the choice of explanatory theorems.

Another approach to getting a common ground was described by Wilson (1980). At the end of a seminar, he told his students about the literature they could choose to read next. He also provided an overview of the key names in the field and schools of thought to which they belong. At the beginning of the new seminar, the students described one by one

> How would you establish common ground for a discussion in a class and subject matter you might teach?

what they had read, their opinions of it, and whether they would recommend it to other students. Then,

> We create a pattern. . . . The topic for the session is placed at the centre, and then I will say something like, "So what are some of the things that we need to look at today?"—and the ideas will start to emerge. As they emerge I may say something like, "Is that a separate item, or does it belong with this idea we've already got?"—and so the main headings are identified, and subheadings placed with them.
>
> When we are running out of suggestions I will then usually ask a student to draw lines enclosing points that could be dealt with together. Often the other students will suggest how to do this. Then we can easily place these chunks in order ready for the discussion.
>
> *(Wilson, 1980, p. 83)*

During the Meeting

Once you have settled the questions of objectives and common ground and have arranged an appropriate physical setting, the discussion can begin. What do you do now? How should you behave during the meeting? How do you want your students to behave? When should you intervene?

The Teacher's Role   If you want, you can do almost all of the talking. Or, you can just remain silent. Or, you can interject comments here and there. The choice is yours because your role as teacher gives you authority.

The more you talk, the less your students talk, of course, and the less they benefit—a good reason to minimize your participation. Once you get the discussion started, you should become a listener and observer, though you might also choose to be chairperson, giving students the floor by calling their names or pointing or nodding at them. Some teachers delegate the role of chairperson in order not only to be freer to listen but also to keep students from directing remarks to the teacher instead of one another.

Ideally, with the teacher simply listening, the students proceed to the topic—explaining it, agreeing on definitions and assumptions, questioning the adequacy of statements or the relevance of examples and analogies, and gradually arriving at a consensus, on a noncontroversial topic, or sharpening the issue, on a controversial one. The teacher, although silent, is working hard: making notes and following, analyzing, and evaluating the discussion, its logic, its relevance, and its facts. Sharing these thoughts with students is important, but such feedback should not contain personal criticisms or take much of the group's time.

Often students resist a teacher's silence by addressing questions to him or her. Should the teacher answer? Probably not. If the teacher gives in and responds, the discussion can easily become a ritualized check-with-the-expert process, and the notion of mutual aid is lost. So early in the history of a group, when the first questions come to the teacher, a technique must be devised to get students to help answer one another. As the teacher, you may well have some good ideas on the discussion,

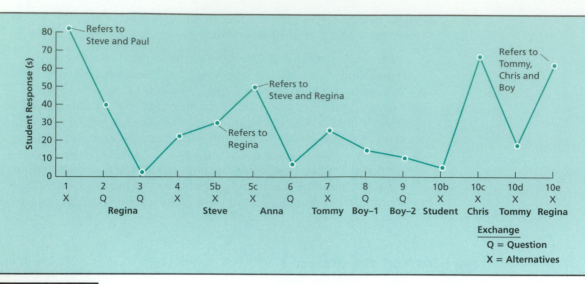

Refers to
Steve and Paul

Refers to
Steve and Regina

Refers to
Regina

Refers to
Tommy,
Chris and
Boy

Student Response (s)

| 1 | 2 | 3 | 4 | 5b | 5c | 6 | 7 | 8 | 9 | 10b | 10c | 10d | 10e |
| X | Q | Q | X | X | X | Q | X | Q | Q | X | X | X | X |

Regina ... Steve ... Anna ... Tommy ... Boy–1 ... Boy–2 ... Student ... Chris ... Tommy ... Regina

Exchange
Q = Question
X = Alternatives

FIGURE 10.1

Questions versus alternatives in a 40-minute eleventh-grade U.S. history class of 30 students, half of each gender, seated rectangularly, discussing nationalism. The vertical axis shows the duration of a student's response in seconds (s). The horizontal axis shows the nature of the teacher's utterance (X = nonquestion; Q = question) immediately preceding the student response whose duration is shown.

Reprinted from Teaching and Teacher Education, *Volume 1, J. T. Dillon, "Using Questions to Foil Discussion," p. 116. Copyright 1985, with permission from Elsevier Science Ltd., The Boulevard, Langford Lane, Kidlington OX5 1GB, UK.*

but save them; you will have time to get them in later. As a discussion group gets under way, students learn about your role more from what you do and don't do than from what you say about it.

To help yourself judge how well students are interacting with one another as well as with you, you can observe eye-contact patterns. When students are talking or when they finish a statement, do they look to you for approval? When no one is talking, do all eyes turn in your direction? If the answer is yes, you are probably in control of the group process even though you are not very talkative.

After a while, particularly if the discussion begins to bog down in confusion, repetition, or irrelevance, you may want to step in. With a minimum of words, try to get the discussion back on track. Offer a distinction, a fact, or a perspective. Or offer just a part of one of these, so that the students can have the pleasure of finishing it. Then sit back, listen, and watch.

The Effects of Teachers' Questions   Here is a surprising, counterintuitive point about the effects of teachers' questions on discussions: *Frequent questioning may not be effective if a teacher wants to foster discussion.* Dillon (1985) found evidence in many classrooms that "questions foil discussion" and "nonquestions foster discussion" (p. 109). Figure 10.1 shows typical results in one of the classes studied.

Dillon (1985) discussed this figure as follows:

Regina's initial contribution of 83 seconds diminishes to 39 seconds and then to one second in response to questions, then rises to 23 seconds after a statement. Student talk continues to increase, with Steve and Anna at 30 and 50 seconds, respectively; then it decreases to seven seconds after a question. Next, after a statement, student talk again rises to 24 seconds, again falls to 14 and 12 in response to questions, and once again recovers to 66 seconds after a statement.

But students do not merely talk more; they talk *differently* when not responding to questions. Their talk has a pronounced flavor of exploration, personal revelation, interpretation of experience, questioning, and interconnectedness. More students join in. Students refer to one another's contributions. Students combine, elaborate, and build upon previous contributions. (p. 115)

So whenever the teacher asked a question, the duration of the student response tended to be shorter than when the teacher uttered a **nonquestion alternative.**

According to Dillon, the same results appeared regardless of grade level, class size, length of class period, seating arrangement, subject matter, teacher gender, student gender, student social class, student ethnicity, required or elective nature of the course, academic or social nature of the subject, "touchy" or neutral nature of the topic, amount of teacher talk, number of teacher questions, pace of teacher questions, or cognitive level of the teacher question.

Even when a teacher in one case study urged students to participate, discussion did not result. Why? Because the teacher had been asking questions and students were simply answering them. And we do mean "*simply!*"

> How would you explain Dillon's findings on the effects of teachers' questions and nonquestions on classroom discussions?

APPLICATION

Experimenting with Using Questions versus Nonquestion Alternatives

In your classroom or practice teaching, conduct some of your own research by trying out these two different means of fostering group discussion. For one class lesson, deliberately use teacher questions as a primary means of interaction with your students. In another lesson, avoid questioning and make a concerted attempt to implement as many nonquestion alternatives as you can.

You might do this on a few different occasions to allow for the fact that you or your students might be having a "bad day." But remember that, according to the research quoted in the text, nonquestion alternatives tend to produce more and more varied student responses regardless of other variables. So in this case you do not have to be concerned with carefully factoring in and balancing out all possible variables.

Monitor the discussions. Which seem more lively and thoughtful? in which ones do students seem most engaged and most willing to contribute? Are clear differences discernible between the occasion(s) in which you employed many teacher questions versus those in which you used nonquestion alternatives? What implications for your own future teaching do you find here?

Under these circumstances:

Students speak briefly, for three to four seconds on average. They do not ask questions, they do not comment on their classmates' contributions, they do not speak to or about one another. All they do is answer questions, because the teacher is asking questions. The questions are asked to get a discussion going, but they work to keep it from getting started.

(Dillon, 1985, p. 111)

And when a discussion does get started, questions frustrate it: "They turn it away and gradually diminish it" (p. 111).

Nonquestion alternatives should be used if teachers want to foster discussion. What exactly should they do instead of asking questions? They can (Dillon, 1988, p. 132)

1. *state their own selected thought* in response to what a student has just said (e.g., I don't look at it that way), or

2. *call for a student question* related to the speaker's contribution, or

3. *acknowledge what a speaker has said* without themselves taking and holding the floor, or

4. *say nothing at all* but maintain a deliberate approach to silence.

Also, the teacher can (E. D. Wong, 1991)

5. *summarize* what a student has just said, or

6. *make a short comment* (Right, or O.K.).

These types of responses may work best after a question has been asked, to point the discussion in the direction a teacher wants.

Remember, though, that all of this applies to the goal of stimulating student discussion. If a teacher's purpose is something other than fostering a discussion, teacher questions remain a valuable tool.

The Students' Role   One way to improve your own teaching role is to give students an explicit understanding of what their role should be. In a discussion group, students should be able to state their own solution to a problem and be led by you and other students to elaborate on it, defend it against attack, relate it to other ideas, and modify it, if necessary, in light of those other ideas.

Students' comments should, if possible, be evaluated by their fellow students, and every student should participate in evaluating the comments of others. The students themselves should see to it that communication has been adequate by asking a fellow student to clarify a point and by asking questions of one another when necessary. When a teacher has to assume these responsibilities because the students do not, the teacher should point out that students are expected to ask their own questions. Unless students are told that these roles are proper, they may not develop them.

When Should the Teacher Intervene?   There is a fine balance here. Too much teacher participation can limit the effectiveness of small-group discussion, and so can too little. But a discussion that has gotten side-

POLICY, RESEARCH, AND PRACTICE

How Do a Teacher's Actions Stifle or Stimulate Student Discussion?

A LOOK INSIDE THE CLASSROOM

Ms. Yamashita's eighth-grade social studies class had just been dismissed. She stood alone for a moment, looking at the desks clustered into small circles, and shook her head. My, had that lesson fallen flat! She'd expected an engaged buzz to fill the room for this discussion. Instead, there had been long pauses and an almost stifled quality to the discussion. This seemed to happen especially when she had wandered over to a group and tried to stir things up. And it wasn't the first time. She'd noticed this before with discussion groups in her classroom. It certainly wasn't her own preparation; she loved American history and always made sure that she was as informed as she could be about a particular topic. And she'd set the groups up well; she knew they were capable of good work together. So she took a few moments now to reflect on what else could be going on. Something was nagging her about the way the interactions she tried to encourage seemed to stop in mid-air. Let us look at some factors Ms. Yamashita might analyze.

A LOOK AT THE RESEARCH

Many factors can affect the length of students' contributions (E. D. Wong, 1991). One is the type of question a teacher asks. Yes-no questions encourage short answers, and non–yes-no questions encourage longer responses. So if a teacher asks a question beginning with *Is, Was, Did,* and so on, and the student can logically answer yes or no, the student is likely to do so—and a discussion is stymied. Also, a teacher's straight factual questions, requiring a particular date or piece of information in response, can stop the flow of a discussion. In addition, such factors as students not having enough background knowledge or not especially caring about the topic at hand can also derail group interactions and contributions.

Nonetheless, as Dillon (1991) emphasized, student responses to non-questions tend to be longer than those to questions, regardless of the type of question—opinion or fact, yes-no or non–yes-no—and regardless of the topic and the average length of student utterances on that topic. Dillon also contended that students not only talk more but show more complex thought, more initiative (elaborate responses, voluntary contributions, ideas), more participation, more questioning, more student-

continues

student exchanges, and more student-student references when the teacher uses nonquestion alternatives. In every case, "not only was student initiative greater overall when teachers questioned less, but also the initiative in every case was greater in response to alternatives than to questions—two and three times greater." (Dillon, 1991, p. 164) In other words, cognitive activity is maximized in classrooms that reject the Socratic idea we all once thought was the "proper" basis on which to instruct.

REFLECTIONS FOR YOUR OWN CLASSROOM

In her reflection, Ms. Yamashita came to see that she had engaged in a number of the practices described above. She realized that she intervened with questions that do not provoke or even permit thoughtful responses. And she almost never used provocative statements instead of specific questions. She vowed to work on her approach to discussion group interactions. More specifically, good recommendations for stimulating classroom discussion that you should keep in mind are as follows:

- Make frequent use of nonquestion alternatives (see text explanation). This is the best advice available, and more compatible than questioning strategies, especially for people from non-schooled cultures and Native American cultures. Try teaching with a dinner conversation as your model of discourse, and forget the courtroom!
- If you do ask questions, avoid yes-no questions. Try asking questions that begin, "How would you explain . . . ?" or ". . . analyze?" or ". . . evaluate?" or ". . . apply?"
- Avoid simple questions of fact. Try to pepper your interactions with opinion questions, which are likely to bring forth longer answers.
- Be sure that your students are prepared for the discussion and that they have background knowledge on the topics you give them.
- Try to choose discussion topics that are of particular interest to students.

tracked lowers students' motivation for learning. So the teacher needs to judge correctly and quickly when intervention is necessary. If it comes too soon or too often, students may be deprived of the opportunity to learn how to get themselves out of blind alleys. If it comes too late, students become frustrated.

How does a teacher decide when to intervene? Here are some suggestions:

- *Is a digression taking too much time?* If several contributions in a row are too far afield, insert a brief reminder of the topic and the part of it being discussed.
- *Are pauses between contributions becoming too long?* Lengthy pauses may mean that participants are too bewildered to speak, or hesitate to speak in the face of mounting confusion. If pauses grow too long, intervene to find out why.
- *Is an outright error of fact being accepted?* If so, and if the error is having a serious effect on the validity of the discussion, step in and correct it. It is better, of course, if a student corrects an error. But

you should not let an error do great damage before putting the discussion back on a valid factual basis. This assumes, of course, that you know the difference between opinions and values on the one hand, and facts on the other. Research (Zeigler, 1967) with hundreds of teachers at the high school level suggested that around half might agree that the following statement is factual: "The form of government in the United States may not be perfect, but it is the best form of government yet devised by mankind." Teachers should understand that this is a statement of opinion.

■ *Are serious logical fallacies going undetected?* Fallacies may be subtle and hard to detect, but they can damage the validity of a discussion in even the most mature groups. Piaget pointed out that at early ages students can be expected to be only moderately logical (see Chapter 4). A teacher can do a great service to students—one with lasting and general value—by pointing out instances of the kinds of errors in logic that have been known to philosophers for many centuries.

What are **logical fallacies?** For a full explanation, you should take a look at a logic textbook or a good encyclopedia. Table 10.1 lists some of them briefly and gives an example of each. These kinds of logical errors may occur frequently in class discussions (and in your lectures as well). So it is good policy for you to keep them in mind and use them as the focal point of a discussion at least once in a while. By pointing them out,

> Give examples of some of the logical fallacies shown in Table 10.1—if possible, fallacies you have actually heard from politicians or others.

TABLE 10.1

Some Logical Fallacies and an Example of Each

Confusing what is accidental (that is, incidental) with what is essential. Example: Thinking all mammals are land animals.

Arguing from a general rule to a particular case, or vice versa, without noting special circumstances. Example: If it is wrong to kill, then capital punishment is necessarily wrong.

Diverting attention to an extraneous fact instead of proving the fact in dispute. Example: Attacking the speaker personally instead of his or her ideas; or appealing to fear or sentiment, not logic.

Begging the question—for instance, demonstrating a conclusion by means of premises that presuppose the conclusion. Example: Condemning a proposed social policy on the grounds that it is "un-American" and anything un-American is bad.

Arguing that a result is caused by any prior condition. Example: A student does her homework regularly and gets an A on a test. Therefore, if she gets an A on a test, she must do her homework regularly.

Basing a conclusion on an insufficient or erroneous reason. Example: If a woman is wealthy, she must have worked hard.

Combining several questions into one in a way that conceals the fact that more than one question is involved. Example: Do you still cheat on tests? Here, two questions—Did you ever cheat on tests? and Do you cheat on tests nowadays?—are combined, so that either a yes or a no answer is an admission of having at one time cheated on tests.

you model logical analysis for your students. You will know you have done so successfully when you yourself are stopped by a student for faulty reasoning in your discussions or lectures.

After the Meeting

The teacher's activity after the discussion consists of making notes, keeping records, and evaluating the discussion.

Notes and Records   After the meeting, the teacher (or a student) should make notes about anything unanticipated that emerged during the discussion. Such things might be used as part of the discussion of that topic by other students in subsequent years. For example, suppose in a discussion of the Bill of Rights, a teacher offers, without having planned to do so, an example from the Declaration of Independence. That the teacher did so should be entered into the postmeeting notes. Or suppose during a discussion of *The Music Man* a student suggests that certain repetitions in the author's style are similar to Gertrude Stein's or Ernest Hemingway's. Again, this idea should be written down.

The teacher should also make note of points, issues, definitions, or logical fallacies that gave difficulty during the discussion. Calling these to the attention of the students at the beginning of the next session can help them see how their discussion has moved along, and it can help them become more aware of discussion as a process.

Evaluations   Evaluation is another postmeeting procedure. You may decide to hand out a simple reaction sheet, a rating scale such as that illustrated in Figure 10.2. Make sure the students realize their ratings are to remain anonymous. Then compute the average rating for the session. By charting the averages from one session to the next, you can check your own impressions, relating the cues you have observed during a discussion to the students' mean rating. Over time, you can learn to predict ratings and, as you are learning, you can begin to govern your own behavior to improve ratings. Low ratings may turn out to be associated with too much participation on your part or that of a particular student, or with too much or too little insistence on sticking to the topic.

Students' anonymous comments on a postmeeting rating sheet are another source of information. (But students may think that their handwriting will reveal their identity! If so, the students should discuss the value of the discussion with the teacher not present, and one student should give the teacher a summary of the discussion.) Here students can

FIGURE 10.2 Postdiscussion rating scale	*How valuable did you find today's meeting?*					
	A complete waste of time (0)	Somewhat valuable but not much (1)	Valuable but often weak (2)	Valuable but sometimes weak (3)	Valuable almost all the time (4)	Completely valuable all the time (5)

note the reason for their high or low ratings. Although students' opinions should not be the only indicator of the value of a discussion, they can give you insight into how much your values are shared by the students.

One obstacle to collecting and using students' ratings and comments is teachers' understandable reluctance to be criticized. But teachers cannot choose whether they or their discussion sessions are going to be evaluated. Their only choice is whether they want to know those evaluations.

Intellectual Pitfalls

Broadly speaking, the pitfalls in teaching by the discussion method are of two kinds: intellectual and social-emotional. The intellectual pitfalls include biasing the discussion, encouraging yielding, withholding crucial information, and sticking to a dead topic. To avoid these pitfalls, a teacher should occasionally tape-record discussions. Listening to them later helps to identify problem areas.

Biasing the Discussion   Biasing the discussion means giving the students cues that tend to subvert their objectivity. Bias is often the end product of a teacher's expressing opinions in ways that close discussion or force students to conform. Students cannot discuss the problem of population control sensibly, for example, if the teacher gives them a set of fixed assumptions about how food production can be improved. And students cannot discuss the dramatic value of Hamlet's soliloquy honestly if they know that their teacher thinks everything Shakespeare wrote is perfect. Think about your own experiences. Could you answer honestly if your teacher were to ask, "How many of you enjoyed my husband's guest lecture last week?" (Many hands raised) "Oh, how nice! Would you like to have him take over another class session?"

Teachers at all grade levels must be constantly aware of their enormous power in the classroom. With the reward-and-punishment power of grades, even casual mention of teachers' own opinions, attitudes, and beliefs can influence some class members. Students are perceptive; they are very quick to zero in on what they think their teacher wants.

Of course, a teacher's biases do not always limit student behaviors. They can enliven discussions if students feel free to challenge the teacher. Most of us have values and biases—strong convictions about rationality, about people's obligations to others. Teachers do not have to conceal them. They can try in *rational ways*, never using grades or ridicule, to guide students' beliefs.

To decide on which of your values to share, you have to rely on judgment about your proper role in relation to students at a certain grade level, in a certain subject matter. You need to know what is accepted as ethical teaching in your profession and community. You need to know the law concerning the teaching of controversial issues—evolution, for example, which is still controversial in some states, or secular humanism—and also to have worked out your own values in relation to the law. When deciding what to teach there is no substitute for your best judgment as a citizen of a democracy and a responsible member of a profession.

Encouraging Yielding If a group of people agree about an issue, fact, or opinion and someone goes along with them even though he or she thinks they are wrong, it is called **yielding.** Groups exert an inordinate amount of power over individuals, some of it quite subtle. In a classic study by Asch (1956), replicated many times, subjects individually joined groups of seven other people. The others were actually assistants working with the experimenter, but the subjects did not know this. On certain trials of what was supposed to be a perceptual test, the groups were shown the two cards pictured in the margin. The seven other members of the group—actually confederates of the researcher—unanimously agreed that line A was the same length as the standard line. In these test trials, the subjects had to decide whether to yield (go along with the majority consensus) or to be independent (give what was actually the correct answer). Asch found that about 37 percent of his subjects yielded. In postexperimental interviews, the subjects described the intense discomfort and stress they had felt in the situation, but they yielded nevertheless.

In similar studies over the years, subjects under pressure to yield have ended up agreeing that the average American eats six meals per day, that Americans average four to five hours of sleep per night, and that the average number of children in a family is between five and six, among other falsehoods. Not every subject has agreed to statements of this kind, but some have, particularly when they believed they were the only group member who differed.

Of the important findings in studies of yielding and conformity to a group, two stand out for teachers. First, the phenomenon of conformity is widespread. The teacher and a group of students, or any coalition of people, may agree to something false or unwise and "force" at least some members of a minority into conformity with the rest of the group. School groups usually have well-established mechanisms for dealing with deviants who do not go along with the majority. The majority can ignore them, physically attack them, keep them out of games by not choosing them, and so on.

Second, if just one other person supports a minority opinion, yielding is markedly reduced. So teachers must see to it that diverse positions are heard and that alliances are formed. A minority position is not likely to change a majority opinion, but if at least one other person agrees with it, at least the minority opinion will be preserved.

Withholding Crucial Information Sometimes teachers withhold crucial information in order to maximize the amount of participation by students. But a discussion can reach a point where it cries out for a fact, a definition, a distinction, a concept, or a principle. There are no clear guidelines for teachers in this situation. Certainly it is not wrong to share expertise and experience when a discussion can profit from it. On the other hand, it is wrong if the sharing stems merely from teachers' need to establish their own competence in the eyes of the students.

Sticking to a Dead Topic Sticking to a dead topic is a pitfall that also requires quick perceptiveness on the teacher's part. A *dead topic* is one whose value for promoting achievement of educational objectives has

Standard

A B C

Describe an occurrence of conformity in a discussion you witnessed. Why did it occur?

been exhausted. Signs that a topic has reached a dead end are repetition of points already made, longer pauses between contributions, irrelevant contributions, and an air of boredom and inattention. Well before these signs appear, the topic should be changed, or a new aspect of the topic should be introduced. Sometimes students themselves change the topic to something more worthwhile.

Social-Emotional Pitfalls

The social and emotional pitfalls of teaching by the discussion method arise from the attitudes of students toward themselves, other students, and the teacher. These pitfalls can greatly reduce the value of the discussion method. They include nonparticipation, uneven rates of participation, and the danger of hurting students' feelings.

Nonparticipation   Sometimes nonparticipation is a problem. The teacher finishes the introductory remarks or question, and none of the students says anything. What should he or she do? Here are some alternatives:

1. *Wait the silence out.* Silence is discomforting so some student may break it eventually. Of course, waiting too long may create an embarrassing or hostile atmosphere. But allowing a reasonable period of silence—thirty seconds or even longer—indicates that students' taking time to think about what they want to say is acceptable.

2. *Ask what the silence means.* Allow students to indicate confusion, worries about seeming irrelevant or foolish, or need for time to think about the issue at hand.

3. *Guess out loud what the silence means.* The teacher can say something like, "It's risky to be the first to talk," freeing students to take that risk.

4. *Break the group into smaller groups,* dividing a class of, say, thirty into six groups of five each. Smaller groups seem to increase the likelihood that students will participate and decrease their anxiety about speaking up.

5. *"Go around the table,"* that is, require everyone to speak up, without calling on and so "threatening" any individual. This means asking for ideas, reactions, and the like, from everyone in the order students are seated around the table (or circle). The next time this device is used, the teacher can begin at the other end so that the same students are not always first and last.

Uneven Participation   Uneven distribution of participation occurs in almost all discussion groups. Some students talk a lot; others never do. Uneven participation is not necessarily a bad thing. On any given topic, students differ in knowledge and interest, and these differences may justifiably affect their participation. But if certain students participate a great deal, whatever the topic, and other students fail to participate week after week, the teacher should suspect that irrational social and emotional factors are at work.

Status affects participation. Higher-status members of groups often control the discussion, at least at the start. So males tend to dominate females, older children tend to dominate younger children, and Anglo students tend to dominate minority-group members. All these phenomena probably reflect differences in status.

Racial and gender differences in participation show up even when participants are matched on task-related competence. This is so because a member's status in the group depends not on actual competence but rather on other members' *perceptions* of his or her competence. And in the absence of information to the contrary, perceptions may be influenced by a student's gender or ethnicity.

Accordingly, Cohen and Lotan (1995) examined ways in which African-American and other minority-group students are influenced by interaction processes to participate more or less in classroom discussions. Their work suggests that teachers can increase the participation and influence of low-status students in their own eyes and the eyes of others by increasing their status. To do this, teachers can

1. *assign roles* that lead to more positive expectations of the competence of low-status students. For example, have a low-status student be the "teacher," instructing higher-status students on a new task.

2. *introduce a referent actor,* someone from outside the group who belongs to the low-status group but is highly competent at the task. In schools, minority-group members in positions of authority (principals, teachers) can serve as referent actors. Or a teacher can show a videotape of low-status group members taking the lead in a game.

3. *act as a high-status evaluator,* raising the expectations of both minority- and majority-group members. Praise the competence, performance, and contributions of minority-group students.

4. *create equal-status expectations* for the group, expectations that call for equal participation by all members. Tell the group that everyone should be listened to and that everyone should have a chance to talk.

5. *(a) build tasks that require multiple-abilities and (b) assign competence in these tasks to low-status students.* To build **multiple-ability tasks,** Cohen and Lotan (1995) had teachers arrange for their class to discuss the many different abilities such as—reasoning, creativity, and spatial problem solving required for certain collective tasks. The teachers also pointed out that no one student had all of these abilities but each student had some of them. "Theoretically this intervention produces a mixed set of expectations for competence for each student rather than uniformly high or low expectations" (p. 102).

To assign competence to low-status students, the researchers had teachers watch for and positively evaluate *publicly* instances of good performance by low-status students on tasks (e.g., "observing astutely, being precise, or being able to use visual thinking") *relevant to success* on the multiple-ability group tasks. One teacher said, for example,

> Luis is really looking at the [activity] card when he is building this structure and following the diagram on the card. He puts one straw across like this to make it stronger. . . . You [classmates] need to

How do these approaches to improving the participation of low-status students relate to the goals of integrated education and equalizing educational opportunity?

tell Luis what you want to do because he is the one who is the resource here.

(Cohen & Lotan, 1995, p. 103)

Teachers who more frequently built multiple-abilities tasks and assigned competence to low-status students succeeded in increasing the participation rates of low-status students without lowering the rates of high-status students. Also, the teachers who used these treatments more often tended to lower the degree to which students' participation rates were correlated with their reading pretest scores. In short, the results supported these methods of equalizing students' participation rates and, according to some evidence, also improving their achievement.

In racially integrated schools, education can remain unequal despite physical proximity unless steps are taken to bring about greater social and psychological equality and togetherness. The five approaches listed above promise to improve equality of opportunity in such schools. But these approaches also have been successful in reducing gender and age differences in participation rates; so they are recommended for all schools.

That group size can also affect participation was first shown in work done decades ago (Hare, 1962; Applegate, 1969). Groups of about five students provide opportunity for participation to all, with enough participants for variety. And students feel they can participate in discussions more readily in groups of 15 or less than in larger groups.

What about students who do not participate whatever the size of the group? They usually give one of two reasons: not being able to say

Discussions can demand thoughtfulness and hold attention in ways that lectures cannot.

(© Elizabeth Crews/ Stock Boston)

what they mean and the possibility of being wrong. The remedy here is threefold:

1. Make discussion groups smaller.
2. Help students, carefully and unobtrusively, to say what they mean.
3. Create a climate of trust so that there is no penalty (ridicule) for being wrong.

Using reinforcement can also modify the rate of responding for individual students. But teachers cannot reinforce until a response is made. How do we get a student to respond in the first place? Here again, one relatively unobtrusive procedure is to announce at the beginning of a discussion, and repeatedly thereafter, "We'll now go around the table and let everyone take a minute or two to comment on the topic."

Once a student responds, the teacher can immediately reinforce his or her contribution. How? By acknowledging the student's ideas, thanking the student, or (if appropriate) praising the student's insights. Also, tying someone's ideas to other ideas and referring to them can be a kind of positive reinforcement that has repeatedly been found to promote achievement.

Operant conditioning (see Chapter 6) works. Provided often enough, contingent reinforcement should increase the frequency of responding in children who tend not to participate. As most operant psychologists would predict, changing the reinforcement contingencies in the environment can turn a follower into a leader. The necessary environmental changes consist of positive reinforcement of the target person's participation, but because positive reinforcement alone is not likely to be effective, mild punishment and ignoring of the verbal output of frequent responders may also be required. The mild punishment (frowning while the student talks, cutting the student off, commenting negatively about the student's contribution, and so forth) may be necessary in order to give the target student "room" to contribute.

Both verbal and nonverbal communication probably serve as green lights. Head nods and positive exclamations ("Good point! That's interesting!") reinforce the target student's contributions. Conversely, frowns and cuing remarks ("Let's hold it, Johnny, and hear again from Myra; she was making a lot of sense.") can serve as red lights, suppressing the responding of other group members. Teachers can prevent a criticism from seeming like a personal attack by introducing it with a positive note: "I'm glad you brought that up, but . . . ."

Hurting Students' Feelings   Stories have been written about the charm, humor, and educational values that flowed from the biting style of George Lyman Kittredge, a famous professor at Harvard:

> He had a violent temper and an undisguised contempt for the average student. White-bearded, cigar-puffing, loud-voiced, he commanded their respect rather than attracted their affection. They laughed at him once when he strode too far and fell off his platform.

He glared at them, and said: "This is the first time I have ever reduced myself to the level of my audience."
(Highet, 1955, pp. 218–219)

But teachers like Kittredge, and students who feel secure enough not to be harmed by such teachers, are rare. Sarcasm and ridicule are weapons that almost no teacher and no students should be allowed to use.

And what should teachers do about a student whose arguments are shown in a discussion to be false, irrelevant, or illogical? They have to correct the statements without attacking the student. There is a difference between saying, "Ariel, you're wrong," which refers to Ariel, and saying, "Ariel, I don't agree with your statement," which refers to Ariel's statement. Learning to receive criticism or correction without taking it personally is a major goal of the discussion method. Students should learn that their primary concern is the solution of the problem or task, not the protection of their self-esteem.

This goal may be hard to achieve, however. Teachers can help by inviting challenges to their own ideas and then reacting rationally and unemotionally. Here again you see the importance of teachers' opening their ideas to criticism.

Cooperative Learning

We have been talking so far about the discussion method, a method often used for teaching groups of two to about twenty students. Now we turn to one of the most important other methods for teaching small groups, **cooperative learning**—getting students to work together.

Research (e.g., Shachar & Sharan, 1994) has shown that, compared with traditional whole-class teaching, teaching by arranging cooperative learning can

- *reduce prejudice and hostility* between individuals and groups, including ethnic groups.
- *increase low-status students' participation* in social interaction, so that they take a more equal role in group tasks.
- *improve student facility in speaking,* that is, increase frequency and duration of speaking to fellow students.
- *improve student achievement* of cognitive objectives as measured with tests.

To arrange cooperative learning, a teacher gives assignments and projects to groups of four to six students. The students divide the labor among themselves, help one another (especially the weaker members), and praise or criticize each other's efforts and contributions. Liking and respect typically (but not always) develop among group members as a result of cooperative learning experiences.

Some Cooperative Learning Schemes

Of the many possible cooperative learning schemes (see Sharan, 1994), we describe here only those in which groups study the same thing (with no task specialization) and receive rewards based on how well its individual members perform. Those described have often been subjected to experimental research.

The **Student Teams and Achievement Divisions** (STAD) method seems at first glance to involve merely studying together. But it has a twist that makes it more motivating. Developed by Slavin (1983), STAD has the teacher assign four or five students to each learning team. Each team should, if possible, have both high- and low-achieving students, both girls and boys, and both minority- and majority-group members.

After the teacher introduces a new unit of content, team members study worksheets or other printed matter on the content. They work together in pairs a good part of the time, trading roles (tutor and tutee, "quizzer" and "quizzee") and using other forms of problem solving. The students have free access to the answers to the problems, so they realize that their goal is understanding, not just getting the answers right. They continue to work until all of them believe they grasp the concepts.

After this team-learning effort, students are tested on the unit. Here they work alone, independently. The teacher or a student scores the tests (percent of correct answers) as soon as possible, then derives the team scores. At this point, the method takes an unusual turn:

> The amount each student contributes to his or her team [score] is determined by the amount the student's quiz score exceeds the student's own past average. A base score is set five points below each student's average, and students earn points, up to a maximum of ten, for each point by which they exceed their base scores. Students with perfect papers always receive the ten-point maximum, regardless of their base scores. This individual improvement score system gives every student a good chance to contribute maximum points to the team if (and only if) the student does his or her best, and thereby shows substantial improvement or gets a perfect paper. This improvement point system has been shown to increase academic performance even without teams . . . , but it is especially important as a component of STAD since it avoids the possibility that low performing students will not be fully accepted as group members because they do not contribute many points.
>
> (Slavin, 1983, p. 24)

Rewards are given on a team basis. Each week the teams with the highest scores are listed in a weekly newsletter, and individual improvement is also recognized in the newsletter.

Teams-Games-Tournaments (TGT) (Slavin, 1983) sets up groups of three students, all from approximately the same achievement level, to play a game. Each group member serves in turn as Reader, Challenger 1, or Challenger 2. The Reader chooses a numbered card from a deck of cards, finds the problem or question with the same number as that on the card, reads the problem or question out loud, and then tries to solve or answer it. Next Challenger 1 chooses either to challenge, by giving a different answer, or to pass. Then Challenger 2 looks up the correct answer.

Whoever (Reader, Challenger 1, or Challenger 2) was right keeps the card. If the Reader was wrong, there is no penalty; if Challenger 1 or 2 was wrong, he or she must return a previously won card, if any, to the deck.

Weekly tournaments of this kind get students competing against others with similar previous achievement records from the various STAD teams. The competing trios change every week, but they remain homogeneous. "The high scorer at each table is moved to the next higher table for the next tournament, and the low scorer at each table is moved to the next lower table" (p. 26). So all students, regardless of their performance level, can conceivably win points for their teams. Team scores are again recognized in the weekly newsletter.

Team-Assisted Individualization (TAI) (Slavin, 1983), which is used for teaching mathematics, sets up heterogeneous four- or five-member groups. Each student first studies with one other student of his or her choosing, using programmed instructional materials, doing the necessary reading and worksheets, and then taking subunit tests and a final unit-mastery test. Students working together exchange answer sheets for scoring; the unit-mastery test is scored by a student monitor.

Team scores are derived by totaling members' test scores and number of tests taken each week. If the team score exceeds a preset team standard, team members are rewarded with a certificate. Here, teams do not compete against other teams but against their own predetermined team standard. And the teacher, free of test scoring and monitoring, can tutor and give other individualized help to single students or groups of students as necessary.

TAI uses individualization rather than group instruction. It is especially useful, then, for extremely heterogeneous classes, particularly those with children who have learning disabilities or retardation.

Complex Instruction is a cooperative learning scheme used by Cohen and Lotan (1995) to produce equal-status interaction in heterogeneous classrooms. In this case teachers formed small groups of boys and girls differing in achievement and English proficiency. Using Finding Out/ Discrubrimiento, an English-Spanish math and science curriculum for elementary schools, the teachers also applied the two treatments— multiple-ability and assigning competence to low-status students—described above.

The tasks called upon students to use a wide range of abilities in solving problems, sometimes with manipulatives (physical objects) such as rods. "Aside from reading, writing, and computing, these abilities included reasoning, hypothesizing, visual and spatial thinking, careful observing, precision in work, and interpersonal skills" (p. 106). Teachers had to be trained in ways of management that would bring about a high level of student talking and working together.

Group Investigation (Sharan & Sharan, 1992) provides specific procedures for enabling students to produce a summary report and presentation from which a whole class can learn. Students interact, with teacher guidance, to decide on a topic and a purpose and method for investigating it. They divide the tasks among themselves, plan their activities, bring their results together to form an integrated whole, design and prepare the report, and carry out the presentation.

It has been argued persuasively that such group-project methods (Blumenfeld et al., 1991) are among the most powerful ways to motivate students; provide them with authentic tasks of appropriate duration, breadth, and complexity; and foster deeper learning of the subject matter.

The Role of Computers in Cooperative Learning

Although we discuss how computers can assist instruction primarily in Chapter 11, we note here that computers have an important and increasing place in cooperative learning (e.g., Male, 1994). Computers are so expensive that most schools cannot purchase one for each student. But designers have successfully created computer-aided instruction for groups of students working together. So teachers should not think of computers as learning devices only for individuals.

The Effectiveness of Cooperative Learning

How effective is cooperative learning? The answer comes from experiments in which children taught by cooperative learning methods have been compared with children taught by conventional methods. Comparisons have been made on (a) achievement, (b) self-esteem, (c) intergroup relationships (friendships among African-American, white, Hispanic, and other students), and (d) relationships between students with learning disabilities or mental retardation and those without.

Because of the variety of cooperative learning methods used in the research, generalizations across methods are less valuable than those concerning specific methods. And of course the effectiveness of any of the methods depends—as is true of any teaching method—on how well teachers use (implement) it.

Positive Effects   Keeping these cautions in mind, Slavin (1990b), who has been a major participant in the cooperative-learning movement, finds that the evidence is, on the whole, favorable. Six outcomes of instruction have been studied:

1. *Achievement* is higher in most comparisons. And the proportion of positive results was even higher in a study where two requirements were met: there was a group goal, and individual students were **accountable** for their own achievement. The benefits for high- and low-achieving students tend to be about equal.

2. *Self-esteem* tends to rise. Students who participate in cooperative learning tend to change toward better regard for themselves on several dimensions, including academic competence.

3. *Interethnic relationships* show desirable effects. Interaction under equal-status conditions makes students change toward more favorable attitudes. When they are asked to name their friends, they choose members of other ethnic groups more often after a period of cooperative learning. Some studies have also found that these changes last for

Contrast the small-group method called *discussion* with that called *cooperative learning*. What are the advantages of each over the other?

POLICY, RESEARCH, AND PRACTICE

Computers and Cooperative Learning

How can computers be used to enhance cooperative learning among students?

WHAT THE RESEARCH TELLS US

Computers can facilitate cooperation between students in the same class or in different classes. Students can interact while sharing the same computer, or they can interact and cooperate via two or more computers linked together. Brown, Ash, et al. (1993) described how their students have interacted with others via e-mail. The students

make use of a commercially available, child-friendly electronic mail package called *QuickMail.* With QuickMail, students can send messages electronically to members of the classroom, to their teacher, and to mentors at the university and elsewhere in the community. . . . The child needs only to "click" on an icon visually depicting the target—for example, a picture of a peer or an adult, or a [symbol] of a group (e.g., a dolphin for the Dolphins). (p. 211)

Computers can provide even very young students easy access to a tremendous range of resource, reference, and library materials—printed words, pictures, maps, diagrams, oral speech, music, and film. So it is now possible to find teaching in which students

plan their research activities and gather information using books, videos, and their own field notes, all with the help of Browser. . . , an electronic card catalog . . . that

Teams of students, rather than individuals, are more economical users of computers—and they learn quite well in groups.
(© Michael Zide)

continues

enables children to find materials via cross-classification (e.g., "Find me all examples of insect mimicry in the rain forest").
(Brown, Ash, et al., 1993, p. 198)

The systems-thinking program, described by Mandinach and Cline (1994), is an example of how groups of students can learn to understand complex systems and the many variables that go into a scientifically sound prediction. For example, a group of four or five students may try predicting the population of the world in the year 2050. They learn to do so using a number of different estimates for birth rates, based on fertility trends. Then they compute a number of different estimates for death rates, using different assumptions about medical improvements. They add in still more variables and watch as the computer automatically plots the trends over time on a graph. They see the effects of different assumptions on the trend lines. This program seems to have powerful effects on students' ability to think in terms of interacting variables—which is what systems thinking is all about.

There are also many computer writing programs and other computer-linked learning programs that are based on constructivist approaches, particularly the Vygotskian perspective. All use group processes to facilitate learning, and most can cite supporting evidence of beneficial changes in behavior (see Cognition and Technology Group at Vanderbilt, 1996).

The constructivist writing programs try to involve students in group writing projects, sometimes as collaborators, sometimes just as reviewers of and commentators on each other's writing. Early evidence is positive. Writing quality seems enhanced, and students seem to regard writing as a valuable communication tool, not drudgery (Scardamalia, Bereiter, & Lamon, 1994).

REFLECTIONS FOR YOUR OWN CLASSROOM

Computers (hardware) and their programs (software) are improving rapidly, so virtually anything specific we might want to write here would be out of date by the time you read it. That means that specific programs and software are also likely to be obsolete within a few years. Teachers need to keep abreast of new developments by consulting specialized books (e.g., Grabe & Grabe, 1998) and sharing information and needs among themselves and their consultants.

Our point, however, is that group games, simulations, and problem-solving activities that require cooperation strongly motivate students, improve attitudes about schooling, and usually are considered great fun. This is what every teacher hopes will happen in his or her class. The instructional materials result in gains in achievement as well. But measuring that achievement is not so simple. Gains in achievement may not always be evident on standardized achievement tests. What does a student learn from e-mail communication with an adult in England about a finding that dates the origin of *Homo sapiens* hundreds of thousands of years earlier than was previously thought? What is learned when a student participates in an electronic bulletin board devoted to discussion of the Hale-Bopp comet, and the student gives weekly reports to the class on scientific findings that week and where Hale-Bopp can be seen in the sky? These really are wonderful learning experiences for young people. Nevertheless, teachers may need to defend such learning experiences to parents and other educators because they are probably only tenuously related to improved test scores. Teachers using computers in group learning activities have to be prepared to convince others of the usefulness of the activities, independent of any direct relationship to achievement tests.

months and apply to members of ethnic groups with whom students have not been fellow group members or even classmates.

4. *Relationships with mainstreamed students* have been found to be more positive in three cooperative-learning studies that examined this kind of outcome.

5. Time-on-task tends to be higher, and academic standards are more often attained.

6. Cooperation, altruism, and ability to take another's perspective seem to improve.

Criticisms   The picture is not, however, without blemishes. Cooperative learning methods sometimes require more skill than teachers can muster.

> Teachers who are trained in managing cooperative groups are not necessarily successful in promoting cooperative exchanges among students; negative interactions among students are common. . . . Finally [it has been] found that frequent use of small groups that have low-quality interactions resulted in negative student outcomes.
> *(McCaslin & Good, 1996, p. 647)*

Without appropriate teacher care, students may

- give one another false knowledge.
- come to value pleasant group processes more than the truth or the right answer.
- come to depend too much on fellow students.
- fail to participate enough or, equally undesirable, "take over" a discussion.
- learn from fellow students that they are "incompetent."

These possibilities mean that teachers cannot lower their guard over what goes on while teaching with cooperative learning methods.

S U M M A R Y

1. The rationale for small-group teaching draws upon social learning theory, particularly the ideas of Vygotsky (Chapter 4) and Bandura (Chapter 6), and the concept of distributed cognition.

2. The most widely used small-group method is discussion. Its primary objectives are to promote critical thinking ability, skills of democratic participation, and other cognitive abilities and skills. It is typically effective for teaching problem-solving skills and fostering speaking ability, in low-consensus fields, and for teachers who can tolerate a low degree of structure. It is less efficient for communicating information.

3. Before a discussion begins, you must choose a topic. The things to think about are different for noncontroversial and controversial topics. Then you and your students need to establish some common ground—a shared experience with an article or book, television program, visit to a museum, or whatever—from which to work on the topic. It is also important to let students know the specific problem or question the discussion is to center around.

4. During the meeting, your role must be clearly defined. Too much teacher participation can limit the effectiveness of students' discussion. Too little can be frustrating for them. A teacher's knowing when and how to intervene—watching for digressions, pauses, errors of fact, and logical fallacies, and adjusting for them—is critical to the success of a discussion. Teaching students their roles—such as ways to evaluate the comments of other students and how to attack and defend positions—is also important.

5. After the meeting, you should make notes about unanticipated ideas that emerged and difficulties that arose. Keep a record for future years. You may also find it helpful to evaluate discussion, combining your thoughts with students' ratings and comments.

6. Discussion-group teaching is not without pitfalls, either intellectual or social-emotional. To avoid the intellectual pitfalls, try not to bias the discussion in ways that lower its educational value. Do not encourage students to yield to group pressure. Do not withhold crucial information when it is needed. And be sensitive to signals that a topic has been exhausted.

7. Nonparticipation is a primary symptom of the social and emotional pitfalls. Often participation is linked to students' status—their gender, social class, or ethnic group. Group size can also be a factor. Reinforcement techniques are effective for correcting uneven participation. Another problem here is hurting students' feelings. Do not use sarcasm or ridicule to correct students. Although learning to accept criticism is a key part of discussion, criticism should not come in the form of a personal attack by the teacher or other students.

8. Cooperative learning is another important method of small-group instruction. A variety of ingenious schemes, some involving the use of computers, have been developed and subjected to research on their effectiveness. In general, the effective methods use learning teams with group goals and individual accountability to motivate students' learning. Research reviews have found cooperative learning to be effective in improving achievement and self-esteem, combating status differences and prejudices among students, and increasing acceptance of mainstreamed students.

Individual Instruction

Overview

A RATIONALE FOR INDIVIDUAL INSTRUCTION

Promoting Independent Learning

Adapting to Individual Differences

WAYS OF PROMOTING INDEPENDENT LEARNING

Homework

Study Skills and Strategies Training

Independent Study

WAYS OF ADAPTING TO INDIVIDUAL DIFFERENCES

Ability Grouping

Forms of ability grouping

Effects on achievement

Effects on self-esteem

Mastery Learning

Rationale

The approach at work

Effectiveness of mastery learning

Criticisms of the mastery approach

Tutoring

Diagnosis

Remedial work

Positive reinforcement

POLICY, RESEARCH, AND PRACTICE
What Are the Benefits of Peer Tutoring?

Effectiveness of tutoring

Cost-effectiveness analysis of tutoring

USING COMPUTERS FOR LEARNING IN THE CLASSROOM

Programmed Computer-Assisted Instruction (CAI)

Advantages of CAI

Limitations of CAI

Evaluating instruction using CAI

Cost-effectiveness analysis of CAI

Further Uses of Computers in Today's Classrooms

Word processors in instruction

Databases and spreadsheets

Multimedia applications

Telecommunications: The Internet and the World Wide Web

APPLICATION
Making the Computer Work for You

The Teacher's Role with Computers

Summary

OVERVIEW

Are there times when students learn best working individually with a teacher? Are there times when they learn best working alone? If students differ from one another, shouldn't teaching try to fit each one's particular characteristics? If one of the primary objectives of teaching is that students be able to go on learning when formal schooling is over, don't teachers have to give students opportunities to be independent, to learn on their own? **Individual instruction** involves one-on-one teaching and tutoring, and independent study. It allows, but does not ensure, **individualized** (adaptive) **instruction.** That is, individual instruction—its goals, materials, subject matter, and methods—may or may not be adapted to the single student. Individualized instruction may be carried out with one student at a time or with groups of similar students at the same time. In this chapter, we talk about individual instruction, some of which is individualized.

We begin by looking at the rationale for individual instruction: promoting independent learning and adapting to individual differences. Then we go into ways of promoting independent learning: homework, study skills, and independent study. Next we turn to ways of adapting to individual differences: ability grouping; tutoring; mastery learning; and various uses for the computer in the classroom, including computer-assisted instruction.

A Rationale for Individual Instruction

The rationale for individual instruction has two main concerns: promoting independence in learning and adapting to individual differences.

Promoting Independent Learning

The first rationale for individual instruction developed out of the concern of educational theorists with the need for students to work and continue to learn after they have left school. "Learning how to learn" is regarded as a major objective in its own right. This ideal was expressed in 1873 by the British philosopher Herbert Spencer, who wrote that

In your high school years, did you do enough independent learning? Too much? Too little? Can you remember a good experience with such learning? What was it like?

> In education, the process of self-development should be encouraged to the fullest extent. Children should be led to make their own investigations, and to draw their own inferences. They should be *told* as little as possible and induced to *discover* as much as possible. Humanity has progressed solely by self-instruction; and . . . to achieve the best results, each mind must progress somewhat after the same fashion.
>
> *(Spencer, 1873, pp. 24–25)*

Adapting to Individual Differences

The whole body of knowledge about individual differences implies that instruction should often address those differences. In Part Two we examined in detail the ways in which students differ in their cognitive and linguistic abilities, in personality, and in their cultural background, including that associated with gender. We examined ways in which those differences were related to other important aspects of students' lives. But knowledge about student differences in all these ways emerged systematically only in the twentieth century, with the development of testing methods—first for cognitive abilities and eventually for all the other characteristics. The testing movement revealed large differences in cognitive ability and achievement among students, even within a single typical classroom. Studies showed that the most able students in the regular classroom were capable of learning both more and faster than the least able students.

Individual differences of this magnitude may complicate the teacher's task. What is more appropriate for some students may be less appropriate for others. This can be true of assignments, learning materials, explanations, topics, discussions, and many other ingredients of classroom work.

One major example: For less able students, highly **structured teaching** works better; for more able students, less structure tends to work better (Snow & Lohman, 1984). A high degree of structure means that the teacher controls

> the sequence of pacing, feedback, and reinforcement. . . . The instructional tasks are broken down into small units, and presentations are concrete and explicit. . . . [and instructional methods are] expository, direct instruction, teacher-controlled, or drill-and-practice. [A low degree of structure means that] learners must act more independently . . . must on their own contribute inferences and generalizations that are not explicitly provided, [and the teaching is] indirect, inductive, discovery-oriented or learner-controlled.
> *(Gustafsson & Undheim, 1996, p. 227)*

So one style of teaching is not best for all students.

Focus on individual differences obviously calls into question the lecture method. Even classroom discussion, in which students can participate in different ways, centers at any moment on a single process and a single topic—the same topic for all students regardless of their individual differences. It seems that any attempt to teach students in a group may miss the mark for some of them. So what individual differences imply for teaching is that students differ in how they should be taught—in the level, speed, degree of structure, and other dimensions of instruction. This means teachers should find ways to individualize instruction: to set each student to work on *tasks* appropriate to his or her particular abilities, prior achievement, and interests; to use *techniques and styles of learning* appropriate to the student's abilities, prior achievement, and interests; and to let each student move ahead at his or her own appropriate *rate*. But this is not an easy task when class size is large.

> Were you ever in a class that was inappropriate for you because you knew either too much or too little about the subject? Can you think of what might have been a good solution to the problem for you?

Ways of Promoting Independent Learning

Given this rationale, the obvious problem is how to address students' needs for independent learning. Over much of the twentieth century, many approaches have been developed and tried: homework, independent study, and contracting. Let us look at each of these methods.

Homework

Homework consists of work assigned to students by teachers to be done outside of school. By this definition, Cooper (1989a, 1989b) excluded in-school guided study, home study courses, and extracurricular activities.

Objections to homework have included the arguments that it can
- satiate and fatigue students
- reduce leisure-time activities

- bring about parental interference in how things are taught and parental pressure on students
- encourage cheating
- increase differences between high and low achievers.

These arguments may be justified some of the time. But the question on which many people want research-based answers is whether homework in general improves achievement.

Cooper (1994a, 1994b) synthesized 17 reports yielding 48 comparisons of student achievement with and without homework. Of these, about 70 percent documented positive effects. But grade level made a big difference. In high school, homework tended to raise an average student's achievement to a level exceeding that of 69 percent of the no-homework students. The advantage produced by homework was smaller in junior high school, and nonexistent in grades 4 to 6. Not surprisingly, the benefits of homework were less than those of supervised in-class study. And there were no subject-matter differences in homework effectiveness as long as the work was not too difficult and did not require skills that were new to students.

The desirable upper limit on amount of homework in junior high school is perhaps one to two hours per day, but it is a matter of judgment. The proper amount is probably greater at the senior high school level, but again judgment should determine how much is too much. Certainly, U.S. teachers and parents would not tolerate what occurs in Japan and South Korea: In Japan nearly 60 percent of junior high school students go to high-priced, intensive after-school "cram" schools for five hours three days a week; and South Korean students are even more driven (Bracey, 1996).

Even though homework does not improve achievement in elementary

Teacher and student alike expect learning to go on while working alone.

(© Peter Menzel)

schools, it can have good effects on study habits, especially if it is easy enough to allow students to feel successful at it. Cooper recommended a mixture of required and interesting voluntary homework at the junior high level.

Reasonable suggestions based on experience are that teachers should

- be sure that assignments are related to what is being taught. If not, benefits to achievement in the curriculum are unlikely.
- plan homework assignments carefully, discuss them with students, and revise them in the light of that discussion if necessary.
- be sure assignments often require non-routine work, but rather require thinking, planning, and problem solving appropriate to the students and the subject.
- hold students accountable for doing homework correctly, or it will be less effective; and "count" the completion of homework in grading. But teachers should not grade the homework itself; instead they should use homework primarily to diagnose individual students' problems with the subject matter. It is better to think of homework as a basis for formative evaluation rather than summative evaluation of achievement (see Chapter 13).
- comment on completed assignments orally or in writing.
- ask parents for their help in seeing to it that students do their homework, if necessary. (But, in Cooper's view, parents should not have a formal instructional role.)
- provide, with help of the school administration, a suitable place for students to do homework if those from very low-income families have none.

How does the value of homework relate to the differences among students' home environments? Can you see here a part of the explanation for income-level differences in achievement?

What about homework for students with learning disabilities (Bursuck, 1994)? These are students who "(a) scored within the normal range of intelligence but (b) showed significant underachievement in one or more areas of [subject matter] not primarily due to emotional disturbance, economic disadvantage, or lack of educational opportunity" (Cooper, 1994b, p. 474). For such students also, the small amount of evidence suggests, homework has positive effects. But here parental involvement in setting schedules and tutoring, and teachers' monitoring of assignments, become more important.

Study Skills and Strategies Training

Exactly how students spend their time doing homework depends on their study skills and strategies. Teachers can help students learn on their own by suggesting better study skills based on research findings. Experimentally tested learning strategies were brought together by Pressley et al. (1989; see also Chapter 7). Their list included only strategies that students could learn to use themselves without a lot of time or effort on the teacher's part.

1. **Summarization** consists of deleting trivial information and redundant information, substituting overall terms for lists of items, using an overall action term to cover a series of events, and selecting, or inventing, a topic sentence. In addition, students can use headings, subheadings, and paragraphs to guide their summaries. These pro-

cesses can be done first for paragraphs and then for longer passages of text. Spatial devices (outlines, "maps" with boxes) can help.

2. **Mental imagery** calls for students to imagine a picture of what the prose is saying. The image can be representational (literal images of the prose) or mnemonic (substitute images). This strategy includes the keyword method whereby a well-known word is selected to stand for an image useful in remembering, such as *tailor* for Taylor or *scales* for justice (see p. 267).

3. **Story-grammar training** gives students a structure (e.g., when? where? who?) for a story's beginning, then its beginning event, then the goal or problem, then the steps taken to solve the problem, then how the main character felt. Children taught this structure tended to remember much more than those not so taught about the stories they read (see pp. 268–269).

4. **Question generation** calls for formulating broad overall questions while reading. Then, of course, the learner tries to answer them. In doing so, the student finds out how well he or she understands the material and whether something needs to be done to improve comprehension. "In the process of generating questions, students need to search the text and combine information, and these processes help students comprehend what they read" (Rosenshine, Meister, & Chapman, 1996, p. 182). But students may need to be taught how to generate broad questions. To do this, teachers can give several "procedural prompts," demonstrating their use first. Some of these (see Rosenshine, Meister, & Chapman, 1996, pp. 186–187) are:

Signal words—who, what, when, where, and how
Generic question stems—How are . . . and . . . alike? What is the main idea of . . .?
Main idea—Identify the main idea of each paragraph.

Overall, the 26 studies reviewed by Rosenshine, Meister, and Chapman (1996) showed that the skill of question generation can be taught and that question generation improves reading comprehension substantially on standardized tests and even more so on tests made specifically for the study.

5. **Question answering,** or answering questions presented at the end of the reading matter, improves learning by adults but less so for children. Perhaps adults reread the material after finding themselves unable to answer a question, and children do not tend to do so. But when children are taught how to find such answers, they do improve in their ability to recall the information.

How do these study skills and strategies compare with those you have found useful in your own work as a student? Are there some good ones not mentioned here? What makes you think so?

These relatively easy-to-teach learning strategies can be supplemented by one that takes more time and effort to teach:

6. **Prior knowledge activation** means students use what they already know to help them comprehend and remember new material. When children have been trained in relating text material to their own knowledge and experience, they remember more of the story than children not given such training. They are also better able to answer questions requiring inferences from what they have read. But when text material contradicted their prior knowledge, they tend to misremember the text passages.

Thus we have presented study strategies that have been effective with students of various ages (Wade et al., 1990; Pressley et al., 1989). Helping students acquire these broad, general strategies is likely to improve student achievement in all grades from third on up.

Independent Study

Teachers can help students become independent learners, to take more responsibility for their own education, through programs of **independent study.** Such independent work has been done throughout the centuries by mature scholars and scientists, journalists, and artists. Independent study puts teacher and student in a one-to-one relationship.

In elementary and secondary schools, promoting independence is a primary objective of individual instruction. Among the methods teachers use for this purpose are giving a student an assignment that lasts over several days or weeks and freeing him or her from attending formal classes during that period. In this case the students should

- consider the work worthwhile and personally significant.
- be able to organize themselves to do the work.
- be able to use human and material resources.
- succeed in doing a better job than they were originally capable of.

Contracting is one method of organizing a student's work for independent study. Together, the teacher and the student write a contract that specifies (1) what is to be learned, (2) the way in which the student is to demonstrate achievement, (3) the resources the student should use, (4) the steps or tasks to be carried out, (5) the intermediate points at which progress is to be judged, and (6) a schedule. Contracting in elementary school has been effective in improving academic productivity, performance accuracy, study skills, school attendance, and social behavior (Murphy, 1988). Many students have also developed greater motivation for schooling when they have had a voice in determining their own course of study (see Chapter 8).

Degree of independence can vary in independent study. The teacher can supervise and guide students fairly closely, or the teacher and students can plan the work cooperatively, with students receiving less supervision and feedback. Or students can work almost entirely on their own, identifying and selecting problems, planning activities, and turning in finished products.

The right degree of independence depends, of course, on the student's maturity and on selecting objectives that are suitable for the student. Even children in the earliest grades should experience independent study at some level. And even the most mature students should at times learn from lectures, discussions, tutoring, and other nonindependent methods. That is, independent study ought to be mixed into school activities at all stages of education. Under the labels "the integrated day" and "open education," many features of independent study have been introduced in the primary grades.

It is important, however, to realize that not every student thrives under independent study. How can teachers tell the level of independent study a student will profit from? One way is to estimate how well the student can perform these four tasks:

- Identify the topic or project for independent study
- Outline what is to be done
- Identify resources to be used
- Set deadlines

In a conference with the student, the teacher can probe his or her ability to formulate an independent study project. This can be done informally, or a rating scheme like the one shown in Figure 11.1 can be used. Notice that under each of the four tasks of independent study—identifying a topic, outlining a project, identifying resources, and setting deadlines—there are three levels of independence:

- *Guided study,* where students have little ability to direct their own work or to be self-disciplined. The teacher needs to spend considerable time helping them.
- *Cooperative planning,* where students can direct their own activities but need help during the project in monitoring progress.
- *Individual pursuit,* where students can already define topics, make decisions, locate resources, and hold to deadlines. They need the teacher only to be a facilitator, critic, audience, guide, and colleague. The teacher's challenge is to help students move from guided study to cooperative planning, and from cooperative planning to individual pursuit.

Independent study usually requires more resources than are needed in the regular classroom. Teachers may have to set up **resource centers** for science, mathematics, social studies, art, and so forth. Ideally this might mean breaking down a wall or building a small alcove in the classroom. But you may be able to get by with less drastic measures. You could band together with other teachers, pooling your instructional re-

FIGURE 11.1

A system for estimating students' level of independence
Adapted from Ward (1973).
Note: Numbers under names are overall estimates of students' level of independence. 3 = high; 2 = medium; 1 = low.

Overall estimate of level of independence for students	Area of Independent Study											
	Identifying a study topic			Outlining what is to be done			Identifying resources			Setting deadlines		
	Guided Study	Cooperative Planning	Individual Pursuit	Guided Study	Cooperative Planning	Individual Pursuit	Guided Study	Cooperative Planning	Individual Pursuit	Guided Study	Cooperative Planning	Individual Pursuit
Alexander S. 2		X			X		X					X
Manuel B. 3			X			X		X				X

sources and creating resource centers in closets, hallways, storerooms, and the backs of classrooms. A resource center can contain instructional materials, books, audio- and videotapes, reference works, films and filmstrips, workbooks, and lists of community volunteers who are willing to work with students on a given project.

Although many teachers and students enjoy and benefit from contracting for independent study, some do not. As is true of all techniques for teaching and learning, independent study should be comfortable and make sense for both teachers and students. Sometimes a method simply takes getting used to. Give yourself a few weeks or even months to get a program running smoothly. Some surprisingly good things can happen once these systems have been functioning for a while.

Ways of Adapting to Individual Differences

Students differ not only in relatively stable characteristics (scholastic abilities, interests), but momentarily in the degree to which they understand an explanation, are ready to move on to another problem or topic, or need more practice on a particular concept or skill. So teachers often feel the need to custom-tailor teaching to both stable and momentary individual differences, while working with numbers of students. Meeting that need has always been a source of tension for teachers. In this section we present several approaches to help you meet the challenges of individualizing and adapting teaching to individual differences. They are ability grouping, tutoring, mastery learning, and computer-assisted instruction.

Ability Grouping

An intermediate step toward adapting to individual differences is **ability grouping,** or **homogeneous grouping,** which puts students together with others of about the same ability or level of achievement. The idea behind the grouping is that teaching has better effects when it is done with students of similar ability.

Forms of Ability Grouping   Grouping may take one or more of five forms (Kulik, 1993):

1. *Between-class grouping,* in which students of different levels of ability are put into separate classes in different rooms.

2. *Cross-grade grouping,* in which children from different grades but similar achievement levels are put into the same class in their own classroom.

3. *Within-class grouping,* in which students of differing ability in a single classroom are put into separate ability groups.

4. *Accelerated classes,* in which students of high ability are taught separately so as to allow them to move ahead more rapidly through the curriculum and grades.

5. *Enrichment classes,* in which high-ability students receive a curriculum that goes into greater depth and more varied content.

Despite much research and repeated meta-analyses (Kulik, 1992; Slavin, 1990b), ability grouping remains controversial. The many studies of the effects of ability grouping have led to far from unanimous conclusions. There are conflicting data on the effects of grouping on achievement, self-concept, attitudes toward others, and behavior (Gustafsson & Undheim, 1996; Stipek, 1996). It is clear, however, that whatever the ability grouping method used, individual differences *within* each group continue to be substantial.

Effects on Achievement   These effects depend on what the teacher does with the high- and low-ability groups. If the teacher enriches or accelerates the curriculum and instruction of the high-ability students, they benefit accordingly. Meanwhile there are no effects, good or bad, on the achievement of average- or low-ability students. These results remain the same for both within- and between-class grouping. These effects may be due to a tendency for teachers of high-ability groups to favor them with better content and instruction, higher expectations, and more favorable teacher-student interactions (Oakes, 1985).

Ability grouping often leads to the placement of economically disadvantaged and culturally different (i.e., less literate in English) students into low-ability groups, especially if they are less literate in English. These groups tend to get lower-quality instruction, provided by less experienced and less well-trained teachers, who have higher rates of turnover and larger classes (Portes, 1996). Such students might well achieve better in heterogeneous groupings. So it becomes hard to tell whether it is the grouping itself or these correlated factors that causes the benefits of grouping for high-ability groups.

Effects on Self-Esteem   These effects are also controversial. What Marsh et al. (1995) call the **big-fish-little-pond effect** (BFLPE) may operate. That is, students in high-ability groups tend toward lower self-esteem, while students in low-ability groups tend toward higher self-esteem. The BFLPE, though, changes only self-concept related to the basis for the grouping. So being put into an academically-gifted group lowers *academic* self-concept but not self-concept concerning physical characteristics, appearance, or relations with fellow students and parents. For within-class grouping, the BFLPE probably depends on how much the teacher calls attention to the grouping and the differences between the groups (Stipek, 1996). But Kulik (1993) concluded that these effects on self-esteem are small; high-ability students do not become smug, and lower-ability students show no big drop in self-esteem. But individual students vary in how much they react to being homogeneously grouped. So it is necessary to be vigilant if ability grouping occurs.

Mastery Learning

Two influential movements in individualized teaching are Benjamin Bloom's (1968) **mastery learning** and Fred Keller's (1968) personalized system of instruction (PSI). Although the two plans were derived from

> Ability grouping has been regarded as putting low-ability students at a disadvantage while improving the learning of high-ability students. What should be done about the ethical dilemma here?

different theoretical perspectives, they are alike in many ways. But because Keller's PSI is aimed at the college level and requires teaching assistants, we do not discuss it here.

Rationale Mastery learning (based on Carroll, 1963) defines some major factors in learning in terms of time. *Student aptitude* is defined as the amount of time ordinarily required by a student for learning in some domain, say mathematics or science, other things being equal. *Student motivation* is defined as the amount of time a student is willing to spend on learning, other things being equal. *Task difficulty* is defined as the amount of time needed to learn a particular task, other things being equal. Other factors are *instructional quality* and *time allowed for learning.*

Bloom's major insight was that, if students do not master a unit of the curriculum on their first attempt, they should be given additional time and a variety of instructional aids until they do master it. He claimed that, using this program, between 80 and 90 percent of students can achieve at the A or B levels otherwise achieved by less than half the students.

The Approach at Work The mastery approach has been used primarily in grades 1 through 12. It is based on three fundamental conditions: that initial instruction be given, that instruction be mastery-oriented, and that help be available when needed.

- *Initial instruction.* Initial instruction is group-based, whole-class, more or less conventional classroom teaching.
- *Mastery orientation.* Until students demonstrate mastery of a particular area of instruction, they do not go on to new material. There is no penalty for failure. Parallel forms of short tests must be designed in advance. Then, after a first failure and a new effort at studying, students are tested again. Students continue the cycle of studying and testing until the criterion for acceptable work—usually 80 or 90 percent correct responses—has been reached.
- *Supplementary help as necessary.* The classroom teacher or aide provides remedial instruction as needed—helping with problems, talking about the subject matter, exploring the implications of particular points, going over missed items, and of course providing encouragement and support. This attention is usually individual (one-on-one) instruction.

Effectiveness of Mastery Learning Meta-analyses of research have shown that mastery learning improves achievement substantially, raising average achievement from the 50th percentile rank to about the 65th (e.g., Guskey & Pigott, 1988; Slavin, 1987b). But the effectiveness of the mastery approach depended on the duration of the experiment and the kind of achievement test used (i.e., whether it was made by the experimenter or was a standardized, commercially available test). Slavin (1987b) found that longer-term experiments (lasting from four weeks to a full school year) yielded much lower estimates of effectiveness than did briefer ones. (He actually considered briefer experiments—those shorter than four weeks—irrelevant to the practical value of mastery learning.) He also found, as did others (Kulik, Kulik, & Bangert-Drowns, 1990a), that standardized achievement tests showed less effectiveness for the approach than did experimenter-made tests. Perhaps the latter tests emphasize the material in the mastery-approach curriculum more than those in the control (conventionally taught) curriculum. But, "even when the curriculum is held constant, it seems likely that the mastery-learning procedures hold teachers more narrowly to the mastery objectives, whereas control teachers may be teaching material that is useful or important but is not assessed on the final test" (Slavin, 1990b, p. 301).

Slavin's meta-analysis focused exclusively on cognitive achievement, in precollege-level experiments. But it may not be inappropriate to look also at affective outcomes and college-level experiments (Kulik, Kulik, & Bangert-Drowns, 1990). Those concluded that mastery learning improves achievement fairly substantially at the college level, and improves attitudes toward the subject matter as well. Moreover, the mastery-learning approach increased the amount of time students spent on a course (a "good" outcome) but decreased the percentages of college students who completed the course (a "bad" outcome).

Bloom (1968) claimed that one particular benefit of the mastery approach is motivational. Once students realize they can achieve at the same level as anyone else in class, even if it takes them more time, they are motivated by their successful experiences.

Criticisms of the Mastery Approach   Mastery learning is said (Mueller, 1976; Cox & Dunn, 1979) to have the faults that it

- takes much of the responsibility for learning away from students, who may end up not knowing how to learn independently.
- requires nonfixed-time instructional units or greatly liberalized time allocations.
- makes faster learners "wait around" while slower learners catch up, unless the faster learners are motivated to spend their time achieving objectives beyond the prespecified ones. (This is also called the "Robin Hood effect," because Robin Hood robbed from the rich to give to the poor.)
- commits a major part of instructional resources—corrective effort, teaching aides, peer tutoring, and alternative learning materials—to slower students.
- assumes that everything in an instructional unit must be learned equally well by almost all students. This assumption is hard to defend except for learning basic skills and hierarchical subjects (such as mathematics).

Accordingly, Mueller (1976) claimed that the approach is most useful in the elementary grades with basic skills, and for slow learners at all levels, and that it is less effective in maximizing learning for fast learners, especially in subject areas where there are fewer prespecifiable objectives, and in the higher grades.

Where is the teacher in the mastery approach? Besides preparing or selecting reading assignments and unit quizzes and supervising the course, does the teacher bow out? For Bloom, "feedback and correctives" were to be provided by the teacher. But little research has been done on alternative ways of carrying out these parts of the approach. The added paperwork needed for grading the frequent quizzes used in the approach calls for teachers' commitment to that over the explaining, discussing, and demonstrating they might value more. "It is time to welcome the teacher back into the mastery-learning classroom, not just as a paper-pusher or student-tutor or sitter, but as an active creator of learning" (Martinez & Martinez, 1988, p. 29). In addition, teacher differences of some unidentified kinds have influenced the effectiveness of mastery-learning approaches. Future research should unmask these factors.

Discussion of mastery learning would not be complete without recognition of the kinds of questions raised by Jaynes (1975) about PSI, since they also apply to mastery learning:

> I can see it in chemistry, mathematics, cooking, physics, engineering, harmony, law, auto repairing. But what of the subject where there is a huge variety of ways of teaching, of materials to be taught . . . ? Literature, history, philosophy—these subjects, if they are anything, are intercommunications between human beings. No one should learn [them] by rote. . . . I object to the too arrogant standardization that it imposes upon the mind. . . . What the Keller Method in complex subjects does is to grind down the individual student's particular style of going over things. It rebukes his wish to insert his own importances. (p. 631)

> Overall, how do you regard the mastery-learning approach now that you have read about it? Why would you be willing or unwilling to try it?

Tutoring

Tutoring can be used to help students at any age level. In most programs, the tutors have been nonprofessional teachers. They may be students the same age as, or just a few years older than, those being tutored. Or they may be adults with no special training in education beyond that received as part of the tutoring program. At times the purpose of the tutoring is as much or more to help the tutor as it is to help the tutee. That is, tutoring is often used to increase the tutor's self-esteem and competence as much as to help the tutee. Several different tutor-tutee combinations—older student–younger student, teacher–student, adult teacher's aide–student, more competent age mate–less competent age mate—have been tried. There appear to be no inherently bad combinations.

Diagnosis Diagnosis is aimed at finding out as specifically as possible what is blocking a tutee's progress. It can take the form of casual conversation, in which the tutee tries to describe his or her problem. Or the tutor can ask the tutee to do a sample of work—for example, read aloud or try to solve an arithmetic problem—so that the tutor can observe where the tutee seems to be going wrong. Or the tutor can give a diagnostic test—one that reveals objectively what kinds of errors the tutee is making and where help is needed. The tutor can also consult the tutee's regular teacher for information on the nature of the problem, suggestions on how it can be solved, and materials with which to work.

Remedial Work Once a tutor has formed some ideas about the causes of a student's problems, he or she gives the tutee opportunities to prac-

The tutor should diagnose and then remedy while providing encouragement.

(© Elizabeth Crews)

tice correctly the skills found to be deficient. The tutor asks questions, waits for answers, and praises correct responses or furnishes them if it is appropriate to do so. A correct response cues the tutor to stay at the same level or skill for additional practice or, if evidence of learning is already adequate, to go on to the next skill or problem. An incorrect response often means that the tutor should give the right answer (not a cue or a prompt). It also means that the tutor needs to vary the instruction, offering the explanation in new words, with new examples. Then the tutor repeats the question, problem, or practice exercise.

Positive Reinforcement   Most tutors should furnish lots of positive reinforcement. Many tutees have a history of what they perceive as failure, and schooling may have become a bad experience. For the tutee, the relationship to a respected and valued tutor can give the learning situation a saving warmth. Here are some guidelines to remember:

- Compare the student's performance only with his or her own past performance.
- Report progress, however slight by other standards, in positive, encouraging terms.
- Keep tutoring sessions short enough so that they do not tire out or bore the tutee.
- Use a style that is appropriate to your age and status and to the tutee's. If you tutor a child, make a game of it and season the game with comfortable humor.
- Do not encourage a tutee by saying that a task is easy. In fact, we recommend that you say the task is fairly difficult. If the tutee succeeds, the reward is greater; and if the tutee fails, the tutor has salvaged the student's self-esteem (see attribution theory in Chapter 8).

POLICY, RESEARCH, AND PRACTICE

What Are the Benefits of Peer Tutoring?

Annis (1983) studied the effects of peer tutoring on both tutors and tutees, randomly assigning 120 college women to five groups. The read-only group read material for a test. The read-to-teach group read material in preparation for tutoring but did not actually teach it. The read-and-teach group read material in preparation for teaching it, then actually taught a tutee. The taught-only group was taught the material by a tutor. The read-and-taught group read the material, then was taught it by a tutor.

The material consisted of a three-page article on the Lisbon earthquake of 1755, introduced into a college course in world history. A posttest a week later was made up of 48 multiple-choice and essay questions evenly divided over the six main levels of the cognitive taxonomy (see Chapter 2).

On the subtests of comprehension and evaluation, the five groups did not differ more than chance might allow. But on the subtests of knowledge, application, analysis, and synthesis the differences were statistically significant. On these subtests, the taught-only students scored lower than those in the read-to-teach and read-and-teach groups; in that case the tutor received the greater advantage. Moreover, the benefits of teaching resulted from the preparation stage of teaching in itself. Students in the read-to-teach group scored higher than the read-only students in both the content-specific and more general achievement measured by the application and analysis subtests. And the read-and-teach students scored higher than the read-to-teach students, so that the actual teaching had value beyond that of preparing to teach. "*Peer tutoring thus appears to be a potentially powerful technique for increasing all levels of student learning*" (Annis, 1983, p. 46; italics added).

Effectiveness of Tutoring   Overall, the research on tutoring shows positive results for achievement. A set of five meta-analyses of the effectiveness of students' tutoring other, less mature students, consistently demonstrated improvements in achievement (Lipsey & Wilson, 1993). The average of the averages in these compilations showed that being tutored typically raised average achievement in elementary and secondary school classrooms and special education classes (where special education students tutored other special education students) from about the 50th percentile rank to about the 69th. Furthermore,

tutoring effects were larger in [a] more structured programs, . . . [b] in tutoring programs of shorter duration, . . . [c] when lower level skills were taught and tested in examinations, . . . [d] when mathe-

matics rather than reading was the subject of the tutoring . . . [and e]
on locally developed tests [rather than] on nationally standardized
tests.

(Cohen, Kulik, & Kulik, 1982, p. 243)

Liking for the subject matter is almost always improved by tutoring,
though the effect is small. Effects on self-concept were positive in seven
of nine studies of this effect, but again the effect was small.

What about effects on the tutors? In 33 of 38 studies, tutors did better (by about 13 percentile ranks) than nontutors on examinations in
the subject taught. The effect on tutor achievement tended to be higher
for mathematics tutors than for reading tutors. In 12 of 16 studies, the
tutors' self-concept improved more than that of nontutors. And in four
out of five studies, attitude toward the subject matter was more favorable for tutoring students than for students who had not been tutored.

Cost-Effectiveness Analysis of Tutoring   The desirability of any method
of improving educational results depends not only on its effectiveness
but also on its costs. For this reason, educators have studied the cost-
effectiveness of various educational changes. One such analysis (Levin,
Glass, & Meister, 1984) compared the cost-effectiveness of four ways of
improving mathematics and reading achievement of elementary school
children: (a) reducing class size, (b) increasing the length of the school
day, (c) computer-assisted instruction, and (d) peer and adult tutoring. The most cost-effective approach was peer (not adult) tutoring, followed in turn by computer-assisted instruction, reducing class size, and
lengthening the school day. The fact that the elementary school student
tutors were assumed to cost nothing was not responsible for this result.
Rather, it was the greater effectiveness of the tutoring.

Using Computers for Learning in the Classroom

Technology has a long history of enthusiasm followed by disuse in education. Radio, movies, and television, including videocassette recorders (VCRs), have all been predicted to improve radically what goes on in
schools. Most of them have not succeeded. But the computer, after more
than a generation of research and development, seems to be gaining ever
wider use, more so than any of the previous technologies.

Computers have surged into all areas of present-day life—business,
industry, agriculture, science, engineering, medicine, entertainment, *and*
education. In education, use of computers began in the late 1950s with
the now-primitive teaching machines designed for **programmed instruction.** By 1997, it was estimated that 98 percent of all U.S. public
schools had computers, and 28 percent had over 50 computers in their
buildings. On average, there was one computer for every 8.7 students in
high school and one for every 11.8 students in elementary school (Coley
et al., 1997). Today computers have become so user-friendly that learning how to use one is possible even for preschoolers and kindergartners.

Since tutoring seems
to help tutors as well
as tutees, would you
be willing to try it
in your work as a
teacher? What issues
do you think about
as you decide?

The *cost* in cost-
effectiveness analysis
is usually measured
in terms of dollars.
What other kinds of
cost can you think of?

Programmed Computer-Assisted Instruction (CAI)

The simplest important use of computers for instruction is at the programmed-instruction level. Here **computer-assisted instruction** (CAI) presents and corrects a series of content-question-feedback steps. Each step presents three things:

a. *Content* to be read by the student, but only a small amount, ranging from a single line to perhaps a whole page

b. *A question* or problem to be answered by the student

c. *Immediate feedback* to the student as to whether the answer is correct

Each a-b-c combination makes up *one step* in the program.

Each step is followed by another that builds on its predecessors. The steps are arranged in a sequence that leads students from the entering level of knowledge and understanding to the full knowledge, understanding, and skill in the subject matter.

Some instructional programmers hold that a program should be written so that most students—say, 90 percent—can respond correctly to most frames—say, 90 percent. In this way most students experience mostly positive reinforcement as they proceed through the program. The positive reinforcement should also strengthen motivation to learn with the program.

Advantages of CAI   CAI has certain advantages:

1. *Activity.* It makes each student active; the student must participate in the teaching-learning process.

2. *Individualized pace.* It allows each student to learn at his or her own pace.

3. *Individualized treatment.* It makes individualized treatment of students easier because it reviews each student's most recent response and decides instantly whether the student needs more practice at that level or can move ahead to the next.

4. *Subject-matter flexibility.* It can teach any subject—presumably any high-consensus subject—that can be programmed, or broken down into successive frames that progress through the subject matter from lower to higher levels of achievement.

5. *Summarizable responses.* It statistically summarizes information about an individual's and a group's responses.

6. *Response-speed information.* It obtains information about the speed of students' responses.

7. *Stimulus-form adaptability.* It can present many kinds of stimuli—both verbal and nonverbal (e.g., mathematical equations, maps)—both visual and auditory (e.g., musical or spoken), both still pictures (e.g., paintings) and motion pictures, and both black-and-white and color images.

8. *Touch responding.* It can allow students to respond simply by touching the computer screen to identify the right answer (e.g., the isosceles triangle or the Rococo statue).

Computer-assisted instruction continues to be the basis of a vigorous research and development movement.
(© Elizabeth Crews)

9. *Widespread availability.* Millions of individuals have CAI available to them at home and in school.

Limitations of CAI   Early in the history of CAI, Suppes (1966) identified three levels: drill-and-practice, tutoring, and dialogue. The discussion above describes drill-and-practice. Only with much effort can CAI be made capable of tutoring, which requires branching from the main program to take account of a student's response history. But, as with other aspects of CAI, this limitation is disappearing—and *intelligent tutors* may be on the way. Intelligent tutoring systems (ITS) are in the forefront of current research on CAI. These systems "attempt to mimic the capabilities of human tutors . . . [in] the ability to meaningfully analyze each student's responses (not just determine whether they are correct by matching predefined answers) and the ability to interact with the student—give advice when a mistake is made and answer students' questions" (Rosenberg, 1987, p. 7). The research on ITSs ultimately aims at doing everything human tutors would do, including the social and emotional aspects of it. The review by Holt and Wood (1990) pointed to the contributions by computer scientists, psychologists, and educators. Designing these systems has proved more difficult than was expected, but business and military organizations have some in operation, and eventually intelligent tutoring systems may become widespread in education (Derry & Lesgold, 1996).

As for the dialogue level, CAI cannot yet respond adequately to students' spoken language or written sentences, paragraphs, or essays. That is, it cannot engage in much dialogue. But that is changing as well. New writing programs conduct dialogues with students learning to write essays (Zellermayer et al., 1991). Dialogue is also uniquely suited to teachers' needs. It is the basis for the Higher-Order Thinking Skills program (H.O.T.S.) used in several hundred schools, with apparent success. Teachers using this program learn to engage students working on CAI and educational games in instructional dialogues. It lets the computer create a microworld in which to make decisions, and it reserves for teachers the capability to ask the right question at the right time of a particular student (Pogrow, 1996).

Evaluating Instruction Using CAI   How effective is computer-assisted instruction? For achievement, the results of 12 meta-analyses of hundreds of studies comparing CAI with non-CAI instruction were brought together by Lipsey and Wilson (1993). All 12 showed positive average effects of CAI on achievement. More specifically, the average achievement of the CAI students, measured from the 50th percentile rank for the non-CAI group, ranged from the 60th to the 85th percentile rank with an average at the 64th percentile rank. More recent meta-analyses (Fletcher-Flinn & Gravatt, 1995; Liao, 1992) have supported this average improvement. Roughly the same results appeared for elementary and secondary school students, college students, and students with retardation and learning disabilities.

Does the improvement in achievement result from CAI method itself, or does it result from "better-quality instruction" contained in the CAI material (Fletcher-Flinn & Gravatt, 1995)? Further research is necessary to hold quality of instruction constant between CAI and non-CAI students to resolve this question.

Students' attitudes toward their classes improved to about the 61st percentile with CAI (Kulik, 1994). Students' attitudes toward computers were more favorable than those of about 63 percent of students who learned without computers. So experience in using CAI made students like computers more. Students' attitudes toward the subject matter were unchanged.

Because the studies reviewed in these meta-analyses ranged from elementary and secondary school to college and adult levels, over many uses of computers and over many subject matters, these results justify broad generalizations. They indicate that the use of computers in instruction tends to have moderately favorable effects on achievement and attitudes.

Cost-Effectiveness Analysis of CAI   These gains may not come at low cost, however, either financially or organizationally—that is, in terms of changes in established ways of running schools and classrooms. As noted above, the **cost-effectiveness** of computer-assisted instruction was lower (improved achievement less per dollar spent) than that of peer tutoring but higher than extending the school day or reducing class size. And peer tutoring proved more cost-effective not, as we noted above, because it was less expensive but because it was much more effective in improving achievement (Levin, Glass, & Meister, 1984). So it was no surprise when Lewis, et al. (1990) found that a computer-assisted instructional program yielded higher gains per unit of cost than a tutor-based program in teaching basic reading to adults.

The findings of these studies on the relative cost-effectiveness of CAI are merely suggestive in the absence of many additional studies. But they indicate some of the complexities facing the computer revolution in education or any other innovation in ways of teaching. The revolution is moving more slowly than was predicted in the 1960s. Some writers (e.g., Noble, 1996) question the whole enterprise. In the meantime, the role of the human teacher continues to predominate in the ways we describe throughout this book.

Nonetheless, any inspection of high-quality programs is likely to impress teachers and parents with the positive value of CAI. The material reflects careful analysis of objectives, content, and instructional activity and is presented in a colorful, attention- and activity-inducing style.

Further Uses of Computers in Today's Classrooms

A category of computer applications that goes beyond the tutorial role of CAI includes word processing software, databases, spreadsheets, telecommunications—the Internet and World Wide Web—and multimedia software such as CD-ROM. With these tools, students and their teachers engage in a host of activities and gain access to vast amounts of information and resources.

Word Processors in Instruction With word processing programs, students can do the following basic functions: input text, store and retrieve, edit, format, insert graphics, check spelling, and print. Word processing programs are available for students from the primary grade level through secondary level. Software especially designed for students in the primary grades can include a default to a large-size font and print-out on the kind of paper used in the primary grades. Word processors change the conditions of writing, making it easier and faster to manipulate text (edit) and compose and create documents such as reports, stories, and letters. The writing process (Graves, 1983), which includes the stages of planning, drafting, editing and revising, and publishing, especially lends itself to instruction with word processing software.

Databases and Spreadsheets With electronic tools, users can easily store, retrieve, and manipulate abundant amounts of data. As a way of thinking about the power of computing, recall (from Chapter 7 on cognitive processes) that the metaphor for the description of the theory of information processing is that of the computer's memory, storage, and retrieval system. With computerized database applications, students can use dictionaries, thesauruses, encyclopedias, and libraries of all kinds: print and media (film, video, art). With databases, students use the skills needed for doing research: reading, following directions, gathering and categorizing data for their own purposes, taking notes, summarizing, and posing questions. Databases are widely available as software for computers and by telecommunications through the Internet and the World Wide Web, discussed below.

Like databases, spreadsheets provide a convenient way to store and manipulate data, particularly numerical data. While spreadsheets are used widely in business, they also have multiple uses in education. Users can categorize data, perform calculations, and display the results in graphic formats, such as charts or tables. For example, if you were teaching a history lesson and wanted to display and compare migration and demographic patterns during several periods, a spreadsheet would give you a method for demonstrating and asking questions about trends. Spreadsheets are often used by teachers for administrative tasks of keeping student scores and performing complex weighting formulas for the assignment of grades. Students learn to use and interpret information in tabular formats as charts and tables—a necessary skill for reading newspapers and magazines as well as academic materials such as reports, articles, and textbooks.

Multimedia Applications   With multimedia applications, students can work with sound (audio), images (art, photos, and graphics), *and* text. Many of the applications described above—CAI, word processing programs, databases—can be delivered with multimedia systems. One example of a multimedia CAI program is *The Journey Inside,* developed and produced by Intel Corporation to provide instruction on what computers are made of and how they function. Other multimedia applications in classrooms are electronic books, simulations, and games available on CD-ROM.

Electronic or "talking books" provide students opportunities to interact with text, make predictions, select and study vocabulary, and hear and study pronunciation. Electronic "talking books" multimedia are a relatively new tool, which require evaluation and research regarding its efficacy for teaching literacy. Teachers should carefully and critically evaluate literacy software considering their own instructional objectives as well as the quality of electronic products. With simulations and games developed by experts in many fields, students can use computers to learn about other historical periods, other cultures, other spheres of human activity—whether scientific, aesthetic, political, or economic. Students can face the dilemmas of peasants in the France of Louis XIV, the puzzles of scientists testing hypotheses about the nature of combustion, the problem of an art critic judging a painting.

Another form of multimedia is hypermedia, a nonlinear form of multimedia. A key distinction between hypermedia and other forms of multimedia is that hypermedia applications give the user considerable freedom to choose and sequence the possible links. Hypermedia is often referred to as an authoring tool because students, in essence, become programmers or developers of their own work. A popular form of hypermedia is *HyperStudio* (Roger Wagner Publishing, Inc.). As a departure from traditional learning materials, hypermedia requires that students learn both basic skills and higher-order thinking skills.

Telecommunications: The Internet and the World Wide Web   Telecommunications refers to a powerful network linking individuals and groups with each other, with information, and with services. The Internet is an international network or community of computers that share resources and transfer information. Today, most users gain access through "server" computers and a modem—equipment that allows signals from your computer to be sent to another computer over a link, most commonly a telephone line. Users can get onto the Internet by using browsers such as Netscape Navigator or Microsoft Internet Explorer. Search engines on the Internet such as Yahoo!, Lycos, or Webcrawler make it possible for users to locate information and services. Teachers need to be linked to the Internet to get the information they need about such resources.

Direct access to people through electronic mail, called e-mail, is one of the most popular and powerful uses of technology. This communication tool instantaneously puts people in touch with other people regardless of geographic location. Thus, a wide range of interactions between individuals—teachers and students, students and students—now expands the ways education can be extended and supported.

The World Wide Web is a special type of Internet tool, permitting links of information and resources by a special hypertext or hypermedia. The Web is rapidly evolving and growing. Access to Web sites and Web "home pages" of virtually any institution, organization, and many individuals is changing the information and communications landscape. For example, teachers and students can go to the Library of Congress site by entering the Internet address or URL (Uniform Resource Locater) (www.loc.gov). For another example, teachers and students can go into the popular government education site AskERIC by entering the URL (www.ericsp.org). A useful source of information on current research on learning with technology has been provided by Grabe and Grabe (1998).

APPLICATION

Making the Computer Work for You

The more knowledgeable you are about the computer yourself, the easier it will be to teach your students about its uses and to instill enthusiasm for its possibilities. With this in mind, try out a miniresearch project on the Internet. Choose a topic of particular interest from this chapter or another of the chapters in this Part. Through your own, a friend's, or your university's access to the 'Net, do a search for your topic and list how many sources you can find for information about it. What can you learn about your topic in this manner? Do you see ways in which it might lead to further avenues or subtopics? If possible, start an e-mail conversation with someone who is making information on the topic available. How does the interaction with this person augment or modify the information you have previously gained? Is there some specific knowledge (either from your own prior knowledge of the topic or from something you have just learned by doing this research) that you can in turn share with others? In this way, you might start a dialogue. Finally, summarize the steps you went through in a brief report for your own subsequent use in the classroom.

The Teacher's Role with Computers

The rapidly growing use of CAI leads to an important and intriguing question: Where do teachers fit into all this?

In the early years of the computer revolution, some educators expected CAI to take over the teacher's role. "There won't be schools in the future. I think the computer will blow up the school. That is, the school defined as something where there are classes, teachers running exams, people structured in groups by age—all of that" (Papert, 1984).

That expectation has since vanished. The human teacher cannot be replaced—at least not in elementary or secondary schools or colleges and universities. In business, industrial, and military training programs, however, the picture differs. In those settings, a substantial amount of teaching and learning does go on without much involvement of teachers. The reasons are that (1) those programs are for *training* (as against education) in that they generally have highly specific and practical objectives, primarily concerning tools and techniques that apply to the needs of specific organizations; and (2) learners in such organizations are typically adults who do not need as much of the kind of assistance and facilitation that teachers can provide.

The teacher using computers in the classroom will need to

1. *Become knowledgeable about computers.* Here *knowledgeable* means (a) knowing how to do word processing, get into databases, use the World Wide Web, send and receive e-mail, and bring up and use CDs; and (b) having acquired some information about the ever-increasing storehouse of software (programs) and hardware (computers and their accessories) that may have value for achieving your educational objectives. Obviously, you pass this knowledge along to your students at the level they are capable of handling.

2. *Facilitate students' use of the technology* by helping them to select research topics, guiding their search for information, helping them learn the use of various information-management tools, providing feedback on the writing and sequencing of ideas, organizing discussion groups and assigning roles to group members, and keeping track of their progress (Carey, 1993).

Teachers may think that this role calls upon them merely to observe, look over students' shoulders, sometimes put in a question, and give clues to the answers to their own questions. This facilitation role may come hard for teachers accustomed to the role of dispenser of knowledge. One teacher, for example, used a video disc concerning real-life dilemmas by "showing the class how she would lead the discussion and operate the computer to make various choices. . . . The system was seldom used by individuals." Other teachers "were unwilling to manage a computing environment in which student groups worked on different problems or curriculum units" (Carey, 1993, p. 110).

Because the teacher-as-facilitator approach goes against much of the traditional conception of the teacher's role, it may be hard for many to adopt. Major changes in teacher education programs may be necessary before teachers can be comfortable in this role.

449

3. *Ensure emphasis on the educational objectives* (knowledge, understanding, and skill in important kinds of content), and regard the technology as a *tool* for achieving those objectives. Of course, the computer can help do this. Computers can make possible a broadening and deepening of objectives by exploiting the data bases and other resources students can use.

SUMMARY

1. Individual instruction helps teachers adapt to students' individual differences and teach them to learn independently.

2. For promoting independent learning as well as improving achievement, homework is an important tool. Training in study methods and strategies can make independent learning more efficient. Independent study projects and contracting give students structured opportunities to develop skills that will be useful when they no longer can depend on teachers for help.

3. For adapting to the abilities and needs of individual students, teachers can use ability grouping. But its effects on achievement and fairness, to both higher- and lower-ability students, are still highly controversial despite much research.

4. The mastery-learning approach—adjusting the time allowed for attainment of objectives and the teacher's assistance to the individual student's needs—raises overall class achievement. But here again, questions concerning the fair use of resources for more-able students have been raised.

5. Tutoring has a good record of effectiveness in raising the achievement of both tutees and tutors.

6. Peer tutoring can be an especially effective means of individualizing instruction, with benefits to both tutors and tutees.

7. Computer-assisted instruction (CAI) has become a way of supplementing instruction on certain subject matter. CAI has moderately better effects than conventional teaching methods on student achievement and attitudes. The method's cost-effectiveness is still an unresolved question. Dialogue programs and intelligent tutoring systems that mimic human tutors may become useful for teaching but are not yet available.

8. Apart from CAI, computers can be useful in fostering independent study. Students can learn word processing, gain access to databases and reference works, use e-mail, explore the World Wide Web, and learn through simulations and games.

9. The teacher's role in CAI and other ways of using computers in the classroom differs from the traditional role as dispenser of knowledge, questioner, source of feedback, and controller of learning. The teacher needs to become more a facilitator of students' learning as he or she works with computers—a role that may be hard for teachers to accept and carry out.

A couple of things to think about: First, because teachers and students are individuals, no single method works for everyone all the time. For this reason, innovation is valuable. It can give teachers new ways to handle problems or reach a student who is not responding to traditional methods. But second, innovation is difficult. Implementation (putting innovations into effect) can be demanding and success slow, if it comes at all. Adopting something new, then, means a commitment in time and patience—for teachers, students, and the school boards responsible for the educational programs and the funds to support them.

Classroom Teaching: The Orchestration of Methods

Overview

THE PATTERN OF CLASSROOM TEACHING

Distinguishing Characteristics of Classroom Teaching

Two phases: Planning and interaction

The flexibility of recitation

Inclusion of both direct instruction and constructivist teaching

An orchestration of methods

Reasons for the Prevalence of Classroom Teaching

Adaptability

Reinforcement and feedback

Class size

Suitability to basic tasks

POLICY, RESEARCH, AND PRACTICE

Does Smaller Class Size Improve Achievement?

THE PLANNING PHASE OF CLASSROOM TEACHING

Types of Planning Needs

Planning for Classroom Discipline and Management

Factors beyond the teacher's control

Two categories of problem behavior: The teacher's role

Strategies for too much unwanted behavior

Strategies for too little wanted behavior

Planning for control of bias

APPLICATION

Becoming Aware of Your Own Unintentional Biases

Planning to use pedagogical content knowledge

Planning for scaffolds (instructional supports)

Planning for variety and flexibility

THE INTERACTIVE STAGE OF CLASSROOM INSTRUCTION

Direct Instruction

The importance of judgment in using research findings

Teacher structuring

Teacher soliciting

Teacher reacting

POLICY, RESEARCH, AND PRACTICE

Redirecting Questions and Probing

Seatwork

Criticisms of direct instruction

POLICY, RESEARCH, AND PRACTICE

How Can Teachers Improve the Academic Learning Time (ALT) of Students?

Constructivist Teaching

The nature of constructivist teaching

The effectiveness of constructivist teaching

Criticisms of constructivist teaching

A Synthesis of Direct Instruction and Constructivist Teaching

Summary

OVERVIEW

What can we tell you about classroom teaching that you do not already know? After all, you have been surrounded by the process for at least 20 hours a week, 40 weeks a year, for more than 12 years. What we do in this chapter is introduce you to the process from two new points of view: the teacher's and the educational psychologist's.

From the teacher's point of view, you look at classroom teaching as an activity in which you have the power to shape the process. You probably had little of that power when you were in the student's role; then you did pretty much what your teacher wanted you to do. But, as a teacher, you will have a determining role and the responsibility that goes along with it.

From the educational psychologist's point of view, you examine classroom teaching through the concepts and principles we have talked about throughout this book. You also come across some new concepts developed expressly for the purposes of understanding and improving classroom teaching and fostering good outcomes.

After we explore the key planning phase of classroom teaching, we emphasize the phase of teaching that has received the most attention from researchers—the interactive aspects of teaching in the classroom. This is what most of us think of as typical teaching because it is what we have most often experienced. We introduce you to a diverse set of teaching behaviors that can help you plan and be more effective, whatever the subject or grade. For the most part, these behaviors have been shown to be effective through research. In a look at direct instruction, we talk about how the teacher's use of structuring and question-asking and probing skills helps students learn. The effects on student achievement of teachers' praise, the use of students' ideas, and high rates of criticism and disapproval by teachers are also noted. Next, we examine seatwork, presenting the relationship between academic learning time and student achievement and suggesting how academic learning time can be improved. We also look at a newer perspective—constructivist teaching—and consider the possible advantages and disadvantages of this kind of instruction. We conclude with a brief discussion of the potential benefits of combining elements of direct instruction and constructivist teaching in the classroom.

The Pattern of Classroom Teaching

Classroom teaching is what many people mean by the word *teaching*. It is the classical model of teaching method, and for that reason it has been the subject of more research than have any other major teaching methods.

At times, classroom teaching combines elements of the lecture, discussion, and independent-study methods. Occasionally, short (five- to fifteen-minute) lectures are part of the program. Usually, however, the teacher allows more interruption by students' questions than is typical in lectures. If the interruptions become frequent enough and take the form of questions and responses to statements the teacher or other students have made, this kind of lecturing shades off into discussion. *Independent study* may go on too, especially in elementary and secondary school classrooms, where teachers frequently assign **seatwork**—assignments for students to work on by themselves or with one or two other students.

Classroom teaching has several distinguishing characteristics, each of which we briefly define and examine. We then look at the reasons for the prevalence and popularity of classroom teaching.

Distinguishing Characteristics of Classroom Teaching

Classroom teaching consists of two phases: (1) planning to meet a hierarchy of needs and (2) interaction with students. The interactive phase typically includes **recitation,** which usually consists of a series of short interactions between the teacher and a student. In the presence of the whole class, the teacher calls on the student to answer a question, comment, read something, give an answer to homework, or some similar response. As you will see, recitation is far more flexible than many educators have realized; it allows the teacher considerable freedom in arranging lessons, and is an inclusive, rather than exclusive, format for instruction. There is room in classroom teaching for both **direct instruction**—in which the teacher leads the learning process—and **constructivist teaching**—in which the learner does more of the leading. Finally, in its essence, classroom teaching is a synthesis of methods—a true orchestration in which the whole is larger than the sum of its parts.

Two Phases: Planning and Interaction The classroom teacher's work goes on in two phases: planning and interaction. In the planning phase, teachers work alone (or, in team teaching, with other teachers), preparing their teaching. They think about objectives and about their students. They organize course materials and schedules. They plan assignments, exercises, learning experiences, field trips, demonstrations, visual aids, audiotapes, discussion outlines, and tests of achievement. They consider the class as a whole, its interests and ability level, and individual students, their achievements and problems. In the interactive phase, the teacher is actually face to face with students, interacting with them in the give-and-take of learning. This is social interaction—two or more people stimulating and responding to one another.

The Flexibility of Recitation The recitation component of classroom teaching is a key part of the interactive phase of classroom teaching. In primary grade mathematics and social studies lessons observed by Stodolsky et al. (1981), recitations took up about a third of instructional time. In high school grades the proportion may be greater. Contrary to what many educators and students believe, recitation can take almost innumerable forms, but basically it consists of four categories of behavior, listed below. In using these categories, teachers are adhering to what Bellack et al. (1966) called the "rules of the classroom language game." (See Table 12.1.)

1. *Structuring*—Setting the context for classroom behavior by starting or ending an interaction and indicating its nature

2. *Soliciting*—Seeking a response

3. *Responding*—Fulfilling the expectation set by the soliciting behavior

4. *Reacting*—Modifying or evaluating a previous response

Before going further, write down as much as you can about the nature of objectives. Then reread the presentation in Chapter 2 to check the accuracy of your knowledge.

12.1

Comparisons between Selected Mean Measures of Classroom Bahavior in Two Studies

	Percentage of Talking			
	Bellack et al.		Hoetker & Ahlbrand	
	Teacher	Student	Teacher	Student
Structuring	14.5	3.0	22.4	3.4
Soliciting	20.3	2.5	20.6	1.2
Responding	5.0	15.6	4.3	13.1
Reacting	24.8	5.1	31.4	0.6
Total	64.6	26.2	78.7	18.3
Totals	90.8		97.0	

Source: Adapted from J. Hoetker and W. P. Ahlbrand, "The Persistence of the Recitation," American Educational Research Journal, 6, pp. 145–167 and 589–592. Copyright 1969 American Educational Research Association, Washington, D.C. Used by permission.

Note: Percentages within studies add to less than 100 because some talking fell into other categories of classroom behavior.

Teachers tend to be highly consistent with themselves in their patterns of behavior from one class session to another. And the structuring-soliciting-responding-reacting formulation of recitation has been useful in many countries for describing teaching at all grade levels in subjects as varied as reading, English, mathematics, business, science, teaching, and nursing; and even in describing individualized instruction and early-education programs (Bellack, 1976). Another investigator (Mehan, 1979) calls the pattern *initiation-reply-evaluation.*

Stodolsky et al. (1981) identified some of the positive features of the recitation. Students typically pay relatively good attention, they seem to learn more easily from recitation than from seatwork, they are not highly anxious, and they receive some attention from the teacher. But recitation can be boring and dull—for example, when children spend significant amounts of time taking turns reading aloud. This may explain why the high-SES districts in Stodolsky's study did not use recitations so much in social studies classes: They had other curricula and materials available (Stodolsky et al., 1981).

One major study (Rosenshine, 1980) showed that the amount of recitation or "the substantive interaction which took place—explanations, questions and answers, and feedback" (p. 121) correlated more highly than the amount of group work (children working together) with overall time-on-task, a good predictor of classroom achievement. (We talk more about time-on-task later in this chapter.)

A few of the possible variations on recitation should be noted at the outset. Teachers need not use only a restricted and narrow version of it. It is important to note that at times one or two of the four links in the chain of behaviors described above can be omitted. Although teacher questioning and student responding almost always occur, structuring and reacting may happen only occasionally. The functions of recitation can also vary. It can be used for review, introducing new material, checking answers, practice, and checking understanding of materials and ideas. Often more than one purpose can be served in a single recitation session. And along with these different functions come differences in students' opportunity to participate.

Each of the behaviors in recitation has various alternatives, which may or may not take place in any single recitation sequence. Just to illustrate, suppose we say that each of the three parts of a recitational sequence under teacher control can take five forms—five ways of structuring, five ways of soliciting, five ways of reacting. Then there would be 125 ($5 \times 5 \times 5$) possible combinations, each one representing a different form of the episode. Surely, with 125 possibilities in any one episode, and the many episodes that constitute a single recitation lesson, this kind of teaching can be extremely flexible.

A sampling of some specific variations: Structuring can readily relate the subject matter to the objectives or to students' background knowledge or both. Soliciting can consist of a recall question or a higher-level question requiring more than recall. Student responding can be correct, irrelevant, or incorrect. Reacting can consist of praise or build on what students have contributed. And recitations need not be conducted only with the whole class so that individual students get little attention; they can involve subgroups of students who may differ greatly in previous achievement and current readiness for a particular topic.

But remember as you study the rest of the chapter that this great flexibility may not show up in practice. Recitation can become a series of unrelated teacher questions that require only factual answers and display of (presumably) known information, too many yes-no questions, too few questions related to students' ideas, too little elaboration of ideas. Clearly, such recitations fail to take advantage of the great variety of possible forms, and they are exactly what you should strive to avoid in your own teaching.

Inclusion of Both Direct Instruction and Constructivist Teaching

Classroom teaching can incorporate both direct instruction and constructivist teaching. The distinction between these two approaches to teaching has been clarified in recent decades. *Direct instruction* is the term applied to a host of teaching practices that emerged from decades of "process-product" research on teaching—the search for relationships between processes (what goes on in the classroom by way of teacher and student behavior) and products (what students learn, typically but not necessarily measured with achievement tests and with attitude questionnaires and observations of student conduct). As the findings of process-product studies, both correlational and experimental, have converged, a set of teaching practices have showed up fairly consistently as causally related to higher achievement and better attitudes and conduct.

More recently an emphasis on constructivist teaching has developed to fit in with the concept of constructivist learning described in Chapter 7. As you recall, the constructivist conception of learning holds that knowledge is built—rather than passively absorbed—by learners as they interact with the world and other people. Learners start out afresh at every moment with a set of facts, concepts, understandings, preconceptions, expectations, and the like about what is true. If what they then observe, hear, read, and otherwise experience is compatible with that initial state of knowledge and understanding, it is accommodated, that is, fitted into the existing knowledge structure. If the new experience is not easily accommodated, learners have to construct a new state, and that construction process results in learning. This means that constructivist teaching should sometimes be less direct—sometimes take different forms and display different emphases than those that characterize direct instruction.

Which type of teaching has been predominant in your own experience as a student?

An Orchestration of Methods   Classroom teaching is inclusive and flexible; it uses different forms of various methods at different times, for certain purposes, for all or certain students in the class. It consists in large part of a synthesis of lecturing and explaining (Chapter 9), the discussion method (Chapter 10), and individual instruction (Chapter 11). This combination makes sense. Teachers and students are working to achieve more than one objective in any unit of instruction. And for any of the objectives, for any group of students, some teaching methods are more effective than others.

But classroom teaching is even more than a combination of teaching methods. Think for a minute about orchestration, the way music is arranged for an orchestra. The composer weaves musical themes and sections of the orchestra together to achieve artistic effects. The composition is more than the separate themes and instruments. It is also the connections, relationships, and transitions between them. And it is this sequencing that determines the effect of the whole. It is the relationship between notes and themes, not the individual notes and themes themselves, that determines the melody. That is why a change in key, which changes all the notes, does not change the melody.

Similarly, in classroom teaching the relationships among methods (notes and themes) are just as important as the teaching methods themselves. The time teachers give to each method—and the sequences, rates, structures, and variations used—all determine the character of teaching. It is not enough to study the component parts of the method; teachers have to look at the "symphony" as a whole.

Reasons for the Prevalence of Classroom Teaching

Why has classroom teaching been so prevalent for so long? As we look at some answers to this question, examine the excerpt from a recitation

FIGURE 12.1

Example of recitation in a ninth-grade class

Adapted from Nystrand & Gamolan (1991, pp. 264–265).

Setting

Discussion of the book *Roll of Thunder, Hear My Cry*. John (a student) has summarized chapter four, while the teacher has tried to write his key points on the chalkboard.

Transcript

Teacher [to the class as a whole]: Wow! What do you think about that?

Student: It was very thorough.

Teacher: Yeah, pretty thorough. I had a lot of trouble getting everything down [on the board], and I think I missed the part about trying to boycott. [Reads from the board]: ". . . and tries to organize a boycott." Did I get everything down, John, that you said?

John: What about the guy who didn't really think these kids were a pest?

Teacher: Yeah, okay. What's his name? Do you remember?

John: [indicates he can't remember]

Another student: Wasn't it Turner?

Teacher: Was it Turner?

Students: Yes.

Teacher: Okay, so Mr. Turner resisted white help. Why? Why would he want to keep shopping at that terrible store?

John: There was only one store to buy from because all the other ones were white.

Teacher: Well, the Wall Store was white too.

Another student [addressed to John]: Is it Mr. Holling's store? Is that it?

John: No. Here's the reason. They don't get paid till the cotton comes in. But throughout the year they still have to buy stuff—food, clothes, seed, and stuff like that. So the owner of the plantation will sign for what they buy at the store so that throughout the year they can still buy stuff on credit.

Teacher [writing on board]: So "he has to have credit in order to buy things, and this store is the only one that will give it to him."

John: [continues to explain]

Teacher: [continues to write on board]

Another student: I was just going to say, "It was the closest store."

Teacher [writing on board]: Okay—it's the closest store; it seems to be in the middle of the area; a lot of sharecroppers who don't get paid cash—they get credit at the store—and it's very hard to get credit at other stores. So it's going to be very hard for her to organize that boycott; she needs to exist on credit. Yeah? [nods to another student]

[Discussion continues]

Analysis by Nystrand and Gamolan

Noteworthy is the seriousness with which the teacher treats the students' ideas. She summarizes their points and notes for clarifications. She shows meticulous interest in John's thinking. She is genuine in her interest. She models the kinds of questions and issues germane to a realistic discussion of literature. Her questions are authentic—not "test" questions.

in Figure 12.1. This example of a good recitation may explain in part why the method flourishes.

Adaptability   First, classroom recitation is highly adaptable to varied objectives. To teach knowledge or understanding of facts, concepts, and principles, the classroom teacher can lecture, more or less formally, for a few minutes or more, depending on the students' maturity. To teach the ability to examine ideas critically, the teacher can promote recitation in which students' own points of view and values can be expressed.

Just how much lecturing, discussion, and individual study actually go on in classrooms can be estimated from the findings summarized in Table 12.2. The table is based on extensive observation in 18 mathemat-

TABLE 12.2

Average Percentages of Segments* Used for Various Instructional Formats in Grade 5

Format Type	Mathematics			Social Studies		
	Low SES	Middle SES	High SES	Low SES	Middle SES	High SES
Seatwork	42.6	19.5	21.9	17.2	15.0	4.9
Diverse seatwork	0.6	2.1	7.8	1.5	2.8	6.2
Individualized seatwork	1.2	13.6	20.3	—	—	—
Recitation	37.7	27.1	18.8	29.1	17.7	5.6
Discussion	—	—	3.1	3.7	3.3	3.1
Lecture	2.5	1.7	—	—	1.1	—
Demonstration	—	0.4	1.6	0.7	1.7	0.6
Checking work	6.2	7.6	1.6	3.0	3.9	—
Test	3.7	3.8	1.6	1.5	2.2	1.2
Group work	—	2.1	4.7	26.9	28.9	58.0
Film/audiovisual	—	—	—	3.7	2.8	5.6
Contest	0.6	14.0	1.6	0.7	3.3	—
Student reports	—	—	—	0.7	2.8	—
Giving instructions	4.3	5.9	6.2	7.5	10.6	8.6
Preparation	—	1.7	1.6	0.7	3.3	1.2
Tutorial	—	0.4	9.4	—	—	—
Other	0.6	—	—	2.2	0.6	—
Total instructional segments	100%	100%	100%	100%	100%	100%

Adapted from S. S. Stodolsky et al., "The Recitation Persists But What Does It Look Like," Journal of Curriculum Studies, 13:121–130. Copyright 1981. Used by permission.

* *"A segment is defined as a unique time-block in a lesson which possesses one instructional format, a specified curriculum content and student participants, and occurs in a fixed physical setting" (p. 122).*

ics and 17 social studies classes in the fifth grade, in schools in 22 school districts in the Chicago area. The data show that

- lectures were used infrequently, as would be expected in the fifth grade.
- recitation tended to be more frequent in mathematics than in social studies, and in low-SES classes than in high-SES classes.
- seatwork was more frequent in mathematics and in low-SES classes.
- small-group work was much more frequent in social studies classes, especially in high-SES classes.

The nature of the subject matter makes the differences between mathematics and social studies classes easier to understand. But what about the differences among SES groups? These differences may reflect teachers' perceptions of their students' ability levels, which are correlated with SES. They may also reflect the fact that wealthier districts can afford richer curriculum materials and better prepared teachers, both of which may encourage alternatives to recitation.

Also, some teachers were far above and some were below these percentages. This variability suggests that classroom teaching is useful not only for recitations but also for lectures, discussions, and individual study in just the ways that might help us understand the widespread use of the method.

Reinforcement and Feedback Second, classroom recitation can reinforce the teacher through providing a way of finding out whether students are learning—by asking questions. Students provide not only correct answers but, through the attention they pay the teacher, social reinforcement.

Correct answers come forth only if the questions can readily be answered, if they are not too complex for the class. This can lead to asking only simple "fact questions." But teachers can also learn to be reinforced by asking questions that elicit more complex answers. Whatever the nature of the questions, recitation may be prevalent because it provides teachers with reinforcement that is relatively easy to obtain. And even when answers to questions are incorrect, teachers obtain information for modifying their lessons. Thus, compared to lecture method, recitations allow more opportunities for teachers to obtain feedback about how they are doing in promoting learning.

Class Size Third, class size can promote the use of classroom recitation. The vast majority of public schools in the United States are organized into classes of approximately 30 students (plus or minus 15). Research generally shows that class size, within the range of about 20 to 45 students, makes only slight difference in academic achievement.

Although smaller classes are more effective, particularly in the early grades, creating them is costly. In a large-population state, a reduction in class size of just *one student throughout the state* would cost many millions of dollars each year in teacher salaries and additional classrooms. And reducing class size at all grades from 30 to 15—the class size at which a substantial improvement in education would be likely to result (Finn & Achilles, 1990)—would increase the cost much, much more.

Suitability to Basic Tasks Fourth, classroom recitation allows teachers to perform three basic tasks:

- Present what they want to teach (the structuring phase when the teacher can give a brief explanation)
- Give students opportunities to practice the material (the responding phase, when teachers ask and students answer questions)
- Set up conditions for ensuring that students are prepared for and interested in learning (the reacting phase, when teachers can give positive reinforcement and encouragement)

POLICY, RESEARCH, AND PRACTICE

Does Smaller Class Size Improve Achievement?

Class size is a major determiner of educational costs. For one million students, classes of 15 students require 66,666 teachers, classes of 16 students require 62,500 teachers, and classes of 25 students require 40,000 teachers. At an annual salary of $35,000 per teacher, the reduction of class size from 25 to 16 would cost an additional $787,500,000! Providing additional classrooms would cost additional large amounts.

So class size reduction is expensive. Much research has investigated whether such reductions are worthwhile in improved achievement, attitudes, and long-range outcomes, such as employability and life adjustment.

Research on class size has seldom been conducted with randomized experiments—where students are assigned at random to smaller classes, say, 15–17 pupils, and larger classes, say, 23–27 pupils. Perhaps because of this shortcoming, results and meta-analyses have yielded ambiguous and controversial results.

In 1984, however, a highly respected randomized experiment on class size was begun in Tennessee (Mosteller, et al., 1996). Seven thousand kindergartners were assigned at random to (1) smaller classes (N = 13–17), (2) regular classes (N = 23–27), or (3) regular classes with full-time teacher aides. The results obtained from kindergarten through grade 3 showed consistent advantages in achievement for the small classes over the regular classes without or with aides. In addition to higher achievement, the small classes had fewer retentions, more on-task time for teachers, a higher level of student engagement, and smaller differences in test scores between white and nonwhite students.

Apart from random assignment, the experiment may have succeeded because the "treatment" (smaller classes) began in kindergarten and first grade rather than later.

Many citizens and educators would react to the Tennessee results with further questions. Do the improvements last into the grades beyond the fifth? Into life beyond school? Would similar results be obtained from replications in other localities—elsewhere in Tennessee, elsewhere in the United States? Should cost-benefit analysis be applied to determine whether the much greater costs would be justified by greater benefits—educational, economic, and social?

The Planning Phase of Classroom Teaching

The importance of planning cannot be overestimated. Decisions made by teachers while planning instruction have a profound influence on their classroom behavior and on the nature and outcomes of the education children receive. Teachers' instructional plans serve as "scripts" for carrying out interactive teaching.

(Shavelson, 1987, p. 483)

Planning goes on both before and after the interactive phase. Preinteractive reflection and planning come before a course or term begins and before each class meeting. Postinteractive reflection and planning take place after each class meeting and after a course is over.

Decision making is a critical part of planning. Teachers spend a good deal of time deciding on textbooks and other curricular materials; on schedules for rates of progress, examinations, report cards, and the like; and on out-of-class assignments and activities (homework, field trips). And they spend a good deal of time modifying those decisions. Most educators believe that teachers should organize their teaching as much as possible before they meet their students. But they also think teachers should stay ready to revise their plans once they learn about their students' abilities, interests, previous learning, and experience.

In Chapter 2 we described a model of the instructional process. This model identifies five primary teaching tasks: (1) choosing objectives,

> Think of other aspects of your life that might have this same structure—for instance, hosting a party or taking a trip. How important was the planning phase? If you did not plan, do you believe the overall experience would have been more successful if you had?

Decisions made by teachers while planning instruction have a profound influence on students.

(© Jean-Claude Lejeune)

(2) determining student characteristics, (3) understanding and using ideas about the nature of learning and motivation, (4) selecting and using methods of teaching, and (5) evaluating student learning. The model is prescriptive—it defines the ways teachers *should* begin to plan. But is it also descriptive? Does it say how teachers actively go about planning teaching?

> While this prescriptive model of planning may be one of the most consistently taught features of the curriculum of teacher education programs, the model is consistently not used in teachers' planning in schools. Obviously there is a mismatch between the demands of classroom instruction and the prescriptive planning model. The mismatch arises because teachers must maintain the flow of activity during a lesson or face behavioral management problems.
>
> *(Shavelson & Stern, 1981, p. 447)*

Another possible reason for the mismatch between the model and what teachers actually do may be that they do formulate objectives, as the model prescribes, but only implicitly, almost unconsciously. It may be that research techniques for describing what teachers do have not been subtle and searching enough to reveal the objectives that teachers really have in mind when they teach.

So what do teachers actually do? They focus on activities and tasks— what they want their students to do and how to get them to do it. Shavelson (1987) notes that these tasks are made up of

- content, often in a textbook
- materials, including things to manipulate
- activities—the things to be done in the lesson, in sequence, with a given pace and timing
- goals, or general aims, which are less specific than objectives
- references to students whose characteristic needs must be considered, especially early in the year
- references to the class as a whole, including groups of students within it.

Planning entails *problem finding or problem formulation*—the process by which a teacher becomes aware of a problem that needs to be solved— and problem solving. In teacher planning, problem finding is the discovery of a potential instructional idea that requires further planning and elaboration. *Problem solving* goes on through the "progressive elaboration of plans" (Yinger, 1980). Finally, the plan is put into effect and evaluated. If it works, it becomes part of the teacher's routine.

Planning is "nested." That is, planning for days takes place within weeks; planning for weeks is determined by plans for units of subject matter; planning for units, within planning for a semester and the year. The amount of detail increases in going from the larger timeblocks to the smaller ones. Teachers revise plans at each level, each revision being based on the previous day's or year's experience. Teachers use unit notebooks containing notes, handouts, worksheets, audiovisual aids, quizzes, and tests—all based on previous experience and revised to fit the current year's students and schedule. Textbooks, the school calendar, the district curriculum guide, and less often, the state's statement of objectives are taken into account. Plans take the form of sketchy outlines of content and activities, lists, notes, homework assignments, textbook exercises, and reminders about things to tell students about procedures (D. S. Brown, 1988).

Types of Planning Needs

Classroom planning needs fall into several categories:

1. Discipline, control, and management
2. Control over biases so as to deal with all students fairly
3. Use of pedagogical content knowledge
4. Provision of scaffolding—instructional supports that help students learn
5. Variety and flexibility

Planning for Classroom Discipline and Management

Many teachers and principals believe that the problems of discipline, classroom control, and management are the most important cause of teacher failure. "The most common type of failure is weakness in maintaining discipline. This particular form of failure is the leading cause for dismissal in studies of teacher failure which have been conducted over the past seventy years" (Bridges, 1986, p. 5). When students misbehave or disrupt activities in any of a hundred different ways, the teacher has failed to create the environment necessary for classroom teaching and learning.

Factors beyond the Teacher's Control   Problem behavior in the school— tardiness, truancy, insubordination, profanity, vandalism, and violence—is widespread. Teachers are affected by violence and vandalism, but they are often not responsible for causing it. Some causes reside in the same societal factors that produce crime outside the schools— parental rejection of children, poverty, violence in the media, peer and gang influences, and the frustration that accompanies low scholastic aptitude or achievement (correlations between achievement and aggression are $-.39$ for boys and $-.36$ for girls) (Feldhusen, 1979).

Also, usually beyond the control of the teacher are the causes of behavior problems stemming from school structures that force students to take courses that are inappropriate for their individual needs or level of achievement. This kind of structure breeds failure and threatens self-esteem. Delinquent behavior is one way of escaping that failure and threat.

Family and neighborhood play a much larger role than the school in causing delinquency. Yet schools do play a significant role. Schools that are impersonal and overcrowded, and that have weak administrative leadership, low expectations concerning student achievement, inadequate emphasis on thinking skills, large classes that prevent teachers from helping or even identifying students who need special attention, poor communication between school and home—schools that operate under these conditions contribute to the crime, delinquency, and problem behavior that exist in them.

By and large these problems lie beyond the scope of educational psychology alone. These are problems that need the attention of all the social and behavioral sciences—in particular, economics, political science, sociology, and social psychology. Political and economic forces operating at levels far beyond the local community create conditions that cause poverty, alienation, and a commercialism that disregards the welfare of children and youth. Commercialism, for example, leads television and other entertainment media to emphasize the seductive, degrading violence that, as we noted in Chapter 7, much research shows is a cause of aggression among children (e.g., Boyatzis et al., 1995; Molitor & Hirsch, 1994; Paik & Comstock, 1994).

Two Categories of Problem Behavior: The Teacher's Role   Of course, there are things the individual teacher can do when students misbehave in the classroom. The strategies for coping with problem behavior depend on the kind of problem behavior: too much unwanted behavior or too little wanted behavior. The first category includes physical aggression, moving around the room at inappropriate times, making too much noise, challenging authority at the wrong time or in the wrong way, and making unjust or destructive criticisms and complaints. The second category includes failing to: pay attention, show interest in work, interact appropriately with other students, attend school, be prompt, and be sufficiently independent. Teachers find two clusters of behaviors intolerable: aggression and poor cooperation. These behaviors are outer-directed or disruptive, having an effect on other pupils.

The difference between the two kinds of problem behaviors determines how teachers plan to handle them. They approach the "too-much" kind with prevention, extinction, strengthening incompatible behavior, or punishment strategies. The too-little kind calls for reinforcement, which strengthens behavior. (Extinction, punishment, strengthening incompatible behavior, and reinforcement are discussed in detail in Chapter 6.)

Strategies for Too Much Unwanted Behavior   In general, the strategies for dealing with too much of an unwanted behavior are to prevent it, to extinguish it, to elicit and strengthen incompatible behavior, or to punish it.

Prevention   Certain managerial skills of teachers tend to prevent unwanted behavior. Kounin (1970) identified several of these skills:

1. *Withitness*—the knack of seeming to know what is going on all over the room, of having "eyes in the back of your head." A teacher's awareness, and the students' awareness of it, make a difference. Teachers with high withitness make few mistakes in identifying which student is misbehaving, in determining which of two misbehaviors is the more serious, or in timing an effort to stop a misbehavior.

2. *Overlappingness*—attending to two or more activities or problems at the same time without getting confused or losing awareness of all that is occurring

As you envision facing your own class, what are your greatest concerns about classroom discipline? Using the ideas in this section as a starter, you might keep a journal of specific strategies that you glean from various sources to use as a personal resource when you step into your own classroom.

3. *Maintaining momentum*—not allowing classes to slow down

4. *Smoothness*—maintaining a continuous flow of activities without being distracted or distracting students during changes

5. *Group-alerting skill*—managing recitations in ways that keep students involved, attentive, and alert, perhaps by maintaining suspense about the kinds of questions that are going to be asked next or who is going to be called on

These carefully derived measures of teacher's sensitivity and behavior are based on Kounin's analyses of videotape recordings. They correlate positively with students' involvement in their work and with the absence of misbehavior in the classroom. Also, the more teachers were observed behaving in these ways in the early elementary school grades, the higher their students' achievement in reading tended to be.

Having managerial skills is obviously an important part of the prevention process. But so is knowing when to use them. The beginning of the school year is especially important for classroom management. One study of third-grade teachers showed that in the first three weeks of the year the more effective classroom managers (1) achieved more workable systems of rules, (2) were better in touch with their students' needs and problems, and (3) gave clearer directions and instructions (Emmer, Evertson, & Anderson, 1980).

In effective junior high school classrooms observed during the first three weeks of the school year, there was less emphasis on the direct teaching of rules and procedures. Rather, these teachers became more effective by (1) communicating clearly what they expected of their students, (2) checking up on whether students did what was expected, (3) providing information to help correct deviant behavior, and (4) giving students responsibility for getting their own work done.

Extinction Extinction—withholding reinforcement—is one way of stopping misbehavior. This usually means not paying attention to it—a strategy that may seem paradoxical but has repeatedly been found to work. When feasible, simply ignore a misbehaving student. Turn your back, pay attention to a student who is behaving properly, walk away. Do not give the student the attention that has often been found to result in unintentional reinforcement of unwanted behavior.

What if a student's misbehavior is being reinforced by other students' amusement or admiration? You can ask the other students to ignore the behavior too. Model the ignoring behavior for them, and keep them occupied with interesting tasks so that ignoring their classmate is that much easier. If other students call your attention to their classmate's misbehavior, simply change the subject and continue with whatever you were doing or talking about before the misbehavior occurred.

Extinction takes time. It may be a while before a child's misbehavior begins to decrease. But be careful: Even an occasional unintentional reinforcement can undo the whole process. That is, by changing from a continuous nonreinforcement schedule to a variable schedule (see Chapter 6), you can make it extremely difficult to extinguish behavior. So you and your students must consistently ignore the unwanted behavior.

There are exceptions to the extinction approach. Some behaviors (defiance, obscenity, hostility to the teacher) are too disruptive to be ignored. And ignoring behavior may make the misbehaving student think his or her behavior is acceptable when it is not.

When to intervene depends on which student is misbehaving and the nature and timing of the misbehavior. If the student is a frequent misbehaver or the misbehavior is serious and highly inappropriate, intervention is appropriate. When misbehavior takes place during an important instructional sequence or learning activity, teachers are more likely to intervene as well.

Strengthening Incompatible Behavior This approach involves reinforcing a wanted behavior that is incompatible with the unwanted behavior. For example, if a student has been blurting out, without raising his hand and getting permission, you can call on him before he talks without permission, and you can call on him whenever he does raise his hand and praise him for doing so. If a student has been fighting with others who have been calling her names on the playground, you can ask her to make a competing response, say, to write down the name-caller's name on a slip of paper and ignore the name calling (Clarizio, 1971). The writing is incompatible with the fighting. You can also replace stimuli that have come to trigger unwanted behavior with stimuli that bring forth acceptable behavior. If fighting breaks out primarily during certain games, substitute other games. If fighting breaks out whenever two students get together, put each of them with another student he or she gets along with.

Punishment Punishment should be used only as a last resort—only when you have tried everything else and have not been able to reduce the unwanted behavior to a level that permits effective teaching. But if punishment is necessary, do not be afraid to use it. If the education of other students suffers too much because of the misbehavior of one or two, your responsibility is to do what is needed, including punishing, to make effective teaching possible.

Punishment can take the form of (1) soft reprimands, (2) reprimands coupled with praise and prompts to behave appropriately, (3) social isolation, (4) response cost or point loss, and (5) corporal punishment. A soft reprimand is one heard only by the student concerned, and is often (but not always) more effective than one that other students can hear.

Also, teachers whose classes are extremely disruptive can use negative attention. This means responding quickly to unwanted behavior with words indicating that the student is misbehaving; such as an emphatic "That's enough," or "Not now," or comparable facial expressions and gestures. Important here, too, are quick positive attention and reinforcement when the student begins behaving appropriately. Time-out—depriving the student of time for having fun (see Chapter 6)—can also be used.

Corporal punishment is controversial. Most psychologists (American Psychological Association, 1975) and educators (e.g., Oklahoma State Department of Education, 1994) oppose corporal punishment in regular classrooms. Still, it has been widespread in American and British education. Apart from ethical, legal, and medical considerations (see Wessel, 1981, for a pediatrician's view), the psychological aspects are best summarized in the 1975 resolution of the American Psychological Association, which stated that

- corporal punishment tends to reduce the likelihood of employing more effective, humane, and creative ways of interacting with children;
- socially acceptable goals of education, training, and socialization can be achieved without the use of physical violence against children, and that children so raised, grow to moral and competent adulthood;
- corporal punishment intended to influence "undesirable responses" may create in the child the impression that he or she is an "undesirable person"; and an impression that lowers self-esteem and may have chronic consequences;
- to a considerable extent children learn by imitating the behavior of adults, especially those they are dependent upon; and the use of corporal punishment by adults having authority over children is likely to train children to use physical violence to control behavior rather than rational persuasion, education, and intelligent forms of both positive and negative reinforcement;
- the effective use of punishment in eliminating undesirable behavior requires precision in timing, duration, intensity, and specificity, as well as considerable sophistication in controlling a variety of relevant environmental and cognitive factors, such that punishment administered in institutional settings, without attention to all these factors, is likely to instill hostility, rage, and a sense of powerlessness without reducing the undesirable behavior;
- the American Psychological Association opposes the use of corporal punishment in schools, juvenile facilities, child care nurseries, and all other institutions, public or private, where children are cared for or educated.

(American Psychological Association, 1975, p. 632)

Strategies for Too Little Wanted Behavior Many behavior problems take the form of a student's doing too little of something good—too little volunteering to recite, standing up for his or her own opinion, paying attention to what is being explained or discussed in class. These unobtrusive kinds of behavior, in the opinion of psychiatrists and clinical psychologists, can be symptomatic of something more seriously wrong than obvious kinds of misbehavior. A child who is unusually withdrawn or inattentive may need referral to a psychiatric social worker, school or clinical psychologist, or psychiatrist, who can decide whether a teacher ought to continue to work on the problem alone, or whether the student needs professional help.

One way to decide whether the problem is too serious for you to handle is to see whether behavior-modification techniques do any good. Those techniques are eliciting, modeling, reinforcing, and shaping wanted behaviors (see Chapter 6).

Eliciting and Modeling   You can try eliciting wanted behavior by calling on the student, providing opportunities for engagement or involvement in interesting school tasks, and giving assignments that require the wanted activity. You can model the wanted behavior by showing a film, a videotape of a television program, or otherwise depicting appropriate behavior.

Reinforcing   You can supply reinforcement immediately (but not too obviously) when the student responds to being called on. When the student volunteers, call on him. When the student shows signs of interest or involvement, give her your attention by talking to her, accepting her ideas, falling in with her plans. When the student expresses an opinion, agree if you can do so honestly, or at least take the opinion seriously and treat it respectfully. (We deal further with praise later in this chapter.)

You can reinforce on-task behavior by providing (1) contingent positive verbal feedback ("You read well, John," "I like your poster") and (2) free time during the time remaining after academic work is completed.

Shaping Successive Approximations   This technique (see Chapter 6) takes time. You cannot expect a new behavior to show up immediately or in complete form. When the student *almost* volunteers, reinforce the tentative behavior. When the student shows a fleeting spark of interest, seize the opportunity to reinforce again with attention and praise. When the student offers a hesitant, tentative opinion, accept the offer immediately and use the student's idea in your next remark. As these kinds of wanted behaviors grow a little stronger, you can begin—but not too quickly!—to demand a little more before you reinforce. Gradually, as much experience (Strayhorn & Rhodes, 1985) has shown, your patience will be rewarded. Moreover, your own strategy for shaping student behavior will be shaped by the increasingly close approximations of the behavior to that of an active, involved, participating, attentive, and self-respecting student.

Contracting   Setting up contracts with students (see Chapters 6, 8, and 11) is another possible strategy. You can, for example, agree that the student is to volunteer once each day for a week. If the contract is met, the reward will be something (within reason) the student wants—perhaps time with a book or computer game or, for an older student, a chance to use the school's new microscope. After the contract expires, make a new one for, say, volunteering twice a day for three days in a row. Again, when the student completes the contract, give the agreed-on reward. Soon the contract becomes unnecessary as the intrinsic rewards of volunteering—being an accepted and active member of the classroom group—begin to provide the reinforcement that maintains the student's volunteering.

> Try using a contract system if you are currently tutoring or practice teaching. Keep a record of how and why it's effective or not effective and how it might be improved.

An Experiment in Improving Student Behavior   Do such techniques for improving student behavior work? An experimental group of seventeen teachers in grades 3 through 6 was trained to use a set of these teaching skills. At the same time, a randomly equivalent control group, made up of another seventeen teachers, went through an irrelevant (self-

Teachers can enlist students in their plans to increase wanted behavior and decrease unwanted behavior.
(© Sieplinga/HMS Images/ The Image Bank)

concept) training program. In the nine-week training program, the experimental group studied pamphlets describing the skills, applied the skills in simulated situations, practiced them in their own classrooms, and checked on their progress with partners by discussing tape recordings of their performances. Observers looked for the set of specific classroom behaviors among both the experimental- and the control-group teachers before and after the training. They found that the training was by and large effective: it resulted in the wanted changes in teaching behavior on 14 of the 17 teaching-behavior variables studied. And the payoff was that the students in the classes of the experimental-group teachers did better in showing on-task behavior and avoiding both mildly and seriously deviant behavior (Borg & Ascione, 1982).

Planning for Control of Bias   If you plan and use procedures for maintaining order in your classroom, you have the opportunity to teach toward your cognitive and other objectives. But you also need to control your biases—common human failings that are especially important in teaching.

As an observation exercise, we once gave a group of new teachers the task of classifying the students involved in some teacher-student interactions of experienced teachers. They were asked to use the following categories:

- Seated in the front half of the class versus seated in the rear half of the class
- Seated on the left-hand side of the class versus seated on the right-hand side of the class
- Minority-group members versus majority-group members
- Nice-looking students versus average-looking students
- Girls versus boys
- More able students versus less able students (based on IQ scores)

By simple calculations, we were able to determine the distribution of interactions expected by chance. For example, if teacher and students had 100 interchanges, we would expect about half to be with students on the left-hand side of the class and half with students on the right-hand side. If a class had 10 minority-group students and 20 majority-group students, we would expect the minority students to receive about 33 and the majority students to receive about 67.

We used observation to determine the actual distribution of interactions. And we found that *every observed teacher showed some bias.* Some worked mainly with students in the front of the room. Some worked predominantly with girls; others, with boys. Some worked almost exclusively with the more-able students. Surely some of these biases are harmful.

Bias in teacher interaction with minority-group students is particularly harmful. The Civil Rights Commission (1973) report on Mexican-American and Anglo students' interactions with their teachers (observed in 429 classrooms throughout the Southwest) clearly revealed this kind of bias (see Figure 12.2). Ethnic bias almost certainly still exists in many communities, and it affects achievement, attendance, school completion, and rate of college entrance among minority-group students (Valencia, 1991).

Another kind of bias relates to students' achievement or ability level. It is sometimes more satisfying to address questions to students who are more likely to give you correct answers. It may also be easier to listen more carefully to the contributions of such students. But that kind of

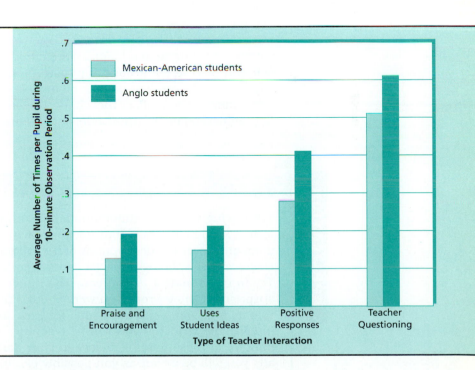

FIGURE 12.2

Teacher interactions with Mexican-American and Anglo students

Source: U.S. Civil Rights Commission (1973).

bias puts the other students at a disadvantage. Your bias becomes a kind of self-fulfilling prophecy: your low expectations of students (unintentionally) tends to make lower-achieving students fulfill your low expectations.

Even the facial attractiveness of students is related to how some teachers judge or interact with them. In one study, photographs of an attractive or an unattractive 5th grade student were attached to a report card, and teachers were asked to make judgments about the student's IQ, peer relationships, parental interest in the child's academic achievements, and the student's potential educational attainments. The teachers made more favorable judgments about all four measures for the attractive students (Clifford & Walster, 1973).

Similarly, teachers in grades 4 and 5 in one school were observed in their interactions with eighty boys and girls (Algozzine, 1977). The interactions were classified as positive, negative, or neutral. After the observations had been made, the teachers themselves categorized the students in several ways, including most and least attractive. The attractive boys and girls were involved in more positive interactions than were the unattractive boys and girls. Unattractive girls received more negative interactions, while there was no difference in negative interactions related to the attractiveness of the boys.

Teachers differ in their susceptibility to bias. Some differentiate much more than others in how they evaluate essays or drawings produced by students varying in ethnicity, social class, achievement level, or attractiveness. To overcome your biases requires planning.

First, you must become aware—make yourself conscious—of your unintentional biases. Then, if you have been short-changing a student, you have to make a conscious effort to interact with him or her. Try pairing your favorite student with the one you find most difficult to work with so that interaction includes them both. Make coded notes to yourself and place them around the room. Some teachers put a small sign saying "G > B" on their desk or on a clipboard, as a reminder to call on a few more girls to offset their bias. The same idea can work with "LA" (low achievers) or "R" (right side) or "LI" (lower-income) as a reminder to

Becoming Aware of Your Own Unintentional Biases

Try testing your own unintentional assumptions. Locate the yearbook from a local high school (but not your own). Choose a few pages at random, and cover the descriptions of the students' activities and interests. Using only the photographs, jot down a few impressions of each student. Try to be as honest as you can. Then uncover the captions. If you are surprised by how wrong you were about a few individuals, you can use this as a lesson—and a warning for how you might find yourself prejudging the students you will be teaching. Try to make yourself more mindful of these possible biases in your daily thinking so that eventually you will be as fair as you possibly can in your own classroom.

counteract biases. Even more than other people, teachers have a responsibility to confront and compensate for their biases to avoid harming students.

Planning to Use Pedagogical Content Knowledge   Everyone agrees that teachers ought to know the subject matter of their teaching. Recently, however, educators have realized that this knowledge should take a special form: What Shulman (1987) called *pedagogical content knowledge* (PCK). PCK consists of that which anyone trained in a subject matter possesses, *plus* the ways that content can and should be taught. Since it includes the latter, PCK is now recognized as a kind of knowledge specific to teachers. It includes ways of representing for students

> the structure of the field
> the relative importance for students of different parts of that structure
> the most useful sequence of topics for promoting student comprehension
> the strengths and weaknesses of different conceptions or emphases within the field.

These relatively general concerns are accompanied by more specific ones, such as the best

> analogies for explaining a given concept
> diagrams for illustrating a certain relationship
> examples of a given phenomenon.

PCK also includes knowing the areas of the content that create *puzzlements* for most students and the best way of coping with them.

Content knowledge itself also makes a difference. For example, teachers who know a lot of math present the subject as one permitting flexibility in ways of solving problems. They comprehend why different approaches succeed or fail. But teachers who know little math present the subject as something that is fixed and has to be accepted, not necessarily understood. In history, more knowledgeable teachers tend to emphasize its uncertainty and need for interpretation, whereas those less knowledgeable tend to stress its facts, dates, and settled character.

Also, teachers tend to avoid teaching content when their own knowledge of the area is weak. In other words, their knowledge level affects how they teach a subject. In one study, science teachers who knew the subject well used whole-group teaching more often, and less knowledgeable teachers used small-group approaches more often—presumably so that students would have something useful to do, since they were unsure of what to teach. The more knowledgeable teachers also permitted more student talk, except that, when they felt less secure with the topic, they "tended to dominate the discussions" (Grossman, 1991, p. 207). Similar relationships were found between the teachers' knowledge level and their questions: those with less knowledge asked more lower-order questions.

PCK reminds teachers that knowledge of the subject alone is not enough. You will benefit from knowing (1) your students—their typical abilities and backgrounds at their age; (2) the best learning strategies to

What are some ways you can build your PCK during your professional life? Think of as many resources as you can that will help foster continual growth.

use with them; and (3) how your subject is formulated in the curriculum you are using and how it fits into your school system. Combined and integrated, these kinds of knowledge constitute your PCK. As you might guess, your PCK will build slowly. It is a rare teacher who, during the first year of teaching, has the proper metaphor at her fingertips, or can provide just the right example for a student unlike herself. Postinteractive reflection is the time for deciding what should be kept and what should be changed the next time a particular topic is taught.

PCK seems important in its own right. But in the long run teachers want to know how it connects with student learning. So the next step in research on teachers' PCK is to investigate its connection to students' learning and achievement.

Planning for Scaffolds (Instructional Supports)   Teachers often want to help students acquire relatively general, widely useful skills, such as summarizing a story, taking notes, or writing a term paper. So researchers have done experiments to try out and evaluate ways of helping students along these lines. Rosenshine and Meister (1992) extracted tentative lessons for teachers from the ways in which the successful experiments helped students acquire such relatively unstructured skills as reading expository and narrative text, or generating questions, summarizing, and taking tests. They developed "scaffolds," or "forms of support provided by the teacher . . . to help students bridge the gap between their current abilities and the intended goal" (p. 135), which the teachers taught to students. Scaffolds are considered temporary and adjustable, to be abandoned after a skill (e.g., writing expository essays or laboratory reports, producing a news story) is acquired.

Teachers who use scaffolds engage in modeling—thinking aloud (while students listen)—and give prompts, aids, suggestions, and guidance. Providing students with examples of finished work by experts, to compare with their own, is another scaffold. Checklists for use by students in evaluating their work are still another kind of scaffold.

The findings from successful studies were put by Rosenshine and Meister (1992) into the categories shown in Table 12.3. In Component 1, the "concrete prompts" referred to are such things as guides, analogies, question-generating skills (see Chapter 11), summarizing, audience identifying (in writing), and phrases or cues useful in getting ideas for elaborating or improving (e.g., "An even better idea is . . ."). Then the teacher demonstrates the technique, guides students' initial practice, provides a variety of situations for practicing the strategy, gives students feedback and ways of evaluating their own work, gradually lets students do more of the task by themselves, and finally lets them work on their own.

Planning for Variety and Flexibility   Once you have done the types of planning discussed above, you are ready to plan for variety and flexibility in your teaching. Such variety and flexibility are desirable because no single way of doing things in teaching is best for all kinds of content and objectives, for all students, under all circumstances. Variety allows a teacher to take advantage of the strengths of various alternatives and

TABLE 12.3

Components for Teaching Higher-Order Cognitive Strategies

1. Locate or develop a concrete prompt that can guide students' processing.

2. Demonstrate use of the prompt through modeling and thinking aloud.
   a. Model the process of using the concrete prompt.
   b. Think aloud as choices are made.

3. Guide initial practice through techniques that reduce the difficulty of the task.
   a. Start with simplified material.
   b. Complete part of the task for the student, when appropriate.
   c. Provide cue cards to help them use the concrete prompt.
   d. Present the new material in small steps.
   e. Anticipate student errors.

4. Provide a variety of contexts for student practice.
   a. Provide teacher-led practice.
   b. Collaborative social dialogue.

5. Provide feedback and self-checking procedures for the student.
   a. Offer teacher-led feedback.
   b. Provide checklists.
   c. Provide models of expert work.
   d. Suggest fix-up strategies.

6. Increase student responsibility as they master the strategy.
   a. Diminish prompts and models.
   b. Gradually increase the complexity and difficulty of the material.
   c. Diminish student support.
   d. Practice putting all the steps together (consolidation).
   e. Check for student mastery.

7. Provide independent practice.
   a. Provide extensive practice.
   b. Facilitate application to new examples.

Caution: This list offers only suggestions for consideration when teaching cognitive strategies. It is not intended to be used as a tool for evaluation.

Source: B. Rosenshine & C. Meister (1992). The use of scaffolds for teaching higher-level cognitive strategies. Educational Leadership, 49 *(7), 26–33.*

overcome the shortcomings of any single approach. Variety also has a kind of "wake-up" value; it provides relief from the routine and humdrum quality of anything always done the same way. Several studies (Rosenshine, 1971b) have yielded positive correlations between the amount of short-segment variation and students' attention to their learning tasks. Teachers who are not oriented toward variety and flexibility tend to do what comes most readily, turning their teaching into deadly monotony.

Types of Variety Teachers can create variety by changing the ways in which they carry out any of the components of teaching. They can

- change content and objectives (Chapter 2)
- find out more about what teaching is compatible with different aspects of students' cognitive abilities (Chapter 3), development

(Chapter 4), and background (Chapter 5) so as to be able to vary teaching methods appropriately

- alter the kinds of learning arranged for students to experience (Chapters 6 and 7)
- try different ways of motivating students (Chapter 8)
- use different teaching methods (Chapters 9 to 12), materials (e.g., games, projects), or media (films, videotapes, audio recordings)
- employ different ways of assessing students' achievement (essay tests, performance tests, multiple-choice tests) (Chapters 13 and 14)

In thinking about variety, you need to be clear about the segments of behavior or teaching that can vary. First, the size of segments can vary. Short segments are parts of teaching that take only a minute or two, such as asking a question, gesturing, giving an explanation, using an intonation, or speaking loudly. Variety in long segments, lasting an hour, a day, or a week, can take the form of something new such as a field trip, film, debate, role-playing, tutoring session, or lecture.

Second, variation in classroom teaching can refer to style and method. Style is the way a teacher expresses her- or himself; it is reflected in gestures, movement about the room, tone and volume of voice, warmth, humor, and enthusiasm. Method refers to the more formal and self-conscious aspects of teaching—the ways the teacher interacts with students, the kinds of questions asked, how questions are addressed to students, the sequence of questions, the pacing or tempo of the lesson, the social arrangement (competition or cooperation between students), the activities students are required or allowed to take part in (for example, reading silently, reading aloud, listening to tapes or records, working in a laboratory in a science or a foreign language), the amount and kind of decision making the teacher allows, and when and how often the teacher emphasizes direct instruction or constructivist teaching.

Third, variation can apply to teaching materials and facilities. Different themes—political, seasonal, geographic, national, cultural, and others—can be used as bases for changes in instructional materials, that is, books, films, projects, bulletin boards, and so on. Facilities outside the classroom—parks, observatories, factories, museums—can be used to vary the learning environment. And classroom seating can be varied by arranging students in circles or small clusters.

Administering Classroom Variety You can plan these kinds of variety around traditional classroom recitation. But to carry them out you must develop administrative skills. You are going to have to schedule and budget your time; anticipate needs for materials, equipment, transportation, and other resources; and have a supply of alternatives and supplements on hand to meet unforeseeable turns of events, either in the logic of the discussion or in the equipment and materials. Only experience and practice can improve your skills in the administrative aspects of planning and organizing for variety. Educational psychologists can only point to the theory and research underlying the idea that variety improves classroom teaching. Acting on that idea is your responsibility.

What teaching style has most appealed to you during your years as a student? Why do you think this is so? Do you plan to emulate it?

The Interactive Stage of Classroom Instruction

After you have planned as thoroughly as possible, you are ready to engage your students in what is really the heart of the matter: the **interactive stage of instruction**. Despite the fact that millions of classrooms are operating around the world every school day, researchers have found remarkable similarities in the way instruction is carried out everywhere. But within the similarities, there have been variations observed among teachers of the same subject matter to the same kinds of students. And those variations have been found to make a difference in student achievement. We next describe two major approaches—direct instruction and constructivist teaching—and how they relate to student achievement.

Direct Instruction

Direct instruction means the teacher does all or most of the following in any single session on a given subject:

1. Reviews the previous lesson's content
2. States the goals of the present session
3. Introduces the new content (knowledge—declarative, procedural, episodic, or the like, as described in Chapter 7, pages 262–263—orally or with printed matter, films, and so forth)
4. Arranges for students to practice using the new content
5. Guides students during practice to correct errors
6. Checks students' oral or written responses, products, or performances for evidence of achievement of the goals of the lesson.

All of this goes on under the teacher's control, typically with the whole class but occasionally with subgroups or individuals. Research has shown that the more the process of direct instruction focuses on subject matter, the higher the students' achievement.

As discussed earlier in this chapter, classroom recitation is a key instructional component of classroom teaching. Below, we examine in detail the three components of the recitation done primarily by teachers: structuring, soliciting, and reacting. And we'll go into how, according to research findings, they tend to relate to student achievement. Our sources of evidence for the findings are largely (but not exclusively) major reviews of the research (e.g., Anderson, 1995; Brophy & Good, 1986; Dunkin, 1987; Gage & Berliner, 1992; Hirsch, 1996; Rosenshine & Stevens, 1986), rather than the primary studies themselves. These reviews provide a more integrated view of the data.

First, however, we need to explore a critical issue that is relevant to the research not only on direct instruction but on any educational topic.

The Importance of Judgment in Using Research Findings   Recommendations on interactive teaching practices are based on research that is sometimes case studies, often correlational, and occasionally experimental. The many aspects of teacher structuring, soliciting, and reacting presented below result from the hard and insightful work of a large number of researchers, who have spent thousands of hours observing and videotaping in classrooms, analyzing what they have seen and heard, and then relating their descriptions and measures of teaching practices to what students have learned. This work, done mostly since the 1960s and still going on, enables present-day teachers to work with the benefit of knowledge much improved over what teachers previously had. They need no longer proceed "in the dark"—without the help of relatively objective and replicated research on teaching.

Nonetheless, it is important—here especially—to remember what we said in Chapter 1, about the need for artistic, practical, and critical thinking in using research findings. Remember that correlations are never perfect, or even close to perfect. Remember that the differences between experimental and control groups are rarely large; the groups' distributions of scores always overlap so that some members of the control group do better than some in the experimental group.

The same is often true to an important degree in such unquestionably successful fields of practice as medicine and engineering (see, e.g., Gage, 1996). For example, the advice physicians often give adults about taking small doses of aspirin every day is based on correlational findings, such as those shown in Table 12.4. Notice that the difference in *percentages* of fatalities is small (5.4 − 1.6 = 3.8). However, this represents a 70 percent reduction (3.8/5.4 = .70) in fatalities. This result is far from perfect—30 percent (1.6%/5.4%) as many fatalities occurred among the aspirin users as among the nonaspirin users. Yet the results are important enough to be taken seriously and acted upon by many physicians, *unless* they have good reason—using their artistic, practical, and critical thinking—not to.

Similarly, in symphony music,

The score . . . is the first word and the last. No performance can be judged acceptable if it flouts the score's prescriptions in any detail:

12.4

TABLE

Incidence of Fatalities from Heart Attacks in Aspirin- and Nonaspirin-Using Patients

Status after Two Years	Aspirin Users (N = 751)	Aspirin Nonusers (N = 185)
Dead	1.6%	5.4%
Alive	98.4%	94.6%
Total	100%	100%

Source: Reproduced with permission from "Reduction in Long-Term Cardiac Deaths with Aspirin after a Coronary Event," by R. E. Goldstein, M. Andrews, W. J. Hall, and A. J. Moss, 1992, Circulation, 86, Supplement 1, p. 535. Copyright 1992 by American Heart Association.

metronome markings must be taken as a guide to tempo; crescendos must start and stop as marked. *Only then can the work of interpretation begin, concerning itself with matters unresolved by the score: nuances of stress, phrasing, dynamics, color, rhythmic flexibility, and so on.*

(Griffiths, P., 1997, italics added).

Likewise, practitioners in many other fields have to use judgment—artistic, practical, and critical thinking—to decide when to go or not to go in the direction implied by available (authoritative or research-based) knowledge.

The correlational result shown in Table 12.4 is no stronger than that on which we typically base the descriptions, given below, of relationships between many teaching-process versus achievement-product relationships in teaching. That is, when we say, "Teaching practice *x* is associated with (or causes) higher achievement," we are referring to results comparable to those in Table 12.4 or Figure 1.1 (page 20), which shows what a correlation of about .40 looks like.

So, in practice, you may often be able to think of good reasons to teach in ways different from—even the opposite of—what we describe below as implied by research findings. There is no substitute for your own good judgment here. But in the long run, over many teachers, in many classrooms, the implications of the research indicate that certain practices pay off better than their opposites. Just as taking small doses of aspirin daily helps prevent heart attacks statistically but not for every individual, so teaching in the ways implied below improves student outcomes statistically but not for every teacher, for every student, in every classroom, at every moment.

At the least, the research findings can make you sensitive to many features of teacher structuring, soliciting, and reacting that you may not have thought of. In that way they can help you reflect better on your own teaching.

Teacher Structuring   "All right, now let's turn from the facts about Nazism and try to see what may have been its causes. No such movement as deep and all-embracing as Nazism could come from nowhere. It had to have causes in the history—the previous economic, political, and social phenomena and processes—of Germany. Let's see what we can find if we look for the reasons why the Nazis came to power." This is one example of teacher **structuring**.

"Structuring moves serve the pedagogical function of setting the context for subsequent behavior by either launching or halting-excluding interaction between students and teachers. For example, teachers frequently launch a class period with a structuring move in which they focus attention on the problem or topic to be discussed during that session" (Bellack et al., 1966, p. 4).

Studies of teacher structuring deal with the following topics: the rate of teacher initiation and structuring, signal giving, organization, and teacher talk.

> Recall the discussion in Chapter 7 on ill-defined vs. well-defined problems. How does the nature of the typical kind of problem faced by a teacher relate to the point that you will frequently need to use your own judgment as a teacher?

479

Having structured the discussion, the teacher solicits responses or requests contributions from students.
(© Paul Conklin/Monkmeyer)

Rate of Teacher Initiation and Structuring How much teacher initiation and structuring is necessary—a lot or a little? The answer is "moderate," which of course, is vague. But during a fifty-minute lesson, very high and very low rates of teacher initiation and structuring were not as beneficial for students as were more moderate rates.

Signal Giving Giving signals indicates a transition from one part of a lesson to another. ("All right, that's enough about the effects of inflation. Now, let's look at its causes"). Fewer student disruptions occurred during transitions from one classroom activity to another when teachers used structured rather than unstructured transitions. Structured transitions are those in which a teacher follows definite rules or procedures for making a transition, such as "OK, we're going to start math in five minutes; you should begin cleaning up your art projects now." Signal giving includes the teacher's emphasizing concepts to be learned. ("Remember the term *selective migration*. It stands for an important kind of argument"). Similarly, the frequency with which teachers used another kind of signal giving, called **verbal markers of importance** ("Now note this . . .") was positively related to achievement. And the use of a well-recognized signal (snapping fingers, "Attention class!") for gaining student attention was one of a set of teaching behaviors that improved achievement.

Organization Another kind of structuring can be measured by obtaining ratings from students on the degree to which brief (ten- to fifteen-minute) teaching exercises were organized. Such ratings have been found to be positively correlated with student achievement. Similarly, students' ratings of *disorganization* were consistently found to be negatively related to measures of student achievement (and interest) in science. In sum, being perceived by students as being organized is likely to be associated with higher achievement.

So how can you make students think a lesson is organized? The perception should not be a false one; it should be based on their seeing and hearing evidence that the lesson has a direction—is going somewhere—and that the steps in that direction have been given some thought. Structuring moves—including signal giving, emphasizing words (concepts) to be learned, and providing verbal markers of importance—can help. It probably also helps to give students evidence of planning, by having materials and demonstrations well arranged before class and by being able to tell them in advance about the structures of the ideas they are going to be learning.

A lesson is also better organized if the teacher uses the self-discipline necessary to avoid digressions or discontinuities—that is, disorderly transitions within a lesson or topic from one point to another. Digressions inject irrelevant subject matter, which tends to reduce not only students' achievement but their perceptions of how well a teacher knows the subject matter.

Teacher Talk   Teacher talk has been the subject of many studies. Teacher talk is the amount of time during which a teacher is speaking, or the number of lines or words spoken by a teacher in a given amount of time. Teacher talk sets the context for student behavior. A good part of it is made up of lecturing and giving directions. Much educational doctrine in recent decades has put a low value on teacher talk, urging teachers to reduce the amount of their own talk and to increase the amount of student talk.

However, teacher talk has had consistently positive but low correlations with student achievement. The number of seconds the teacher lectured before asking a question, regardless of whether the comments referred to the previous discussion or forthcoming questions, has been found to correlate positively with general achievement in grades 3 through 6. "Extended" teacher talk correlated positively with adjusted reading achievement in second grade.

If we assume that teacher talk consists largely of the teacher-structuring component of classroom recitation, we can infer that higher degrees of teacher structuring are associated with higher student achievement. Of course, there probably is an optimum point above which teacher structuring and talk inhibit student growth in some areas. And the idea that quality of teacher talk is definitely more important than its quantity is supported by the consistently positive and *substantial* correlations between rated clarity of teacher talk and student achievement. (See specific ways to be clear in Chapter 9.)

Experiments on Structuring   Several of these types of structuring were manipulated simultaneously in an experiment on teaching a sixth-grade unit on ecology over a nine-day period (Clark et al., 1979). Four teachers were carefully trained to teach eight classes each, yielding sixteen classes with high structuring and sixteen randomly equivalent classes with low structuring. In the high-structuring classes, the teachers

- reviewed the main ideas and facts covered in a lesson, both at the end of the lesson and at the beginning of the next lesson
- stated objectives at the beginning of the lesson
- outlined the lesson content
- signaled transitions between parts of the lesson
- specified important points in the lesson
- summarized the parts of the lesson as it proceeded.

In the low-structuring classes the teachers did not use any of these structuring behaviors. The average score on an ecology achievement test was higher for the high-structuring classes. And the difference was sufficient to make the average high-structuring class rank above about three-fourths of the low-structuring classes. The difference appeared, however, only on the lower-order (knowledge) questions, not the higher-order (reasoning) questions, of the achievement test.

In another experiment, Borg (1975) trained teachers in voice modulation, cueing (calling attention to important points), end-structuring (adding information not previously covered, near the end of a lesson), opening review, and summary review. He found that cueing, terminal structuring, and opening review—all structuring behaviors of one sort or another—caused substantial gains in achievement.

But the research, reviewed by Doenau (1987b), showed enough inconsistencies and complexities in its findings to raise questions about whether educators have learned all they should about structuring. This important component of teaching ought to be something teachers understand well and are ready to use if it is to have consistently good effects on achievement. It may be that how students perceive the structuring is at least as important as the structuring itself. If so, we need to learn to use structuring in ways that students recognize and feel positive about.

Teacher Soliciting   Having structured a teacher-student exchange in a recitation, the teacher solicits a response or requests a contribution, verbal or nonverbal, from one or more students. For example, "Now, class, let's begin with some of the facts about Nazism. When did the Nazis come to power in Germany? What was the situation of the middle class in Germany at that time? What was the big fear of the German industrialists at that time? How did Hitler take advantage of the various aspects of the German situation in 1933?"

Studies of teacher soliciting or questioning deal with the frequency of questions, the cognitive level of questions, wait-time I, directing questions, redirecting questions, and probing.

The Frequency of Questions   The average frequency of teachers' oral questions has been estimated in various studies to be very high—around 150 questions per hour for primary-grade science and social studies teachers, specifically, and several hundred per day for elementary and secondary school teachers. Do students learn more as the number of questions increases? The evidence seems inconsistent. But when the frequencies of academic and nonacademic questions were studied separately, the former correlated positively and the latter negatively with achievement in reading in third grade. A meta-analysis (Walberg, 1991) suggested that there is a moderate but still substantial positive effect of frequency of questioning, particularly in the teaching of science. But remember that a teachers' questioning may not be effective if he or she wants to foster discussion instead of recitation (see Chapter 10).

The Cognitive Level of Questions The cognitive level of questions, or interchanges, also matters. One basis for classifying the cognitive level of questions is the taxonomy described in Chapter 2: knowledge, . . . , analysis, . . . , evaluation. Questions can also be used for purposes other than promoting the intellectual processes set forth in the taxonomy. These other purposes include

- asking students to improve on their first attempts ("Go on. Can you elaborate?").
- arousing curiosity and motivating inquiry ("Why would anyone want to spend billions on getting rocks from Mars when so many people are starving here on earth?")
- guiding students' efforts at acquiring a cognitive or social skill ("What do you think would happen if you applied the Pythagorean theorem at this point?," or "Why do you think Amalia lost her temper?").

The cognitive level of a question depends on students' previous experience. Some questions seem like they are calling for a higher mental process, say, analysis ("What are the main causes of the decrease in voter turnout in recent presidential elections?") or synthesis ("How did the invention of tape recorders and compact discs influence American music-listening habits?"). But if the students have read or heard the answers to these questions, all they have to do is simply remember the responses.

Similarly, some questions that seem to call for simple recall ("When did television come into wide use?") may actually require deductive reasoning, if students have never read or heard the answers. Students may arrive at the answer by reasoning from the facts that President Franklin Roosevelt gave his famous fireside chats over the radio but that President Eisenhower addressed the nation on television. In short, students' previous learning determines which cognitive processes they must use to come to the right answer.

This relationship to previous experience may in part explain why correlations between types of questions and achievement are low and only moderately consistent. The research has been partially motivated by repeated findings that most (up to 80 percent) of the questions teachers ask require only recall, or knowledge, of what was in the textbook or has been read or heard elsewhere; only about 20 percent call for mental processes higher on the cognitive scale. The high percentage of recall questions may be justified, though, because these kinds of questions bring out the raw information on which higher mental processes (analysis, synthesis, and evaluation) can operate. Yet individual teachers have varied around those average percentages; some ask much higher percent-

Choose any major section of any chapter in this book. Make up two sets of higher-order questions for the section—one for learners who have considerable background in the topic and one for students new to the topic.

ages of high-level questions than others. So we are led to an intriguing question: Do variations in student achievement go along with variations in the level of questions asked by their teachers?

Lower-order questions tend to be less difficult than higher-order questions. So it is noteworthy that, in the early grades, the percentage of time spent on low-difficulty material (as determined in the studies of how much time students actively engaged in academic tasks at a low level of difficulty) was positively correlated with achievement, whereas the percentage of time spent on high-difficulty material was negatively correlated with achievement. This finding argues for the greater value of lower-order questions for fostering certain kinds of achievement.

When the difficulty of questions was in general low, so that correct answers were given 80 to 90 percent of the time, *lower-achieving* students in the third grade seemed to achieve more. For such students, the percentage of right answers in the class correlated positively with achievement. But for *high-achieving,* more academically-oriented students, the percentage of correct answers correlated negatively with achievement. You should not misinterpret the latter finding, however; it means only that the percentage of correct answers should be lower—but still quite high.

It could be argued, then, that because questions should be at a low level of difficulty, and because questions at lower cognitive levels tend to be less difficult, teachers are right in asking more questions at lower cognitive levels. Yet experiments show just the opposite. Meta-analyses of the results of relevant experiments showed that greater use of higher level questions during instruction improved achievement. Furthermore, the effect was larger in the more valid and longer lasting experiments (Redfield & Rousseau, 1981; Samson et al., 1987).

How can we explain the apparent contradiction between the effectiveness of low-difficulty-level questions and the effectiveness of higher-cognitive-level questions? The answer may lie in the fact that the findings favoring low difficulty were obtained in grades 1 through 5, whereas those favoring high cognitive level were obtained in higher grade levels. As Winne (1979) pointed out, citing Piaget (see Chapter 4), children at lower grade levels may not yet have reached the stage of cognitive development at which they can deal effectively with questions calling for higher mental processes.

Apart from its effects on achievement, higher-level questioning can also be defended for its influence on what students say in class. All in all, teachers who ask relatively more questions at higher, more complex levels (requiring application, analysis, synthesis, and evaluation) also tend to elicit student responses, or thinking, at relatively higher levels. That is, students' responses to a teacher's questions tend to be at about the same level of cognitive complexity as the teacher's own questions or statements. Higher-order questions tend to make students go through higher-order mental processes—processes that require more than simple recall.

Having said this, we want to add an important caveat: As with all aspects of teaching, judgment is called for here. There are many good reasons why, with a particular class on a particular day, a teacher might decide not to ask higher-order questions. For instance, he or she might be working toward curriculum goals that require rote learning, such as remembering atomic weights or the rhyming pattern of a sonnet. Or the teacher might be working with students who need memory-level questions to gain confidence in responding to questions in class.

Wait-Time I After the teacher asks a question, the interval *before* the student responds is called **wait-time I** (Rowe, 1974). **Wait-time II** (discussed later in this chapter) is the interval *after* a student's response until the teacher speaks. Rowe found that both kinds of wait-time averaged about one second. But Giaconia (1987) found that the average wait-time I of the nine elementary school teachers she studied ranged from 1.5 to 3.9 seconds, and average wait-time II ranged from .63 to 2.15 seconds.

Rowe (1974) suggested that increasing either kind of wait-time from an average of one second to an average of more than three seconds has several beneficial effects on students' responses. Some of these include greater length of responses; more unsolicited but appropriate responses; fewer failures to respond; greater confidence, as reflected in a decrease of students' questionlike tones of voice; and more speculative responses.

If you ask a higher-level question, you need to give students more time to think about the answer. Students need time to process information. Yet Giaconia (1987) found that teachers did not tend to wait longer after they asked higher-order questions. You should not rush a student to get a response.

In addition, Rowe (1974) found that teachers tend to wait longer for an answer from students they think of as more able than from those they think of as less able (one of the common biases mentioned above). But no such tendency was found by Giaconia (1987).

In one experiment (Fagan, Hassler, & Szabo, 1981) trained teachers manipulated *both* wait-time (high and low) and cognitive level of questions (high and low). In this experiment, one of four groups of five teachers of language arts in grades 3, 4, and 5 received training in both wait-time and higher-order questioning. A second group received only wait-time training, a third group received only higher-order-questioning training, and the fourth group received neither kind of training. The length of students' responses in discussions of literature was greater for the teachers who used longer wait-time. Higher-order questioning resulted in more alternative student explanations and a greater number of higher-level student responses. But the longer wait-time *plus* higher-level questioning combination yielded even stronger results. The teachers who received wait-time training asked more higher-level questions but a smaller total number of questions—a finding that makes sense because longer wait-time means that fewer questions can fit into a class period.

A similar experiment (Tobin & Capie, 1982) had 13 teachers conducting eight science lessons in grades 6, 7, and 8. Those researchers also found that longer wait-time (up to three seconds, but not beyond) improved student attending, and that wait-time correlated .69 with the mean achievement scores of the thirteen classes. Furthermore, the effect of three-second wait-time was greatest when it occurred together with questions of higher cognitive level, greater clarity, and higher relevance to objectives.

Since the effects of longer wait-time on achievement are generally positive, you should guard against any tendency to rush students. Allowing substantial wait-time after a question is asked is good teaching practice. But the generally positive effects of wait-time of about three seconds do not mean longer wait-time is *always* a good thing. Shorter wait-time may be desirable when you want students to learn some things by rote memorization or be able to recall certain facts automatically and effortlessly.

Directing Questions   Research data suggest that, at least in the early grades, when directing a question at a specific student, the teacher should call on the child by name before asking the question. This recommendation goes contrary to the argument that asking a question first and then calling a child's name is more effective because it gets all the children thinking about the question.

Similarly, calling on students by "ordered turns" (e.g., in the order in which they are seated) was associated positively with reading achievement in the first grade (Anderson, Evertson, & Brophy, 1979). Perhaps this patterned order is more effective because it reduces anxiety. Of course, a little anxiety helps maintain students' attention. What is more of a problem with random order is that teachers tend to favor the more able students, depriving those who are less able of an equal opportunity to respond.

From all this it follows that teachers should not call on volunteers very often. Doing so decreases the likelihood of all students' getting a fair share of chances to respond. And in two studies, calling on volunteers correlated negatively with reading achievement (Anderson, Evertson, & Brophy, 1979; Brophy & Evertson, 1974).

It also means that teachers should avoid call-outs—answers given by students without waiting for permission to respond. Frequency of call-outs, too, correlated negatively with average class achievement in reading in two studies (Anderson, Evertson, & Brophy, 1979; Brophy & Evertson, 1974). But additional evidence in both studies indicated that call-outs should be permitted for low-achieving children, who often tend to withdraw from opportunities to respond during recitation. Accepting call-outs from these students was positively associated with achievement in reading.

Teacher Reacting   A teacher's reaction to a student's response typically evaluates, clarifies, synthesizes, or expands on that response. Teachers' reactions can be classified according to how quickly they occur (wait-time II) and whether they are positive, negative, or structuring.

Wait-Time II   The second kind of wait-time comes after a student has answered a question, and refers to how long the teacher waits to see whether the student will say something more. Benefits similar to those described for lengthening wait-time I (Rowe, 1974) pertain as well to lengthening wait-time II. As already noted, teachers typically react very

POLICY, RESEARCH, AND PRACTICE

Redirecting Questions and Probing

Suppose you ask a question and a student gives an incorrect or inadequate answer. What should you do? Two alternatives are redirecting and probing.

Redirecting is asking the same question of another student:

T: Carlos, how many degrees are there in an isosceles triangle?
Carlos: 360.
T: Margaret, can you tell us how many degrees there are in an isosceles triangle?

Redirecting makes the class continue thinking about the question. On the face of it, redirecting ought to correlate positively with achievement. And in one study (Wright & Nuthall, 1970), the frequency of the teacher's redirection of nonanswered or incorrectly answered questions indeed correlated positively with student achievement on a test of knowledge. In another study (Brophy & Evertson, 1974), this variable again correlated positively with student achievement for middle-class children. But it correlated negatively with achievement in classes in which low-achieving students predominated. It seems better with low-achieving students, then, not to redirect but to probe for an answer from the student first asked.

Probing is a teacher's continued questioning of the same student. If an answer is incorrect, the teacher repeats the question using different words. If an answer is correct, the teacher asks another question, pursuing the implications of the first answer; then perhaps another and another:

T: Sam, after Hitler made his promise to Chamberlain at Munich, what did he do next?
Sam: Well, he took over Czechoslovakia anyway, in a few months, even though he had promised not to.
T: Okay, Sam, then what happened?
Sam: Well, the Allies saw that nothing would satisfy Hitler. Like they couldn't stop him. Like he was insatiable. War seemed inevitable, and they began to realize that.

Probing can be used to get some kind of creditable response even from low-achieving students. It tends to reduce the frequency of no-response—a frequency that correlates negatively with achievement in low-achieving classes.

Probing to reduce the no-response frequency must be done gently. It can take the form of rephrasing the question, giving clues, or asking a new question. The frequency of each of these procedures correlates posi-

continues

487

tively with the average reading achievement of both low-achieving and average-achieving classes (Brophy & Evertson, 1974; Anderson, Evertson, & Brophy, 1979).

Probing can also be used to get extended higher-level responses from higher-achieving students. And probing can be employed, in a nonthreatening way, to get students to clarify their answers. Probing for clarification has been found to be one of a set of related behaviors correlating positively with student achievement in mathematics and reading (Soar, 1966; Spaulding, 1965).

One additional concept, called *simple reciprocation* (back-and-forth exchanges), involves teaching cycles made up of either (1) soliciting, responding, and reacting or (2) soliciting and reacting. In this case, soliciting means questioning, redirecting, or probing. In one study, the frequency of either simple-reciprocation teaching cycle was found to be positively correlated with student achievement (Wright & Nuthall, 1970).

It appears, then, that both redirection and probing are associated with higher student achievement. But this conclusion is based on a small number of "votes," or studies, done in too few situations to allow great confidence in the conclusion. If for no other reason, we recommend redirecting and probing of both kinds—to get any acceptable answer and to get a better answer—because they keep students involved in the lesson. Active student involvement always allows for the possibility of a positive effect on achievement.

quickly (within one or two seconds) to students' responses. But by increasing this wait-time to at least three seconds, they can change the nature of recitations, making them less "inquisitional" and more "conversational." And such changes can improve students' attending and achievement. That is, as the teacher waits longer, the students tend to elaborate and otherwise raise the level of their response. Giaconia (1987) found, however, that the cognitive level of questions was even more important than wait-time II as a correlate of the cognitive level of students' responses.

Positive Reactions   Positive reactions can take the form of (1) giving verbal praise, (2) accepting students' ideas, and (3) using tokens. All of these are kinds of positive reinforcers. According to operant-conditioning theory, this kind of reinforcer should strengthen whatever student behavior it follows.

Praise of students has been studied as to its frequency. Observational studies found that praise was actually quite rare on average—perhaps about 6 percent of the time, or less than five times per hour. But negative reactions are also rare. Most reactions by teachers are neutral.

Do teachers who praise their students more often have students who achieve at higher levels? Evidence from many studies has yielded no consistent relationship. A small amount of evidence suggests that, in the

Pedagogically, reacting moves serve to evaluate, clarify, or expand on a student's performance.

(© Michael Weisbrot)

early elementary grades, praise rates do correlate weakly with student achievement in low-achieving classes, but not at all or slightly negatively in average-achieving classes.

How do we explain these results? Brophy (1981) found that, instead of being used as a reinforcer, teacher praise was often (1) a "spontaneous expression of surprise or admiration," (2) a "balance for criticism" or a justification of a teacher's earlier reproof, (3) "attempted vicarious reinforcement" (when the teacher praises one student in an effort to control the behavior of others), (4) positive guidance in trying to foster warmth, (5) an "ice breaker or peace offering," (6) "student-elicited stroking," (7) a "transition ritual," or (8) a "consolation prize or encouragement" (pp. 17–18).

The effect of praise depends on what students see as the cause of it. If they believe that praise is something received only by students of low ability—that is, as a kind of "overpraise"—then it loses its effectiveness. And if praise is given too often, it loses its value, particularly in the upper grades. For praise to be effective, it should follow the guidelines in Table 8.5 on page 355.

It is probably best if teachers have an intrinsically favorable attitude toward people of all sorts. In questionnaires, teachers who expressed warm, accepting, sympathetic attitudes toward other people in general tended to be better regarded by others, including students (Ryans, 1960). Such teachers have little difficulty finding reasons to praise students, seeking out what is laudable in even the poorest student's performance.

Accepting students' ideas is the second positive teacher reaction. It means using students' contributions in subsequent discussion, and may consist of acknowledging, modifying, applying, comparing, or summarizing what a student has said. Acceptance of an idea tells the student that

Before reading the next section, describe how students might be affected adversely by a teacher's negative attitudes toward people in general.

the teacher considers the idea worth taking seriously. So acceptance presumably has reinforcing, or motivating, effects in addition to the cognitive value of repeating and reprocessing an idea:

> *T:* After the Nazis had come to power, what did they do? Katya?
> *Katya:* They began a program of putting down the opposition. They went after everybody in Germany who had raised any questions about them.
> *T:* Right, Katya. They installed one of the most efficient, thorough, and ruthless systems of suppression in human history. They used scientific methods to seek out and wipe out their opposition.

Using student ideas during teaching is associated with higher achievement and more positive student attitudes toward the teacher. But it is possible that the correlation occurs because higher-achieving classes express ideas that are more acceptable in the sense of relevance and validity. Nonetheless it seems safe, in the absence of experiments that would settle the question, to act on the assumption that a teacher's acceptance causes the higher achievement. Of course, students' ideas should be accepted only if they contribute to the academic focus of the recitation.

Tokens, the third positive reaction, are effective even when they are not part of an extensive system such as a token economy (see Chapter 8). Tokens can also be effective when used more casually as reinforcers for appropriate behavior. They can be exchanged for activities, such as time to read for pleasure or play computer games.

Research on the use of tokens in classrooms has dealt mostly with student behavior, especially problem behavior in the primary grades. Tokens for wanted behavior (and their withdrawal for unwanted behavior) have been found useful in changing certain behaviors. But in general, a token system can be used to react to any students in a way that shows approval of their responses.

Negative Reactions   When students respond or behave incorrectly, some teachers tend to disapprove, reprove, criticize, and rebuke: "That's not right." "Wrong!" "Stop that!" "You didn't do that very well." Such negative reactions have rarely been observed in most of the studies of classroom processes. But a large majority (13 of 16) of the studies of the relationship between a teacher's use of criticism and disapproval and student achievement have yielded a negative relationship. In other words, teachers who more frequently criticize their students tend to have students who do less well on achievement tests.

Which is cause and which is effect? Does more frequent criticism cause lower achievement? Or does lower achievement cause the teacher to criticize more? Or do lower-achieving students also misbehave more often, and so get the teacher to criticize more often? Because boys achieve less well than girls in the elementary school grades, where all of the studies of teacher criticism were conducted, and because boys tend to receive more criticism, the negative correlation between teacher criticism and student achievement may arise from the association of *both* variables with the gender of the student. That is, classes with more boys may tend to achieve less well *and* to receive more teacher criticism and disapproval.

To settle the question of whether disapproval causes lower achievement, or vice versa, experiments in which teacher criticism is manipulated would be needed. A randomly-assigned group of teachers would be trained to criticize less often, while another group would receive no such training, presumably criticizing in their usual ways. Then the behavior of the two groups of classes would be measured and compared. That kind of evidence is hard to get.

Meanwhile, it seems safe to say that teachers should be careful about using criticism and disapproval too freely. In fact, too much criticism and disapproval probably indicates that something is wrong—with the teacher's attitudes or teaching methods, the curriculum, the school's organization, the schedule, the student's home environment, or any of the other factors we have talked about, except the student. To say that the cause of excessive disapproval is the student is fruitless, because it is the teacher's responsibility to do what is needed to see that criticism is not necessary.

Reactions with Structuring   What do we do when students answer incorrectly? Our alternatives to criticism and disapproval include

- redirecting the question to another student
- end-structuring (giving more information or directions) at the end of an episode (a section of recitation that begins with a solicitation and ends with the next solicitation).

Both of these amount to a kind of mild criticism that communicates higher expectations.

Redirecting and *end-structuring* tend to be positively related to student achievement, especially with high-achieving students. Studies of these kinds of structuring-reaction variables are few, so the evidence is merely suggestive. Riley (1981) had science teachers in the primary and intermediate grades vary (1) high cognitive questioning (0%, 50%, or 100% high cognitive level) and (2) questioning strategy (directed, redirected). The redirected strategy resulted in slightly higher achievement overall and very much higher achievement on the comprehension subtest as against the knowledge and analysis subtests. In another study (Crawford, 1983), redirecting was less well correlated with low-income students' achievement than its opposite: sustained feedback to the same student. Thus, a sequence like the following, where the teacher's structuring behavior is indicated in italics, is probably associated with higher achievement only weakly.

T: Name a country where it is colder in August than in December, John.

John: Sweden.

T (redirecting the question): Hal? Where is it colder in August?

Hal: Australia

T (giving praise and thanks): Good. Thank you, Hal. *(Providing end-structuring):* So, class, in August, when it's hot here in the United

States in the Northern Hemisphere, it's cold in Australia and New Zealand and other countries in the Southern Hemisphere.

These structuring reactions make sense because the teacher makes no direct criticism of the student who has answered incorrectly. The teacher implicitly corrects John's error by accepting and praising Hal's answer. Praise is given only for correct responding, which is as it should be. And by end-structuring, the teacher repeats and elaborates the correct response. Without the repetition of Hal's correct response, some members of the class might learn John's incorrect response.

Academic feedback—informing students about the correctness of their answers or statements—as a form of structuring reaction has a fairly clear positive correlation with student achievement. But responses to low-achieving students need special attention. What happens when a student repeatedly answers incorrectly, so that any honest response by the teacher becomes a sign of student failure? How should teachers deal with low-achieving students? If teachers consistently ask easier questions of these students—questions that will almost certainly be answered correctly—low achievers are at a disadvantage. Here are some suggestions to help you avoid communicating low expectations to low-achieving students. For low-achieving students you should, just as frequently as for high-achieving students,

- Call on them
- Seat them close to you
- Wait for an answer
- Be willing to repeat the question, provide a clue, or ask a new question
- Withhold praise for unacceptable answers
- Avoid criticizing
- Confirm correct answers
- Praise correct answers

It is your responsibility to keep aware of your interactions with low- and high-achieving students, and to reduce or eliminate as much unintentional bias as possible.

Seatwork   Reasonable estimates suggest that elementary school students, at least in the early grades, work alone much of the time and participate in recitations much less of the time. So the variables in seatwork may be quite as important as those in recitations as correlates, and possible determiners, of achievement.

Why do we see so much seatwork in the early elementary school grades? Probably because early-grade teachers make such frequent use of small groups in teaching reading and other subjects. While teachers are working with groups of, say, five to eight students in oral reading or mathematics instruction, the rest of the students are assigned seatwork—preferably academically relevant and appropriate to a high success rate for each student.

Some teachers misuse seatwork for mindless, inappropriate purposes, as a way to keep students busy at any cost. Like any other teaching prac-

> Jot down a brief reason explaining why you think each of these suggestions works well with low-achieving students.

tice, seatwork can be overused, abused, and subverted. But it can also be put to good purposes: (1) drill and practice on skills (e.g., in addition and multiplication) that students should learn to perform automatically, (2) test-taking skills, (3) skills in problem solving without the teacher's immediate assistance, (4) writing on lively subjects, and so on.

Variables in Seatwork One major variable in seatwork takes the form of **academic learning time** (ALT)—the time a student attends to the learning tasks relevant to academic objectives that permit high success rates. Notice that this variable comprises several other variables: content covered, task orientation, academic focus, and engaged time. Classes differ greatly on measures of ALT. In one set of four second-grade classes, for example, the amounts of ALT on mathematics for the whole school year were estimated to be 33, 30, 50, and 58 hours. Similarly, in four fifth-grade classes in reading, the estimates were 60, 78, 140, and 148 hours.

These variations are important because they affect achievement. The evidence that ALT is positively related to achievement in reading and mathematics comes from careful observational and correlational studies in second- and fifth-grade classes (Berliner, 1990).

Criticisms of Direct Instruction Despite the successes documented by the research reviews, direct instruction has received a full share of criticism. It has been charged with fostering "mere" knowledge and discouraging the higher levels of cognitive achievement. Students, it is said, learn by rote and acquire no deep understanding of the subject matter. Students are treated as if they only can learn from being told, as if they are passive recipients of knowledge. One critic held that most curricula and teaching methods (presumably direct instruction) have the following effect:

> Most students have command of lower-level, rote skills, such as computation in math, recalling facts in science, decoding words in reading, and spelling, grammar, and punctuation in writing. Most students can remember facts, solve routine textbook problems, and apply formulas. Many fewer can use what knowledge they have to solve more complex problems—problems that might take several steps and have no obvious, immediate answer. Many if not most students have difficulty using what they know to interpret an experiment, comprehend a text, or persuade an audience. They can't rise above the rote, factual level to think critically or creatively. They can't apply what they know flexibly and spontaneously to solve ill-structured, ambiguous problems that require interpretation.
> (Bruer, 1993, p. 5)

Whether this indictment is justified is debatable. And even if it is justified, it is possible that the shortcomings are due not to direct instruction but to many other defects in American education. Improved direct instruction, benefiting from research findings like those we have described, might remedy the shortcomings in achievement.

POLICY, RESEARCH, AND PRACTICE

How Can Teachers Improve the Academic Learning Time (ALT) of Students?

One answer is simply to *allocate more time* to academic activities. In planning their daily schedules, teachers can set aside 45 minutes instead of 30 minutes for reading or mathematics. It may be possible to do so without sacrificing something that, on careful examination, is truly valuable. It turns out that teachers differ greatly in the efficiency with which they use class time. And it also turns out that more efficient ways of using time—or avoiding waste of time—are associated with higher student achievement.

What are these more efficient ways of using teaching time? Studies of the teaching behaviors found to correlate with class achievement in reading in the early grades made it possible to identify behaviors that seemed effective because they reduced wasted time and increased academic learning time. Teachers should:

1. *Have a system of rules* that allows students to attend to their personal and procedural needs without having to obtain the teacher's permission.

2. *Move around the room* to monitor students' seatwork and communicate awareness of their behavior.

3. *See to it that assignments are interesting, worthwhile, and still easy enough* to be completed by each student working without teacher direction.

4. *Be sure to provide, but keep to a minimum, such activities as giving directions and organizing* the class for instruction. Teachers can do this by writing the daily schedule on the board, ensuring that students know where to go and what to do. Some nonengaged activities—transitions before and after breaks, housekeeping tasks, and waiting between activities—are inevitable but should be done quickly.

5. *Make abundant use of textbooks, workbooks, and other paper-and-pencil activities.* Using such materials—as opposed to use of nonacademic games, toys, and machines—has been found to be associated with higher student achievement.

6. *Avoid "timing errors."* That is, teachers should prevent misbehavior from continuing long enough to increase in severity or spread to and affect other children.

7. *Avoid "target errors."* That is, teachers should attempt to direct disciplinary action accurately—at the student who is the primary cause of a disruption.

These teaching practices for seatwork seem effective on the basis of correlational studies. They make good sense as well. Even if they were obvious, it would not mean that teachers do not need this information or that they are already behaving in these ways. These teacher-behavior variables would not have correlated with student achievement if teachers did not vary a lot in doing these things.

Yet these ways of improving seatwork may not be as effective as simply reducing (*not eliminating*) the amount of seatwork. This idea makes sense, not because seatwork is trivial or without value, but because students have been found in various studies to be academically engaged less often during seatwork (about 70 percent of the time) than during teacher-led group work (about 84 percent of the time).

CULTURAL DIFFERENCES IN ALT

The importance and meaning of some of the ideas about academic learning time can be seen in how time is spent in mathematics classes in three countries: Japan (J), Taiwan (T), and the United States (U.S.) (Stigler, Lee, & Stevenson, 1987). Based on a very small non-random sample, it appears that the two Asian countries have significantly higher average mathematics achievement than the United States from kindergarten all the way through high school. The differences in how time is spent in mathematics classes appear in Table 12.5.

It also seems highly likely that teaching-practice differences among nations are at least some of the causes of these differences in achievement. In the table there is a much greater effectiveness in fostering ALT among students in Japan and Taiwan. That is, the United States is consistently higher (worse) than Japan and Taiwan in the various indices of off-task behavior, and Japan and Taiwan are consistently higher in the on-task behaviors. Given what we know about the relationship between ALT and achievement, we should not be surprised that the two Asian countries do better on average in mathematics than the United States.

We also have evidence, from the United States and other countries, that the relationship between ALT-related teaching practices and achievement is a causal one. Fifteen experiments have been performed in several countries in grades 1 to 13 over a semester or school year with regular teachers and regular curricula. The experiments used randomly assigned control and experimental groups of teachers, with the latter receiving training enabling them to understand and use practices of the kind described in the list above. The classes of the trained teachers consistently did better than those of the control groups on measures of achievement, attitude, and behavior (Gage & Needels, 1989; Needels & Gage, 1991).

In addition, a comprehensive and careful study (discussed on pages 499–
continues

TABLE

12.5

Observed Differences between Mathematics Classrooms in Grades 1 and 5 in Japan (J), Taiwan (T), and the United States (U.S.)

Class organization, total class	J, T > U.S.
Leader of activity, teacher	T > J > U.S.
On-task behaviors: attending	T > J > U.S.
Ask academic question	T > J > U.S.
Seatwork	U.S. > T, J
Off-task behaviors	
Out of seat	U.S. > T, J
Out of seat and off-task	U.S. > T, J
Inappropriate peer interaction	U.S. > T, J
Other inappropriate action	U.S. > T, J
Total inappropriate	U.S. > T, J
Who teacher works with	
Class	J, T, > U.S.
Group	U.S. > J, T
Individual	U.S. > J, T
No one	U.S. > J, T
Teaching behaviors	
Imparting information	T > J > U.S.
Ask academic question (individual)	U.S. > J, T
Ask academic question (group)	J, T > U.S.
Ask nonacademic question	U.S. > J, T
Giving directions	U.S., J > T
Academic feedback	
Praise	U.S. > J, T
Correct	U.S., J > T
Behavior feedback	
Physical correction	T > U.S., J
Punishment	T, J > U.S.
Use of audiovisual	U.S., T > J

Source: Adapted from Stigler, Lee, and Stevenson, "Mathematics Classrooms in Japan, Taiwan, and the United States," Child Development, 58, 1987, pp. 1272–1285. Reprinted by permission.

500) has indicated that many U.S. eighth-graders rank lower in mathematics and science achievement than do those in other countries (Beaton et al., 1996a; 1996b). It seems likely that at least part of the lower U.S. standings could be overcome by educating teachers in practices of the kinds described in this chapter.

Constructivist Teaching

A different kind of classroom teaching has received much attention from educators in recent decades: constructivist teaching. How does constructivist teaching differ from direct instruction? The answer should follow from the constructivist view of learning (see Chapter 7), which holds

Do you remember how "constructivist learning" is defined? Write a brief explanation in your own words; then check the presentation in Chapter 7.

that students learn not by passively receivi
structing, or reconstructing, knowledge on th
ence interacts with their previous knowledge.
is remembered according to how it fits in
knowledge. So it is summarized, distorted, or
structed—rather than merely recorded verb
when we hear a lecture, we remember few of
Rather, we remember its gist, which we construct as it interacts with our previous knowledge, interests, expectations.

If students are to do this constructing, they need opportunities to resolve differences between their initial knowledge and their new experience. Constructivist teaching seeks to provide those opportunities.

The Nature of Constructivist Teaching   To engage in constructivist teaching, the teacher must relinquish some of his or her control over what students do, to enable them to do more on their own. Some of the ways of doing this have been to

- bring out what students already know, believe, expect, and are capable of doing. This can be done by asking students questions, having them bring forth ideas in a group discussion, or brainstorming.
- arrange for discovery learning, in which the various approaches described in Chapters 7 and 11 are used. The teacher gives students a problem, a set of phenomena, or a series of results (as in science or math) and asks an individual student or group of students to find the concept or principle that explains the phenomena or solves the problem.
- ask students to identify their own problems in the subject matter being studied and define "projects" that would help them resolve those problems. The problems can take an unlimited variety of forms, such as:

Why are blue reflectors placed on the pavement in the middle of streets in some cities? (A: Students visit streets and discover inductively that the reflectors are used to mark the location of fire hydrants so that firefighters can more easily locate them at night.)

Why did the U.S. Senate play no role in the impeachment of President Nixon? (A: By consulting the U.S. Constitution, students discover that the House of Representatives always does the impeaching; the Senate conducts the trial. But because Nixon resigned after the House Judiciary Committee adopted two articles of impeachment, there was no impeachment and no trial.)

Why do we indent each subproduct by one digit after multiplying by each successive digit in a multidigit multiplier? (A: Students discuss this question and finally realize that each successive multiplier digit stands for 10 times its amount as it moves one space to the left, so that its product has 10 times the value and should be indented accordingly.)

Confrey (1990) described the implications of constructivism for teaching mathematics. But they apply to any subject. They call for "promotion of autonomy and commitment in the students; development of students' reflective processes; construction of 'case histories'; identification and negotiation of tentative solution paths with the students; retracing the solution paths; and adherence to the intent of the materials" (p. 1

Promoting autonomy and commitment means such things as getting students to make a commitment to their answers, questioning students answers whether they are right or wrong, asking students to explain what they have tried, staying with students long enough to give them a good start, walking away from students if they are being too dependent, and encouraging students to take credit for their successes.

Developing students' reflective processes takes such forms as getting students to face a problem in the subject matter, asking them to restate it in their own words, getting them to explain how they are trying to solve the problem, and asking them to justify the strategy they are trying.

Construction of "case histories" refers to the teacher's coming to an understanding of each student's characteristic ways of approaching problems. One student, for example, might usually reject the use of diagrams and rely on poorly understood rules, and another student may tend to give up altogether. The teacher tries to understand the reasons for these tendencies.

Identification and negotiation of a tentative solution path means the teacher uses the "case histories" to anticipate and analyze students' inadequacies in solving problems and then works out with them possible ways of overcoming their difficulties. Options include "relating ideas to other concepts, . . . pushing toward consistency with other concepts, . . . or exploring the idea from multiple perspectives" (Confrey, 1990, p. 121).

Retracing and reviewing the solution path involves going back over the problem after it has been correctly solved, giving the student an understanding of what he or she has achieved and time to think about the whole problem and its solution.

Adherence to the intent of the materials—that is, the constructivist method—refers to having an approach that does not require remaining silent but permits "telling" the students, on occasion, what they need in order to make progress. It is the intent of the method—helping students make sense of the content on their own as much as possible—not any iron-clad rule, that is important.

The Effectiveness of Constructivist Teaching. This kind of learning takes more time than direct instruction per unit of content (concept, principle, or the like), which means that less content can be covered in a given amount of time. But it may also mean that students develop a deeper understanding of the topic, one that they will be better able to apply in new learning and problem solving. So some breadth of learning may be sacrificed for greater depth.

Is greater depth of understanding better than greater breadth of knowledge? Here we get into matters of *values*—what is important in education. And how does the *breadth of knowledge*—the amount of knowledge of facts, word meanings, concepts, principles, and so forth—of students taught "constructively" in a given part of the curriculum compare with that of students taught the same subject matter for the same amount of time by direct instruction? Do "constructively" taught stu-

The constructivist teacher attempts to have children develop their knowledge for themselves.

(© Elizabeth Crews/ The Image Works)

dents have a deeper understanding of the desired *propositional knowledge?* Are they more skillful with desired *procedural knowledge?*

What about retention and transfer? That is, do constructively taught students remember longer what they learned? Are they better in school and in the "real world" at applying their knowledge to the solution of new kinds of problems in the subject matter?

Such questions can in fact be resolved, but only in part, through empirical research. So far, however, persuasive research-based answers to these questions are not available, at least not in any abundance. We sketch some tentative evidence in what follows.

TIMSS   Despite the lack of definitive answers, some hints can be seen in the results of a set of international comparisons made by TIMSS— the Third International Mathematics and Science Study (Beaton et al., 1996a; 1996b). Using careful sampling and control methods in 41 countries to maximize the comparability of the results across nations, TIMSS obtained average scores on achievement tests in mathematics and science of 13-year-olds (eighth-graders in the U.S.). The United States ranked slightly below the average of the TIMSS countries in mathematics, and slightly above the average in science. Japan, by contrast, ranked third in both mathematics and science. Comparing the United States and Japan bears on constructivist teaching because the evidence based on analyses of teaching in the two countries suggests that Japanese teachers teach in a more constructivist way than U.S. teachers do. For example, when teachers reported how often they ask students to do reasoning tasks in math, the percentages shown in Table 12.6 were obtained. (Data on this question were unavailable for U.S. teachers of science.) They show a distinct tendency for Japanese teachers to ask students to do reasoning tasks more often. These data do not, of course, necessarily mean that using more reasoning tasks *causes* higher achievement. It is conceivable that Japanese teachers can give more reasoning

TABLE

12.6

12.6

Mathematics Teachers' Reports on How Often They Ask Students to Do Reasoning Tasks

	Never or Almost Never	Some Lessons	Most Lessons	Every Lesson
Japan	0	7	55	37
U.S.	0	24	50	26

Source: Beaton et al. (1996a, p. 160).

tasks to their students because they are already achieving better, so that they can handle such tasks.

International Observational Comparisons Other suggestive evidence on teaching comes from an investigation of mathematics and science teaching in six countries, including the United States and Japan (Schmidt et al., 1996). Using the concept of **characteristic pedagogical flow** (CPF)—"recurrent patterns of instruction and classroom activity" (p. 71), the study described CPF in the United States as follows:

> Lessons from the US were characterized by teachers presenting information and directing student activities and exercises. The multiplicity and diversity of both topics and activities were a unique feature of US lessons. Both teacher and student activity tended to emphasize the basic definitions, procedures and concepts of subject matter. Consistent with the cognitive emphasis found in textbooks, the preponderance of lesson discussion involved information about procedures, exercises and basic facts. Content complexity in lessons stemmed from an emphasis on knowing technical vocabulary and definitions. Periods of independent student practice were common. . . . Such periods contributed to the low content visibility in some observed lessons. These general characterizations seem to have held despite greater variability and diversity among the US lessons than among those from any other country.
>
> *(Schmidt et al., 1996, pp. 131–132)*

On the other hand,

> Japanese lessons were characterized as built around a consideration of multiple approaches to carefully chosen practical examples or activities through which the teacher led students into an understanding of subject matter concepts and relationships. Subject matter complexity was primarily due to the way in which topics were developed and sequenced in the curriculum, and to the relatively focused and coherent development of them within lessons. Topic development in lessons generally occurred through subtly directed class discus-

sions interspersed with periods for individual or small group reflection or practice.

(Schmidt et al., 1996, p. 130)

It is possible to see in these descriptions a more constructivist approach on the part of Japanese teachers. And again, the association of that approach with higher achievement in Japan is suggestive. But there are many other possible reasons (student characteristics, socio-cultural factors, and so forth), that could have brought about the higher achievement of Japanese students.

An experiment provides another hint. It comes from an experiment (reported in Bruer, 1993) by Case and Griffin, who designed material for teaching first-graders the number line and basic operations on it: "forward and backward counting, making one-to-one comparisons, comparing numbers, and . . . moving up and down one unit on the number line" (p. 89). The material provided games that up to five children could play together—rolling dice and deciding who had more dots, deciding how many cookies were in a bag if one was added or removed. Low-achieving children from low-SES homes were put into either the experimental group or the control group; the latter "received only the standard classroom math instruction." On the posttest, 87 percent of the experimental group passed, while only 25 percent of the control group did so. If the experimental and control treatments may be regarded as examples of constructivist teaching and direct instruction, respectively, the evidence clearly favors the constructivist approach.

These samples of the kind of research available on the effectiveness of constructivist teaching are far from conclusive. Much more evidence, based on careful experiments, replicated and summarized by meta-analysis, is necessary before a constructivist "revolution" in teaching is justified. But positive evidence on its effects is growing.

> As with all aspects of teaching, you will need to use your judgment about how much emphasis you give constructivist teaching approaches in your own classroom. What do you believe now about how constructivist a teacher you would like to be, and why?

Criticisms of Constructivist Teaching   The idea of constructivist teaching is relatively new. But it has predecessors: the romanticist education of French philosopher Rousseau (see Hirsch, 1996), progressive education, the project method, humanistic education, open education, discovery learning, and student-centered education. These ideas were based on different theories, but led to similar teaching practices. Although they have been the basis of major reform movements in twentieth-century American education, none has ever prevailed.

The history of how teachers taught during the years from 1890 to 1980 was examined by Cuban (1992). More specifically, he looked into the degree to which teacher-centered or student-centered instruction prevailed. By *teacher-centered*, he meant instruction where teachers do most of the talking, usually teach the whole class rather than individually or small groups, determine the use of time, and arrange students' desks in rows facing the chalkboard. In the student-centered classroom, students talk as much or more than the teacher, are usually taught individually or in small groups, may have a voice in choosing and organizing learning and the rules of classroom conduct, have available a variety of materials, and often have a voice in determining how the materials are used. The student-centered classroom is also arranged to allow students to move around and work together. Cuban's teacher-centered instruction looks a lot like what is called traditional, conventional, or direct classroom teaching. And his student-centered instruction bears some resemblance to constructivist education.

To write his history, Cuban could not refer to systematic observational research on what went on in classrooms from 1890 to 1980—such observation was extremely rare until about 1960. So he used an ingenious array of evidence: photographs of teachers and students in class, textbooks and tests teachers used, students' recollections of their experiences in classrooms, and the like (Cuban, 1984).

Cuban discovered that teacher-centered instruction predominated from 1890 to 1980 despite major reform efforts on the part of progressive, open, and discovery-oriented educators. Teacher-centered instruction has been extremely viable over the years. Student-centered education has seldom been adopted, and when it was, it was eventually again replaced by the teacher-centered instruction reformers had struggled to change.

An attempt to understand "what went wrong" with the open-education approach was made by Rothenberg (1989). He found that this type of student-centered education was "very demanding" and did not seem to improve achievement (on average). It was often inadequately prepared, used without integrating its elements into a unified approach, and often so poorly monitored that it allowed students to neglect important parts of the curriculum, especially the basic skills. Perhaps the student-centered movement promised more than it could deliver. It was often opposed by low-income and minority-group parents who saw it as neglecting basic skills and experimenting on their children.

Criticism of constructivist teaching has not been absent either. Although student-centered teaching and constructivist teaching are not identical, they are similar. If nothing else, they both call for radical departures from traditional, teacher-centered, direct instruction.

Hirsch (1996) accepts the premise that people construct (rather than receive passively) the meaning of what they read, hear, or otherwise experience. "But," he says, "constructivism is not only desirable, it is also universal" (p. 134). That is, it is true of everything meaningful that we experience, and so it does not require any special kind of experience or teaching. Furthermore, "the amount of *useful* construction and learning that occur depends chiefly on the amount of relevant background the student already possesses rather than on the mode of instruction" (p. 134). Even if discovery learning is better retained, Hirsch continues, it takes more time. And it sometimes leads to learning that is beside the point, unrelated to the purposes of the teaching, and even incorrect.

Criticisms of discovery learning also have a history. Ausubel (1963), in particular, cogently expounded the "psychological and educational limitations of learning by discovery." He questioned, among other things, whether "all real knowledge is self-discovered"; whether meaning is exclusively the product of creative, nonverbal discovery; and whether the discovery method is adequate for transmitting subject-matter content.

Highly persuasive evidence on the effectiveness of constructivist, or discovery, learning is not yet in. "Educators are too hasty in concluding that constructivism justifies 'MORE experiential, inductive, hands-on learning, MORE active learning with all the attendant noise of students doing, talking, collaborating'" (Hirsch, 1996, p. 135). As noted in Chapter 7, however, teaching from a discovery-learning perspective has some distinct advantages. Chief among them are its motivational effects and the fact that information learned through genuine discovery is rarely forgotten. Perhaps the best route for teachers is one combining elements of both approaches—what we referred to as *guided discovery* in Chapter 7. Let us explore this idea further.

A Synthesis of Direct Instruction and Constructivist Teaching

> Draw up a sample lesson plan in your content area, using both direct instruction and constructivist teaching methods and procedures. Do you see how they can work in tandem?

To minimize the disadvantages and emphasize the advantages of both direct instruction and constructivist teaching, one solution would be to combine the two approaches in the classroom. To do so, the teacher would use one or the other at any given time, depending upon everything from curriculum goals to time constraints. This would be necessary because even if the effectiveness of constructivist teaching were to become well established, it would still likely be impracticable to use exclusively. The well-established efficacy of direct instruction—especially when structuring, soliciting, and reacting are conducted according to the abundant research results described above—continues to make it useful for a good portion of teaching.

But since it certainly does not address all needs at all times, a synthesis and an alternation of the two approaches probably serves best. Such a synthesis is seen in college courses where, in addition to teacher-directed listening and reading, students engage in laboratory experiences, and write term papers on topics and with methods and resources of their own choosing, with the guidance of their instructor. Similar combinations of the direct and constructivist approaches seem feasible at the elementary and secondary school levels. Children come in many different varieties, and their parents hold many different goals for schooling. So a teacher wedded to a single approach to education may do injustice to many students and displease many parents. A professional eclecticism would seem to be a wise compromise.

S U M M A R Y

1. Classroom teaching, the most common kind of teaching, has several distinguishing characteristics.

2. There are two phases of classroom teaching: the planning phase and the interactive phase. Planning deals with what goes on before the

teacher faces the students and before the assessment of achievement. The interactive phase, the heart of teaching, goes on during the actual instructional time, when teacher and students are talking, listening, and attending to one another.

3. Classroom teaching typically includes an instructional segment called *recitation.* Although recitation usually comprises four kinds of predictable behaviors, it is far more flexible than commonly believed and can go on in a great variety of ways.

4. Within classroom teaching, there is room for different approaches to instruction. Among them are the more teacher-controlled direct instruction and the more student-centered constructivist teaching.

5. Along with recitation, classroom teaching combines lecturing, discussion, and individual instruction. It is more than the sum of these parts, however; it is more like an orchestration of teaching methods in which the relationships among the methods are just as important as the methods themselves.

6. Classroom teaching has remained prevalent for centuries for many reasons, including its adaptability, the reinforcement value of questioning to the teacher, the requirements imposed by customary class size, and its suitability to the basic tasks of instruction.

7. The planning phase follows a hierarchy of planning needs. Teachers plan for (1) discipline, control, and management; (2) eliminating biases in dealing with individual students; (3) using pedagogical content knowledge; (4) providing scaffolding; and (5) variety and flexibility.

8. In planning for classroom discipline and control, teachers must deal with behavior problems of two kinds: too much unwanted behavior and too little wanted behavior.

9. For the "too-much" kind, prevention is best. If that does not work, teachers can withdraw attention (their own and that of the other students), strengthen incompatible behavior, or use punishment.

10. The "too-little" kind, although less disruptive, can actually be more serious. Teachers should consider referring an extremely shy or withdrawn child to a mental health professional. To increase wanted behaviors, a teacher can elicit the behaviors, provide positive models, and use reinforcement and shaping techniques. (Contracts can also help.)

11. Research has shown that bias is widespread in classroom teaching. To control it, teachers must compensate for their tendencies to treat students differently, and often unfairly, according to their gender, social class, achievement, intelligence, race, ethnic background, physical attractiveness, or even location in the classroom. Everything a teacher does at school—choosing a student to call on, waiting for a student to answer, reacting to the student's answer—is affected by biases. Giving yourself cues and reminders to control these biases may be helpful here.

12. Planning to use your pedagogical content knowledge helps you to teach the main ideas and the structure of the field, and to use the right analogies and examples for the content, in response to the context of the classroom and your students' abilities.

13. Planning to provide scaffolds helps students learn what they should in less structured areas of the curriculum.

14. Planning for variety and flexibility, which have been found to be associated with higher student achievement, helps in developing and choosing among alternative ways of carrying out instructional tasks. Variety can apply to almost everything about instruction—teaching style, use of materials, methods of motivation, content and objectives, ways of assessing student achievement, and so on.

15. Recent major reviews of studies on and experiments in direct instruction have made possible a research-based examination of the kinds of teacher behaviors that are more and less effective. The groupings of these behaviors—structuring, soliciting, and reacting—are based on the three links in the classroom recitation chain that the teacher controls.

16. Structuring behaviors include the rate of teacher initiation and structuring, signal giving, organization, and teacher talk. Research evidence suggests that teacher initiation and structuring should be at moderate or intermediate levels, that signal giving is effective, that at least the perception of organization is probably associated with student achievement, and that amount of teacher talk relates positively to achievement.

17. The frequency of teachers' soliciting behaviors (typically, asking questions) has no consistent relationship to student achievement. The cognitive level of teachers' questions is positively related to the cognitive level of students' answers, and somewhat to student achievement. Wait-time I, how long teachers wait after asking a question, is important; it should be about three seconds. It seems, too, that less academically-oriented students should be asked slightly less difficult questions. Research on the targeting of questions to particular students—predictable or random—shows a positive association between predictable targeting and higher achievement, at least in the lower grades. Redirecting questions and probing also seem, on the basis of a few studies, to be associated with higher achievement.

18. Reacting behaviors can be quick or less quick, positive or negative. Increasing wait-time II—the time between the student's response and the teacher's next utterance—to about three seconds has beneficial effects.

19. Of the positive reactions, the frequency of praise in itself has inconsistent relationships with achievement. But some evidence suggests that contingent, or appropriate, praise is associated with higher achievement, especially for less academically-oriented students. Accepting and using students' ideas goes along fairly consistently with higher achievement, as does the reinforcing use of tokens for appropriate student responses.

20. Of the negative reactions, criticism is consistently associated with lower achievement, but the question of which of the two variables causes the other is much in doubt. Structuring reactions—redirecting questions and end-structuring—seem, on slight evidence, to be positively associated with achievement. Responses to low-achieving students need to be monitored carefully. Many teachers have been found to unintentionally discriminate against low-achievers in a variety of subtle ways.

21. Seatwork is effective to the degree that it fosters academic learning time (ALT)—time actually spent engaged with academic tasks in

which the student is successful. Ways to increase ALT include using systems of rules and schedules, teacher monitoring, using academic materials (not overdoing the use of toys and games), and avoiding disciplinary errors. Experiments in which some teachers have been trained to use these and similar practices have resulted in substantially improved class achievement, compared with that of teachers who have not received the training. The experiments support the causal efficacy of these practices in improving achievement.

22. Constructivist teaching, recently emerged by that name, calls upon teachers to give students autonomy and freedom to discover and formulate their own meanings of phenomena and solutions to problems. Only suggestive evidence of its effectiveness has so far appeared. Its basic premise—that a special kind of teaching is needed in order for students to engage in constructing meanings—has been questioned. It does seem, however, that students in constructivist learning environments enjoy their education more.

23. Perhaps the best way of realizing the advantages of both constructivist teaching and direct instruction is a synthesis of the two approaches, in which teachers combine elements of both approaches in particular instructional situations.

PART FIVE

Assessment

All your life you have been taking tests. They have brought you success or failure, joy or sorrow, a sense of justice done or outrage suffered. In this part, we introduce you to the theory and practice of testing—or, speaking more broadly, the processes of educational assessment in whose service tests are often used.

In Chapter 13 we deal with basic concepts and distinctions you should understand if you are going to have a professional grasp of the subject. We also give you some insights into standardized testing, an industry that has developed to help teachers, administrators, and parents make better decisions about the promise of a child's success in courses, schools, and jobs, and to make judgments about the effectiveness of school, city, and state educational programs. Standardized tests, however, have some negative side effects, and you need to know those, too. In Chapter 14, we look at ways for you to make your own tests—the instruments with which you can best evaluate your students' achievement of the objectives you have been aiming toward in your own class. Some of these forms of testing are newly created, so you might never have been exposed to them yourself. We also go into the complex, touchy, and controversial subject of grading, where the spectrum of opinion ranges from those who favor outright abolition of grades to those who favor more frequent testing and stricter grading.

Basic Concepts in Assessment and the Interpretation of Standardized Testing

Overview

ASSESSMENT WITH TESTS
  Systematic Procedures
  Measuring
  Behavior
  Sample
  Evaluation
  Standards and Norms
NORM-REFERENCED TESTING
  Using a Local Norm Group
  Using a National Norm Group
CRITERION-REFERENCED TESTING
RELIABILITY
  Test-Retest Reliability
    Norm-referenced tests
    Criterion-referenced tests
  Internal-Consistency Reliability
  The Standard Error of Measurement
  Improving Reliability
VALIDITY
  Content Validity

  Criterion Validity
  Construct Validity
EVALUATION
  Formative Evaluation
  Summative Evaluation
STANDARDIZED TESTS IN THE ASSESSMENT PROCESS
  Advantages and Special Uses of Standardized Tests
  Disadvantages of and Concerns about Standardized Tests
  Types of Standardized Tests Used in Schools
    Achievement tests
    Aptitude tests

POLICY, RESEARCH, AND PRACTICE
Is It Fair to Publish Standardized Achievement Test Scores?

    Differences between aptitude and achievement tests

APPLICATION
Taking a Test to Understand It

  Administering Standardized Tests
  Interpreting Standardized Tests

POLICY, RESEARCH, AND PRACTICE
High-Stakes Standardized Testing Can Have Some Very Undesirable Consequences

  What Does the Future Hold for Standardized Testing?

Summary

OVERVIEW

Assessment is the process of collecting, interpreting, and synthesizing information in order to (1) make decisions about students; (2) give students feedback about their progress and their strengths and weaknesses; (3) judge instructional effectiveness; and (4) inform educational policy (American Federation of Teachers, et al., 1990).

Teachers make decisions about their students virtually every few minutes of the day. They may be concerned about whether their class understands a particular concept. Or whether Sandra can complete the assignment within the time allowed. They ask questions like these: "Is Tony adjusting to the front row?" "Am I going too fast or too slow?" So assessment—making information-based decisions—is an everyday activity for teachers.

Assessment of student characteristics or achievement can be informal, to obtain general information about a student. In such cases few records are kept; most of the information is stored in the teacher's mind. Assessment can also be formal, in which case it usually involves assignments, quizzes, reports, and tests. Sometimes the formal evaluations are used for official purposes, such as giving grades or placing students in special programs. Formal evaluations are mainly assessments of cognitive achievement, and records are kept of such assessments.

This chapter discusses the basic concepts of assessment: the nature of tests, how standards and norms are created for judging test performance, how tests are linked to those norms or to criteria set in advance, and how tests must show reliability and validity. We cover also the ways in which educational evaluation takes place, both to improve curriculum, instructional methods, or projects, and to judge their usefulness and cost-effectiveness. In addition, we examine the ways in which educators select, administer, and interpret standardized tests in order to provide better assessments. The differences between standardized aptitude and achievement tests are pointed out, and the serious side effects of "high-stakes" standardized testing are discussed.

Assessment with Tests

A test is a systematic procedure for measuring a sample of a person's behavior in order to evaluate that behavior against standards and norms. Tests generally come in two forms: norm-referenced and criterion-referenced. Good tests of either type must be reliable and valid. Let us take a closer look at some of the concepts about tests that were used in these three sentences.

Systematic Procedures

We are all observers, constantly watching the world around us. But most of our observations are unsystematic, and what they tell us may well turn out to be untrue or only partially true. Suppose you are watching some young children playing on swings. Yes, you can see what they are doing, but you can't judge their psychomotor skills. To do that, you would have to hold constant the kind of swing, the chain or rope holding the swing, how the children get started (with a push or by themselves). Your observations would have to follow some standardized procedures, rules, and schedules—a system—so that all the children have an equal chance to show their psychomotor ability. Anything less would result in some kinds of bias and unfairness.

In the same way, you cannot judge problem-solving ability by just

When we want estimates of a student's achievement, we have to use systematic procedures to obtain those estimates.
(© Mimi Forsyth/Monkmeyer)

Arrange with a friend to do an informal observation of children on the playground. Compare your notes afterward. Are there any important discrepancies between your sets of observations?

watching. Suppose your brother and his friend are both trying to figure out a way to get a raise in their allowances. If your brother manages to get a raise and his friend does not, does this mean his friend has less problem-solving ability? Without systematic procedures, you cannot tell. Maybe he does, or maybe your parents had a different attitude than the friend's parents to begin with.

The point is that casual, unsystematic observation is not enough for teachers. For feedback to students and their parents, and for examining the effectiveness of their own teaching, irregular, unsystematic observation is much too fallible. Too much is at stake! When we want estimates of a student's achievement, as we surely do a great many times each school year, we have to use systematic procedures to obtain those estimates. A test is a method for obtaining trustworthy estimates of achievement. A test, when designed correctly, provides the same stimuli (e.g., questions) for all students. Tests are not substitutes for observations. They are themselves observations of behavior—observations that are more efficient, more refined, and less biased than other ways of observing. Tests are also easier to summarize and interpret than most other kinds of observation. Perhaps it is for this reason that, in surveys of test use, about 90 percent of elementary school teachers and 99 percent of high school teachers said they used tests as part of their assessment of students. In fact, 16 percent of the teachers reported using tests daily, 95 percent used them weekly, and 98 percent reported at least biweekly use of tests (Gullickson, 1990). Overall, a reasonable estimate is that teachers spend 20 to 30 percent of their time in assessment, and that time is often connected to testing activities. So it is important to learn about testing procedures.

Measuring

One reason for the popularity of tests is that they give teachers a quantitative estimate of ability or achievement—they tell us how much. In education, the attributes that interest us emphasize the abilities and achievements of students, including such things as intelligence, creativity, spelling ability, science knowledge, and interest in art. When we quantify a student's social studies achievement, academic aptitude, or appreciation of poetry, we are measuring.

Some tests are objectively scoreable in that it is easy to get different judges to agree about the score or measure yielded by the test. **Objectively-scoreable tests** can be scored by clerks or machines. **Subjectively-scoreable tests** require expert judgment, and it is harder to get the experts to agree exactly or closely because the criteria each expert uses when scoring the tests either are not described or cannot be described. The objectivity or subjectivity of a test depends on the scoring, not on the test's content.

Behavior

Tests are designed to elicit behavior from students. Educators cannot deal with what students are thinking when they solve problems unless we can observe that thinking through their thinking aloud, their writing, or their solutions to problems. We cannot study students' creativity unless we can see its processes and its product—that is, the creative behaviors. That we must rely on what is observable is an important point. How else can a teacher know what that silent boy in the back row is really thinking about and taking in? How else to know whether a young child turning the pages of a book is actually capable of reading? Whether it is thoughtfulness, physical prowess, understanding, or a host of other characteristics we want to examine, we must first convert them into observable behaviors before we can measure them.

Sample

We must remember that a test samples behavior. We do not test all of a student's mathematics knowledge or ability to understand French. We use only a small number of the many possible tasks or problems to determine whether the student knows how to add or knows the meaning of common French words. From that sample, we estimate how well the student can use information or apply ideas. That is, we generalize from a small sample of behavior to the larger domain of behavior we are really interested in—from items about such things as World War I to knowledge of history. So the chosen sample of behavior should be as unbiased as possible, should cover important areas of the curriculum, and should provide many ways for the student to demonstrate competence. When certain students perform poorly on a test, the fault may lie with our sampling procedure, not their ability. Every one of us has at some time or other felt ready to take a test—only to find we knew the answers

Describe an experience from your own schooling in which a test did not fairly assess your knowledge. How did you feel about it?

to a lot of questions the teacher did not ask! (We describe some methods to raise the probability that a test is a fair sampling of behavior relevant to achievement in Chapter 14.)

Evaluation

Evaluation is the process by which we attach value to something. We use our values to make judgments about the quality of something—a student or a teacher, a movie or a play, a computer program or a school system (Baker & Niemi, 1996). We may measure a sample of a student's observable behavior to estimate how much of a given attribute that student has. But evaluating the measures—attaching value to and judging their meaning—is an altogether separate process. For example, suppose a student scores 40 points on a reading comprehension test. What does this measurement tell us about the student's reading comprehension? Is it good enough or weak, commendable or regrettable? In the process of evaluating, we determine how well a student has mastered the material. Or an evaluation can tell us whether a student should be recommended for acceleration, or whether a class is doing poorly, or whether a school is achieving at an excellent level. Measurement gives us numbers. Human judgment and interpretation turn those numbers into evaluations.

Standards and Norms

Standards and norms are both means of comparison. When educators talk about standards, they mean that people have made a judgment about what is minimally acceptable and reasonable performance for an individual or a group of individuals on a specific test. If you meet the standard for a driver's license, you are an acceptable driver, not necessarily an excellent one. A student's numerical score is evaluated differently depending on the standards used to interpret it. We might want to know whether a score of 40 points on a reading comprehension test is above or below the established criterion for acceptable competence in reading.

A standard is different from a norm, which is used to interpret a student's score in relation to the scores of other students. Norms require comparisons among students. Some norms, such as those based on students in the same class or in the same school district, are called *local norms*. Other norms, such as those derived from a sample of students representing the whole state or country, are called *state* or *national norms*. Both of these kinds of norms are used to interpret the scores obtained in norm-referenced testing. Standards, on the other hand, are used in criterion-referenced testing.

Next we define and examine the nature of these two markedly different forms of testing. Later in this chapter we look at norm-referenced tests and criterion-referenced tests in terms of their use as published, standardized tests in our schools.

Norm-Referenced Testing

Norm-referenced tests (NRT) are those that use the test performance of other people on the same measuring instrument as a basis for interpreting an individual's test performance. A norm-referenced measure allows us to compare one individual with other individuals. Although such comparison provides some very useful information, it can be the cause of a great deal of student misery. Since students differ in ability, there are always winners and losers when norm-referenced testing is used in evaluation.

Using a Local Norm Group

Suppose Lisa received the highest score, an A, on her test in auto mechanics class (her peer group). Gloria, with a B, was seventh highest in the class. In this norm-referenced situation, using the scores of their immediate peer group as our norms, we can say that Lisa knows more about auto mechanics than Gloria knows, at least as measured by this test. But unfortunately the scores by themselves tell us nothing about what the two girls really know.

Suppose the test they took was used as a basis for admission to an advanced class in auto mechanics. If only six openings were available, Lisa would get into the class and Gloria would not. It may be that even Lisa does not know enough to be able to benefit from the advanced class, but we could not determine this fact from the norm-referenced test because it does not necessarily tell us what Lisa knows about how cars work. It tells us only where she ranks in comparison with others who took the same test.

So norm-referenced tests give us a way to distinguish between higher-achieving and lower-achieving students in a particular subject matter area. When the norm group is a student's own class or fellow students in the same grade at school or within the district, the local peer group provides the norms by which we judge performance.

Using a National Norm Group

Let us say that Perry and Lisa both take a national test on knowledge of auto mechanics. Perry scores at the 74th percentile in comparison with thousands of others around the nation who have taken the same test. That is, his knowledge of auto mechanics is equal to or better than 74 percent of the students who took this test. We could also say that only 26 percent of the other students know more about auto mechanics than Perry does. The other students, a representative norm group against which Perry's score can be judged, are like a distant, somewhat invisible peer group. To the degree that the distant peer group is meaningful—that is, appropriate as a basis for comparison—we can interpret Perry's score in light of the group's scores.

Now suppose that Lisa receives a score that places her at the 54th percentile rank on the national norms. Although Lisa's knowledge, when compared with that of her local peer group, was at the 99th percentile rank, she seems clearly less knowledgeable when compared with the distant peer group that made up the national norming group. If we learn, however, that the national norm group—the norm group for the test—contains mostly boys, we can evaluate Lisa's score differently. In many cultures, males tend to know more about the workings of cars than do females, so the comparison *may* not be a fair one. This is the same problem that many African Americans, Hispanic Americans, and Native Americans face with norm-referenced testing when the norms are based on distant, but supposedly representative, peer groups. Minority-group students who show excellent performance relative to their local peers often seem to perform poorly on nationally standardized tests—tests with a national norm group. Why? Perhaps because the national norm group used to judge their scores is not really representative; it may not include enough members of minority groups. For certain purposes, then, the norm group is biased. And a biased norm group can unfairly penalize a minority-group student who has a different cultural background.

In the case of Lisa, if the test is being used as a basis for admission to an auto mechanics course, perhaps her performance should be compared only with that of other women. That is, we might want to use different norms to evaluate performance on a test if we are concerned about equal opportunity, as we are in an admissions test. Here social class, gender, race, and ethnicity can all be relevant considerations. But if the test Lisa took was an evaluation of competency in the course work on auto mechanics and we want highly competent rather than mediocre auto mechanics, then social class, gender, race, and ethnicity are probably irrelevant.

Criterion-Referenced Testing

If we really want to determine the content of what Lisa knows about cars, we would have to abandon the norm-referenced approach and turn to **criterion-referenced evaluation.** No matter what we learn about a person's standing relative to his or her peers, in the norm-referenced approach we can never learn whether the person really knows a certain thing, such as how to diagnose problems with automobile transmissions. Except when the purpose of testing is to select a fraction of students for scarce positions (for example, enrollment in a highly competitive college or a small honors class), a student's achievement would be better assessed through criterion-referenced rather than norm-referenced approaches. For most school purposes, criterion-referenced testing markedly improves assessment and evaluation, though these tests are not used nearly as much as we think they should be. We discuss performance tests, which have recently become so popular, in Chapter 14. Here it is worth noting that performance tests—driving a car, giving a piano recital, building a science project—are used primarily as criterion-referenced tests (Hambleton, 1996).

Criterion-referenced tests measure an individual's ability with respect to some content-based standard or objective. The standard, or criterion, is determined in advance by knowledgeable people in the field. Automobile driving tests are not norm-referenced (who wants the best of a group of bad drivers?); they are criterion-referenced performance tests. Someone's competence is judged against the standards of content knowledge or performance that have been determined in advance. Comparison among students is not a factor here. The criterion-referenced measure is used when we want to know what students know or can do, rather than how they compare with nearby or distant peer groups (Airasian, 1991, 1996). The criterion-referenced test is deliberately constructed to give information that is directly interpretable in terms of an *absolute* criterion of performance.

The absolute criterion is usually based on a teacher's experience with students, on the particular curriculum area, on records of past performance, and also on the teacher's intuition and values. Suppose a teacher decides that students must be able to answer correctly five out of six questions of the following kind for her to believe that they have the comprehension skills she wants them to have:

Which title best describes the following paragraph?
(a) Jessie had a dog
(b) Dogs run away
(c) Why Jessie feels sad

In this case the students would read some short paragraphs and try to give them a title that demonstrated that they comprehend what they read. If a student can answer correctly five or six items such as this, the teacher can conclude that reading skills of the type that were tested have been mastered. Failure to reach the teacher-set criterion, or performance standard, is defined as four or fewer items correct.

In this kind of testing, teachers learn what a particular student can or cannot do. Comparing Enrique's test score with Ann's test score does not meet a big part of a parent's or teacher's need for information about reading comprehension. It is too bad that parents do not always recognize this. They often want information about how their child compares to others rather than information about the actual knowledge and skills their child has learned. Teachers need to educate parents that the criterion-referenced approach is often more in tune with classroom needs than is the norm-referenced approach.

Usually criterion-referenced tests are graded on a pass-fail basis. An example is your state's test of your knowledge of auto-driving laws. You either pass or fail, and in principle everyone taking the test might pass or might fail. You do not get a score comparing you with other people. Teachers' concern here is whether each student has mastered the material, not how much each student knows in relation to what other students know. One student may do more work in an area than another. One student may be quicker to finish work than another. But when it comes to judging proficiency in certain curricular areas, criterion-referenced tests allow us to determine how well students are meeting the criterion. Perhaps all the students will pass a test; perhaps none of them will. If there are several standards for different letter grades (say, 7 out of 10 = C, or 8 or 9 out of 10 = B) perhaps all students will receive a C, or none will.

It is important that the criteria of performance be set before students take a test. Then the criteria cannot be influenced by how well the students do on the test. And then it is impossible for the teacher to adjust standards so that some predetermined percentages of the students receive grades of A, B, and so on. The choice of either norm-referenced or criterion-referenced testing, then, has important consequences for your classroom and school (Gronlund, 1993). Table 13.1 lists some pros and cons of criterion-referenced testing and norm-referenced testing.

> Before studying Table 13.1, make a list from your own experience and knowledge of the pros and cons of each type of testing. Then use the table to check your agreement with it.

TABLE 13.1

Pros and Cons of Criterion- and Norm-Referenced Measurement

Criterion-Referenced Measurement (CRM)

Description

A criterion-referenced test measures whether a student has or has not reached a standard criterion, or specified level of achievement. Test scores depend on specifying an *absolute standard of quality*. This standard is independent of the scores achieved by other students taking the same test and completing the same course.

Applications

Criterion-referenced measurement is useful
- when instruction is guided by standards and objectives.
- for evaluating individualized learning programs.
- for diagnosing student difficulties.
- for estimating a student's ability in a particular area.
- for measuring what (not how much) a student has learned.
- for certification of competence.
- for controlling entry to successive units of instruction.
- whenever mastery of a subject or skill is of prime concern.
- wherever quota-free selection is being used.
- whenever we want to encourage students to cooperate rather than to compete with one another.

Criticisms

Educators tend to disagree about the value of CRM. The following arguments are those that commonly appear in the literature:
- Criterion-referenced measurement tells us what a student knows or can do but does not tell us the degree of excellence or deficiency of the student's performance in relation to peers. So CRM provides only part of the information required to judge a student's performance.
- It is unrealistic to expect a teacher to provide the degree of detail necessary to write instructional objectives or content standards so that reliable criterion-referenced measures can be obtained.
- Knowledge and understanding do not lend themselves to clear definition. It is extremely difficult, then, to establish adequate criteria of achievement.
- Criterion-referenced measurements may discourage the use of authentic tests or problem-solving questions and encourage the use of questions with clearer right or wrong answers. Responding is not problem solving; it is simply choosing from among another person's solutions.

continues

TABLE

13.1

(continued)

Norm-Referenced Measurement (NRM)

Description

A norm-referenced score measures the student's performance against the scores achieved by others completing the same test. It measures individual differences among students, particularly over broad areas of content.

Applications

Norm-referenced measurements are particularly useful for

- classifying students.
- selecting students for fixed quota requirements.
- making decisions as to *how much* (more or less) a student has learned in comparison to others.

Criticisms

The following criticisms of NRM have been drawn from those that commonly appear in the literature:

- If NRM is used in a classroom, the final grade received by a student in a subject conceals the student's misunderstandings, inadequate study skills, and potential limitations in the subject. For any interpretation to have meaning, each individual's score needs to be related to the content of the test.
- Any given mark does not signify a definite amount of knowledge and so has little relevance to content or meaning for those who try to have absolute standards.
- Over a period of time, some students who are continually exposed to NRM decrease their level of motivation. Although they master everything they are supposed to, if they are not among the very highest scorers in the class, they may never get the As (see Chapter 8).
- With everyone out for the top marks, students are pitted against one another. They do not tend to cooperate with others.
- Tests constructed to provide NRM sample only a small number of the course objectives.
- Use of NRM in classroom tests hides the fact that some courses are very good while others are very bad, or that teachers set different standards or teach to different objectives.
- The setting of frequency limits in failure and pass rates (that is, "grading on the curve," a process associated with NRM that is impossible with CRM) can become an administrative necessity that overrides individual, educational, and even statistical considerations.

Source: Adapted from N. Gronlund (1993); and J. C. Clift & B. W. Imrie (1981).

Reliability

There are two major criteria for judging the quality of the tests we use: reliability and validity. A good test is both reliable and valid. Here we examine test reliability; in the next section, we look at test validity.

Suppose we are interested in the academic performance of a student named Carmine. She has just finished a test of knowledge about botany. The test had 40 items, each worth 1 point. Carmine received a score of 24. To interpret Carmine's test performance in terms of norms, we would find it useful to know that the mean, or average, score of the class was 29. To interpret her test performance in terms of criteria, we would have

"Children who may be gifted in real-life settings are often at a loss when asked to exhibit knowledge solely through decontextualized paper-and-pencil exercises. . . . If we do not have some knowledge of children's lives outside of the realms of paper-and-pencil work, and even outside of their classrooms, then we cannot know their strengths. Not knowing students' strengths leads to our "teaching down" to children from communities that are culturally different from that of the teachers in the school."

Lisa Delpit, *Other People's Children*, 1995.

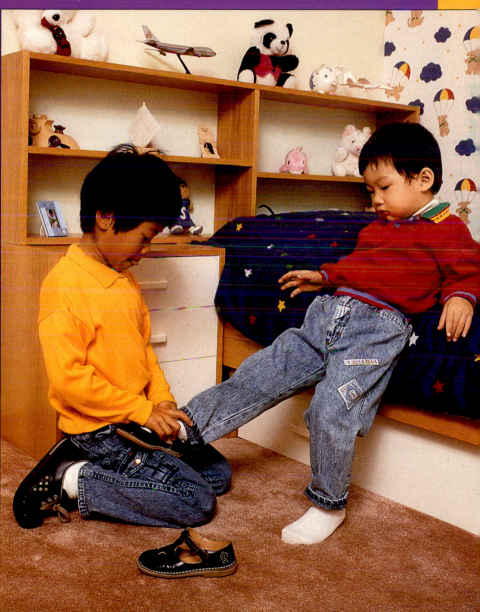

© Lawrence Migdale/Stock Boston

"Anyone who has prepared a multiple-choice test realizes that it is indeed much easier . . . to write factual items than items that require infer-ence, analysis, interpretation, or analysis of a principle.**"**

N. Fredericksen, "The real test bias: Influences of testing on teaching and learning," *American Psychologist*, 1984.

The abstract structure representing the knowledge we have stored in memory is called

  a. metaphonic knowledge.
  b. scaffolding.
*c. a schema.
  d. a learning hierarchy.

Rationale: Schemata are abstract structures of knowledge in which we place our experience.

Julie has more intellectual ability than Matthew. Nevertheless, they both learn to recite a poem equally well. What would you predict about these students' retention of the poem six months later?

  a. They will both retain the same amount since they had the same initial level of learning.
  b. Matthew will remember more of the poem since he had to rehearse it more times before learning it.
*c. Julie will remember more of the poem since she is intellectually more able than Matthew.
  d. They will both have completely forgotten the poem.

Rationale: The rate of retention of information over time is different for students of varying ability. Brighter students retain more than less bright students even when they have the same initial level of learning.

"[In our high school] every student must complete the requirements of fourteen different "portfolio" areas: literature, history, ethics, science, math, media, and so on, and present seven of them to [an outside committee] for questioning and defense.

The essence of our notion of standards is . . . publicness. It's like the old one-room schoolhouse evening performance, where kids got up before the whole community and recited poems, were quizzed on history, and so on. It's like a well-done Bar Mitzvah. There's both showmanship and authenticity to it. It's why we're so hostile to the idea of imposed "standards" via tests.

I like our system because the conversation about the test is part of the test . . . and the [students] can always try again."

Deborah Meier, *The Power of Their Ideas*, 1995.

© Bob Daemmrich/The Image Works

"Education, at best, is ecstatic."

George B. Leonard, *Education and Ecstasy*, 1963.

© David Lassman/The Image Works

to know that the teacher had set 80 percent or more items correct as the criterion of competence or mastery. So 32 items correct (.80 × 40) was the cut-off score to determine who has or has not mastered the domain of botany being assessed. Given this information and either a norm-referenced or criterion-referenced perspective, you might think we could say that Carmine's performance is somewhat below average, or that she has not reached the mastery criterion.

But the issue is not this simple. With any test, we must ask whether we would make the same decisions about Carmine's performance if she took the same or a similar test again within a short period of time. We must consider how dependable, consistent, or stable her test performance is. To do so, we need to know Carmine's performance over different testings and time spans. The dependability, consistency, and stability of a score are different aspects of what we call *test reliability,* one of the fundamental characteristics of tests. If we believe that the decisions we make about people on the basis of a test will be the same from one time to another, we are assuming that the test is reliable.

Test-Retest Reliability

How do we know whether a test gives us reliable information about a student? One way is to retest Carmine (with the same test or a parallel test), at a later time. Then we could see whether her score is about 24 on the retest. If it is, our evaluation that Carmine is slightly below average in knowledge of botany or has not mastered botany seems to hold. The test appears to be a reliable instrument—or has **test-retest reliability.** Moving from one student to a class of thirty, we see that reliability refers to the degree to which the scores received by students on one test occasion are about the same as the scores they would receive if tested again on a different occasion.

Norm-Referenced Tests   When we are interested in norm-referenced interpretations of scores, reliability becomes a question of the degree to which the rank-ordering of individuals is the same from one time to the next. If students' ranks according to their scores are about the same from one test occasion to another, the test may be considered reliable in the sense that it is highly stable.

One estimate of reliability for norm-referenced tests is the correlation between the ranks obtained on a first testing occasion and the ranks obtained on a second testing occasion. Remember that a correlation tells us the degree of relationship between two things. Suppose we had five students take a test and then retake it, and the results of the second testing were those listed in column A or column B of Table 13.2. If we obtained the results in column A, we would not be too surprised. There have been some changes in ranks: The first- and second-ranked students switched ranks, and so did the third- and fourth-ranked students. But the least able student on the first test remained fifth on the second test. So in this case the test has some stability in terms of how it orders people from lowest to highest in ability, although it clearly is not perfect.

TABLE

13.2

Hypothetical Student Rankings on Two Tests

Student	Rank on First Testing	(A) Rank on Second Testing	or	(B) Rank on Second Testing
Jeana	1	2		4
Thu	2	1		3
Alison	3	4		1
Bobby	4	3		5
Henry	5	5		2

(The rank-difference **coefficient of correlation** for this case is +.80.) But with the results in column B, the ranks correlate −.20 with those on the first testing. People who ranked low on the first occasion ranked high on the second occasion, and some who ranked high on the first occasion ranked low on the second. This is much too quirky for us to trust the test; it cannot be considered stable, dependable, or reliable. A correlation that is low, near zero, or negative, indicates little or no reliability from one testing occasion to another. The correlation in this case is low and negative, indicating undependable test scores or rankings.

In sum, the coefficient of correlation between the ranks (on the same test given twice or on two parallel tests) obtained by students in a class can be used to estimate stability, dependability, or reliability, giving us a numerical value to use for interpreting a test's reliability. If two rank orderings of test scores were exactly the same, the correlation would equal 1.00, which would mean the test was perfectly reliable. If the correlation equals .90 or .84, the reliability is considered high, because the rank orderings are pretty much the same on the two testing occasions. That is, the information we get from a score, which we then use to make decisions, stays relatively constant from one testing occasion to another.

Generally, we need reliability coefficients above .80 to make *important* decisions about students from norm-referenced tests. Lower reliabilities generally are not acceptable. But if a student scores extremely high or low on a test, some decisions become safe even if the reliability is lower than .80. That is, even with low test reliability, say about .60, we would not expect the top- and bottom-scorers to switch places completely. Perhaps the low-scorers move up a bit and the high-scorers move down a bit, but those at the extremes of a distribution move around a lot only if reliability is down closer to .00.

Criterion-Referenced Tests When educators deal with criterion-referenced tests, reliability has a different meaning. The precision of the score is less important to us than the dependability of our decision about whether Carmine has or has not mastered the botany unit. In a way, Carmine's exact score is not very important—all scores under 32 are grouped together as failures, and all scores at or above 32 are grouped together as passes. The interpretive decision, not the actual score, is what matters.

The test-retest method can also be used to estimate the reliability of our decision about Carmine. If she were retested and we found once again that she had not mastered the unit, the test shows some reliability. For a group of students, we would analyze the decisions made about them each time they were tested. We might ask how we classified Carmine, Enrique, Phyllis, Herman, and the other members of the class on each test. Inspecting these data tells us whether or not the decisions are being confirmed.

The numerical indices of test-retest reliability for criterion-referenced tests provide either correlational information, which is what we have been discussing, or probability estimates (Berk, 1980; Sweezy, 1981; Hambleton, 1990). If one criterion-referenced test has a probability of .82 for correctly classifying "masters" and "nonmasters," it is more reliable than a test that has a probability of only .55. Both correlational and probability estimates of reliability can have numerical values between 0 and 1.00 and are interpreted in a similar way: the closer to 1.00, the higher the estimate of reliability.

Internal-Consistency Reliability

To determine test-retest reliability, we have to give students the same test (or a parallel form of the same test) on a second occasion. But most teachers do not have the time to retest students. They have to be able to determine reliability from a single administration. **Internal-consistency reliability** does not reflect stability over time; it indicates how precisely a single test measures whatever it measures, at a single time.

How does it work? What we do is estimate the correlation between the test we are giving and some hypothetical test that would be given at the same time. The statistical procedures for computing internal-consistency reliability are too complicated to discuss here. An introductory textbook on testing or measurement can give you the information you need if you want to estimate the internal-consistency reliability for your own norm-referenced tests. But procedures for determining the reliability of criterion-referenced tests from a single administration are still too difficult for classroom teachers to use easily.

It is important to note that when educators study the reliability of teacher-made tests, either with test-retest methods or by estimating the correlation using internal-consistency measures, the reliability is usually low. These facts suggest that any one test, particularly a short one, provides a teacher with untrustworthy information about students' performance. The sum of several teacher-made tests, each of low reliabilty, however, may yield a total score that has substantial reliability.

How might this information affect the assessment system you set up in your own classroom?

The Standard Error of Measurement

The ability to actually compute reliability estimates is much less important to teachers than is the conceptual understanding that scores from tests have less than perfect stability and internal consistency. Reliability estimates for tests in education are always less than 1.00, and often less than .80. Therefore, the scores for individuals fluctuate a little (or a lot) from one occasion to the next. Be sure to remember, then, if you ever have to make decisions based on a single score for a student—say, assigning all those who have scored above 45 on a certain test to the gifted program, or giving Ds to all those who have scored below 18 on a certain test—that the scores you are using to characterize each student are not all that precise. The lack of precision in scores—their lack of perfect reliability—is reflected in a statistic called the **standard error of measurement.**

Any score on any test is made up of "error" as well as the "true" level of the attribute we want to measure. When we require students to take the SAT, ACT, or ASVAB (Armed Services Vocational Aptitude Battery), as part of an application for admission to college or the military, we place them in a standardized testing situation where we can measure their aptitude for performing certain intellectual tasks we think are needed in their future work. But that measurement is affected on the day of the test by several factors: the person's health, emotional state, motivation, rapport with the examiner, recent practice in the area being tested, attention, coordination, memory, fatigue, and luck in guessing on any given test occasion.

So, an observed score on any test—say, Carmine's 24 points on the botany test—is made up of true score and error score. The estimated amount of the error in a person's score is what we want to know. After we estimate the error, we can estimate a **confidence interval** around the observed score and be pretty sure that a person's true score is within that confidence interval or band. The standard error of measurement (further described, with its formula, in almost all introductory testing and measurement texts) provides us with the information we need to develop a confidence interval for the observed scores we get for individuals. By tradition we usually talk of 68, 95, or 99 percent confidence in estimating true scores.

Suppose we learn from the use of the statistical formula that the standard error of measurement was 4 points for the botany test that Carmine took. Then we would know that Carmine's true score was probably somewhere in the range from 4 points below to 4 points above the score she actually received (often described as plus or minus 1 standard error). That is, her true score on the test would probably be between 20 and 28. This is the confidence interval, and from our statistics we would have confidence that we were right 68 percent of the time. If we used 2 standard errors to build our confidence interval, we would say that Carmine's true score lay somewhere in the range of 24 plus or minus 8, or between 16 and 32, and we would be accurate in that prediction 95 percent of the time.

There is an important point here for teachers to learn: Errors of measurement always occur. So we must learn to think of Carmine's score, and those of all our other students, as falling within ranges, not at precise points, on our tests. Knowing there is a standard error of measurement also keeps us on guard when we compare two or more students whose observed scores seem different. Suppose Enrique's observed score on the botany test was 31. At first glance, it would appear that he is slightly above and Carmine below the average for the class, and that Enrique scored 7 points higher than Carmine. But when we use the standard error of measurement to determine confidence intervals, we find a situation like the one shown in Figure 13.1. Thinking in terms of confidence intervals, not precise scores, leads us to different interpretations. First, we notice that the two confidence intervals overlap. So we probably do not want to conclude too quickly that Enrique's true score is higher than Carmine's. If his true score is at the low end of the confidence interval determined for his observed score and Carmine's true score is at the high end of the confidence interval around her observed score, Carmine would actually be performing better on the botany test than Enrique!

Because scores are not precise points but rather indicators of bands, many people who use criterion-referenced tests add a third category to "mastery" and "nonmastery"—a category called "no decision." To reflect the acknowledged lack of precision in the scores on the botany examination, it might pay to designate 30 to 33 items correct as a band within which we need more information before classifying someone as showing "mastery" or "nonmastery." The size of the band we choose reflects how much we are concerned about the size of the standard error of measurement.

FIGURE 13.1

Determining confidence intervals around observed scores by using the Standard Error of Measurement (68 percent confidence)

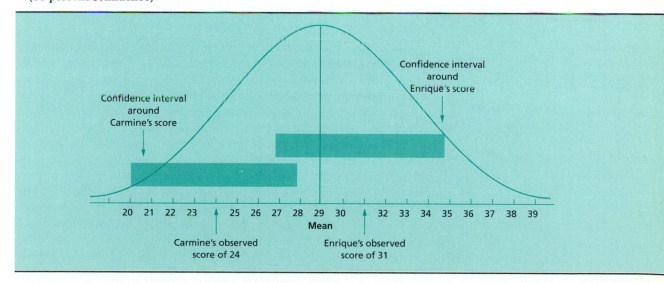

All this discussion of unreliability and error of measurement is designed to keep you cautious. In any testing you are involved with, in any tests you interpret, in any selection or grading you do, remember that each score has associated with it a confidence interval that defines the range of error for that particular score. If reliability is less than 1.00, as it surely will be, the obtained score contains some error. Do not think of numerical scores as God-given. They are fallible, as are the teachers who must interpret them.

Improving Reliability

One way to improve test reliability, and so reduce the standard error of measurement, is to increase the length of a test. This is true for both norm-referenced and criterion-referenced tests. You should remember that all tests sample behavior. Of the hundreds of test questions that could be asked in an area of arithmetic or about a novel, only a subset (or sample) of items are used to make up a test. If a student has a momentary lapse in attention or makes a careless error on one question, he or she is hurt more if the test is short. If a student does not remember one character or incident in a novel, and that is what all the questions on a test are about, again the student is in trouble. A greater number of items which sample more widely from a domain of knowledge really work to a student's advantage when taking a test. Although students and teachers both complain about the tedium of lengthy examinations, the relation between reliability and test length is clear. If you had a 5-item test with reliability of .20, adding 5 items of the same type would increase the estimated reliability coefficient to .33. If you add 15 items of the same type, the reliability estimate increases to .50. Adding 88 items of the same type would yield a reliability estimate of .85. When the reliability of a test is low, adding items of the same kind increases the reliability coefficient. When reliability is already high, adding items does not have much effect.

Validity

Test **validity** is the degree to which testing procedures and interpretations help teachers assess what we want to assess. It is the single most important issue to consider when evaluating a test (Committee to Develop Standards for Educational and Psychological Testing, 1985). This is because so many tests really do not measure what they claim to measure. A highly reliable test of verbal ability, for example, may not identify the most creative students in art, only those who have learned art terms. Or a test may identify students for an art program who are really no better at art than the ones who were not picked. Reliability is important, but ultimately what we most want in a test is validity. We want the test to measure what we intend it to measure—intelligence, or achievement of a certain kind, or the promise of various candidates for scarce positions, or the creativity of students, and so forth. There are many different kinds of validity, but we concentrate here on just three: content validity, criterion validity, and construct validity—the three Cs (Cronbach, 1971; Messick, 1980, 1989; Shepard, 1993).

Content Validity

Teachers must be sure when they put together, say, a geology test that they are really measuring geology knowledge and skills. They have to be sure that the questions pertain to what they have taught, whether the entire curriculum or just the content in one class. We have to know that the questions are representative of the content taught and that there are enough questions to sample adequately the different kinds of knowledge and skill taught in that particular content domain.

If a social studies test asks questions that could be answered on the basis of general intelligence, test wiseness, or regular newspaper reading, the course content in social studies is not being tested adequately. The items on an achievement test should be tied to an instructional domain that students have had an opportunity to learn. If independent experts agree that a test in eighth-grade social studies is measuring the common curriculum in that subject area, the test has **content validity.** As the social studies subject matter changes or as new subtopics are stressed, the content sample for the eighth-grade social studies test must also change if it is to remain valid.

Content validation is a logical procedure and it is based on good sense. (In Chapter 14 we describe how to define a domain and sample from it.) Content validity is a special problem for norm-referenced tests; it is less of a problem with criterion-referenced tests, in which instructional objectives are tied directly to test items.

Criterion Validity

If you are using a test for selecting students for admission to a school, curriculum, course, or job, you must make sure that it is valid for the purpose. Suppose in your district you have a program for academically gifted students and are using a creativity test for selection. Does the test actually select students who are more likely than others to profit from the program? To estimate the **criterion validity** (sometimes also called *concurrent* or *predictive validity*) you need to test a group of students and then let all of them, whatever their scores, into the program. You would then correlate scores on the selection test with scores on a criterion measure that reflects success in the instructional program. This correlational procedure allows you to see the degree to which the high-scorers on the selection test profit more from the program than the low-scorers on the selection test. If they do profit more from instruction, and if in the future you want to choose students who will get the most from the special program, you can use that test for selection. In other words, the test is valid for predicting who will do well on the criterion. This is why college admissions offices want applicants to take the SAT or ACT tests and supply a transcript of high school grades. Over the years, it has been established that these tests and grades have predictive validity. When the criterion is first-semester grades in college, the SAT or ACT and high school grades predict with well-above-chance accuracy how well students do.

Once again, a warning: Criterion validity coefficients provide a useful basis for selecting and counseling students in various curriculum areas, but only when a particular student is like the students who were in the sample on which the validity coefficient was determined. Along with school psychologists, curriculum specialists, or special educators, you may someday be part of a committee responsible for making important decisions about students. If so, you should always ask whether a particular test has a substantial criterion-validity coefficient—you need to know whether the group used to determine that coefficient is like the group to which the information is now to be applied. Selection for special programs can be helped by valid tests, but selection should also take into account the unique circumstances of a particular student, the student's motivation, and the implications of wrong decisions.

Construct Validity

Our third C is **construct validity,** which may be the most difficult kind of validity to understand. But it may also be the most important. Construct validity deals with the questions of whether a test measures the attribute or characteristic it claims to measure, whether interpretations of the test scores are sensible, and whether the consequences of using the test are acceptable. These are extremely complex issues, and they tie test validity to issues within the culture of which the test is a part (Shepard, 1993).

We call certain abstract characteristics or attributes of people *constructs.* Intelligence is a construct. So are creativity, anxiety, and many other things. We cannot measure these attributes, characteristics, traits, or constructs directly, the way we can measure height, weight, or the less abstract attributes, such as arithmetic achievement or spelling ability. So people invented the idea of intelligence or creativity or anxiety to talk about a complex set of behaviors that, all together, seem to indicate that a person can or will act intelligently, creatively, or anxiously. But how can we tell whether a test we are using to measure, say, scientific aptitude, is really measuring the construct of scientific aptitude? Maybe it is measuring only knowledge of science, general intelligence, reading comprehension, or all of these. This is a tricky question. Too many tests pass as tests of creativity, art aptitude, or mechanical aptitude when they do not measure the attribute they claim to measure.

How do we check for construct validity then? One way is to use correlations. If we have a test of art aptitude and a rating of how well students did in art, the two measures ought to be related. The same would be true for a test of mechanical aptitude and performance in auto mechanics, or any other aptitude test and a criterion measure of the corresponding kind of performance. Even a moderate correlation would be reassuring. We can also correlate one test of, say, IQ with another. For example, a new short IQ test had better correlate substantially with the Stanford-Binet and Wechsler IQ tests, both well-accepted tests of the construct of IQ. If the new measure of IQ does not have much in common (i.e., correlates low) with these tests, then what it measures is not what we usually mean by intelligence, regardless of what the test is intended to measure.

Another way to check a test for construct validity is to test hypotheses about how high-scorers and low-scorers should act. When we test leadership, self-concept, attitude toward mathematics, or other constructs, high-scorers and low-scorers on these tests should act differently. If they do in fact behave the way we expect them to, the tests have a claim to construct validity.

One particular aspect of construct validity is often overlooked. This is the interpretation associated with a test. A test of career interests may validly identify students who will or will not enjoy engineering as a career. But if that test is used to counsel students out of a drafting course in high school, it is being used inappropriately. The construct of drafting achievement was never examined; the test purports to measure only interest in engineering. This erroneous interpretation of the test destroys its construct validity.

So a test's consequences must be thought about if we are to judge a test's construct validity. If the interest-in-engineering construct is more often associated with males or middle-class white students and the construct results in counseling women and minority-group members away from courses (such as high school drafting) that lead toward engineering careers, then the test has unacceptable social consequences.

In each case, when we are determining whether a test measures what it is supposed to, whether it is interpreted correctly, or whether it is having unanticipated and negative consequences, we must ask about the construct validity of the test, which is really a way of asking about the use, interpretation, and consequences of tests. These are tough and controversial issues in present-day society.

Claims about how drugs affect people are carefully checked by federal and state agencies, and physicians' prescriptions for drugs are monitored, even if only casually. When a drug is actually approved for use, it is not just on the basis of its effectiveness, but on its freedom from undesirable side effects (Shepard, 1993). But there is no such monitoring of educational and psychological tests. The claims associated with tests, including their interpretation and their consequences—their side effects—are not checked by an independent board. The field of education is filled with people who make up tests, advocate their use without looking carefully at their validity, and then disclaim any responsibility for the interpretations of the tests or the consequences of using the tests. This is unethical. Teachers, then, have to be careful about the tests they use and the interpretations and consequences associated with their use. Teachers, more than anyone else in education, must be protectors of children and keep them away from tests that are inappropriately used or interpreted. To do so requires that you learn more about test and measurement issues, as your career progresses, than we can give you here.

> How might an intelligence test be used inappropriately? an SAT test? a reading achievement test?

Evaluation

As discussed earlier in the chapter, **evaluation** is the part of the assessment process having to do with attaching value to data that have been collected and interpreted. Although we have focused primarily on student assessment, many different elements in education can be assessed, and ultimately evaluated. In this section, we look at how school programs, curricula, teaching methods, and other school activities are evaluated (see Baker & Niemi, 1996; McLaughlin & Phillips, 1991). This kind of evaluation plays a key role in educational **accountability**—holding educators accountable for the success of their efforts in product development and curriculum development. It is usually carried out by trained evaluators, who address these kinds of questions:

- How have the new attendance boundaries in the district affected segregation?
- How can I change the reading program to help students learn more?

How nice it is when tests provide information to grow on, not punishment or a lowering of self-concept.

(© David Pratt/Positive Images)

- How do students like the food since we hired the new cafeteria manager?
- Should this teacher get a merit raise?
- Is the new curriculum on patriotism doing what it should?

Evaluators are educators who help members of a policy-shaping community (a committee, school board, legislature) to recognize their own interests, weigh the consequences of alternative approaches, and discover new ways to perform their tasks (Cronbach & Associates, 1980). Evaluators are detectives looking for evidence to shed light on some problem. The evidence they must collect to help others make decisions may include such things as teacher-made and standardized-test assessments of student achievement, observations of teacher and student behavior, surveys of parent opinion, interviews with school-board members, and financial-cost records.

Whatever is being evaluated—whether it be student performance or instructional programs and materials—ordinarily requires two kinds of evaluation: formative evaluation and summative evaluation. Our focus here is on how these two kinds of evaluation are used by evaluators to judge materials and programs.

Formative Evaluation

Formative evaluation is what educators use as a basis for revising materials or programs. It is the responsibility of not only the developers of the materials or programs but teachers and administrators as well. Is the new film on mitosis effective the way it is, or do we need more instructional time? Are the inductive methods we are using to teach the concept of "peninsula" working as we want? How can we improve them? How can the instructional games we developed for use with Native American youngsters in the Southwest be made to do what we intended? Whenever teachers try out new materials, teaching methods, or programs, they should also put into use a system for monitoring their innovation. Teachers can work alone or with other teachers, but a formative evaluation should be the basis for improving or abandoning the program.

> Using information in this section and other sources, create an evaluative checklist and assess instructional materials you find in a resource library or that you are using in practice teaching. Can they be improved?

Summative Evaluation

After a product, program, or activity has been refined and modified through formative evaluations, and used as intended in some educational settings, a **summative evaluation** may be called for. A good summative evaluation examines competing methods or programs, too, to see whether they can produce the same or better results for less money or in less time. The usual summative evaluation is like a horse race: Curriculum A is pitted against curriculum B; textbook C is pitted against textbook D.

The evaluation of materials or activities must also take into account factors other than educational effects, namely, cost-effectiveness (see

Levin, 1986), time required, ease of use, needs met by the program, attitudes of students, preferences of teachers, judgments of specialists, and so on. Summative evaluation is complex because many sources are used to obtain information for making decisions about keeping or abandoning materials or activities. Teachers are rarely involved in summative evaluation. This is a job for unbiased evaluators from outside a school system.

Teachers have a right and a responsibility, however, to demand summative evaluation reports. When consumers want information about washing machines, automobiles, or cameras, they can get it from local consumer groups, agencies of the federal government, or *Consumer Reports*, a magazine that offers summative evaluations of many products each year. What do teachers do? Where do they get the information they need about the effectiveness of textbooks, curricula, and other educational products? They have to begin to ask product developers to answer questions such as these:

- Which of my students will profit from these materials—the brightest only, middle-class students only, or others as well?
- What skills and knowledge will my students have after using the materials? What would a final test look like?
- What is the cost per student? Are the materials reusable?
- How much of my time will be needed? of students' time? What are the prerequisites for students and teachers who want to use these materials?
- Can you give me the name of someone in the area who is using these materials?

Teachers have a responsibility for helping improve educational quality as much and as quickly as possible. One way to meet that responsibility is to demand summative evaluations—to be a good consumer—of new teaching programs and materials. A lot of people are selling things to educators—computers, textbooks, curriculum units, tape recordings—and making outrageous claims about their effectiveness (Molnar, 1996; Noble, 1997). It would be nice to know *before* a purchase is made whether the educational claims associated with materials have been evaluated.

Standardized Tests in the Assessment Process

All through your schooling you have been dealing with **standardized testing.** Such tests become some of the evidence schools collect about you. But you have always been on the student's side of this aspect of assessment. Now we talk briefly about the other side: the teacher's and, more generally, the educator's.

Advantages and Special Uses of Standardized Tests

First, a standardized test is one that has been given to a large, representative sample of some **population** so that someone else's scores, such as your students' scores, can be compared with those of the people in that sample. That is, norm-referenced standardized tests provide norms that make possible the comparison of any student's score with those of many other students. Whenever you want to evaluate a student against criteria that go beyond a single teacher's classroom and that teacher's conception of what should be taught, you need a standardized test.

Second, standardized tests usually have detailed instructions about how the test should be administered—the exact directions to be given the students, the time limits (if any), and the ways in which the teacher should handle any special problems that may arise. It is primarily for these reasons that the tests are called *standardized*—all the procedures and test-taking conditions are the same (that is, "standard") for all the students taking the tests, wherever and whenever they take them, and all answers are evaluated according to the same scoring standards.

Third, standardized tests are usually more carefully constructed than teacher-made tests since they are constructed by experts using the technical, statistical, and research knowledge of the testing field.

Fourth, standardized tests usually come with more or less detailed background information about the test—its rationale, its purposes, and the ways in which its content and items were chosen. This information also includes evidence about the test's reliability and validity (discussed above).

Criterion-referenced standardized tests, both the paper-and-pencil and performance kinds, are becoming more popular, particularly because of demand by the states. These tests yield direct information about how well a student has performed in relation to some specific criterion, rather than the performance of other students. Some tests of reading disabilities, the Red Cross lifesavers' tests, the requirements for merit badges in the Boy Scouts—all are criterion-referenced standardized tests being used today in educational programs. Criterion-referenced tests are rapidly being developed to measure achievement in many other areas of the curriculum. Figures 13.2 and 13.3 are examples of the information a teacher receives from a well-known norm-referenced standardized test and a criterion-referenced standardized test.

One reason for the growing popularity of criterion-referenced standardized tests has to do with problems inherent in the use of norms over time. Think of it this way: you want the norm group to be up-to-date for interpreting the present-day performance of your students. Teachers say that students do not differ much from one year to another, but when they look back after 10 or more years they see great shifts in their students as well as their curriculum. So norms need to be somewhat current to interpret current performance.

There is, however, a great problem associated with current norms. Invariably, students appear to perform better when judged by older norms. As teachers become familiar with what is in a test, they tend to teach those very things. And students, naturally, do better on the test over time. In fact, today's students do better on norm-referenced achievement tests than did those of the 1980s; but we have also raised the performance

Find copies of standardized tests from the 1950s and 1960s and compare them with the most recent versions available. Note all the differences and similarities you can discern.

ACHIEVEMENT TEST SERIES, EIGHTH EDITION
WITH OTIS-LENNON SCHOOL ABILITY TEST, SIXTH EDITION

STUDENT SKILLS ANALYSIS
FOR
JOHN A SNYDER

TEACHER:	CESTERO	1988 NORMS:	STANFORD GRADE 04	OLSAT GRADE 04
SCHOOL:	NEWTOWN ELEM	GRADE: 04	PERIOD 12 NATIONAL	NATIONAL
		TEST DATE:	LEVEL: INTERMED 1 E	
DISTRICT:	NEWTOWN	05/89	FORM: J	1

TESTS	NO. OF ITEMS	RAW SCORE	SCALED SCORE	NATL PR-S	NATL NCE	GRADE EQUIV	AAC RANGE	NATIONAL GRADE PERCENTILE BANDS
Total Reading	94	64	630	57-5	53.7	5.0	HIGH	
Vocabulary	40	33	661	81-7	68.5	7.2	HIGH	
Reading Comp.	54	31	611	41-5	45.2	4.0	MIDDLE	
Total Math	118	37	569	13-3	26.3	3.1	LOW	
Concepts of No.	34	15	595	30-4	39.0	3.8	MIDDLE	
Computation	44	8	537	4-2	13.1	2.4	LOW	
Applications	40	14	575	20-3	32.3	3.2	MIDDLE	
Total Language	60	42	628	53-5	51.6	4.7	HIGH	
Lang Mechanics	30	20	616	40-5	44.7	4.1	MIDDLE	
Lang Expression	30	22	640	61-6	55.9	5.6	HIGH	
Spelling	40	19	603	31-4	39.6	3.6	MIDDLE	
Study Skills	30	15	601	30-4	39.0	3.1	MIDDLE	
Science	50	38	650	87-7	73.7	8.2	HIGH	
Social Science	50	35	631	71-6	61.7	5.8	HIGH	
Listening	45	35	654	88-7	74.7	7.8	HIGH	
Using Information	70	46	627	54-5	52.1	4.8	HIGH	
Thinking Skills	101	55	607	45-5	47.4	4.4	MIDDLE	
Basic Battery	387	212	605	35-4	41.9	3.9	MIDDLE	
Complete Battery	487	285	614	45-5	47.4	4.4	MIDDLE	

National Grade Percentile Bands scale: 1 10 30 50 70 90 99

OTIS-LENNON SCHOOL ABILITY TEST	RAW SCORE	SAI	AGE PR-S	AGE NCE	SCALED SCORE	NATL GRADE PR-S	NATL GRADE NCE	
Total	72	25	81	12-3	25.3	574	27-4	37.1	
Verbal	36	14	87	21-3	33.0	583	36-4	42.5	
Nonverbal	36	11	80	11-3	24.2	565	21-3	33.0	

Scale: 1 10 30 50 70 90 99

AGE 11 YRS 6 MOS	READING GROUP Comprehension	LANGUAGE ARTS GROUP Study Skills	MATHEMATICS GROUP Computation	COMMUNICATIONS GROUP Average

CONTENT CLUSTERS	RAW SCORE/ NUMBER OF ITEMS	BELOW AVERAGE	AVERAGE	ABOVE AVERAGE
Reading Vocabulary	33/ 40			✓
Synonyms	20/ 24			✓
Context	6/ 8		✓	
Multiple Meanings	7/ 8			✓
Reading Comprehension	31/ 54		✓	
Recreational	11/ 18		✓	
Textual	9/ 18		✓	
Functional	11/ 18		✓	
Literal	10/ 21		✓	
Inferential	16/ 26		✓	
Critical	5/ 7		✓	
Concepts of Number	15/ 34		✓	
Whole Numbers	7/ 16		✓	
Fractions	1/ 4		✓	
Decimals	2/ 3		✓	
Operations and Properties	5/ 11		✓	
Mathematics Computation	8/ 44	✓		
Add and Subtract/Whole Nos	3/ 12	✓		
Multiplication/Whole Numbers	3/ 12	✓		
Division/Whole Numbers	1/ 10	✓		
Add and Subtract/Decimals	1/ 6	✓		
Add and Subtract/Fractions	0/ 4	✓		
Mathematics Applications	14/ 40	✓		
Problem Solving	5/ 22	✓		
Graphs and Charts	5/ 6		✓	
Geometry/Measurement	4/ 12	✓		

CONTENT CLUSTERS	RAW SCORE/ NUMBER OF ITEMS	BELOW AVERAGE	AVERAGE	ABOVE AVERAGE
Language Mechanics	20/ 30		✓	
Capitalization	6/ 7			✓
Punctuation	6/ 11		✓	
Applied Grammar	8/ 12		✓	
Language Expression	22/ 30		✓	
Sentence Correctness	14/ 20		✓	
Sentence Effectiveness	8/ 10		✓	
Spelling	19/ 40		✓	
Study Skills	15/ 30		✓	
Library/Reference Skills	8/ 17		✓	
Information Skills	7/ 13		✓	
Science	38/ 50			✓
Physical Science	12/ 16			✓
Biological Science	14/ 20			✓
Earth/Space Science	12/ 14			✓
Social Science	35/ 50		✓	
Geography	8/ 13		✓	
History	8/ 8			✓
Political Science	8/ 10			✓
Economics	6/ 10		✓	
Psych/Sociol/Anthro	5/ 9		✓	
Listening	35/ 45			✓
Vocabulary	11/ 15			✓
Listening Comprehension	24/ 30			✓
Using Information	46/ 70		✓	
Thinking Skills	55/101		✓	

COPY 02

PROCESS NO. 18904271-8909-03356-2

Abbreviations used: GR = Grade Equivalent, PR = Percentile, S = Stanine, RS/NP = Raw Score/National Percentile.

FIGURE 13.2

The information received by a teacher on a student's performance on a norm-referenced standardized test

OBJECTIVE MASTERY DETAIL BY STUDENT

TEST BOOKLET NUMBER 59009-4
GRADE 05   LEVEL J

DISTRICT   JEFFERSON SCHOOL DISTRICT
SUPERINTENDENT   CHARLES CUFFIE
PRINCIPAL   RICHARD FISCHER
SCHOOL   GARY MEMORIAL
TEACHER   KIP SEARS

DATE TESTED 01-02-83
SUBJECT READING/LANGUAGE ARTS
NO. OF OBJECTIVES TESTED   21
OBJECTIVE MASTERY CRITERIA = 3 OUT OF 4
(BASED ON 4 OPTION ITEMS)
PROBABILITY OF MASTERY BY GUESSING IS
LESS THAN 100 IN 1000
STUDENTS TESTED   25

OBJECTIVES TESTED	MASTERY CRITERIA	% NATIONAL MASTERY	% CLASS MASTERY
STRUCTURAL ANALYSIS			
SUFFIXES, MEANINGS CF	3 OF 4	40	37
PREFIXES, MEANINGS CF	3 OF 4	32	31
VOCABULARY			
WORD MEANING: IDENTIFICATION	3 OF 4	53	69
MULTIPLE MEANINGS	3 OF 4	58	46
LIFE/STUDY AND REFERENCE			
USING COMBINED DICT SKILLS	3 OF 4	33	26
READING MAPS	3 OF 4	32	17
CARD CATALOG, SELECT CARD TYPE	3 OF 4	46	49
COMPLETING AN OUTLINE	3 OF 4	38	31
LITERAL COMPREHENSION			
DETAILS, RECOGNIZING	3 OF 4	59	60
INFERENTIAL COMPREHENSION			
DRAWING CONCLUSIONS	3 OF 4	54	54
CAUSE AND EFFECT, IMPLIED	3 OF 4	52	46
MAIN IDEA, PARAPHRASED	3 OF 4	38	29
COMPARISON OR CONTRAST	3 OF 4	50	49
CONTEXT CLUES	3 OF 4	46	43
CRITICAL COMPREHENSION			
ANALOGIES	3 OF 4	53	46
DISTINGUISH FACT/OPINION	5 OF 6	54	51
SPELLING			
PLURAL SPELLINGS, S IES VES	3 OF 4	64	69
*M-CONTROLLED VOWEL SPELLINGS	3 OF 4	63	60
MECHANICS			
PUNCTUATION: COMMAS	3 OF 4	16	20
CAPT AND PUNCT: QUOTATIONS	3 OF 4	30	23
USAGE			
IRREGULAR VERB FORMS	5 OF 6	64	77
PERCENT OF OBJECTIVES MASTERED			

Notice that for every objective either a number or a letter indicates how many items each student got right or whether the student has mastered (M the area.

A printout like this is a source of valuable diagnostic information for teachers, students, and parents.

FIGURE 13.3

Information from a criterion-referenced test

Reprinted from Curriculum Referenced Tests of Mastery Reports Catalog by permission of Psychological Corporation.

level needed to score at the 50th percentile rank on these tests (Linn, Graue, & Sanders, 1990; Berliner & Biddle, 1995). So higher scores are needed today to be judged average in achievement than 10 years ago.

This is the reason many educators advocate criterion-referenced systems of assessment. They avoid the sliding scale of accomplishment inherent in norm-referenced standardized testing. Norms are unimportant if we specify what level of performance we want on tests that are referenced to the standards and objectives identified as important.

Disadvantages of and Concerns about Standardized Tests

Except for concern about using current norms, what we have discussed so far are the advantages and positive aspects of standardized-test use. There are also disadvantages of using standardized tests, and a few of the concerns you need to keep in mind are the following:

1. The developers of most standardized tests hold a behavioral viewpoint. So learning is seen as a sequence of small steps, with basic skills considered prerequisites for later learning. Complex learning is believed to come about after prerequisites are mastered. Both criterion-referenced and norm-referenced tests often have this quality. They all assume that achievement can be broken down into isolated knowledge skills, and that information can be taken out of the context of the situations in which it was learned. These underlying assumptions are now seriously questioned in the light of contemporary learning theories. Resnick and Resnick (1990) and Shepard (1991) caution against using tests that treat learners and learning in this way.

2. Sometimes norm-referenced standardized tests do not cover well what is taught through the textbooks and instructional activities used in classes. For example, a careful comparison of three leading textbooks in fourth-grade mathematics with five frequently used norm-referenced standardized tests yielded startling results (Institute for Research on Teaching, 1980). According to this comparison, in the best match between what a textbook taught and what a test measured, only 71 percent of the topics tested were actually in the textbook! In the worst case, only 47 percent of the topics tested were covered in the textbook. Such mismatches between curriculum and tests cause gross underestimates of what students learn in school. Curriculum and tests must be in alignment; otherwise there is no coherence between the taught and the assessed curriculum (Smith & Levin, 1996).

3. The number of test items per behavior measured is typically very small. That is, it is customary in both norm- and criterion-referenced tests to have only a few items per objective. And in order to cover a broad curriculum, a nationally-normed standardized test may have only one or two items for each area in a language-arts or other program.

In order to clarify both the advantages and disadvantages of standardized tests and how they compare to teacher-made achievement tests (discussed in Chapter 14), a chart of attributes is shown in Table 13.3.

TABLE

13.3

Comparison of Standardized and Teacher-Made Tests of Achievement

Criterion	Standardized Tests	Teacher-Made Tests
Reliability	Reliabilities usually high, often around .90 for norm-referenced tests	Reliabilities rarely estimated; when estimated, average about .60
Validity	Criterion validity generally determined; construct validity discussed	Construct and criterion validity unknown
	Content validity generally high for criterion-referenced tests; difficult to assess in the case of norm-referenced tests, but can be estimated	Content validity generally high if systematic procedures used to construct test
Measurement of content taught	Measured content common to a majority of American schools but may not always reflect local curriculum	Measures content unique to local curriculum
		Continual adaptation of test possible
	Measurement of basic skills and complex outcomes adaptable to many local situations	Tests adaptable to changes in emphases; can rapidly reflect new curriculum
		Tend to stress knowledge rather than higher-order outcomes
Student preparation	Studying usually does not help obtain a better score unless test is tied closely to local curriculum	Studying usually helps obtain a better score
Quality of test items	Quality generally very high; items written by test experts, tried out, and revised before included in test	Quality unknown, varied; test-item files of variable quality often available from publishers of texts in use
Item type	Usually multiple-choice	Various kinds of items used
Administration and scoring of test	Procedure standardized and constant from class to class	Procedures for testing are flexible
		Teacher scored
	Specific instructions given	
	Machine scored	
Interpretation of scores	Scores usually compared with state or national norms	Scores interpretable on basis of immediate peer group, or local norms
	Scores often have confidence bands	
	Test manuals provide help in interpreting information and making decisions	

■ Types of Standardized Tests Used in Schools

The two main kinds of standardized tests used in schools are achievement and aptitude tests. About 80 percent of the tests used are achievement tests, and most of these are norm-referenced, multiple-choice tests. Almost half of all the standardized tests used are designed by only three testing companies (United States General Accounting Office, 1993).

Achievement Tests   The kinds of standardized tests that teachers more frequently come in contact with measure achievement, not aptitude. These tests are used to assess students' achievement of instructional objectives in a given course or curriculum area. There are standardized achievement tests in, say, third-grade reading, fifth-grade arithmetic, seventh-grade social studies, ninth-grade algebra, and eleventh-grade chemistry. The tests have been constructed by specialists in the curriculum areas and administered to large samples of students in the appropriate grade levels and courses. They tell us how well any particular student, class, school, school district, county, or state has done in comparison with the norm group.

You often see newspaper articles reporting that the students of a certain city have fallen above (or below) the norm for the state as a whole in reading achievement. Or an article may conclude that, within a given city, certain schools do better and others do worse than the citywide average in achievement in sixth-grade arithmetic. And every few years 13-year-olds, eighth graders, or some other group in the United States is compared with students in other nations. In these comparisons, U.S. children usually do well on tests of literacy, and less well on tests of mathematics and science (Berliner & Biddle, 1995; Third International Mathematics Science Study, 1996). Such comparisons among nations are possible only with standardized tests of achievement. But as we said above, you can most meaningfully compare *students* in one school or nation with those in another if (1) each is similar in relevant respects to the norm group that was used, or (2) each is similar to the other on important dimensions such as social class, quality of the schools, expenditures per pupil, and so forth.

Aptitude Tests   Aptitude tests often cover broad areas of intellectual functioning and are called *intelligence tests, scholastic aptitude tests, academic aptitude tests,* or *general-ability tests.* When they are aimed at more specific kinds of intellectual ability, they are called *special ability* or *special aptitude tests.* The most frequently used tests of this kind are verbal, mathematical, spatial, mechanical, and clerical aptitude tests.

In general, aptitude tests are norm-referenced and provide information for student guidance and counseling. In colleges, business, and industry they are used for selection and placement. Students have been put into special classes, or treated differently in regular classes, on the basis of their scores on aptitude tests. As we saw in Chapter 3, controversies rage over whether such tests (in the form of intelligence tests) in the schools do more harm than good. Certainly when Spanish-speaking children are classified and treated as mentally retarded because they do poorly on scholastic aptitude tests printed in English, it is easy to see that these tests are harmful. But, as we saw in Chapter 3, some critics think that the tests also do harm by influencing teachers' expectations of their students. They argue that teachers act on their expectations, treating some of their students inappropriately—calling on them less often, "staying with" them in classroom recitations less often, giving them enriched assignments less often, and the like (see Good, 1993). It

POLICY, RESEARCH, AND PRACTICE

Is It Fair to Publish Standardized Achievement Test Scores?

Newspapers in many areas publish the scores of schools and districts on state standardized achievement tests. Is this fair? Don't people have a right to know how the schools they support are doing? We think the public does have a right to know how schools are doing on these tests, but newspapers usually do not provide enough information to tell people much at all.

Newspapers should not publish standardized test results in a state or region unless they are willing to provide as well some explanations of poverty rates in the various schools, language difficulties, social-class differences, mobility rates of the population, and expenditures per pupil in each district. It is not fair to present uninterpreted, raw data because it is so misleading. Is it likely that a school with 80 percent turnover or a large bilingual population will look as good as a school with 20 percent turnover or no recent immigrants? Of course not! Perhaps the students in the school with high turnover *who stay at that school* for at least three years are doing well. But newspapers seldom tell about that; they just present raw data, with no explanations of how schools differ. Without comparative data on other school and community characteristics, a legitimate comparison of instructional effectiveness at different schools cannot be made.

This concern also holds for international comparisons. If students in the United States are like those in Singapore, Hungary, Korea, Japan, or Slovakia, then the international comparisons are interpretable. But if the lives of children in the various countries differ in terms of parental support, days of schooling per year, coverage by the curriculum of what is on the test, qualifications and planning time of the teachers, time engaged in sports, time engaged in dating, hours of after-school employment, and so forth, then the comparisons are much harder to make. And some of the international comparisons of achievement are very difficult to interpret because of how these cultural differences affect the lives of children in the various countries.

If newspapers provide the unexplained scores that purportedly represent the performance of schools on standardized achievement tests, perhaps they should also print the unexplained annual death rates per thousand admissions to hospitals in the same area. Death rates per hospital vary too, and people want to live in areas where the hospitals are doing well, just as they want to live in areas where the schools are doing well.

continues

537

Why not print those rates? This is important information since about 4 percent of medical interventions have adverse outcomes, leading to 1.3 million medical injuries, 180,000 deaths, and a cost to the nation of about $50 billion per year (Levy, 1996). Is it possible that newspaper editors believe it is acceptable to attack teachers but not physicians? But of course, hospitals vary in the people they admit—their age levels, diseases, injuries, income levels, the quality of their staff and resources, and so forth. Each hospital is different, some specializing in oncology cases and others in coronary care. But this is precisely the point educators must make: Each school is different as well. Unless people learn about the special circumstances of each school, newspapers act irresponsibly when they simply print standardized test scores.

Some people worry also about the 20 million school days per year spent by schoolchildren in the United States taking standardized and teacher-made achievement tests (National Commission on Testing & Public Policy, 1990). It is likely that an additional 300 million school days are spent in preparation for achievement tests, and something approaching one billion dollars is spent annually on purchasing, administering, and scoring such tests (Paris et al., 1991). Although the total expenditures are large, the costs in time and money *per pupil per year* seem more reasonable. The approximately 52 million students in kindergarten through grade 12 spend an average of about one half day taking standardized tests per year, spend 4.4 to 6.7 days specifically in preparation for the tests, and the tests cost something around $20 per child. Moreover, if the tests are "good" ones (the kind teachers can defend, high in content validity), then the time spent in test preparation is not wasted. These less alarming numbers suggest that the problem is not nearly a crisis overall, although in particular districts testing programs can result in squandering scarce instructional time and tax dollars.

is argued that any measurement of any student characteristic that is thought of as an aptitude measure—a predictor of future learning or performance—is in effect a prophecy that teachers may then unconsciously fulfill, to the detriment of the students who have done poorly on the test. This may be particularly true for students who come to schools in the United States from foreign and minority cultures (Garcia & Pearson, 1994).

Others argue that knowledge of a student's general or special ability can help the teacher adjust teaching, explanations, assignments, and overall treatment so as to challenge the more able and avoid frustrating and discouraging the less able. To us, both arguments have some truth. A thoughtful and skilled teacher must learn to use knowledge of the test scores of a student in ways that are helpful, not harmful, to that student.

Differences between Aptitude and Achievement Tests How do aptitude tests differ from achievement tests? They differ primarily in func-

At this point, where do you stand in this debate? Do you believe that aptitude tests are more beneficial than they are potentially harmful? Why or why not?

In colleges, business, and industry, norm-referenced aptitude tests are used for selection and placement.
(© George Zimbel/ Monkmeyer)

What do you remember of the characteristics of the aptitude and achievement college entrance tests? Did the former seem to be truly testing your typical abilities and the latter your learning? Why or why not?

tion: Aptitude tests are used to predict achievement, or the outcomes of future learning experiences. Achievement tests are used to measure and evaluate achievement, or the outcomes of past learning experiences. But achievement tests often predict future achievement as well as, if not better than, aptitude tests do. So the distinction between the two kinds of tests in terms of function does not always hold up well.

We can also make a distinction in terms of content. In an achievement test, the content should, and usually does, deal with what is taught directly and intentionally in schools. Here we ask questions about content that has been read in textbooks, discussed in class, practiced in homework and at the chalkboard, and explained by the teacher. Achievement test content should always be high in what we might call "taughtness"; aptitude test content need not be. We would not usually ask questions about the geography of a state or French vocabulary on an aptitude test, and we would not usually include questions that measure spatial ability (which is not taught in most schools) on an achievement test. But such inappropriate questions are sometimes included in each type of test, and when they are, confusion reigns.

Even experts have trouble with the distinction between aptitude and achievement (Anastasi, 1980; Ebel, 1980; D. R. Green, 1974). For our purposes here, it is enough for you to remember that aptitude tests should have validity for selection and prediction, and that achievement tests should be high in "taughtness" and content validity. Remember too, though, that aptitude tests, which predict future performance, cannot be criterion-referenced. We do not expect a future astronomer or jet engine mechanic to meet the criteria for acceptable performance in those fields today. We only want to find the best candidates for training pro-

Taking a Test to Understand It

If you want to understand a standardized achievement test, take it yourself and make judgments, item by item, as to its content validity and the adequacy of its coverage of the things you teach in your class and your school. If a particular test requires timing and reading directions aloud to students, have another teacher or a family member administer the test to you. This procedure, along with a careful reading of the test manual on how the test was developed and what evidence is available regarding its validity, should help you make an intelligent decision about whether the test can provide enough useful information to make it a worthwhile investment in time and money for the district or state in which you work.

Be sure to score your test and interpret your score, using the norms and other materials provided. And keeping in mind our earlier warning about the possible difficulties in currency of norms, check whether the norms are up to date. You should always be as informed as possible about any test you are giving your students.

grams in astronomy or engine repair and this means relying on norm-referenced tests. Achievement tests, on the other hand, can be either norm- or criterion-referenced.

Administering Standardized Tests

The term *standardized* refers in part to the way the tests are given. Unless directions are followed carefully, the results are meaningless. You should prepare students as necessary, depending on their age and the kind of test involved. Motivate them, but do not make them anxious—and watch for signs of parent-induced anxiety. A survey of teachers in one state reported many cases of children crying, misbehaving, vomiting, and soiling themselves during standardized testing (Haas, Haladyna, & Nolen, 1989). Older students, who know more about what the tests mean, motivate themselves to the extent that they want to do well in school. But they too can feel debilitating anxiety or a sense of meaninglessness. In fact, there are many reports of older students making random designs on their answer sheets because they believed that standardized test results had no impact on their grades, were unrelated to what they were learning, and were of no interest to their parents or teachers. Concerning standardized testing, then, your challenge as a teacher is to alleviate anxiety in younger students and to build motivation among older ones.

You must also see to it that students know how to take the test. Some youngsters may not be familiar with the format of a test; others may not be accustomed to working alone. Still others may not understand that they should not move ahead in a test when each section is timed. New

How would you react to a colleague who refuses to do any coaching for standardized testing and feels that such coaching is always wrong?

students in a district may also need coaching, especially if others in the group have taken a similar test before.

It is a good idea to teach students to understand test-item formats that are strange to them. It is now clear that an allocation of study time for developing familiarity with item types and test formats does improve student performance on standardized tests. One commercial course for preparing students for the Scholastic Aptitude Test takes about eighteen hours and costs hundreds of dollars. Students who are motivated and can afford to take the course have reported as much as a 200-point gain in SAT scores (Owen, 1985). If the reports are true, there is a moral question for American society to consider: Should this kind of advantage be available primarily to the wealthy? That wealth is the issue here is evident from research showing that coaching minority-group and low-income students can lead to dramatic test score improvements (Anastasi, 1981; Messick, 1982).

Giving a standardized test is not particularly difficult for teachers who are prepared. But it can be a nightmare for teachers (and their students) who discover too late that they are not prepared. Confusion, unclear directions, unobserved time limits, and inability to answer questions about what is (and is not) permissible can make students do much more poorly (or meaninglessly better) than they otherwise would.

So, prepare yourself. Read a copy of the test, the manual, and the directions for administering the test at least a few days in advance. You might even try a trial run, with another teacher or a family member acting as a student, to help you do justice to your students and to the standardized test itself.

Interpreting Standardized Tests

Although you have taken many standardized tests, you may have only a partial understanding of their interpretation. As a teacher you need to be able to make sense of test data presented as raw scores, stanines, grade-equivalents, and so forth, so that you, your students, and their parents can benefit from the information they provide. Below we present four common questions, as if asked by parents when given their child's norm-referenced, standardized achievement test score. These questions are meant to be only representative; you should take the time to study the materials and manuals accompanying any test you administer.

Use this section as a kind of minitest. After reading and studying it, cover the answer section of each question and write out your own answers. How well did you learn the material from one reading? from rereading?

Q: What is the raw score?

A: The raw score is the number of right answers. But that turns out not to be very useful. If a student gets a 36 or a 56 as a raw score, we cannot tell much about his or her performance vis-à-vis others. If we learn that the test has 60 items, it might seem that 36 is a marginally acceptable score and 56 is high. But if the test is a hard one, 36 might really indicate very good performance; and if the test is easy, then 56 no longer seems as good a score. Raw scores are not easy to interpret for these reasons.

Q: What is the percentile rank?

Teachers can pool their judgment in arriving at decisions about the content validity and overall suitability of standardized achievement tests.

(© Walter S. Silver)

A: The percentile rank is a way to judge the raw score with respect to local, state, or national norms. It is the most commonly used score in standardized achievement tests. If Tommie gets a score of 36, we would find out what percent of students in the norm group (district, state, or nation) scored below that score. On a difficult 60-item test of mathematics, Tommie's score of 36 might be at the 86th percentile. Tommie then would have scored better than 86 percent of the norm group (though worse than 14 percent), and his percentile rank would be 86. If the test was easy, the raw score of 36 might be equivalent to the 12th percentile rank. Then Tommie's performance was better than only 12 percent of those in the norm group, and he was exceeded in performance on the test by about 88 percent of the students in the norm group. Percentiles allow us to judge relative performance—at least if the norm group is like the student whose score is being interpreted.

Q: What is the **stanine** score?

A: Stanines (from "standard nine") are scores on a nine-point scale, from 1 (the lowest) to 9 (the highest). They are matched to percentile ranks but cover broader ranges (see Table 13.4). A stanine of 5 covers the percentile ranks of 41 to 60, or approximately the middle 20 percent of the distribution of the raw scores that occurred in the norm group. Table 13.4 presents the stanine scores and their associated percentile ranks. A stanine of 3 for a raw score of 56 would indicate performance at about the 17th percentile rank—that is, below-average achievement in comparison to a particular norm group. Generally, teachers regard stanines 1, 2, and 3 as low; 4, 5, and 6 as average; and 7, 8, and 9 as above average in achievement. While stanines are quite imprecise, they are handy to use to get a rough estimate of performance relative to the norm group.

POLICY, RESEARCH, AND PRACTICE

High-Stakes Standardized Testing Can Have Some Very Undesirable Consequences

A LOOK INSIDE THE SCHOOL

The stakes are high when tests are used to judge teachers, schools, districts, the curriculum in use, or even whole states. Corporations may not relocate to a particular area because of the company officers' perception that the schools are not very good in that area. Real estate prices in a neighborhood can change because of schools' test scores. And people move into and out of geographic areas because of their beliefs about the performance of schools in that area. So a lot of decisions rest on test scores, and there have been some unexpected consequences for teachers.

Among other negative effects, standardized tests can narrow a teacher's range of curriculum choices. Listen to what one teacher had to say to an interviewer:

Interviewer: Do the [standardized test] scores ever get used against you?

Teacher: Well, the first year I used Math Their Way [a program designed for conceptual understanding of math concepts through the manipulation of concrete materials], I was teaching a second-grade class and they scored at grade level. But other second grades in that school scored higher than grade level, and I had to do an awful lot of talking before they allowed me to use that program again.

Interviewer: So they were willing to throw out the program on the basis of the scores. How did you feel?

Teacher: I was angry. I was really angry because so many of the things I had taught those children about math were not on the test—were not tested by the test. And, indeed, the following year they did extremely well in the third grade. I had no children who were in any of the low math classes, and a great many of my children were in the advanced classes doing better than some of the children who had scored higher than they had on the [test]. But it's very hard to start a new program knowing that the [test] may be used against you.
(Smith, 1991, p. 8)

What are some other potential effects of high-stakes testing and what can you do about them as a teacher?

A LOOK AT THE RESEARCH

Following are additional findings from Smith (1991) when she interviewed teachers documenting their concerns about **high-stakes testing:**

- The publication of average and low standardized achievement test scores produces feelings of shame, embarrassment, guilt, and anger in some teachers. So some do whatever is necessary to avoid such feelings, including teaching items on the test, breaking standardized test administration

continues

543

procedures, sending their least able students on field trips during test times, or changing answers on answer sheets. Smith alleges that teachers' cheating, fudging, violating rules, and the like have become widespread. And why not? some teachers ask. Those teachers feel the scores are used as hammers against them by principals, superintendents, and the public, who do not understand the effects on test performance of the child-rearing practices in the students' homes, malnutrition, lead poisoning, child abuse and neglect, and repeated moving from school to school.

- Some teachers believe test scores to be invalid, and so feel alienated from the system they are part of. As one teacher put it, "Why worry about test scores when we all know they are worthless?" This teacher may have seen a mismatch between what she taught and what was tested (a content validity issue). Or the diagnostic information the test provided about students' performance came too late to use. Or if the diagnostic information was timely and revealed that a child was performing below the norm group on identifying initial consonants, say, it still may have been inadequate; in norm-referenced tests such a diagnosis may be based on only one test item. Or that particular diagnosis may be of no interest to the teacher, who shuns tests and expects the problem to take care of itself as the child reads more and more genuine literature.

- Some teachers feel guilty and anxious because the tests have harmful effects on their students. Though not all teachers and administrators believe this is the case, enough reports exist to indicate that standardized testing disturbs teachers, who see how the tests cause stress in young children or alienation in older students.

- Some teachers resent the instructional time lost. State-mandated achievement testing and preparation for the tests in the schools Smith studied resulted in the loss of about 100 hours of instructional time per class. School weeks are about 30 hours, so more than three weeks of instructional time were lost in these schools through yearly standardized achievement tests—nearly 10 percent of the entire school year!

- One class Smith studied went from 40 minutes of writing per day before January to no writing afterward, as the test became of paramount importance. The time allocated for social studies and health disappeared as the test drew nearer. And drill and practice rather than critical inquiry came to dominate the curriculum as the test came closer.

- Multiple-choice standardized testing can lead to multiple-choice instruction. Some teachers narrow the methods they use, and some teaching becomes more testlike, with many more short questions, worksheets, problems, and drill-and-practice activities. In some districts where pressure to do well on the tests is heavy, what may go out of the curriculum is problem solving; math with manipulatives; science as a process; free-reading time; social studies discussions; extended art, music, or physical education instruction; and anything else that requires time or creative thought. The pressure to answer multiple-choice items has made teachers in some districts more like technicians than professional educators. This trend may be dangerous. Smith (1991, p. 11) says: "A teacher who is able to teach only that which is determined from above and can teach only by worksheets is an unskilled worker." So the high-stakes standardized achievement-testing movement may have some consequences for teachers that are not pleasant to contemplate.

WHAT THIS MEANS FOR YOU AS A TEACHER

These effects of large-scale standardized testing should be weighed against the benefits of such testing programs at the international, national, state, or district levels. These benefits consist of making possible the comparison of student achievement across those levels and the revelation of possibly important strengths and problems through such comparisons. Unless feasible methods other than standardized multiple-choice testing for such large-scale programs can be invented, opposition to such testing programs implies their abandonment.

The solution may lie in educating teachers, educational administrators at all levels (national, state, etc.), political leaders (governors, mayors), and the general public as to the valid and invalid interpretations of the results of large-scale standardized testing programs. It may be possible to retain the values of such testing without the bad effects described by Smith (1991).

We believe that testing is in a time of transition and that teachers can make a difference. The problems caused by the use of standardized tests are being weighed against their benefits. It is hard to read the future, but multiple-choice standardized tests have been found to have so many negative side effects that their use in education will probably decrease. New tests or new ways of using such tests need to be found.

Q: What is a **grade-equivalent score?**

A: The grade equivalent is a widely used way of reporting scores, and one that teachers and parents have much trouble with. Suppose Leticia, a fifth-grader, receives a grade equivalent score on a mathematics achievement test of 8.6. What does it mean? Airasian (1991) believes 95 out of 100 teachers would answer as follows:

- Leticia does as well in mathematics as an eighth-grade student in the sixth month of school.
- Leticia can do the mathematics expected of an eighth-grader.
- Leticia's score indicates that she could succeed in an eighth-grade mathematics curriculum.
- Leticia could be placed in an eighth-grade mathematics class now and succeed.

In fact, every one of these interpretations is wrong! Leticia took a fifth-grade achievement test. It covered fifth-grade material. The fact that she answered as many items as an eighth-grader in the sixth month might have is simply a way of saying that she really has a great grasp of fifth-grade mathematics. No eighth grader ever took that test, only fifth graders did. Leticia's performance was indeed very good—estimated to be where an eighth grader might be. But it does not mean that Leticia has mastered eighth-grade material! She has not yet had sixth-grade mathematics, or seventh-grade mathematics, or any eighth-grade mathematics. If Leticia had to take an eighth-grade mathematics test, she would

545

probably perform poorly in comparison to eighth graders. Leticia has mathematics skills—of that there is no doubt. She has mastered fifth-grade mathematics at a level equivalent to the estimated performance of the average child in the sixth month of the eighth grade.

This distinction is subtle, but you need to understand it so that you know how to communicate with parents who want their child skipped because his or her performance is at the eighth-grade level, despite being only in fifth grade. What we really know about Leticia is that when we compare her to the fifth graders for whom the test was intended and on whom the test was normed, she performs quite a bit above the average. Grade-equivalent scores are a popular way of communicating performance to parents, but they are also quite confusing to them.

What Does the Future Hold for Standardized Testing?

Of the many questions surrounding the uses and abuses of standardized testing today, we deal here with the two we believe are of most concern to you as a teacher: (1) Should present-day standardized multiple-choice tests be replaced by other kinds of standardized tests?; and (2) Should any standardized tests be used, even those that would measure achievement of instructional objectives much more directly and with greater validity?

Current thinking on the first question seems to be crystallizing. Multiple-choice tests are typically biased against higher-level-thinking kinds of educational objectives. They seldom require in any genuine way the kinds of writing, reading, mathematical problem solving, extended analysis and synthesis of ideas, creation of curriculum-relevant products, and so on, that educators are increasingly emphasizing (Fredericksen, 1984; Resnick & Resnick, 1990). Even if multiple-choice tests of ability to edit prose, for example, correlated substantially with assessments of students' writing ability, they would be undesirable because of their side effects on teaching and learning. "You get what you assess, you do not get what you do not assess," so you should "build assessments toward which you want educators to teach" (Resnick & Resnick, 1990, p. 66). In other words, if we want teachers to aim at their students' ability to write, read, do math, understand history, think about political issues, and grasp the nature of science and its methods, we should assess these kinds of achievement directly. Assessing them indirectly, as is now typically attempted through multiple-choice tests, misses the mark too widely and pulls teachers toward "multiple-choice teaching" rather than the real-life forms of these kinds of achievement.

So it seems clear that American education, after a movement toward multiple-choice testing that began in the 1920s, is now ready to move to a system that is closer to the real-life, authentic forms of testing urged by many contemporary researchers (Resnick & Resnick, 1990; Baron & Wolf, 1996). Some of these new kinds of assessments are discussed in Chapter 14.

On the second question—whether any standardized testing should be done—opinion seems more sharply divided. Would much of the distress teachers feel in present-day standardized testing situations disappear if they had great respect for what was being measured by the tests? Probably (see Smith & Levin, 1996). Or would teachers still feel anxious and resentful because any standardized tests would still evaluate the achievement of their students in ways that inevitably made possible comparisons with other teachers? As we know, teachers of students from low-income homes very often have classes with lower average scores on achievement tests. These teachers then seem to be ineffective to uninformed observers, unfamiliar with the nonteacher factors, especially those in the home background, that affect achievement.

Can we assume that authentic evaluations of student achievement with standardized procedures might be more acceptable to teachers than the multiple-choice tests now so popular? Some teachers say no, because they believe any such evaluation must inevitably measure achievement in a way inappropriate for the emphases, styles, and approaches of their teaching, which are different from those of any other teacher. Other teachers, however, recognize the value of such authentic standardized testing. It can reveal schools and teachers who are helping students overcome the obstacles faced in minority-group, non-English-speaking, low-income homes. And identification of effective teaching and schooling can provide important lessons for other schools and teachers. But it is also true that such testing might identify teachers and schools with, say, relatively advantaged, middle-class students who are not doing as well as expected on the authentic achievement tests. It is the possibility of such negative evaluations that understandably arouses teacher anxiety.

Our own position is that standardized testing can be a desirable tool for assessment when the tests used are those that

1. most teachers consider to be valid, authentic approaches to the kinds of knowledge, thinking, reasoning, problem solving, and creativity they value

2. representative groups of teachers have had substantive involvement in creating

3. are accompanied by education of the press and the public concerning the factors, other than those controlled by teachers and schools, that affect achievement so that the public does not unjustifiably criticize teacher and school effectiveness

4. are accompanied by thoughtful and strong efforts to understand *and remedy* the low performance of any teachers and schools that cannot reasonably be attributed to factors outside the control of the teacher or school involved

5. are accompanied by sufficient financial resources to meet the much higher costs of authentic assessment compared to those of standardized multiple-choice testing

> What do you think it would mean if your students consistently did well on your own tests but came out poorly on standardized achievement tests? How do you think you would feel? Are there any steps you might take in response?

SUMMARY

1. A primary function of teachers is the assessment of students, materials, and programs.

2. Tests are often used in the assessment process. A good test relies on systematic procedures for observing student performance and quantifies that performance. A test samples only a small amount of what students have learned, but that small amount can provide a meaningful indicator of what has been learned. Educators measure the observable behavior of students, assign a score, and use that—the student's score—to evaluate learning.

3. Norms allow us to interpret a student's score in relation to the scores of other students—in a local area or the nation as a whole. Norm-referenced testing tells us how a student's knowledge compares with that of other students; it does not tell us what the student actually knows. For this kind of interpretation, we have to use criterion-referenced testing—tests that allow us to compare student behavior with some preset standard of performance.

4. A good test must be both reliable and valid.

5. Reliability has to do with stability. No test is ever perfectly reliable. As a result, we must take account of the standard error of measurement and think of a student's score, not as a precise point, but as a range—a confidence band around the observed score.

6. Validity—the degree to which a test measures what we intend it to measure—is the most important element in the assessment process. An achievement test has content validity when it tests material that students have had an opportunity to learn. Criterion validity tells us how well a test predicts success in an instructional program or a job. Construct validity is more difficult to determine because it deals with the degree to which a test measures an abstraction. Here the question is whether a test in fact measures the construct (ability, trait, or tendency) it is intended to measure. A test must also be interpreted sensibly, and the consequences of its use must be anticipated and acceptable. A test fails to achieve sufficient construct validity if we are not comfortable about its meaning in the educational context in which it is used.

7. In addition to assessing students' learning, teachers are responsible for evaluating the programs and materials they are using or plan to use. Formative evaluation gives teachers and others the information they need to improve programs or curricular materials. Summative evaluation, which is usually conducted by outside experts, tells us whether programs and products are providing what they were intended to provide at reasonable costs in money, effort, and time. Teachers should demand more evaluation information from curriculum developers and those who sell educational materials.

8. Use of standardized tests has both advantages and disadvantages in the overall assessment process. There are both norm-referenced and criterion-referenced standardized tests. Norm-referenced are the most commonly used.

9. Because standardized tests are constructed by experts, they are usually more carefully designed than are teacher-made tests. They also come with important information—on test reliability and validity and administration procedures and problems. The procedures by which they are administered and their scoring standards are the same for all students.

10. Some of the disadvantages of standardized-test use include the typical assumption that learning is behaviorally-based and can be broken down into discrete skills; a frequent mismatch with the curriculum actually covered in class; and too few items to accurately test a concept or knowledge.

11. Standardized tests should not be used for grading students or evaluating a teacher's performance.

12. Schools use two kinds of standardized tests: aptitude and achievement tests. Aptitude tests give us information for student guidance and counseling. They are used to predict achievement—a source of controversy among educators, some of whom believe that teachers accept the predictions as fact and act accordingly with students. Achievement tests, which can sometimes be better than aptitude tests as predictors of future learning, are used primarily to measure past learning.

13. Administration is a critical part of the standardized testing process. Preparation is twofold here. Teachers should (1) talk to students about how to take the test—about the rules, format, item types, and time requirements, (2) try to reduce anxiety among students, and (3) try to increase their motivation to do well. And teachers should prepare themselves, by reading the test and the directions, doing a trial run, and collecting any necessary materials ahead of time.

14. Teachers also have to be able to interpret test results. Results are usually reported as raw scores, percentile ranks, stanines, or grade equivalents. Grade equivalents are easily misunderstood; they are not indicative of the grade level a student can perform at. Regardless of the form scores are reported in, teachers must remember that scores are not perfectly reliable.

15. Reliance on standardized tests has had some negative side effects. Teachers may be embarrassed about performance and anxious for their students, falsify data, resent the time lost to testing, and unnecessarily restrict what and how they teach. Standardized achievement testing may contribute to the deskilling of teachers. Unanticipated problems with standardized testing now have become obvious.

16. There are at least two major questions about standardized testing that concern teachers. The first is whether present-day multiple-choice tests should and can be replaced by more authentic, direct, and valid kinds of achievement tests. The second is whether even the latter kinds of standardized testing are defensible. On the first issue, we say yes. On the second, we also say yes, provided that five conditions are met: teachers respect the test, teachers have helped compose the test, the public is helped to interpret the test appropriately, teachers are helped to deal with low achievement, and funds are provided to meet the higher costs of authentic testing.

17. Be sure to remember that this chapter on assessment concepts and standardized tests (and the next chapter on teacher-made tests) can give you only the briefest glimpse of a highly technical field. We live in an age of evidence, and you need technical skills to collect and interpret usable data. So we urge you to take a specialized course in testing and to read some of the recent literature on the subject.

CHAPTER 14

The Teacher's Assessment and Grading of Student Learning

Overview

INFORMAL ASSESSMENT
  Sizing-Up Assessments
  Assessment during Interactive Teaching
FORMAL ASSESSMENT: DETERMINING WHAT KINDS OF ACHIEVEMENT ARE IMPORTANT
  Domain-Referenced Testing
  The Table of Specifications
TYPES OF FORMAL TESTS AND TEST ITEMS
  Performance Tests
    Scoring performance assessments
    Portfolios of performance

  POLICY, RESEARCH, AND PRACTICE
  What Are the Problems and Prospects of Performance Assessment?

    Prompts in performance testing
  Essay Tests
    Writing essay-test questions
    Scoring essay tests

Short-Answer Tests
    Types of short-answer questions
    Multiple-choice questions at all levels of cognition
    Writing multiple-choice questions

  APPLICATION
  Using Guidelines to Write Good Multiple-Choice Questions

    Refining multiple-choice tests
  Getting the Advantages of Using All Kinds of Questions
  Using the Computer in Classroom Assessment
FROM ASSESSING TO GRADING: A DIFFICULT TRANSITION
  Establishing a Frame of Reference for Grading Judgments
    Absolute standards
    Pseudoabsolute standards
    Relative standards
  Two Common Questions about Testing, Grading, and Marking

  POLICY, RESEARCH, AND PRACTICE
  How Can Tests and Grades Be Used Sensibly and Humanely in the Assessment Process?

  Sources of Information for Grading Decisions
    Formal assessments
    Informal assessments

  POLICY, RESEARCH, AND PRACTICE
  What Factors Actually Go into Teachers' Grading Decisions?

  Considering the Toughest Grade of All: Nonpromotion
  USING PORTFOLIOS IN THE ASSESSMENT PROCESS
  Summary

OVERVIEW

We turn now to one of your most important functions as a teacher: evaluating your students' achievement of your instructional objectives. Standardized tests measure achievement of objectives that are presumably common to many classes, teachers, and schools; they are not tailored to your class. So informal and formal assessments are made *by you* to evaluate students against the objectives you hold. You decide what it is important to learn, and you decide what and how to assess the achievement of that learning during and after instruction. Most assessments actually take place during instruction, though these are the informal kind. Formal assessment, usually by means of tests, often takes place after instruction has occurred.

Formal assessment by teachers in the classroom is designed to measure important and relevant kinds of achievement—and only those kinds of achievement. Differentiating among students is altogether beside the point. Students' test scores and grades should reveal how well they have achieved objectives, not how well they have performed as compared with their fellow students. If every student does perfectly on a test, that's wonderful. Teachers should not worry that a test was too easy or ineffective because it failed to differentiate among students. If every student fails a test, we conclude that they have not been taught adequately and have not learned well enough, not that the test was too difficult. Formal assessment of this kind relies on criterion-referenced or standards-based achievement tests.

To develop satisfactory teacher-made achievement tests that are referenced to criteria and standards, you need to know how to (1) determine what kinds of achievement are important, (2) elicit student performance or behavior that reveals those kinds of achievement, and (3) interpret that performance or behavior in ways that can be communicated to your students and also help you do a better job with your students. In this chapter we go into each of these areas. In addition, we look at two relatively new developments in assessment: performance tests and portfolio systems of assessment.

We also talk about some of the pros and cons of evaluation systems, the ways teachers gather and combine information about students, and the kinds of standards on which grading systems are based. Throughout the chapter we advocate good sense, kindness, and awareness that grades are a serious matter and that our own biases and those of our testing instruments call for a special generosity toward our students.

Informal Assessment

There are two kinds of informal assessment to which teachers devote a lot of time each year. These are **sizing-up assessments** and **instructional assessments.** Both are considered informal in that records of these assessments are not usually kept. Rather, the information is stored in teachers' heads and influences their actions and opinions as the year progresses. They are also considered informal because teachers use subjective criteria for these assessments, though their judgments should be based on experience and made carefully.

Sizing-Up Assessments

Sizing-up assessments provide teachers with practical knowledge of students' cognitive, affective, and psychomotor skills. Such assessment occurs primarily during the first two weeks of the school term, when teachers naturally begin to understand their students as helpful, highly motivated, athletic, bright, shy, sassy, sad, emotionally needy, tricky, or describable in some other way. In fact, such assessments may start even before school begins, as when one teacher says to another, "I hear you have Jimmy Schott next year—boy that one's a handful!" It is worth noting that expert teachers tend not to pay attention to such comments, nor do they usually check school records at the start of the year to learn about their students. They want all children to have a chance to behave differently in their classes than they might have behaved before. Expert teachers recognize that every student acts differently in different environments. Accordingly, expert teachers tend to hold off using records or other information about students longer than do beginning teachers (Carter, et al., 1987). Perhaps that is a good policy for all teachers to follow.

There are a number of pitfalls in making sizing-up assessments (Airasian, 1991). One problem to beware of is that early impressions can become permanent, leading to self-fulfilling prophesies. Teachers can hold on to beliefs that a child is unmotivated, or very bright, long after his or her classroom behavior indicates otherwise. A second problem is the validity of the impressions. Teachers tend to be good judges of cognitive ability and much poorer judges of things like interest, self-concept, and emotional stability. Third, these affective attributes of children are far less stable than are the cognitive characteristics they display. Fourth, sizing-up assessments, because they are unspoken and subjective, are prone to all the cultural stereotyping that teachers naturally bring to their classrooms (Combs & Gay, 1988; Doherty & Hier, 1988). This stereotyping occurs subtly, for example, by interpreting Carolyn's low mathematics score on a review test as due to the fact that she cannot do math because she's a girl rather than to the fact that Carolyn forgot her math over the summer. Or it shows up when you see Rodney (an African-American boy) hit Ben (an Asian boy) and decide that Rodney is aggressive and needs extra watching, when what really happened is that Ben stole Rodney's watch just before their dispute caught your attention. In sum, the validity and reliability of sizing-up assessments are questionable, so teachers must be careful about the permanence of such assessments.

> Did any teacher hold a belief about you that was not accurate? How did you feel?

Assessment during Interactive Teaching

The second kind of informal assessment, taking up much time throughout the school year, is instructional assessment during interactive teaching. While teaching, teachers, like other performers such as actors, dancers, and musicians, must "read" their audience. They must constantly assess their performance (Should I give more examples? Am I beating a dead horse? Should I write that out on the board?). It has been found that during interactive instruction the greatest proportion of a teacher's thoughts deal with how well instruction is being received by students (Clark & Peterson, 1986; Calderhead, 1996). Experienced teachers seem to be adept at reading cues about the comprehension of

Informal assessments and remediation are common classroom events.

(© Jean-Claude Lejeune/Stock Boston)

instruction of their own students, in their own classrooms, but the skill may not be generalizable. Accurate interpretation of cues about the comprehension of a lesson may depend upon a teacher's knowing the subject matter being taught, the ability of the students, the events that preceded instruction, and so forth (Stader, Colyar, & Berliner, 1990). With experience, then, comes a "feel" for how instruction is going in the classroom—but perhaps only a teacher's own classroom.

The problems with informal assessment during instruction are the basic problems of all assessment: reliability and validity. Problems with reliability have to do with the rapidly changing nature of classroom instruction, such that dependable estimates of instructional effectiveness and student involvement are not easy to get when the teacher is on-the-run. And teachers may not "read" the cues from all students. Some students not monitored by the teacher may or may not be learning and enjoying the lesson in the same way as the few who are observed. Teachers often are found to have *steering groups*—about four or five students they monitor carefully—to gauge the cognitive and motivational effectiveness of their instruction. So they may have too small a sample (similar to too few test items) to get a reliable reading of what is going on in the classroom.

The validity of informal assessment during instruction is questionable, since most teachers are biased—they are seeking ways to confirm that their marvelous instruction is working well and fully appreciated by their students. Because of this all-too-human need to feel competent, teachers sometimes give away answers to questions by tipping off the students, skip hard topics, or attribute wrong answers to students' inadequate sleep or motivation instead of to faulty instruction. Problems of validity also arise in the judgments made about how a lesson is being received when a student nods at appropriate times, has his or her eyes

Did you ever con a teacher by purposefully looking attentive and engaged while your mind wandered?

on the teacher, is taking notes, and has a thoughtful facial expression. Even with all that, the student could still be on Mars! It is hard to know what students—particularly older students—are thinking.

Airasian (1991) offered three suggestions to improve the validity and reliability of assessment during interactive instruction:

1. Include a broad sample of students when gathering information about instructional success. (For example, do not just call on volunteers when asking questions.)

2. Try to assess the progress of learning, not just whether or not students are paying attention. (For example, ask many higher-order questions as you proceed; do not just monitor whether students are participating actively.)

3. Supplement informal assessment with more formal means. (For example, use homework assignments, review exercises, and worksheets that accompany a text, so that you can obtain some written records to analyze how instruction is progressing.)

Experience and thoughtfulness will help you get better at sizing-up and on-the-run instructional assessments. These assessments can be improved by delaying your evaluations of students, and ensuring that those evaluations are open to change. Instructional assessments need to be monitored to ensure adequate sampling of students, and they must also be focused on instructional progress rather than just participation in activities, as gratifying as that might be. You must also be on your guard not to let your own need to see everything go well bias your observations.

Formal Assessment: Determining What Kinds of Achievement Are Important

Formal assessment occurs periodically throughout the school year. The performance of students—on a test, an essay, homework, a project—has some permanence and the assessment of it is made permanent by writing it down in record books or storing it in portfolios or files. Formal assessments, unlike sizing-up assessments, are mostly concerned with the cognitive domain. They provide records for making decisions about the progress of students, and—very important to teachers—grading students. Formal assessment requires you, first, to decide what kinds of achievement are important for your students—that is, what should they know (What declarative knowledge should they possess?) and what should they be able to do (What procedural knowledge should they possess?). This issue is basically the same one we dealt with in Chapter 2 concerning specifying educational objectives and standards.

We concentrate in this chapter on test development, but the procedures to be described hold for homework, review exercises, projects, and any other assignment you give. You must *always* keep in the forefront of your mind what it is your students need to know and be able to do. Otherwise, the homework, tests, projects, and all your other assignments will be seen by your students, and rightly so, as time fillers with little educational significance.

Domain-Referenced Testing

In certain fields it is possible to map the whole domain of achievement with some confidence. The multiplication of one- and two-digit numbers up to twelve—the multiplication tables we all learned as children—is a prime example. Homework assignments, review exercises, or an achievement test could be based on a large, representative sample of the 144 possible combinations. The kind of sample of multiplication items we would develop from the multiplication tables would give us a domain-referenced as well as a criterion-referenced test. If a student does the multiplications in this sample correctly, we can infer that he or she can do the whole domain correctly, and we would evaluate the student's achievement positively. Whether the student's classmates did as well or much less well is irrelevant to our evaluation of this particular student's achievement.

Did you ever have a homework assignment that seemed merely busywork? How did that make you feel?

The Table of Specifications

When the domain of achievement is not finite and unarguable, teachers have to analyze and outline the content. The outline of topics acts as one dimension of a table. The other dimension sets forth what students should be able to do with each topic. Do we want them simply to *know* the facts, definitions, concepts, and conventions? Or do we also want students to *comprehend* them? Or should they be able to *apply, analyze, synthesize,* or *evaluate* material within each of the topics? You may recognize these italicized terms as major headings of the taxonomy of the cognitive domain described in Chapter 2. They help us define what students should be able to do with any given part of the content.

Crossing the two dimensions—content and types of cognitive performance—yields a *table of specifications* for an achievement test, much like the behavior-content matrix we talked about in Chapter 2. Into each cell of the table, where a given behavior intersects with a given topic, we can put the percentage of questions that, in our judgment, should deal with that particular behavior-content combination.

Two examples of tables of specifications are shown in Table 14.1: one for a test on four novels by two American authors and one on educational assessment and evaluation. Notice how these tables organize the test material. They help us avoid asking too many questions about some topics and too few about others, or too many recall or recognition questions and too few "thought" questions.

We recommend that you take the time to develop these kinds of organizers for constructing your tests. To do so is time consuming, but they help not only in designing a test but in analyzing the scores obtained. We can score the questions in the various cells separately to see whether students have mastered a particular topic or type of cognitive performance. If these part-scores are reliable enough—if they are based on large enough samples of items on the topic or the behavior—they can serve a diagnostic function, helping teacher and student pinpoint specific areas that call for further instruction.

It is also possible to design a test for just one cell in a table of spe-

TABLE

14.1

Tables of Specifications for Two Teacher-Made Tests

Behavioral Competence	Novels Studied				
	A Farewell to Arms	The Sun Also Rises	The Great Gatsby	Tender Is the Night	Total
Knowledge of facts about characters and plot	5%	5%	5%	5%	20%
Ability to identify various literary devices	5	5	5	5	20
Ability to relate novel to social history of its time	5	5	5	5	20
Ability to apply criteria to evaluations of novel as a whole	10	10	10	10	40
Total	25%	25%	25%	25%	100%

Subject Matter Category	Educational Assessment and Evaluation			
	Knowledge of Facts, Definitions, and Principles	Understanding of Basic Concepts and Considerations	Ability to Apply Principles and Rules to Practical Problems	Total
Basic concepts in assessment and evaluation	10%	10%	10%	30%
The teacher and standardized testing	5	5	5	15
The teacher's assessments and grades	10	10	35	55
Total	25%	25%	50%	100%

cifications—say, skill in the solution of mathematical problems dealing with chemical energy and changes. Obviously a student's score on this kind of focused criterion-referenced test could be used to determine whether he or she has mastered this part of the course.

It is important to share the objectives of instruction with students. In our opinion, it is also a good idea, when students are old enough, to share the table of specifications with them. It can help them understand what they should be learning.

How do you decide on the number of questions for each cell? How do you determine the relative emphasis on each behavior-content combination? Your decision should reflect the relative amount of effort, time spent in class and out, and importance of each cell in the total array of objectives. Educational values are involved here, and your judgment,

Did you ever study for a test that did not cover what you studied? How did that make you feel?

influenced by what you read and learn from experts, is usually more useful than any scientific data.

How many questions should you ask? Other things being equal, more questions mean greater reliability and therefore greater assurance that the judgments you make about a student are accurate. But other things are not always equal, and sometimes you have to compromise. You may choose to use essay and short-answer questions in your formal assessment, in which case only a small number of items can be used on each testing occasion. You may choose a performance test, such as requiring students to conduct a simple science experiment. Generally, performance tests take a long time, so they may consist of only one item, a single exercise that might be broken down to provide various sub-scores. Otherwise students' ages and abilities, difficulty of questions, and available time determine the number of questions you can ask. If you use multiple-choice items, as many teachers do, experience will tell you how many items of a certain kind your students can handle per minute. The range is probably from 15 to 30 seconds per item for able, older students attempting to answer easy items, and 100 or more seconds per item for less able, younger students working on more difficult items. Younger students can sometimes sustain attention to test taking for only about 15 minutes, whereas twelfth graders, if motivated, can handle up to 120 minutes of test taking at a time. What you can do is use frequent short tests, written to objectives, and add the scores together to give you the greater reliability of longer tests. But also keep in mind what some critics assert—that in contemporary classrooms too much time is spent on testing and too little on actual instruction!

Something to think about before we go on: Your tests are deeds that speak louder than words about your educational values. You may claim proudly that you want your students to learn to think about a subject—to learn how to analyze, or synthesize, or evaluate. But if your tests measure verbatim knowledge of what is in the textbook or what has been said in class, your students will learn what your deeds—not your words—have told them.

How fast can you do multiple-choice items? How many are your less able students likely to be able to do in 20 minutes?

Types of Formal Tests and Test Items

After you have made a table of specifications, you have to choose the kinds of test items you want to use. There are three major categories:

1. *Performance tests,* or various forms of authentic performance, such as a driving test, a spelling contest, or products such as a work of art, or a written story. Records of these performances can be kept in portfolios (files of significant accomplishments by students, discussed on pages 593–597).

2. *Long-answer questions*—essays or paragraph-length constructed responses to questions.

3. *Short-answer questions,* which can in turn be divided into (a) **supply questions** and (b) **select questions.** With supply items the answer is a written word, phrase, or sentence. Select items require a choice

from a set of alternatives, and select types can be further divided into multiple-choice, true-false, and matching questions.

Your choice of question types largely determines the kinds of cognitive processes students will need to use to answer them. In general, performance tests, long-answer questions, and supply questions are easier to compose so as to tap higher-level cognitive processes. Although experts are capable of writing multiple-choice questions that measure processes more complex than knowledge (recall or recognition), even they find it difficult to do so. Most teachers do better in measuring various kinds of reasoning and problem-solving achievement when they use essay questions or short-answer supply questions. Besides, a multiple-choice item reflects the fact that you believe knowledge is fragmented into independent little pieces, and you probably do not want to teach that way. Nor do you want knowledge to be decontextualized—seen as isolated chunks of information out of context—as is often the case when short-answer select-type items are presented. For example, think about the true-false item "Eisenhower was the president at the end of World War II." But that item calls for a mere isolated chronological fact. It is certainly important to know about the Roosevelt presidency, the Truman presidency, the beginning of the cold war, the war in Korea, Eisenhower's presidency, and other events of the period. But is it sensible to pick out little bits of information about that time period, without their surrounding meanings? Some views of education and knowledge hold that it is appropriate to learn just the facts. But contemporary cognitive psychologists and educators believe that we may have gone overboard in fragmenting and decontextualizing the knowledge to be learned. Too many of the tests we use to assess learning reflect that problem. No doubt our students should know who was president at the end of World War II and when Eisenhower became our president; knowledge of this type *is* important. But we should worry if that is all they know and remember about that entire time period of American history.

Performance tests, long-answer questions, or supply questions are more likely to teach students that knowledge is made up of sets of related ideas, of large integrated networks of facts, concepts, principles, opinions, and feelings. Also, in the real world, craftspersons, business people, and professionals have to be able to solve problems and write descriptive reports, informative letters, and other communications. Performance tests, long-answer questions, and supply questions are a form of practice that can develop these kinds of abilities. Short-answer select questions seldom do that. The real world rarely presents its problems in a multiple-choice, select-the-right-alternative form.

Multiple-choice and the other kinds of select questions work best in measuring knowledge—the ability to recall or recognize what has been learned. The most common form of test bias, noted Fredericksen (1984), results from the influence of multiple-choice tests on teaching and learning, since there is a tendency for such tests to get at knowledge rather than the ability to reason. This bias has been present for a long time, but its pernicious effects have only recently been fully appreciated. It

How did you feel after a test with memory-only, multiple-choice questions?

implies that as the twentieth century progressed American educators may have made a mistake in moving so heavily toward short-answer select questions in their tests. We are already seeing a swing toward long-answer questions on achievement tests, and even more recently has come the rediscovery of performance tests for assessing higher levels of student achievement in an authentic way.

Performance Tests

If you have a license to drive a car, you have successfully passed a performance test. There was nothing new about such tests even in 1943 (see Remmers & Gage, 1943, Chapter 11, "Product and Procedure Evaluation"), but in recent years they have been brought back into education as an alternative to traditional testing, particularly multiple-choice testing. More scholars now believe that an assessment of intellectual achievement requires the performance of exemplary tasks (Wiggins, 1989; Baron & Wolf, 1996; Marzano & Kendall, 1996). Assessments must be designed to present or simulate as closely as possible the kinds of tasks performed by individuals who really write, conduct business, engage in scientific experiments, calculate numbers, and so forth. Such tasks are authentic in that they match what is expected of people in life outside of school settings. Even if such **authentic tests** are not easily judged, they represent the kind of tasks that should be done to be sure someone has the skills needed to be successful in the real world. Performance tests, then, ensure that a person can translate his or her knowledge and understandings into action. Neither essay exams nor multiple-choice exams can make that claim. Would you like to employ a reporter who knows how to find misspelled words in a paragraph and can tell you the meaning of the prefix *anti,* or would you prefer to hire someone who can write a news story? How would you compare one candidate's test results against another who brought you a portfolio of his or her exemplary news stories? Clearly, authentic examples of writing are more desirable for potential employers or faculty advisors to the school newspaper than the proxies we sometimes use to assess writing skill. Performance tests can be used to find the writer we want; multiple-choice tests are inherently less adequate for our purposes.

Why is it that in athletics, the arts and crafts, the professions, we accept performance tests as appropriate but hold no such requirement for most academic subjects? The game, recital, play, debate, science fair, and school newspaper article are performance measures of skill and ability that we all acknowledge to be legitimate. Moreover, for these performances we allow coaching and tell students in advance the criteria and standards for judgment. These tests are transparent; that is, the test takers know what is coming and how to prepare for it. There are few surprises.

> If we wish to design an authentic test we must first decide what are the actual performances that we want students to be good at. We must design those performances first and worry about . . . grading

Can you think of some performance tests in the area or grade you are to teach?

them later. Do we judge our students to be deficient in writing, speaking, listening, artistic creation, finding and citing evidence, and problem solving? Then let the tests ask them to write, speak, listen, create, do original research, and solve problems. Only then need we worry about scoring the performances, training the judges, . . . [and providing] useful feedback to students about results.

(Wiggins, 1989, p. 705)

Traditional tests are like drills in athletics or exercises on the violin or piano. Performance tests, however, are like games and recitals; they are the real thing. If we break out of our mind-set about what a test is supposed to look like, we might start making academic tests more like public performances. For example, advocates of performance tests believe that doing and presenting to a class or panel of judges one piece of original research, with all its ambiguities and unstructured aspects, is probably a better indicator of scientific knowledge than an efficient 50-item, multiple-choice, end-of-semester examination. Certainly a multiple-choice exam can measure some components of scientific knowledge. But performance-test advocates say that students need more sophisticated and authentic tests of ability to prepare for the real world and to stay interested in the evaluative process.

Performance tests, however, need not be just end-of-semester tests. Engaging and complex standardized assignments can be used for instruction and assessment; they can be an integral part of classroom life, embedded in instruction rather than separate from it. Figure 14.1 presents two examples of performance tests. One, the history examination, is integrated into classroom instruction; the other, the economics examination, is an end-of-semester test, though it may require weeks to prepare for it.

As the examples in Figure 14.1 make clear, these assessments differ sharply from the kinds most people have had throughout their school careers. In fact, performance tests have unique characteristics (Marzano & Kendall, 1996; Baron, 1990, 1991). They generally

- are grounded in the real world
- involve sustained work that may extend over several days, both in and out of school
- deal with the major or "big" ideas in a discipline
- are more loosely structured than other types of tests, often requiring students to identify some of the subproblems that exist as well as to find strategies for their solution
- are problems that can be brainstormed, so that multiple perspectives are brought to bear on the problem through collaboration with other students
- require students to figure out for themselves what data are needed, as well as how to collect, analyze, portray, report, and critique the data
- require the use of a wide range of skills useful in the real world, not just the skills needed to succeed at school work

How many tests like these have you had in school? How do you think you would feel if these kinds of tests were used in your schooling?

Oral History Project, 9th Grade (Developed in Hope High School, Providence, Rhode Island)

You must complete an oral history based on interviews and written sources and present your findings orally in class. The choice of subject matter will be up to you. Some examples of possible topics include: your family, running a small business, substance abuse, a labor union, teenage parents, or recent immigrants. You are to create three workable hypotheses based on your preliminary investigations and come up with four questions you will ask to test each hypothesis.

To meet the criteria for evaluating the oral history project described above, you must:

- investigate three hypotheses;
- describe at least one change over time;
- demonstrate that you have done background research;
- interview four appropriate people as sources;
- prepare at least four questions related to each hypothesis;
- ask questions that are not leading or biased;
- ask follow-up questions when appropriate;
- note important differences between fact and opinion in answers that you receive;
- use evidence to support your choice of the best hypothesis; and
- organize your writing and your class presentation

Economics Project (Developed in Brighton High School, Rochester, New York)

You are the chief executive officer of an established firm. Your firm has always captured a major share of the market, because of good use of technology, understanding of the natural laws of constraint, understanding of market systems, and the maintenance of a high standard for your product. However, in recent months your product has become part of a new trend in public tastes. Several new firms have entered the market and have captured part of your sales. Your product's proportional share of total aggregate demand is continuing to fall. When demand returns to normal, you will be controlling less of the market than before.

Your board of directors has given you less than a month to prepare a report that solves the problem in the short run and in the long run. In preparing the report, you should: 1) define the problem, 2) prepare data to illustrate the current situation, 3) prepare data to illustrate conditions one year in the future, 4) recommend action for today, 5) recommend action over the next year, and 6) discuss where your company will be in the market six months from today and one year from today.

The tasks that must be completed in the course of this project include:

- deriving formulas for supply, demand, elasticity, and equilibrium;
- preparing schedules for supply, demand, costs, and revenues;
- graphing all work;
- preparing a written evaluation of the current and future situation for the market in general and for your company in particular;
- preparing a written recommendation for your board of directors;
- showing aggregate demand today and predicting what it will be one year hence; and
- showing the demand for your firm's product today and predicting what it will be one year hence.

FIGURE 14.1

Examples of performance tests in history and economics at the high school level

Adapted from Wiggins (1989, p. 707).

- require students to make explicit their assumptions, to generalize, and to connect what they do to other topics and concepts
- require students to become self-critical of what they (and others) do so that performances can be improved.

Some states and districts are trying to develop performance measures because they share the hope that more authentic performance tests will improve the nature of teaching and learning in our schools. Initial evidence (Sheingold, Heller, & Paulukonis, 1995) tells us that teachers and their instructional practices do indeed change when they engage fully in the development and scoring of performance assessments. Some teachers' comments about this process are reported in Table 14.2.

Scoring Performance Assessments   Writing is one of the easiest curriculum areas in which to develop performance assessments. Scales to judge

14.2

Teachers' Comments on Performance Test Development and Scoring

On using new sources of evidence; shifting from exclusive reliance on traditional tests: "It has made me not as caught up in the teach-test, teach-test cycle. I can accept a sketch, an oral report, a group product as the acceptable project instead of thirty little quizzes. Assessment can be brainstorming previously learned material" (Middle school history–social science teacher).

On sharing responsibility for learning and assessment; helping students take control of their own learning: "Because of my involvement (in the assessment design) . . . I have empowered students completely to establish their own performance standards. They not only did a thorough job on standards, but they did well on scoring each other's performances (High school English–language arts teacher).

On changing the goals of instruction; learning what is essential for each discipline: "In planning lessons and assessing learning, I'm looking more at the important, big ideas like meaning-making and critical thinking (Elementary school English–language arts teacher).

On deciding how to evaluate evidence; learning about the inferences that can be made from what students are asked to do: "What the heck am I doing? [Before joining the discussion] I put up all kinds of stuff on the board the kids have done. I looked at it— I know that's evidence, [but] I don't know what it means. . . . I am just at the beginning stage of looking at [student work] and trying to figure out "What does this really show and how can I prove to myself and someone else that this shows that?" (High school history–social science teacher).

On changing views about the relationship between assessment and instruction; how separation is unneccessary and undesirable: "I have become more aware that every-thing I do is tied to assessment and that every mode of response from my students can inform me as to how to refine my practice and use my students as my guide." (High school English–language arts teacher).

From Sheingold, Heller, and Paulukonis, "Actively seeking evidence: Teacher changes through assessment development," Center for Performance Assessment MS #94-04, 1995, pp. 17–22. Reprinted by permission of Educational Testing Service, the copyright owner.

Is student teaching a performance test?

the quality of writing have been in use for decades. Oral reading scales are also easy to construct. Levels of performance—say, excellent, good, average, and poor—can be described using examples from previous performances to illustrate the categories. Checklists can also be used to judge performance (as in driving tests), or rating scales of key elements can be used, just as judges do when rating diving or ice skating at the Olympics. But what seems easy is often hard to do. As Stiggins (1987) reminds us, "If you do not have a clear sense of the key dimensions of sound performance—a vision of poor and outstanding performance—you can neither teach students to perform nor evaluate their performance" (p. 37).

The development of **scoring rubrics**—model performances illustrating different levels of quality and rules for evaluating those different levels of performance—is required for scoring to be reliable. Two kinds of rubrics for scoring performance tests are illustrated in Table 14.3. These

14.3

Scoring Rubrics for Performance Assessments

Eighth-Grade Scale for Oral Performance

LEVEL FIVE

The student is aware of the importance of both content and delivery in giving a talk. The content is powerfully focused and informative. The issue is clearly defined, and detail is judiciously selected to support the issue. The talk is delivered in a style that interests and persuades the audience. Questions, eye contact, facial expressions and gesture engage the audience. The student displays evidence of social, moral and political responsibility, and offers creative solutions. Causes and effects are elaborated. The second version of the talk reveals significant changes based on revision after viewing. The student may make effective use of cue cards. The student is confident and takes risks.

LEVEL FOUR

The student is aware of the importance of both content and delivery in giving a talk. The student's talk is well shaped and supported with pertinent information. The student supports conclusions with facts, and makes connections between cause and effect. The talk is delivered in a style that may interest and persuade the audience. Questions, eye contact, facial expressions, and gesture are used occasionally to engage the audience. Delivery is improved after viewing the first draft of the talk. The student is fairly confident and can self-evaluate.

LEVEL THREE

The student is aware of the importance of both content and delivery in giving a talk. The talk displays a noticeable order and some organization, primarily through lists. The student includes some specific information, some of which supports or focuses on the topic. The conclusion may be weak. The student may show personal involvement with topic and concern about the consequences of not dealing with the issues. There is evidence of revision as a result of viewing the first version of the talk. The student is fairly confident and can self-evaluate.

LEVEL TWO

The student's talk contains some specific information with some attempt at organization. The main idea is unclear and facts are disjointed. Some paraphrasing of text is evident. The student uses no persuasive devices, has little eye contact or voice inflection and does not take a clear stand on the issue. The delivery is hesitant and incoherent. Little improvement is shown in the talk after watching the first version. The student demonstrates little confidence.

LEVEL ONE

The student chooses one or two details to talk about but the talk lacks coherence. The talk is confused and illogical. There may be no response.

General Scale Designed for Mathematics Performance Tasks

EXEMPLARY RESPONSE—Rating = 6

Gives a complete response with a clear, coherent, unambiguous, and elegant explanation; includes a clear and simplified diagram; communicates effectively to the identified audience; shows understanding of the open-ended problem's mathematical ideas and processes; identifies all the important elements of the problem; may include examples and counterexamples; presents strong supporting arguments.

COMPETENT RESPONSE—Rating = 5

Gives a fairly complete response with reasonably clear explanations; may include an appropriate diagram; communicates effectively to the identified audience; shows understanding of the problem's mathematical ideas and processes; identifies the most important elements of the problems; presents solid supporting arguments.

SATISFACTORY RESPONSE

Minor Flaws But Satisfactory—Rating = 4
Completes the problem satisfactorily, but the explanation may be muddled; argumentation may be incomplete; diagram may be inappropriate or unclear; understands the underlying mathematical ideas; uses mathematical ideas effectively.

continues

TABLE

14.3

(continued)

SATISFACTORY RESPONSE
Serious Flaws But Nearly Satisfactory—Rating = 3
Begins the problem appropriately, but may fail to complete or may omit significant parts of the problem; may fail to show full understanding of mathematical ideas and processes; may make major computational errors; may misuse or fail to use mathematical terms; response may reflect an inappropriate strategy for solving the problem.

INADEQUATE RESPONSE
Begins, But Fails to Complete Problem—Rating = 2
Explanation is not understandable; diagram may be unclear; shows no understanding of the problem situation; may make major computational errors.

UNABLE TO BEGIN IMMEDIATELY—Rating = 1
Words do not reflect the problem; drawings misrepresent the problem situation; copies parts of the problem but without attempting a solution; fails to indicate which information is appropriate to problem.

NO ATTEMPT—Rating = 0

From Wiggins (1996, pp. 152–153); and Herman, Aschbacher, & Winters (1992).

rubrics are for an oral performance and a mathematics problem to be solved (Wiggins, 1996; Herman, Aschbacher, & Winters, 1992).

Examples of a clear vision of performance and criteria for reliable scoring are given in Table 14.4. This example is from the performance assessment in mathematics given as part of the National Assessment of Educational Progress (NAEP). The problem is one that requires a constructed response to a real-world problem consumers might be faced with, such as the following:

> Treena won a 7-day scholarship worth $1,000 to the Pro Shot Basketball Camp. Round-trip travel expenses to the camp are $335 by air or $125 by train. At the camp she must choose between a week of individual instruction at $60 per day or a week of group instruction at $40 per day. Treena's food and other expenses are fixed at $45 per day. If she does not plan to spend any money other than the scholarship, what are *all* choices of travel and instruction plans that she could afford to make? Explain your reasoning.
> *(Dossey, Mullis, & Jones, 1993, p. 116)*

> Is this an authentic task? Is it a good assessment of mathematical reasoning?

In Table 14.4 are the NAEP recommended solutions and the performance scoring key with six categories of proficiency.

Portfolios of Performances Some performances—dancing, piano playing, a speech—are fleeting unless they are recorded. But when recorded they are products to be evaluated like other products of instruction, such as paintings, essays, mathematical solutions, or science projects. Performances in art, writing, mathematics, science, and so forth can be stored in portfolios—repositories of a student's achievements over a span of time. These allow teachers, at grading time and at parent conferences, to examine and assess an entire body of work and to document growth over time. Portfolios are described later as a way of improving grading.

TABLE

14.4

Scoring for Mathematics Performance Assessment

Treena's fixed expenses will be $45 \times 7 = \$315$ for the seven days. Therefore, she has $\$1{,}000 - \$315 = \$685$ to spend on travel and instruction. Travel costs are either train ($\$125$) or plane ($\$335$). Instruction costs are either group ($\$40 \times 7 = \$280$), or individual ($\$60 \times 7 = \$420$).

The four choices Treena has are:

1. Travel by train, group instruction, and fixed expenses: $\$125 + \$280 + \$315 = \$720$
2. Travel by plane, group instruction, and fixed expenses: $\$335 + \$280 + \$315 = \$930$
3. Travel by train, individual instruction, and fixed expenses: $\$125 + \$420 + \$315 = \$860$
4. Travel by plane, individual instruction, and fixed expenses: $\$335 + \$420 + \$315 = \$1{,}070$

Students must realize that Treena cannot choose the individual plan and travel by plane because the total expenses ($\$1{,}070$) would be greater than the allotted scholarship. Any full credit response must clearly communicate that Treena has three options that do not exceed $\$1{,}000$, what the three options are, and how the student arrived at the three options.

Level	Description	Student Example	Commentary on Student Example
No response	0. No response		
Incorrect	1. The work is completely incorrect or irrelevant, or the response states, "I don't know."	Add everything other than scholarship and you will get 230.	This INCORRECT response appears to be somewhat on task, but the work shown does not warrant credit even at the minimal level.
Minimal	2a. Student indicates one or more options only (such as group and train) with no supporting evidence, or 2b. Student work contains major mathematical errors and/or flaws in reasoning (e.g., the student does not consider Treena's fixed expenses).	She could take the train to camp, have individual instruction, and eat every day and not run out of money.	This MINIMAL response does illustrate one valid budget option but does not show any supporting calculations.

Partial	3. The student (a) indicates one or more correct options; additional supporting work beyond the minimal level must be present, but the work may contain some computational errors; or (b) demonstrates correct mathematics for one or two options, but does not indicate the options that are supported by his or her mathematics.	train at $125
		 goup at $280
		         $315
		         $720
		
		 40 45
		 ×7 ×7
		 280 315
		
		 $720 would she all spend
		
		 She just took the cheapest ones of her choices; now she has money left over.
			This PARTIAL response illustrates one acceptable budget alternative (group and train) and the corroborating computational work.

Satisfactory	4a. The student shows correct mathematical evidence that Treena has three options, but the supporting work is incomplete; or 4b. The student shows correct mathematical evidence for any two of Treena's three options and the supporting work is clear and complete.	$125 + 420 + 315 = \$860$ $\$1{,}000 > \$860$ If $1,000 is more than $800 she has money left over, so she could take private lessons, a train and her food. $325 + 315 + 280 = \$930$ $\$1{,}000 > \$930$ She could take a plane, her food, and group lessons.	This SATISFACTORY response illustrates two appropriate budget options (both individual and train and group and plane) as well as the correct supporting calculations.

Extended	5. The correct solution indicates what the three possible options are and includes supporting work for each option.	(1) 1000 (2) 1000 (3) 1000
		  −335 −125 −125
		   665 875 875
		  −280 −280 −420
		   385 595 455
		  −315 −315 −315
		  $ 70 $280 $140
		 (1) Air, group, food
		 (2) Train, group, food
		 (3) Train, individual, food
			This outstanding EXTENDED response provides the correct calculations in terms of the excess dollars that remain from the $1,000 scholarship, for the three acceptable budget options.

Adapted from Dossey, Mullis, & Jones (1993, pp. 117–120).

POLICY, RESEARCH, AND PRACTICE

What Are the Problems and Prospects of Performance Assessment?

Do you think performance tests are more appropriate than traditional tests for the measurement of ability among low-income and minority children?

Educators have learned that the student who does well on a traditional test may not do well on a performance measure, and vice versa. Because of the difference in the nature of the tasks and the requirements for success, different people are often identified as talented by a performance test than by a traditional test (Shavelson, 1991). This may be bad, because any identification of who is and is not knowledgeable that depends on which kind of test we use seems unfair. On the other hand, performance tests *may* be more equitable than traditional tests in identifying talent among minorities and low-income students. Many unlicensed contractors, landscape architects, auto mechanics, plumbers, and electricians who cannot pass the state multiple-choice examinations perform impressively on the job. Perhaps more low-income, minority, and linguistically and culturally different students will be able to show their talents through performance assessment than would be able to do so with traditional tests (Gordon & Bonilla-Bowman, 1996). We still do not know enough about these issues to make any definitive statement.

Sometimes a single performance is altogether convincing, all we need to make a valid judgment. But it also seems apparent that a single performance measure may not be a good indicator of what a student knows and can do—a single performance measure may not assess reliably (dependably/consistently) enough (Lane et al., 1996; Linn 1994; Shavelson, Baxter, & Gao, 1993). So a substantial number of performance tasks might be needed to reliably assess students, just as adding many more items to a short select-type multiple-choice test increases reliability. But unlike multiple-choice tests, performance assessments are much more costly to administer, perhaps as much as twenty times more costly (*Education Daily,* 1996). This problem has not yet been resolved.

Although costs and reliability issues are currently preventing their greatly increased use in education, performance assessments are an exciting returned movement in education. After the public, teachers, and students get to understand them, they will come to like them because of their four admirable characteristics (Stiggins, Backland, & Bridgeford, 1985). (1) They require students to demonstrate what they have been taught or learned. (2) What is demonstrated has to be specified in advance (that is, the test must be transparent). This particular advantage of performance assessment means that after a teacher works hard on developing scales, checklists, or descriptions for holistic scoring of oral presentations, written products such as book reports, science, or social studies projects, and so forth, they can give them to students and their parents. So a teacher can make the testing process transparent. (3) There is a public component to performance assessment (that is, the test must be observable). (4) The performance is assessed by experienced, well-trained judges with clear conceptions of standards for performance at different levels of accomplishment. You can even remove yourself from being a judge of your students. You can evaluate students' performances in another class or school, and other teachers can evaluate your students' performance. This allows teachers to separate their instructional, motivational, and coaching roles from their evaluational role, which is good because it may be difficult to be both teacher and judge of student performance.

The construction and use of performance assessments are not beyond the ability of most classroom teachers (Airasian, 1991). And as criticisms of traditional means of assessment continue, teachers will be asked, singly and in teams, to develop more authentic ways of assessing students. This stimulating movement promises to revolutionize educational assessment.

> Is it a problem if you have to both instruct and assess your students? Could this cause you trouble?

But portfolios are a natural accompaniment of performance assessments. They constitute the archives for documenting growth in areas representing genuine achievement.

Prompts in Performance Testing   In many performance assessments, prompts are provided by a tester to see if only a momentary lapse of memory or judgment is involved, or whether genuine lack of understanding is the root of a problem. (Remember the discussion, in Chapter 4, of Vygotsky's zone of proximal development? In traditional testing it is ignored; in performance assessment it can be integrated into the assessment process.) The British have had mathematics performance assessment for years, and when a student has difficulty, the assessor is asked to prompt the student: "Is there a way to check your answer?" "Would it help you here to measure the diameter of the circle?" The student's responses are scored using categories such as

1. success without aid
2. success after one prompt
3. success after a series of prompts
4. success after teaching by the tester; prompts did not work
5. unsuccessful response even after prompting and teaching by the tester.

Such testing seems more humane and insightful than a multiple-choice test of whether the student can tell which term is missing in determining the circumference of a circle.

Essay Tests

Essay tests should be used primarily to measure the kinds of achievement that cannot readily be tested with multiple-choice items. These include higher-order cognitive processes such as application, analysis, synthesis, and evaluation. Essay tests are much less efficient for getting at simpler kinds of knowledge and comprehension.

Writing Essay-Test Questions   Some experts argue that an **essay-test** question should be highly structured. They would have you say, "Discuss the Articles of Confederation in terms of *a, b,* and *c.*" Others claim you learn more about what your students know and how they think if you leave the question unstructured, simply saying, "Discuss the Articles of Confederation." Then the students must supply their own *a, b,* and *c.* The less structured the topic or question, the harder it is to evaluate the answer reliably, but these kinds of questions require students to provide their own structure and focus. The length of the answer required is related to the breadth of the topic. Longer answers can call for greater complexity, but they are again harder to evaluate consistently.

The verbs you use in your questions are important. Explain them to your students. Tell them that when you say "compare and contrast," you are asking them to point out the likenesses and unlikenesses of two or more things. When you say "identify," you are not usually looking for a long answer, just information about a person, place, or thing. When you say "analyze," you want students to break some subject down into parts. And when you say "argue," you are asking for advocacy, as a lawyer might do when defending or prosecuting. *Discuss, define, justify, explain, summarize*—all imply more or less specific tasks. Choose among them carefully, and be sure your students understand them.

Although giving students a choice among questions usually makes them feel better, it gives you the problem of seeing to it that achievement is expressed just about as well in answering one alternative question as in answering another. This is usually impossible to do. So it is probably best to have all students answer the same essay questions.

You may want to get at the students' ability to write fairly long (more than one or two pages) essays under test conditions, whether at home or in the classroom. But you gain certain advantages if you ask for relatively short—say, five-line to half-page—answers. First, you can ask more shorter questions per unit of time and therefore broaden your sample of student achievement. Second, you can probably evaluate shorter answers more reliably.

Scoring Essay Tests   You may have noticed that our discussion of writing essay questions alluded several times to their scoring as well. This is inevitable because, owing to the open-ended nature of essay-test questions, you need to keep their ultimate evaluation in mind even as you generate them. In other words, the main advantage of essay questions— the complex response they require of the student—is also their major fault: complex answers are harder to score reliably.

Here *reliability* means agreement among teachers scoring the same essay tests. We have known since about 1910 that reliable scoring is a problem with essay tests. To see how large a problem, look at Table 14.5, which shows how one hundred different English teachers scored the same composition. Percentage grades ranged from the low 60s to the high

TABLE 14.5

Assigned Percentage Grade and Estimated Grade Level of Same Composition Submitted to 100 English Teachers

| Percentage Grade Assigned | Estimated Grade Level of Paper | | | | | | | | | | |
| | Elementary | | | | High School | | | | College | | |
	5th	6th	7th	8th	9th	10th	11th	12th	13th	14th	15th
95–99		1		3	3	1	2	3	2		2
90–94			1	4	4	7	5	2	1		
85–89		1	2	3	4	4	6				
80–84		1	2	2	8	8		1			
75–79					2	2	1	3			
70–74					2	1	1	2			
65–69											
60–64	1	1			1						

90s—or from roughly a D− to an A+. And when the teachers were asked to guess the grade level of the student who wrote the paper, their estimates ran from the fifth grade to the junior year in college! The same teacher's grading over time has also been studied. A teacher re-marked the same ten essay examinations after two months, and the correlation between the grades assigned the first time and those assigned the second time was only about .45. Clearly reliability is a problem if even the same teacher's grades do not agree from one scoring to another! To get high reliability in grading essay tests requires careful and question-specific training for the grader.

Unfortunately, even irrelevant variables, including the physical attractiveness of the writer, penmanship, and the student's name, can influence the grader. Yet another problem with essay questions, which also stems from their complexity, is inadequate coverage, or sampling, of the domain of achievement. As with performance tests, because each question is relatively time consuming, only a few can be asked. So a test may cover too little, neglecting important parts of the subject matter, raising questions about the test's validity as well as its reliability.

In any case, you might write out a model answer to guide yourself in grading the students' answers. Unless a question is intentionally vague to force students to do the structuring, you can then indicate to yourself in advance (and later to your students) what you intend the question to call for. The technique used for such broad questions is **holistic scoring,** in which a single score is provided, based on a reading of the essay as a whole. Such scoring is quick and amazingly reliable if (1) model answers are available for broad categories of scores (for example, unac-

> Did you ever argue with a teacher over an essay-test-question score? Why was there disagreement?

Did you ever wonder if your teacher really read your essays, reports, or homework assignments? What can you do to ensure that your students know you read everything they hand in?

ceptable, marginally acceptable, good, exceptional; see also Table 14.3, for the scoring of performance tests), and (2) the essay readers have had practice in scoring with these models. Also similar to performance tests, the development of scoring rubrics—the model answers and rules for evaluating responses to constructed-response tests—are required for holistic scoring to be reliable.

If your model answer can be analyzed into separate points (for example, one that civil liberties are provided in the Bill of Rights, one that the First Amendment provides for freedom of speech and press, one a recent news story that involved the First Amendment, and so on), you can use this list of points in grading the answers. The different points allow you to do **analytic scoring,** which is much more useful for providing feedback to students. But it is more time consuming as well, because essays may need to be read more than once.

Whether you engage in holistic or analytic scoring, you should take one crucial step before you give an essay to your class. You should write a model answer and have your scoring rubrics prepared *in advance.* An essay examination is in some ways like a performance test, so it is not surprising that the guidelines presented earlier for performance tests (see Table 14.3) can also be used for developing rubrics for rating essay answers.

Remember that biases in scoring essay tests are common. Research has shown that you can reduce such biases by not looking at the student's name when you score essay exams; by scoring answers to each question separately if there are two or more questions on a test; and by reading the essays a second time, if you can spare the time, to check your two semi-independent assessments of their worth.

After you do your best to score an essay test objectively, you must remember that your feedback to students should contain positive elements—no matter how poor the overall performance. If students never receive anything but criticism and faultfinding, they can develop crippling anxiety about writing and may stop writing altogether as soon as possible. When corrective criticism is needed, you should provide it, but you should also give well-placed, sincere praise whenever you can.

Short-Answer Tests

Short-answer questions have the advantage of enabling you to pinpoint the particular fact, concept, or principle that you want to test your students on. They also have the advantage of being relatively easy to score, as your judgment of an answer's correctness can be made relatively simply and reliably. Teachers agree, with themselves and one another, much more closely in scoring short-answer questions than full-fledged essay questions. That is why short-answer questions are often called *objectively scorable questions.*

But do not misunderstand. Short-answer questions, if good, can test more than knowledge or memory. *Given enough effort, ingenuity, and command of your subject matter,* you can devise short-answer questions that call for higher-order cognitive processes.

Types of Short-Answer Questions When using short-answer questions, you need to choose between the supply and select types. In supply types, the student supplies the answer; in select types, the student selects the answer from given alternatives. Supply types take the form of direct questions, such as "What is the definition of a sonnet?" or incomplete statements, such as "A sonnet is defined as _____." Three select types will be discussed here: **multiple-choice** forms, such as "A sonnet is a verse form consisting of (a) six lines; (b) eight lines; (c) ten lines; (d) twelve lines; (e) fourteen lines"; **true-false** statements, like "T F—A sonnet is a verse form consisting of six lines"; or **matching** forms, such as the following:

1. Sonnet	a. five lines
2. Sestina	b. seven lines
3. Limerick	c. fourteen lines
	d. sixteen lines
	e. thirty-nine lines

The *supply type* has the advantage of requiring students to recall or create the correct answer. But at the same time—unless the correct answer can take one and only one form—the teacher may have trouble deciding whether a student's answer is correct. A bewildering array of synonyms, arguable alternatives, and debatable misinterpretations of the correct answer is bound to show up. Also, supply questions tend to make the teacher resort to asking for the *one* correct word, term, or name that fits the question. This kind of knowledge is important. But if teachers use only short-answer supply questions, their tests tend to neglect the abilities to make important distinctions and to do subtle reasoning.

Two of the *select types* have distinct disadvantages. True-false questions tend to be misused. Many teachers pick sentences out of a textbook and use them as they are (for true statements), or insert *not* (for false statements), or in other ways use these questions to measure verbatim knowledge rather than understanding. In addition, people have a tendency—to differing degrees—to say "true" when they are in doubt. This variability in acquiescence tendency clouds the meaning of scores on true-false tests.

Matching items also tend to be limited in usefulness. They are usually appropriate only for measuring ability to match up relatively discrete facts; they do not lend themselves to the measurement of more complex and subtle kinds of knowledge or comprehension.

Overall, we believe that to measure the ability to make important distinctions and do subtle reasoning, you should use well-constructed multiple-choice questions. Next we present examples of multiple-choice questions written for different cognitive levels, and then we discuss the writing of multiple-choice questions.

Multiple-Choice Questions at All Levels of Cognition To illustrate how multiple-choice questions can require all kinds of cognitive responses, including higher-order thinking, some examples of items at each level of the taxonomy of cognitive objectives are shown in Table 14.6. Your tests

14.6

Examples of Multiple Choice Items Representing All Levels of the Taxonomy of Cognitive Objectives

Knowledge (memory): Under typical conditions, which of the following is likely to have the highest reliability?

*a. A lengthy multiple-choice test
 b. Two performance tests on the same domain
 c. An essay test consisting of a few different topics to write on
 d. A short-answer test with around a dozen recall items

Comprehension: Which of the following is used to measure content validity?

 a. Correlations between the test and a criterion
*b. Inspection of test items and the curriculum
 c. Correlations between the test and other similar tests
 d. Inspection of the test manual and test reviews

Application: On the basis of a series of observations in school, and multiple-choice tests and essays in class, Tyrone was judged aggressive, extremely knowledgeable, and creative. Which one of these judgments is likely to be the most valid?

 a. Aggressive
*b. Knowledgeable
 c. Creative

Analysis: Without having any other information, which of the following standardized tests of spelling would you choose to see how well your fifth-grade class was doing in relation to a national sample?

 a. The Smith test of medical terminology: test-retest reliability, .92; correlation with general intelligence, .35; test time, 72 min.
 b. The Jones test of frequently used words: test-retest reliability, .63; norms from a representative set of urban schools; correlation with the Brown reading test, .41; test time, 60 min.
 c. The Michigan test of spelling ability: test-retest reliability, .79; complete state norms; correlation with spelling grades, .35; test time, 35 min.
*d. The Hardy test of spelling: parallel-form reliability, .89; words selected from a sample of newspapers; norming group, a 5 percent random sample of all elementary schoolchildren in the U.S.; test time, 40 min.

Synthesis: Given the following elements,

1. construct a table of specifications for an achievement test.
2. determine whether essay or short answers are called for.
3. determine whether supply or select items are called for.
4. assign weights to reflect the importance of different content areas.
5. list objectives.

What would be the appropriate sequence to use in developing a classroom test?

*a. 5, 1, 4, 2, 3
 b. 2, 3, 4, 1, 5
 c. 5, 3, 2, 4, 1
 d. 4, 5, 1, 2, 3

Evaluation: Using everything you have learned about the ways in which the following things would affect the environment, rank them in order of their danger to the world's future:

1. Overpopulation
2. Leakage from nuclear-energy power plants
3. The extinction of the grizzly bear, bald eagle, and other endangered species

*a. 1, 2, 3
 b. 1, 3, 2
 c. 2, 1, 3
 d. 2, 3, 1
 e. 3, 1, 2
 f. 3, 2, 1

Note: Asterisks indicate correct choice.

A good multiple-choice question can demand higher-order thinking skills. But most do not!
(© Jean-Claude Lejeune)

should measure higher levels of cognitive processing even when you use multiple-choice items.

Writing Multiple-Choice Questions   Writing multiple-choice questions can be intellectual fun, but it is also time consuming. Just the opposite of essay questions, multiple-choice questions take a lot of time to make up and little time to score. The task of writing good multiple-choice items is demanding enough that major test-construction organizations expect their item writers to produce no more than about ten items in an eight-hour workday. And they expect to heavily revise or ultimately reject most of those.

Multiple-choice items have two main parts: (1) the **stem,** which is either a question or an incomplete statement that comes first and states the topic or problem with which the item is concerned; and (2) the *alternatives,* which require students to demonstrate their achievement by choosing the best or correct one and rejecting the others, called **distractors.** The effectiveness of a multiple-choice item depends on how you deal with each of these parts, individually and together. Over time, some rules have grown out of experience in writing multiple-choice items (see Application, p. 574), and they should be checked every time you have to write such tests.

There is an interesting procedure that almost ensures that you can write multiple-choice achievement-test items measuring comprehension rather than rote memory (R. C. Anderson, 1972). *Comprehension* here is defined as a student's ability to answer a question based on a *paraphrase* of a statement that appeared in the learning materials. A paraphrase is related to the original material with respect to meaning, but not related with respect to the sounds of words, shapes of letters, or any other dimension that provides cues for rote memory. A statement is a paraphrase of another if none of the substantive words (modifiers, verbs, nouns) is com-

Using Guidelines to Write Good Multiple-Choice Questions

Try your hand at writing multiple-choice items. First, study each of the following guidelines and examples carefully. Then, using your own subject area, write a set of items that incorporates as many of the guidelines as possible. Try giving your questions to a fellow student as a mock test, and then take some time together afterward to discuss what worked and what did not work about your questions.

1. *The stem should focus on and state a meaningful problem rather than simply lead into a collection of unrelated true-false statements.*

> Poor: The United States
> a. has more than 300 million people.
> b. grows large amounts of rubber.
> c. has few good harbors.
> d. produces most of the world's automobiles.

> Better: The population of the United States is characterized by
> a. stable birthrate.
> b. people of varied national backgrounds.
> c. its even distribution over the area of the country.
> d. an increasing movement from suburbs into cities.

> Still better: The birthrate of the United States during the 1990s could be characterized as
> a. rising.
> b. staying fairly stable.
> c. falling.

2. *The distractors should be plausible enough that students who do not have the achievement being evaluated (knowledge, comprehension, and so on) tend to select them rather than the correct answer.* You can get plausibility by making the distractors familiar, reasonable, and relevant.

3. *Use as many distractors, up to five, as can be logically created.* But do not just fill the page and waste students' valuable reading time.

4. *Do not hesitate to change the number of distractors from item to item.* Where it is sensible, you might want to use four distractors; for another item, only two may be appropriate.

5. *Use direct questions (rather than incomplete statements) in the stem when it seems appropriate to do so.* Questions are not as likely to lead to your shifting point of view in the middle of an item or its response alternatives. Usually direct questions make it easier to express ideas because incomplete statements make the alternatives come at the end of the statement, where they may not fit as well.

> Poor: In analyzing the cost of living in the United States, we find that its largest component is
> a. food.
> b. housing.

CONTINUED

c. clothing.
d. health care.
e. recreation.

Better: Which of the following is the largest component of the cost of living in the United States?
a. Food
b. Housing
c. Clothing
d. Health care
e. Recreation

6. *When possible, avoid repeating words in the alternatives; put them in the stem.*

Poor: Which of the following is the best brief description of this novelist's writing?
a. A flowery approach to characterization
b. A psychiatric approach to characterization
c. An inner-feeling approach to characterization
d. An overt-action approach to characterization

Better: Which of the following is the best brief description of this novelist's approach to characterization?
a. Flowery
b. Psychiatric
c. Inner feeling
d. Overt action

7. *Do not vary the length and precision of the choices systematically with their correctness.* Careless item writers tend to make the correct choice the longest one.

8. *Vary the correct response alternative from item to item.* Careless writers tend to build a bias into their tests by favoring, say, option *a* and rarely using, say, option *d*.

9. *Make all choices grammatically consistent with the stem and one another.*

Poor: The Judiciary Committee's impeachment deliberations resulted in a resolution in favor of
a. no impeachment.
b. the majority voted for three articles.
c. a sharp division between the two parties.
d. one article cited obstruction of justice.

Better: The Judiciary Committee's impeachment deliberations resulted in resolutions in favor of how many articles of impeachment?
a. None
b. One
c. Two
d. Three
e. Four

10. *There should be one and only one choice that experts would con-*

continues

sider best. Otherwise, students will question the scoring of an item and the fairness of a test. One way to observe this rule is to have other teachers check your test and scoring key, preferably before you give the test.

11. *It is probably best to avoid using "none of these" as an alternative.* Some experts accept its use, but only with a qualification: an absolutely correct answer to a stem should be possible. In mathematics or science tests, where answers can often be absolutely right or wrong, a response alternative such as "none of these" may be acceptable. But in tests of aesthetic judgment, where answers are only "best," this kind of alternative is confusing.

12. *Do not make tests so long that they become speed rather than power tests.* A multiple-choice test that requires a lot of thinking can easily exceed the time allotted for the test. Teachers usually want students to show their power by having time to attempt all the items. We rarely want to judge students' cognitive achievement by their speed. You should remember that some very able students have been very slow test takers.

mon to both statements and the statements are equivalent in meaning.

For example, if you have used the statement "Rising air cools and releases water" in a lecture, your test item might read,

When ocean winds go over the coastal mountains, they are likely to
a. pick up moisture.
b. increase in velocity.
c. bring rain.

In this item, we have not only paraphrased but also used an example of the phenomenon we are interested in. Paraphrasing is always a good way to get at comprehension of principles, because items with specific paraphrased examples of principles are usually easy to answer if the principle is understood but hard to answer if the principle is simply memorized.

Another approach to writing multiple-choice items was developed by Brown and Burton (1979). They saw the choice of distractors as rich sources of information if the test items were designed with diagnosis in mind, not just as ways to assess knowledge. A good example of **diagnostic** testing comes from mathematics, but this kind of test can also be built in other areas such as reading comprehension, physics, and music. To construct a diagnostic test, a teacher must know the subject matter well and keep in mind all the tasks and subtasks necessary to solve particular kinds of problems. For example, to test subtraction we might build an item like this: $327 - 48 = ?$ The response alternatives could be (a) 389, (b) 321, (c) 279, and (d) 189. Response (c) is correct. If a student chose response (a), we would hypothesize that she correctly "borrowed" 10 from the appropriate number on top but forgot to reduce the number in the column she borrowed from by 1, a common and easily corrected error. If she chose (b), we would infer that the student subtracted the smaller number from the larger number regardless of whether it was on top or on the bottom. And if the student chose (d), we would assume that she borrowed twice from the left-most digit on top, and never from the adjoining column. So we can learn much about a student's difficulties if we construct a diagnostic test, where the errors tell us the nature of a student's problem. Piaget and others have reminded teachers that they should not always try to judge student responses as right or wrong. Instead, they should use them as pieces of information that reveal what a child is thinking—an approach that allows for much better diagnosis of problems.

In sum, writing multiple-choice items is a kind of art form. Making up these items takes time. But the process is challenging and can be fun. And the collection of items can be built up over a number of years, not done all at once.

Refining Multiple-Choice Tests   After a multiple-choice test is completed, you can use students' responses as feedback for revising the test. This process is called *item analysis.* It is beyond this introductory text to teach you the many item-analysis procedures available; some further coursework or independent reading is needed to learn them. When item-analysis methods are applied, though, you can determine which items to keep, which to modify, and which to throw out, based on your students' performance. You can learn which distractors draw low-achieving students' responses, and which do not. You can learn which items are most sensitive to instruction, and which hardly show instructional effects at all. You can learn which items are too difficult and which are too easy to be useful. And you can learn which items really discriminate well (that is, pick out the high scorers) and which items do not discriminate well (that is, are answered in the same way by the higher and lower scorers). When a teacher, district, or state keeps refining the items in the test pool of items, a technically sound test can be built after a few administrations. And that is why security is maintained on many tests. When you have spent a few years refining test items to get a short, reliable, and valid multiple-choice test, you do not want students to have access to it, forcing you to start again.

Getting the Advantages of Using All Kinds of Questions

As you have just seen, multiple-choice testing allows you to measure your students' knowledge and understanding over a broader range of ideas than essay testing can, and makes possible checks on knowledge that performance tests may miss. However, both kinds of tests have advantages.

Many teachers get the advantages of both types of questions by using both essay and short-answer select questions. In this way they motivate students to do a different kind of studying, to look at a subject as a whole so that they can discuss it intelligently in their own terms (essay questions); and they get broader coverage and motivate students to focus on details and specifics (short-answer questions). If you think both kinds of learning are good, you should use both kinds of questions.

14.7

TABLE

Relative Advantages of Performance, Essay, and Short-Answer Tests

Consideration	Type of Test Having the Advantage		
	Performance	Essay	Short-Answer
Integrative	+	+	
Closest to real-world skills wanted	+		
Potentially most valid	+		
Potentially most interesting to take	+		
Tasks to be performed and standards of performance known in advance	+		
Capable of calling for higher levels of cognitive processes	+	+	
Eliminates effects of guessing	+	+	
Easier and quicker to prepare		+	
Useful for testing writing ability		+	
Adequately samples whole domain of achievement			+
Reliable scoring or grading			+
Easier and quicker to score			+
Eliminates effects of bluffing by writing or talking "around" topic	+		+
Eliminates effects of writing ability, quality of handwriting, quality of speech, and appearance of testee			+

Table 14.7 summarizes the relative advantages and disadvantages of performance, essay, and short-answer testing, and lists their key characteristics as well.

Using the Computer in Classroom Assessment

Computers are excellent aids for test developers. They allow you to store items by objectives, a process called *item banking.* Anytime you call up an objective, you can get a printout of the multiple-choice items, essay questions, and performance tests that have been used to assess learning of that objective in the past. Item analyses, including difficulty level, are available for each multiple-choice item, and the data can be updated each time the item is administered. The software allows you to estimate the reliability of a test before administering it (based on past history with the item), and to compute total reliability after you administer it. More and more, optical scanning systems (which count the black pencil marks located in the correct places on special answer sheets) are within reach in terms of cost and reliability, removing even the drudgery of scoring select-type items.

For entire academic departments—English, history, sciences, music, mathematics—where substantially the same curriculum is taught to many students year after year, this technology can easily be used to improve testing. But even the individual teacher can build, over a few years, an item bank that eventually saves time and increases test quality. Dozens of item-bank programs are available for all kinds of computers. The most comprehensive of these programs also do complete item analyses, store information on each student in separate files, and then even help prepare report cards.

Simulations and testing on computers, particularly in science, where it is expensive to set up real performance tests, are increasingly common. With a computer the test problem can be simulated. For example, a series of fluids representing certain chemicals can appear on the screen, and the student is asked to do certain things with them. Then, on the basis of what gets done, the student is asked to identify the chemicals. This process could be very time consuming, messy, and costly if done in a laboratory as a genuine performance test of inquiry in chemistry. Once the test has been programmed and the simulation made to appear real, the cost per pupil to assess knowledge is low, it is not messy, and less time is taken to assess chemical knowledge. But such tests depend for their validity upon their realism, and not all of them are as authentic appearing as they claim to be. And as noted above, the student who does well in a simulation of this kind may not do well on traditional tests or genuine performance tests, since each method reveals a different picture of who is and is not a master of the material (Shavelson, 1991).

Because we do not yet know everything we need to about how to choose among the available alternative approaches to assessment, we should use a wide range of assessment devices to make our decisions. The wide range of assessments will provide for the display of ability in a student body that has a wide range of individual and cultural variation.

All assessment is a political act. It lets people know if doors are open or closed to them, and it typically opens doors for some people and closes them on others. It is also an assertion of power—one person tells another what to read and study, how to respond, what constitutes an appropriate answer, how much time she has, and so forth. Those with the power to make these decisions are not usually the ones that are having the difficulties with schooling—immigrants, poor children, racial or linguistic minorities (Delpit, 1988). And this leads to conflicts and resentment that are harmful to our society. A wide range of assessment tools helps in identifying, as best we can, at least some of the talent among people who are not powerful economically, socially, or politically (Garcia & Pearson, 1994).

Do you agree or disagree with the claim that assessment is intimately tied to politics and power?

From Assessing to Grading: A Difficult Transition

Grading students is one of the teacher's hardest tasks. Because many teachers think of their students as friends, they shrink from the job of standing in judgment of them. The two roles—friend and judge—seem incompatible. But however painful the process, formal evaluation is a necessary part of education. Schools are designed to transmit the values of a society. And because classroom teachers are agents of the society, their value judgments about students' school behavior and achievement must in some degree represent what is considered important and good by the society. That is why schools set up regular procedures for communicating teachers' value judgments to students, parents, and others, who use them to make decisions about past performance and future courses of action.

Grading is a kind of summary evaluation; it helps identify students' strengths and weaknesses. Teachers can use this evaluation to help students make immediate decisions (say, counseling a student to take remedial writing), long-term plans (helping a student decide whether to choose or reject a college preparatory program), and vocational plans (suggesting career possibilities that seem to fit students' aptitudes and interests).

Summary evaluations are also a source of information for parents, other teachers, and employers. For instance, a person who judges applicants for admission to medical school or a job as a laboratory technician needs to know the candidates' achievement in chemistry. Teachers' grades and marks also serve as a basis for honors, promotion, graduation, probation, and other selection, retention, and sorting functions. And sometimes grading is done simply to provide an incentive for greater effort by students.

Evaluating students is one of a teacher's hardest tasks.
(© Spencer Grant/The Picture Cube)

In short, considering all the purposes that grades and marks serve, it does not make sense to abolish them. Despite the stress and anxiety that grades may cause, too many people need too many of the functions they provide. But if we do not abolish grades then we must engage in the grading process with all the seriousness of purpose and all the humanity we are capable of.

Establishing a Frame of Reference for Grading Judgments

The purpose of grading, marking, observing, and other assessment activities is to provide information to students, their parents, and school officials about performance and achievement. To make such assessments you must first establish a frame of reference for your value judgments. For this purpose, you can use either absolute or relative standards.

Absolute Standards   When you decide to use absolute standards to interpret a student's performance, you imply that you know what is and what is not an acceptable level of performance. Any student's performance can be judged in relation to the standard you have chosen. Criterion-referenced standards are absolute standards. They are easily communicated—a student does or does not meet the standard to show mastery of addition of fractions, or use of participles, or applications of Newton's third law. Whenever teachers' expectations of performance are clear, whenever we are willing to give all As or all Fs, we are using absolute standards as a reference for judging student performance.

Pseudoabsolute Standards   But, in many instances, grades or percentage letter grades are used as absolute standards when they are really relative standards. For example, if a teacher always gives As to just 10 percent of a class or has a record of never failing anyone, his grading system is probably not based on preset standards of performance. He juggles the composite scores until they "fit" some wanted distribution.

Percentage grades that are not tied explicitly to achievement are also misleading. For example, a 75 percent in reading comprehension implies that some total amount of reading comprehension exists at this age level and that this student has only three-fourths of it. But such a 75-percent grade is usually only a global rating on a scale from 60 to 100. A teacher often talks about percentage scores as if they were absolute standards, stating that a score of 60 percent or better is needed to pass the course. But then he adjusts the distributions and scoring standards of particular tests to fit the cutoff point and get most students over that point. So the apparently absolute system is really a relative system; overall ratings are adjusted to fit loosely into a preconceived distribution with so many 90s, 80s, 70s, and 60s. The students are actually being compared with one another rather than with absolute standards of performance. This kind of system prevails in the United States.

We urge teachers to think about ways to make the pseudoabsolute standards they use truly absolute. This could be done by administering more criterion-referenced tests and more transparent performance tests with clear scoring rubrics describing different levels of performance. Percentage systems of the type described on pages 586–590 need not predetermine the numbers of students getting certain grades. They can be designed to be more like absolute standards than relative standards, which we discuss next.

Relative Standards   Relative standards are more commonly used than are absolute standards. Here individual students are evaluated on the basis of how well they are doing relative to other students in the class, grade, age group, or ability level. If a student ranks high, he or she is likely to get an A or B letter grade. If a student ranks low, he or she may receive a C, a D, or even an F. Relative standards do not necessarily mean that a teacher is marking "on the curve." (To do that, you would take a distribution of student scores and assign, say, 7 percent As, 24 percent Bs, 38 percent Cs, 24 percent Ds, and 7 percent Fs.) Relative standards simply mean that students are being evaluated in relation to other students. The difficulties inherent in this system are most noticeable in selective colleges, where the freshman class represents the best high school students in the country. Some freshmen find themselves getting Ds, Fs, or no credit for courses, because they are being evaluated in relation to their brilliant classmates. Use of relative standards for these talented students inevitably and often unjustifiably lowers the self-esteem of many of them. (See the Big Fish-Little Pond effect on page 436.)

Another problem with relative standards is one noted in our discussion of norm-referenced tests. These standards do not really tell us what students know, just how much they know in relation to other students. A student may be the best mathematician in the fifth grade but still not be doing very well in multiplication. The top test taker in American history may be doing better than her peers but still not know much about this country's past.

Two Common Questions about Testing, Grading, and Marking

You can find interesting attacks on traditional testing, grading, and the dangerous effects of competition in Covington (1992), Eisner (1991), Glasser (1969), Hoffman (1962), Holt (1969), and Krumboltz & Yeh (1996). A good defense of student evaluation by traditional methods was offered by Ebel (1974). Here we discuss two of the most common questions about grading and testing that beginning teachers ask us. Some of the answers are matters of logic and values, but others are directly addressed by empirical research.

Do grading and testing practices interfere with or help learning? If students see the whole assessment and grading system as threatening and arbitrary, they might work more for grades than for any learning. Teachers need to watch carefully that their marking and grading methods do not simply force students to learn what they would otherwise shun.

Unfair testing and grading programs can reduce students to frenzied seekers of what the tester wants. Even a casual observer can see this situation in many schools today.

Some critics argue that school testing and grading are much like wages for labor. They claim that classrooms are economic systems where student performance is exchanged for grades—where students are earners, not learners. These critics are not surprised to find that students forget what they have learned after being tested. This kind of learning is not intrinsically driven. One proposal to remedy this problem is for teachers to act as critics, not markers, of student work. This is one of the virtues of performance measures, discussed above. Personal oral or written criticism communicates serious concern for the quality of a student's work. Marks, like wages, may not be as personally motivating for many students. That is, genuine criticism may motivate; marks may not work as well.

On the other hand, if the marks earned in a subject matter indicate progress toward mastery of that area, then working for marks actually furthers the purposes of education. This condition clearly holds for criterion-referenced programs. The mark or symbol P (for pass) stands for the mastery of some educational material, so working for mastery and working for marks become the same thing. It is not a problem if students are working for a mark because the mark means that the material has been learned. Even in norm-referenced programs, a mark should be a valid indication of important educational outcomes. An A in a course in educational psychology should signify a student's ability to state objectives, describe the concept of intelligence, list several motivational techniques, and so forth.

Testing and grading practices can also improve learning and performance. For example, Nungester and Duchastel (1982) had high school students study a history text. One group, the control group, simply read the text; a second group was given time for review after reading the text; a third group was tested after reading the text, with the test taking about the same amount of time as the review. All students were tested (or retested) one week later. The review group scored 10 percent higher than the control group. The tested group, however, scored 25 percent higher than the control group! And the effect held for both supply- and select-type items. So a test can facilitate retention. Moreover, the simple knowledge that a test is going to be given affects study habits and the time students spend studying (Halpin & Halpin, 1982). From this information you might predict that a course with frequent quizzes would produce greater amounts of learning than a course with no quizzes. This relationship has in fact been shown many times. One study even checked the frequently made claim by graduate students that they are already as highly motivated as they can be and therefore do not need the extrinsic incentives offered by tests and grades (D. C. Clark, 1969). But these graduate students at Stanford were wrong. They were found to work harder and score higher when tests and grades were used to motivate them. The evidence is clear that testing and grading affect student achievement in a

Do you agree that marks are not as motivating as comments or criticisms? Why is that?

POLICY, RESEARCH, AND PRACTICE

How Can Tests and Grades Be Used Sensibly and Humanely in the Assessment Process?

We have evaluated several pros and cons, and we still think tests and grades have a valuable role. But they are by no means harmless assessment devices. Assessments should give information that individual students and those concerned with their well-being can use. As an integral part of effective teaching, assessment experiences should lead to feelings of success by both teachers and students. As noted by Shavelson, Baxter, and Pine (1992, p. 22), "A good assessment makes a good teaching activity, and a good teaching activity makes a good assessment." A good teaching activity satisfies both teacher and student.

If you give tests, you should try to embed them in instruction, announce them in advance, clearly specify the areas you are to test, and indicate how much the tests will count in some summary marking system. You should also provide for individual student's problems—say, absences and makeup tests. If you have students who did not understand instructions, studied the wrong material, or were nervous or tired, you should arrange to give them special or individual attention.

Always keep private your collection of students' tests and written papers, and your observations and notes about them. By maintaining privacy, you reduce the competition among students or among parents—competition that can penalize slower or less able students. You can share your records with the student, and sometimes with parents, guidance counselors, or medical personnel. But by law, only students or their parents are able to authorize access to school records, so maintaining privacy is not just desirable, it is required.

When grading student achievement, use only relevant information. Do not include students' tardiness records in your evaluation of their English compositions. Try to provide feedback to a student on each area of concern to you and the student, independent of his or her behavior in any other area of concern. Separate effort from achievement. Achievement is achievement; attendance, effort, and what the student's father wants are separate issues. Don't ignore them; just keep them separate.

Efforts are constantly being made to improve marking and reporting practices through cooperation among teachers, students, parents, and school administrators. In elementary schools, parent conferences are being used more and more to supplement the information on report cards, and portfolios can become the basis for fruitful parent-teacher conferences. And report cards themselves are being designed for each grade

Did you ever miss a test? How was that handled by the teacher? What will you do when that happens with your students?

level, using standards and objectives as a framework for each curriculum area.

There is perennial debate in educational circles about how to improve marking and reporting. Clearly, the information teachers give students should be helpful to them and their parents. Because our society places so much emphasis on grades, teachers must take the process of grading seriously. When you are unsure about a grade, be lenient. Students deserve the benefit of the doubt, given the imprecision of our instruments and the importance of the decision. Kindness is likely to do more good than harm, particularly in norm-referenced grading. Fewer moral dilemmas arise when we use criterion-referenced standards for traditional tests and performance tests because the criteria of success—acceptability and passing—are much clearer.

Grading, marking, and reporting systems should not be abolished. If teachers think about them carefully and apply them humanely, these systems work well. But we must change such systems if grades are used punitively, give rise to too much anxiety, and produce unhealthy levels of competition. What we need is to apply grades sensitively and tie reporting systems to defined levels of achievement.

positive way. But there is a side effect: Students sometimes rate instructors who test them lower than those who do not test them (Halpin & Halpin, 1982).

Does leniency or strictness in grading affect the attitudes and motivation of students? Lenient or strict grading policies apparently have little or no effect on students' subsequent test performance. Strict grading, however, has other consequences. Sometimes it determines whether a student chooses a particular course or curriculum area. Science courses, for example, are noted for being graded harder than humanities courses. Students, of course, want high grades and therefore do not choose science courses as frequently as they do some other courses, nor do they as frequently continue in science after experiencing the difficulty of getting a high grade in an introductory course. In particular, if science courses were graded less stringently, female enrollment would be expected to increase dramatically (Bridgham, 1972a; 1972b). This does not mean that science teachers would need to lower grading "standards" beneath those maintained in other academic subjects. Just setting standards of performance so that more people could receive some positive reinforcement would probably increase science enrollments.

Another aspect of grading severity is seen in pass–no credit or pass–fail grading systems. It turns out that motivation—or the performance of students from which we infer motivation—is somewhat lower when pass–no credit grading is used instead of conventional letter grades (A, B, C, D, F). Most teachers and students believe that students do not work as hard or as well for pass–no credit grades. But students and faculty frequently mention the positive consequences of this kind of grading system: less pressure on students, healthy experimentation in new areas, and healthier attitudes toward the course. These benefits may outweigh the slightly lower amount and quality of student achievement under pass–no credit grading. In any case, the data show the motivational importance of grades and grading systems.

Sources of Information for Grading Decisions

When grading a student in any curriculum area, you should use a wide range of relevant and appropriate sources of information. This is because each individual source of evidence is fallible, with different weaknesses and strengths. In this section we look at a variety of sources and a systematic means of combining data.

Formal Assessments During a semester or a year, student achievement is usually evaluated several times in several ways—by multiple-choice tests, essay tests, projects, oral reports, homework assignments, and performance tests. Most of these assessments result in a score, grade, or summary mark. A mark could be a letter grade (A, B−, D+), a percentage grade (78 percent), a proportion (8/13), the number right (+43), the number wrong (−7), or simply information about whether someone's performance passes or fails (P or F).

When teaching with standards and objectives, you can use criterion-referenced testing, so you may not need to combine scores or marks. Each score is itself an example of some definable achievement. It makes no sense to combine achievement on a test of multiplication of two-digit numbers with achievement on a test of multiplication of decimals. All you want to know is whether a student has achieved each objective. But because parents want letter grades, not a report of objectives achieved, you may need to provide summary grades as well.

When norm-referenced testing is used, or when trying to get a summary grade for criterion-referenced assignments and tests, you may need to combine the scores on various tests to obtain an overall grade. For example, a final grade in biology may be based on the average score on 16 weekly tests. Or you may have to combine scores on a midterm exam, a term paper, and a final examination to determine a student's grade in social studies.

Merging information from many diverse sources is a problem. You might have scores on essays, multiple-choice tests, class presentations, and projects—all of which had very different mean scores and altogether different measures of variability. How do you combine these data?

Combining Data Some advanced coursework in assessment can teach you the most technically sound procedures for doing this. But if your district has no guidelines, and you need a simple and reasonably sound way to get started, we can offer some advice. Think about putting all student products you receive into a pass-fail system that uses percent. A passing score is any percent you assign between 60 and 100 percent. Failure is any score you assign under 60 percent. Or you might assign letter grades to student products as follows (see Airasian, 1991):

A = 94 or higher	C = 74–76
A– = 90–93	C– = 70–73
B+ = 87–89	D+ = 67–69
B = 84–86	D = 64–66
B– = 80–83	D– = 60–63
C+ = 77–79	F = less than 60

If you do not like so many gradations, you might instead use: A = 90–100, B = 80–89, C = 70–79, and so forth.

If you put all the assessment information you collect throughout a semester or marking period into percentages, you can weight and average the evidence at the time you must assign grades. Otherwise you will have trouble combining information from several sources. For example, how would you make sense of your assessments in, say, social studies if, during a school term, you gave an essay exam of three questions, four homework assignments, three short-answer multiple-choice tests, and an exercise calling for an oral report? If the essays were holistically scored A–F, then a B grade would be translatable into something in the 80–89 range of percentages, say 85. A B– would be worth 81 or 82 percent. The homework assignments you required of your students could be given grades too—Excellent (worth 95), Good (worth 85), Acceptable (worth 75), Failure (worth nothing; must be redone until acceptable). The short-answer multiple-choice tests could be graded in percentages right from the start, and if your tests are criterion-referenced, then you could specify in advance what percentage is equivalent to excellent, good, acceptable, and unacceptable performance. Perhaps you could consider excellent performance to be 90–100, good to be 80–89, and acceptable, which is the minimum mastery level that you accept, to be 70–79. If some performance is deemed unacceptable—at the nonmastery level—it would be worth no points until the performance is tried again and becomes at least acceptable. In this case everyone in the class would eventually have a score of between 70 and 100, despite some students' having initially scored at the nonmastery level. This system, of course, imposes more work on teachers. But it avoids having to fail any student.

Oral reports or term projects, holistically scored, could also be given letter grades corresponding to some percentage system. Then, at the end of a grading period, you might have records such as those displayed in Table 14.8. This simple percentage system for combining scores allows you to average different pieces of information and provide a letter grade for the marking period.

The system allows for the weighting of scores as well. For example, suppose you want to weight an oral presentation 50 percent higher than the other evidence you collected, and you want to weight the fourth homework assignment three times more than other sources of evidence because it covered more material, took a longer time to finish, and was more complex. You would then multiply the percentage given to the oral examination by 1.5 and the percentage given on the fourth homework assignment by 3. Using Tyrone Adams as an example, you can see that his unweighted semester-average percentage score was 90, equivalent

14.8

Example of a Simple Combination of Percentages for Grading

Names	Homework Assignment #1	Homework Assignment #2	Multiple-Choice Test #1	Homework Assignment #3	Multiple-Choice Test #2	Homework Assignment #4	Multiple-Choice Test #3	Essay Test	Oral Presentation	Semester Average	Semester Grade
Adams, Tyrone	Exc. 95	Good 85	Exc. 95	Good 85	Exc. 95	Accept. 75	Exc. 95	A 97	B+ 88	90	A−
Bestor, Edwina	Accept. 75	Accept. 75	Unaccept. Accept. 75	Good 85	Accept. 75	Good 85	Unaccept. Accept. 75	B 85	C 75	78	C+
Corleone, Thomas	Accept. 75	Accept. 75	Good 85	Unaccept. Accept. 75	Accept. 75	Good 85	Accept. 75	C− 72	C+ 78	77	C+
…	…	…	…	…	…	…	…	…	…	…	…
Zandejas, Zulin	Good 85	Exc. 95	Good 85	Good 85	Good 85	Exc. 95	Good 85	B+ 88	B− 82	87	B+

in this grading scheme to an A−. Recalculating his oral presentation to be worth 1.5 × 88, or 122, and his fourth homework assignment to be worth 3 × 75, or 225, we get a higher sum of the 9 scores than before. But now, instead of dividing that sum by 9 we divide it by 11.5 (the weights of 3 + 1.5 added to the other 7 scores). Now Tyrone's semester average is 86, and his semester grade would drop from an A− to a B. Weighting may result in grades different from those resulting from equal weights, but that is appropriate if your sources of evidence about students are not all of equal importance in your judgment.

This system is simple and flexible, it allows weighting and combining, and it is understandable to students, their parents, and employers. If you have no standards-based evaluation system in place, you might do well to start your teaching career with this kind of system. If you have a standards-based system in science, history, or any other subject matter, and you have degrees of proficiency to describe student performance against the standards (say, novice, basic, proficient, and advanced), you might record student data as displayed in Table 14.9. Students may start out at the novice level until they do more or better work. Then you would record that they reached the basic level, and onward until they are at least proficient if not advanced. This sensible, but time-consuming

TABLE 14.9

Reporting Student Performance by Standards (for Recordkeeping and Report Cards)

Science	Novice (1)	Basic (2)	Proficient (3)	Advanced (4)
Science Standard 1: Earth and Space				(4)
Science Standard 2: Life Sciences			(3)	
Science Standard 3: Physical Sciences				(4)
Science Standard 4: Science and Technology				(4)
Overall Science: 3.75				

History	Novice (1)	Basic (2)	Proficient (3)	Advanced (4)
History Standard 1: Civilization and Society		(2)		
History Standard 2: Exploration and Colonization			(3)	
History Standard 3: Revolution and Conflict				(4)
History Standard 4: Industry and Commerce		(2)		
History Standard 5: Forms of Government		(2)		
Overall History: 2.6				

From R. Marzano and J. Kendall (1996), A Comprehensive Guide to Designing Standards-Based Districts, Schools, and Classrooms. *Aurora, CO: Mid-continent Regional Educational Laboratory. Reprinted with permission of McREL.*

Ongoing classroom-based assessment occurs in several situations including teachers' one-on-one interactions with students in conferences.

(Tony Freeman/PhotoEdit)

system requires that you have descriptions of performance for each level of proficiency and each standard or objective that you describe. On the other hand, once you have those, the records are easily converted into highly informative report cards, with little additional work. Your records actually become the students' report cards.

Informal Assessments   Much of the information you need in order to know a student well can be obtained from simple observations, often called *kid watching.* By watching children playing on the playground, working with counting blocks, or learning to use a dictionary, by observing adolescents in the laboratory, on the dance floor, or in a discussion group, you can get considerable insight into their academic and social behavior. When you see students tackling a problem, you are seeing intelligence in use!

Of course, seeing is not enough. You also have to *remember* Maria's brilliant analysis of Robert Frost's poetry in front of the class, John's kindness to Caitlin, Alice's achievements in three-dimensional tic-tac-toe. And since informal assessments are not usually written down, you may not remember all the incidents that helped you size up Maria, John, and Alice. Perhaps you need to write little notes about salient events you have witnessed and put them into files or portfolios for each student. Notes can help you remember the incidents much later, which is helpful because you will be assisting students in planning their future or you will be asked to recommend students for some school, club, or honor. Your informal observations can give you more insight into a student than can test scores alone, and notes help recall those insights. So take the time to watch your students playing, studying, solving problems, flirting, or debating. You are sure to form opinions about them in more than the cognitive areas. And in elementary and middle schools you may in fact

POLICY, RESEARCH, AND PRACTICE

What Factors Actually Go into Teachers' Grading Decisions?

What exactly are the ways in which teachers make judgments from all the data they have? Whitmer (1982) studied teachers' thoughts while grading and found that they make heavy use of their grade book—the record of achievement, number of tasks completed, absences, behavior problems, and so forth. Overall, the study concluded that most grading is classroom-bound. That is, most grading is based on classroom events, not judgments about children's out-of-class behavior and background. This is as it should be. However, the most important variable in the grade book was rate of task completion—the speed with which students move through the curriculum. This was a disappointing finding. Certainly rate of task completion should not be given the greatest weight in assigning grades to elementary school students. The study also showed that when a student's grade was not clear, teachers marked up or down depending on their own ratings of the student's ability and effort. Furthermore, they also used their own ratings of home support, classroom behavior, physical maturity, and difficulty of each task to be learned.

Sometimes outside-the-classroom factors also enter into a teacher's grading decisions. For example, in a study by Di Gangi et al. (1991), teachers claimed they did not allow information about parental involvement in school activities to influence their grades. Nevertheless, it was found that a big factor in grading was whether parents participated in school activities as teacher's aides, members of the parent-teacher group or community board for the school or district, and so forth. Students who would have received a C or C+ grade for their work often received a B or B+ if their parents were active; they often received a D or D+ if their parents were inactive, judged by teachers to be unconcerned about school activities. Obviously, some children receive poorer grades in part because their parents, especially their mothers, cannot participate in the life of the school. This grading bias is patently unfair and needs to be guarded against.

In sum, whatever teachers do—grading essay tests or observing students in a discussion group—they bring to the task certain biases. Zillig (1928) was one of the first to demonstrate how biases affect grading. In that case, notebooks containing written assignments of students judged to be bright by their teachers were examined and compared to those of students judged to be much less competent by their teachers. The number of errors that had not been noted by the teachers was found to be higher

continues

Have you ever experienced any of these kinds of bias in grading? How will you guard against such biases?

for the students judged to be brighter. Teachers seemed to expect, then actually found, more errors in the notebooks of the students they judged less competent. Errors made by the brightest students were less likely to be caught. The teachers misperceived reality because they believed that the brighter students were less likely to make errors.

In addition, students can learn how to take advantage of teachers' biases. In extensive studies of grading (Stiggins, 1997) it was found that a stereotypic personality type appears among high school students, one that teachers regard favorably. Students who seem attentive and aggressive in class receive higher grades than others, apparently just because they've learned to act as if they are learning more. They did not, objectively, learn any more than others. The implicit message these students receive is that they don't have to learn much if they just act like they are trying. They learned they can control their teachers' assessments of their motivation. This is dangerous because white, male students may be socialized to fit this stereotype better than females or members of some minority groups. If this is so, unfairness in assessment and grading will result.

We have already talked about bias many times in this book. We raise the issue again because it comes up in all kinds of teaching activities—and particularly in assessing students. The grades you give can greatly influence your students' future. It is critical that you be acutely aware of your own frailties when you sit in judgment of the strengths and weaknesses of others.

be asked to record your perceptions of some noncognitive aspects of behavior, say, motivation or the ability to get along with others, on student report cards.

Considering the Toughest Grade of All: Nonpromotion

In these times of public demand that schools uphold high academic standards, the pressure to retain students in grade has increased. Because of students' academic failure or emotional immaturity, teachers in the United States will probably recommend that well over a million students not be promoted this year. Principals and superintendents have pointed to increased rates of nonpromotion as evidence of "tougher" schools. The annual cost to the nation of these recommendations is in the billions of dollars. While all this is happening, research is accumulating to suggest that this educational trend goes against the best interests of the vast majority of students who are held back. There is indeed research evidence that nonpromotion can have a positive effect on some retained children (Sandoval & Hughes, 1981), but the preponderance of evidence suggests that most students do *not* benefit from being retained in grade.

A meta-analysis of 44 independent studies of retained versus promoted students showed great consistency (Holmes & Matthews, 1984). The studies covered elementary and junior high school grade levels, comparing in total 4,208 students who were not promoted with 6,924 similar students who were promoted. The meta-analysis showed that, if there were two students of similar academic achievement, the achievement of the one who was retained in grade would measure the next year 17 percentile ranks below that of the one who was promoted. Furthermore, the nonpromoted student would be about 11 percentile ranks lower in social adjustment, 14 percentile ranks lower in emotional adjustment, and 12 percentile ranks lower in other behavioral ratings. In attitude toward school, the nonpromoted student would measure 6 percentile ranks lower and be absent more frequently by 5 percentile ranks.

Those who retain students in grade without recommending special programs for them are simply asking them to repeat an experience at which they have already done poorly. Those who retain students in grade because special programs are delivered to them would do better to think about promoting the students and still providing the special programs. This policy would allow students to stay with their age-mates. We certainly do not recommend "social promotion"—a policy that might let students reach high school without being able to read or do mathematics. But we hold that it makes good sense to promote students and offer special services, whenever possible, to bring them up to grade level.

Of course there are also economic factors here. Obviously the special services would raise costs. But promoted students do not lose a year of employability by remaining in school a year longer, and society does not have to bear the costs of an extra year of schooling. So it is hard to understand why a decision that costs over $5,000 per year per child (the cost of an extra year of schooling in a typical state) and mostly produces worse results than promotion should be considered effective. For the problems arising from low-achieving students, retention in grade is seldom the solution.

Using Portfolios in the Assessment Process

Educators are still learning what should go into portfolios and how to assess them. But they still seem to make sense, and we will never find out how to use them intelligently if we do not just start working with them. We do know they have a number of uses in the assessment process, and we will focus here primarily on their great potential as a way to report achievement.

Good models of what a **portfolio assessment** system might look like can come from writing and language arts classrooms in Pittsburgh, Pennsylvania (Camp, 1990). Teachers there collect many samples of classroom writing over a long period, and the samples include students' drafts and rewrites so that improvement may be seen. The students also can select which pieces to put into the portfolio, as examples of their best works and works showing how they have improved over time. If they think they can determine what is inadequate about a piece, they willingly put their comments in the portfolio, without embarrassment. They learn that they have control of their portfolio and that it is appropriate to show poor work *if* they know how it can be improved.

Portfolios also allow students to reflect on what they have learned, to remember the writing strategies they have tried out. By reflecting, they "make explicit much that is ordinarily hidden from student writers and their teachers. [Reflection] makes visible certain aspects of students' perceptions and purposes that are not accessible from their written products alone" (Camp, 1990, p. 13). The teachers hope that through such reflection on their portfolios, students will learn to be more self-evaluative—a skill everyone needs to develop.

Some evidence for that is apparent in a sample of a ninth grader working on writing dialogues, who looked at his work and wrote:

I feel like my writing formed two hills, like this

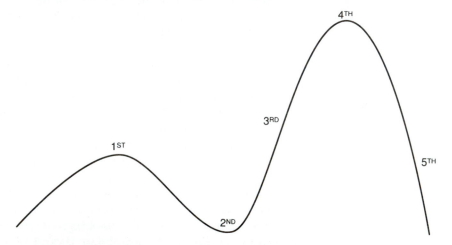

I was writing good, to my standards, then it started lacking what I thought made it good. Then I started climbing again, this time greater than my first one. Finally, my last dialogue was terrible.

(Camp, 1990, p. 27)

This student sees the evolution of his work; he is well aware of his writing. Even though not a fluent writer himself, he has developed standards by which to judge his work. This kind of self-assessment, over time, cannot happen without portfolios to work with.

The teachers in Pittsburgh learned that negotiating with students about what should go into the portfolio is a good way to understand what students think they have learned, what they think is important, and why portfolios are useful to teachers in making instructional decisions and individualizing those decisions as well. A body of work is always more revealing to a teacher than any single specimen—performance, assignment, project, test, or piece of volunteered work—can ever be.

When assessing a full writing portfolio, a rubric for scoring it might consist of the following three categories (LeMahieu, Gitomer, & Eresh, 1995):

1. *Accomplishment in writing*—Evidence of a student's ability to meet worthwhile challenges; establish and maintain purpose; use appropriate techniques for the genre; control conventions, vocabulary,

and sentence structure; be aware of the needs of the audience; creatively use language, sound, images, tone, and voice; use humor and metaphor; be playful.

2. *Use of processes and strategies for writing*—Evidence of effective use of prewriting strategies; drafts to discover and shape ideas; conferencing opportunities to refine ideas; revision.

3. *Growth, development, and engagement as a writer*—Evidence of investment in the writing task; increased engagement with writing; development of a sense of self as a writer; evolution of criteria for self-evaluation (as in the quote from the ninth grader above); demonstration of risk taking and innovation in writing; variation in purposes and genres; progress from early to late pieces.

Rubrics such as these make evaluations of portfolios more reliable, a problem inherent in portfolios since they are designed to be unique. In one study of hundreds of portfolios, inter-rater agreement was very acceptable, but such reliability can occur only after extensive investment of time by the raters. A key to high reliability seems to be a lot of discussion of the rubrics by the raters and having the rubrics decided on collaboratively by the teachers involved. In this case, rubric construction becomes a form of teacher in-service education, designed to develop shared interpretive frameworks for evaluation. These discussions seem to improve instruction as well as evaluation (LeMahieu, Gitomer, & Eresh, 1995).

Portfolios can also be developed in science, history, mathematics, and other areas of the curriculum. Performances, tests, projects, reports, homework, and so forth, can be collected. The material can be used by students for reflection on what was learned and by teachers for discussion of progress with students' parents (Newman & Smolen, 1993). Figure 14.2 shows an item in a science portfolio that would allow a teacher to understand whether students got the concept being taught; and would let parents see evidence that their children are indeed learning (Gitomer & Duschl, 1995). A typical science portfolio might include photos and reports of experiments, questions about the science texts, journal entries and observations, and descriptive essays about key concepts as illustrated in the figure.

Portfolios can serve also as the basis for narrative feedback to students and their parents from the teacher. Instead of giving a letter grade, which hides much of what is done, a teacher can write a narrative report about students' accomplishments over the long haul because the records are there to help create the narrative. Table 14.10 contains an example of comments in narrative reports of teachers in Edmonton, Alberta (Bailey & McTighe, 1996). Whether supplementary or stand-alone, such report cards can be a more complete and satisfying form of assessment for teachers, students, and parents than the traditional ones in use today.

An especially useful characteristic of portfolios is that they help promote conversations about student work among the teacher, the student, and the student's parents. A common language for discussing what students are learning, and the criteria for evaluation, can be anchored in real products of the students if portfolios are used (Sheingold & Fredrick-

How would you feel if you had a portfolio for your educational psychology class? What might go in it?

FIGURE 14.2

An example of a science portfolio entry

From Shawn Glenn & Reinders Duit, Learning Science in the Schools. *Copyright © 1995 by Lawrence Erlbaum Associates, Inc. Reprinted by permission of Lawrence Erlbaum Associates, Inc., and the author.*

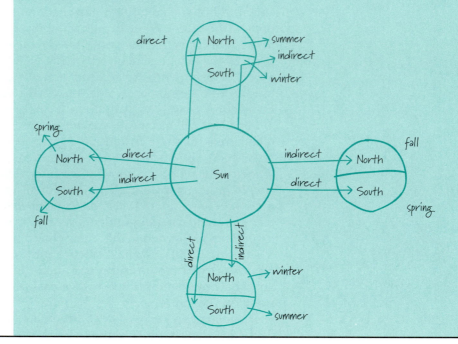

Science 6—1   Revolution   5—8—92

1. What is revolution and what does it cause?

Revolution is when something goes around something like a racecar going around a racetrack or the earth going around the sun. Revolution causes the seasons. The earth is tilted on its axis ($23\frac{1}{2}°$). The rays from the sun are either direct or indirect and they depend if the southern Hemisphere is facing more toward the sun or if the Northern Hemisphere is facing more toward the sun. When it's spring in the Northern Hemisphere it's fall in the Southern Hemisphere. The Northern Hemisphere and Southern Hemisphere always have the opposite seasons. It takes the earth 365 days (1 year) to go around the sun.

son, 1995). And these conversations can provide the motivation for both teachers and students to improve what they do. For all these reasons, portfolios are expected to become common in assessment.

Of course there are problems with portfolios. As mentioned earlier, without extensive training teachers do not always judge them reliably. This means undependable assessment (see Mills, 1996; Koretz et al, 1992). Portfolios have sometimes been standardized through rigid rules about what goes into them. Such rules compromise portfolio uniqueness, and they can be abused by students who pay them little attention (Gong & Reidy, 1996). But all in all, portfolios represent a promising innovation in getting a full picture of students' progress, they provide a way

TABLE

14.10

Narrative Comments about a Student (Mander)

Mathematics

This term Mander has studied the basic skills of algebra. In particular, he has studied units on the operations of polynomials, equation solving and factoring polynomials. Class time is used wisely. He organizes work effectively. He aims for excellence. Keep up the good work, Mander!

Spanish

In our Spanish class we have been studying basic concepts of grammar and syntax. We have continued working on building a basic vocabulary to be used for meaningful oral and written expression. We have researched and discussed some cultural traits of various Spanish-speaking countries. Mander has had the opportunity to participate in a variety of activities designed to enhance his appreciation and ability to communicate in Spanish. He makes a positive contribution to the class. Mander is always willing to participate and help his peers in class. Caramba, hombre, que bien!

Art

In Art 10, Mander developed techniques in watercolor and acrylic painting. He applied knowledge of color theory and painting techniques in several compositions. We also had a guest artist visit us. Next term's projects will include stretching a canvas and creating a composition in acrylics. Mander is improving in the area of acrylic color blending and should concentrate on brush technique and careful attention to assignment requirements and problem solving. Mander is a talented artist and is enjoyable to have in class.

From J. Bailey & J. McTighe, Communicating Student Learning, ASCD Yearbook 1996 (figure pp. 132–133) by T. R. Guskay (ed.). Alexandria, VA: Association for Supervision and Curriculum Development. Copyright © ASCD. Reprinted by permission. All rights reserved.

for teachers to talk about what they do, and they give parents an unsurpassed view of how their children are growing and what they are accomplishing.

S U M M A R Y

1. Informal assessment is done to size up students and to monitor learning and motivation during instruction.

2. Formal assessment in the classroom usually requires tests of some sort, and these must be constructed by the teacher. A standardized test will not do.

3. The first step in creating a test is preparing a table of specifications, which lists the number of questions that should deal with each behavior-content combination of instruction.

4. The next step is choosing among types of tests and test items.

5. Performance tests have a number of advantages, particularly their authenticity and transparency.

6. Teachers need also to consider essay tests for getting at complex kinds of achievement. Writing essay-test questions is relatively simple, but scoring them is far more complex.

7. The advantages of short-answer tests are primarily in enabling greater breadth of coverage and higher reliability in scoring. In choosing between supply- and select-type questions, the teacher should be aware of the advantages of each type. Supply questions require students to recall or create answers; select questions can offer flexibility and the opportunity for students to do subtle reasoning.

8. Among the possible types of short-answer tests, multiple-choice items offer the greatest potential for covering the range of cognitive skills and levels of thinking. Good multiple-choice questions can be written, but only with considerable ingenuity and effort, for all levels of the cognitive taxonomy.

9. Overall, the best solution for most teachers is probably a combination of performance tests, essays, and multiple-choice questions, with an emphasis on the first two forms of testing.

10. Computer technology can play a role in the assessment process, especially in test construction and performance assessment with simulations.

11. Because the role of grades in students' lives is so important, teachers have a responsibility to make the assessment process and grading system as effective and just as possible. This means reducing errors, bias, and unreliability in marking systems, making grades reflect actual achievement, and finding a balance between maintaining standards and minimizing anxiety created by grading.

12. To make evaluations, you must first choose between absolute and relative standards. Criterion-referenced assessments use absolute standards—standards based on a predetermined level of acceptable performance—and are common when standards and objectives are used to guide instruction. Pseudoabsolute standards are often part of the letter-grade or percentage-grade systems used by many schools. Relative standards are used to evaluate each student's performance in relation to the other students' performances. They are particularly helpful when criterion-referenced standards are hard to define and complex learning outcomes are expected.

13. Grades should not be dropped from an educational program simply because they do not work to everyone's satisfaction. Rather, the process used to arrive at them needs to be improved.

14. Combined with effective teaching, grading systems should, whenever possible, lead to feelings of success and provide students with suggestions for improving performance. Also important are understanding any students' special circumstances, keeping students' records confidential, and minimizing irrelevant influences on judgments of students' achievement.

15. Assessment should rest on a wide range of sources of information, such as scores from tests and other formal evaluations (papers, projects), supplemented with careful observations of students in social and academic settings.

16. An undesirable element enters into grading decisions: teacher biases of various kinds. It is very important for teachers to watch for and eliminate, as much as possible, their biases, to prevent them from influencing judgments of student achievement.

17. The most difficult decision many teachers have to make is whether to retain a student in grade. Despite a trend toward more nonpromotions each year, research evidence shows that retention is usually not beneficial for the student. Beyond the academic, emotional, and social costs of nonpromotion are major economic costs to the student and society.

18. Grading and reporting student performance are serious matters. But they can probably be improved with portfolio systems set up to keep track of student performances and products over each marking period. Portfolios encourage conversations about student work among teachers and students, which leads to better instruction. No reporting system, however, is free of problems. So teachers need to give students the benefit of the doubt in recognition of the fact that they and the assessment instruments we use are fallible.

Appendix: Standard Deviation

The scores on a test can spread over a considerable range, or their distribution can be narrow, with most scores near the mean, or average. Figure A.1 presents examples of these two kinds of distributions. The preferred measure of this kind of variability or dispersion in scores is the *standard deviation*. It has special meaning for certain distributions called *normal curves*. Such distributions have the bell shape shown in Figure A.1. They are mathematically defined abstractions that approximate the actual distribution of many variables, such as the height of adult white females in the United States. Often test scores have distributions that are fairly normal.

The standard deviation is a statistic that, for curves that are normal or approximately normal, marks off the distribution of scores into intervals that contain a known percentage of the cases. In both distributions shown in Figure A.1, the interval between the mean and 1 standard deviation above the mean contains 34 percent of the cases. Similarly, the interval between the mean and 1 standard deviation below the mean contains 34 percent of the cases. When a particular score falls anywhere within 1 standard deviation of the mean, we know it is grouped with about 68 percent of the other scores in that normal distribution. If a score falls 2 standard deviations below the mean, it is exceeded by about 98 percent of the scores in that normal distribution. If a score falls 1 standard deviation above the mean, it is exceeded by about 16 percent of the scores and exceeds 84 percent of the scores. All this information is known because of the mathematical properties of normal distributions. The percentage of cases associated with various standard-deviation distances from the mean, as determined by mathematicians, is given in Figure A.1.

Here is a numerical example. Suppose a student receives a score of 33 points on the test whose distribution is displayed on the left in Figure A.1. Since we know that the mean is 29 and the standard deviation is 2, we know that this student is 2 standard deviations above the mean. Because the standard deviation marks off interpretable percentages of cases in the distribution, we can estimate that this student's score falls at about the 98th percentile, exceeded by only about 2 percent of the scores in that distribution. Now, suppose that the same score is received by a student whose test comes from the distribution presented on the right in Figure A.1. The mean is the same as in the first distribution, but the variability of scores is more than twice as great. The test score of 33 does not quite reach the point that is 1 standard deviation above the mean. This score certainly falls lower than the 84th percentile, and we can estimate that it is at about the 80th percentile, exceeded by about 20 percent of the scores. So we see that, even when the mean is the same, the same score has very different meanings, depending upon the dispersion, or standard deviation, of scores in the distribution in which it occurs. In one case the score of 33 is practically the best score one could obtain; in another case it is above average, but hardly exceptional.

The standard deviation, along with the mean, provides some of the most important information you can obtain about a test. The mean tells you about the central tendency of the distribution, and the standard deviation tells you about the variability of the scores. The smaller the standard deviation, the more closely the scores are clustered around the mean. Knowing the standard deviation and the mean, and assuming that the scores are approximately normally distributed, you can tell almost immediately the percentile rank of a score. You can accurately estimate (or use tables provided in most testing and statistics books) how this score compares with other scores in the distribution. For example, suppose you learn that a friend received a score of 390 on the verbal part of the Graduate Record Examination. Since the Graduate Record Examination has a mean of 500 and a standard deviation of 100, we know immediately that the person's score is more than 1 standard deviation below the mean. Therefore, the score of 390 is almost at the 16th percentile, exceeded by over 84 percent of the scores received by other students.

Although information of this kind is often important, it still tells us nothing about what that particular test taker knows or what he or she can do. The interpretation of a score by reference to the mean and standard deviation is a norm-referenced approach to evaluation.

FIGURE A.1

Two distributions of test scores with the same mean and different standard deviations

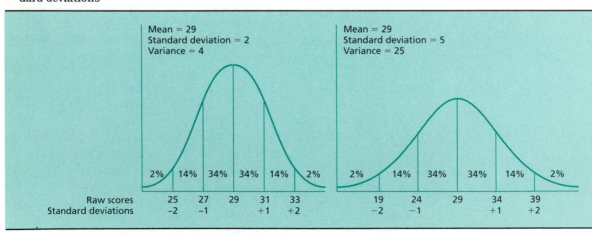

602

Glossary

Ability grouping The practice of putting students of roughly similar levels of ability together, either within groups in a classroom, sometimes called homogeneous grouping, or in separate classrooms, sometimes called tracking.

Academic engaged time The time a student attends to learning tasks relevant to academic objectives.

Academic learning time (ALT) The time that students are engaged, have high success at what they are doing, and do things related to desired outcomes.

Acceleration Moving students ahead faster than is normal or customary because they are presumably capable of learning faster. Example: letting students skip a grade.

Accommodation As used by Piaget, the modification of an already existing cognitive structure to permit understanding of a new concept or experience. A change in *schema*. Compare *assimilation*.

Accomplishment vs. inferiority After Piaget, the stage of development between kindergarten and puberty, in which children become able to do things or, failing, experience feelings of inferiority or inadequacy.

Accountability Being responsible for something. Example: holding administrators and teachers responsible for the quality of instruction and student achievement.

Achievement motivation A desire for or interest in success in general or in a specific field of activity. A need to excel at something.

Achievement test A test that measures a student's achievement of educational objectives, usually in the *cognitive domain* and in a specific subject matter.

Adaptation After Piaget, describes both *accommodation* and *assimilation,* which are related processes.

Adaptive behavior The social and cognitive skills needed to get along in a particular environment. Often used to judge retardation because IQ scores alone can be misleading.

Advance organizer As used by Ausubel, a beginning section, usually verbal and abstract, about the structure of a body of subject matter, intended to facilitate its comprehension and retention.

Affective domain That part of human behavior characterized by attitudes, emotions, feelings, interests, and values. See also *cognitive domain* and *psychomotor domain. Educational objectives* are written in this domain.

Affective objectives Those goals of instruction dealing with the *affective domain.* Examples: appreciating music, enjoying reading, caring about others.

Affiliation motive The degree to which people want and need friendly relationships with other people.

Aggression Behavior intended to express hostility or do harm to another, symbolically or physically.

Allocated time The time set aside by the state, district, or teacher for instruction in a particular area. Example: a second-grade teacher sets aside 40 minutes per day for mathematics.

Alterable variable A variable under the teacher's control, such as choice of content or allocated time. Compare *unalterable variables*.

Analogy items Test items in which the student is asked to infer the relationship between two initial concepts and then apply that relationship to the selection of a fourth concept that has the same relationship to a given third concept. Example: Hand is to glove as foot is to _____.

Analysis Breaking down a subject into its components. A part of the cognitive domain of the *Taxonomy of Educational Objectives.*

Analytical scoring   Breaking down a total test score into scores on particular parts, sections, or themes.

Anxiety   A sense of vague or specific fear that may be either a *state* or a *trait*.

Application   Using concepts and principles in the solution of problems or in new situations.

Appreciation   A tendency to see value in something, and understand its subtleties, often in the arts.

Aptitude   Primarily used to refer to an ability to acquire skills given an opportunity to learn, often measured with an aptitude test. Example: identifying a student for a special course in auto mechanics because she has an *aptitude* for mechanical subjects.

Aptitude test   See *aptitude*.

Aptitude-treatment interaction (ATI)   The phenomenon whereby a given treatment (typically an instructional method or practice) has different effects on a dependent variable (typically achievement or attitude) for students at different points on the scale of some characteristic (ability, aptitude, gender, social class, etc.).

Aspiration   What one wants to achieve.

Assessment   The process of determining, estimating, and evaluating a broad range of evidence concerning student achievement and other characteristics.

Assimilation   After Piaget, the process of fitting concepts or experiences into already existing cognitive structures. Compare *accommodation*.

Assimilationist ideology   The system of ideas that call upon minority group members to adapt to the mainstream culture and abandon their native culture.

Associativity   The idea that the sum is independent of the order in which things are added.

Attention   The focusing of the mind on one thing.

Attitude   A feeling for or against something, having both cognitive and affective aspects and being more or less long-lasting.

Attribution   Assigning responsibility for one's success or failure to oneself (typically ability or effort) or something outside oneself (typically task difficulty or luck).

Authentic assessment   Assessment procedures and tools that come close to the way in which educational achievement would be manifested under real-life conditions. Example: using tasks requiring extended written matter rather than multiple-choice tests.

Authentic tests   Tests that call for behavior or performance matching that expected of persons actually engaged in such "real-world" performance outside the school setting.

Autonomy versus shame and doubt   As used by Erikson, the second stage of development, during which children begin exploring the environment.

Aversive stimulus or situation   One that an organism finds unpleasant and avoids.

Avoidance learning   See *escape learning*.

Baseline   The frequency of a behavior before any systematic *behavior modification* begins.

Behavior   The activity of an organism. Usually refers to the overt or visible but also can refer to covert, invisible, or internal processes, such as thinking.

Behavior modification   The application of the principles of learning theory, particularly operant conditioning and social learning theory, to the changing of behavior. Example: using a *token economy* to improve student performance.

Behavioral objective   An *educational objective* stated in terms of observable (visible or audible) behavior.

Behaviorism   A philosophical and scientific orientation toward psychology, one that restricts scientific effort to the study of observable events and that excludes mental phenomena.

Behaviorists   Psychologists who believe in *behaviorism*.

Bias   The tendency to interact with others with a frequency or an attitude that differs from what would be expected on the basis of statistical probability or the concept of fairness to all.

Big-fish-little-pond effect (BFLPE)   The tendency for students placed in high-ability groups to develop lower academic self-esteem, and for students in low-ability groups to develop higher academic self-esteem.

Big Five Factors of Personality   The five currently accepted broad clusters of traits, factor-analytically derived: hostile vs. agreeable, introverted vs. extraverted, impulsive vs. conscientious, neurotic vs. emotionally stable, intellectually narrow vs. intellectually open.

Bloom's taxonomy   See *Taxonomy of Educational Objectives*.

Bottom-up processing   Constructing meaning primarily from external stimuli. Example: making sense of prose primarily from what is read, not from past experience. Compare *top-down processing*.

CAI   See *computer-assisted instruction.*

Causal relationship   A relationship between two variables such that different values of one bring about, determine, or cause different values of the other.

Characteristic pedagogical flow   Recurrent patterns of instruction and classroom activity.

Classical conditioning   The type of conditioning, formulated by Pavlov, whereby previously *neutral stimuli* become capable of eliciting responses similar to *unconditioned responses*. The *conditioned stimulus* acquires this capability by being paired with, or presented frequently just prior to, the *unconditioned stimulus.*

Classification   After Piaget, the process of grouping objects into various categories, especially during the concrete operational stage. Involves the ability to classify entities according to one or more characteristics.

Classification hierarchy   A lecture-organization scheme that shows how higher-level categories include lower-level categories.

Classroom management   The process of ensuring that, in classroom teaching, sufficient order and freedom from disruption are maintained.

Classroom teaching   The predominant approach to teaching in which the teacher works with a group of students, usually about 15 to 40 in number, and sequentially or simultaneously uses such methods as large-group lecturing, small-group discussion and cooperative learning, recitation, and seatwork.

Coefficient of correlation   The numerical value of a *correlation.* May run from -1.00 through 0 to $+1.00$. High correlation coefficients (e.g., .83, $-.75$) indicate tight relations between two variables. Low correlation coefficients ($-.07$, .15) indicate loose relationship between variables.

Cognition   The process whereby the mind comes to know facts, concepts, principles, etc. In general, all the ways in which people think.

Cognitive development   The process whereby individuals acquire more complex and adaptive ways of thinking and problem solving as they grow from infancy to adulthood.

Cognitive domain   Those aspects of behavior that call primarily on cognitive processes. Distinguished from *affective domain* and *psychomotor domain. Educational objectives* are written in this domain. They are concerned with *cognitive outcomes.*

Cognitive load   The amount of mental effort required by the learner in comprehending, problem solving, and other activities related to a given teaching-learning situation.

Cognitive objectives   Used to refer to the intellectual processes that a learner uses, say, in translating a mathematics word problem into mathematical symbols in appropriate ways and in carrying out the appropriate intellectual subtasks to reach a solution.

Cognitive outcomes   Those outcomes of instruction dealing with the *cognitive domain.* Examples: spelling, mathematics, reading skill.

Cognitive psychology   A philosophical and scientific conception of psychology that deals with cognition. It focuses on the internal, not directly observable, mental processes by which human beings acquire, remember, and use information about their internal and external environments. Contrasted with the psychological position of *behaviorism,* which denies the scientific validity of references to unobservable mental processes.

Cohort   A specified set of individuals. Examples: All first-graders or all mainstreamed children in one year are Cohort I; the first-graders or mainstreamed children studied in the next year are Cohort II, etc.

College Board score   A standard score on a scale with a mean of 500 and a standard deviation of 100. Used by the College Entrance Examination Board for its Scholastic Assessment Test (SAT).

Combinatorial device   A scheme for showing how two or more sets of categories can be combined to yield a larger set of categories.

Co-membership   Membership in the same group or culture as that in which another person is a member, so that cultural norms and values are shared.

Common ground   A body of information (definitions, issues, orientations, and so forth) shared by a group prior to a discussion and providing the focus of the discussion.

Communicational channel   The medium, such as words, pictures, graphs, and audio- or video-recordings, by which ideas are conveyed.

Comparison   A lecture organization that shows how two or more things are similar and different on various bases.

Complex Instruction   A cooperative-learning scheme, developed by Cohen and Lotan, to produce equal-status interaction. It requires *multiple-ability tasks* and assigning competence to low-status students.

Component (part-whole) relationship   A lecture-organization scheme that shows the parts of a whole, such as a concept, phenomenon, or principle.

Composition   The idea that whenever two elements of a system are combined (e.g., gasoline-engine cars, A, and other cars, A′), another element of the system (i.e., cars, B) is obtained. Or if we combine cars (B) and other means of transportation (B′), we obtain means of transportation (C).

Comprehension   The ability to understand without necessarily being able to analyze or apply information. The lowest level of understanding in the *Taxonomy of Educational Objectives.*

Computer-assisted instruction (CAI)   Instruction mediated by a computer, either mainframe or desktop, which presents content, asks questions, and records and reacts to responses. May provide drill and practice, tutoring, a simulation, or a game.

Concept   An idea that embodies what is common to a whole set of things that have one or more properties in common. May be concrete or abstract. Examples: dog, reinforcer, development.

Conceptual model   The words or diagrams used in instruction to help learners build mental models of subject matter.

Concrete operational stage   After Piaget, the third major stage of *cognitive development* covering approximately the elementary school years. Refers to the nature of children's thought, which is concrete and logical but not abstract.

Conditioned response   A response elicited by an originally ineffective or *neutral stimulus* that has become effective through being presented repeatedly just prior to the presentation of an originally effective *unconditioned stimulus.* A conditioned response is a learned response.

Conditioned stimulus   An originally ineffective or *neutral stimulus* that has become effective in eliciting a response by being repeatedly paired with, or presented just prior to, an originally effective or *unconditioned stimulus.*

Conditioning   Changed relationships between stimuli and responses, between responses, or between stimuli, resulting from practice, contiguity, or *reinforcement.* Includes *classical conditioning* and *operant conditioning.*

Confidence interval   A student's test score plus and minus the standard error of measurement, providing a band, not a point, for thinking about scores.

Con-pro sequence   A lecture-organization scheme that first presents the arguments against a position and then the arguments supporting it.

Consequence   The stimulus or event that follows a response and that controls the strength or frequency of the response. Example: Getting a gold star or having a sad face drawn on your worksheet by a teacher is the consequence associated with doing worksheets in class.

Conservation   After Piaget, the process whereby a person considers the mass, weight, or volume of some matter, solid or liquid, to stay the same despite changes in its shape, configuration, or placement.

Construct validity   The degree to which a test measures the construct, or psychological concept or variable, at which it is aimed (e.g., intelligence, anxiety). Inferred from all of the logical arguments and empirical evidence available.

Constructivism   The doctrine that people construct their own understandings and interpretations of the "stimuli" (situations, problems, events, discourses, etc.) to which they are exposed.

Constructivist teaching   Teaching that allows for and fosters the student's own constructions, or sense-making processes.

Content   The body of knowledge, skills, values, and the like, that instruction deals with.

Content validity   The degree to which an achievement test's content contains a representative and appropriate sample of the content (subject matter) contained in the instructional objectives whose attainment the test is intended to measure.

Contextualization   Understanding an idea, word, skill, event, etc., in the context, or setting, in which it occurs. Example: understanding percentages in the context of baseball batting averages.

Contiguity learning   The learning that results from the presentation of two or more stimuli very close together in time or space, so that subsequently the presentation of one of the stimuli calls forth, as a response, the other stimulus. Association of the events in mind is considered a natural process.

Contingency   The dependence of a reinforcement on the occurrence of a specific response.

Contingency contract   A commitment that is mutually agreed on, often in writing, such that on completion of certain tasks or on achieving certain levels of proficiency, a specific *reward* is given.

Contingency management   The systematic use of *contingencies* and the development of *contingency contracts* to achieve particular goals.

Continuous reinforcement   A schedule whereby every response of a certain kind is reinforced.

Contracting   An approach to independent study that specifies what a student is to learn, in what way, with what resources and schedule, etc.

Control   The capability of bringing about change in a *dependent variable* by manipulating the causally related *independent variable.*

Control group   The subjects in an *experiment* who either receive no treatment or receive their usual treatment, not the experimental treatment. It is used to measure the level of the *dependent variable* in the absence of the experimental treatment. Example: In an experiment to see if a "new" music curriculum is associated with outcomes different from those of an "old" music curriculum, the group receiving the "old" curriculum is the control group.

Conventional level of morality   After Kohlberg, the middle of three stages, focused on maintaining rules and order and pleasing others.

Convergent questions   Questions for which there is a single right answer.

Convergent thinking   Thinking that leads to a single correct or customary answer to a question or problem.

Cooperative learning   An approach to learning, arranged by the teacher, that requires two, or a small group of, students to work together to achieve an educational objective.

Correlation   A statistical description of the closeness and direction of the relationship between variables. May be positive, where being low or high on one variable means being low or high on another. (Example: the correlation between high school GPA and number of hours spent studying.)

May also be negative, indicating that being low or high on one variable means being the opposite on the other variable. (Example: high school GPA and number of hours spent watching television.)

Correlational relationships   Relationships between variables described or measured as they occur naturally, i.e., without any manipulation or intervention by a researcher.

Cost-effectiveness   The relationship (such as the ratio) between the cost or expenditure and attainment of a given effect on, say, student achievement.

Covering-law model   A model for explanations whereby a teacher shows that something is an example of a broader, more general principle.

Creativity   The process or ability that results in the formulation or production of new ideas, approaches, or products that have some artistic or scientific merit.

Criterion   A basis or means for judging something, such as the validity of an intelligence test.

Criterion validity   The degree to which the score on a test predicts the individual's score or performance in some other area. Example: If correlated, a test of scholastic achievement can be used to predict job success.

Criterion-referenced evaluation   The process of determining the degree to which a performance or achievement fits prespecified standards or criteria. Distinguished from *norm-referenced evaluation.*

Criterion-referenced tests   Tests with a prespecified standard, so that students succeed when they exceed the standard. No comparison with other students, as with *norm-referenced tests,* is required.

Crystallized intelligence   The kind of intelligence, after R. B. Cattell, that is expressed in well-structured forms by a given culture (e.g., school achievement, vocational skills). Distinguished from *fluid intelligence.*

Cue   A stimulus that, through previous experience, indicates a situation where, if a correct response is made, a reinforcer will or will not follow.

Cultural literacy   After Hirsch, specific, communally shared information, rarely detailed or precise, but needed by every member of a society to be able to participate fully in its affairs.

Culture   The information, ideas, and ways of thinking and behaving of a social group, large (e.g., Navajos) or small (e.g., the Jones family).

Culture-free test   A test that calls for skills or attitudes that have been minimally, or not at all, influenced by the culture in which the individual being tested has grown up. Sometimes called a culture-fair test. An ideal that may not be achievable.

Decay   The fading or disappearance of information from *short-term memory.*

Declarative knowledge   Knowledge or memory of factual things; includes *episodic memory* and *semantic memory.*

Decontextualize   Understanding an idea, word, event, etc., in any context or at least outside of any single context or field or environment. Example: understanding words (e.g., percentage) in more than one, or in any, context (e.g., baseball batting average, interest on a loan, etc.).

Deficit model of education   An approach to education for poor minority-group children based on the assumption that they are "disadvantaged" and need education that will compensate for their disadvantage.

Dependent variable   The variable in a research investigation that is considered to be influenced by one or more other variables that are either being manipulated or are varying freely, within the context of the study.

Desensitization   A conditioning procedure whereby strong emotional responses are progressively weakened by pairing stimuli that elicit those responses with pleasant events. Example: For a person scared of algebra, you develop a hierarchy of fearful stimuli and pick the weakest of them to pair with an antagonistic response to anxiety (say, pairing thoughts about two-column addition with relaxation responses). Then you move up the hierarchy, progressively removing or weakening fear responses.

Development   Physical or psychological change over time, as from infancy to old age.

Developmental crises   After Erikson, referring to the struggles individuals have at various points in the life cycle. Example: Learning how to live with and share life with another, versus maintaining autonomy and living alone, is a crisis every young adult faces in our society.

Diagnostic testing   Testing that yields information as to the cause of difficulties in comprehension, problem solving, etc.

Differential reinforcement   Used in conditioning, refers to a process of reinforcing some responses and not others.

Direct instruction   A set of instructional practices in which the teacher controls student behavior fairly closely by presenting the material to be learned, soliciting and reacting to students' responses, and generally keeping instruction tied to objectives.

Disadvantaged   A term applied to children who have economic and social handicaps. Usually refers to low-income minority children who have experiences different from those of middle-class suburban white children.

Discipline   Refers both to the control of a class by teachers and the dispensing of punishment by teachers.

Discovery learning   A kind of learning in which the student must induce concepts or principles fairly independently of *direct instruction,* i.e., by observation and analysis of events and processes. Usually entails relatively free exploration by the student but may be guided by the teacher.

Disequilibrium   After Piaget, the process that occurs when events cannot be handled by existing knowledge and skill, requiring *adaptation* by the organism. When cognitions are characterized by disequilibrium, new learning takes place, so cognitive *equilibrium* can be reestablished.

Disinhibition   The release of behavior that had been suppressed or inhibited. Example: the violence of ordinary people in a lynch mob.

Distractor   An incorrect response alternative in a multiple-choice test item.

Distributed cognition   A cognition (idea, concept, principle, problem solution, and the like) located among a group of persons or things (such as books or films) produced by a group.

Divergent questions   Questions for which many answers or unique answers are acceptable.

Divergent thinking   Thinking that leads to a variety of desirable or relevant responses or to unusual responses to a particular problem situation. Regarded as a form of *creativity.*

Domain   As used in the *Taxonomy of Educational Objectives,* a major category of educational objectives: cognitive, affective, or psychomotor. Can also refer to a clearly defined body of knowledge or skill. Examples: two-column addition, the Federalist Papers, stick handling in hockey.

Domain-specific knowledge   Knowledge about a particular area, such as an occupation, a unit of instruction, or a sport. Can correlate more highly than IQ with achievement in that area.

Dual-coding   The coding of information in long-term storage in a verbal or symbolic form and a pictorial or iconic form.

Educational objectives   The goals and desired outcomes of education. Can be broad, as in specifying that all children should become good citizens; or narrow, as in a *behavioral objective,* such as specifying that all children can recognize the Bill of Rights.

Educational psychology   The study of learning, teaching, schooling, and related areas, using the concepts and methods of the discipline of psychology.

Educational standards   Statements of the minimal, or lowest, acceptable level of achievement, or levels that all students should be required to attain, insofar as possible.

Effect size   The magnitude of the result of an investigation; for correlational studies, the correlation coefficient; for experiments, the standardized difference between the means of experimental and control groups.

Egocentrism   An inability to take the view of others, characteristic of children's thinking. Also, a belief that others experience events in the same way as oneself.

Elicited response   A response brought about by a stimulus. Example: salivation after sight of food, feelings of hunger. See *classical conditioning.*

Emitted response   A response made by an organism, for which the eliciting factors are unknown. See *operant conditioning.*

Emotional stimuli   Stimuli that elicit an emotional reaction. Examples: words like "blood" or "pizza" or "danger."

Empathy   The ability to put oneself in the psychological place ("shoes") of another person or group.

Empirical   Relying on experience, as in observation or experimentation. Compare *logical.*

Enactive stage   After Bruner, the first stage of *cognitive development,* characterized by motor responses—touching, grasping, feeling, chewing, etc.—through which the child comes to know the objective world. Followed by *iconic stage* and *symbolic stage.*

Encoding   Transforming verbal, visual, musical, and other forms of sensory information into some system for processing and storing that information.

Engaged time   That part of allocated time during which students are actually paying attention to, or involved in, an activity.

Enrichment   Offering additional learning opportunities in some area to gifted students. May be used instead of *acceleration.*

Episodic memory   Storage of personal, dated, autobiographical memories.

Equalization effect   A characteristic of students to use all available resources when studying for a test, thus making it difficult to evaluate the effects of different teaching methods. Example: The difference in effects of teaching one class via small groups and the other as a large group may be wiped out if the two classes study hard.

Equilibrium   After Piaget, a balance between *accommodation* and *assimilation.* Maintaining equilibrium is the force behind cognitive growth.

Escape conditioning   The avoidance of *aversive stimuli* by leaving or escaping from an aversive situation before the aversive stimuli appear (called *avoidance learning*) or right after the aversive stimuli occur.

Essay tests   Achievement tests that call on the student to write a relatively lengthy response typically based on comprehension, application, analysis, synthesis, or evaluation.

Esteem needs   From the hierarchy of motives, after Maslow, the need to belong to and be accorded status in some group. If not fulfilled, one will not reach higher levels of the hierarchy.

Ethnicity   The identification of an individual, a group, or a society in terms of its culture: ways of thinking, customs, values, beliefs, etc.

Evaluation   A cognitive process calling for judgments of either the goodness or correctness (i.e., for the valuing) of something. Also, a procedure whereby observations and measurements are compared with norms or criteria in order to arrive at a recommendation concerning a decision or policy. Examples: calling a score of 24 superb; using all available data to determine whether a citizenship program is having its intended effect.

Exceptional children   Children who are not in the typical range on some characteristic. Physically handicapped, learning disabled, mathematically precocious, and artistically gifted are all exceptional children.

Expectancy   A prediction or prophecy about performance, sometimes coming true, as in the *self-fulfilling prophecy.*

Experiment   A method of investigation or research in which one variable, the independent or experimental variable, is manipulated and the subsequent value of another, or dependent, variable is measured to determine whether changes in the independent variable cause changes in the dependent variable.

Explain   In teaching, the clarification of the meaning of a term, concept, process, or event. More specifically, in philosophy, the explanation of something by showing that it is an instance of a more general ("covering") law or accepted relationship.

Explaining links   Linkages between clauses, sentences, or paragraphs that help tie them together and make their implications clear. Words like "because," "therefore," "thus," and others clarify a message.

Experience   An interchange with the environment whereby stimuli become meaningful and related to responses.

Experimental group   The group of subjects that receives the treatment in an experiment intended to determine the treatment's effects; contrasted with the "control group," which does not receive the treatment.

Explanation   Accounting for a relationship between variables by showing that it is logical.

Expository teaching   Teaching that sets forth, presents, and explains the material to be received, as against discovered, by the student.

External   See *locus of control.*

Extinction   The disappearance, more or less rapid, of a previously conditioned response. In classical conditioning, it results from presentation of the conditioned stimulus without subsequent presentation of the unconditioned stimulus. In operant conditioning, it results from unreinforced occurrences of the operant behavior.

Extrinsic motivation   Motivation that results from reinforcers that are not inherent in the activity.

Extrinsic reinforcement   Reinforcement that is external to an activity, not from within, as in the difference between grades versus self-satisfaction for finishing a term project.

Face validity   The extent to which a test appears to laypersons to measure what it is supposed to measure. Example: A test of first-aid ability would be judged to have some face validity if it has items on setting splints and tying tourniquets. It would have less face validity if it has items on arthritis—a chronic disease.

Factor analysis   A statistical method for identifying the common dimensions underlying a set of variables that correlate more or less highly with one another. Used in identifying primary abilities, or types of intelligence, such as verbal, numerical, spatial. Also applicable to attitudes and other types of variables.

Fear of failure   Anxiety about undertaking certain kinds of tasks, often leading to choices of tasks that are too easy or too difficult, so as to maximize success or avoid personal responsibility for failure.

Fear of success   Anxiety about losses of friendship and love relationships owing to high levels of achievement.

Feedback   Information about performance. Examples: Teachers receive feedback about their teaching by watching students and assessing their test performance; students receive feedback from their teachers in the form of grades and personal comments.

Fixed-interval schedule   A *schedule of reinforcement* whereby reinforcers occur at points equally separated in time from one another.

Fixed-ratio schedule   A *schedule of reinforcement* whereby reinforcers occur after equal numbers of specified responses have been made since the preceding reinforcement.

Flexibility   In creativity, the ability to use many different procedures, concepts, or strategies in solving problems.

Fluency   In creativity, the ability to rapidly and steadily come up with alternative and relevant views or solutions.

Fluid intelligence   A kind of intelligence, after R. B. Cattell, which has not been closely shaped by cultural forces, or learned in formal educational settings, but rather has developed through free and unstructured interaction with the environment. Distinguished from *crystallized intelligence.*

Formal operational stage   As used by Piaget, the stage of *cognitive development* in which the adolescent becomes capable of dealing with and manipulating abstractions and logical relationships.

Formative evaluation   A kind of *evaluation* intended to provide information for the improvement of teaching, curricula, or instructional materials. Compare *summative evaluation.*

Frame   A segment of programmed instructional material in which content is presented and a question or problem calls on the student to respond.

Fraternal twins   Twins resulting from simultaneous fertilization of two ova by two sperms and hence no more similar genetically than ordinary siblings. Compare *identical twins.*

Frequency distribution   A table in which, for each value or group of values of a variable, the number of persons or entities possessing that value is indicated.

Frustration   An emotional response, leading to aggressiveness or regression, stemming from an inability to obtain reinforcement.

g   See *general factor.*

Gatekeeper   A person who influences or determines the entrance of other persons into an occupation, organization, opportunity, etc.

General factor   A factor that includes all the variables, such as intelligence test scores. Revealed by a factor analysis and results from the positive intercorrelations of scores on all cognitive ability tests.

Generative model of learning   After Wittrock, the idea that students learn through generating, or developing more or less on their own, the meanings inherent in what they are studying.

Generativity versus stagnation   After Erikson, the stage of development in which an adult reaches out beyond personal concerns toward broader societal problems as against being preoccupied with one's own interests.

Genetic determination   The informal or intuitive notion that, in a normal environment, a characteristic is coded, and caused, by the genes. Applies to individuals, compared with "heritability," which applies, like correlation, only to groups.

Grade-equivalent score   A way of interpreting test scores such that a given raw score is translated into the grade level of the average student who has received that raw score in a specified norm group. For example, a grade equivalent score of 4.3 means that the student's raw score equals the average score expected from students in the third month of the fourth grade.

Group differences   Differences between groups (racial, ethnic, community, etc.) in some described or measured characteristics. Contrasted with "individual," or intragroup, differences.

Group Investigation   A cooperative-learning scheme, developed by Sharan and Sharan, that requires a small group of students to inquire into a challenging problem, interact with one another, interpret the gathered information, make a presentation and, with the teacher and other students, evaluate their work.

Group tests   Tests that can be given to more than one person at a time, as against *individual tests.*

Heritability   The proportion of the variation in a characteristic that is accounted for by variation in heredity.

Heterogeneous grouping   The practice of grouping students without regard for their ability or achievement.

Hidden curriculum   The portion of the schooling process not easily noticed but part of what is learned. Examples: the ways schools sort children by achievement scores and social class; how society's gender expectations become part of the school culture; or the fact that the history of nonwhite people is rarely presented.

Hierarchical structure   After Gagné, the arrangement of learning tasks so that early tasks are prerequisites to, or facilitative of, learning the next task, and so on.

High-consensus field   Subject matter areas where there is great agreement about the facts, concepts, principles, and methods that should be taught to students. Examples: mathematics in the elementary grades, introductory biology in high school.

Higher-level questions   Questions that call for thinking, or cognitive processing of ideas. Often refers to levels above knowledge when using the *cognitive domain* of the *Taxonomy of Educational Objectives.*

High-inference variables   Variables in teaching that can be judged only by using much inference, interpretation, or extrapolation from cues. Examples: clarity, warmth.

High-stakes testing   Standardized testing whose results, as interpreted by school administrators, political officials, business enterprises, and others, can have important effects on the status of students and their teachers.

Holistic scoring   Giving a single test score to a product or performance on the basis of an overall, general impression of its quality.

Holophrastic language   Language in which single words are used to express complete thoughts, typically in infancy; when, for example, "Go" means "I want to go now."

Homework   Work assigned by teachers to be done outside of school. Excludes in-school guided study, home study courses, and extracurricular activities.

Homogeneous grouping   See *ability grouping*.

Humanistic   An orientation toward those characteristics that are the essence of being human— love, grief, laughter, caring, sharing, embarrassment, self-worth, and so forth. Humanistic psychologists and humanistic education emphasize these aspects of the human condition.

Hypothesis   A statement of the predicted relationship between two or more variables, awaiting validation on the basis of research.

Iconic stage   After Bruner, the stage of human development in which the child responds to information conveyed by visual or auditory imagery, such as pictures, diagrams, speech, and melodies.

Ideational scaffolding   Providing or calling forth a cognitive structure within which to fit new experience. Used to account for the effectiveness of *advance organizers.*

Identical elements   The theory that transfer depends on the degree to which the new situation resembles, or has identical elements with, the original situation in which a skill was acquired.

Identical twins   Twins resulting from fertilization of a single ovum by a single sperm and hence carrying the same genes. Compare *fraternal twins.*

Identity   After Piaget, the idea that the quantity of something stays the same unless some amount is added or subtracted. Also, more generally used to refer to the sense of self, a particularly important concern of adolescents who may suffer an "identity crisis."

Identity versus confusion   After Erikson, the stage of development in school in which adolescents deal with their roles in society and the nature of their own selves.

Identity versus role diffusion   After Erikson, the stage of development in which adolescents deal with their roles in society and the nature of their own self.

Imagery   A mental representation of information in pictorial, diagrammatic, or iconic form. An aid to memory.

Imitation   To behave in the same way as a *model.* To copy another's behavior. An important part of *social learning theory.*

Incentive   Something that can satisfy a motive. Example: Money is an incentive for those who want to be rich; they can be motivated by the promise of money.

Incidental learning   Learning that takes place unintentionally, while doing other things. Examples: learning a good deal about driving a car, while a passenger; learning probability while playing poker.

Independent study   Studying, doing research, writing, and other intellectual activities done by a student with relatively great autonomy and self-direction.

Independent variable   The variable in a relationship that freely takes on different values or is manipulated so that subsequent values of another variable, the *dependent variable,* can be studied to see if they are a function of the independent variable.

Individual differences   Variations among individuals that have psychological significance. Examples: *intelligence,* personality, learning rate, *anxiety,* etc.

Individual instruction   Teaching one student at a time. May or may not be *individualized instruction.* Examples: tutoring, computer-assisted instruction.

Individual tests   Tests that can be given to only one person at a time, as against *group tests.* Example: Stanford-Binet Intelligence Scale.

Individualized education program (IEP)   A program of educational experiences specifying objectives and means for achieving them. Required by law for handicapped students.

Individualized instruction   Instruction that has been adjusted to be appropriate to the abilities, interests, and needs of specific students.

Industry versus inferiority   After Erikson, the stage of development in which children learn to obtain satisfaction from doing productive work independently.

Information processing A cognitive conception of learning describing how individuals attend to, store, code, and retrieve information.

Inhibition In conditioning, the blocking of a response.

Initiative versus guilt After Erikson, the stage of development in which children first try to see how well they can handle adult problems and roles.

Instructional assessments Informal assessments that are made during interactive teaching so that teachers can assess their own performance.

Instructional objectives The ways of behaving—thinking, feeling, and moving—that are set forth as the goals of teaching.

Instrumental conditioning See *operant conditioning.*

Integrated ends-means model Used to describe teacher planning where ends are not always specified before means are picked. Ends can arise from activities (means).

Integrity versus despair After Erikson, the stage of development in which old persons look back on and evaluate their careers, with more or less satisfaction.

Intelligence The ability of an organism to solve problems, usually involving abstractions and general knowledge of the kind acquired through informal interaction with the environment as against formal educational processes. Often regarded as a single *general factor,* but also considered as a set of *special abilities* (verbal, mathematical, spatial, etc.), or multiple intelligences, after Howard Gardner, or made up of trainable components, after Robert Sternberg.

Intelligence quotient (IQ) Originally the ratio of mental age to chronological age × 100. Now typically measured differently but still a scale with a *mean* of 100 and a *standard deviation* of about 16, for quantifying general intelligence or mental ability.

Interactive stage of instruction The time in which teachers and students are working together for instructional purposes. Examples: lecturing, recitation, small-group work. Contrast with *preactive stage of instruction.*

Interference In studying memory, the problem that new learning sometimes prevents the recall of old learning; a blocking of the information already in storage.

Interlecture structuring Tying a lecture to the preceding and subsequent lectures in a series.

Intermittent reinforcement The process whereby responses are sometimes but not always reinforced. Compare *continuous reinforcement.*

Internal See *locus of control.*

Internal consistency reliability A measure of the dependability or consistency of a test based on the average intercorrelation of the items of the test.

Interpretive research The study of some phenomena, usually using qualitative, ethnographic, or naturalistic methods of investigation, and relying on the interpretive powers of the investigator. Describes events and the meanings of those events to the participants involved.

Interval schedule A schedule of reinforcement based on time; may be a *fixed interval* or *variable interval.*

Intimacy versus isolation After Erikson, the stage of development in young adulthood in which attempts to form an intimate relationship with another person take on great importance.

Intrinsic motivation Motivation due to reinforcers that are inherent in the activity being performed.

Intuitive phase After Piaget, the preoperational stage of development in which the child reaches conclusions on the basis of vague impressions and nonverbal perceptual judgments.

Item stem See *stem.*

Keller plan A system of personalized instruction in which the subject matter is broken up into one- or two-week units. The student studies the material independently and takes a test of her mastery of the subject matter. If she passes the test, she goes on to the next unit. If not, she is given assistance through tutors and supplementary material. The process continues until all of the units have been mastered. Developed by Fred Keller.

Keyword method A mnemonic method in which students can use visual imagery of a word to think of another word. Example: "vin" ("wine" in French) is associated with a "van," with a bottle of wine in it. When a student hears "vin," the key word and visual image appear and a translation is possible.

Knowledge The ability to recall or recognize something: a fact, definition, concept, principle, custom, etc. The lowest level of achievement in the *Taxonomy of Educational Objectives, cognitive domain*. Requires little cognitive processing of information.

Knowledge of results Information, preferably given immediately, about the correctness or incorrectness of a person's responses.

Knowledge structures Sets of related ideas, concepts, facts, etc., into whose relationships new information must be fitted.

Large-group instruction Ways of teaching 15 to 20 or more students at a time. Example: lecturing.

Law A principle so strongly supported by logic and evidence that it cannot be doubted without much new evidence.

Learned helplessness A chronic condition of failure to deal effectively and energetically with the inevitable challenges one faces. Giving up quickly in mathematics problem solving, perseverance at inane tasks, low levels of aspiration, etc., characterize the student with learned helplessness.

Learning A change in behavior as a result of experience. The change is not attributable to physiological forces, such as fatigue or drugs, or to mechanical forces, such as stumbling. It occurs in all of life's settings, including schools and classrooms. Although an internal change, learning is inferred from changes in observable behaviors.

Learning strategy One of a family of procedures with which a student can improve her comprehension of a body of content. Includes self-questioning, summarizing, reviewing, and underlining.

Least restrictive environment The requirement that handicapped children be placed in environments as close to normal as possible. Thus many physically, mentally, and emotionally handicapped children have been removed from special schools and classes, where they were segregated, and returned to regular classrooms. See *mainstreaming*.

Level of aspiration The level of achievement or performance that an individual wants and expects to attain.

Libido After Freud, the life force, springing from a person's sexual energy.

Loci method A mnemonic device whereby the person aids memory by visualizing the to-be-remembered things as occupying places in a familiar or well-known setting, such as a home or school.

Locus of control The *attribution* for behavior. May be internal, as when one attributes success or failure to ability or effort. May be external, as when one attributes success or failure to luck or the nature of the task. Persons with internal or external loci of control differ in many ways, particularly in taking responsibility for their own actions.

Logical Relying on consistency in reasoning. Compare *empirical*.

Logical fallacies The subtle, hard-to-detect but logically erroneous arguments that can mislead an audience or a participant in a discussion.

Longitudinal study An investigation in which the same individuals are observed, interviewed, questioned, or tested at several points in time, usually separated by one or more years.

Long-term memory (LTM) The hypothetical repository of information that has been coded so that it can be retrieved after months or years.

Lookback strategy A learning strategy by which students look back in text when they have questions.

Low-consensus field Subjects where there is a wide range of acceptable ideas about what should be taught to students. Examples: literature, art, social studies.

Low-inference variables Variables in teaching that can be judged without much inference, interpretation, or extrapolation from cues. Examples: frequencies of smiles, chalkboard diagrams.

Mainstreaming The practice of putting handicapped children in regular classrooms, whenever possible, so that they will experience the *least restrictive environment* for their development.

Mastery learning An approach to learning through instruction that divides the subject matter into many units of one or a few weeks' duration, gives students tests of their mastery after each unit, provides supplementary instruction through tutors and varied materials to students who do not attain mastery on the first attempt, and continues this process until all students have achieved mastery, usually defined as getting between 80 and 90 percent of the total possible achievement score. The initial instruction usually takes place in a regular classroom, rather than through independent study, as in the *Keller plan*, but subsequent and supplementary instruction is conducted individually or in small groups. Developed by Benjamin S. Bloom.

Matching items   A type of objectively scorable test item requiring the student to match a set of, say, three items with the appropriate member of a class of, say, five alternatives.

Maternal effect   After Devlin et al., the effect on IQ resulting from variations in the intrauterine environments provided by different mothers.

Mean   The arithmetic mean, popularly called the average, equal to the sum of scores divided by the number of scores. Affected by extremely high or low scores.

Measurement   The process of determining the amount or quantity of something, such as height or, in education, ability, achievement, or attitude.

Median   The middle score when all of the scores are arranged in rank order from high to low; used as a measure of central tendency or the point around which scores tend to fall. Unaffected by a few extremely high or low scores.

Mediation   Mental processes that occur between a stimulus and a response. Also, a way to increase meaningfulness by associating items to be learned with each other. Example: To remember that Sacramento is the capital of California, you might remember that Sacramento is where the Gold Rush began and that was in California. The information about the Gold Rush is a mediator.

Mental age   A measure of mental ability determined by the average chronological age of the persons who attain that level of develoment in intelligence. Thus, if a 10-year-old child can answer questions typically answerable only by 12-year-olds, the 10-year-old would be said to have a mental age of 12.

Mental imagery   Imagining a picture or diagram of what reading matter or speech is presenting.

Mentoring   A relationship between a person who is an experienced and excellent performer and a relative newcomer in the same field. Examples: seasoned baseball players for rookies; established scientists for graduate students; experienced teachers for new teachers.

Meta-analysis   The quantitative synthesis of the results of two or more studies of roughly the same relationships or phenomena. Originated by Gene V Glass and applied to large bodies of research results in the behavioral and other sciences.

Metacognition   The mental processes whereby one monitors one's cognitive processes in thinking, learning, and remembering. Thus metacognition allows one to be aware of whether one has understood a paragraph after reading it.

Metalinguistic awareness   Knowing and being able to talk about language and its rules and customs.

Microcomputer   A computer small enough to fit on a desk and be used in a classroom or home for personal word processing, computation, problem solving, learning, etc.

Misperceptions   In *cognitive psychology*, the kind of intractable naive beliefs people hold, in spite of what they learn in school. Example: belief that light travels farther at night than during the day.

Mnemonics   Memory devices that make the task of remembering easier, particularly when the to-be-remembered information has little intrinsic structure or meaning.

Model   In *social learning theory*, someone or something that one can *imitate*. A person, a videotape, a prose description can all serve as models for new learning. In science, a mathematical or diagrammatic portrayal of some concept or process.

Moral dilemmas   Descriptions of situations where the proper or right moral course of action is unclear. Used to study moral development.

Moral judgment   Beliefs about proper and improper behavior when faced with a *moral dilemma.*

Motivation   The hypothetical internal process that energizes and directs behavior.

Multidimensional class   A classroom or other educational setting in which individuals or groups of students work at different tasks.

Multiple intelligences   After Howard Gardner, the conception that intelligence takes perhaps six highly distinct forms (verbal, spatial, musical, etc.) identified on neurological, pathological, and other bases, in addition to the traditional psychometric, factor-analytic research.

Multiple-ability tasks   Tasks that require many different abilities, preferably not all possessed by any one student.

Multiple-choice tests   Tests of ability, achievement, aptitude, or attitude in which the individual is required to choose a correct, best, or preferred response from two or more presented alternatives.

Nature-nurture   The argument about the contributions to variations in intelligence of variations in heredity (nature) or environment (nurture).

Need for approval   The need to be considered good, attractive, meritorious, etc., according to some standard.

Need for power   The need to have influence, control, or dominance over other people.

Needs   What an individual requires, subjectively or objectively, for physical or psychological comfort.

Negative reinforcement   The process of reinforcing behavior by the withdrawal of an aversive stimulus. Example: discontinuing criticism after a student begins to behave properly.

Neutral stimulus   A stimulus that is ineffective in producing an *elicited response*. A stimulus to which the organism pays no particular attention.

Noncognitive tests   Tests of interests, attitudes, values, motor skills, and so forth. Tests classified outside the *cognitive domain*.

Nonquestion alternative   Something, other than a question, a teacher can do or say during a discussion. Includes making a statement, acknowledging a student statement, building on a student remark, or nonverbally inviting a student to speak.

Normal curve   See *normal frequency distribution*.

Normal frequency distribution   A mathematically defined bell-shaped *frequency distribution*. Approximated by actual data when the values, or scores, are determined by many independently operating factors, each with only a small influence.

Norm-referenced evaluation   Any system of testing, grading, rating, or evaluation in which an individual's or group's measure is judged by comparisons with that of other individuals or groups, who constitute the norm group.

Norm-referenced tests (NRT)   Tests with no prespecified standards. Comparisons are made between a student and other students who constitute a comparison or norm group.

Object permanence   A child's awareness that objects exist even when out of sight.

Objective   Desired outcome, goal, aim, purpose. Choosing objectives is often considered the first step in the educational process.

Objective tests   Tests that can be graded or scored objectively, even by machine, such as multiple-choice or true-false tests.

Observational learning   Learning resulting from the observation of another individual (a *model*).

Obvious reaction   A tendency to regard the findings of social and educational research as obvious, regardless of whether they are the actual findings or the opposite of the actual findings.

Operant   See *emitted response*.

Operant behavior   Behavior controlled by its consequences.

Operant conditioning   The learning resulting from the reinforcement or nonreinforcement of an *emitted response*.

Operation   After Piaget, a logical thought process, carried out mentally, without need of physical manipulations. Example: learning $3 + 2 = 2 + 3$ without having to check each time that this is true.

Operational thought   After Piaget, logical, scientific, rational thought. A characteristic of children from about early elementary-school age is *concrete operational* thought. Older children become capable of *formal operational* thought.

Opportunity to learn   A powerful predictor of learning. Related to *allocated time*, exposure to content, pace of instruction, practice, and many other terms referring to whether or not students have had a sufficient chance to learn what we want them to learn.

Organism   A term used in psychology to refer to living animals, such as rats, pigeons, human babies and adults.

Organizational network   A scheme that shows how a set of things are related to one another so as to form an interconnected set of relationships.

Orienting response   Attention or arousal to changes in the stimulus situation.

Originality   The infrequency or rarity of a response. Used as a measure of creativity.

Origins   After Richard DeCharms, persons who feel that they control their own success or failure. Compare *pawns*. See also *locus of control*.

Overachiever   A student whose classroom performance or achievement test scores are quite a bit higher than would be expected given his or her aptitude or intelligence test scores.

Overlapping distributions   Frequency distributions in which some of the members of the distribution with the lower mean have measures (e.g., scores) higher than some members of the other distribution.

Overlearning   The continuation of practice or rehearsal beyond the point at which a perfect performance first occurs.

Overregularization   In language learning, the application of a rule to cases where it is inappropriate. Example: "He gived me candy."

Participant structure   The rules that govern turn taking in a discussion, conversation, classroom recitation, and other settings.

Pawns   After Richard DeCharms, persons who feel their success or failure is out of their own control. Compare *origins*. See *locus of control*.

Pedagogical content knowledge   Knowledge of the content to be taught and how it should be taught.

Percentile   The raw score that has a given *percentile rank*. Example: On the Blank Test, the 50th percentile is 39; so a score of 39 has a percentile rank of 50.

Percentile rank   The percentage of persons in a norm group whose scores are exceeded by any specific raw score, which then is assigned that percentile rank. Often (and inappropriately) called percentile.

Perception   The process of assigning meaning to a sensation, something seen, heard, touched, etc.

Performance   Another term for *behavior*. Changes in performance are the basis for judging that *learning* has taken place.

Performance-content matrix   A two-dimensional table, with one dimension consisting of categories of the subject matter being taught or learned and the other dimension consisting of types of cognitive, affective, or psychomotor process to be applied to the types of subject matter. Used in formulating objectives and the structure of achievement tests. The cells of the table, where the dimensions intersect, define specific ways of processing specific kinds of content.

Personalized system of instruction (PSI)   See *Keller plan*.

Pivot words   Words used by children in combination with other words to express several complex ideas. Examples: "No eat" and "No car" meaning "I do not want to eat now" and "The car is gone."

Population   All members of a group or groups about whom it is desired to make a generalization. Examples: all fifth-graders in the United States, all third-grade classes in City C.

Portfolio assessment   Assessment based on a collection of the student's or candidate's work over a period of, perhaps, a school term or year—work in whatever forms are authentic for the kinds of achievement or ability being assessed. Compare *authentic assessment*.

Positive reinforcement   The process of strengthening a response through the presentation, after a response, of a stimulus that has that effect, as when food is presented to a hungry organism or when information that a response is correct is presented to a student.

Postconventional stage of morality   After Kohlberg, the highest two levels of moral development where ethical principles, the welfare of society in general, and other complexities are taken into account when making *moral judgments*.

Poverty circle   The process in which parents who are low in income and educational level produce children low in income and educational level, who then grow up and, as parents, repeat the process with their own children. A form of "vicious circle."

Preactive stage of instruction   The planning, choosing, reflecting, analyzing kinds of activities of teachers that occur before they meet their students during the *interactive stage of instruction*.

Preconventional stage of morality   After Kohlberg, the lowest two levels of moral development, characterized by concerns for authority or rewards and punishment when *moral judgments* are made.

Predict   To state, with better than chance accuracy, the future value of a variable on the basis of prior knowledge of the value of the same or other variable.

Prediction   Foretelling the subsequent values of a variable with better than chance accuracy on the basis of knowledge of the earlier values of the same or some other variable.

Predictive validity   The *validity* of a test that is used to predict performance in some other area. See *criterion validity*.

Predictor   A *variable* used to foretell values of another variable. Example: The number of hours spent in paid nonacademic work can predict, to some extent, high school grade point average.

Premack principle   The idea that behaviors that occur more frequently under natural conditions can be used as reinforcers for behaviors that occur less frequently. Example: using computer games to reinforce computer drill-and-practice programs.

Preoperational phase After Piaget, the stage of development in childhood in which the child cannot do *operations*. The child is learning language and gaining experience but is still incapable of understanding relational terms and multiple classifications; in the intuitive phase, from about ages four to seven, child relies on vague impressions and unverbalized perceptual judgments.

Prerequisite capabilities The knowledge and skills required of students before they can learn in a given teaching-learning situation.

Primary reinforcers Stimuli that act as *positive reinforcers* for an organism without having been learned. Examples: food, drink, sexual activity.

Principle A relationship between two or more *concepts* established through scientific methods of observation, correlation, and experimentation.

Prior knowledge What a student already knows about a topic or subject to be learned. Regarded by some as the most important factor influencing new learning. Compare *prerequisite capabilities*.

Probing Continuing to question a student after an initial response to bring out more knowledge or clarify points that the student made.

Problem solving The application of principles to the solution of a problem that is new to the student.

Procedural knowledge Knowledge about how to perform a physical or cognitive activity.

Processing The general term applied to the many cognitive activities concerned with information, including receiving, rehearsing, storing, and retrieving the information.

Programmed instruction Instruction that proceeds by presenting the learner with an organized series of *frames,* each presenting information, a question calling for a response, and immediate knowledge of the correctness of the response. Permits self-pacing.

Projective tests Tests consisting of unstructured stimuli that, when interpreted by the individual, yield information useful in understanding the individual's personality, including needs. Examples: Thematic Apperception Test, Rorschach Test.

Psychomotor Consisting of bodily movements, from fine finger movement to whole-body activity, governed by the individual's awareness of his own position or movements and evaluation,

given what is intended. Examples: typewriting, violin playing, high diving, ice skating, sewing, dancing.

Psychomotor domain Those aspects of human behavior characterized by *psychomotor* behavior, and one of three domains in which educational objectives are often written. See also *affective domain* and *cognitive domain.*

Psychomotor objectives Objectives consisting of ways of moving, from fine finger movement to whole-body activity. Examples: typewriting, violin playing, dancing.

Punishment 1 The presentation to an organism of an aversive ("unpleasant") stimulus resulting in a decrease in the strength or frequency of responses that preceded the punishment. Example: sharp criticism of a student's behavior.

Punishment 2 The withdrawal from an organism of a pleasant or wanted stimulus resulting in a decrease in the strength or frequency of the responses that preceded the punishment. Example: removal of a child from the playground. See also *response cost* and *time-out.*

Qualitative research Forms of research in which the observational and interpretive skills of the researcher play an important role and the assignment of numerical values to variables is less frequent.

Quantitative research Forms of research in which measurement and statistics play an important role.

Question generation Formulating questions while reading, to improve comprehension and retention.

Random assignment The assigning of individuals or groups in an *experiment* to the experimental or *control group* on the basis of chance alone, thus maximizing the likelihood of the initial equivalence of the experimental and control groups of subjects.

Random selection In research studies, the selection of respondents in such a way that all individuals in a population have an equal probability of being included in the sample, thus maximizing the degree to which the *sample* is representative of the *population.*

Ratio schedule A schedule of *reinforcement* based on the proportion of correct responses that are made, as when 1 out of 20 correct responses is reinforced. May be a *fixed ratio* or *variable ratio* schedule.

Raw score   The original or actual score obtained on a test before it has been transformed to a more interpretable form. Example: A raw score of 52 on a mathematics test may equal a *College Board score* of 500 or a *stanine* of 5.

Reacting   Commenting or otherwise responding to a student's response in *recitation*.

Reciprocal teaching   A form of instruction in which students learn to ask questions of other students and the teacher in order to learn what comprehension questions might be asked on tests and what comprehension monitoring they must engage in if they are to show they understand the material.

Recitation   A component of classroom teaching in which the teacher engages in *structuring* (introduces or presents a topic) and *soliciting* (presents a question and seeks a response from a student), with a student *responding,* and the teacher *reacting* to the student's response.

Recognition test   A testing format where the correct answer is presented and must be recognized, as in multiple-choice or matching tests. Distinguished from test formats where recall of information (as in fill-in-the-blank) is required or memory and production are required (as in essay examinations).

Redirection   Channeling a question that has been unanswered or partially answered by one student to another student, and so on, until all the requisite information is brought out.

Rehearse   Continued practice. Example: repeating a phone number over and over to remember it.

Reinforcement   The process of presenting a reinforcing stimulus to an organism after the organism has made a response. Result: increasing the strength of that class of responses.

Reinforcer   An event or stimulus that strengthens a class of responses.

Relevance relationship   A lecture-organization scheme that presents ideas in order of their increasing or decreasing connectedness to the matter at hand.

Reliability   The degree to which a test or other measurement device yields consistent, dependable, stable measures across time, test administrations, forms of the test, items of the test, judges, or raters.

Replication   The repetition of an investigation—observational, correlational, or experimental—to determine the consistency of findings or to confirm previously obtained results.

Resource center   A place where learning materials, books, supplies, reference materials, games, videotapes, computer programs, and so forth, are brought together for use in independent study.

Respondent conditioning   See *classical conditioning.*

Responding   Typically by a student, answering a teacher's solicitation or request.

Response   Originally a behavior either *elicited* by a stimulus (as in *respondent conditioning*) or *emitted* by an organism to no known stimulus (as in *operant conditioning*). The behavior involved the action of either muscles or glands. More recently, with the growth of *cognitive psychology,* also refers to cognitive responses, where covert not overt processes are at work. Thus, today, a response is any behavioral or cognitive change.

Response cost   A version of *punishment 2,* where reinforcers are taken away when unacceptable behavior occurs. Examples: speeding tickets—the taking away of money for violation of traffic laws; the 15-yard penalty in football for unnecessary roughness.

Retention   Used to describe delayed recall of knowledge, as in a retention test, and to be differentiated from an immediate test of learning.

Retrieve   Bring forth information from memory.

Reversibility   After Piaget, an *operation* that allows a child to work backward and forward, rotate objects in mind, work from either direction on a problem, and undo activities that have been completed in actuality or in thought.

Reward   An outcome or event that is perceived by the organism as enjoyable and thus acts as a *positive reinforcer.* Examples: food pellets for rats, gold stars for children, money for adults, etc.

Rhetoric   The study of the elements used in composition or lecturing, including hyperbole, irony, and the like.

Rhetorical device   A use of words to convey a nonliteral meaning that has a persuasive or literary effect.

Role   The set of behaviors expected of a person occupying a position in a social group or organization. Examples: the teacher's role, the student's role, women's roles in the family.

Rote learning   Memorization without attempting to make the material meaningful.

Routines   Well-rehearsed, virtually automatic patterns of behavior. Examples: doing figure eights in ice skating, driving a car almost automatically. In classrooms routines are used to hand in papers, take roll, check homework, etc. Routines may differentiate between expert and novice teachers.

Rule-example-rule   In lecturing or writing, the presentation of a principle or generalization, followed by positive examples of it, and then, the repetition of the principle or generalization.

Sample   A portion of a total *population*, perhaps representative of the population. Example: 500 children randomly selected for a study of reading habits in a Chicago suburb are a sample of the total population of children living in that suburb.

Scaffolding   A mental device or process that identifies the way in which new information is ordered and related to other information.

Scatterplot   A graphic representation of cases, each with two values, plotted on a two-dimensional graph to show the relationship of two variables. Used to portray a correlation—high or low, positive or negative. Example: a scatterplot in which each "dot" represents a student and the two scores obtained by that student on two tests.

Schedule of reinforcement   The way in which reinforcement is presented to an organism, as in *ratio schedules* and *interval schedules* of reinforcement.

Schema   (plural: schemata) The abstract but organized set of ideas that reflect an individual's understanding of a phenomenon, situation, or event. Example: All the ideas one possesses about Africa, or dining out, are in separate schemata. Schemata intersect as in understanding dining out in an Ethiopian restaurant.

Scoring rubric   A model or category for evaluating different levels of performance on a test.

Seatwork   In classroom teaching, the setting in which students work at their seats on problems or assignments received from the teacher.

Secondary reinforcers   Stimuli that through learning act as *positive reinforcers*. Contrast *primary reinforcers*. Examples: kind words, money, hugs.

Select questions   Test questions that require a choice of the correct response from two or more choices; e.g., multiple-choice, true-false, or matching questions.

Selective migration   The hypothesis used to account for the finding that, say, urban or suburban people have higher average achievement than rural people. Refers to the best or worst of some group leaving, such that the remaining group is less or more talented.

Selective placement   Placing adoptive children in families whose socioeconomic status is similar to that of the children's biological parents. A hypothesis offered as a partial or complete explanation of the positive correlation between IQs of children and those of their adoptive parents.

Self-actualization   After Maslow, the stage of motivational development at which the individual fulfills his or her potential for personal achievement.

Self-concept   A person's definition of his or her own characteristics and worth in general and in specific contexts (mathematics, dating, hockey).

Self-efficacy   One's own ability to succeed in a particular task.

Self-fulfilling prophecy   A prediction that, if believed, tends to make itself come true. Example: The teacher's overt or covert communication of a prediction that a pupil will succeed tends to make the pupil try harder and thus succeed. Works, as well, in the opposite manner, promoting failure.

Self-regulation   The ability to keep track of one's own behavior and to control it.

Semantic maps   Visual and verbal maps of *declarative knowledge* and *procedural knowledge*, created as an aid to organization for the purpose of learning and remembering.

Semantic memory   Storage of concepts, principles, and characteristics of objects without personal involvement.

Sensorimotor stage   After Piaget, the stage of development in which the infant is learning to use its sense organs and muscles.

Sequential relationship   A lecture-organization scheme that arranges ideas in some chronological, logical, magnitude, or other sequence.

Shaping   The process of reinforcing *successive approximations* to a desired complex behavior.

Short-term memory (STM)   The component of *information processing* models in which information from the *short-term sensory store* is either forgotten or coded and transferred to *long-term memory*. Sometimes called *working memory*.

Short-term sensory storage (STSS) Also called the sensory register. A component of models of *information processing* in which sensations are stored very briefly before being either forgotten or transferred to the *short-term memory* for further processing.

Signals of transition A set of words or other devices that tell students that a lecturer is changing the subject or some aspect of the subject.

Significance In statistics, the probability that the results of an *experiment* or of a correlational study are not due to chance. Thus, to say the results were significant is to say that the probability is very small that the result obtained, such as the difference between two means, is just due to unsystematic events; therefore, the results can probably (but not certainly) be accepted as not due to chance.

Sizing-up assessments Informal assessments providing teachers with practical knowledge of students' cognitive, affective, and motor skills, primarily during the first weeks of schooling.

Small-group instruction Ways of teaching appropriate for 2 to 20 or so students at a time. Examples: discussion, cooperative learning methods.

Social climate The beliefs held by members of a school or classroom about the fairness, humor, academic orientation, permissiveness, opportunities for personal choice, and other social dimensions of that place.

Social interaction Repeated cycles of stimulation by one person of one or more other people and the responses of those people.

Social learning The theory concerning the process by which individuals learn from the observation of other individuals.

Socioeconomic status (SES) The status of an individual or group that is determined by educational level, financial wealth, place of residence, material possessions, occupational level, general prestige, and the like.

Soliciting Questioning or otherwise inviting a rseponse from a student.

Special abilities The group factors that are found when factor analyzing *intelligence*—verbal ability, spatial ability, mathematical ability, etc. These abilities show low correlations with each other but are positively related, indicating a *general intelligence* or *g factor* as well for intelligence.

Stability The degree to which two or more scores on a single test or equivalent tests tend to stay the same over time.

Standard Either the minimally acceptable level of achievement of an educational objective, because of society's requirements, or the level considered by authorities or general consent to be desirable.

Standard deviation A measure of the variability of a set of measures around the average (arithmetic mean) of the measures.

Standard error of measurement A statistical and psychometric quantity, determined by the reliability and standard deviation of test scores, which tells how much a score would be expected to vary if a very large number of repeated measurements were made with the same instrument under the same conditions; the higher the reliability, the smaller the standard error of measurement; the larger the standard deviation or variability of the test scores, the larger the standard error of measurement. Used in determining the *confidence interval.*

Standardized tests Tests of ability, achievement, attitude, or interest that are commercially available, intended for widespread use, equipped with directions for administration and interpretation, presumably constructed by experts, and usually *norm-referenced*, although *criterion-referenced* standardized tests are increasingly available.

Stanine A standard score on a scale ranging from 1 to 9, with a mean of 5 and a standard deviation of approximately 2.

State A condition of an individual that is relatively temporary and specific to a given situation. Example: Anxiety over a particular test is state anxiety. Anxiety that appears for almost every test is *trait* anxiety.

Statistically significant The characteristic of a statistical measure's being so large as to be unlikely to have resulted from chance fluctuations in a random sampling; applies to correlation coefficients, differences between means, and other statistical measures.

Stem The component of a multiple-choice test item that states the task, either as a question or as an incomplete statement.

Stimulus (plural: stimuli) Anything in the environment that activates a sense organ.

Stimulus control The condition in which a response's occurrence or magnitude is determined by the organism's experiencing a prior stimulus, which does not elicit but sets the occasion for the response.

Stimulus generalization   Responding in the same way to stimuli that differ more or less widely.

Stimulus variation   A change in what students see or hear to increase their attention.

Stimulus-response (S-R) learning   Refers to *classical* and *operant conditioning* and *contiguity learning.*

Story grammar   The way in which stories are organized. Learning is enhanced if students are aware that stories are organized in certain recurring ways.

Stratum III factor   After Carroll, the general factor running through all tests of mental ability. Also called *general intelligence* or *g factor.*

Structural support   Something, such as an outline or graph, shown to students to display the organization, or structure, of a lecture.

Structure   The organization, or set of relationships, that underlies something, such as a subject matter, an intellectual discipline. Also, as a verb, the statements by the teacher in introducing and laying out a new topic.

Structured teaching   The degree to which teaching has controlled sequence and pacing, small units, concreteness, directness, expositoriness, and feedback and reinforcement.

Student Teams and Achievement Divisions (STAD)   Developed by Slavin, whereby heterogeneous small groups cooperate to achieve and compete against other groups to obtain group rewards.

Study skills   Skills helpful in studying, such as summarization and question generation.

Subjectively scored tests   Tests scored on the basis of expert judgment, typically of a complex response or performance.

Subjects   The people or animals that are studied in a research project. Also, the content studied in schools.

Successive approximations   Responses that come closer and closer to the desired complex response. *Shaping* results from reinforcing successive approximations as they occur.

Summarization   A learning strategy that involves identifying the main information, deleting incidental and redundant information, and relating main to supporting information.

Summative evaluation   Evaluation at the end of a program or project to determine the degree to

which it has achieved its purposes. Compare *formative evaluation.*

Supply-type items   Test items that require furnishing the correct response, such as short-answer completion or essay-test items.

Symbolic stage   After Bruner, the third and final stage of development, which begins with the systematic use of language and is characterized by use of symbol systems, as in language, mathematics, and science. See *enactive stage* or *iconic representation.*

Synesthesia   A condition in which the experience of a stimulus or object is regularly linked with images in a different sensory mode. Example: experiencing sounds as colors.

Synthesis   One of the higher levels of the *Taxonomy of Educational Objectives,* referring to cognitive processes that require putting pieces of things together to form a whole. Example: synthesizing the causes of the Civil War.

Targeting error   Identifying or disciplining the wrong person when calling attention to student misbehavior.

Task analysis   The process used for identifying the step-by-step procedures needed to accomplish something. Example: The precise steps, skills needed, and prerequisite knowledge to multiply three-digit numbers by three-digit numbers.

Taxonomy   A system of classification. Often applied to educational objectives, such as the *Taxonomy of Educational Objectives.*

Taxonomy of Educational Objectives   Developed by Benjamin Bloom and his colleagues, sometimes referred to as Bloom's taxonomy, classifies objectives of education from the lowest levels of cognition (knowledge, rote memory) through to the higher levels of cognitive activity (analysis, synthesis, evaluation).

Teaching method   A recurrent pattern of teaching behavior, applicable to various subject matters, characteristic of more than one teacher, and relevant to learning.

Teaching practice   A component of a *teaching method.* Examples: questioning during recitation, using overheads during lectures.

Team-Assisted Individualization (TAI)   Developed by Slavin, whereby students in heterogeneous small groups study together and test each other, freeing the teacher from many monitoring and testing duties. Scores for teams and students are evaluated against preset standards.

Teams-Games-Tournaments (TGT) Developed by Slavin, an achievement game whereby teams of three students, matched on ability, compete against each other for rewards that go to their teams.

Terminal performance Behavior indicating that an educational objective has been achieved. It is the end at which an instructional effort is aimed. Examples: reciting the alphabet, solving a quadratic equation.

Test One or more questions or problems used for estimating a person's ability, achievement, or aptitude and calling on the person to perform at the highest level of which he or she is capable.

Test bias The degree to which a test contains content or requires behavior that is more frequently found in one cultural group than another. Often considered as a possible explanation of group differences in average test scores.

Test-retest reliability One method of estimating the *reliability* of a test, obtained by administering the same test to the same individuals two or more times. The *coefficient of correlation* obtained is the estimate of reliability.

Thematic Apperception Test (TAT) A projective test developed by Henry A. Murray for the measurement of psychological needs, e.g., need for achievement, affiliation, power. Consists of ambiguous pictures about which the person being tested is asked to create stories.

Theory A set of organized ideas—concepts and their relationships, or principles—used to describe systematically a set of phenomena or to provide an explanation of those phenomena. Examples: attribution theory, operant conditioning theory, measurement theory.

Theory of identical elements See *identical elements*.

Time-on-task (time-on-target) The amount of time a student is actually attending to the tasks that were assigned or are appropriate for that subject matter. More than *engaged time*. This is engaged time on the appropriate task.

Time-out A form of *punishment 2* consisting of keeping a person from access to desirable things or activities for a specified time.

Timing error Intervening in student misbehavior at the wrong time. Examples: intervening too soon, when misbehavior might have stopped by itself; intervening too late, after the misbehavior is out of hand and affecting others.

Token economy An economic system (wages for work) using tokens to strengthen the display of appropriate behavior.

Token reinforcement Reinforcement by means of physical or symbolic things, such as coins, disks, or stars, which the students can exchange for other desired things or activities, such as toys or free time.

Top-down processing A way of cognitive functioning that imposes organization by examining information with a broad and inclusive schema and then uses more specific and less inclusive ideas to comprehend events. In reading, it emphasizes that what the reader brings to the text is at least as important as what is in the text for making sense of what is there. Contrast *bottom-up processing*.

Tracking See *ability grouping*.

Trait A stable and general way of behaving that manifests itself in a wide variety of situations. Trait anxiety is anxiety that the individual experiences more or less continuously regardless of the situation.

Transfer The process whereby learning in one situation influences subsequent behavior in a more or less different situation. Substantive transfer refers to the number of identical elements present in each situation (driving a car, driving a truck). Procedural transfer refers to the principles that are present in each situation (playing hockey, playing soccer). Transfer may be positive, facilitating learning or desirable behavior, or negative, interfering with learning or desirable behavior.

Transitional (connective) relationship A lecture organization that shows how one idea provides a basis for moving on to another.

True score The hypothetical mean of the scores that an individual would receive if he or she took a test an infinite number of times under the same conditions.

True-false items Test items in the form of statements to which the individual responds "true" or "false."

Trust versus mistrust After Erikson, the crisis in infancy in which one learns the degree to which other persons can be counted on.

T-score A standardized score scale, with a mean of 50 and a standard deviation of 10, derived from *z-scores*. $T = 50 + 10z$ eliminates the negative values and decimals that characterize *z*-scores.

Tutoring   Teaching one student at a time. Tutor may be a teacher, aide, older student, or peer.

Unalterable variable   A variable such as gender, *intelligence, socioeconomic status,* motor coordination, that is not easily if at all alterable by teachers or schools. Contrast *alterable variable.*

Unconditioned response (UR)   The response, muscular or glandular, that an individual makes when presented with an *unconditioned stimulus (US).* The US-UR connection is built into the individual's nervous system. Example: pupillary contraction when the eye is stimulated by light. The concept of UR is used in *classical conditioning* theory.

Unconditioned stimulus (US)   A stimulus event that naturally elicits an *unconditioned response (UR).* The US-UR connection is built into the organism's nervous system. Example: food in the mouth (US) increases salivation (UR). See *classical conditioning.*

Underachiever   A student whose classroom performances or achievement test scores are quite a bit lower than would be expected given his or her aptitude or intelligence test scores.

Unintentional reinforcement   Reinforcement, as by a teacher, of behavior that the teacher did not intend to reinforce. Example: attention to misbehavior such that the misbehavior is reinforced or strengthened.

Validity   The degree to which a test measures what it is intended to measure (see *construct validity, content validity,* and *criterion validity*).

Variability   The degree to which the measures, scores, or values of a variable cluster or spread widely around the average, or central tendency, of the measures. Example of variability measures: *standard deviation.*

Variable   A concept that can take on different qualitative or quantitative values. Examples: gender (male, female), IQ.

Variable-interval schedule   A system of reinforcement whereby the amount of time between reinforcers varies. Example: one reinforcer for a correct response every 30 seconds, then one reinforcer for a correct response every 60 seconds, then one every 25 seconds, etc.

Variable-ratio schedule   A system of reinforcement whereby the ratio of reinforcers to desired responses changes from one set of responses to another. Example: one reinforcer for each response, one reinforcer for every five responses, then one reinforcer for every three responses.

Variance   The standard deviation squared. A measure of variability. Compare *standard deviation, variability.* (Has advantages over the standard deviation for some statistical purposes. Sometimes used as a synonym for variability.)

Verbal intelligence   Skill in answering questions or solving problems requiring knowledge of word meanings and their relationships, as in synonyms, antonyms, analogies, and paragraph comprehension.

Verbal markers of importance   In lectures, indicating which points are important and should be attended to in more depth. Example: "Now this is a key factor . . ."

Vicarious reinforcement   Effects on behavior from observing the *reinforcement contingencies* of another person. An important concept in *social learning theory.*

Wait time I   The time between the end of a teacher's thought-provoking question and a student's being called on to answer the question.

Wait time II   The time between the end of a student's response and the beginning of the teacher's commenting on that response.

Withitness   After Kunin, a characteristic of teacher behavior whereby the teacher exhibits awareness of what is going on in the classroom even when not obviously looking at or listening to the students being attended to.

Working memory (WM)   Used in information-processing models of memory to describe the focus of attention. Sometimes viewed as identical to *short-term memory (STM),* sometimes distinguished from STM.

Yielding   Going along with a group even though you believe them to be wrong.

Zone of proximal development   From Vygotsky, the difference between what children can do on their own and what they can do under adult guidance and tutelage.

z-score   A standardized score, with a mean of 0 and a standard deviation of 1. $z = (X - M)/\text{SD}$, where X = raw score, M = arithmetic mean, and SD = standard deviation.

Author-Reference Index

Number following dash indicates page on which work is cited. Some major entries are annotated. "MP" citations refer to the four-color Multiple Perspectives sections.

Airasian, P. W. (1991). *Classroom assessment.* New York: McGraw-Hill.—516, 545, 552, 554, 567, 586

Airasian, P. W. (1996). *Assessment in the classroom.* New York: McGraw-Hill.—516

Algozzine, R. F. (1977). Perceived attractiveness and classroom interactions. *Journal of Experimental Education, 46,* 63–66.—472

Allen, M., & Bourhis, J. (1995). *The relationship of communication apprehension to communication behavior: A meta-analysis.* ERIC Document Reproduction Service No. ED379706.—373

Alloway, N. (1984). *Teacher expectations.* Paper presented at the meeting of the Australian Association for Research in Education, Perth.—70

Allport, G. W., & Odbert, H. S. (1936). Trait-names: A psycholexical study. *Psychological Monographs, 47*(211).—136

Alschuler, A. S. (1967). *The Achievement Motivation Development Project: A summary and review* (Occasional Paper No. 3). Cambridge, MA: Center for Research and Development on Educational Differences, Harvard University. (Cooperative Research Project of the Office of Education, Department of Health, Education, and Welfare, Contract No. OE5–10–239.)—340

Alschuler, A. S. (1968). *How to increase motivation through climate and structure* (Working Paper No. 8). Cambridge, MA: Achievement Motivation Development Project, Graduate School of Education, Harvard University.—345, 346, 347

American Association on Mental Retardation. (1992). *Mental retardation: Definition, classification, and systems of support workbook.* Washington, DC: Author.—185

American Federation of Teachers, National Council on Measurement in Education, National Education Association (1990). Standards for teacher competence in educational assessment of students. *Educational Measurement: Issues and Practice, 9*(4), 30–32.—509

American Psychological Association. (1975). Proceedings for the year 1974: Minutes of the annual meeting of the Council of Representatives. *American Psychologist, 30,* 620–651.—467–468

Ames, C., & Ames, R. (1984). Goal structures and motivation. *Elementary School Journal, 85,* 39–52.—329

Ames, R. (1982). Teachers' attributions for their own teaching. In J. M. Levine & M. C. Wang (Eds.), *Teacher and student perceptions.* Hillsdale, NJ: Erlbaum.—326

Anastasi, A. (1958). *Differential psychology* (3d ed.). New York: Macmillan. *A comprehensive, lucidly written textbook on differences (gender, race, class, and the like) between individuals and groups in intelligence and many other dimensions. Newer editions are available.*—85

Anastasi, A. (1980). Abilities and the measurement of achievement. In W. B. Schrader (Ed.), *New directions for testing and measurement* (No. 5). San Francisco: Jossey-Bass.—539

Anastasi, A. (1981). Coaching, test sophistication and developed abilities. *American Psychologist, 36,* 1086–1093.—541

Anastasi, A. (1986). Intelligence as a quality of behavior. In R. J. Sternberg & D. K. Detterman (Eds.), *What is intelligence?* Norwood, NJ: Ablex.—51

Anastasiow, N. J., Hanes, M. P., & Hanes, M. L. (1982). *Language and reading strategies for poverty children.* Baltimore: University Book Press.—118, 121

Anderson, L. (Ed.). (1995). *International encyclopedia of teaching and teacher education* (2d ed.). Oxford: Pergamon.—477

Anderson, L. M., Evertson, C. M., & Brophy, J. E. (1979). An experimental study of effective teaching in first-grade reading groups. *Elementary School Journal, 79,* 193–223. *A carefully performed experiment, with real teachers, showing that teachers can be trained to help students improve achievement.*—9, 486, 488

Anderson, R. C. (1972). How to construct achievement tests to assess comprehension. *Review of Educational Research, 42,* 145–170. *Provides a method for changing memory questions into higher-order questions.*—573

Anderson, R. C. (1974). Concretization and sentence learning. *Journal of Educational Psychology, 66,* 179–183.—266

Anderson, R. C., & Pearson, P. D. (1985). A schema theoretic view of basic processes in reading comprehension. In P. D. Pearson, R. Barr, M. Kamil, & P. Mosenthel (Eds.), *Handbook of reading research.* White Plains, NY: Longman.—298

Anderson, R. C., & Pichert, J. W. (1978). Recall of previously unrecallable information following a shift in perspective. *Journal of Verbal Learning and Verbal Behavior, 17,* 1–12.—294

Anderson, R. C., Reynolds, R. E., Schallert, D. L., & Goetz, E. T. (1977). Frameworks for comprehending discourse. *American Educational Research Journal, 14,* 367–381.—293

Anderson, R. C., Spiro, R. J., & Anderson, M. C. (1978). Schemata as scaffolding for the representation of information in connected discourse. *American Educational Research Journal, 15,* 433–440.—293

Andrews, G. R., & Debus, R. L. (1978). Persistence and the causal perception of failure: Modifying cognitive attributions. *Journal of Educational Psychology, 70,* 154–166.—341–342

Angoff, W. H. (1988). The nature-nurture debate, aptitudes, and group differences. *American Psychologist, 43,* 713–720. *Points out that high heritability is compatible with the high alterability of a human characteristic.*—65

Annis, L. F. (1983). The processes and effects of peer tutoring. *Human Learning, 2,* 39–47.—441

Applebee, A. (1981). *Writing in the secondary schools: English and the content areas.* Urbana, IL: National Council of Teachers of English.—257

Applegate, J. R. (1969). Why don't pupils talk in class discussions? *The Clearing House, 44,* 78–81.—417

Arias, M. B., & Casanova, U. (1993). *Bilingual education: Politics, practice, and research: Ninety-second yearbook of the National Society for the Study of Education* (Pt. 2). Chicago: University of Chicago Press.—124

Aronoff, J., Raymond, N., & Warmoth, A. (1965). *The Kennedy-Jefferson school district: A report of neighborhood study in progress.* Unpublished manuscript, Graduate School of Education, Harvard University, Cambridge, MA.—340

Asch, S. E. (1956). Studies of independence and conformity. A minority of one against a unanimous majority. *Psychological Monographs, 70* (9, Whole No. 416). *A seminal study demonstrating the powerful effect of group opinion on personal judgment.*—414

Ashton, P. T., & Webb, R. B. (1986). *Making a difference: Teachers' sense of efficacy and student achievement.* White Plains, NY: Longman.—351

Ausubel, D. P. (1960). The use of advance organizers in the learning and retention of meaningful verbal learning. *Journal of Educational Psychology, 51,* 267–272.—377

Ausubel, D. P. (1963). *The psychology of meaningful verbal learning.* New York: Grune & Stratton.—502

Ausubel, D. P. (1968). *Educational psychology: A cognitive view.* New York: Holt, Rinehart, & Winston.—289

Ausubel, D. P. (1978). In defense of advance organizers: A reply to the critics. *Review of Educational Research, 48,* 251–257.—289, 290

Ayers, S. J. (1987). *Gifted and talented evaluation: Practices, problems, and recommendations.* ERIC Document Reproduction Service No. ED334795.—199

Azrin, N. H., & Holz, W. C. (1966). Punishment. In W. K. Honig (Ed.), *Operant behavior: Areas of research and application* (pp. 380–447). New York: Appleton-Century-Crofts.—228

Bailey, J., & McTighe, J. (1996). Reporting achievement at the secondary level: What and how. In T. R. Guskey (Ed.), *Communicating student learning. ASCD yearbook, 1996* (pp. 119–140). Alexandria, VA: Association for Supervision and Curriculum Development.—595, 597

Baker, E. L., & Niemi, D. (1996). School and program evaluation. In D. C. Berliner & R. C.

Calfee (Eds.), *Handbook of educational psychology* (pp. 926–944). New York: Macmillan.—000

Bandura, A. (1963). The role of imitation in personality development. *Journal of Nursery Education, 18,* 207–215.—235

Bandura A. (1969). *Principles of behavior modification.* New York: Holt, Rinehart, & Winston. *An authoritative development of operant conditioning, observation, and other theories of learning and their application to a variety of practical problems.*—234, 237

Bandura, A. (1977). *Social learning theory.* Englewood Cliffs, NJ: Prentice-Hall.—208, 237, 239

Bandura, A. (1978). The self system in reciprocal determinism. *American Psychologist, 33,* 344–358.—243

Bandura, A. (1986a). From thought to action: Mechanisms of personal agency. *New Zealand Journal of Psychology, 15,* 1–17.—241

Bandura, A. (1986b). *Social foundations of thought and action: A social-cognitive theory.* Englewood Cliffs, NJ: Prentice-Hall. *The melding of social learning theory with cognitive psychological concerns to provide, among other things, a picture of how competence and efficiency are learned.*—237, 241, 245

Bandura, A. (1989). Regulation of cognitive processes through perceived self-efficacy. *Developmental Psychology, 25,* 729–735.—245

Bandura, A. (1993). Perceived self-efficacy in cognitive development and functioning. *Educational Psychologist, 28,* 117–148.—348, 352

Bandura, A., & Schunk, D. H. (1981). Cultivating competence, self-efficacy, and intrinsic interest through proximal self-motivation. *Journal of Personality and Social Psychology, 41,* 586–598.—354

Banks, J. A. (1993). Multicultural education: Characteristics and goals. In J. A. Banks & C. A. M. Banks (Eds.), *Multicultural education: Issues and perspectives* (2d ed., pp. 3–28). Needham Heights, MA: Allyn & Bacon.—151, 152, 155

Banks, J. A., & Banks, C. A. M., Eds. (1993). *Multicultural education: Issues and perspectives* (2d ed.). Needham Heights, MA: Allyn & Bacon. *Chapters by many who see the United States as a pluralistic society, strengthened by its diversity, not weakened by it.*—165

Barabasz, M., & Barabasz, A. (1996). Attention deficit disorder. Diagnosis, etiology and treatment. *Child Study Journal, 26*(1), 1–37.—231

Baratz, D. (1983). *How justified is the "obvious reaction"?* Unpublished doctoral dissertation, Stanford University, Stanford, CA.—10

Barker, R. G., Dembo, T., & Lewin, K. (1943). Frustration and regression: An experiment with young children. In R. G. Barker, J. S. Kounin, & H. F. Wright (Eds.), *Child behavior and development.* New York: McGraw-Hill.—339

Baron, J. B. (1990). Performance assessment: Blurring the edges among assessment, curriculum, and instruction. In A. B. Champagne, B. E. Lovitts, & B. J. Calinger (Eds.), *Assessment in the service of instruction* (pp. 127–147). Washington, DC: American Association for the Advancement of Science.—560

Baron, J. B. (1991). Strategies for the development of effective performance exercises. *Applied Measurement in Education, 4,* 305–318.—561

Baron, J. B., & Wolf, D. P. (Eds.). (1996). *Performance-based student assessment: Challenges and possibilities: Ninety-fifth yearbook of the National Society for the Study of Education.* Chicago: University of Chicago Press.—546, 559

Bar-Tal, D. (1979). Interactions of teachers and pupils. In I. H. Frieze, D. Bar-Tal, & J. S. Carroll (Eds.), *New approaches to social problems: Applications of attribution theory.* San Francisco: Jossey-Bass.—326

Bar-Tal, D. (1982). The effects of teachers' behavior on pupils' attributions: A review. In C. Antaki & C. Brieson (Eds.), *Attribution and psychological change: A guide to the use of attribution theory in the clinic and the classroom.* London: Academic Press.—342

Bar-Tal, D., & Darom, E. (1979). Pupils' attributions of success and failure. *Child Development, 50,* 264–267.—323

Bar-Tal, D., Raviv, A., & Bar-Tal, Y. (1982). Consistency of pupils' attributions regarding success and failure. *Journal of Educational Psychology, 74,* 104–110.—325

Bauer, P. J. (1996). What do infants recall of their lives? *American Psychologist, 51,* 29–41.—107

Beaton, A. E., Martin, M. O., Mullis, I. V. S., Gonzalez, E. J., Smith, T. A., & Kelly, D. L. (1996a). *Science achievement in the middle school years. IEA's Third International Mathematics and Science Study (TIMSS).* Chestnut Hill, MA: Boston College.—496, 499

Beaton, A. E., Mullis, I. V. S., Martin, M. O., Gonzalez, E. J., Kelly, D. L., & Smith, T. A.

(1996b). *Mathematics achievement in the middle school years. IEA's Third International Mathematics and Science Study (TIMSS).* Chestnut Hill, MA: Boston College.—496, 499

Beck, I. L., & Carpenter, P. A. (1986). Cognitive approaches to understanding reading. *American Psychologist, 41,* 1098–1105.—298

Beilin, H. (1980). Piaget's theory: Refinement, revision, or rejection? In R. H. Kluwe & H. Spada (Eds.), *Developmental models of thinking.* New York: Academic Press.—109

Beilin, H. (1992). Piaget's enduring contribution to developmental psychology. *Developmental Psychology, 28,* 191–204.—98, 109

Bellack, A. A. (1976). *Studies in the language of the classroom.* Paper presented at the First International Conference on Research and Teaching, Memorial University of Newfoundland, St. John's.—455

Bellack, A. A., Kliebard, H. M., Hyman, R. T., & Smith, F. L. (1966). *The language of the classroom.* New York: Teachers College Press. *The classroom "game" described on the basis of thorough analyses of what was said by teachers and students in 15 tenth- and twelfth-grade economics classes.*—454, 479

Bellezza, F. S. (1981). Mnemonic devices: Classification, characteristics and criteria. *Review of Educational Research, 51,* 247–275.—267

Bereiter, C. (1994). Constructivism, socioculturalism, and Popper's world 3. *Educational Researcher, 23*(7), 21–23.—256

Bergquist, W. H., & Phillips, S. R. (1989). Classroom structures which encourage student participation. In R. A. Neff & M. Weiner (Eds.), *Classroom communication: Collected readings for effective discussion and questioning* (pp. 19–23). Madison, WI: Magna.—400

Berk, R. A. (1980). *Criterion-referenced measurement: The state of the art.* Baltimore: Johns Hopkins University Press.—521

Berk, R. A. (Ed.). (1982). *Handbook of methods for detecting test bias.* Baltimore: Johns Hopkins University Press.—85

Berliner, D. C. (1968). *The effects of testlike events and note taking on learning from lecture instruction.* Unpublished doctoral dissertation, Stanford University, Stanford, CA.—390

Berliner, D. C. (1982). Instructional variables. In D. E. Orlosky (Ed.), *Introduction to education.* Columbus, OH: Merrill.—353

Berliner, D. C. (1990). What's all the fuss about instructional time? In M. Ben-Peretz & R. Bromme (Eds.), *The nature of time in schools* (pp. 3–35). New York: Teachers College Press.—14, 493

Berliner, D. C. (1992). The nature of expertise in teaching. In F. K. Oser, A. Dick, & J.-L. Patry (Eds.), *Effective and responsible teaching* (pp. 227–248). San Francisco: Jossey-Bass.—44

Berliner, D. C. (1994). Expertise: The wonders of exemplary performance. In J. N. Mangieri & C. C. Block (Eds.), *Creating powerful thinking in teachers and students* (pp. 161–186). Fort Worth, TX: Holt, Rinehart, & Winston. *An overview of what we know about expertise in teaching.*—279, 280, 281, 283

Berliner, D. C. (1997). Educational psychology meets the Christian Right: Differing views of children, schooling, teaching, and learning. *Teachers College Record, 98*(3), 381–415.—278

Berliner, D. C., & Biddle, B. J. (1995). *The manufactured crisis.* New York: Longman. *Defends against recent criticisms of American education, in part, on grounds that they ignore or distort the results of recent valid research.*—32, 61, 319, 352, 534, 536

Berliner, D. C., & Biddle, B. J. (1996). Standards amidst uncertainty and inequality. *School Administrator, 53*(5), 42–45.—32

Berliner, D. C., & Calfee, R. C. (Eds.). (1996). *Handbook of educational psychology.* New York: Macmillan. *This first handbook in the field contains 33 authoritative chapters in its 1,071 pages.*—22

Berlyne, D. E. (1965). Curiosity and education. In J. D. Krumboltz (Ed.), *Learning and the educational process* (pp. 67–89). Chicago: Rand McNally.—356

Bigler, R. S., & Liben, L. S. (1992). Cognitive mechanisms in children's gender stereotyping: Theoretical and educational implications of a cognitive-based intervention. *Child Development, 63,* 1351–1363.—173

Bligh, D. A. (1972). *What's the use of lectures?* (2d ed.). Harmondsworth, Eng.: Penguin.—370, 379

Block, C. C. (1994). Developing problem-solving abilities. In J. N. Mangieri & C. C. Block (Eds.), *Creating powerful thinking in teachers and students* (pp. 141–160). Fort Worth, TX: Harcourt Brace.—288

Block, N. J. (1995). How heritability misleads about race. *Cognition, 56,* 99–128. *Distinguishes between heritability and genetic determination.*—64–65, 83

Block, N. J., & Dworkin, G. (Eds.). (1976). *The IQ controversy.* New York: Random House.—61

Bloom, B. S. (1964). *Stability and change in human characteristics.* New York: Wiley. *Puts forth the thesis that most of what we call intelligence is determined by age eight; a technical report that provides a rationale for early childhood education programs.*—55

Bloom, B. S. (1968). Learning for mastery. *Evaluation Comment, 1*(2). University of California Center for the Study of Evaluation, Los Angeles.—436–437, 438

Bloom, B. S. (1980). The new direction in educational research: Alterable variables. In *The state of research on selected alterable variables in education* (Mesa Seminar, 1980). Chicago: Department of Education, University of Chicago. *The provocative statement by a ranking scholar concerning advantages of research on variables that we can do something about.*—12

Bloom, B. S. (Ed.). (1985). *Developing talent in young people.* New York: Ballantine. *Case studies of high-achieving people in very different fields, and the commonalities in their education and training.*—143

Bloom, B. S., Engelhart, M. D., Furst, E. J., Hill, W. H., & Krathwohl, D. R. (1956). *Taxonomy of educational objectives. The classification of educational goals,* Handbook 1: *Cognitive domain.* New York: Longmans, Green. *"Bloom's taxonomy," the classic attempt to bring order into the welter of what teachers say they want their students to learn.*—41

Bloome, D., & Lemke, J. (Eds.). (1995). Special Issue: Africanized English and education. *Linguistics and Education, 7.*—122

Blumenfeld, P. C., Pintrich, P. R., & Hamilton, V. L. (1986). Children's concepts of ability, effort, and conduct. *American Educational Research Journal, 23,* 95–104.—324

Blumenfeld, P. C., Soloway, E., Marx, R. W., Krajck, J. S., Guzdial, M., & Palincsar, A. (1991). Motivating project-based learning: Sustaining the doing, supporting the learning. *Educational Psychologist, 26*(3 & 4), 369–398.—422

Boden, M. A. (1980). *Jean Piaget.* New York: Viking.—107

Borg, W. R. (1975). Protocol materials as related to teacher performance and pupil achievement. *Journal of Educational Research, 69,* 23–30.—482

Borg, W. R., & Ascione, F. R. (1982). Classroom management in elementary mainstreaming classrooms. *Journal of Educational Psychology, 74,* 85–95. *A demonstration of the possibility and value of significant experiments in real classrooms.*—470

Bouchard, T. J., Jr. (1993). The genetic architecture of human intelligence. In P. A. Vernon (Ed.), *Biological approaches to the study of human intelligence* (pp. 33–93). Norwood, NJ: Ablex.—63

Bouchard, T. J., Jr., Lykken, D. T., McGue, M., Segal, N. L., & Tellegen, A. (1990). Sources of human psychological differences: The Minnesota study of twins reared apart. *Science, 250,* 223–228.—65

Bough, J. (1983). *Black street speech: Its history, structure and survival.* Austin: University of Texas Press.—122

Bower, G. H., Karlin, M. B., & Dueck, A. (1975). Comprehension and memory for pictures. *Memory and Cognition, 3,* 216–220.—261

Boyatzis, C. J. et al. (1995). Effects of "The Mighty Morphin Power Rangers" on children's aggression with peers. *Child Study Journal, 25,* 45–55.—465

Bracey, G. W. (1996). The sixth Bracey report on the condition of public education. *Phi Delta Kappan, 78,* 127–138.—430

Brainard, C. J. (1978a). *Piaget's theory of intelligence.* Englewood Cliffs, NJ: Prentice-Hall.—100, 107

Brainard, C. J. (1978b). The stage question in cognitive-developmental theory. *Behavioral and Brain Sciences, 2,* 173–213.—100

Bransford, J. D., & Johnson, M. K. (1972). Contextual prerequisites for understanding. Some investigations of comprehension and recall. *Journal of Verbal Learning and Verbal Behavior, 11,* 717–726.—294

Braswell, L., & Bloomquist, M. L. (1991). *Cognitive-behavioral therapy with ADHD children.* New York: Guilford Press.—195

Bridgeman, B., & Shipman, V. C. (1978). Preschool measures of self-esteem and achievement motivation as predictors of third-grade achievement. *Journal of Educational Psychology, 70,* 17–28.—146

Bridges, E. M. (1986). *The incompetent teacher: The challenge and the response.* Philadelphia: Palmer Press. *An approach to the problem of how a school administration can cope with an incompetent teacher.*—464

Bridgham, R. G. (1972a). Ease of grading and enrollments in secondary school science, Pt. 1: A model and its possible tests. *Journal of Research in Science Teaching, 9,* 323–329.—585

Bridgham, R. G. (1972b). Ease of grading and enrollments in secondary school science, Pt. 2: A test of the model. *Journal of Research in Science Teaching, 9,* 331–343.—585

Brigham, F. J., Scruggs, T. E., & Mastropieri, M. A. (1992). Teacher enthusiasm in learning disabilities classrooms: Effects on learning and behavior. *Learning Disabilities Research and Practice, 7*(2), 68–73.—393

Broadwell, M. M. (1980). *The lecture method of instruction,* D. G. Langdon (Ed.). Englewood Cliffs, NJ: Educational Technology Publications.—MP 3, Chapter 9

Brody, N. (1992). *Intelligence* (2d ed.). San Diego: Academic Press.—90

Brophy, J. E. (1981). Teacher praise: A functional analysis. *Review of Educational Research, 51,* 5–32. *The most comprehensive and circumspect analysis of an age-old topic, based on careful observation and research to an unprecedented degree.*—354, 489

Brophy, J. E. (1987). On motivating students. In D. C. Berliner & B. V. Rosenshine (Eds.), *Talks to teachers: A Festschrift for N. L. Gage* (pp. 201–245). New York: Random House.—352

Brophy, J. E., & Evertson, C. M. (1974). *Process-product correlations in the Texas teacher effectiveness study: Final report* (Research Rep. No. 74–4). Austin: Research and Development Center for Teacher Education, University of Texas.—486, 487–488

Brophy, J. E., & Evertson, C. M. (1976). *Learning from teaching: A developmental perspective.* Boston: Allyn & Bacon.—358

Brophy, J. E., & Good, T. L. (1986). Teacher behavior and student achievement. In M. W. Wittrock (Ed.), *Handbook of research on teaching* (3d ed., pp. 328–375). New York: Macmillan.—9, 477

Brophy, J. E., Rohrkemper, M. M., Rashad, H., & Goldberger, M. (1983). Relationships between teachers' presentations of classroom tasks and students' engagement in those tasks. *Journal of Educational Psychology, 75,* 544–552.—352

Broudy, H. S. (1963). Historic exemplars of teaching method. In N. L. Gage (Ed.), *Handbook of research on teaching* (pp. 1–43). Chicago: Rand McNally. *A brief but scholarly introduction to great thinkers about teaching from the Sophists (fifth century B.C.) to Herbart (1893).*—388

Brown, A. L. (1978). Knowing when, where, and how to remember: A problem of metacognition. In R. Glaser (Ed.), *Advances in instructional psychology.* Hillsdale, NJ: Erlbaum.—270

Brown, A. L. (1980). Metacognitive development and reading. In R. J. Spiro, B. C. Bruce, & W. F. Brewer (Eds.), *Theoretical issues in reading comprehension.* Hillsdale, NJ: Erlbaum.—270

Brown, A. L. (1994). The advancement of learning. *Educational Researcher, 23*(8), 4–12.—108, 286

Brown, A. L., Armbruster, B. B., & Baker, L. (1985). The role of metacognition in reading and studying. In J. Orasanu (Ed.), *Reading comprehension: From research to practice.* Hillsdale, NJ: Erlbaum.—272

Brown, A. L., Ash, D., Rutherford, M., Nakagawa, K., Gordon, A., & Campione, J. (1993). Distributed expertise in the classroom. In G. Salomon (Ed.), *Distributed cognitions: Psychological and educational considerations* (pp. 188–228). New York: Cambridge University Press.—286, 423, 424

Brown, A. L., Bransford, J. D., Ferrara, R. A., & Campione, J. C. (1983). Learning, remembering, and understanding. In J. H. Flavell & E. M. Markman (Eds.), *Handbook of child psychology,* Vol. 3: *Cognitive development* (4th ed.). New York: Wiley.—272

Brown, A. L., & Campione, J. C. (1986). Psychological theory and the study of learning disabilities. *American Psychologist, 41,* 1059–1068.—298

Brown, A. L., & Palincsar, A. S. (1982). Inducing strategic learning from texts by means of informal, self-control training. *Topics in Learning and Learning Disabilities, 2*(1), 1–16.—271

Brown, D. S. (1988). Twelve middle school teachers' planning. *Elementary School Journal, 89,* 69–87.—464

Brown, J. S., & Burton, R. R. (1979). Diagnostic models for procedural bugs in basic mathematical skills. In R. W. Tyler & S. H. White (Eds.),

Testing, teaching, and learning. Washington, DC: National Institute of Education.—576

Brown, J. S., Collins, A., & Duguid, P. (1989). Situated cognition and the culture of learning. *Educational Researcher, 18,* 32–42.—286, 305

Bruer, J. T. (1993). *Schools for thought: A science of learning in the classroom.* Cambridge, MA: MIT Press.—286, 493, 501

Bruner, J. S. (1960). *The process of education.* Cambridge, MA: Harvard University Press.—274, MP 2, Chapter 5

Bruner, J. S. (1966). *Toward a theory of instruction.* Cambridge, MA: Harvard University Press. *Insightful comments about teaching by a distinguished developmental psychologist.*—97, 109–111

Bruner, J. S. (1973). *The relevance of education.* New York: Norton.—109

Bruner, J. S. (1990). *Acts of meaning.* Cambridge, MA: Harvard University Press. *Essays on education by one of the seminal psychologists of our times.*—114

Bruner, J. (1996). *The culture of education.* Cambridge, MA: Harvard University Press, p. 127.—MP 3, Chapter 9

Bullivant, B. M. (1993). Culture: Its nature and meaning for educators. In J. A. Banks & C. A. M. Banks (Eds.), *Multicultural education: Issues and perspectives* (2d ed., pp. 29–47). Needham Heights, MA: Allyn & Bacon.—151

Bullough, R. V., Jr. (1989). *First-year teacher: A case study.* New York: Teachers College Press.—283

Bullough, R. V., Jr., & Baughman, K. (1997). *A teacher's journey: First-year teacher revisited.* New York: Teachers College Press.—283

Bursuck, W. D. (Ed.). (1994). Special series on homework. *Journal of Learning Disabilities, 27,* 466–509.—431

Butler, R., & Nisan, M. (1986). Effects of no feedback, task-related comments, and grades on intrinsic motivation and performance. *Journal of Educational Psychology, 78,* 210–216.—335

Byrne, B. M. (1984). The general/academic self-concept nomological network: A review of construct validation research. *Review of Educational Research, 54,* 427–456.—146

Cahan, S., & Cohen, N. (1989). Age versus schooling effects on intelligence development. *Child Development, 60,* 1239–1249.—68

Calderhead, J. (1996). Teachers: Beliefs and knowledge. In D. C. Berliner & R. C. Calfee (Eds.), *Handbook of educational psychology* (pp. 709–725). New York: Macmillan.—552

Cameron, J., & Pierce, W. D. (1994). Reinforcement, reward, and intrinsic motivation: A meta-analysis. *Review of Educational Research, 64,* 363–423.—335

Camp, R. (1990, March). *Presentations on arts propel portfolio explorations: Seminar on alternatives to multiple-choice assessment.* Princeton, NJ: Educational Testing Service.—593, 594

Campbell, F. A., & Ramey, C. T. (1995). Cognitive and school outcomes for high-risk African-American students at middle adolescence: Positive effects of early intervention. *American Educational Research Journal, 32,* 744–772.—91, 92, 93

Campione, J. C., & Armbruster, B. B. (1985). Acquiring information from texts: An analysis of four approaches. In J. W. Segal, S. F. Chipman, & R. Glaser (Eds.), *Thinking and learning skills.* Vol. 1: *Relating instruction to research* (pp. 317–359). Hillsdale, NJ: Erlbaum.—112

Campione, J. C., Brown, A. L., & Jay, M. (1992). Computers in a community of learners. In E. De Corte, M. C. Linn, H. Mandle, & L. Verschaffel (Eds.), *Computer-based learning environments and problem solving.* Berlin: Springer.—298

Capron, C., & Duyme, M. (1989). Assessment of the effects of socio-economic status on IQ in a full cross-fostering study. *Nature, 340*(6234), 552–554.—80, 88

Carey, D. M. (1993). Teacher roles and technology integration: Moving from teacher as director to teacher as facilitator. *Computers in the Schools, 9,* 105–118.—449

Carey, S. (1985). Are children fundamentally different kinds of thinkers and learners than adults? In S. F. Chipman, J. W. Segal, & R. Glaser (Eds.), *Thinking and learning skills.* Vol 2: *Research and open questions.* Hillsdale, NJ: Erlbaum.—107

Carey, S. (1986). Cognitive science and science education. *American Psychologist, 41,* 1123–1130.—297

Carpenter, T. C., Fennema, E., Peterson, P. L., Chiang, C., & Loef, M. (1989). Using knowledge of children's mathematics thinking in classroom teaching: An experimental study. *American*

Educational Research Journal, 26, 499–532.—295

Carroll, J. B. (1963). A model of school learning. *Teachers College Record, 64,* 723–733. *An early statement of the model of learning that underlies the mastery approach in instruction.*—437

Carroll, J. B. (1993). *Human cognitive abilities: A survey of factor-analytic studies.* New York: Cambridge University Press. *A major synthesis of the empirical studies of the organization of human intelligence.*—56, 75, 78

Carter, D. B., & Levy, G. D. (1988). Cognitive aspects of children's early sex-role development: The influence of gender schemas on preschoolers' memories and preferences for sex-typed toys and activities. *Child Development, 59,* 782–793.—169

Carter, K., Sabers, D., Cushing, K., Pinnegar, S., & Berliner, D. C. (1987). Processing and using information about students: A study of expert, novice, and postulant teachers. *Teaching and Teacher Education, 3,* 147–157.—143, 552

Casanova, U. (1996). Parent involvement: A call for prudence. *Educational Researcher, 25*(5), 30–32.—168

Case, R. (1978). A developmentally based theory and technology of instruction. *Review of Educational Research, 48,* 439–463.—107

Case, R. (1993). Theories of learning and theories of development. *Educational Psychologist, 28,* 219–233.—108

Case, R. (Ed.). (1991). *The mind's staircase: Stages in the development of human intelligence.* Hillsdale, NJ: Erlbaum.—108

Case, R., & Griffin, S. (1990). Child cognitive development: The role of central conceptual structures in the development of scientific and social thought. In C. A. Havert (Ed.), *Developmental psychology: Cognitive, perceptual, motor, and neuropsychological perspectives.* Amsterdam: Elsevier/North Holland.—108, 501

Ceci, S. (1991). How much does schooling influence general intelligence and its cognitive components? A reassessment of the evidence. *Developmental Psychology, 27,* 703–722. *A defense of how schooling—an environmental factor—influences intelligence test performance.*—67, 68, 83

Champagne, A. B., & Bunce, D. M. (1991). Learning theory–based science teaching. In S. M. Glynn, R. H. Yeany, & B. K. Britton (Eds.), *The psychology of learning science* (pp. 21–41). Hillsdale, NJ: Erlbaum.—298

Cheong. See **Lau Kam Cheong.**

Chi, M. T. H. (1985). Interactive roles of knowledge and strategies in the development of organized sorting and recall. In S. F. Chipman, J. W. Segal, & R. Glaser (Eds.), *Thinking and learning skills.* Vol 2: *Research and open questions.* Hillsdale, NJ: Erlbaum.—107

Chi, M. T. H., Glaser, R., & Rees, E. (1982). Expertise in problem solving. In R. Sternberg (Ed.), *Advances in the psychology of human intelligence.* Hillsdale, NJ: Erlbaum.—284

Chilcoat, G. W. (1989). Instructional behaviors for clearer presentations in the classroom. *Instructional Science, 18,* 289–314.—374

Chipeur, H. M., Rovine, M., & Plomin, R. (1990). LISREL modeling: Genetic and environmental influences on IQ revisited. *Intelligence, 14,* 11–29.—64

Chipman, S. F., Segal, J. W., & Glaser, R. (Eds.). (1985). *Thinking and learning skills* (Vol. 2). Hillsdale, NJ: Erlbaum.—270

Chomsky, N. (1957). *Syntactic structures.* The Hague: Mouton.—118

Chomsky, N. (1968). *Language and mind.* New York: Harcourt Brace Jovanovich. *One of the most important books on language.*—118

Chukovsky, K. (1968). *From two to five* (M. Morton, Trans.). Berkeley: University of California Press.—120

Clandinin, D. J., & Connelly, F. M. (1992). Teacher as curriculum maker. In P. W. Jackson (Ed.), *Handbook of research on curriculum* (pp. 363–401). New York: Macmillan.—34

Clarizio, H. F. (1971). *Toward positive classroom discipline.* New York: Wiley.—467

Clark, C. M., Gage, N. L., Marx, R. W., Peterson, P. L., Stayrook, N. G., & Winne, P. H. (1979). A factorial experiment on teacher structuring, soliciting, and reacting. *Journal of Educational Psychology, 71,* 534–552.—481

Clark, C. M., & Peterson, P. K. (1986). Teachers' thought processes. In M. C. Wittrock (Ed.), *Handbook of research on teaching* (3d ed., pp. 255–296). New York: Macmillan.—552

Clark, D. C. (1969). Competition for grades and graduate-student performance. *Journal of Educational Research, 62,* 351–354.—583

Clark, J. M., & Paivio, A. (1991). Dual coding theory and education. *Educational Psychology Review, 3,* 149–210.—261

Clement, J. (1982). Students' preconceptions in introductory mechanics. *American Journal of Physics, 50*(1), 66–71.—297

Clifford, M., & Walster, E. (1973). The effect of physical attractiveness on teacher expectations. *Sociology of Education, 46,* 248–258.—472

Clift, J. C., & Imrie, B. W. (1981). *Assessing students, appraising teaching.* New York: Wiley.—518

Cobb, N. L. (1995). *Adolescence* (2d ed.). Mountain View, CA: Mayfield Publishing.—132

Cognition and Technology Group at Vanderbilt. (1990). Anchored instruction and its relationship to situated cognition. *Educational Researcher, 19,* 2–10.—305

Cognition and Technology Group at Vanderbilt (1996). Looking at technology in context: A framework for understanding technology and education research. In D. C. Berliner & R. C. Calfee (Eds.), *Handbook of educational psychology* (pp. 807–840). New York: Macmillan.—279, 288, 424

Cohen, E. G., & Lotan, R. (1995). Producing equal-status interaction in the heterogeneous classroom. *American Educational Research Journal, 32,* 99–120.—416–417, 421

Cohen, H. L. (1973). Behavior modification and socially deviant youth. In C. E. Thoresen (Ed.), *Behavior modification in education: Seventy-second yearbook of the National Society for the Study of Education* (Pt. 1). Chicago: University of Chicago Press. *Shows the powerful effects of a behavior modification program.*—343–344

Cohen, J. (1994). The earth is round (p < .05). *American Psychologist, 49,* 997–1003.—22

Cohen, P., Kulik, J. A., & Kulik, C. C. (1982). Educational outcomes of tutoring: A meta-analysis of findings. *American Educational Research Journal, 19,* 237–248.—442

Cohen, R. L. (1989). Memory for action events: The power of enactment. *Educational Psychology Review, 1,* 57–80.—264

Cole, M., & Bruner, J. S. (1971). Cultural differences and inferences about psychological processes. *American Psychologist, 26,* 867–876.—114

Coleman, J. S., Campbell, E. Q., Hobson, C. J., McPartland, J., Mood, A. M., Weinfeld, F. D., & York, R. L. (1966). *Equality of educational opportunity.* Washington, DC: Government Printing Office. *The well-known Coleman report that led to questions about the efficacy of schools in reducing inequalities of educational achievement. Much reanalyzed, defended, and challenged.*—82, 86

Coley, R. J., Cradler, J., & Engel, P. K. (1997). *Computers and classrooms: The status of technology in U.S. schools.* Princeton, NJ: Policy Information Center, Educational Testing Service.—442

Collins, A., Brown, J. S., & Newman, S. E. (1989). Cognitive apprenticeship: Teaching the craft of reading, writing, and mathematics. In L. B. Resnick (Ed.), *Knowing, learning, and instruction: Essays in honor of Robert Glaser.* Hillsdale, NJ: Erlbaum.—286

Combs, R. C., & Gay, J. (1988). Effects of race, class, and IQ information on judgments of parochial school teachers. *Journal of Social Psychology, 128,* 647–652.—552

Comer, J. P. (1986, February). Parent participation in the schools. *Phi Delta Kappan,* 442–446.—168

Comer, J. P. (1991). Home, school and academic learning. In J. Goodlad and P. Keating (Eds.), *Access to knowledge: An agenda for our nation's schools* (pp. 23–44). New York: College Entrance Examination Board.—168

Committee to Develop Standards for Educational and Psychological Testing. (1985). *Standards for educational and psychological testing.* Washington, DC: American Psychological Association. *The recommended criteria for testing, test development, using information, and rights of test takers, as developed by three professional associations.*—524

Confrey, J. (1990). What constructivism implies for teaching. In R. B. Davis, C. A. Maher, & N. Noddings (Eds.), *Constructivist views on the teaching and learning of mathematics* (pp. 107–124). Reston, VA: National Council of Teachers of Mathematics.—256, 276, 497–498

Cooper, H. M. (1994a). *The battle over homework.* Thousand Oaks, CA: Corwin Press. *Reports on a meta-analysis of experiments that study whether and how homework affects achievement.*—430

Cooper, H. M. (1994b). Homework for students with learning disabilities: The implications of research for policy and practice. *Journal of Learning Disabilities, 27,* 470–479.—430, 431

Cooper, H. M. (1989a). *Homework.* White Plains, NY: Longman. *A meta-analysis of many experiments.*—23, 429

Corno, L. (1993). The best laid plans: Modern conceptions of volition and educational research. *Educational Researcher, 22*(2), 14–22.—349

Corno, L., Mitman, A., & Hedges, L. (1981). The influence of direct instruction on student self-appraisals: A hierarchical analysis of treatment and aptitude-treatment interaction effects. *American Educational Research Journal, 18,* 39–61.—146

Covington, M. V. (1984). The self-worth theory of achievement motivation: Findings and implications. *Elementary School Journal, 85,* 5–20.—329, 331

Covington, M. V. (1992). *Making the grade.* Cambridge: Cambridge University Press. *A persuasive argument about the damage done to millions of students by the grading systems in common use in the United States*—141, 142, 143, 144, 146, 327, 329, 331, 582

Covington, M. V., Crutchfield, R. S., Davies, L., & Olton, R. M. (1974). *The Productive Thinking Program: A course in learning to think.* Columbus, OH: Merrill.—141

Cox, W. F., Jr., & Dunn, T. G. (1979). Mastery learning: A psychological trap? *Educational Psychologist, 14,* 24–29.—438

Crawford, J. (1983). *A study of instructional processes in Title I classes.* ERIC Document Reproduction Service No. ED247282.—491

Crawford, J. (1992). *Hold your tongue: Bilingualism and the politics of "English Only."* Reading, MA: Addison-Wesley. *A readable and valid critique of the critics of bilingual education.*—124

Crawford, J., Gage, N. L., Corno, L., Stayrook, N. G., Mitman, A., Schunk, D., & Stallings, J. (1978). *An experiment in teacher effectiveness and parent-assisted instruction in the third grade* (Vols. 1–3). Stanford, CA: Center for Educational Research, Stanford University. ERIC Document Reproduction Service No. ED160648.—146

Cronbach, L. J. (1971). Test validation. In R. L. Thorndike (Ed.), *Educational measurement* (2d ed., pp. 443–507). Washington, DC: American Council on Education.—525

Cronbach, L. J., & Associates. (1980). *The reform of program evaluation.* San Francisco: Jossey-Bass.—529

Cronin, M. W., Grice, G. L., & Olsen, R. K. (1994). The effects of interactive video instruction in coping with speech fright. *Communication Education, 43*(1), 42–53.—373

Cuban, L. (1992). *How teachers taught: Constancy and change in American classrooms* (2d ed.). White Plains, NY: Longman.—502

Culross, R. R. (1996). *Concepts of inclusion in gifted education.* Paper presented at the annual meeting of the American Educational Research Association, New York, April 8–12. ERIC Document Reproduction Service No. ED395404.—200

Cummins, J. J. (1986). Empowering minority students: A framework for intervention. *Harvard Educational Review, 56*(1), 18–36.—177

Cushner, K., McClelland, A., & Safford, P. (1996). *Human diversity in education: An integrative approach* (2d ed.). New York: McGraw-Hill.—152, 156, 157

Dacey, J., & Kenny, M. (1994). *Adolescent development.* Dubuque, IA: Brown & Benchmark.—129, 130

Dacey, J. S. (1989). *Fundamentals of creative thinking.* Lexington, MA: D. C. Heath.—141

DaRosa, D., Kolm, P., Follmer, H. C., Pemberton, L. B., Pearce, W. H., & Leapman, S. (1991). Evaluating the effectiveness of the lecture versus independent study. *Evaluation and Program Planning, 14,* 141–146.—371

Davey, B., & McBride, S. (1986). The effects of question generation training on reading comprehension. *Journal of Educational Psychology, 78,* 256–282.—268

Davis, M., & Hull, R. E. (1997). Effects of writing summaries as a generative learning activity during note taking. *Teaching of Psychology, 24*(1), 47–49.—389

Davis, R. B. (1990). Discovery learning and constructivism. In R. B. Davis, C. A. Maher, & N. Noddings (Eds.), *Constructivist views on the teaching and learning of mathematics* (pp. 93–106). Reston, VA: National Council of Teachers of Mathematics.—274

DeCharms, R. (1976). *Enhancing motivation.* New York: Irvington Press/Wiley.—340

DeCharms, R. (1980). The origins of competence and achievement motivation in personal causation. In L. J. Fyans, Jr. (Ed.), *Achievement motivation.* New York: Plenum Press.—340

DeCharms, R. (1984). Motivational enhancement in educational settings. In R. Ames & C. Ames (Eds.), *Research on motivation in education,* Vol. 1: *Student motivation* (pp. 275–310). New York: Academic Press.—340

Deci, E. L. (1975). *Intrinsic motivation.* New York: Plenum Press.—335

Deci, E. L., & Ryan, R. (1985). *Intrinsic motivation and self-determination in human behavior.* New York: Plenum Press.—335

De Corte, E. (1996, August). *Learning bad and good things from instruction: A European perspective.* Paper presented at the meeting of the American Psychological Association, Toronto, Canada.—295

De Corte, E., Greer, B., & Verschaffel, L. (1996). Mathematics teaching and learning. In D. C. Berliner & R. C. Calfee (Eds.), *Handbook of educational psychology* (pp. 491–549). New York: Macmillan.—274, 295

de Groot, A. (1965). *Thought and choice in chess.* The Hague: Mouton.—283

Delpit, L. D. (1988). The silenced dialogues: Power and pedagogy in educating other people's children. *Harvard Educational Review, 58*(3), 280–298.—579

Delpit, L. D. (1995). *Other people's children: Cultural conflict in the classroom.* New York: New Press.—MP 4, Chapter 13

de Ribapierre, A., & Rieben, L. (1995). Individual and situational variability in cognitive development. *Educational Psychologist, 30,* 5–14.—98

Derrickson, D. A. (1995). At-risk ninth-grade students and the perception of success. *Teaching and Change, 2,* 352–368.—340

Derry, S., & Lesgold, A. (1996). Toward a situated social practice model for instructional design. In D. C. Berliner & R. C. Calfee (Eds.), *Handbook of educational psychology* (pp. 787–806). New York: Macmillan.—444

Devlin, B., Daniels, M., & Roeder, K. (1997). The heritability of IQ. *Nature, 388,* 468–471.—64, 67

Diaz, R. M. (1983). Thought and two languages: The impact of bilingualism. In E. W. Gordon (Ed.), *Review of research in education* (Vol. 10). Washington, DC: American Educational Research Association.—123

Diaz, S., Moll, L. C., & Mehan, H. (1986). Sociocultural resources in instruction: A con-text-specific approach. In Bilingual Education Office (Ed.), *Beyond language: Social and cultural factors in schooling language minority students.* Los Angeles: California State University at Los Angeles.—162

Dickinson, D. (1974). But what happens when you take the reinforcement away? *Psychology in the Schools, 11,* 158–160.—344

Diener, C., & Dweck, C. (1978). An analysis of learned helplessness: Continuous changes in performance, strategy, and achievement cognitions following failure. *Journal of Personality and Social Psychology, 36,* 351–362.—342

Di Gangi, S. A., Faykus S. P., Powell, J. H., Wallin, M., & Berliner, D. C. (1991). *Novice and experienced teachers' decisions about grading.* Paper presented at the meeting of the American Psychological Association, San Francisco.—591

Dillon, J. T. (1985). Using questions to foil discussion. *Teaching and Teacher Education, 1,* 109–121.—406–408

Dillon, J. T. (1988). *Questioning and teaching.* New York: Teachers College Press.—408

Dillon, J. T. (1991). Questioning the use of questions. *Journal of Educational Psychology, 83,* 163–164.—409–410

Doenau, S. J. (1987). Structuring. In M. J. Dunkin (Ed.), *International encyclopedia of teaching and teacher education* (pp. 398–407). Oxford: Pergamon.—482

Doherty, J., & Hier, B. (1988). Teacher expectations and specific judgments: A small-scale study of the effects of certain non-cognitive variables on teachers' academic predictions. *Educational Review, 40,* 333–348.—552

Dole, J. A., Duffy, G. G., Roehler, L. R., & Pearson, P. D. (1991). Moving from the old to the new: Research on reading instruction. *Review of Educational Research, 61,* 239–264.—257

Dossey, J. A., Mullis I. V. S., & Jones, C. O. (1993). *Can students do mathematical problem solving? Results from constructed-response questions in NAEP's 1992 mathematics assessment.* Washington, DC: U.S. Department of Education, Office of Educational Research and Improvement.—564, 565

Doyle, W. (1992). Curriculum and pedagogy. In P. W. Jackson (Ed.), *Handbook of research on curriculum* (pp. 486–516). New York: Macmillan.—35

Duin, A. H., & Graves, M. F. (1987). Intensive vocabulary instruction as a prewriting technique. *Reading Research Quarterly, 22,* 311–330.—299

Duncker, K. (1945). On problem-solving. *Psychological Monographs, 58* (5, Whole No. 270). *A classic description of a series of studies about how humans solve complex problems.*—357

Dunkin, M. J. (Ed.). (1987). *International encyclopedia of teaching and teacher education.* Oxford: Pergamon.—477

Dunkin, M. J., & Biddle, B. J. (1974). *The study of teaching.* New York: Holt, Rinehart, & Winston. *Still a comprehensive introduction to research approaches and issues, but no longer useful as a summary of research on teacher behavior and its correlates.*

Durkin, D. (1979). What classroom observations reveal about reading comprehension instruction. *Reading Research Quarterly, 14,* 481–538.—257

Dusek, J. B. (Ed.). (1985). *Teacher expectancies.* Hillsdale, NJ: Erlbaum.—35

Dweck, C. S. (1975). The role of expectations and attributions in the alleviation of learned helplessness. *Journal of Personality and Social Psychology, 31,* 674–685.—341

Dweck, C. S., & Leggett, E. L. (1988). A social-cognitive approach to motivation and personality. *Psychological Review, 95,* 256–273.—327

Eaton, C. B. (1992). Relation of physical activity and cardiovascular fitness to coronary heart disease, Pt. I: A meta-analysis of the independent relation of physical activity and coronary heart disease. *Journal of the American Board of Family Practice, 5*(1), 31–42.—18

Ebel, R. L. (1974). Should we get rid of grades? *Measurement in Education, 5*(4), 1–5.—582

Ebel, R. L. (1980). Achievement tests as measures of developed abilities. In W. B. Schrader (Ed.), *New directions for testing and measurement* (No. 5), San Francisco: Jossey-Bass.—539

Education Daily (1996, January 4). Educators weigh high price of performance assessments. *Education Daily, 29*(3), 1–3.—566

Effros, E. G. (1989, February 14). Give U.S. math students more rote learning. *New York Times* (editorial page).—43

Eisenberg, N., Martin, C. L., & Fabes, R. A. (1996). Gender development and gender effects. In D. C. Berliner & R. C. Calfee (Eds.), *Handbook of educational psychology* (pp. 358–398). New York: Macmillan.—169, 170, 171

Eisenberger, R., & Cameron, J. (1996). Detrimental effects of reward. *American Psychologist, 51,* 1153–1166.—335

Eisner, E. W. (1991). *The enlightened eye.* New York: Macmillan. *A reminder that psychological science is only one way to know or make sense of the world or to obtain a basis for important decisions. Explains the value of qualitative methods and ways of knowing.*—582

Elawar, M. C., & Corno, L. (1985). A factorial experiment in teachers' written feedback on student homework: Changing teacher behavior a little rather than a lot. *Journal of Educational Psychology, 77,* 162–173.—354

Elkind, D. (1976). *Child development and education.* New York: Oxford University Press.—117

Elsen, A. (1969). The pleasures of teaching. In *The study of education at Stanford: Report to the university,* Pt. 8: *Teaching, research, and the faculty* (pp. 21–23). Stanford, CA: Stanford University.—368

Emmer, E., Evertson, C., & Anderson, L. (1980). Effective classroom management at the beginning of the school year. *Elementary School Journal, 80,* 219–231.—466

Ericsson, K. A. (Ed.). (1996). *The road to excellence.* Mahwah, NJ: Erlbaum.—264, 279

Erikson, E. (1963). *Childhood and society* (2d ed.). New York: Norton. *One of the finest psychoanalysts of our time literately describes the development of children.*—127

Erikson, E. (1968). *Identity, youth and crisis.* New York: Norton.—97, 127–130

Eron, L. (1992, June 18). Testimony before the Senate Committee on Public Affairs. *Congressional Record.*—240

Estes, W. K. (1982). Learning, memory, and intelligence. In R. J. Sternberg (Ed.), *Handbook of human intelligence.* New York: Cambridge University Press.—51

Evans, W. E., & Guyman, R. E. (1978). *Clarity of explanation: A powerful indicator of teacher effectiveness.* Paper presented at the annual meeting of the American Educational Research Association, Toronto.—387

Fagan, E. R., Hassler, D. M., & Szabo, M. (1981). Evaluation of questioning strategies in language arts instruction. *Research in the Teaching of English, 15,* 267–273.—485

Fantuzzo, J. W., Rohrbeck, C. A., Hightower, A. D., & Work, W. C. (1991). Teachers' use and children's preferences of rewards in elementary school. *Psychology in the Schools, 28*(2), 175–181.—222

Feldhusen, J. F. (1979). Student behavior problems in secondary schools. In D. L. Duke (Ed.), *Classroom management: Seventy-eighth yearbook of the National Society for the Study of Education.* Chicago: University of Chicago Press.—464

Fergusson, D. M., Lloyd, M., & Horwood, L. J. (1991). Family ethnicity, social background, and scholastic achievement: An eleven-year longitudinal study. *New Zealand Journal of Educational Studies, 26,* (1), 49–63.—80

Fernandez-Balboa, J.-M., & Stiehl, J. (1995). The generic nature of pedagogical content knowledge among college professors. *Teaching and Teacher Education, 11,* 293–306.—372

Ferster, C. B., & Skinner, B. F. (1957). *Schedules of reinforcement.* New York: Appleton-Century-Crofts. *Portrays in detail the lawfulness of animal behavior under various reinforcement schedules.*—217–218

Finn, J. D., & Achilles, C. M. (1990). Answers and questions about class size: A statewide experiment. *American Educational Research Journal, 27,* 557–577.—460

Fitzgerald, J., & Markham, L. R. (1987). Teaching children about revision in writing. *Cognition and Instruction, 4,* 3–24.—270

Flannery, M. C. (1993). Making science a laughing matter. *Journal of College Science Teaching, 22,* 239–241.—393

Flavell, J. H. (1963). *The developmental psychology of Jean Piaget.* Princeton, NJ: Van Nostrand. *One of the major presentations of Piaget's thoughts about the development of cognitive processes; a technical but accurate interpretation.*—98

Flavell, J. H. (1976). Megacognitive aspects of problem solving. In L. B. Resnick (Ed.), *The nature of intelligence.* Hillsdale, NJ: Erlbaum.—270

Flavell, J. H. (1985). *Cognitive development* (2d ed.). Englewood Cliffs, NJ: Prentice-Hall.—103

Fleischman, H. L., & Hopstock, P. J. (1993). *Descriptive study of services to limited English proficient students,* Vol. 1: *Summary of findings and conclusions.* Arlington, VA: Development Associates, Inc.—123

Fletcher-Flinn, C. M., & Gravatt, B. (1995). The efficacy of computer-assisted instruction (CAI): A meta-analysis. *Journal of Educational Computing Research, 12,* 219–242.—445

Flynn, J. R. (1987). Massive IQ gains in 14 nations: What IQ tests really measure. *Psychological Bulletin, 101,* 171–191. *A fascinating look at large increases in intelligence test scores in several industrial nations over the period of a generation. Questions whether those scores measure intelligence or only a "weak correlate" of intelligence.*—66–67, 83

Fordham, S. P. (1988). Racelessness as a factor in black students' success: Pragmatic strategy or pyrrhic victory? *Harvard Educational Review, 58,* 54–84. *Provocative review of what it means to achieve well in school when African-American.*—130, 332

Fosterling, F. (1985). Attributional retraining: A review. *Psychological Bulletin, 48,* 495–512.—341, 342

Fowler, J. W., & Peterson, P. L. (1981). Increasing reading persistence and altering attributional style of learned helplessness children. *Journal of Educational Psychology, 73,* 251–260.—342

Fraser, S. (Ed.). (1995). *The Bell Curve wars.* New York: Basic Books. *Contains essays for and against* The Bell Curve, *the controversial book by Richard Herrnstein and Charles Murray.*—49

Fredericksen, N. (1984). The real test bias: Influences on teaching and learning. *American Psychologist, 39,* 193–202.—546, 558, MP 4, Chapter 13

Freire, P., & Macedo, D. (1987). *Literacy: Reading the word and the world.* South Hadley, MA: Bergin & Garvey.—MP 1, Chapter 2

Frieze, I. H., & Snyder, H. N. (1980). Children's beliefs about the causes of success and failure in school settings. *Journal of Educational Psychology, 72,* 186–196.—323

Furnham, A., Johnson, C., & Rawles, R. (1985). The determinants of belief in human nature. *Personality and Individual Differences, 6,* 675–684.—84

Fyans, L. J., Jr., & Maehr, M. L. (1980). Attributional style, task selection and achievement. In L. J. Fyans, Jr. (Ed.), *Achievement motivation.* New York: Plenum Press.—323

Gage, N. L. (1991). The obviousness of social and educational research results. *Educational Researcher, 20*(1), 10–16.—10, 380–381

Gage, N. L. (1996). Confronting counsels of despair for the behavioral sciences. *Educational Researcher, 25*(3), 5–15, 22. *Defends the possibility of social science against various criticisms and on the empirical grounds that many highly replicated generalizations exist.*—25

Gage, N. L., & Berliner, D. C. (1989). Nurturing the critical, practical, and artistic thinking of teachers. *Phi Delta Kappan, 71,* 212–214.—25

Gage, N. L., & Berliner, D. C. (1992). *Educational psychology* (5th ed.). Boston: Houghton Mifflin.—447

Gage, N. L., & Needels, M. C. (1989). Process-product research on teaching: A review of criticisms. *Elementary School Journal, 89,* 253–300.—15, 18, 495

Gagné, R. M. (1985). *The conditions of learning* (4th ed.). New York: Holt, Rinehart, & Winston. *Especially noteworthy for the hierarchy of types of learning, by a leading theorist of instructional technology.*—290

Gall, M. D., & Gall, J. P. (1976). The discussion method. In N. L. Gage (Ed.), *The psychology of teaching methods: Seventy-fifth yearbook of the National Society for the Study of Education* (Pt. 1, pp. 166–216). Chicago: University of Chicago Press.—402

Gallagher, J. J. (1992). Gifted persons. In M. C. Alkin (Ed.), *Encyclopedia of educational research* (6th ed., Vol. 2, pp. 544–549). New York: Macmillan.—199

Garber, H. L. (1988). *The Milwaukee Project: Preventing mental retardation in children at risk.* Washington, DC: American Association on Mental Retardation.—91

Garcia, G. E., & Pearson, D. (1994). Assessment and diversity. In L. Darling-Hammond (Ed.), *Review of Research in Education, 20,* 337–392. Washington, DC: American Educational Research Association.—538, 579

Garcia, O., & Baker, C. (Eds.). (1995). *Policy and practice in bilingual education.* Clevedon, U.K.: Multilingual Matters, Ltd.—124

Gardner, H. (1983). *Frames of mind: The theory of multiple intelligences.* New York: Basic Books. *Departing from the factor-analytic paradigm, this book, using a variety of kinds of evidence, reopened the area of the structure of cognitive abilities. It provides evidence for a theory of multiple semi-independent intelligences.*—75, 76–78, 110, 111

Gardner, H. (1985). *The mind's new science.* New York: Basic Books. *A tour de force by a gifted writer on the history, problems, achievements, and future of cognitive science.*—199, 288, 292

Gardner, H. (1993). *Multiple intelligences: The theory in practice.* New York: Basic Books. *Seeks to replace general intelligence (g) with seven intelligences derived from several kinds of evidence.*—79

Garner, R., Hare, V. C., Alexander, P., Haynes, J., & Winograd, P. (1984). Successful use of a text lookback strategy among unsuccessful readers. *American Educational Research Journal, 21,* 789–798.—268

Garner, R., Macready, G. B., & Wagoner, S. (1984). Readers' acquisition of the components of the text-lookback strategy. *Journal of Educational Psychology, 76,* 300–309.—268

Gearheart, B. R., & Weishahn, M. W. (1984). *The exceptional student in the regular classroom* (3d ed.). Columbus, OH: Merrill.—179

Gelman, R. (1985). The developmental perspective on the problem of knowledge acquisition: A discussion. In S. F. Chipman, J. W. Segal, & R. Glaser (Eds.), *Thinking and learning skills* (Vol. 2). Hillsdale, NJ: Erlbaum.—107

Getzels, J. W., & Jackson, P. W. (1962). *Creativity and intelligence.* New York: Wiley.—141

Giaconia, R. (1987). *Teacher questioning and wait-time.* Unpublished doctoral dissertation, Stanford University, Stanford, CA.—485, 488

Gibson, S., & Dembo, M. H. (1984). Teacher efficacy: A construct validation. *Journal of Educational Psychology, 76,* 569–582.—351

Gick, M. L., & Holyoak, K. L. (1987). The cognitive basis for knowledge transfer. In S. M. Cormier & J. D. Hagman (Eds.), *Transfer of learning* (pp. 9–57). New York: Academic Press.—301

Gilligan, C. (1982). *In a different voice.* Cambridge, MA: Harvard University Press. *A feminist critique of a well-researched area: moral development.*—133–134

Gilligan, C., & Antanucci, J. (1988). Two moral orientations: Gender differences and similarities. *Merrill Palmer Quarterly, 34,* 223–237.—133

Gilligan, C., Ward, J. V., & Taylor, J. M. (1988). *Mapping the moral domain.* Cambridge, MA: Harvard University Press.—133

Ginsburg, H., & Opper, S. (1988). *Piaget's theory of intellectual development* (3d ed.). Englewood Cliffs, NJ: Prentice-Hall.—98

Gitomer, D. H., & Duschl, R. A. (1995). *Moving toward a portfolio culture in education.* Center for Performance Assessment, MS 94–07. Princeton, NJ: Educational Testing Service.—595

Glass, G. V (1976). Primary, secondary, and meta-analysis of research. *Educational Researcher, 5,* 3–8.—23

Glasser, W. L. (1969). *Schools without failure.* New York: Harper & Row. *Outlines plans for making schools more responsive to children's affective needs.*—582

Gleason, J. J. (1991). Developing a humor unit for the gifted: A dianoetic ditty a day. *Gifted Child Today, 14*(1), 60–61.—393

Glynn, S. M., Yeany, R. H., & Britton, B. K. (1991). A constructivist view of learning science. In S. M. Glynn, R. H. Yeany, & B. K. Britton (Eds.), *The psychology of learning science* (pp. 3–19). Hillsdale, NJ: Erlbaum.—298

Gold, M. W., & Ryan, V. M. (1979). Vocational training for the mentally retarded. In I. H. Frieze, D. Bar-Tal, & J. S. Carroll (Eds.), *New approaches to social problems: Applications of attribution theory.* San Francisco: Jossey-Bass.—342

Gong, B., & Reidy, E. F. (1996). Assessment and accountability in Kentucky's school reform. In J. B. Baron & D. P. Wolf (Eds.), *Performance-based student assessment: Challenges and possibilities: Ninety-fifth yearbook of the National Society for the Study of Education* (Pt. 1, pp. 215–233). Chicago: University of Chicago Press.—596

Good, T. L. (1987). Teacher expectations. In D. C. Berliner & B. V. Rosenshine (Eds.), *Talks to teachers: A Festschrift for N. L. Gage* (pp. 157–200). New York: Random House.—69

Good, T. L. (1993). Teacher expectations. In L. Anderson (Ed.), *International encyclopedia of education of teaching and teacher education* (2d ed.). Oxford: Pergamon.—536

Goodlad, J. I. (1984). *A place called school.* New York: McGraw-Hill.—367

Gordon, E. W., & Bonilla-Bowman, C. (1996). Can performance-based assessments contribute to the achievement of educational equity? In J. B. Baron & D. P. Wolf (Eds.), *Performance-based student assessment: Challenges and possibilities: Ninety-fifth yearbook of the National Society for the Study of Education* (Pt. 1, pp. 32–51). Chicago: University of Chicago Press.—566

Gottfried, A. W. (1984). Home environment and early cognitive development: Integration, meta-analysis, and conclusions. In A. W. Gottfried (Ed.), *Home environment and early cognitive development: Longitudinal research.* Orlando, FL: Academic Press.—89

Grabe, M., & Grabe, C. (1998). *Integrating technology for meaningful learning* (2d ed.). Boston: Houghton Mifflin.—424, 448

Graham, S. (1986). Teacher feelings and student thoughts: An attributional approach to affect in the classroom. *Elementary School Journal, 85,* 91–104.—324

Graham, S., & Barker, G. P. (1990). The down side of help: An attributional-developmental analysis of helping behavior as a low-ability cue. *Journal of Educational Psychology, 82,* 7–14.—242, 324

Graham, S., Doubleday, D., & Guarino, P. (1984). The development of relations between perceived controllability and the emotions of pity, anger, and guilt. *Child Development, 55,* 561–565.—324

Graham, S., & Weiner, B. (1996). Theories and principles of motivation. In D. C. Berliner & R. C. Calfee (Eds.), *Handbook of educational psychology* (pp. 63–84). New York: Macmillan.—321

Graves, D. (1983). *Writing: Teachers and children at work.* Exeter, NH: Heinemann.—446

Green, D. R. (Ed.). (1974). *The aptitude-achievement distinction.* Monterey, CA: CTB/McGraw-Hill.—539

Green, J. L. (1983). Research on teaching as a linguistic process: The state of the art. In E. W. Gordon (Ed.), *Review of research in education* (Vol. 10). Washington, DC: American Educational Research Association. *A comprehensive review describing a decade of research in relatively new areas.*—126

Greeno, J. G. (1994, August). *The situativity of learning.* Paper presented at the meeting of the American Psychological Association, Los Angeles.—285

Greeno, J. G., Collins, A. M., & Resnick, L. B. (1996). Cognition and learning. In D. C. Berliner & R. C. Calfee (Eds.), *Handbook of educational psychology* (pp. 15–46). New York: Macmillan. *Contrasting views of the major learning theories and their implications for teaching, curriculum, and assessment.*—284

Griffiths, P. (1997, August 12). What's the score (Review of *The Compleat Conductor*). *New York Times Book Review,* p. 11.—479

Gronlund, N. E. (1993). *How to make achievement tests and assessments* (5th ed.). Needham Heights, MA: Allyn & Bacon.—517, 518

Grossman, P. (1991). Mapping the terrain: Knowledge growth in teaching. In H. C. Waxman & H. J. Walberg (Eds.), *Effective teaching: Current research* (pp. 203–215). Berkeley, CA: McCutchan.—473

Gruber, H. E., & Vonèche, J. J. (Eds.). (1977). *The essential Piaget: An interpretive reference and guide.* New York: Basic Books. *The difficulty of reading Piaget still exists, but these editors have chosen the most important passages and articles. Truly the essential Piaget.*—98

Gugliotta, G. (1993, March 16). An impromptu "dream" becomes a national model. *Washington Post,* p. A6.—315

Gullickson, A. R. (1990). Teacher education and teacher perceived needs in educational measurement and evaluation. *Journal of Educational Measurement, 23,* 347–354.—511

Guskey, T. R., & Pigott, T. D. (1988). Research on group-based mastery learning programs: A meta-analysis. *Journal of Educational Research, 81,* 197–216.—437

Gustafsson, J.-E. (1992). Stability and change in broad and narrow factors of intelligence from ages 12 to 15 years. *Journal of Educational Psychology, 84,* 141–149.—55

Gustafsson, J.-E., & Undheim, J. O. (1996). Individual differences in cognitive functions. In D. C. Berliner & R. C. Calfee (Eds.), *Handbook of educational psychology* (pp. 186–242). New York: Macmillan. *A thorough treatment of a central concern.*—56, 429, 436

Haas, N., Haladyna, T. M., & Nolen, S. B. (1989). *Standardized testing in Arizona: Interviews and written comments from teachers and administrators* (Technical Report 89–3). Phoenix: Authors, Arizona State University.—540

Hakuta, K. (1986). *Mirror of language: The debate on bilingualism.* New York: Basic Books. *A comprehensive and scientific look at the evidence for concluding that bilingual children are cognitively advantaged in comparison with monolingual children.*—123, 124

Hakuta, K., & McLaughlin, B. (1996). Bilingualism and second language learning: Seven tensions that define the research. In D. C. Berliner & R. C. Calfee (Eds.), *Handbook of educational*

psychology (pp. 603–621). New York: Macmillan.—123

Hall, G. S. (1887). *How to teach reading and what to read in school.* Boston: D. C. Heath.—MP 3, Chapter 9

Hall, R. V., & Hall, M. C. (1980a). *How to select reinforcers.* Lawrence, KS: M & M Enterprises.—222

Hall, R. V., & Hall, M. C. (1980b). *How to use time out.* Lawrence, KS: M & M Enterprises.—230

Hall, V. C. (1976). *Review of research on classroom communication patterns, leading to improved student performance.* ERIC Document Reproduction Service No. ED127292.—158

Hallinan, M. T. (1996). Race effects on students' track mobility in high school. *Social Psychology of Education, 1,* 1–24.—199

Halpin, G., & Halpin, G. (1982). Experimental investigation of the effects of study and testing on student learning, retention, and ratings of instruction. *Journal of Educational Psychology, 72,* 32–38.—583, 585

Hambleton, R. K. (1990). Criterion-referenced testing methods and practices. In T. B. Gutkin and C. R. Reynolds (Eds.), *Handbook of school psychology* (pp. 388–415). New York: Wiley.—521

Hambleton, R. K. (1996). Advances in assessment models, methods, and practices. In D. C. Berliner & R. C. Calfee (Eds.), *Handbook of educational psychology* (pp. 899–925). New York: Macmillan.—515

Hamilton, R. J. (1985). A framework for the evaluation of the effectiveness of adjunct questions and objectives. *Review of Educational Research, 55,* 47–86.—38

Hare, A. P. (1962). *Handbook of small group research.* New York: Free Press.—417

Harrison A. (1995). Using knowledge decrement to compare medical students' long-term retention of self-study reading and lecture materials. *Assessment and Evaluation in Higher Education, 20*(2), 149–159.—371

Harrow, A. J. (1972). *A taxonomy of the psychomotor domain.* New York: David McKay.—41

Hartigan, J. A., & Wigdor, A. K. (1989). *Fairness in employment testing: Validity generalization, minority issues, and the General Aptitude Test Battery.* Washington, DC: National Academy Press.—60

Hartley, J. (1976). Lecture handouts and student note-taking. *Programmed Learning and Educational Technology, 13,* 58–64.—394

Hartley, J., & Davies, I. K. (1977). *Notetaking.* Unpublished manuscript, University of Keele, Keele, Eng.—394

Hartley, J., Goldie, M., & Steen, L. (1979). The role and position of summaries: Some issues and data. *Educational Review, 31,* 59–65.—395

Hartshorne, H., & May, M. A. (1928). *Studies in the nature of character,* Vol. 1: *Studies in deceit.* New York: Macmillan. *Classic experiments showing the relative specificity of honesty, deceit, and other traits.*—138

Hatano G., & Inagaki, K. (1991). Sharing cognition through collective comprehension activity. In L. Resnick, J. M. Levine, & S. D. Teasley (Eds.), *Perspectives on socially shared cognition* (pp. 331–348). Washington, DC: American Psychological Association.—403

Hattie, J., & Rogers, H. J. (1986). Factor models for assessing the relation between creativity and intelligence. *Journal of Educational Psychology, 78,* 482–485.—141

Heath, R. W. (1992). *Native Hawaiian hearing project: Counteracting the negative educational effects of otitus media in native Hawaiian preschoolers.* Final Report to the Institute on Disability and Rehabilitation Research, grant no. H33A9001. Washington, DC: U.S. Department of Education.—180

Heath, S. B. (1983). *Ways with words: Ethnography of communication, communities, and classrooms.* Cambridge: Cambridge University Press. *An insightful long-term study of children's acquisition of language and community norms.*—159–160

Heath, S. B., & McLaughlin, M. W. (Eds.). (1993). *Identity and inner-city youth: Beyond ethnicity and gender.* New York: Teachers College Press. *Documents the important positive role played by clubs and other after-school groups serving poor and minority youth.*—319

Heckhausen, H., Schmalt, H. D., & Schneider, K. (1985). *Achievement motivation in perspective.* Orlando, FL: Academic Press.—321, 330, 340–342

Hedges, L. V. (1987). How hard is hard science, how soft is soft science? The empirical cumulativeness of research. *American Psychologist, 42,* 443–455.—25

Heller, K. A., Holtzman, W. H., & Messick, S. (1982). *Placing children in special education: A strategy for equity.* Washington, DC: National Science Foundation/National Academy Press.—176–177

Helmstad, G., & Marton, F. (1992). *Conceptions of understanding.* Paper presented at the annual meeting of the American Educational Research Association, San Francisco.—384

Herman, J. L., Aschbacher, P., & Winters, L. (1992). *A practical guide to alternative assessment.* Alexandria, VA: Association for Supervisor and Curriculum Development.—564

Herrnstein, R. J., & Murray, C. (1994). *The bell curve: Intelligence and class structure in American life.* New York: Free Press. *The blockbuster that got more attention and aroused greater controversy than any other work of the 1990s in the social and behavioral sciences.*—49, 62, 91–92

Hiebert, E. H., & Raphael, T. E. (1996). Psychological perspectives on literacy and extensions to educational practice. In D. C. Berliner & R. C. Calfee (Eds.), *Handbook of educational psychology* (pp. 550–602). New York: Macmillan.—294, 296, 298

Higgins, A., & Barna, G. (1994, April). *An analysis of community development in a democratic moral education program.* Paper presented at the meeting of the American Educational Research Association, New Orleans.—135

Highet, G. (1955). *The art of teaching.* New York: Vintage. *A beautifully written discussion of teaching by a classicist, with no use of, or reference to, the behavioral sciences.*—419

Hiller, J. E. (1968). *An experimental investigation of the effects of conceptual vagueness on speaking behavior.* Unpublished doctoral dissertation, University of Connecticut, Storrs. *Initiated a line of research on vagueness, subsequently applied by others in several studies of teaching.*—387

Hirsch, E. D., Jr. (1987). *Cultural literacy: What every American needs to know.* Boston: Houghton Mifflin. *A defense of the importance of knowledge and the curriculum that will produce it.*—43

Hirsch, E. D., Jr. (1993, September 8). *International Herald Tribune.*—MP 1, Chapter 2

Hirsch, E. D., Jr. (1996). *The schools we need and why we don't have them.* New York: Doubleday. *Continues the defense of knowledge and also, in part, criticizes the supposed need for constructivist teaching.*—34, 477, 501, 502, 503

Hodgkinson, H. L. (1985). *All one system: Demographics of education—kindergarten through graduate school.* Washington, DC: Institute of Educational Leadership.—152

Hoffman, B. (1962). *The tyranny of testing.* New York: Crowell-Collier-Macmillan.—582

Hokoda, A., & Fincham, F. D. (1995). Origins of children's helpless and mastery achievement patterns in the family. *Journal of Educational Psychology, 87,* 375–385.—327

Holmes, C. T., & Matthews, K. M. (1984). The effects of nonpromotion on elementary and junior high school pupils: A meta-analysis. *Review of Educational Research, 54,* 225–236.—592

Holt, J. (1969). *On testing.* New York: Pitman.—582

Holt, P., & Wood, P. (1990). Intelligent tutoring systems: A review for beginners. *Canadian Journal of Educational Communication, 19*(2), 107–123.—444

Homme, L. E., Csanyi, A. P., Gonzales, M. A., & Rechs, J. R. (1970). *How to use contingency contracting in the classroom.* Champaign, IL: Research Press. *A first-rate guide to the use of behavior modification in the classroom.*—223

Homme, L. E., & Tosti, D. T. (1971). *Behavior technology.* San Rafael, CA: Individual Learning Systems.—145

Hudgins, B. B. (1977). *Learning and thinking.* Itasca, IL: F. E. Peacock.—304

Huesmann, L. R., Eron, L. D., Klein, R., Brice, P., & Fischer, P. (1983). Mitigating the imitation of aggressive behaviors by changing children's attitudes about media violence. *Journal of Personality and Social Psychology, 44,* 899–910.—240–241

Hunt, E. (1995). *Will we be smart enough? A cognitive analysis of the coming workforce.* New York: Russell Sage Foundation.—61

Hunter, D. (1996). *The ritalin-free child: Managing hyperactivity and attention deficits without drugs.* Fort Lauderdale, FL: Consumer Press.—195

Hunter, J. E. (1986). Cognitive ability, cognitive aptitudes, job knowledge, and job performance. *Journal of Vocational Behavior, 29,* 340–362.—59–60

Husén, T., & Tuijnman, A. (1991). The contribution of formal schooling to the increase in intellectual capital. *Educational Researcher, 20*(7), 17–25.—67–68

Hutchins, R. M. (1952, December 8). Testimony. *Time.*—MP 1, Chapter 2

Huxley, A. (1940). *Words and their meanings.* Los Angeles: Jake Zeilin (The Ward Ritchie Press).—MP 1, Chapter 2

Hyde, J. S., & Linn, M. C. (1988). Gender differences in verbal activities: A meta-analysis. *Psychological Bulletin, 104,* 53–69.—171

Idol, L. (1987). Group story mapping: A comprehension strategy for both skilled and unskilled readers. *Journal of Learning Disabilities, 20,* 196–205.—269

Igoa, C. (1995). *The inner world of immigrant children.* New York: St. Martin's Press.—163, 164

Institute for Research on Teaching. (1980, Winter). *Communication Quarterly* (Michigan State University, East Lansing).—534

Jacobs, J. E. (1991). Influence of gender stereotypes on parent and child mathematics attitudes. *Journal of Educational Psychology, 83,* 518–527.—171

Jacoby, R., & Glauberman, N. (1995). *The Bell Curve debate: History, documents, opinions.* New York: Random House.—49

Jaynes, J. (1975). Hello, teacher . . . A review of Fred S. Keller, "The history of psychology: A personalized system of instruction" and Fred S. Keller, "Selected readings in the history of psychology: A PSI companion." *Contemporary Psychology, 20,* 629–631.—439

John, O. P. (1990). The "big five" factor taxonomy: Dimensions of personality in the natural language and in questionnaires. In L. A. Pervin (Ed.), *Handbook of personality: Theory and research* (pp. 66–100). New York: Guilford Press.—136

Johnson, D. (1981). Naturally acquired learned helplessness: The relationship of school failure to achievement behavior, attributions, and self-concept. *Journal of Educational Psychology, 73,* 174–180.—327

Johnson, D. K. (1988). Adolescents' solutions to dilemmas in fables: Two moral orientations—two problem solving strategies. In C. Gilligan, J. V. Ward, & J. M. Taylor (Eds.), *Mapping the moral domain.* Cambridge, MA: Harvard University Press.—134

Johnson, D. W., & Johnson, R. T. (1979). Conflict in the classroom: Controversy and learning.

Review of Educational Research, 49, 51–70.—403–404

Johnston, J. M. (1972). Punishment of human behavior. *American Psychologist, 27,* 1033–1054.—228

Jones, E. E., & Nisbett, R. E. (1971). *The actor and the observer: Divergent perceptions of the causes of behavior.* Morristown, NJ: General Learning Press.—143–144

Kazdin, A. E. (1989). *Behavior modification in applied settings* (4th ed.). Homewood, IL: Dorsey. *One of the best examples of the power of operant conditioning to change people's behavior.*—223, 224, 226

Keller, F. S. (1968). Good-bye teacher! *Journal of Applied Behavioral Analysis, 1,* 79–84. *The paper that started the movement toward personalized systems of instruction.*—436–437

Keogh, B. K., & MacMillan, D. L. (1996). Exceptionality. In D. C. Berliner & R. C. Calfee (Eds.), *Handbook of educational psychology* (pp. 311–330). New York: Macmillan.—199, 200

Kessler, C., & Quinn, M. E. (1987). Language minority children's linguistic and cognitive creativity. *Journal of Multilingual and Multicultural Development, 8*(1 & 2), 173–186.—124

Kifer, E. (1975). Relationships between academic achievement and personality characteristics: A quasi-longitudinal study. *American Educational Research Journal, 12,* 191–210.—146

Kilbourn, B. (1991). Self-monitoring and teaching. *American Educational Research Journal, 28,* 721–736.—246

King, A. (1992). Comparison of self-questioning, summarizing, and note taking–review as strategies for learning from lectures. *American Educational Research Journal, 29,* 303–323.—391

Klahr, D. (1980). Informational processing models of intellectual development. In R. H. Kluwe & H. Spada (Eds.), *Developmental models of thinking.* New York: Academic Press.—108

Klauer, K. J. (1984). Intentional and incidental learning with instructional texts: A meta-analysis for 1970–1980. *American Educational Research Journal, 21,* 323–339.—38

Klausmeier, H. J., Sorenson, J. S., & Ghatala, E. S. (1971). Individually guided motivation: Developing self-direction and prosocial behaviors. *Elementary School Journal, 71,* 339–350.—347

Kohlberg, L. (1963). The development of children's orientations toward moral order, Pt. 1: Sequence in the development of moral thought. *Vita Humana, 6,* 11–33.—131–132

Kohlberg, L. (1984). *The psychology of moral development* (Vol. 2). San Francisco: Harper & Row.—132

Kohn, A. (1993). *Punished by rewards.* Boston: Houghton Mifflin. *The strongest arguments about the negative effects of positive reinforcement on motivation and achievement.*—335

Kohn, A. (1996). By all available means: Cameron and Pierce's defense of extrinsic motivators. *Review of Educational Research, 66,* 1–4.—335

Koretz, D., McCaffrey, D., Klein, S., Bell, R., & Stecher, B. M. (1992). *The reliability of scores from the 1992 Vermont portfolio assessment program: Interim report.* Washington, DC: RAND Corporation.—596

Kornhaber, M., Krechevsky, M., & Gardner, H. (1990). Engaging intelligence. *Educational Psychologist, 3 & 4,* 177–199.—72, 78, 79

Kounin, J. S. (1970). *Discipline and group management in classrooms.* New York: Holt, Rinehart, & Winston. *A sensible view of classroom management by one who sat, watched, recorded, and categorized what he saw.*—465–466

Kozulin, A., & Presseisen, P. Z. (1995). Mediated learning experience and psychological tools: Vygotsky's and Feuerstein's perspectives in a study of student learning. *Educational Psychologist, 30*(2), 67–75.—114

Krathwohl, D. R., Bloom, B. S., & Masia, B. B. (1964). *Taxonomy of educational objectives. The classification of educational goals, Handbook 2: Affective domain.* New York: McKay. *The affective counterpart of the well-known taxonomy of cognitive objectives.*—41

Krumboltz, J. D. (1990 Jan.–Feb.). Do schools teach kids to hate learning? *Stanford Observer,* p. 10.—329

Krumboltz, J. D., & Yeh, C. J. (1996, December). Competitive grading sabotages good teaching. *Phi Delta Kappan, 78*(4), 324–326.—330, 552

Kulik, J. A. (1992). *An analysis of the research on ability grouping: Historical and contemporary perspectives.* ERIC Document Reproduction Service No. ED350777.—436

Kulik, J. A. (1993, Spring). An analysis of the research on ability grouping. *National Research Center on the Gifted and Talented Newsletter.*

ERIC Document Reproduction Service No. ED367095.—435, 436

Kulik, J. A. (1994). Meta-analytic studies of findings on computer-based instruction. In E. L. Baker (Ed.), *Technology assessment in education and training.* Hillsdale, NJ: Erlbaum.—445

Kulik, J. A., & Kulik, C-L. C. (1984). Synthesis of research on effects of accelerated instruction. *Educational Leadership, 42*(2), 85–89.—199

Kulik, J. A., Kulik, C-L. C., & Bangert-Drowns. (1990). Is there better evidence on mastery learning? A response to Slavin. *Review of Educational Research, 60,* 303–307.—437–438

Lambiotte, J. G., Dansereau, D. F., Cross, D. R., & Reynolds, S. B. (1989). Multirelational semantic maps. *Educational Psychology Review, 1,* 331–368.—290

Lane, S., Liu, M., Ankenmann, R. D., & Stone, C. A. (1996). Generalizability and validity of a mathematics performance assessment. *Journal of Educational Measurement, 33*(1), 71–92.—566

Larkins, A. G., McKinney, C. W., Oldham-Buss, S., & Gilmore, A. C. (1985). Teacher enthusiasm: A critical review. In H. S. Williams (Ed.), *Educational and psychological research monographs.* Hattiesburg, MS: University of Southern Mississippi.—392–393

Lattal, K. A., & Neef, N. A. (1996). Recent reinforcement-schedule research and applied behavior analysis. *Journal of Applied Behavior Analysis, 29*(2), 213–230.—221

Lau Kam Cheong (1972). *Augmenting lecture presentation with structural support.* Unpublished doctoral dissertation, University of Malaya, Kuala Lumpur.—387

Lave, J. (1988). *Cognition in practice: Mind, mathematics, and culture in everyday life.* New York: Cambridge University Press.—277

Lave, J., & Wenger, E. (1991). *Situated learning: Legitimate peripheral participation.* New York: Cambridge University Press. *A strong statement in support of the power and limitations of the context in which learning takes place.*—277, 286

Lazarsfeld, P. F. (1949). The American soldier—an expository review. *Public Opinion Quarterly, 13,* 377–404.—10

LeMahieu, P. G., Gitomer, D. H., & Eresh, J. T. (1995). *Portfolios beyond the classroom: Data quality and qualities.* Center for Performance Assessment, AMP-95-3872. Princeton, NJ: Educational Testing Service.—594–595

Leonard G. (1987). *Education and ecstasy: With the great school reform hoax.* Berkeley, CA: North Atlantic Books.—MP 4, Chapter 13

Lepper, M. R., & Chabay, R. W. (1985). Intrinsic motivation and instruction: Conflicting views on the role of motivational processes in computer-based education. *Educational Psychologist, 20,* 217–230.—359

Lepper, M. R., & Greene, D. (1975). Turning play into work: Effects of adult surveillance and extrinsic rewards on children's intrinsic motivation. *Journal of Personality and Social Psychology, 31,* 479–488.—334–335

Lepper, M. R., Greene, D., & Nisbett, R. E. (1973). Undermining children's intrinsic interest with extrinsic rewards: A test of the overjustification hypothesis. *Journal of Personality and Social Psychology, 28,* 129–137.—334

Lepper, M. R., & Hodell, M. (1989). Intrinsic motivation in the classroom. In C. Ames & R. Ames (Eds.), *Research on motivation in education* (Vol. 3). San Diego: Academic Press.—336, 357

Lepper, M. R., Keavney, M., & Drake, M. (1996). Intrinsic motivation and extrinsic rewards: A commentary on Cameron and Pierce's meta-analysis. *Review of Educational Research, 66,* 5–32.—335, 336

Lerner, J. W. (1997). *Learning disabilities: Theories, diagnosis, and teaching strategies* (7th ed.). Boston: Houghton Mifflin.—187

Levin, H. M., Glass, G. V, & Meister, G. R. (1984). *Cost-effectiveness of four educational interventions.* Stanford, CA: Institute for Research on Educational Finance and Governance (Project Report No. 84–A11).—445

Levin, H. M., Glass, G. V, & Meister, G. R. (1987). Cost-effectiveness of computer-assisted instruction. *Evaluation Review, 11,* 50–72.—442

Levin, J. R. (1981). The mnemonic 80s: Keywords in the classroom. *Educational Psychologist, 16,* 65–82.—267

Levin, M. E., & Levin, J. R. (1990). Scientific mnemonics: Methods for maximizing more than memory. *American Educational Research Journal, 27,* 301–321.—268

Levine, M. (1996). *Viewing violence.* New York: Doubleday.—240

Levy, D. (1996, November 5). Examining the casualty count. *USA Today,* p. 6D.—538

Lewis, D. R., et al. (1990). Cost-effectiveness of micro-computers in adult basic reading. *Adult*

Literacy and Basic Education, 14(2), 136–149.—445

Liao, Y.-K. (1992). Effects of computer-assisted instruction on cognitive outcomes: A meta-analysis. *Journal of Research on Computing in Education, 24,* 367–380.—445

Linguistic Society of America. (1997). *Resolution on the Oakland "Ebonics" issue.* Chicago: The Society.—122

Linn, M. C. (1986). Science. In R. F. Dillon & R. J. Sternberg (Eds.), *Cognition and instruction* (pp. 155–204). New York: Academic Press.—297

Linn, R. L. (1994). Performance assessment: Policy promises and technical measurement standards. *Educational Researcher, 23*(9), 4–14.—566

Linn, R. L., Graue, M. E., & Sanders, N. M. (1990). Comparing state and district test results to national norms: The validity of claims that "Everyone is above average." *Educational Measurement: Issues and Practice, 9,* 5–14.—534

Linscheid, T., Iwata, B., Ricketts, R., Williams, D., & Griffin, J. (1990). Clinical evaluation of the Self-Injurious Behavior Inhibiting System (SIBIS). *Journal of Applied Behavior Analysis, 23*(1), 53–78.—229

Lipsey, M. W., & Wilson, D. B. (1993). The efficacy of psychological, educational, and behavioral treatment: Confirmation from meta-analysis. *American Psychologist, 48,* 1181–1209.—441, 445

Lubinski, D., & Humphreys, L. G. (1996). Seeing the forest from the trees: When predicting the behavior or status of groups, correlate means. *Psychology, Public Policy, & Law, 2,* 363–376.—80

Luborski, D., & Benbow, C. P. (1995). An opportunity for empiricism (Review of book *Multiple intelligences: The theory in practice*). *Contemporary Psychology, 40,* 935–938. *A brief criticism, by mainstream psychometricians, of the theory of multiple intelligences.*—78

Luiten, J., Ames, W., & Ackerman, G. (1980). A meta-analysis of the effects of advance organizers on learning and retention. *American Educational Research Journal, 17,* 211–218.—290, 377

Luria, A. R. (1979). Cultural differences in thinking. In M. Cole & S. Cole (Eds.), *The making of mind: A personal account of Soviet psychology.* Cambridge, MA: Harvard University Press.—113

Lynn, R. (1993). Nutrition and intelligence. In P. A. Vernon (Ed.), *Biological approaches to the study of human intelligence* (pp. 243–258). Norwood, NJ: Ablex.—67

Maccoby, E. E., & Jacklin, C. N. (1974). *The psychology of sex differences.* Stanford, CA: Stanford University Press.—170

MacMillan, D. L., & Balow, I. H. (1991). Impact of Larry P. on educational programs and assessment practices in California. *Diagnostique, 17*(1), 57–69.—69

Maehr, M. L. (1976). Continuing motivation: An analysis of a seldom considered educational outcome. *Review of Educational Research, 46,* 443–462.—354

Maehr, M. L., & Midgley, C. (1991). Enhancing student motivation: A schoolwide approach. *Educational Psychologist, 26,* 399–428.—352

Mager, R. F. (1975). *Preparing instructional objectives* (2d ed.). Belmont, CA: Fearon Publishers.—37

Male, M. (1994). Cooperative learning and computers. In S. Sharan (Ed.), *Handbook of cooperative learning methods* (pp. 267–280). Westport, CT: Greenwood Press.—422

Mandinach, E. B., & Cline, H. F. (1994). *Classroom dynamics: Implementing a technology-based learning environment.* Hillsdale, NJ: Erlbaum.—424

Marks, C. B., Doctorow, M. J., & Wittrock, M. C. (1974). Word frequency and reading comprehension. *Journal of Educational Research, 67,* 259–262.—275

Marliave, R., & Filby, N. N. (1985). Success rate: A measure of task appropriateness. In C. W. Fisher & D. C. Berliner (Eds.), *Perspectives on instructional time.* White Plains, NY: Longman.—338

Marsh, H. W. (1988). *The failure of academically selective high schools to deliver academic benefits: The importance of academic self-concept and educational aspirations.* ERIC Document Reproduction Service No. ED300403.—201

Marsh, H. W., Chessor, D., Craven, R., & Roche, L. (1995). The effects of gifted and talented programs on academic self-concept: The big fish strikes again. *American Educational Research Journal, 32,* 285–319.—201, 436

Martens, R. L., Portier, S. J., & Valcke, M. M. A. (1995). *Comparing study outcomes from different learning environments for statistics.* Heerlen, Netherlands: Centre for Educational Technical

Innovation, Open University (ERIC Document Reproduction Service No. ED383745).—371

Martin, C. L. (1991). The role of cognition in understanding gender effects. In H. Reese (Ed.), *Advances in child development and behavior* (Vol. 23, pp. 113–149). New York: Academic Press.—169

Martin, C. L., & Halverson, C. F. (1983). The effects of sex-typing schemas on young children's memory. *Child Development, 54,* 563–574.—169

Martin, J. (1993). Episodic memory: A neglected phenomenon in the psychology of education. *Educational Psychologist, 28,* 169–183.—263

Martinez, J. G. R., & Martinez, N. C. (1988). "Hello, teacher": An argument for reemphasizing the teacher's role in PSI and mastery learning. *American Journal of Education, 97,* 18–33.—439

Marzano, R. J., & Kendall, J. S. (1996). *Designing standards-based districts, schools, and classrooms.* Alexandria, VA: Association for Supervision and Curriculum Development.—559, 560, 589

Maslow, A. H. (1954). *Motivation and personality.* New York: Harper & Row.—317

Maslow, A. H. (1971). *The farther reaches of human nature.* New York: Viking.—318

Mastropieri, M. A., & Scruggs, T. E. (1989). Constructing more meaningful relationships: Mnemonic instruction for special populations. *Educational Psychology Review, 1,* 83–112.—267

Matson, J. L., & DiLorenzo, T. M. (1984). *Punishment and its alternatives.* New York: Springer.—228

Matthew, J. A. D. (1991). Cartoons in science. *Physics Education, 26,* 110–114.—393

Mayer, R. E. (1983). Can you repeat that? Qualitative effects of repetition and advance organizers on learning from science prose. *Journal of Educational Psychology, 75,* 40–49.—265

Mayer, R. E. (1986). Mathematics. In R. F. Dillon and R. J. Sternberg (Eds.), *Cognition and instruction.* New York: Academic Press.—295

Mayer, R. E. (1989). Mathematics. In R. F. Dillon & R. J. Sternberg (Eds.), *Cognition and instruction.* New York: Academic Press.—302–303

Mayer, R. E., & Wittrock, M. C. (1996). Problem solving transfer. In D. C. Berliner & R. C. Calfee (Eds.), *Handbook of educational psychology* (pp. 47–62). New York: Macmillan.—271, 275, 301

McCaslin, M., & Good, T. L. (1996). The informal curriculum. In D. C. Berliner & R. C. Calfee (Eds.), *Handbook of educational psychology* (pp. 622–670). New York: Macmillan.—331, 400, 425

McCaslin, M., Tuck, D., Ward, A., Brown, B., LaPage, J., & Phyle, J. (1994). Gender composition and small group learning in fourth-grade mathematics. *Elementary School Journal, 94,* 467–482.—263

McCombs, B. L., & Pope, J. E. (1994). *Motivating hard-to-reach students.* Washington, DC: American Psychological Association. *A primer for K–12 teachers on how to seek information to better motivate students.*—338

McEwan, B., & Nimmo, G. (1995). *Effective management practices for severely emotionally disturbed youth: A collaborative study on democratic practices in inclusive classrooms.* ERIC Document Reproduction Service No. ED385045.—193

McGue, M., Bouchard, T. J., Jr., Iacono, W. G., & Lykken, D. T. (1993). Behavioral genetics of cognitive ability: A life-span perspective. In R. Plomin & G. E. McLearn (Eds.), *Nature, nurture, and psychology* (pp. 59–76). Washington, DC: American Psychological Association.—64

McKeachie, W. J. (1994). *Teaching tips: Strategies, research, and theory for college and university teachers* (9th ed). Lexington, MA: D. C. Heath. *A primer of educational psychology for new teachers in higher education settings.*—370

McKeachie, W. J., Pintrich, P. R., Lin, Y.-G., & Smith, D. A. F. (1990). *Teaching and learning in the college classroom: A review of the literature.* Ann Arbor, MI: National Center for Research to Improve Postsecondary Teaching and Learning.—371, 399

McKey, R. H., & Smith, A. H. (1985). *The impact of Head Start on children, families, and communities.* DHHS Publication No. (OHDS) 90–31193. Washington, DC: U.S. Government Printing Office.—91

McKinney, C. W., Larkins, A. G., Kazelskis, R., Ford, M. J., Allen, J. A., & Davis, J. C. (1983). Some effects of teacher enthusiasm on student achievement in fourth-grade social studies. *Journal of Educational Research, 76,* 249–253.—393

McLaughlin, M. W., Irby, M. A., & Langman, J. (1994). *Urban sanctuaries.* San Francisco: Jossey-Bass. *The effects of after-school affilia-*

tions on student achievement and identity are described.—319

McLaughlin, M. W., & Phillips, D. C. (Eds.). (1991). *Evaluation and education at quarter century: Ninetieth yearbook of the National Society for the Study of Education* (Pt. 2). Chicago: University of Chicago Press.—528

McLeish, J. (1976). The lecture method. In N. L. Gage (Ed.), *The psychology of teaching methods: Seventy-fifth yearbook of the National Society for the Study of Education* (Pt. 1). Chicago: University of Chicago Press.—370, 371

McNeil, D. (1970). *The acquisition of language.* New York: Harper & Row.—118

Mehan, H. (1979). *Learning lessons: Social organization in the classroom.* Cambridge, MA: Harvard University Press.—126, 455

Mehan, H. (1982). The structure of classroom events and their consequences for student performance. In P. Gilmore & A. A. Glatthorn (Eds.), *Children in and out of school.* Washington, DC: Center for Applied Linguistics.—126

Meier, D. (1995). *The power of their ideas: Lessons for America from a small school in Harlem.* Boston: Beacon Press. *One of America's most successful school administrators describes her successful school.*—MP 4, Chapter 13

Messick, S. (1980). Test validity and the ethics of assessment. *American Psychologist, 35,* 1012–1028.—525

Messick, S. (1982). Issues of effectiveness and equity in the coaching controversy: Implications for educational and testing practice. *Educational Psychologist, 17,* 67–91.—541

Messick, S. (1989). Validity. In R. L. Linn (Ed.), *Educational measurement* (3d ed., pp. 13–103). New York: American Council on Education/Macmillan.—525

Metcalf, K. K. (1992). The effects of a guided training experience on the instructional clarity of preservice teachers. *Teaching and Teacher Education, 8,* 275–286.—364

Midgley, C., Feldlaufer, H., & Eccles, J. S. (1989). Student/teacher relations and attitudes toward mathematics before and after the transition to junior high school. *Child Development, 60,* 375–395.—351

Mills, R. P. (1996). Statewide portfolio assessment: The Vermont experience. In J. B. Baron & D. P. Wolf (Eds.), *Performance-based student as-*
sessment: Challenges and possibilities: Ninety-fifth yearbook of the National Society for the Study of Education* (Pt. 1, pp. 192–214). Chicago: University of Chicago Press.—596

Mischel, W. (1973). Toward a cognitive social learning reconceptualization of personality. *Psychological Review, 80,* 252–283.—138

Mischel, W. (1990). Personality dispositions revisited and revised: A view after three decades. In L. A. Pervin (Ed.), *Handbook of personality: Theory and research* (pp. 111–134). New York: Guilford Press.—138

Moely, B. E., Hart, S. S., Santulli, K., Leal, L., Johnson-Barron, T., Rao, N., & Burney, L. (1986). How do teachers teach memory skills? *Educational Psychologist, 21,* 55–72.—257, 265

Moldavan, C. (1993). Tips for beginners: Attention getters. *Mathematics Teacher, 86,* 297.—393

Molitor, F., & Hirsch, K. W. (1994). Children's toleration of real-life aggression after exposure to media violence: A replication of the Drabman and Thomas studies. *Child Study Journal, 24,* 191–207.—465

Moll, L. (Ed.). (1990). *Vygotsky and education.* Cambridge, England: Cambridge University Press.—111

Molnar, A. (1996). *Giving kids the business.* Boulder, CO: Westview Press.—530

Moore, J. C. (1968). Cueing for selective note taking. *Journal of Experimental Education, 36,* 69–72.—394

Morgan, M. (1984). Reward-induced decrements and increments in intrinsic motivation. *Review of Educational Research, 54,* 5–30.—354

Morine-Dershimer, G. (1987). Can we talk? In D. C. Berliner & B. V. Rosenshine (Eds.), *Talks to teachers: A Festschrift for N. L. Gage* (pp. 37–53). New York: Random House.—126–127

Morine-Dershimer, G., & Tenenberg, M. (1981). *Participant perspectives of classroom discourse* (Final Report, Executive Summary, NIE–G–78–0161). Washington, DC: National Institute of Education.—126

Mosteller, F., et al. (1996). Sustained inquiry in education: Lessons from skill grouping and class size. *Harvard Educational Review, 66,* 797–842.—461

Mueller, D. J. (1976). Mastery learning: Partly boon, partly boondoggle. *Teachers College Record, 78,* 41–52.—438

Mugleston, W. F. (1989). Turning them on the first day of class. *OAH Magazine of History, 4,* 7–8.—393

Murphy, C. A., & Walls, R. T. (1994). *Concurrent and sequential occurrences of teacher enthusiasm behaviors.* ERIC Document Reproduction Service No. ED375128.—392

Murphy, J. J. (1988). Contingency contracting in schools: A review. *Education and Treatment of Children, 11,* 257–269.—433

Murray, H., et al. (1938). *Explorations in personality: A clinical and experimental study of fifty men of college age.* New York: Oxford University Press. *Raised the study of personality to a much higher level of sophistication, ingenuity, and insightfulness.*—317

Myers, D. G. (1993). *Social psychology.* New York: McGraw-Hill.—10

Nagoshi, C. T., & Johnson, R. C. (1986). The ubiquity of *g. Personality and Individual Differences, 7,* 201–207.—60

Nagy, P., & Griffith, A. K. (1982). Limitations of recent research relating Piaget's theory to adolescent thought. *Review of Educational Research, 52,* 513–556.—107

National Center for History in the Schools. (1994). *National standards for United States history.* Los Angeles: The Center, University of California at Los Angeles.—32

National Commission on Testing and Public Policy. (1990). *Reforming assessment: From gatekeepers to gateway to education.* Chestnut Hill, MA: Boston College.—538

National Council of Teachers of Mathematics. (1989). *Curriculum and evaluation standards for school mathematics.* Reston, VA: National Council of Teachers of Mathematics.—32

National Research Council. (1996). *National Science Education Standards.* Washington, DC: National Academy Press.—32

Needels, M., & Gage, N. L. (1991). Essence and accident in process-product research on teaching. In H. C. Waxman & H. J. Walberg (Eds.), *Effective teaching: Current research* (pp. 3–31). Berkeley, CA: McCutchan.—15, 18, 495

Neill, A. S. (1960). *Summerhill: A radical approach to child rearing.* New York: Hart. *The first of the wave of writings by the humanistic educators of the 1960s.*—36

Neisser, U. (1976). General, academic, and artificial intelligence. In L. Resnick (Ed.), *The nature of intelligence.* Hillsdale, NJ: Erlbaum.—71

Neisser, U. (1996). Intelligence: Knowns and unknowns. *American Psychologist, 51,* 77–101. *Report of a committee of the American Psychological Association appointed, in part, as a response to* The Bell Curve *by Richard Herrnstein and Charles Murray.*—71

Nelms, B. C. (1989). Emotional behaviors in chronically ill children. *Journal of Abnormal Child Psychology, 17,* 657–668.—182

Nelson, K. (1973). Structure and strategy in learning to talk. *Monographs of the Society for Research in Child Development, 38*(149).—119

Nesher, P. (1986). Learning mathematics. *American Psychologist, 41,* 1114–1122.—295

Newby, T. J. (1991). Classroom motivation strategies of first year teachers. *Journal of Educational Psychology, 83,* 195–200.—352–353, 358

Newman, C., & Smolen, L. (1993). Portfolio assessment in our schools: Implementation, advantages, and concerns. *Mid-Western Educational Researcher, 6*(1), 28–32.—595

Nicholls, J. G. (1984). Achievement motivation: Conceptions of ability, subjective experience, task choice, and performance. *Psychological Review, 91,* 328–346.—353

Nickerson, R. S., & Adams, M. J. (1979). Long-term memory for a common object. *Cognitive Psychology, 11,* 287–307.—260

Nilsson, I., & Ekehammar, B. (1989). Social attitudes and beliefs in heredity: A replication and extension. *Personality and Individual Differences, 10,* 363–365.—84

Noble, D. D. (1996). Mad rushes into the future: The overselling of technology. *Educational Leadership, 54*(3), 18–23.—446

Noble, D. D. (1997). A bill of goods: The early marketing of computer-based education and its implications for the present moment. In B. J. Biddle, T. L. Good, & I. Goodson (Eds.), *International handbook on teachers and teaching.* Boston: Kluwer.—530

Noddings, N. (1990). Constructivism in mathematics education. In R. B. Davis, C. A. Maher, & N. Noddings (Eds.), *Constructivist views on the teaching and learning of mathematics* (pp. 7–18).

Reston, VA: National Council of Teachers of Mathematics.—255, 276

Noddings, N. (1992). *The challenge to care in schools.* New York: Teachers College Press. *An important counterpoint to the achievement-at-any-cost philosophy that determines how we evaluate schools.*—135–136

Nungester, R. J., & Duchastel, P. C. (1982). Testing versus review: Effects on retention. *Journal of Educational Psychology, 74,* 18–22.—583

Nuthall, G., & Snook, I. (1973). Contemporary models of teaching. In R. M. W. Travers (Ed.), *Second handbook of research on teaching* (pp. 47–76). Chicago: Rand McNally.—232

Oakes, J. (1985). *Keeping track: How schools structure inequality.* New Haven, CT: Yale University Press. *A thoughtful review of the harmful effects of teaching, and some alternatives.*—201, 331, 436

Oakes, J. (1992). Can tracking research inform practice? Technical, normative, and political considerations. *Educational Researcher, 21,* 12–21.—331

O'Day, J. A., & Smith, M. S. (1993). Systemic reform and educational opportunity. In S. Fuhrman (Ed.), *Designing coherent policy: Improving the system* (pp. 250–312). San Francisco: Jossey-Bass.—32

Ogbu, J. U. (1987). Variability in minority school performance: A problem in search of an explanation. *Anthropology and Education Quarterly, 18,* 312–334.—130

Ogbu, J. U. (1991). Low school performance as an adaptation: The case of blacks in Stockton, California. In M. A. Gibson & J. U. Ogbu (Eds.), *Minority status and schooling: A comparative study of immigrants and involuntary minorities.* New York: Garland Press.—332

Oklahoma State Department of Education (1994). *A handbook of alternatives to corporal punishment* (4th ed.). ERIC Document Reproduction Service No. ED370174.—468

Ornstein, R., & Ehrlich, P. (1989). *New world, new mind: Moving toward conscious evolution.* New York: Doubleday.—MP 3, Chapter 9

Ortega y Gasset, J. (1930). *The revolt of the masses.* New York: W. Norton.—MP 2, Chapter 5

Ortony, A. (1975). Why metaphors are necessary and not just nice. *Educational Theory, 24,* 45–53.—294

Oser, F. (1986). Moral education and values education: The discourse perspective. In M. C. Wittrock (Ed.), *Handbook of research on teaching* (3d ed., pp. 917–943). New York: Macmillan.—135, 404

Oser, F. K. (1994). Moral perspectives on teaching. In L. Darling-Hammond (Ed.), *Review of Research in Education, 20,* 57–128.—135

Page, E. B. (1958). Teacher comments and student performance: A seventy-four classroom experiment in school motivation. *Journal of Educational Psychology, 49,* 173–181.—354–356

Paik, H., & Comstock, G. (1994). The effects of television violence on antisocial behavior: A meta-analysis. *Communication Research, 21,* 516–546.—465

Paivio, A. (1986). *Mental representations: A dual-coding approach.* New York: Oxford University Press.—266

Palincsar, A. S., & Brown, A. L. (1981). *Training comprehension-monitoring skills in an interpretive learning game.* Unpublished manuscript, University of Illinois, Urbana.—271

Papert, S. (1984). New theories for new learning. *School Psychology Review, 13*(4), 422–428.—449

Paris, S. G., & Cunningham, A. E. (1996). Children becoming students. In D. C. Berliner & R. C. Calfee (Eds.), *Handbook of educational psychology* (pp. 117–147). New York: Macmillan.—122

Paris, S. G., Lawton, T. A., Turner, J. C., & Roth, J. L. (1991). A developmental perspective on standardized achievement testing. *Educational Researcher, 20*(5), 12–20.—538

Paris, S. G., Wixson, K. K., & Palincsar, A. S. (1986). Instructional approaches to reading comprehension. In E. Z. Rothkopf (Ed.), *Review of research in education.* Washington, DC: American Educational Research Association.—298

Pascual-Leone, J. (1980). Constructive problems for constructive theories: The current relevance of Piaget's work and a critique of information-processing simulation psychology. In R. H. Kluwe & H. Spada (Eds.), *Developmental models of thinking.* New York: Academic Press.—108

Pastore, N. (1949). *The nature-nurture controversy.* New York: Kings Crown Press, Columbia University.—83–84

Pederson, P. (1988). *A handbook for developing multicultural awareness.* Alexandria, VA: American Association for Counseling and Development.—156

Pekrun, R. (1994, April). *Academic emotions in students' self-regulated learning.* Paper presented at the meeting of the American Educational Research Association, New Orleans.—263

Perez, C. M., & Widom, C. S. (1994). Childhood victimization and long-term intellectual and academic outcomes. *Child Abuse and Neglect, 18,* 617–633.—85

Perfetti, C. A., & Curtis, M. E. (1986). Reading. In R. F. Dillon & R. J. Sternberg (Eds.), *Cognition and instruction.* New York: Academic Press.—298

Peterson, P. L., Clark, C. M., & Dickson, W. P. (1990). Educational psychology as a foundation in teacher education: Reforming an old notion. *Teachers College Record, 91,* 322–346.—275

Petty, M. F., & Field, C. J. (1980). Fluctuations in mental test scores. *Educational Research, 22,* 198–202.—55

Pfiffner, L. J. (1996). *All about ADHD: The complete practical guide for classroom teachers.* Jefferson City, MO: Scholastic Professional Books.—194

Phillips, D. C. (1995). The good, the bad, and the ugly: The many faces of constructivism. *Educational Researcher, 24*(7), 5–12.—256, 276

Phillips, S. U. (1983). *The invisible culture: Communication in classroom and community on the Warm Springs Indian Reservation.* White Plains, NY: Longman. *Describes how the participant structures in two cultures can be different and clash, yet be practically invisible to the people in each culture.*—126

Piaget, J. (1926). *The language and thought of the child* (M. Worden, Trans.). New York: Harcourt, Brace.—98

Piaget, J. (1928). *Judgment and reasoning in the child* (M. Worden, Trans.). London: Routledge & Kegan Paul.—98

Piaget, J. (1932). *The moral judgment of the child* (M. Worden, Trans.). New York: Harcourt, Brace.—98

Piaget, J. (1951). *The child's conception of physical causality* (M. Gabain, Trans.). New York: Humanities Press. (Original work published 1930.)—98

Pinnell, G. S., Lyons, C. A., DeFord, D. E., Bryk, A. S., & Seltzer, M. (1994). Comparing instructional models for the literacy education of high-risk first graders. *Reading Research Quarterly, 29,* 8–38.—348

Pogrow, S. (1996). HOTS: Helping low achievers in grades 4–7. *Principal, 76*(2), 34–35.—445

Portes, P. R. (1996). Ethnicity and culture in educational psychology. In D. C. Berliner & R. C. Calfee (Eds.), *Handbook of educational psychology* (pp. 331–357). New York: Macmillan.—114, 436

Powell, J. P., & Andresen, L. W. (1985). Humour and teaching in higher education. *Studies in Higher Education, 10,* 79–90.—392

Prawat, R. S. (1989). Promoting access to knowledge, strategy, and disposition in students: A research synthesis. *Review of Educational Research, 59,* 1–41.—265

Premack, D. (1965). Reinforcement theory. In D. Levine (Ed.), *Nebraska Symposium on Motivation* (Vol. 13, pp. 123–180). Lincoln: University of Nebraska Press.—222–223

Pressley, M., Burkell, J., Cariglia-Bull, T., Lysynchuck, L., McGoldrick, J. A., Schneider, B., Snyder, B. L., Symons, S., & Woloshyn, V. E. (1990). *Cognitive strategy instruction.* Cambridge, MA: Brookline. *A practical guide for teachers. Describes in detail the available strategies for increasing learning in reading, mathematics, writing, and other academic subjects.*—268, 270

Pressley, M., Johnson, C. J., Symons, S., McGoldrick, J. A., & Kurita, J. A. (1989). Strategies that improve children's memory and comprehension of text. *Elementary School Journal, 90,* 3–32.—431, 433

Pressley, M., Levin, J. R., & Delaney, H. D. (1982). The mnemonic keyword method. *Review of Educational Research, 52,* 61–91.—267

Pressley, M., Levin, J. R., & McDaniel, M. A. (1987). Remembering versus inferring what a word means: Mnemonic and contextual approaches. In M. McGeown & M. E. Curtis (Eds.), *The nature of vocabulary acquisition* (pp. 107–127). Hillsdale, NJ: Erlbaum.—267

Pressley, M., & McCormick, C. B. (1995). *Advanced educational psychology.* New York: HarperCollins.—257, 266, 275, 297

Pressley, M., Woloshyn, V., Lysynchuck, L. M., Martin, V., Wood, E., & Willoughby, T. (1990). A primer of research on cognitive strategy instruction: The important issues and how to address them. *Educational Psychology Review, 2,* 1–58.—256

Pugh, R. C. (1995). *Interactive television in distance education settings.* ERIC Document Reproduction Service No. ED389264.—387

Ramirez, D. J., Yuen, S. D., Ramey, D. R., & Pasta, D. J. (1991). *Longitudinal study of structured-English immersion strategy: Early-exit and late-exit transitional bilingual educational programs for language minority children* (Vols. 1 and 2). San Mateo, CA: Aquirre International.—123, 124

Raphael, T. E., & Wonnacott, C. A. (1985). Metacognitive training in question-answering strategies: Implementation in a fourth-grade developmental reading program. *Reading Research Quarterly, 20,* 282–296.—268

Rappaport, M. D., Murphy, M. A., & Bailey, J. E. (1982). Ritalin vs. response cost in the control of hyperactive children: A within-subject comparison. *Journal of Applied Behavior Analysis, 15,* 205–216.—230

Redfield, D. L., & Rousseau, E. W. (1981). A meta-analysis of experimental research on teacher questioning behavior. *Review of Educational Research, 51,* 237–245.—484

Reed, S. K. (1987). A structure-mapping model for word problems. *Journal of Experimental Psychology: Learning, Memory, and Cognition, 13,* 124–139.—301

Reed, S. K. (1989). Estimating answers to algebra word problems. *Journal of Experimental Psychology: Learning, Memory, and Cognition, 10,* 778–790.—295

Remmers, H. H., & Gage, N. L. (1943). *Educational measurement and evaluation.* New York: Harper.—559

Resnick, L. B. (1987). Constructing knowledge in school. In L. S. Liben (Ed.), *Development and learning: Conflict or congruence.* Hillsdale, NJ: Erlbaum.—257

Resnick, L. B., Levine, J. M., & Teasley, S. D. (Eds.). (1993). *Perspectives on shared cognition.* Washington, DC: American Psychological Association.—398

Resnick, L. B., & Resnick, D. P. (1990). Tests as standards of achievement in schools. In *Proceedings of the 1989 ETS Invitational Conference: The uses of standardized tests in American education* (pp. 63–80). Princeton, NJ: Educational Testing Service. *A criticism of current practices in standardized achievement testing and a sketch of standardized testing approaches that would not have deleterious side effects on curriculum and instruction.*—534, 546

Rest, J. R., Thoma, S., Volker, J., Yong, L. M., Getz, I., Deemer, D., & Berndt, T. (1985, March). *Research on moral development.* Symposium presented at the meeting of the American Educational Research Association, Chicago.—133, 134

Rest, J. R. & Narvaez, D. (Eds.). (1994). *Moral development in the professions: Psychology and applied ethics.* Hillsdale, NJ: Erlbaum.—134–135

Reynolds, C. R., Chastain, R. L., Kaufman, A. S., & McLean, J. E. (1987). Demographic characteristics and IQ among adults: Analysis of the WAIS-R standardization sample as a function of the stratification variables. *Journal of School Psychology, 25,* 323–342.—60

Rife, R. M., & Karr-Kidwell, P. J. (1995). *Administrative and teacher efforts for elementary emotionally-disturbed and behaviorally-disordered students: A literature review and recommendations for an inclusion program.* ERIC Document Reproduction Service No. ED396497.—192

Riley, J. P. (1981). The effects of preservice teachers' cognitive questioning level and redirecting on student science achievement. *Journal of Research in Science Teaching, 18,* 303–309.—491

Riley, M. S., Greeno, J. G., & Heller, J. I. (1983). Development of children's problem-solving ability in mathematics. In H. P. Ginsburg (Ed.), *The development of mathematical thinking.* New York: Academic Press.—295

Rimland, B. (1990, October 2). Personal communication to N. L. Gage.—228

Roehler, L. R., & Duffy, G. G. (1986). What makes one teacher a better explainer than another? *Journal of Education for Teaching, 12,* 273–284.—385

Rogoff, B. (1990). *Apprenticeship in thinking.* New York: Oxford University Press. *Thought-provoking views about how tailors or mathematicians come to acquire the habits of mind and the skills to function well in their environments.*—237

Rohrkemper, M. M. (1986). The functions of inner speech in elementary school students' problem-solving behavior. *American Educational Research Journal, 23,* 303–314.—342

Romberg, T. A., & Collis, K. F. (1987). Different ways children have to add and subtract. *Journal for Research in Mathematics Education,* monograph no. 2.—295

Rose, M. (1995). *Possible lives.* Boston: Houghton Mifflin.—MP 2, Chapter 5

Rosenbaum, M. S., & Drabman, R. S. (1979). Self-control training in the classroom: A review and critique. *Journal of Applied Behavior Analysis, 12,* 467–485.—247

Rosenberg, M. S., Wilson, R., Maheady, L., & Sindelar, P. T. (1997). *Educating students with behavior disorders* (2d ed.). Needham Heights, MA: Allyn & Bacon.—190

Rosenberg, R. (1987). A critical analysis of research on intelligent tutoring systems. *Educational Technology, 27*(11), 7–13.—444

Rosenholtz, S. J., & Simpson, C. (1984). Classroom organization and student stratification. *Elementary School Journal, 85,* 21–38.—331

Rosenshine, B. V. (1971a). Objectively measured behavioral predictors of effectiveness in explaining. In I. D. Westbury & A. A. Bellack (Eds.), *Research into classroom processes* (pp. 51–98). New York: Teachers College Press.—386, 389

Rosenshine, B. V. (1971b). *Teaching behaviours and student achievement.* London: National Foundation for Educational Research in England and Wales. *Brings together, clusters, and summarizes about 50 studies.*—475

Rosenshine, B. V. (1980). How time is spent in elementary classrooms. In C. Denham & A. Lieberman (Eds.), *Time to learn.* Washington, DC: National Institute of Education.—455

Rosenshine, B. V., & Meister, C. (1992). The use of scaffolds for teaching higher-level cognitive strategies. *Educational Leadership, 49*(7), 26–33.—275, 474

Rosenshine, B. V., Meister, C., & Chapman, S. (1996). Teaching students to generate questions: A review of the intervention studies. *Review of Educational Research, 66,* 181–221.—432

Rosenshine, B. V., & Stevens, R. (1986). Teaching functions. In M. C. Wittrock (Ed.), *Handbook of research on teaching* (3d ed., pp. 376–391). New York: Macmillan.—338, 477

Ross, J., & Lawrence, K. A. (1968). Some observations on memory artifice. *Psychonomic Science, 13,* 107–108.—267

Rosser, R. (1994). *Cognitive development: Psychological and biological perspectives.* Boston: Allyn & Bacon.—118

Roth, V. J., & Anderson, C. W. (1990). Promoting conceptual change in learning from science textbooks. In P. Romsden (Ed.), *Improving learning: New perspectives.* New York: Nichols.—297

Rothenberg, J. (1989). The open classroom reconsidered. *Elementary School Journal, 90,* 69–86.—502

Rowe, M. B. (1974). Wait-time and rewards as instructional variables: Their influence on language, logic, and fate control, Pt. 1: Wait-time. *Journal of Research in Science Teaching, 11,* 81–94.—485, 486

Royce, J. (1891). Is there a science of education? *Education Review, 1,* 15–25, 121–132.—25

Rumelhart, D. E. (1980). Schemata: The building blocks of cognition. In R. J. Spiro, B. C. Bruce, & W. F. Brewer (Eds.), *Theoretical issues in reading comprehension.* Hillsdale, NJ: Erlbaum.—292

Rumelhart, D. E., & Ortony, A. (1977). The representation of knowledge in memory. In R. C. Anderson, R. J. Spiro, & W. E. Montague (Eds.), *Schooling and the acquisition of knowledge* (pp. 99–135). Hillsdale, NJ: Erlbaum.—292

Runnheim, V. A., et al. (1996). Medicating students with emotional and behavioral disorders and ADHD: A state survey. *Behavioral Disorders, 21*(4), 306–314.—231

Russell, B. (1916). *Principles of social reconstruction.* London: G. Allen & Unwin.—MP 2, Chapter 5

Russell, B., & Branch, T. (1979). *Second wind.* New York: Ballantine.—77

Ryan, J. J., Paolo, A. M., & Dunn, G. E. (1995). Analysis of a WAIS-R old-age-normative sample in terms of gender, years of education, and preretirement occupation. *Assessment, 2,* 225–231.—60

Ryan, R. M., & Deci, E. L. (1996). When paradigms clash: Comments on Cameron and Pierce's claim that rewards do not undermine intrinsic motivation. *Review of Educational Research, 66,* 33–38.—335

Ryans, D. G. (1960). *Characteristics of teachers.* Washington, DC: American Council on Education. *Factor analyses of ratings of teacher and* *student behavior; still one of the most comprehensive and careful studies of teaching.*—489

Salomon, G. (Ed.). (1993). *Distributed cognitions: Psychological and educational considerations.* New York: Cambridge University Press. *Explorations on what it means to define intelligence as residing outside the individual as well as a characteristic of the individual. Thus, ability to use computers and work in communities of learners are intelligence-enhancing activities.*—398

Salomon, G., & Globerson, T. (1987). *Skill is not enough: The role of mindfulness in learning and transfer* (Report No. 11). Tel Aviv: Tel Aviv University, School of Education, Unit for Communication and Computer Research in Education.—305

Salomon, G., & Perkins, D. N. (1989). Rocky roads to transfer: Rethinking mechanisms of a neglected phenomenon. *Educational Researcher, 19,* 2–10.—305

Samson, G. E., Strykowski, B., Weinstein, T., & Walberg, H. J. (1987). The effects of teacher questioning levels on student achievement: A quantitative synthesis. *Journal of Educational Research, 80,* 290–295.—484

Sandoval, J., & Hughes, G. P. (1981). *Success in nonpromoted first-grade children.* Davis: Department of Education, University of California.—592

Sawyer, R. J., Graham, S., & Harris, K. R. (1992). Direct teaching, strategy instruction, and strategy instruction with explicit self-regulation: Effects on the composition skills and self-efficacy of students with learning disabilities. *Journal of Educational Psychology, 84,* 340–352.—247

Saxe, G. B. (1988). Candy selling and math learning. *Educational Researcher, 17,* 14–21.—295

Saxe, G. B. (1990). *Culture and cognitive development: Studies in mathematical understanding.* Hillsdale, NJ: Erlbaum.—277

Scandura, J. M., & Scandura, A. B. (1980). *Structural learning and concrete operations.* New York: Praeger.—107

Scardamalia, M., & Bereiter, C. (1991). Higher levels of agency for children in knowledge building: A challenge for the design of new knowledge media. *Journal of the Learning Sciences, 1,* 37–68.—286

Scardamalia, M., Bereiter, C., & Lamon, M. (1994). The CSILE Project: Trying to bring the classroom into world 3. In K. McGilly (Ed.), *Classroom lessons: Integrating cognitive theory and classroom practice* (pp. 201–228). Cambridge, MA: MIT Press.—286, 424

Scarr, S., & Weinberg, R. A. (1976). IQ test performances of black children adopted by white families. *American Psychologist, 31,* 726–739.—87–88

Schacht, S., & Stewart, B. J. (1990). What's funny about statistics? A technique for reducing student anxiety. *Teaching Sociology, 18*(1), 52–56.—393

Schiff, M., Duymé, M., Dumaret, A., Stewart, J., Tomkiewicz, S., & Feingold, J. (1978). Intellectual status of working-class children adopted early into upper-middle-class families. *Science, 200,* 1503–1504.—88

Schlaefli, A., Rest, J. R., & Thoma, S. J. (1985). Does moral education improve moral judgment? A meta-analysis of intervention studies using the Defining Issues Test. *Review of Educational Research, 55,* 319–352.—134

Schlieper, A. (1985). Chronic illness and school achievement. *Developmental Medicine and Child Neurology, 27*(1), 75–79.—182

Schmeiser, C. B. (1982). Use of experimental design in statistical item bias studies. In R. A. Berk (Ed.), *Handbook of methods for detecting test bias* (pp. 64–95). Baltimore: Johns Hopkins University Press.—86

Schmidt, F. L., & Hunter, J. E. (1992). Development of a causal model of processes determining job performance. *Current Directions in Psychological Science, 1,* 89–92.—60

Schmidt, F. L., & Hunter, J. E. (1993). Tacit knowledge, practical intelligence, general mental ability, and job knowledge. *Current Directions in Psychological Science, 2,* 8–9. *Criticizes the concepts of tacit knowledge and practical intelligence.*—74

Schmidt, W. H., Jorde, D., Cogan, L. S., Barrier, E., Gonzalo, I., Moser, U., Katsuhiko, S., Sawada, T., Valverde, G. A., McKnight, C., Prawat, R. S., Wiley, D. E., Raizen, S. A., Britton, E. D., & Wolfe, R. G. (1996). *Characterizing pedagogical flow: An investigation of mathematics and science teaching in six countries.* Boston: Kluwer.—500–501

Schneider, W., Körkel, J., & Weinert, F. E. (1989). Domain-specific knowledge and memory performance: A comparison of high- and low-aptitude children. *Journal of Educational Psychology, 81,* 306–312.—61

Schultz, J. J., Florio, S., & Erickson, F. (1982). Where's the floor? Aspects of cultural organization of social relationships in communication at home and in school. In P. Gilmore & A. A. Glatthorn (Eds.), *Children in and out of school.* Washington, DC: Center for Applied Linguistics.—126

Schumaker, J. B., & Deshler, D. D. (1992). Validation of learning strategy interventions for students with learning disabilities: Results of a programmatic research effort. In B. Y. L. Wong (Ed.), *Contemporary intervention research in learning disabilities: An international perspective* (pp. 22–46). New York: Springer-Verlag.—257

Schunk, D. C. (1981). Modeling and attributional effects on children's achievement: A self-efficacy analysis. *Journal of Educational Psychology, 73,* 93–105.—238

Schunk, D. H. (1991). Self-efficacy and academic motivation. *Educational Psychologist, 26,* 207–231.—349

Schunk, D. H. (1996). *Learning theories: An educational perspective* (2d ed.). New York: Merrill/Macmillan.—242, 243, 245

Schunk, D. H., & Zimmerman, B. J. (Eds.). (1994). *Self-regulation of learning and performance: Issues and educational applications.* Hillsdale, NJ: Erlbaum.—349

Schweinhart, L. J., & Weikart, D. P. (1980). Young children grow up: The effects of the Perry Preschool Program on youths through age 15. *Monographs of the High/Scope Educational Research Foundation,* No. 7. Ypsilanti, MI: The High Scope Press.—91

Schweinhart, L. J., Barnes, H. V., & Weikart, D. P. (1993). Significant benefits: The High Scope/Perry Preschool Study through age 27. *Monographs of the High/Scope Educational Research Foundation,* No. 10. Ypsilanti, MI: The High Scope Press.—93

Serpell, R. (1979). How specific are perceptual skills? A cross-cultural study of pattern reproduction. *British Journal of Psychology, 70,* 365–380.—162–163

Shachar, H., & Sharan, S. (1994). Talking, relating, and achieving: Effects of cooperative learning and whole-class instruction. *Cognition and Instruction, 12*(4), 313–353.—419

Sharan, S. (Ed.). (1994). *Handbook of cooperative learning methods.* Westport, CT: Greenwood Press. *Presentation of a wide array of group and* cooperative methods and discussions of their efficacy.—419

Sharan, Y., & Sharan, S. (1992). *Expanding cooperative learning through group investigation.* New York: Teachers College Press.—421

Shavelson, R. J. (1987). Teacher planning. In M. J. Dunkin (Ed.), *International encyclopedia of teaching and teacher education* (pp. 483–486). Oxford: Pergamon.—462, 463

Shavelson, R. J. (1991). Performance assessment in science. *Applied Measurement in Education, 4,* 347–362.—566, 579

Shavelson, R. J., Baxter, G. P., & Gao, X. (1993). Sampling variability of performance assessments. *Journal of Educational Measurement, 30,* 215–232.—566

Shavelson, R. J., Baxter, G. P., & Pine, J. (1992). Performance assessments: Political rhetoric and measurement reality. *Educational Researcher, 21*(4), 22–27.—584

Shavelson, R. J., & Stern, P. (1981). Research on teachers' pedagogical thoughts, judgments, decisions, and behavior. *Review of Educational Research, 51,* 455–498.—463

Shea, T. M., & Bauer, A. M. (1994). *Learners with disabilities: A social systems perspective of special education.* Madison, WI: Brown & Benchmark.—180, 183

Sheingold, K., & Fredrickson, J. (1995). *Linking assessment with reform: Technologies that support conversations about student work.* Center for Performance Assessment, MS 94–06. Princeton, NJ: Educational Testing Service.—595–596

Sheingold, K., Heller, J. I., & Paulukonis, S. T. (1995). *Actively seeking evidence: Teacher change through assessment development.* Center for Performance Assessment, MS 94–04. Princeton, NJ: Educational Testing Service.—561, 562

Shepard, L. A. (1991). Psychometrician's beliefs about learning. *Educational Researcher, 20*(7), 2–16.—534

Shepard, L. A. (1993). Evaluating test validity. In L. Darling-Hammond (Ed.), *Review of Research in Education, 19,* 405–450. Washington, DC: American Educational Research Association.—525, 526, 527

Sherwood, J. J., & Nataupsky, M. (1968). Predicting the conclusions of Negro-white intelligence research from biographical characteristics of the investigator (Pt. 1). *Journal of Personality and Social Psychology, 8*(1), 53–58.—84

Shoenfeld, A. H. (1985). *Mathematical problem solving.* Orlando, FL: Academic Press.—295

Short, E. J., & Ryan, E. B. (1984). Metacognitive differences between skilled and less skilled readers: Remediating deficits through story grammar and attribution training. *Journal of Educational Psychology, 76,* 225–235.—269

Shuey, A. (1966). *The testing of Negro intelligence* (2d ed.). New York: Social Science Press.—82

Shulman, L. S. (1987). Knowledge and teaching: Foundations for the new reform. *Harvard Educational Review, 57,* 1–22.—372, 473

Shutes, R. E. (1969). *Verbal behaviors and instructional effectiveness.* Unpublished doctoral dissertation, Stanford University, Stanford, CA.—394

Siegel, L. S., & Brainard, C. J. (Eds.). (1978). *Alternatives to Piaget: Critical essays on theory.* New York: Academic Press.—108

Siegler, R. S. (1991). *Children's thinking* (2d ed.). Englewood Cliffs, NJ: Prentice-Hall. *An authoritative presentation of the major theories, and accompanying data, on the growth of cognition.*—107

Silverman, L. K. (1980, October–November). *How are gifted teachers different from other teachers?* Paper presented at the meeting of the National Association for Gifted Children, Denver.—142

Simpson, R. L. (1992). Children and youth with autism. In L. M. Bullock (Ed.), *Exceptionalities in children and youth* (pp. 168–195). Boston: Allyn & Bacon.—196

Skinner, B. F. (1953). *Science and human behavior.* New York: Macmillan. *The first brave statement of the ways in which operant conditioning can be used in solving many human problems, including those in education.*—214

Skinner, B. F. (1954). The science of learning and the art of teaching. *Harvard Educational Review, 24,* 86–97. *The paper that started the programmed-instruction movement.*—214

Skinner, B. F. (1957). *Verbal behavior.* New York: Appleton-Century-Crofts.—214

Skinner, B. F. (1968). *The technology of teaching.* New York: Appleton-Century-Crofts. *A full treatment of the achievements and promises of operant conditioning for improving instruction.*—214

Skinner, B. F. (1973). The free and happy student. *Phi Delta Kappan, 55*(1), 13–16.—214

Skinner, B. F. (1987). *A statement on punishment.* Cambridge, MA: Author, Harvard University.—213, 221, 229

Slavin, R. E. (1983). *Cooperative learning.* White Plains, NY: Longman. *A clear presentation of a technology that usually accomplishes many goals—academic and social. Written by one of the major theorists and developers of this method.*—420–421

Slavin, R. E. (1984). Students motivating students to excel: Cooperative incentives, cooperative tasks, and student achievement. *Elementary School Journal, 85,* 53–64.—331

Slavin, R. E. (1987a). Ability grouping and student achievement in the elementary schools: A best-evidence synthesis. *Review of Educational Research, 57,* 293–336.—201

Slavin, R. E. (1987b). Mastery learning reconsidered. *Review of Educational Research, 57,* 175–213.—437

Slavin, R. E. (1990a). Achievement effects of ability grouping in secondary schools: A best-evidence synthesis. *Review of Educational Research, 60,* 471–499.—201, 436

Slavin, R. E. (1990b). Mastery learning re-reconsidered. *Review of Educational Research, 60,* 300–302.—422, 438

Slavin, R. E. (1990c). *Cooperative learning: Theory, research, and practice.* Englewood Cliffs, NJ: Prentice-Hall.—331

Slavin, R. E. (1993). Ability grouping in the middle grades: Achievement effects and alternatives. *Elementary School Journal, 93*(5), 535–552.—201

Slavin, R., & Braddock, J. H. (1993). Ability grouping: On the wrong track. *College Board Review, 168,* 11–17.—201

Slavin, R. E., Madden, N. A., Dolan, L. J., & Wasik, B. A. (1996). *Every child, every school: Success for all.* Thousand Oaks, CA: Corwin Press.—348

Smith, L. R., & Cotten, M. L. (1980). Effect of lesson vagueness and discontinuity on student achievement and attitudes. *Journal of Educational Psychology, 72,* 670–675.—387

Smith, M. L. (1991). Put to the test: The effects of external testing on teachers. *Educational Researcher, 20*(5), 8–11.—543–545

Smith, M. S., & Levin, J. (1996). Coherence, assessment, and challenging content. In J. B. Baron & D. P. Wolf (Eds.), *Performance-based student assessment: Challenges and possibilities: Ninety-fifth yearbook of the National Society for the Study of Education* (Pt. 1). Chicago: University of Chicago Press.—534, 547

Smitherman, G. (1994). *Black talk.* Boston: Houghton Mifflin.—122

Smoll, F. L., & Schutz, R. W. (1990). Quantifying gender differences in physical performance: A developmental perspective. *Developmental Psychology, 26,* 360–369.—171

Snow, R. E., Corno, L., & Jackson, D. (1996). Individual differences in affective and conative functions. In D. C. Berliner & R. C. Calfee (Eds.), *Handbook of educational psychology* (pp. 243–310). New York: Macmillan.—136, 138, 139, 144, 263, 349

Snow, R. E., & Lohman, D. F. (1984). Toward a theory of cognitive aptitude for learning from instruction. *Journal of Educational Psychology, 76,* 347–376.—429

Snyderman, M., & Rothman, S. (1987). Survey of expert opinion on intelligence and aptitude testing. *American Psychologist, 42,* 137–144.—51

Soar, R. S. (1966). *An integrative approach to classroom learning.* Philadelphia: College of Education, Temple University.—488

Solomon, D., Watson, M., Schaps, E., Battistich, V., & Solomon, J. (1990). Cooperative learning as part of a comprehensive classroom program designed to promote prosocial development. In S. Sharan (Ed.), *Cooperative learning: Theory and research* (pp. 231–260). New York: Praeger.—135

Spaulding, R. L. (1965). *Achievement, creativity, and self-concept correlates of teacher-pupil transactions in elementary schools.* Hempstead, NY: Hofstra University.—488

Spence, J. T., & Helmreich, R. L. (1978). *Masculinity and femininity.* Austin: University of Texas.—170

Spencer, H. (1873). *Education: Intellectual, moral, and physical.* New York: Appleton & Co.—428

Squire, L. R. (1987). *Memory and brain.* New York: Oxford University Press.—263

Stader, E., Colyar, T., & Berliner, D. C. (1990). *Expert and novice teachers' ability to judge student understanding.* Paper presented at the meeting of the American Educational Research Association, Boston.—553

Steinberg, L. D., Brown, B., & Dornbusch, S. (1996). *Beyond the classroom: Why school reform has failed and what parents need to do.* New York: Simon & Schuster.—317

Sternberg, R. J., & Lubart, T. J. (1995). *Defying the crowd: Cultivating creativity in a culture of conformity.* New York: Free Press.—141

Sternberg, R. J., & Lubart, T. J. (1996). Investing in creativity. *American Psychologist, 51,* 677–688.—140, 141

Sternberg, R., Wagner, R. K., Williams, W. M., & Horvath, J. A. (1995). Testing common sense. *American Psychologist, 50,* 912–927.—72–74

Stevenson, H. W., Lee, S. Y., & Stigler, J. W. (1986). Mathematics achievement of Chinese, Japanese, and American children. *Science, 231,* 693–699.—90

Stiggins, R. J. (1987). Design and development of performance assessments. *Educational and Psychological Measurement, 6*(3), 33–42.—562

Stiggins, R. J. (1997). *Student-centered classroom assessment* (2d ed.). Upper Saddle River, NJ: Merrill.—592

Stiggins, R. J., Backland, P. M., & Bridgeford, N. J. (1985). Avoiding bias in the assessment of communication skills. *Communication Education, 34,* 135–141.—566

Stigler, J. W., Lee, S., & Stevenson, H. W. (1987). Mathematics classrooms in Japan, Taiwan, and the United States. *Child Development, 58,* 1272–1285.—495

Stipek, D. (1996). Motivation and instruction. In D. C. Berliner & R. C. Calfee (Eds.), *Handbook of educational psychology* (pp. 85–113). New York: Macmillan.—336, 436

Stipek, D. J. (1988). *Motivation to learn.* Englewood Cliffs, NJ: Prentice-Hall. *A short but scholarly and practical guide to the field of motivation.*—328, 336

Stodolsky, S. S., Ferguson, T. L., & Wimpelberg, K. (1981). The recitation persists, but what does it look like? *Journal of Curriculum Studies, 13,* 121–130.—454, 455, 459

Strauss, S. (1996, July). *Teachers' and children's mental models of children's minds and learning: Implications for teacher education.* Paper presented at the Second International Conference on Teacher Education, MOFET Institute, Netanya, Israel.—98

Strayhorn, J., & Rhodes, L. A. (1985). The shaping game: A teaching tool. *Pointer, 29*(4), 8–11.—469

Strober, M. (1990, Jan.–Feb.). Kindling students' passion for economics. *Stanford Observer,* 1–3.—356

Sulzer-Azaroff, B. (1981). Issues and trends in behavior modification in the classroom. In S. W. Bijou & R. Ruiz (Eds.), *Behavior modification: Contributions to education.* Hillsdale, NJ: Erlbaum.—226

Sulzer-Azaroff, B., & Mayer, G. R. (1977). *Applying behavior analysis procedures with children and youth.* New York: Holt, Rinehart, & Winston.—216, 222

Sulzer-Azaroff, B., & Mayer, G. R. (1986). *Achieving educational excellence.* New York: Holt, Rinehart, & Winston. *One of the clearest applications of the technology of operant conditioning to contemporary school problems. A wide-ranging book based on a single theoretical position.*—216

Sulzer-Azaroff, B., & Mayer, G. R. (1991). *Behavior analysis for lasting change.* Fort Worth, TX: Holt, Rinehart, & Winston. *A practical guide for using behavioral psychology to achieve school and family goals.*—216, 222, 223, 226

Suppes, P. (1966). The uses of computers in education. *Scientific American, 215*(3), 206–220.—444

Swanson, H. L. (1990). Influence of metacognitive knowledge and aptitude on problem solving. *Journal of Educational Psychology, 82,* 306–314.—271

Sweezy, R. W. (1981). *Individual performance assessment: An approach to criterion-referenced test development.* Reston, VA: Reston.—521

Sweller, J. (1994). Cognitive load theory, learning difficulty, and instructional design. *Learning and Instruction, 4,* 295–312.—374

Teasdale, T. W., & Owen, D. R. (1988). Regional differences in cognitive ability and educational level in Denmark. *British Journal of Educational Psychology, 58,* 307–314.—85

Thielens, W., Jr. (1987). *The disciplines and undergraduate lecturing.* ERIC Document Reproduction Service No. ED286436.—367

Thomas, J. R., & French, K. E. (1985). Gender differences across age in motor performance: A meta-analysis. *Psychological Bulletin, 98,* 260–282.—171

Thomas, J. R., & Thomas, K. T. (1988). Development of gender differences in physical activity. *Quest, 40,* 219–229.—171

Thomas, W. P., & Collier, V. P. (1996). *Language minority student achievement and program effectiveness. Research summary of ongoing study: Results as of September 1995.* Fairfax, VA: Authors, George Mason University.—123, 124

Thoresen, C. E. (1972). Behavioral humanism. In C. E. Thoresen (Ed.), *Behavior modification in education: Seventy-second yearbook of the National Society for the Study of Education* (Pt. 1, pp. 385–421). Chicago: University of Chicago Press.—232

Thorndike, E. L. (1939). *Your city.* New York: Harcourt, Brace.—21

Thorndike, E. L., & Woodworth, R. S. (1901). The influence of improvement in one mental function upon the efficiency of other functions. *Psychological Review, 8,* 247–261, 384–395, 553–564.—300

Tobias, S. (1989). Using computers to study consistency of cognitive processing of instruction. *Computers in Human Behavior, 5,* 107–118.—270

Tobin, K. G., & Capie, W. (1982). Relationships between classroom process variables and middle-school science achievement. *Journal of Educational Psychology, 74,* 441–454.—485

Torrance, E. P. (1967). The Minnesota studies of creative behavior: National and international extensions. *Journal of Creative Behavior, 1*(2), 137–154.—141

Torrance, E. P. (1986). Teaching creative and gifted learners. In M. C. Wittrock (Ed.), *Handbook of research on teaching* (3d ed., pp. 630–647.). New York: Macmillan.—143

Trammel, D. L, Schloss, P. J., & Alper, S. (1994). Using self-recording, evaluation, and graphing to increase completion of homework assignments. *Journal of Learning Disabilities, 27*(2), 75–81.—243, 245, 247

Trudewind, C., & Kohne, W. (1982). Bezugsnorm-Orientierung der Lehrer und motiventwicklung: Zusammenhange mit Schulleistung, Intelligenz und Merkmalen der Hauslichen Umwelt in der Grundschulzeit. In F. Reinberg (Ed.), *Bezugsnormen zur Schulleistungsbewertung: Analyse und Invervoution.* Dusseldorf: Schwann.—330

United States Civil Rights Commission. (1973). *Teachers and students,* Rep. 5: *Differences in teacher interaction with Mexican-American and*

Anglo students. Washington, DC: Government Printing Office.—471

United States Department of Education (1995a). *Digest of educational statistics, 1995.* National Center for Educational Statistics, Publication 95–029. Washington, DC: U.S. Government Printing Office.—152

United States Department of Education (1995b). *101 ways to help children with ADD learn: Tips from successful teachers.* Washington, DC: Office of Special Education Programs, U.S. Department of Education.—194

United States General Accounting Office. (1987). *Bilingual education. A new look at the research evidence.* Washington, DC: U.S. GAO.—123

United States General Accounting Office (1993). *Student testing: Current extent and expenditures, with cost estimates for national examinations.* Washington, DC: U.S. GAO.—535

Urdan, T. C., & Maehr, M. L. (1995). Beyond a two-goal theory of motivation and achievement: A case for social goals. *Review of Educational Research, 65,* 213–243.—332

Valencia, R. R. (Ed.). (1991). *Chicano school failure and success.* London: Falmer Press.—471

Van der Will, C. (1976). The wording of spoken instructions to children and its effect on their performance of tasks. *Educational Studies, 2,* 193–199.—385–386

Verner, C., & Dickinson, G. (1967). The lecture: An analysis and review of research. *Adult Education, 17*(2), 85–100.—370

Violato, C., & Travis, L. (1995). *Advances in adolescent psychology.* Calgary, Alberta, Can.: Detselis Enterprises, Ltd.—129

Vygotsky, L. S. (1978). *Mind in society: The development of higher psychological processes* (M. Cole, V. John-Steiner, S. Scribner, & E. Souberman, Eds. and Trans.). Cambridge, MA: Harvard University Press.—97, 111–114

Vygotsky, L. S. (1986). *Thought and language.* Cambridge, MA: MIT Press. *Major work of the author.*—111

Wade, S. E., Trathen, W., & Schraw, G. (1990). An analysis of spontaneous study strategies. *Reading Research Quarterly, 25,* 147–166.—433

Wadsworth, B. (1989). *Piaget's theory of cognitive and affective development* (4th ed.). White Plains, NY: Longman.—98

Wagner, R. K., & Sternberg, R. J. (1986). Tacit knowledge and intelligence in the everyday world. In R. J. Sternberg & R. K. Wagner (Eds.), *Practical intelligence.* Cambridge: Cambridge University Press.—71

Wainer, H. (1992). Understanding graphs and tables. *Educational Researcher, 21*(1) 14–23.—389, 390

Walberg, H. J. (1986). Synthesis of research on teaching. In M. C. Wittrock (Ed.), *Handbook of research on teaching* (3d ed.). New York: Macmillan. *An organized collection of the results of many meta-analyses of research on teaching.*—313

Walberg, H. J. (1991). Productive teaching and instruction: Assessing the knowledge base. In H. C. Waxman & H. J. Walberg (Eds.), *Effective teaching: Current research* (pp. 33–62). Berkeley, CA: McCutchan.—483

Walters, G. C., & Grusec, J. E. (1977). *Punishment.* San Francisco: Freeman.—231

Ward, B. A. (1973). *Minicourse 15: Organizing independent learning, intermediate level. Teacher's handbook.* New York: Macmillan.—434

Wasik, B. A., & Slavin, R. A. (1993). Preventing early reading failure with one-to-one tutoring: A review of five programs. *Reading Research Quarterly, 28,* 178–200.—348

Webb, N. C., & Palincsar, A. S. (1996). Group processes in the classroom. In D. C. Berliner & R. C. Calfee (Eds.), *Handbook of educational psychology* (pp. 841–873). New York: Macmillan.—331

Weiner, B. (1977). An attributional approach for educational psychology. In L. S. Shulman (Ed.), *Review of research in education* (Vol. 4). Itasca, IL: F. E. Peacock.—327

Weiner, B. (1983). Some methodological pitfalls in attribution research. *Journal of Educational Psychology, 75,* 530–543.—341

Weiner, B. (1986). *An attributional theory of motivation and emotion.* New York: Springer-Verlag.—321, 325, 341

Weiner, B. (1990). History of motivational research in education. *Journal of Educational Psychology, 82,* 616–622.—335

Weiner, B. (1994). Social and personal theories of achievement. *Review of Educational Research, 64,* 557–573.—323

Weiner, B., Graham, S., Taylor, S., & Meyer, W.-U. (1983). Social cognition in the classroom. *Educational Psychologist, 18,* 109–124.—325

Wertsch, J. V., & Tulviste, P. (1992). L. S. Vygotsky and contemporary developmental psychology. *Developmental Psychology, 28,* 548–557.—111

Whisler, J. S., & McCombs, B. L. (1992). *A middle school self-development advisement program.* Aurora, CO: Mid-Continent Regional Educational Laboratory.—338

Whiteside-Mansell, L., & Bradley, R. H. (1996). Early home environment and mental test performance: A structural analysis. *Early Education and Development, 7*(3), 277–295.—89

Whitley, B. E., Jr., & Frieze, I. H. (1985). Children's causal attributions for success and failure in achievement settings: A meta-analysis. *Journal of Educational Psychology, 5,* 608–616.—323

Whitmer, S. P. (1982, March). *A descriptive multimethod study of teacher judgment during the marking process.* Paper presented at the meeting of the American Educational Research Association, New York.—591

Wigfield, A., Eccles, J. S., & Pintrich, P. R. (1996). Development between the ages of 11 and 25. In D. C. Berliner & R. C. Calfee (Eds.), *Handbook of educational psychology* (pp. 148–186). New York: Macmillan.—105, 129, 130, 351, 353

Wiggins, G. (1989). A true test: Toward more authentic and equitable assessment. *Phi Delta Kappan, 70,* 703–713.—559–560, 561

Wiggins, G. (1996). Anchoring assessments with examples: Why students and teachers need models. *Gifted Child Quarterly, 48*(2), 66–69.—564

Williams, I. W., & Buseri, J. C. (1988). Expository teaching styles of Nigerian science teachers, Pt. 2. The explanation appraisal schedule. *Research in Science and Technological Education, 6*(2), 107–115.—387

Wilson, A. (1980). Structuring seminars: A technique to allow students to participate in the structuring of small group discussions. *Studies in Higher Education, 5,* 81–84.—404–405

Winne, P. H. (1979). Experiments relating teachers' use of higher cognitive questions to student achievement. *Review of Educational Research, 49,* 13–50.—484

Wittrock, M. C. (1989). Generative processes of comprehension. *Educational Psychologist, 24,* 325–344. *A report on a series of studies with consistent results: When students have to create their own personal meaning they learn more. Learners must be cognitively active for maximum learning and retention.*—275

Wittrock, M. C. (1991). Generative teaching of comprehension. *Elementary School Journal, 92,* 169–184.—275

Wong, E. D. (1991). Beyond the question/nonquestion alternative in classroom discussion. *Journal of Educational Psychology, 83,* 159–162.—408, 409

Wong, L. Y.-S. (1995). Research on teaching: Process-product research findings and the feeling of obviousness. *Journal of Educational Psychology, 87,* 504–511.—10

Woolfolk, A. E., & Hoy, W. K. (1990). Prospective teachers' sense of efficacy and belief about control. *Journal of Educational Psychology, 82,* 81–90.—351

Wright, C. J. & Nuthall, G. (1970). Relationships between teacher behaviors and pupil achievement in three experimental elementary science lessons. *Educational Research, 7,* 477–491.—487, 488

Wyckoff, W. L. (1973). The effect of stimulus variation on learning from lecture. *Journal of Experimental Education, 41,* 85–90.—389

Yewchuk, C. (1993). The case for ability grouping of gifted students. In C. Yewchuk, L. Wilgosh, D. Rankin, T. Schaufele, S. MacDonald, & D. Chinchilla (Panel Members). *Implications of inclusive education for gifted and talented children* (pp. 75–82). ERIC Document Reproduction Service No. ED371561.—200

Yinger, R. J. (1980). A study of teacher planning. *Elementary School Journal, 80,* 107–127.—463

Ysseldyke, J. E., & Algozzine, B. (1995). *Special education: A practical approach for teachers* (3d ed.). Boston: Houghton Mifflin.—173

Zellermayer, M., Salomon, G., Globerson, T., & Givon, H. (1991). Enhancing writing-related metacognitions through a computerized writing partner. *American Educational Research Journal, 28,* 373–391.—444

Zillig, M. (1928). Einstellung und Aussage. *Zeitschrift für Psychologie, 106,* 58–106.—591

Zimmerman, B. J. (1989). A social cognitive view of self-regulated academic learning. *Journal of Educational Psychology, 81,* 329–339.—243, 354

Zimmerman, B. J. (1990). Self-regulating academic learning and achievement: The emergence of a social-cognitive perspective. *Educational Psychology Review, 2,* 173–201.—242, 247

Zimmerman, B. J. (1995). Self-efficacy and educational development. In A. Bandura (Ed.), *Self-efficacy in changing societies* (pp. 203–231). New York: Cambridge University Press.—349

Zimmerman, B. J., & Kleefeld, C. F. (1977). Toward a theory of teaching: A social learning view. *Contemporary Educational Psychology, 2,* 158–171.—242

Zimmerman, B. J., & Ringle, J. (1981). Effects of model persistence and statements of confidence on children's self-efficacy and problem solving. *Journal of Educational Psychology, 73,* 485–493.—245

Zimmerman, B. J., & Schunk, D. H. (Eds.). (1989). *Self-regulated learning and academic achievement.* New York: Springer-Verlag.—242, 243, 247

Zuckerman, H. (1977). *Scientific elite: Nobel laureates in the United States.* New York: Free Press.—248

Subject Index

A-B-C-D pattern, 354
Abecedarian Project, 91–93, 92(fig.)
Ability: attributions about, 322; teacher sympathy and, 323
Ability grouping, 435; effects on achievement of, 436; effects on self-esteem of, 436; forms of, 435–436
Absolute standards, in grading, 581
Abstract thinking, 51; formal operational stage and, 105, 107; test bias and, 85–86
Academic aptitude tests, 536
Academic competence, language ability and, 162
Academic feedback, 492
Academic learning time (ALT), 11, 13, 493, 494–496
Accelerated classes, 435
Acceleration, gifted students and, 199–200
Acceptance, need for, 356
Accommodation: gifted students and, 200–202; perception and, 105–106
Accomplishment, rewarding, 223–224
Accomplishment vs. inferiority, crisis of, 128–129, 146
Accountability, 422, 528
Achievement: ability grouping and, 436; academic feedback and, 492; academic learning time and, 13, 493, 494–496; accepting students' ideas and, 489–490; affiliation motive and, 332; Asian-Americans and, 90; assessment of, *see* Assessment; changeability of, 65–71; class size and, 461; cognitive ability and, 58–59; cognitive level of questions and, 483–485; computer-assisted instruction and, 445; cooperative learning and, 422; criterion-referenced tests and, 586; cross-cultural differences in, 495, 496; curricular materials and, 172; domain of, 555; effort vs., 584; enthusiasm in lectures and, 393; essay tests and, 567–568, 569; evaluation of, *see* Assessment; evidence of, 32–33; frequency of teachers' questions and, 482–483; grades and, 584, 585; group differences in, 50, 87; handouts and, 394; home environment and, 59, 89; homework and, 430–431; instructional time and, 14; learning strategies and, 256–258; lecture content and, 378; low-income families and, 91–93; non-promotion and, 437–438, 592–593; note taking and, 394; over-, 317; paper-and-pencil activities and, 494; pass–no credit grading and, 585–586; praise and, 488–489; probing and, 488; redirecting questions and, 487; relationship of self-worth and need for, to classroom structure, 328–331; seatwork and, 492–496; self-concept and, 146; teachers' expectations and, 202, 472; teacher structuring and, 479–482; teacher talk and, 481; time spent in academic pursuits and, 315–316; tokens and, 490; tutoring and, 441–442; types of teacher questions and, 483–485; under-, 317; urban-rural differences in, 81–82; variety in teaching and, 475–476
Achievement motivation, 316–317; attributions and, 321–327; autonomous, 319; characteristics of classrooms detracting from, 360t; classroom structure and, 328–331; cooperative learning and, 331; need for performance and, 320–321; self-efficacy and, 348–352; social comparison and, 319–320; training programs, 340–342
Achievement tests, 199, 535, 536–540; aptitude tests vs., 538–540; concerns about, 539; percentile rank and, 542; scholastic success with, 58–59; standardized, 542; table of specifications for, 555–557
Action, understanding environment through, 110
Active learning, 252, 273–276
Activities, motivation and time spent in different, 315–316
Activity reinforcers, 222
Adaptation, perception and, 105–106
Adaptive behavior, 51, 185, 186
Adaptive instruction, 427

Additive approach, in multicultural classroom, 167
Adjective use, developing, 120
Administrative advantages, of lecture method, 368–369
Adolescence/adolescents: confusion crises, 129; formal operational thought and, 104–105, 107; identity crisis, 129; moral training and, 133–134; personality development and, 97; reinforcement and, 344; test anxiety and, 540
Adoption studies, 87–88
Adults: generativity vs. stagnation and, 130; language development role and, 121–122; as learning mediators, 112–114. *See also* Home environment; Parents; Teachers
Advance organizers, 289–290, 377
Aesthetic needs, 318, 319
Affective domain, educational objectives and, 41
Affiliation needs, 332
African-American students: achievement motivation training and, 340; adopted by advantaged white families, 88; early education programs and, 93; environmental disadvantages and, 83; group participation and, 416; IQ tests and, 82–83; and multiculturalism, 165, 168; testing and, 82–83
Aggression, 357, 465; behavior models and, 234; frustration leading to, 339; gender differences in, 170; television and, 240–241
Algebra, 75
Allegory, 388
Allocated time, 14
Alterable variables, 12
Alternatives, multiple-choice items and, 573
Ambiguity, attention-arousing stimuli and, 260
American Indians, *see* Native Americans
Analogies, teaching using, 473
Analysis, 42; essay tests and, 568; multiple-choice tests and, 577; teachers' questions stimulating, 483, 484
Analytic scoring, 570

Anxiety: grading and, 585; parent-induced, 540; performance and, 583; speech fright and, 373; tests and, 212, 215–216, 546; unrealistically high standards and, 245

Application, 42

Apprenticeships, 112; cognitive, 286

Approval, need for, 332–333

Aptitude: scholastic, 55, 58–61; student, 437

Aptitude tests, 535, 536–540

Arithmetic, intelligence in, 75. *See also* Mathematics

Art, spatial intelligence and, 75–76

Articulation, problems in, 180

Arts, the, performance tests and, 559

Asian-American students, 90

Assessment: basic concepts in, 509–530; cultural differences and, 164; eliciting behavior and, 512; evaluation and, 513, 528–530; grades and, 580–593; informal, 510; instructional, 551, 552–554; measuring and, 512; norm-referenced testing and, 514–515; overview of, 509–510; reliability of, 518–524; sampling behavior and, 512–513; standardized procedures and, 510–511; standardized tests and, 530–547; standards and norms and, 513; systematic procedures and, 510–511; teacher's, *see* Teacher's assessment

Assignments, interesting and worthwhile, 494. *See also* Homework assignments; Seatwork

Assimilation, perception and, 105–106

Assimilationism, 154–155

Assimilationist ideology, 155

Associativity, operational thought and, 103

Athletes, 77

Athletics, 170, 359, 559

Attention, 11, 15; conversational recitation and, 488; grading bias and, 591–592; humor in lectures and, 392; incentives for, 237; learning games and, 359; lectures and, 389–394; maintaining, 389–394; questions during lectures and, 390; response-cost procedure and, 230; signal for gaining, 480; variety in teaching and, 475

Attention deficit disorder (ADD), 191–195. *See also* Hypersensitivity

Attention deficit-hyperactivity disorder (ADHD), 191–195

Attitudes: discussion groups and, 401–402; learned through rational processes, 231; transferable, 305

Attractiveness bias, 472

Attributions, 11; achievement, classifying, 321–327; classroom

structure and, 328–331; emotion and, 324–325; external, 324–325, 326–327; internal, 324–325, 326–327, 341–342; self-defeating, 325; students' causal, 323–325; teachers' causal, 326

Attribution training programs, 341–342

Audiovisuals, developing perceptual clarity and, 116

Auditory presentations, *see* Lecture method

Authentic tests, 559

Authority, 131, 132, 402

Autism, pervasive developmental disorder and, 196

Autistic children, 228

Autonomy, 498; vs. shame and doubt, crisis of, 127–128

Aversive stimulus, 216

Avoidance, 229

Bafflement, epistemic curiosity and, 357

Behavior: apparently unrewarded, 333–334; concepts about, 10; consequence of, 213; consistency of, 138; culturally based, 157–162, 158(fig.); decreasing unwanted, 465–468; defined, 209; eliciting, 213, 469, 512; emitted vs. elicited, 213; frustration and, 338; goal, 314–315; ignoring, 227; increasing wanted, 468–470; intelligence as, 51; learned through rational processes, 231; modeling, 469; models disinhibiting/inhibiting, 235–236; motivation and, 313–317; other-regulated to self-regulated, 112; overt, 209; Piaget's stages of, 98; problem, 464–465; punishment and, 138, 227–231; reinforcement of, 214–234; rewards and, 138; sampling, 512–513; segments of, 476; self-regulation of, 243–246; shaping, by successive approximations, 223, 469; social context and, 161; strengthening incompatible, 467; tentative, 469; timing errors and, 494; tokens and, 490. *See also* Behavior changes

Behavioral approach, self-concept and, 145

Behavioral disorders, 188–195

Behavioral humanism, 232–233

Behavioral psychologies: contiguity learning, 212–213; operant conditioning, 213–234; respondent conditioning, 209–212

Behavioral vs. cognitive learning, 253–255

Behavior changes, 213–234; change in cognition and, 241; contingent reinforcement and, 221–224; dis-

cussion groups and, 401–402; learning and, 209; reinforcement schedules and, 217–221; respondent conditioning and, 209–212; as result of experience, 208–209; self-concept changes and, 145

Behaviorists, 209

Behavior models, 234–236, 242–243, 469; high-status, 237; ignoring misbehaviors and, 466–467; motivation and, 238–239; standards learned from, 245; violent, 240–241

Behavior-modification techniques, 230–231; problem behaviors and, 468–470

Between-class grouping, 435

Bias: attractiveness and, 472; group-discussion teaching and, 413; planning for control of, 470–473; test, 85–86

Bicultural students, 125. *See also* Cultural differences

Bidialectism, 122

Big-fish-little-pond effect (BFLPE), 436, 582

Big Five Factors of Personality, 136–138, 137(fig.)

Bilingual education, 123–126. *See also* Multicultural education

Black students, *see* African-American students

Blind students, 177–179

Bodily kinesthetic intelligence, 76, 77, 78, 110

Boredom, 312, 357, 415. *See also* Attention

Brain, hemispheres of, 265

Brain-injured people, 75; exceptional students and, 184

Brain lesions, 197

Brainwashing, 232

Breaks, transitions and, 494

Bribery, reinforcement and, 233

Call-outs, 486

"Case histories," construction of, 498

Case knowledge, 279–280

Causal, or functional, relationships, 15, 17–18, 21–22

Causing-a-change problems, 294

Cerebral palsy, 181

Challenge, 173, 174. *See also* Exceptional students

Characteristic pedagogical flow (CPF), 500–501

Cheating, 138–139, 430

Checklists, instructional supports and, 474

Chess players, expert, 280–283

Children, understanding thinking of, 115

Classical (respondent) conditioning, 207, 209–212

Classification: operational thought and, 103, 104(fig.); problem solving and, 283–284

Classification hierarchy, lectures and, 379

Classroom(s): characteristics of, detracting from achievement motivation, 360; children with emotional disorders in, 192–193; creativity in, 141–143; number of students in, 460, 461; teacher- vs. student-centered, 501–502

Classroom language, rule governed, 126–127

Classroom lessons, structure of, 126

Classroom management: factors beyond teachers' control and, 464–465; political and economic forces and, 465; school structure and, 464; societal factors and, 464; strategies for too little wanted behavior, 468–470; strategies for too much unwanted behavior, 465–468

Classroom structure: attributions and, 328–331; recitation and, 460

Classroom teaching, 452–503; constructivist teaching and, 454, 457, 496–503; control of bias and, 470–473; direct instruction and, 454, 456–457, 477–493; distinguishing characteristics of, 454–457; instructional supports and, 474; interactive phase of, 454, 477–503; method of, 476; orchestration of methods in, 457; pattern of, 453–460; planning phase of, 454, 462–476; planning for scaffolds in, 474; planning for use of pedagogical content knowledge in, 473–474; problem behavior and, 464–470; reasons for prevalence of, 457–460; recitation and, 454–456, 477–503; seatwork and, 453, 492–493, 495; style of, 476; suitability to basic tasks and, 460; variety and flexibility in, 474–476

Climax, as rhetorical device, 388

Cognition: shared, 255; social learning and, 241

Cognitive abilities, 11, 12, 49–95; achievement and, 58–59; adaptive behavior and, 51; conservatism-liberalism and, 84; definition of, 51; differences between jobs, 60; early intervention and, 90–91; environment and, 61–71, 83–84, 85; ethnic differences in, 82–83; gender differences in, 170–171; group differences in, 50, 80–86; group factor abilities and, 56; heredity and, 61–71, 83–84; home environment and, 87–90; improving, 87–93; individual differences in, 50;

intelligence tests and, 69–70; job knowledge and, 59, 60; job success and, 59–61; longitudinal studies and, 54–55; mathematical factor and, 59; measurement of, 51–55, 52(fig.), 53 (fig.); organization of, 55–58; overview of, 49–50; school influences on, 90–93; school success and, 58–59; selective migration and, 84–85; socioeconomic-status differences in, 80–81; stability of, 55; test bias and, 85–86; tests of, 55–56; urban-rural differences in, 81–82. See also Intelligence

Cognitive approaches, motivational patterns and, 340–342

Cognitive development: analyzing errors, 118; bilingualism and, 125; Bruner's theory of, 109–111; enactive stage and, 110; handicapped children and, 107; iconic stage and, 110; independent schoolwork and, 114; instructional implications of Piaget, Bruner, and Vygotsky, 115–118; introducing new experiences and, 117; language and, 97, 109–110; learning pace and, 117; motor experience and, 107; other-regulated to self-regulated behavior and, 112; perceptual clarity and, 116; Piaget's stages, 96–109; self-consciousness and, 109; sequencing instruction and, 115–117; social environment and, 116; symbolic stage and, 111; teacher's questions and, 483–485; Vygotsky's view of, 111–114

Cognitive learning, 251–311; active learning and, 252, 273–276; behavioral vs., 253–255; case knowledge and, 279–280; constructivism and, 252, 255–256, 276–278; developing and enriching schemata, 292–294; discovery learning and, 274–275; distributed expertise/cognition and, 285–286; educational objectives and, 41, 42; expert/novice distinction and, 280–284; generative model of, 275–276; and higher-order thinking, strategies for promoting, 288–299; information-processing model of, 252, 258–264; information storage in memory and, 261–263; instructional design focus and, 289–292; long-term memory and, 261, 263–264; mathematics meaning and, 294–296; mathematics strategies and, 270; mediation/enhancement and, 288–289; metacognition and, 252, 270–273, 301; mindfulness and, 305; mnemonic devices and, 265–

268; orienting stimuli and responses and, 259–260; overlearning and, 264–265; physical activity and, 264; problem-based project learning and, 286–288; problem-solving approach to, 252, 278–284; reading strategies and, 268–269; role of strategies in, 256–258; schemata and reading achievement and, 296–299; shared characteristics and beliefs in, 255–256; short-term memory/forgetting and, 260–261; situated cognition and, 252–253, 284–288; strategies used in, 264–270; student misperceptions in science and, 297–298; transfer of, 299–307 (see also Learning transfer); underlying assumptions of, 253–258; writing strategies and, 270

Cognitive level, of questions, 483–485

Cognitive load, reducing students', 374–375

Cognitively Guided Instruction (CGI), 295

Cognitive processes, 117; teacher's understanding of, 115; variety in teaching and, 475–476

Cognitive psychologists, 209

Cognitive psychology, 108

Cognitive skills, efforts at acquiring, 483

Cognitive tasks, domain-related, 61

Cognitive taxonomy, 42

College: mastery learning and, 438; personalized system of instruction and, 437

College Board scores, 54

Combinational analysis of possibilities, 104

Comments, teacher's: on group discussions, 412; on homework, 431. See also Feedback

Commitment, 498

Common ground, discussion-group teaching and, 404–405

Common sense, see Practical intelligence

Communication, culture and, 158–161

Communication apprehension, 373

Communication channels, changing, 389

Communication disorders, exceptional students and, 180–181

Communities of learners, 255

Community, role of, in multicultural education, 167–168

Comparison, lectures and, 381–382

Comparison problems, 294

Compensatory education, 155

Competence, see Academic competence

Competitive learning: classroom structure and, 328–329; mathematics and, 170–171

Complex ideas, 109, 119

Complex Instruction, 421

Complexity, attention-arousing stimuli and, 260

Component (part-whole) relationships, lecture method and, 379–380

Composition, operational thought and, 103

Comprehension, 42; humor and, 392–393; lecture organization and, 378–379; metacognitive skills and, 272; multiple-choice tests and, 573; note taking in lectures and, 394; paraphrase measuring, 573; of principles, 576

Comprehension questions, 268, 269

Computer-assisted instruction (CAI), 217–218, 443–446; advantages of, 443–444; cost-effectiveness of, 445–446; evaluating instruction using, 445; limitations of, 443–445

Computers: for learning in classroom, 442–450; role of, in cooperative learning, 422, 423–425; in teacher's assessment, 578–579; teacher's role with, 449–450

Concept(s), 10–16; advance organizers and, 377; decontextualization of, 305–306; discussions and, 399; examples and, 387; motivation and, 317–319; schema vs., 292; using language to develop, 99–100

Conceptual models, 301–303

Conceptual structures, changing with age, 108

Concrete information, teaching using, 115

Concrete operational stage, 103–104

Concurrent relationship, 17

Concurrent validity, tests and, 525

Conditioned response (CR), 210–211, 212

Conditioned stimulus (CS), 210–211, 212

Conditioning, awareness and cooperation in, 232

Conferences, teacher-parent, 595; teacher-student, 347

Confidence, 22, 25

Confidence interval, 522–524

Conformist orientation, 132

Conformity: confused with giftedness, 199; need for approval and, 332

Conjunctions, 386

Con-pro sequence, 380–381

Conscience, development of, 128

Conservation, intuitive phase of development and, 100–101, 102(fig.)

Constructivism, 11, 98; cognitive learning and, 252, 255–256, 276–278

Constructivist teaching, 454, 457, 496–503; criticisms of, 501–503; effectiveness of, 498–499; international observational comparisons and, 500–501; nature of, 497–498; synthesis of, 503; TIMSS and, 499–500

Construct validity, tests and, 526–527

Consumable reinforcers, 222

Content of instruction, 28, 29, 34–36; lecture method and, 376–377, 378, 387–388; at national level, 34; at state and local levels, 34; students' role in determining, 36; teacher's role in determining, 34–36

Content knowledge, lecture preparation and, 372–373

Content validity, tests and, 525, 540

Contiguity learning, 207, 212–213, 238

Contingency management, 221–224; contingency contract and, 223–224, 225(fig.); group, 226; Premack principle and, 222–223

Contingent reinforcement, 213, 221–224

Continuous reinforcement, 217, 218

Contracting, 469; contingent, 223–224, 225(fig.); elementary grades and, 345–348; independent study and, 433–435; mathematics and, 345–347; motivation and, 345–348; reading and, 347–348

Contradiction, epistemic curiosity and, 357

Contributions approach, in multicultural classroom, 167

Control, as research objective, 14, 15–16; intrinsic motivation and, 357

Control groups, 15, 21

Controllability, 322

Controversial topics, value of discussing, 402–404

Conventional level of moral development, 131

Convergent thought, 141

Cooperative learning, 11, 419; achievement motivation and, 331; Complex Instruction, 421; cultural differences and, 161–162, 419, 422–425; effectiveness of, 422–425; Group Investigation, 421–422; in multicultural classrooms, 165; role of computers in, 422, 423–425; Student Teams and Achievement Divisions, 420; Team-Assisted Individualization, 421; Teams-Games-Tournaments, 420–421; types of, 419–422

Cooperative planning, 434

Corporal punishment, 467–468

Correlation: causal relationships vs., 16–18; IQ scores and, 63–64; methods for determining, 18–21; negative and positive, 19

Correlation coefficients, 19–21, 520

Cost-effectiveness: of computer-assisted instruction, 445–446; of tutoring, 442

Covering-law model, 384, 385(fig.)

Covert rehearsal, 238

Creativity, 139–140; blocks to, 141; fostering, 141–143; gifted students and, 198; intelligence and, 141; measuring, 512, 526; mentors and, 143; metalinguistic awareness and, 121; testing, 526

Crises, personality development and, 97, 127–130

Criterion-referenced tests, 515–517, 533(fig.); achievement and, 586; pros and cons of, 517t; reliability and, 520–521; standardized, 531

Criterion validity, tests and, 525–526

Criticism, 490–491. See also Comments, teacher's; Feedback

Cross-cultural perspective, developing, 155–165

Cross-grade grouping, 435

Crystallized intelligence, 56

Cuing, 482

Cultural differences, 151–168; in academic learning time, 495–496; aptitude tests and, 536–538; assessment and, 164; cooperative learning and, 161–162, 419, 422–425; curriculum and, 164–165; developing cross-cultural perspective, 155–165; developmental readiness and, 162–163; group participation and, 416; historical background of, 154–155; language development and, 162; norm-referenced testing and, 515. See also Enculturation; Multicultural education

Cultural identity: influences on individual's, 156–157(fig.); non–English speaking students and, 123

Cultural literacy, 43

Culturally based behaviors, impacting teacher-student interactions, 157–162, 158(fig.)

Cultural norms, 163

Cultural pluralism, 154, 155

Cultural shock, of non–English speaking students, 124

Cultural stereotypes, 172; sizing-up assessments and, 551–552

Culture, 151–152; of educational system, understanding, 162–165;

learning from, 112; and readiness to learn in school, 159–161; of school classroom and individual within that culture, understanding, 157–162; understanding individual's acquisition of, 155–157
Culture-fair tests, 86
Curiosity, epistemic, 356–357, 403
Curriculum: cultural differences and, 164–165; gender differences and, 171–172; summative evaluation and, 529
Curriculum guide, planning and, 464
Curriculum materials, 125, 171–172
Cursive writing, 223

Databases, 446
Deaf children, 179–180
Declarative knowledge, 262–263
Decontextualization, 305–306
Defiance, 467
Defining Issues Test, 133
Degree of enculturation, 151
Delinquency: school factors in, 464–465; self-esteem and, 464; token economies and, 343
Democratic skills, small-group teaching and, 400
Dependent variable, 17, 18, 21
Depression, 189, 245
Despair, old age and, 130
Developmental process, 105–106
Developmental readiness, cultural differences and, 162–163
Diagnosis: multiple-choice tests and, 576–577; tables of specification and, 555; tutoring and, 439
Dialogue, computer-assisted instruction and, 444–445
Differential reinforcement, 226–227
Direct instruction, 115, 454, 456–457, 477–493; criticisms of, 493; importance of judgment in using research findings in, 477–479; seatwork and, 492–493; synthesis of, 503; teacher reacting and, 486–492; teacher soliciting and, 482–486; teacher structuring and, 479–482
Directions to students, 494
Disabilities, students with, 173, 174. See also Exceptional students
Disapproval, teacher's, 490–491
Discipline: accurately directing, 494; classroom teaching, 464–470; enthusiasm in lectures and, 393; stifling creativity and, 141
Discovery learning, 115, 274–275, 502–503
Discussion-group teaching, 397, 399; activity after, 412–413; bias and, 413; choosing topic, 402–404; controversial topics and,

402–404; controversiality and attitudes and, 401–402; dead topics and, 414–415; effects of teachers' questions on, 406–408; encouraging yielding and, 414; establishing common ground and, 404–405; evaluations and, 412–413; high-consensus vs. low-consensus fields, 401; intellectual pitfalls, 413–415; large classes and, 400–401; lecture method vs., 370–371; nonparticipation and, 415; notes and records, 412; objectives of, 399–400; planning for, 402–405; reinforcement and, 418; social and emotional pitfalls, 415–419; students' feelings and, 418–419; students' role in, 408; teacher's personality and, 402; teacher's role in, 405–406, 408–412; uneven participation and, 415–418; withholding crucial information in, 414
Disequilibrium, 117
Disinhibition, 235–236
Disruptive behavior, 15
Distractibility, 188
Distractors, 573
Distributed expertise/cognition, 285–286, 398–399
Divergent thought, 141
Diversity, 150–151; cultural differences and, 152; exceptional students and, 173–202; gender differences and, 168–173; general concerns and recommendations for teachers on, 202; teaching from context of, 113–114. See also Cultural differences; Exceptional students; Gender differences
Domain of achievement, 555
Domain-specific knowledge, 43, 61, 108
Doubt, epistemic curiosity and, 357
Drawing, cultural differences and, 163
Drill and practice: computer-assisted instruction and, 444; contiguity learning and, 212; seatwork and, 493
Drug abuse, 197–198
Dyscalculia, 187
Dysgraphia, 187
Dyslexia, 187

Early education programs, argument for, 90–93, 92(fig.)
Economic opportunity, 125
Educable mentally retarded (EMR), 69, 186
Educational accountability, 528
Educational achievement, see Achievement
Education changes, cost-effectiveness of, 442

Educational objectives, 28–46; classifying, 41–42; cognitive domain, 41, 42; computer and, 450; effect of standards-based reform on, 32–33; evaluating achievement of, 30–31; examples of, 40t; general, 37; performance-content matrix and, 44–46, 45t; reasons for stating, 31–32; specific, 37–41; thinking about, in terms of student performance, 36–41
Educational psychology, 3–27; in action, 8–9; concepts of, 10–11; decision-making and, 29–31; defined, 3; as foundational discipline, 8; objectives of, 14; passion and, 8; principles of, 11; purpose of, in preparation of teachers, 4–7; results of research in, 9–10; teaching tasks and, 8
Educational standards, effect of reform of, on objectives, 32–33
Educational system, understanding culture of, 162–165
Education level, moral reasoning and, 134
Effect size, 22
Effort: achievement vs., 584; attributions about, 322; lack of, 327
Electrical shock, for reducing self-injurious behavior, 228–229
Elementary grades: concrete materials for learning in, 115; contracting and, 345–348; homework in, 430–431; mastery learning in, 438; seatwork in, 492
Emotion: attributions and, 324–325; children's speech and, 118
Emotional disorders, 188–195
Emotionality, 339
Empirical methods, 3
Enactive stage, cognitive development and, 110, 116, 263–264
Encoding, 11, 394
Enculturation: degree of, 151; by socializing agents, 152–154
End-structuring, 482, 491–492
English, nonstandard, 122–123
Enhancement, of meaning, 288–289
Enrichment, gifted students and, 200
Enrichment classes, 436
Enthusiasm, 390, 392–393
Environment (nurture): cognitive ability and, 61–71, 83–84; gender differences and, 170; group differences in cognitive ability and, 83–84; language development and, 118; parent's pressure for achievement and, 89; test-taking and, 85–86; training creativity and, 141–143
Environmental approaches, changing motivational patterns and, 343–348

Episodic memory, 262, 263

Epistemic curiosity, 356–357, 403

Equalization effect, 371

Errors, analyzing, 118

Errors of fact, group discussions and, 410–411

Escape conditioning, *see* Negative reinforcers

Essay tests, 567–570, 577, 578*t*

Ethical issues, 231–234

Ethnic differences, in cognitive ability, 82–83. *See also* Cultural differences

Ethnicity, 82, 152

Evaluation, program, 528–530

Evaluation abilities, student's, 42

Evaluation by students: group-discussion teaching and, 412–413; instructional supports and, 474

Evaluation by teacher, special education classes and, 174–176. *See also* Assessment; Feedback; Grades/grading

Examples, used in teaching: familiar material for, 358; generalization and, 307; lectures and, 387

Exceptional students, 151, 173–202; attention deficit disorder (ADD) and attention deficit-hyperactivity disorder (ADHD), 191–195; autism and pervasive developmental disorder, 196; categories of, 177–202; communication disorders, 180–181; emotional and behavioral disorders, 188–195; general concerns of teachers of, 178*t*; gifted and talented, 198–202; hearing impairments, 179–180; labeling and educational relevance and, 176–177; learning disabilities, 187–188; least restrictive environment and, 176; mentally retarded, 184–187; physical health impairment, 181–184; prenatal or early-childhood substance exposure/abuse, 197–198; Public Law 101-476 and, 174–176; in regular education classroom, 192–193; traumatic brain injury, 184; visual impairments, 177–179

Expectations: aptitude tests and, 536; group participation and, 416; language and, 162; sizing-up assessments and, 551–552; teacher bias and, 470–473; teacher-student interactions and, 172–173

Experience(s): cognitive level of questioning and, 483; distal, 117; introducing new, 117; learning and, 209; prompting awareness of relevant, 377; proximal, 117

Experimental group, 15

Experiments: manipulation and, 21; causal relationships and, 17, 21–

22; random assignment and, 21; replication and, 23

Experts: distinction between novice and, 280–284; modeling and, 474; problem solving and, 280–284

Explaining links, 386

Explanation, scientific, 14, 15–16

Explanations to students, 366, 383–384; as minilectures, 383–384; model for organizing, 384, 385(fig.)

Explicitness of lecture method, 385–386

Extinction, 226, 338; problem behavior and, 466–467; variable-interval schedule and, 221; variable-ratio reinforcement and, 218

Extrapolation, lectures and, 373–374

Extrinsic motivation, 333–336

Eye contact, group discussions and, 406

Factor analysis, 56

Factual information: conceptual models and, 303; forgetting, 260–261; values vs., 411

Failure: attributions and, 323–327; competitive setting and, 328–331; resignation to, 341–342

Fairness, 229

Familiarity, learning and, 358

Fantasy, motivation and, 357

Feedback: academic, 492; comprehension questions and, 272; corrective, 272; discussions and, 399; group participation and, 418; instructional supports and, 474; nonjudgmental, 143; programmed instruction and, 443; recitation and, 460; self-efficacy and, 350; teacher-student conferences and, 347. *See also* Comments, teacher's

Feelings, *see* Affective domain; Emotion

Fidgeting, learning disabilities and, 188

Fixed-interval reinforcement schedules, 219–220

Fixed-ratio reinforcement schedules, 217–218

Fluid intelligence, 56–57

Flynn effect, IQ and, 66–67

Foreign language learning: contiguity learning and, 212; keyword method and, 267

Forgetting, 25, 260–261

Formal assessment, table of specifications and, 555–557

Formal discipline, doctrine of, 300

Formal operational stage, 104–105, 107

Formative evaluation, 529

Fraternal twins, 64

Frequency distribution, 53

Frustration, 338–339

Games, 345–347, 359

Gatekeepers, teachers as, 163

Gender differences, 151, 168–173; criticism from teachers and, 490–491; curriculum and, 171–172; group participation and, 415–416; intelligence tests and, 69; mathematical ability and, 170–171; norm-referenced testing and, 515; personality differences and, 170; socialization by parents and, 171; verbal ability and, 171

General ability tests, 536

General intelligence, *see* General mental ability

Generalization(s): examples and, 307; learning transfer and, 300, 305, 307; negative stimuli and, 229; research and, 9–10

General mental ability, 55, 56, 57, 58(fig.), 71

Generative element, 394

Generative model of learning, 275–276

Generativity vs. stagnation, crisis of, 130

Genetic determination vs. heritability, 64–65

Genetics (nature): aggression and, 170; cognitive ability and, 61–71

Gifted and talented students, 198–199; acceleration programs for, 199–200; debate over accommodation of, 200–202; enrichment programs for, 200; grading bias and, 591–592; master teachers of, 142–143; mentors for, 143

Girls, *see* Gender differences; Women

Goal orientation, motivation and, 314–315, 354

Grade equivalent score, standardized tests and, 545–546

Grade level, lecture method and, 369

Grades/grading, 580–593; absolute standards in, 581; anxiety and, 585; assessment and, 584–585; combining data in, 586–590; establishing frame of reference for, 581–582; example of simple combination of percentages for, 588*t*; factors in teachers' decisions about, 591–592; formal assessments and, 586–590; informal assessments and, 590–592; intelligence and, 316–317; learning and, 582–585; lenient vs. strict, 585; motivation and, 353–354, 585–586; nonpromotion and, 592–593; pass-fail, 516–517, 585–586; pseudoabsolute standards in, 581–582; relative standards in, 582; sources of information for, 586–592; using judiciously, 353–354; weighting, 587–589

Grammatical rules, explicit awareness of, 126

Graphics, lectures and, 389

Group: contingency management and, 226; power of, 414. *See also* Discussion-group teaching

Group-alerting skill, preventing problem behavior and, 466

Group differences, 151; explanations of, 84–86; in IQ scores, 64

Group factors, mental abilities tests and, 56

Grouping ability, concrete operational stage and, 103

Group Investigation, 421–422

Group size, participation and, 417

Group work, time on task and, 455

Guidance and counseling, aptitude tests and, 536

Guided discovery, 275, 503

Guided study, 434

Guilt: personality development and, 128; shame vs., 325

Handicapped: attribution patterns and, 325; cognitive development and, 107

Handouts, lectures and, 394

Hands-on experience, 116

Health impairment, 181–184

Hearing impairments, 179–180

Hearing tests, 180

Height, heritability of, 65–66

Helplessness, 340

Heredity, *see* Genetics

Heritability: and ethnic differences in cognitive ability, 82–83(fig.); vs. genetic determination, 64–65; vs. unchangeability, 65–66

Hierarchical structure, 290

High-consensus fields, 401

Higher-order thinking, strategies for promoting cognitive learning and, 288–289

Higher Order Thinking Skills, *see* H.O.T.S.

High-inference variables, 373–374

High schools, *see* Secondary schools

High stakes tests, 543–545

Hispanic students: and cooperative learning, 161; and multiculturalism, 168. *See also* Mexican-American students

History: educational objectives and, 31–32; sample national standards in, 33t; teacher content knowledge and, 473

Holistic scoring, 569–570

Holophrastic speech, 119

Home environment: achievement and, 59, 89; Asian-Americans and, 90; cognitive ability and, 87–90; measuring, 89

Homework assignments, individual instruction and, 429–431

Homogeneous grouping, *see* Ability grouping

Honesty, 138–139

Hope, 127

Hostility, 467

H.O.T.S. (Higher Order Thinking Skills), 445

Housekeeping tasks, 494

Human behavior, *see* Behavior

Humor, 390, 392–393

Hyperactivity, 231, 339. *See also* Attention deficit-hyperactivity disorder (ADHD)

Hyperbole, 388

Hypermedia, 447

Hypotheses, formal operational stage and, 104

Iconic stage, cognitive development and, 110, 116, 264

Ideas, verbally marking important, 387, 480

Identical elements, learning transfer and, 300

Identical twins, IQ and, 62

Identity of procedure, learning transfer and, 300, 301, 310

Identity of substance, learning transfer and, 300, 301, 310

Identity vs. confusion, crisis of, 129

Idiots savants, 75, 78

Imagery, 265–266, 432

Imperatives, young children and, 118–119

Implementation, experiments and, 21

Importance, verbal markers of, 387, 480

Incentives, 337

Incongruity, attention-arousing stimuli and, 260

Independence: instructional supports and, 474; levels of, 434(fig.); reinforcement and, 233

Independent learning, promoting, 428, 429–435

Independent study: classroom teaching and, 72; cognitive development and, 114; contracting and, 433–435

Independent variable, 17–18, 21

Individual differences, 150–151; adapting to, 428–429, 435–442; in cognitive ability, 64; gender differences and, 168

Individual instruction, 427–451; ability grouping, 435–436; adapting to individual differences and, 428–429, 435–442; computer-assisted instruction, 443–446; computers for learning in classroom, 442–450; contracting, 330, 433–435; homework and, 429–

431; independent study, 433–435; mastery learning, 436–439; in multicultural classrooms, 166; personalized system of instruction, 436–437; programmed instruction, 442–446; promoting independent learning and, 428, 429–435; rationale for, 428–429; study skills and strategies training, 431–433; tutoring, 439–442

Individualized (adaptive) instruction, 117, 427; cultural differences and, 166

Individualized Education Plan (IEP), 176

Individually guided motivation, 347–348

Individual pursuit, 434

Individuals with Disabilities Education Act (IDEA), *see* Public Law 101-476

Infants, sensorimotor stage and, 98–99

Inference, lectures and, 373–374

Inferiority, feelings of, 128–129

Inflection, language development and, 120

Information: auditory vs. visual, 389; carried by imagery, 110; retention of meaningful, 262; withholding crucial, in discussion-group teaching, 414

Information processing, 253–254; cognitive development and, 108; and enhancing memory, strategies for, 264–270; model of learning and memory, 252, 255, 258–264

Information-processing theory, Piagetian theory vs., 109

Information storage, in memory, 109, 261–263

Inhibition, 235–236

Initiation-reply-evaluation (IRE), 455; units, 126

Initiative vs. guilt, crisis of, 128

Innovation, monitoring, 529

Instinct, 25

Instruction: content of, *see* Content of instruction; individual, *see* Individual instruction; individualized, *see* Individualized (adaptive) instruction; sequencing, 115–117

Instructional assessment, 551, 552–554

Instructional design, focus on, 289–292

Instructional process, 30(fig.)

Instructional quality, 437

Instructional supports, 474

Instructional time, achievement and, 14

Instructions, explicit, 385–386

Instrumental-relativist orientation, 131, 132

Integrity vs. despair, crisis of, 130

Intellectual abilities: developmental process and, 105–106; hearing impaired and, 179–180; linguistic competence and, 124. *See also* Cognitive abilities

Intellectual agility, 402

Intellectual development, *see* Piaget's stages of cognitive development

Intellectual empathy, teachers and, 115

Intellectual needs, 317, 319

Intellectual processes, 41

Intellectual scaffolding, 114

Intellectual skills, *see* Knowledge-versus-intellectual-skills debate

Intelligence: bodily-kinesthetic, 76, 77, 78, 110; cognitive ability and, 51; creativity and, 141; crystallized, 56; fluid, 56–57; general, 55; grades and, 316–317; interpersonal, 76, 77, 78; intrapersonal, 76, 78; linguistic, 75, 76, 78–79; literary accounts of, 75; logical-mathematical, 75, 76, 77, 78–79; measurement of, *see* Intelligence tests; modular theory of, 78; multiple, 75–80, 111; musical, 75, 76, 77, 78, 79; practical, 71–75; social, 76; spatial, 75–76, 78, 110; symbols and, 76–78; verbal, 75. *See also* Cognitive abilities; IQ; Multiple intelligences

Intelligence tests: advantages and special uses of, 530–534; bilingual students and, 124–125; Binet and, 66; culture-fair, 86; general vs. specific abilities and, 536; getting along without, 69–70; identifying gifted students and, 199; mental retardation and, 185; minority-group members and, 88; normal distribution and, 53–54; percentile ranks and, 54; raw scores and, 52; reliability of, 55; stability of, 54–55; standardized scores and, 54

Intelligent tutoring systems (ITS), 444

Interactive stage of teaching, 454, 477–503; instructional assessment during, 552–554. *See also* Constructivist teaching; Direct instruction; Recitation

Interests, motivation and, 312

Interlecture structuring, 395

Intermittent reinforcement, 217, 218, 226

Internal (mental) representations, *see* Schemata

Internet, 447–448

Interpersonal-concordance orientation, 131

Interpersonal intelligence, 76, 77, 78, 79

Interpretation: formal operational stage and, 104; lectures and, 373–374

Interpretive methods, 22–23

Interracial adoption, 88

Intimacy vs. isolation, crisis of, 129–130

Intrapersonal intelligence, 76, 78, 79

Intrinsic motivation, 328, 333–336, 357

Intuitive phase, of preoperational stage, 100–101

IQ (intelligence quotient), 18, 55; of adopted children, 81t; African-Americans and, 88; Asian-Americans and, 90; changeability of, 66–71; effects of schooling on, 67–68; environment and, 85; Flynn effect and, 66–67; grouping students and, 70; home environment and, 89(fig.), 89–90; nutrition and, 67; teachers' expectations and, 69–70; twins and, 62, 63–64

IQ test(s); items, sample practical, 73(fig.); middle-class bias in, 85–86; normal or bell-shaped curve, 53–54; problems, differences between real-world problems and, 71t; self-fulfilling prophecies and, 69–70

Irony, 388

Isolation, psychological, 129–130

Item analysis, multiple-choice tests and, 577

Item banking, 578

Japan: academic learning time and, 495, 496; characteristic pedagogical flow in, 500–501; TIMSS and, 499–500

Job success, intelligence and, 59–61

Keyword method, 267–268, 432

Kid watching, 590

Knowing, preverbal ways of, 118

Knowledge, 42; activation, prior, 432; breadth of, 498; case, 279–280; declarative, 262–263; domain-specific, 43, 61, 108; episodic, 262, 263; lecture preparation and, 372–373; pedagogical content, 372–373, 473–474; procedural, 263, 499; prompting awareness of relevant, 377–378; propositional, 262, 499; semantic, 262; structures, 293; tacit, 72

Knowledge-versus-intellectual-skills debate, 43–44

Language: acquisition device, 118; cognitive development and, 97, 109–110; complex relational terms and, 100; creative use of, 120–121; expectations and, 162; explicit awareness of rules and, 121; instructional conversation and, 488; mediating events and, 109–110; symbolic mediation and, 100. *See also* Linguistic competence

Language community, 123

Language development, 118–127; bilingualism and, 123–126; cultural differences and, 162; delayed, 180; environment and, 118; and literacy, adults' influence on, 121–122; metalinguistic awareness and, 121; more-than-two-word chains, 120–121; nonstandard English and, 122–123; one-word stage, 118–119; parent's pressure for, 89–90; preoperational stage, 99–100; schools and, 122–127; sociolinguistic competence and schooling, 126–127; two-word stage, 119–120

Language disorders, 180–181

Language laboratory, variable-interval schedule and, 220–221

Larry P. v. Riles, 69

Leaders, group participation and, 418

Learned helplessness, 316, 327, 341

Learning: active, 273–276; behavior change and, 209; cognitive, *see* Cognitive learning; constructionist, *see* Constructivism; contiguity, 212–213; cooperative, *see* Cooperative learning; cross-cultural perspective, 155–157; definition of, 208–209; discovery, 115, 274–275; experience and, 209; familiarity and, 358; generative model of, 275–276; grading and, 582–585; independent, 428, 429–435; information-processing model of, 258–264; mastery, *see* Mastery learning; mathematics and, 170–171; mediated, 112–114; motivation and, 313–317; no-trial, 236; through observation, *see* Observational learning; "occasions" for, 117; paired-associate, 289; performance and, 238–239; perseverance in, 316; readiness, culture and, 159–161; rehearsal in, 260; reinforcing previous, 358–359; setting pace of, 117; social-reference approach for judging, 329, 330–331; social settings and, 234–249; social side of, 117; time allowed for, 437

Learning disabilities, 75, 187–188; cooperative learning and, 422; homework and, 431; learning strategies and, 257; metacognitive deficits and, 271; number identified as having, 188

Learning environments, cooperative, 11, 419–425
Learning games, 359
Learning strategies, 256–258
Learning theories: classical conditioning, 209–212; contiguity learning, 212–213; observational learning, 234–249; operant conditioning, 207–208, 213–234; social learning analysis of observational learning, 237–239
Learning transfer, 11, 299–307; conceptual models for, 301–303; contemporary views of, 301–303; doctrine of formal discipline and, 300; expert-novice differences in problem solving and, 280–284; high-road, 304–306; identity of procedure and, 300, 301, 310; identity of substance and, 300, 301, 310; instructional ideas and strategies for promoting, 306–307; low-road, 304; metacognition and, 301; mindfulness and, 305; negative transfer and, 300–301, 306; positive transfer and, 301; principles and, 301; procedural, 304–306, 310; substantive, 304, 310; teaching for, 303–306; traditional view of, 300–301
Least restrictive environment, exceptional children and, 176
Lecture method, 365–396; administrative advantages of, 368–369; attention and, 389–394; avoiding vagueness in, 387–388; body of, 378–394; clarifying content in, 387–388; clarifying organization of, 385–387; classroom teaching and, 453; cognitive load and, 374–375; combinatorial devices and, 382–383; communication apprehension and, 373; communication channels in, 389; comparisons/contrasts and, 381–382; component (part-whole) relationships and, 379–380; conclusion in, 394–395; con-pro sequence and, 380–381; covering content in, 378; defense of, 367–369; discussion methods vs., 370–371; enthusiasm in, 390, 392–393; essential content in, 376–377; examples in, 387; explaining links in, 386; explanations and, 383–384; explicitness of, 385–386; grade levels and, 369; handouts and, 394; high-consensus fields and, 401; humor in, 390, 392–393; important considerations for using, 371–375; individual differences and, 429; interlecture structuring, 395; introduction to, 375–378; low- vs. high-inference variables and, 373–

374; media for, 373; motivational cues and, 376; note taking and, 391–394; organization of, 377–379(fig.), 385–387; other teaching methods vs., 370–371; outlining forms in, 379–383; paradox, 366–375; pauses in, 389; preparation and, 371–373; previewing, 377; proper uses of, 370; questions in, 377, 390–391; reinforcement and, 368; relevance relationships and, 381; research evidence on effectiveness of, 369–371; rhetorical devices for, 388t; rule-example-rule technique and, 386; sequential relationships and, 380–381; stimulus variation and, 389; structural supports in, 387; students' interests and, 375–376; subject matter and, 369; transitional (connective) relationships and, 381; verbal markers of importance in, 387; visual aids in, 387, 389
Legitimate peripheral participation, 237
Libido, 317
Linguistic community, 119, 121, 123
Linguistic competence, 119, 124–125
Linguistic intelligence, 75, 76, 78–79
Linguistic mediation, 109–110
Literacy: adults' influence on language development and, 121–122; cultural, 43
Local norms, 513, 514
Loci method, 266–267
Locus of control, 321, 326–327, 340
Logic, 111; explanation and, 14, 16; group discussion and, 403–404; Piaget's stages and, 97; sharpening, 403–404
Logical fallacies, 411t, 411–412
Logical-mathematical intelligence, 75, 76, 77, 78–79
Logical operations, 103
Logical relationships, 14, 16
Long-answer questions, 557
Longitudinal studies, intelligence and, 54–55
Long-term memory, 259, 263–264; retrieval from, 261
Lookback strategy, 268
Low-consensus fields, 401
Low-income students: ability grouping and, 436; achievement and, 91–93; attribution patterns and, 325; frequency of no response and, 487; IQ tests and, 69, 85–86; mentors and, 143; performance tests and, 566; redirecting questions and, 487
Low-inference variables, 11, 373–374

Mainstreamed students, cooperative learning and, 425
Maintaining momentum, preventing problem behaviors and, 466
Manipulation, see Experiment
Mapping, 290–292
Mass, conservation of, 100–101, 102(fig.)
Mastery learning, 99, 330, 436–439; criticisms of, 438–439; effectiveness of, 437–438
Matching items, 571
Materials, adherence to intent of, 498
Mathematics, 28; academic learning time and, 493, 494, 495–496; behavior modeling and, 238; competitive learning and, 170–171; contiguity learning and, 212; contracting for, 345–347; creative problem solving and, 139; diagnostic tests and, 576; gender differences and, 170–171; genius and, 75; intelligence and, 59; Japan and, 495, 496; making meaning in, 294–296; performance tests and, 563–564; probing student answers and, 488; sample national standards in, 33t; scaffolds and, 474; seatwork and, 459; strategies in learning, 270; Taiwan and, 495, 496; teacher content knowledge and, 473; team-assisted individualization, 421; tutoring and, 441–442
Matrix, performance-content, 44–46, 45t
Meaninglessness, 540
Measurement, see Assessment
Media, for lecture method, 373
Mediated learning, 112–114
Mediation, 288–289
Melting pot, 155
Memorization, see Rote learning
Memory, 11; episodic, 262, 263; information-processing model of, 258–264; information storage in, 261–263; keyword method and, 267–268, 432; loci method and, 266–267; long-term, see Long-term memory; mnemonics, see Mnemonic devices; note taking and, 394; pictorial representations and, 261–262; short-term, 259, 260–261; strategies for processing information and enhancing, 264–270; visual, 110; working, 259
Mental abilities tests, group factors and, 56
Mental imagery, see Imagery
Mentally retarded, 184–187; attribution patterns and, 342; cooperative learning and, 421; educable, 69, 186; levels of, 185; metacognitive deficits, 271; punishment and, 228; trainable, 186

Mental processes, 10
Mental representations, 283. *See also* Imagery
Mental scaffolding, 290
Mentors, 143, 246–249
Messing around stage, teaching and, 116
Meta-analysis, 23, 59
Metacognition, 252, 270–273, 301, 391
Metalinguistic awareness, 121
Metaphors, 260, 388
Methylphenidate (Ritalin), 230–231
Metonymy, 388
Mexican-American students, 165; bias in teacher interactions with, 471; bilingualism and, 125–126. *See also* Hispanic students
Microlectures, 383–384
Middle-class bias, in tests, 85–86
Mimicry, cultural differences and, 163
Mindfulness, learning transfer and, 305
Minilectures, 383–384
Minority-group students, 123–126; attribution patterns and, 323; bias in teacher interaction and, 471; educable mentally retarded label and, 69; mentors and, 143. *See also* African-American students; Mexican-American students
Mnemonic devices, 256, 265, 303; imagery and, 265–266, 432; keyword method and, 267–268, 432; lectures and, 383; loci method and, 266–267; observational learning and, 238
Modeling, cultural differences and, 163
Molding, cultural differences and, 163
Money, as secondary reinforcer, 216
Monocultural perspective, 155
Monolingualism, 124
Mood, attributions about, 323. *See also* Emotion
Moral reasoning, 97, 131–136
Motivation, 312–362; affiliation and, 332; approval needs and, 332–333; behavior and, 313–317; behavior models and, 238–239; changing, with cognitive approaches, 340–342; changing patterns of, 339–340; competing systems and, 359; conceptions of, 317–319; contracts and, 345–348, 433; controversial topics and, 403; cues and, 376; duality in, 317; environmental approaches to, 343–348; extrinsic, 333–336; frustration and, 338–339; games and, 345–347, 359; goal orientation and, 314–315, 353, 376; grades and, 353–354,

585–586; implications of, for education, 318–319; individually guided, 347–348; intrinsic, 328, 333–336, 357; learning and, 313–317; libido and, 317; Maslow's hierarchy and, 317–319, 318(fig.); multiple, 317; operant conditioning and, 336–339; origins vs. pawns and, 334; power needs and, 332; praise and, 355; reason for, 352–353; reinforcers and, 314; stimulus control and, 337–338; student, 437; teaching techniques and, 352–360; time spent in different activities and, 315–316; token economies and, 343–345; types of, 317–319. *See also* Achievement motivation
Motivators, 337
Motor skills, 98, 99, 118
Multicultural education, 155–156; classroom, developing, 165–168, 166t, 167t; goals of, 156
Multidimensional classrooms, 331
Multimedia applications, 447
Multiple-ability tasks, 416
Multiple-choice tests, 546, 571–577, 572t, 586
Multiple intelligences, 75–78, 111; and factor-analyzed intelligences, 78, 79t; in schools, 78–80; theory of, 75, 80
Multiplication ability, 106
Musical intelligence, 75, 76, 77, 78, 79

National norms, 513, 514–515
Native Americans: looking down while being questioned, 163; multiculturalism and, 165, 168
Nature-nurture issue, social policy and, 83–84. *See also* Environment; Genetics
Needs, motivation and, 317–318(fig.), 319
Negative reinforcers, 215–216
Negative stimuli, punishment and, 227–231
Neo-Piagetians, 108–109
Non-English speaking students, 123–126
Nonpromotion, *see* Retention in grade
Nonquestion alternative, 407
Nonstandard English, language development and, 122–123
Normal distribution, cognitive-ability tests and, 53–54
Norm-referenced tests, 514–515, 531–534, 532(fig.); pros and cons of, 518t; reliability and, 519–520
Norms, test, 513; local, 513, 514; national, 513, 514–515
Note taking: group discussions and, 412; lectures and, 391–394

Novelty, attention-arousing stimuli and, 260
Novices, distinction between experts and, 280–284
Novice teachers, 9
Number, teaching concept of, 115
Nursery schools, 90
Nutrition, IQ and, 67

Obedience, 223–224
Objectively scorable questions, 570
Objectives: affective, 41; cognitive, *see* Cognitive learning; general, 37; planning and, 462, 463; psychomotor, 41; specific, 37–41. *See also* Educational objectives
Object permanence, development of, 99
Objects: classifying, 100; manipulation of, 115
Obscenity, 467
Observation, assessment through, 510
Observational learning, 214, 234–249; analysis of, 237(fig.); attentional phase, 237–238; contiguity and, 238; motivational phase, 238–239; punishment and, 238–239; reinforcement and, 238–239; reproduction phase, 238; retention phase, 238; social learning analysis of, 237–239; television and, 240–241
Obviousness, 9–10
Occupation, intelligence and, 61
Old age, despair and, 130
Open education, 502
Opening review, 482
Operant conditioning, 207–208, 213–234; concept map of, 214(fig.); contingency management and, 221–224; contingent reinforcement and, 213; elimination of responses and, 226–231; ethical issues and, 231–234; extinction and, 226; group participation and, 418; motivation and, 336–339; negative reinforcers, 215–216; positive reinforcers, 215; punishment and, 227–231; rational processes and, 231; reinforcement in, 214–234
Operant level, 213
Operation, 103
Optical scanning systems, 579
Optimism, 127
Oral reports, 587
Ordering problems, concrete operational stage and, 103
Organization: lecture method and, 377–379(fig.), 385–387; teacher structuring and, 480–481
Organizational networks, 382–383(fig.)
Orienting response (OR), 259

Originality, 140, 141. *See also* Creativity

Outlining forms in lecture method, 379–383

Overachievement, 317

Overlappingness, preventing problem behaviors and, 465

Overlearning, 264–265

Overregulation, language development and, 120

Overt rehearsal, in observational learning, 238

Paired-associate learning, 289

Pairing of values, 18

Paper-and-pencil activities, 9–10, 51, 58, 494

Paraphrasing, 573–576

Parents: role of, in multicultural education, 167–168; socialization by, and gender differences, 171. *See also* Home environment

Pass-fail grading, 516–517, 585–586

Patterns, problem solving and, 280–283

Pauses, lecture method and, 389

Pedagogical content knowledge, 372–373, 473–474

Peer groups, student's behavior and, 466

Peer tutoring, 112, 441, 442

Percentile rank, 54, 541–542

Perception(s): accommodation and, 105–106; assimilation and, 105–106; egocentric, 107; of self-efficacy, developing, 349–351; sensorimotor stage and, 98; symbolic mediation and, 100

Perceptual clarity, developing, 116

Performance, 28–29; attributions and, 323; extrinsic rewards and, 335; judging, 243–245; learning and, 238–239; need for, 320–321; observing one's own, 243; personal guidelines, 328–329; rate of, 321; self-generated standards and, 243–245; terminal, 37; thinking about objectives in terms of student, 36–41. *See also* Achievement

Performance-content matrix, 44–46, 45*t*

Performance measure(s), 320–321, 557, 558, 559–567, 577, 578*t*; development and scoring, teachers' comments on, 562*t*; examples of, at high school level, 561(fig.); portfolios of performances, 564–567; problems and prospects of, 566–567; prompts in, 567; scoring, 562–564, 565*t*

Perplexity, epistemic curiosity and, 357

Perseverance, 316

Persistence, 326, 342

Personality: differences, gender differences and, 170; factors, five, 136–138, 137(fig.); gender differences in, 170. *See also* Traits of personality

Personality development, 97, 127–136

Personalized system of instruction, 436–437, 439

Personal space, culture and, 152

Perspective, understanding another person's, 403–404

Physical ability, gender differences in, 171

Physical activity, 264. *See also* Athletics

Physical education, *see* Athletics

Physical impairment, 181–184

Physical needs, 317

Physical reinforcers, 222

Physicists, expert, 283, 284

Physiological needs, satisfying, 216

Piaget's stages of cognitive development, 96–109; alternatives to, 108–109; biological implications of, 106; concrete operational, 103–104; formal operational, 104–105, 107; information-processing theory vs., 108; preoperational, 99–103; questions about, 106–107; sensorimotor, 98–99

Pictorial representations, memory and, 261–262

Pivot words, 119

Planning, 454, 462–476; activities and, 463; for control of bias, 470–473; decision making and, 462; levels of, 463–464; needs, types of, 464; nested, 463; objectives of, 462, 463; postinteractive, 462; preinteractive, 462; for problem behavior, 464–470; for scaffolds, 474; for use of pedagogical content knowledge, 473–474

Policy making, evaluation and, 529

Political ideology, nature-nurture issue and, 83–84

Population, tests and, 530–531

Portfolios, using, in assessment process, 593–597

Positive reinforcement, 215; attention and, 226; contingency contracts and, 223–224; extrinsic vs. intrinsic, 233; primary, 216; secondary, 216; tutoring and, 440

Positive responses to school, conditioning, 210–211

Possibilities, combinational analysis of, 104

Postconventional, autonomous, or principled level of moral development, 131

Power needs, 332

Practical intelligence, 71–72; criticisms of, 74–75; measuring, 72–74; research evidence on, 74

Practice, using research to guide, 23–26

Praise: effective, 354–356, 488–489; expectation of, 337; good vs. bad, 355*t*; group participation and, 418; ineffective, 355*t*; student responses and, 488–489

Preconventional level of moral development, 131

Prediction, 14–16, 17

Predictive validity, tests and, 525

Premack principle, 222–223, 337

Preoperational stage, 99–103

Prepositions, 386

Prerequisite capabilities, 377

Preschool children, concrete materials for learning and, 115

Previewing, in lecture method, 377

Principled reasoning, 132–133, 134

Principles, 11, 13; comprehension of, 576; learning transfer and, 300–301; used in control, 15; used in explanation, 14; used in prediction, 14–15

Prior knowledge activation, 432

Probing, 487–488

Problem-based project learning, 286–288

Problem behavior: categories of, 465; extinction and, 466–467; prevention, 465–466; punishment of, 467–468; strengthening incompatible behavior and, 467

Problem finding or formulation, planning and, 463

Problem solving: approach to learning, 252, 278–284; conceptual models and, 301–303; cooperative learning and, 420; creative, 141–142; experts and, 280–284; gender differences in, 170; ill-defined, 279; intelligence measuring and, 51; lectures and, 380; patterns and, 280–283; planning and, 463; procedural knowledge and, 263; to reduce cognitive load, 374; representation of problem and, 283; routines and, 284; seatwork and, 493; well-defined, 279

Procedural knowledge, 263

Procedural transfer, 304–306, 310

Process-product studies, 456–457

Production of ideas, fluency in, 140

Productive Thinking Program, 141–142

Programmed instruction, 442–446

Project Follow Through, 81

Project Head Start, 81, 91

Prompts, instructional supports and, 474

Propositional thinking, 104–105

Proximal development, *see* Zone of proximal development
Pseudoabsolute standards, in grading, 581–582
Psychological growth, training in, 134
Psychological processes, starting, as social processes, 112
Psychology, 3, 12
Psychomotor knowledge, 41, 110
Psychosocial development, 127–130
Public Law 94-142 (Education for All Handicapped Children Act), 173, 174
Public Law 100-297 (Jacob K. Javits Gifted and Talented Students Education Act [GTSEA]), 198, 199
Public Law 101-476 (Individuals with Disabilities Education Act [IDEA]), 174–177, 180, 184, 189, 191, 196, 198
Punishment, 208, 227–228; attention and, 237; corporal, 467–468; effective, 228; group participation and, 418; negative stimuli and, 227–231; observational learning and, 238–239; as paradoxical reinforcer, 228; presentation, 228–229; problem behaviors and, 467–468; reasoning and, 231; removal, 229–231; response cost, 230; self-, 245–246; taking away something of positive value, 229–231; time-out, 230; vicarious, 236
Punishment-obedience orientation, 131, 132

Qualitative research, 22–23
Qualitative variables, 12
Quantitative variables, 12
Question-and-answer recitation, *see* Recitation
Question(s): cognitive level of, 483–485; creativity and, 143; frequency of, 482–483; generation, study skills and, 432; group discussions and, 406–408; learning to ask, 268; lecturers' asking, 377, 390–391; redirecting and probing, 487–488; rhetorical, 380; students asking themselves, 391; wait-time and, 485–486. *See also* Nonquestion alternatives; Tests
Quizzes, 221, 583

Race differences, intelligence and, 62. *See also* Cultural differences; Ethnic differences
Random assignment, 15; experiments and, 21
Rational processes, operant conditioning and, 231
Ratio schedule of reinforcement, 217
Ravens Progressive Matrices Test, 51–52, 66

Raw scores, 52, 541
Reacting, teacher's, 486; negative reactions and, 490–491; positive reactions and, 488–490; recitation and, 454–456; with structuring, 491–492; wait-time II and, 486–488
Reading: academic learning time and, 493, 494; achievement in, 9, 10, 296–299; comprehension and, 268, 432; contingency management and, 222–223; contracting for, 347–348; early education interventions and, 91; group discussions and, 404; hearing impaired and, 179; learning disabilities in, 187; paper-and-pencil activities and, 9–10; probing student answers and, 488; scaffolds and, 474; schemata and, 296–299; story grammar and, 268–269; strategies in learning, 268–269; tutoring and, 442
Real-world situations, 305, 306
Reasoning ability, 56; language development and, 97
Reasoning with student, as alternative to punishment, 231
Recall questions, 483
Recitation (interactive teaching), 454, 477–503; accepting students' ideas and, 489–490; adaptability of, 458–460; class size and, 460; example of, in ninth-grade class, 458; feedback and, 460; flexibility of, 454–456; praise and, 488–489; reacting and, 454–456, 486–492; reinforcement and, 460, 469; responding and, 454–456; social reinforcement and, 460; socioeconomic status and, 459–460; soliciting and, 454–456, 482–486; structuring and, 454–456, 479–482; suitability to basic tasks and, 460; teacher's assessment during, 552–554; tokens and, 490
Recitations by students, 126
Recognition, need for, 332
Redirecting, 491–492
Referent actor, 416
Referents, children and, 118
Reflective thinking, 232, 462, 498
Regression, frustration leading to, 339
Regression line, 19
Rehearsal, 2, 60
Reinforcement, 208; bribery and, 233; contingent, 213, 221–224; continuous, 217, 218, 226; differential, 226–227; extrinsic, 333–336, 344; fixed, 217–218, 219–220; group discussion and, 418; independence and, 233; intermittent, 217, 218, 226; interval schedule of, 217, 219–221;

learned helplessness and, 341–342; lecture method and, 368; negative, 215–216; non-, 226; observational learning and, 238–239; phasing out, 218; positive, *see* Positive reinforcement; primary vs. secondary, 216; ratio schedule of, 217; recitation and, 460, 469; removal of negative events and, 216; scalloping effect and, 220; schedules, 217–221; self-, 246, 334, 342, 376; stable responses and, 218; strengthening incompatible behavior and, 467; student responses and, 488–490; token system and, 343–345; tutoring and, 440; unintentional, 227; of unwanted behavior, 466; variable, 217, 218, 220–221; vicarious, 239, 240; withholding, 338–339
Reinforcement menu, 337
Reinforcer(s): contingent removal of, 230; defined, 213–214; home-based, 344; motivation and, 314; preferences for, 337–338; punishment as, 228–229; stimulus control and, 337–338; types of, 222–223
Relationships: causal, 17–18, 21–22; correlational, 16–21; qualitative research and, 22
Relative standards, in grading, 582
Relevance relationships, lectures and, 381
Reliability, informal assessment and, 553–554
Reliability of tests, 11, 518–524; cognitive-ability tests and, 55; computers and, 578–579; essays and, 568–569; improving, 524; internal-consistency, 521; test-retest, 519–521
Repetition: contiguity learning and, 212; overlearning and, 264–265
Replication, 23
Research in education: consistency of results, 25; direct instruction and importance of judgment in, 477–479; generalizations from, 9–10; guiding practice and, 23–26; practical intelligence and, 74; purpose of, 9; qualitative, 22–23; replication of, 23
Resource centers, 434–435
Respondent conditioning, *see* Classical (respondent) conditioning
Responding, recitation and, 454–456
Response(s): elimination of, 226–231; orienting stimuli and, 259–260; stimulus relationship, 109; thwarted, as cause of frustration, 338
Response cost, 230

Response set, 300
Responsibility, attributions about, 323
Retarded, *see* Mentally retarded
Retention: educable mentally retarded and, 186; humor and, 392–393; in memory, 262. *See also* Memory
Retention in grade, 592–593
Retrieving information, 261
Reversibility, operational thought and, 103
Rewards: attention and, 237; behavior controlled by, 138; consumable, 337; contingency management and, 223–224; cooperative learning and, 420; extrinsic, 233, 335–336; intrinsic, 233, 334; lecture method and, 368; perseverance and, 316; self-concept and, 145; token economy and, 222, 343–345, 490; verbal vs. tangible, 335; vicarious, 236; volunteering to answer questions and, 469
Rhetorical devices, lectures and, 380, 388t
Ridicule, group participation and, 419
Risk taking, achievement motivation and, 321
Ritalin, *see* Methylphenidate
Robin Hood effect, 438
Rote learning, 212, 255, 485
Routines, problem solving and, 284
Rule-example-rule technique, 386
Rules: classroom language and, 126, 454; system of, 494
Rural-urban differences, in cognitive ability, 81–82

Sarcasm, group participation and, 419
Scaffolds, 275, 290, 474
Scalloping effect, 220
Scatterplots, 19–21, 20(fig.)
Schemata: babies and, 99; cognitive development and, 108; concepts vs., 292; developing and enriching, 292–294; gender, 169; lectures and, 377–378; observational learning and, 238; reading achievement and, 296–299
Scholastic achievement, *see* Achievement
Scholastic aptitude, 55, 58–61
Scholastic aptitude tests, 68, 78, 536, 541
Scholastic fairs, 359
School(s): influences on cognitive abilities, 90–93; language development and, 122–127; moral development in, 134–135; multiple intelligences in, 78–80; self-efficacy of, 351–352

School calendar, planning and, 463–464
Schooling, effects on IQ of, 67–68
School structure, classroom management and, 464
School success, 58–59
Science: computers and, 579; conceptual models and, 301–303; mentoring and, 248; objectives of, 14; overcoming student misconceptions in, 197–198; performance tests and, 560; sample national standards in, 33t; teacher's questions and, 482–483
Scientific principles, 13
Scientific thought, 104–105; domain-specific, 108; metalinguistic awareness and, 121
Scoring rubrics, 562–564, 563–564t
Seatwork, 453, 455, 459, 492–493, 495
Secondary schools: homework and, 430, 431; tests and, 511
Selective migration, 84–85
Select questions, 557–558, 571
Self-actualization, 127, 318
Self-appraisals, goal setting and, 321
Self-concept, 138; achievement and, 146; behavior changes and, 144–145; creativity and, 143; levels of, 144; locus of control and, 327; tutoring and, 442
Self-consciousness, 109
Self-control, 112, 128
Self-criticism, 243
Self-efficacy, 144, 146; achievement motivation and, 348–352; developing perceptions of, 349–351; distorted sense of, 245; of teachers and schools, 351–352
Self-esteem, 128, 144–146; ability grouping and, 436; cooperative learning and, 422; corporal punishment and, 468; delinquency and, 464; perseverance and, 316; tutoring and, 439, 440. *See also* Big-fish-little-pond effect
Self-evaluation, 350
Self-Injurious Behavior Inhibiting System (SIBIS), 228–229
Self-knowledge, 76
Self-monitoring, 243, 246, 342
Self-punishment, 243, 245–246
Self-reflection, training in, 134
Self-regulation, 112–114, 243–246, 247, 272
Self-reinforcement, 243, 246, 334, 342, 376
Self-rewards, 245–246
Self-satisfaction, 243
Self-worth, 144, 146; and need for achievement, relationship of, to classroom structure, 328–331
Semantic maps, 290–292

Sensorimotor stage, of intellectual development, 98–99
Sensory cognitions, behavior model and, 236
Sensory input, information storage and, 261
Sentences, diagramming, 304
Sequential information, cognitive development and, 115–117
Sequential relationships, lecture method and, 380–381
Sex differences, *see* Gender differences
Shame, 327, 329
Shaping, 469
Short-answer questions, 557–558, 570–577, 578t
Short-term memory, 259, 260–261
Short-term sensory storage (STSS), 258
Shyness, 468
Signal giving, teacher structuring and, 480
Similes, 260, 388
Simple-reciprocation teaching cycle, 488
Simulations, 359; computers and, 579
Single-word utterances, 118–119
Situated cognition, 252–253, 284–288
Skinner box, 213
Small-group teaching, 297–298; cooperative learning and, 419–425; discussion groups and, 399–419; large classes and, 400–401; seatwork and, 492; social studies and, 459
Smoothness, preventing problem behaviors and, 466
Social acceptance, 317; attractiveness and, 472; need for, 13, 317
Social-action approach, in multicultural classroom, 167
Social activities, 359
Social advantage, selective migration and, 84–85
Social class: intelligence tests and, 69; recitation patterns and, 460. *See also* Low-income students; Socioeconomic status
Social comparison, achievement motivation and, 319–320
Social constructivists, 252, 255, 277–278, 298
Social context, behavior and, 161
Social-contract legalistic orientation, 131, 132
Social environment, development and, 111–114
Social interaction, 161, 398
Social involvement, 130
Socializing agents, enculturation by, 152–154
Social justice, 87, 134

Social knowledge, 114
Social learning, 208, 214, 234–249, 398; aggression and, 170; mentoring and, 246; self-regulation of behavior and, 243–246
Social needs, 317
Social order, 131, 132
Social policy, nature-nurture issue and, 83–84
Social processes, psychological processes starting as, 112
Social rules, for classroom discourse, 126
Social skills, 483
Social studies, 459
Society's productivity, achievement motivation and, 320
Socioeconomic status (SES): classroom recitations and, 459–460; in cognitive ability, 80–81; and cognitive-ability test scores, 63
Sociolinguistic competence, 126–127
Soliciting, teacher's, 482; cognitive level of questions and, 483–485; directing questions and, 486; frequency of questions and, 482–483; recitation and, 454–456; wait-time I and, 485–486. *See also* Redirecting
Solution paths, 498
Spatial ability, imagery system and, 265
Spatial devices, study skills and, 432
Spatial intelligence, 75–76, 78, 110
Special aptitude tests, 536
Special education: categories of students eligible for, 174–177; non-English speaking students in, 124; students, general teacher accommodations for, 178t
Specifications, *see* Table of specifications
Speech: egocentric, 107; hearing impaired and, 180; left hemisphere and, 265. *See also* Language development
Speech disorders, 180–181
Speech fright, 373
Spelling, contiguity learning and, 213
Spreadsheets, 446–447
Stability, 322
Stability of tests, 55
Standard deviation, 601–602; IQ scores and, 54
Standard error of measurement, tests and, 522–524
Standardized tests, *see* Tests, standardized
Standard score, 54, 542
Standards, tests and, 513, 516–517
Standards for self, 246. *See also* Educational objectives

Stanford-Binet Intelligence Scale, 51, 66(fig.), 527
Stanine score, 54; percentile rank and, 542
Statistical analysis, 21–22
Statistically significant/non-significant, 21–22
Stealing, 138–139
Steering groups, 553
Stem, multiple-choice items and, 573
Stereotypes: attribution patterns and, 342; cultural, 172; gender, 169, 172–173
Stimuli: arousal value of, 356–357; independence of response to, 109; orienting response to, 259–260; predifferentiation, 306; presenting, 215; reinforcing, 337–338; removing, 215–216; unwanted behavior and, 467; variation in, 389
Stimulus generalization, 229
Story grammar, 268–269, 432
Structural supports, lecture method and, 387
Structure, discussion-group teaching and, 402
Structured teaching, 429
Structuring, teacher's, 479; experiments on, 481–482; organization and, 480–481; rate of teacher initiation and, 480; reactions with, 491–492; recitation and, 454–456; signal giving and, 480; teacher talk and, 481
Structuring reactions, 491–492
Structuring-soliciting-responding-reacting units, 126, 454–456, 477–479
Student-centered instruction, 501–502
Student characteristics: cognitive development and, 96–118; cultural differences in, 151–168; educational objectives and, 30; exceptional students and, 173–202; gender differences and, 168–173
Student responses: call-outs, 486; cognitive level of questions and, 483–485; negative reactions to, 490–491; positive reactions to, 488–490; probing and, 487–488; structuring reactions to, 491–492; teachers' reactions to, 486–492; wait-time I and, 485–486; wait-time II and, 485, 486–488
Students: aptitude of, 437; attractiveness of, 472; causal attributions and, 323–325; feelings of, and discussion-group teaching, 418–419; individual differences in, 428–429; interests of, and lecture method, 375–376; misperceptions of, in science, 297–298; motivation of, 437; role of, in de-

terminating content of instruction, 36
Student teaching, 246
Student Teams and Achievement Divisions, 420
Studying: individual instruction and, 431–433; reinforcement schedules and, 220; scaffolds and, 474; tests facilitating, 583
Subject matter, lecture method and, 369
Submissiveness, need for approval and, 332
Substance exposure/abuse, prenatal or early-childhood, 197–198
Substantive transfer, 304, 310
Success, intelligence tests measuring potential, 86. *See also* Job success; School success
Successive approximations, shaping behavior by, 223, 469
Suicides, teenage, 130
Summarization, 268, 431–432; lectures and, 395
Summary evaluations, *see* Grades/grading
Summary review, 482
Summative evaluation, 529–530
Supply questions, 557, 571
Surprise, attention-arousing stimuli and, 356–357
Suzuki method, 75
Symbolic cognitions, behavior model and, 236
Symbolic logic, intelligence and, 76–78
Symbolic mediation, perception and, 100
Symbolic stage, cognitive development and, 111, 116, 264
Symbol system, 109, 118; overriding perception, 100; Piaget's stages and, 98; understanding through, 111
Synecdoche, 388
Synesthesia, 264
Synthesis, as objective, 42; essay tests and, 568; teacher's questions stimulating, 483, 484

Table of specifications, tests and, 555–557; *see also* Performance-content matrix
Tacit knowledge, 72
Taiwan, academic learning time and, 495, 496
Taking turns, rules for, 126
Talented students, *see* Gifted and talented students
Task completion, 321, 591
Task difficulty, 437; attributions about, 322
Task persistence, achievement needs and, 320–321
Tasks: classroom recitation and,

460; interactive elements in, 374; multiple-ability, 416; split-attention requirements in, 374
Taughtness, 539
Taxonomy, 41; cognitive-domain, 42
Teacher attention, unintentional reinforcement through, 227
Teacher-centered instruction, 501, 502
Teacher questions, 482–486; cognitive level of, 483–485; directing, 486; frequency of, 482–483; probing, 487–488; redirecting, 487; wait-time I and, 485–486; wait-time II and, 485, 486–488. *See also* Recitation (interactive teaching)
Teachers: as agents of society, 580; as behavior models, *see* Behavior, modeling; bilingual education role of, 123–124; causal attributions and, 326; expectations, *see* Expectations; expertise developed by, 281–283; as gatekeepers, 163; general concerns and recommendations for, on diversity, 202; grading biases of, 591–592; group-discussion role of, 405–406, 408–412; independent study role of, 434; intellectual empathy and, 115; mastery learning role of, 437–439; minorities as, 152; personality of, and discussion-group teaching, 402; power of, 413; reaction of, in recitation, 486–492; role of, in determining content of instruction, 34–36; role of, with computers, 449–450; self-efficacy of, 351–352; self-regulation and, 246; soliciting by, 482–486; target errors and, 494; timing errors and, 494; trait theory and, 143–144; values of, 413
Teacher's assessment, 550–599; computers and, 578–579; essay tests and, 567–570, 578t; formal, 554–579, 586–590; informal, 551–554, 590–592; instructional, 551, 552–554; during interactive teaching, 552–554; performance tests and, 559–567, 578t; portfolios used in, 593–597; short-answer tests and, 570–577, 578t; sizing-up, 551–552; supply vs. select questions and, 557–558, 571. *See also* Assessment
Teacher's pet, 332
Teacher structuring, interactive teaching and, 479–482
Teacher-student interactions: biases in, 470–473; culturally based behaviors impacting, 157–162, 158(fig.); and expectations, gender differences and, 172–173
Teacher talk, 481

Teaching: concrete materials and, 115; gifted students and, 199; for learning transfer, 303–306; messing around stage and, 116; motivational techniques in, 352–360; objectives of, 28; planning and, 463; segments of, 476; structured, 429; tasks of, 28, 29–31; verbal discussions and, 117
Teaching devices, hearing impaired and, 179
Teaching materials, 476
Teaching methods, 30, 366–367; classroom teaching, 452–503; cooperative learning, 419–425; discussion, 399–419; effective, 15; explanations, 383–384; health impairments and, 182–184; high-inference variables and, 373–374; individual instruction and, 427–451; lecturing, 365–396; low-inference variables and, 373–374; small-group, 397–425; summative evaluation and, 529–530
Team-Assisted Individualization, 421
Teams-Games-Tournaments, 420–421
Team teaching, 454
Technological aids, visual impairment and, 178
Telecommunications, 447–448
Telegraphic speech, 119
Television, aggression and, 240–241
Temporal (time) relationships, 16
Terminal performance, 37
Terminal structuring, 482
Term projects, 587
Test-bias explanation, of group differences in cognitive ability, 85–86
Testing: anxiety and, 212, 215–216, 540; computers and, 578–579; cost of, 538; criterion-referenced, *see* Criterion-referenced tests; domain-referenced, 555; group differences in cognitive ability and, 85–86; intelligence, *see* Intelligence tests; IQ, *see* IQ tests; norm-referenced, *see* Norm-referenced tests; norms, *see* Norms, test; reliability of, *see* Reliability of tests; sampling behavior and, 512–513; validity of, 524–527, 540; variable-interval schedule and, 221. *See also* Assessment
Tests, 510–530; authentic, 559; cramming for, 220; diagnostic, 576–577; equalization effect and, 371; essay, 567–570, 577, 578t; evaluation of, 513; high-stakes, 543–545; lecture method and, 370–371; mastery learning and, 437–438; matching, 571; multiple-choice, 546, 571–577, 572t, 586; number of questions on, 557; objective vs. subjective,

512; performance, 559–567, 577, 578t; short-answer, 557–558, 570–577, 578t; standard error of measurement and, 522–524; standardized vs. teacher-made, 530–534; standards and norms and, 513; supply vs. select, 557–558, 571; surprise, 221; table of specifications and, 555–557; true-false, 571; types of, 557–559
Tests, standardized, 54, 530–547; achievement tests, 535, 536–540; administering, 540–541; advantages and special uses of, 530–534; aptitude tests, 535, 536–540; cognitive-ability, 51–55; culture-fair, 86; disadvantages of and concerns about, 534; future of, 546–547; grade equivalent score and, 545; harmful effects of, 543–545; interpreting, 541–546; percentile rank and, 541–542; publication of scores, 537–538; raw score and, 541; stanine score and, 542; trial run, 540; types of, 535–540
Textbooks: abundant use of, 494; planning and, 463–464; summative evaluation and, 529; teacher's choice of content and, 35
Third International Mathematics and Science Study (TIMSS), 499–500
Thought processes, *see* Cognitive processes
Time allowed for learning, 437
Time on task, 425
Time-out, 230
Token reinforcers or economies, 222, 343–345, 490
Topics: controversial, 402–404; dead, 414–415
Topsy-turvies, 120
Trainable mentally retarded (TMR), 186
Trait names, 136
Traits of personality, 97, 136–146; consistency of, 136; creativity, 139–143; honesty, 138–139; self-concept, 144–146
Trait theory, teacher and, 143–144
Transfer, *see* Learning transfer.
Transformation approach, in multicultural classroom, 167
Transitional (connective) relationships, lecture method and, 381
Transitions: breaks and, 494; signals of, in lectures, 379–380
Traumatic brain injury, exceptional students and, 184
True-false questions, 571
Trust vs. mistrust, crisis of, 127
T-scores, 54
Tutoring, 109, 439–442; computer-assisted instruction and, 444; cost-effectiveness analysis of, 442;

Tutoring (*continued*)
effectiveness of, 441–442; in multicultural classrooms, 165–166
Twins, IQ scores and, 63–64
Two-word utterances, 119–120

Unalterable variables, 12–13
Unconditioned response (UR), 210, 212
Unconditioned stimulus (US), 209, 210–211, 212
Underachievement, 317
Understanding: conceptual models for, 301–303; through symbol systems, 111; three meanings of, 384
Unidimensional classrooms, 331
Unit notebooks, planning and, 463
Universal-ethical-principle orientation, 131, 132
Urban-rural differences, in cognitive ability, 81–82

Vagueness, avoiding, 387–388
Validity, informal assessment and, 553–554
Validity of tests, 524–527, 540
Values, of teachers, 413
Vandalism, societal factors in, 464
Variable-interval reinforcement schedules, 220–221
Variable-ratio reinforcement schedules, 218

Variables, 11–12; alterable and unalterable, 12–13; alternative explanations of correlation between, 17*t*; basis for pairing, 18; causal relationships, 15, 17–18; controlling, 14, 15–16; correlational relationships, 16–18; dependent, 17, 18, 21; direction and strength of relationship between, 19; independent, 17–18, 21; logical relationships, 14; low-inference, 373–374; predictive relationships: *see* Temporal (Time) relationships; qualitative and quantitative, 12
Variety, planning for, 474–476
Verbal ability: coding and, 265; gender differences in, 171
Verbal behavior, 209; self-concepts and, 145
Verbal intelligence, 75
Verbal markers of importance, 387, 480
Verbal material, retention of, 262, 265
Verbal reinforcers, 222, 335
Violence: corporal punishment and, 467–468; societal factors and, 464; television and, 240–241
Visual abilities, coding and, 265
Visual aids, lectures and, 387, 389
Visual images: lectures and, 387, 389; retention of, 110. *See also* Imagery

Visual impairment, 177–179
Vocational plan, grading and, 580
Voice: modulation, 482; speech disorders and, 180
Volume, conservation of, 101, 102(fig.)
Volunteering behavior, 218, 332, 469

Wait-time I, teacher questions and, 485–486
Wait-time II, teacher reactions and, 485, 486–488
Wechsler IQ test, 66(fig.), 527
Weight, conservation of, 101, 102(fig.)
Withdrawal, 339, 468
Within-class grouping, 435
Withitness, preventing problem behaviors and, 465
Women, moral dilemmas and, 133–134. *See also* Gender differences
Word processors, 446
Workbooks, abundant use of, 494
Working memory, 259
World Wide Web, 447–448
Writing strategies in learning, 270

Yielding, 414

Zone of proximal development, 111–112, 114, 117, 398
Z-scores, 54

for Gonville · Bootle

120 g2 L

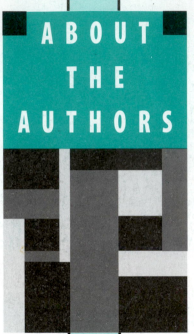

ABOUT THE AUTHORS

Both authors have had a lifelong—from kindergarten through the Ph.D. and beyond—fascination with teaching. When they began to teach educational psychology to undergraduates and graduate students, they quickly realized that their training had been seriously deficient. It had told them much about learning and learners but little about teaching and teachers. It had been particularly lacking in what it provided about what teachers should do face to face with students in the classroom, the lecture hall, the discussion group, and the tutoring session.

Before long, they began trying to remedy that deficiency. Their careers as researchers, authors, editors, and conference organizers—as well as teachers—testify to their conviction that teaching is important, researchable, and improvable through research-based teacher education. The field of educational psychology now pays much more attention to teaching—what teachers should know, understand, and be able to do. The authors would like to think that if they began to teach today with the help of their own book, their work would be much easier and, most important, more effective.

N. L. Gage is the Margaret Jacks Professor of Education and, by courtesy, Professor of Psychology, Emeritus, at Stanford University. He is the author of *The Scientific Basis of the Art of Teaching* and *Hard Gains in the Soft Sciences: The Case of Pedagogy*. He edited the first *Handbook of Research on Teaching*.

David C. Berliner is Dean of the College of Education and Regents' Professor of Educational Leadership and Policy Studies and Psychology in Education at Arizona State University. He is the coauthor (with Bruce J. Biddle) of *The Manufactured Crisis* and coeditor (with Robert C. Calfee) of *The Handbook of Educational Psychology*.

Both authors have taught for many years. Both have been President of the Division of Educational Psychology of the American Psychological Association and recipients of its Thorndike Award for Distinguished Contributions to Psychology in Education. Each has been President of the American Educational Research Association and a recipient of its award for Distinguished Contributions to Educational Research. They have also been Fellows of the Center for Advanced Study in the Behavioral Sciences and members and chairs of the Board of Directors of the National Society for the Study of Education.